ACCOUNTABILITY FOR HUMAN RIGHTS ATROCITIES IN INTERNATIONAL LAW

Beyond the Nuremberg Legacy

Second Edition

ACCOUNTABILITY FOR HUMAN RIGHTS ATROCITIES IN INTERNATIONAL LAW

Beyond the Nuremberg Legacy

Second Edition

STEVEN R. RATNER
JASON S. ABRAMS

OXFORD
UNIVERSITY PRESS

OXFORD
UNIVERSITY PRESS

Great Clarendon Street, Oxford OX2 6DP

Oxford University Press is a department of the University of Oxford.
It furthers the University's objective of excellence in research, scholarship,
and education by publishing worldwide in

Oxford New York

Auckland Bankok Buenos Aires Cape Town
Chennai Dar es Salaam Delhi Hong Kong
Istanbul Karachi Kolkata Kuala Lumpur Madrid
Melbourne Mexico City Mumbai Nairobi
São Paulo Shanghai Taipei Tokyo Toronto

Oxford is a registered trade mark of Oxford University Press
in the UK and in certain other countries

Published in the United States
by Oxford University Press Inc., New York

First published 2001

British Library Cataloguing in Publication Data
Data available

Library of Congress Cataloging in Publication Data
Data available

ISBN 0–19–924833–8
ISBN 0–19–829871–4 (Pbk)

7 9 10 8 6

Typeset in Times by
Cambrian Typesetters, Frimley, Surrey
Printed in Great Britain
on acid-free paper by
Biddles Ltd, King's Lynn, Norfolk

To Nancy, Benjamin, and Isabel
and
Marilyn and Burton Abrams

Acknowledgements

The opportunity to consider systematically the international law governing accountability of individuals for human rights abuses arose somewhat unexpectedly for us. Requested in 1994 by the United States Department of State to write a presumably brief study on the legal options for bringing to justice a particularly horrendous group of government leaders—the Khmer Rouge officials who governed Cambodia in the late 1970s—we found the current literature lacking any comprehensive analysis of this important area of contemporary international law. Hindered in undertaking any analysis of the law with respect to one specific episode, we undertook to study the entire issue of accountability first, and only then reached conclusions about the historical case at issue there. Hoping that the results of this endeavor might be put to use in shedding light on the global problems of accountability, we commenced work on a product for consumption by a larger audience. Our goal was to offer a one-volume treatment of the field as a discrete subject, one integrating international human rights law, international humanitarian law, and international criminal law, and considering the broad range of mechanisms available for holding individuals accountable. The acceleration of developments in the field after 1997 necessitated preparation of this second edition after only three years.

We received important assistance on this book from colleagues in official positions, in non-governmental organizations, and within the academy. At the US Department of State, we thank Alphonse La Porta, Director of the Office of Cambodian Genocide Investigations; Jamison Borek, Dennis Gallagher, and James Hergen of the Office of the Legal Adviser; and Gregory Stanton of the Bureau of International Organizations Affairs. At the Department of Defense, we appreciate helpful suggestions from Col. W. Hays Parks of the Office of the Judge Advocate General of the Army. Our study also benefited greatly from the generous time and valuable input provided by officials of the International Criminal Tribunals for the Former Yugoslavia and Rwanda, including Richard Goldstone, Payam Akhavan, Daryl Mundis, and Reid Bauman. At United Nations headquarters, Virginia Morris and Mahnoush Arsanjani of the Office of Legal Affairs provided us with documents and updates of the work of the International Law Commission and other bodies.

In addition, we thank the Open Society Institute, where one of us (Abrams) wrote the first draft of much of his contribution to this study, including during a leave of absence therefrom, and the Office of Legal

Affairs of the United Nations, where he completed his work on it. The views expressed herein are those of the authors and do not necessarily reflect the views of the Open Society Institute or the United Nations. In July 1995, Neil Kritz and the United States Institute of Peace organized a conference in Washington on the subject of this study, and we appreciate the thoughtful contributions made by the participants, in particular M. Cherif Bassiouni, Anthony D'Amato, David Hawk, Stephen Marks, Theodor Meron, and Diane Orentlicher. An early draft of the first edition received careful review from W. Michael Reisman, M. Cherif Bassiouni, and Hurst Hannum, whom we thank for their many helpful suggestions. Ron Slye of Yale Law School's Schell Center for International Human Rights arranged visits to conferences at Yale for us to share some results of our work in late 1995. At the University of Texas School of Law, we received useful comments from Hans Baade, Douglas Laycock, John Robertson, and Michael Tigar. Theodor Meron agreed to read much of the manuscript in 1996, and we appreciate his many valuable suggestions.

The second edition of the book benefited from ideas shared with us from participants at various conferences and colloquia in 1997, 1998, and 1999, including those sponsored by Hofstra Law School, the UN Department of Political Affairs, the Rijks Universiteit Leiden Faculty of Law, the T.M.C. Asser Institute, the Washington College of Law at American University, and the International Criminal Tribunal for the Former Yugoslavia. Roy Gutman and his colleagues at the Crimes of War Project provided additional suggestions regarding parts of this book that appeared, in abbreviated form, in *Crimes of War: What the Public Should Know.* We took account of useful criticisms of the first edition in various book reviews, in particular those of Jose Alvarez and Payam Akhavan.

Those chapters of the study concerning Cambodia benefited from the assistance of regional experts and others active in assisting that country to understand its past and engender greater respect for human rights in the present and future. We thank in particular Ben Kiernan and Craig Etcheson of Yale University's Cambodian Genocide Program, James Ross of the Human Rights Task Force on Cambodia, Judge Marie Hirigoyen, UN Special Representative Benny Widyono, Brad Adams of the UN Center for Human Rights' Phnom Penh office, and Karen Tse and Christie Warren of the International Human Rights Law Group. The membership of one of the authors (Ratner) in the UN Secretary-General's Group of Experts during 1998 and 1999 provided additional opportunities for addressing this case and numerous interlocutors who shared their views of accountability. We particularly thank David Ashley of the United Kingdom Foreign and Commonwealth Office for his many insights and updates on developments in that country.

We also acknowledge the important contribution made by our student research assistants: Carolina DeOnis, Sophie Fanelli, Jehanne Henry, Nada Ismail, Ondraus Jenkins, Jeffrey Johnston, Amin Kassam, Andrew Keller, Jeffrey Liu, Carla Margolis, Robert McCutchan, Jaykumar Menon, Oliver Metzger, Elizabeth Moorthy, Irina Plumlee, Leila Sayeh, Jennifer Schmid, Michelle Schulz, Leon Schydlower, Elissa Steglich, Shanda Stephenson, Erin Sudbury, and Geoffrey Unger. The final production work was greatly assisted by the wonderful talents of Kelli Baxter, Theresa Pritchard, Paula Perry, and Melonie Alspaugh. Finally, we express our appreciation to the staff of the Tarlton Law Library at the University of Texas School of Law, in particular David Gunn and Jonathan Pratter, and the staff of the Columbia University Libraries, who aided us in many ways with our research.

STEVEN R. RATNER
JASON S. ABRAMS
Austin, Texas, and New York
December 2000

Contents

Abbreviations

ATCA	Alien Tort Claims Act
CCL No. 10	Allied Control Council Law No. 10
ECOSOC	United Nations Economic and Social Council
ICC	International Criminal Court
ICCPR	International Covenant on Civil and Political Rights
ICJ	International Court of Justice
ICRC	International Committee of the Red Cross
ICTR	International Criminal Tribunal for Rwanda
ICTY	International Criminal Tribunal for the Former Yugoslavia
ILC	International Law Commission
IMT	International Military Tribunal at Nuremberg
NGO	Non-governmental organization
TVPA	Torture Victim Protection Act

Shorthand Forms in Footnotes

(for shorthand forms for cases, see the Table of Cases below)

AJIL	American Journal of International Law
All E.R.	All England Reports
ALR	Australian Law Reports
Apartheid Convention	International Convention on the Suppression and Punishment of the Crime of Apartheid, November 30, 1973, 1015 UNTS 243
CCL No. 10	Allied Control Council Law No. 10, December 20, 1945, *reprinted in* 1 CCL No. 10 Trials at xvi
CCL No. 10	Trials of War Criminals before the Nuernberg Military Trials Tribunals under Control Council Law No. 10 (the 'Green Series', US Government Printing Office, 1949–53)
CLR	Commonwealth Law Reports (Australia)
EJIL	European Journal of International Law
ESCOR	Economic and Social Council Official Records
F.2d, F.3d	Federal Reporter Second Series, Federal Reporter Third Series (United States)

F. Supp., F. Supp. 2d	Federal Supplement, Federal Supplement Second Series (United States)
GAOR	General Assembly Official Records
Geneva Convention I	Geneva Convention for the Amelioration of the Condition of the Wounded and Sick in Armed Forces in the Field, August 12, 1949, 75 UNTS 31
Geneva Convention II	Geneva Convention for the Amelioration of the Condition of Wounded, Sick, and Shipwrecked Members of Armed Forces at Sea, August 12, 1949, 75 UNTS 85
Geneva Convention III	Geneva Convention Relative to the Treatment of Prisoners of War, August 12, 1949, 75 UNTS 135
Geneva Convention IV	Geneva Convention Relative to the Protection of Civilian Persons in Time of War, August 12, 1949, 75 UNTS 2
Genocide Convention	Convention on the Prevention and Punishment of the Crime of Genocide, December 9, 1948, 78 UNTS 277
ICCPR	International Covenant on Civil and Political Rights, December 16, 1966, 999 UNTS 171
ICC Statute	Statute of the International Criminal Court, July 17, 1998, UN Doc. A/CONF.183/9
ICJ	Reports of the International Court of Justice
ICTR Rules	Rules of Procedure and Evidence of the International Criminal Tribunal for Rwanda, July 5, 1995, as amended
ICTR Statute	Statute of the International Criminal Tribunal for Rwanda, *in* Security Council Resolution 955, UN SCOR, 49th Year, Res. and Dec., at 15, UN Doc. S/INF/50 (1994)
ICTY Rules	Rules of Procedure and Evidence of the International Criminal Tribunal for the Former Yugoslavia, March 14, 1994, as amended
ICTY Statute	Statute of the International Criminal Tribunal for the Former Yugoslavia, *in* Report of the Secretary-General pursuant to paragraph 2 of Security Council Resolution 808 (1993), May 3, 1993, UN Doc. S/25704
ILC Y.B.	Yearbook of the International Law Commission
ILM	International Legal Materials
ILR	International Law Reports

IMT Charter	Charter of the International Military Tribunal, *in* Agreement for the prosecution and punishment of the major war criminals of the European Axis, August 8, 1945, 82 UNTS 279
IMT Trials	Trials of the Major War Criminals before the International Military Tribunal (the 'Blue Series', IMT Secretariat, 1947–49)
LNTS	League of Nations Treaty Series
Multilateral Treaties	Multilateral Treaties Deposited with the Secretary-General, available at www.untreaty.org
1954 ILC Report	Report of the International Law Commission to the General Assembly, UN Doc. A/2693 (1954), *reprinted in* 1954 [II] ILC Y.B. 140 (containing 1954 Draft Code of Offenses Against the Peace and Security of Mankind)
1956 Slavery Convention	Supplementary Convention on the Abolition of Slavery, Convention the Slave Trade, and Institutions and Practices Similar to Slavery, September 7, 1956, 266 UNTS 3
1996 ILC Report	Report of the International Law Commission on the work of its forty-eighth session, UN GAOR, 51st Sess., Supp. No. 10, UN Doc. A/51/10 (1996), *reprinted in* 1996 [II] [2] ILC Y.B.15 (containing 1996 Draft Code of Crimes Against the Peace and Security of Mankind)
OAS T.S.	Organization of American States Treaty Series
Protocol I	Protocol Additional to the Geneva Conventions of 12 August 1949, and Relating to the Protection of Victims of International Armed Conflicts, December 12, 1977, 1125 UNTS 3
Protocol II	Protocol Additional to the Geneva Conventions of 12 August 1949, and Relating to the Protection of Victims of Non-International Armed Conflicts, December 12, 1977, 1125 UNTS 609
Recueil des Cours	Collected Courses of the Hague Academy of International Law
SCOR	Security Council Official Records
SCR	Supreme Court Reports (Canada)

Statutory Limitations Convention	Convention on the Non-Applicability of Statutory Convention Limitations to War Crimes and Crimes against Humanity, November 26, 1968, 754 UNTS 73
Torture Convention	Convention against Torture and Other Cruel, Inhuman or Degrading Treatment or Punishment, December 10, 1984, 1465 UNTS 85
UNTS	United Nations Treaty Series
U.S.	United States Supreme Court Reports
USC	United States Code
War Crimes Reports	Law Reports of Trials of War Criminals (United Nations War Crimes Commission, 1947–49)

Table of Authorities

TREATIES, CONVENTIONS, AND OTHER INTERNATIONAL INSTRUMENTS

NATIONAL LEGISLATION

Nicaragua

South Africa

Spain

Sweden

United Kingdom

United States

Uruguay

CASES

(Full citations noted here if case is cited in abbreviated form in footnotes)

Australia

Austria

Belgium

Canada

Control Council Law No. 10 Tribunals

Denmark

European Court of Human Rights

France

Germany

Inter-American Court of Human Rights

Hungary

International Court of Justice

International Criminal Tribunal for Rwanda

International Criminal Tribunal for the Former Yugoslavia

International Military Tribunal at Nuremberg

Israel

Netherlands

Other Post-World War II Courts

South Africa

Switzerland

United Kingdom

United States

Introduction to the Second Edition

The goal of this volume since the preparation of our original edition has been to appraise individual accountability for human rights atrocities as a discrete subject of international law and to offer a one-volume treatment integrating its numerous threads. Such a project requires consideration of international human rights law, international humanitarian law, international criminal law, and a range of mechanisms both prosecutorial and otherwise for holding abusers responsible. All must be considered within the political context of various societies whose governments and citizens are contemplating the process of accountability. To limit one's line of inquiry to certain doctrinal categories or one form of sanction is to miss the full picture of this important field.

Our task has been rendered more challenging by significant developments in the international law of individual accountability since the publication of the first edition in 1997. Progress in the field has emanated from three distinct sources. First, societies long reluctant to investigate or prosecute human rights abusers have begun to do so with greater frequency. These include both those inquiring into the abuses of their own officials or former officials, as well as those investigating or prosecuting individuals who have committed abuses in other countries. The former group includes states as different as Indonesia, Guatemala, South Africa, and Chile. Some are revisiting amnesties or other forms of immunity that had shielded former abusers from trials; others have built on the experiment with truth commissions begun in the 1980s. The latter group includes a number of European states that have initiated proceedings against civilian and military officials from Bosnia, Rwanda, Chile, Argentina, Guatemala, and elsewhere. Still others have enacted legislation providing for universal jurisdiction over international crimes. The combined effect of these domestic processes is to chip away, if only incompletely, at the culture of impunity that has characterized much of the modern attempts at accountability.

Second, the United Nations tribunals for the former Yugoslavia and Rwanda, which were just beginning the active processing of cases at the time of our first edition, have now tried a significant number of defendants, with lengthy judgments accompanying each verdict. Prosecutions are proceeding, and the result is the development of an important caselaw in international criminal law. Third, the years 1997–2000 saw the negotiation, conclusion, and preliminary implementation of the Statute of the International Criminal Court. This cooperative effort among many states has yielded both a significant treaty and a potentially valuable new mechanism for bringing individuals to justice.

Each of these three developments bears directly on the first two parts of this book—the substance of the law on accountability and the processes for accomplishing it. New enunciations and interpretations of the law have emerged, and these forays into accountability demand some appraisal, albeit tentative, regarding their promises and limitations. As for the third section of the book, the Cambodia case study, after many years of stalemate on this issue, the last several years have witnessed some moves at the international and domestic level in the direction of accountability of the Khmer Rouge. The twists and turns of the issue since 1997 demonstrate aptly the pitfalls that those seeking accountability can encounter.

Indeed, the Cambodia case highlights our view that it seems premature to speak of a revolution in favor of accountability. Investigation and trial remain the exception rather than the rule; truth commissions often avoid identifying individual perpetrators; and most foreign governments continue to give excessive deference to the affected domestic regimes, especially emerging democracies, regarding their choice of accountability mechanism or even the absence thereof. Moreover, the impact of various processes of individual accountability upon the affected societies remains amorphous. Has the evanescent idea of closure sought by advocates of trials been achieved? Does individual accountability contribute to national reconciliation? One also hastens to add that atrocities by governmental and non-governmental forces continue with impunity, whether in Sri Lanka, Kosovo, Chechnya, Sierra Leone, or the Congo. The result is hardly inexorable progress toward improvement of human dignity.

In considering these latest events, we have remained conscious of our goal of bringing coherence to a field that is metamorphosing before our eyes. In particular, we have done our utmost to avoid seeing the forest for the trees. Secondary literature in this field, especially regarding the international criminal tribunals (the focus, alas, of perhaps too many international lawyers) has mushroomed, with many new issues related to individual accountability now the subject of scholarly inquiry. Our volume does not and cannot address all the developments in this subject area, and the closest we have sought to come is to note significant secondary sources in the footnotes. Instead, this book remains a treatise for understanding the field as a whole by identifying the salient issues, elucidating their essential contours, highlighting areas that remain in flux, and offering our own views on the current state of affairs. Its audience remains the diverse participants in the international community facing decisions on accountability, whether those in governments, international organizations, the human rights community, victims groups, or advocates for targets of inquiry. We hope that this volume will serve them as a core reference for their work.

Introduction to the First Edition

More than a half-century has passed since the victorious Allies brought the leaders of the defeated Axis powers before international tribunals at Nuremberg and Tokyo. The creation of these courts represented the opening act for one of the great developments in international law since World War II—the prescription of an extensive corpus of law designed to protect all individuals from the abuses of their own governments. This law of human rights stands in contrast to the state-centric international law dominant since the late eighteenth century, which safeguarded individuals primarily *vis-à-vis* certain conduct by states other than their own—whether enemy nations (the law of war) or states where they might reside or set up a business (the law of international claims).

The Nuremberg and Tokyo trials were also a watershed for recognizing that individuals, and not merely states, are responsible for violations of human dignity, and that officials who order or commit such abuses must be held accountable. As any student of criminal law knows, such accountability serves important goals in a civil society, whether punishment, deterrence, reform, or a closure that can allow the victims (or their relatives) to move on with their lives. Although some have charged that the Allies retroactively criminalized some acts, Nuremberg and its progeny played a central role in establishing the legitimacy of international criminal law and propelled its development by the legal equivalent of light years. Just as important as their impact on the substantive law, the postwar tribunals also represented a potentially powerful precedent for enforcing that law through international courts.

The years after the war seemed to presage further advances in the international criminal law of Nuremberg, as states negotiated and concluded the Genocide Convention in 1948 and the Geneva Conventions on armed conflict in 1949, and the United Nations International Law Commission began to draft a Code of Offenses against the Peace and Security of Mankind. But the trend soon lost steam. Although the international legal process led to the prescription of an impressive body of human rights law, governments did little to develop any mechanisms for enforcing that law through sanctions against individuals. The penchant of despots and fanatics for such abuse did not, however, abate.

If Nuremberg marked the beginning of the first age of modern international criminal law, it has taken more recent slaughters for the world community to consider a revival of this law to punish human rights atrocities in war and peace. The ebbing of the Cold War unleashed a host of conflicts characterized by brutal acts that flagrantly violated the law crystallized at Nuremberg and elaborated thereafter. Ironically, the decline of Cold War rivalries also opened new opportunities for addressing such crimes, as evinced by the establishment in 1993 and 1994 of international criminal tribunals for the former Yugoslavia and Rwanda. The last few years have also seen governments and others take more seriously the idea of creating a permanent international criminal court. And the spread of democracy since the 1980s has fuelled demands for a reckoning for past human rights abuses in many countries and fostered the development of novel methods of accountability.

Can individual accountability provide a meaningful sanction for atrocities by governments and others in a position of power against those under their control? This volume seeks to shed light on this compelling issue of contemporary international law. It does so by considering the development of this law and assessing current mechanisms of accountability for violations of that law, thereby highlighting both the promises and pitfalls of individual responsibility. In examining accountability, one confronts a moral imperative for punishment, deterrence, and some form of closure; a legal landscape lacking any comprehensive criminal code and enforcement architecture; and a political environment in which governments and domestic constituencies may have sharply differing ideas of both the definition of justice and the costs of administering it to all offenders. The law thus operates within a wholly novel framework in this context compared with routine matters of domestic criminal justice.

The results of such an inquiry will have significant ramifications for transitional societies around the globe emerging from national nightmares and confronting their past, as well as for governments, human rights advocates, and others seeking to prevent, and bring to justice those responsible for, abuses elsewhere. All those involved in the administration of justice require an understanding of the complex legal setting—both the scope of the law and the available mechanisms—before undertaking any policy of individual accountability. Without authoritative guidance, emerging democratic regimes risk missteps that could undermine their credibility with the public, lead to instability as those formerly in power seek to subvert the process for their own ends, or deny due process to those accused of committing offenses. And all societies might fail to realize their legal obligations to hold individuals accountable for abuses as well as their opportunities and limitations in doing so.

Any study of individual accountability must begin with an examination of the substantive law. This requires an assessment of the place of accountability within international law, including the relationship among international human rights law, humanitarian law, and criminal law; and the particular challenges of determining the scope of crimes developed through diverse and often unconnected processes. There we find that some crimes may be well established in treaties, but too narrowly defined to address heinous acts; others may have become criminalized only through customary law, with its manifold barriers to clarity. When applied to the facts of concrete situations, the complex components of the various offenses do not always yield clear findings of criminal liability.

With the law analyzed, the challenge is then to consider the range of mechanisms that might bring justice. This necessitates appraisal of the goals of individual accountability as well as its ramifications for particular states confronting these issues. Of the variety of options available to states, some can proceed at a domestic level, but can fall prey to weak or corrupt governments, unable or unwilling to look too deeply into the past; others can take shape only by a concerted international commitment to the cause. Some offer the prospect of genuine criminal punishment, while others seek accountability through more creative, though less punitive, means. In choosing the proper mechanism for a state, ethical and legal demands must be reconciled with political realities. The results are not in all ways satisfying to our sense of ideal justice.

International human rights law, humanitarian law, and criminal law are not, then, merely a set of academic disciplines. Their value to mankind lies in the difference they might make to confronting past abuses and preventing future atrocities. As a result, an abstruse elucidation of the law and process, all too common in legal discourse, seems insufficient to demonstrate in any useful way either the complexity of the endeavor or its promise. For this reason, we include in the chapters discussing the substantive law sections examining theoretical and practical challenges to the law's application. The chapters analyzing the various mechanisms also include separate appraisals of each forum's opportunities and challenges. Together, these seek to discuss some particularly intriguing normative questions about the adequacy of the state of the law, as well as to provide readers with a sense of the difficulties of invoking and applying the rules and mechanisms of individual accountability to specific cases of atrocities.

Indeed, because of the importance we attach to the solution of contemporary problems using these tools of international law, we believe that inclusion of an individual case study, examined in full detail, is imperative. For this purpose, we analyze one of the most awful chapters of brutality since World War II: the Khmer Rouge rule over Cambodia from 1975 to 1979. This whirlwind of atrocities encompassed the torture and murder of political enemies and ethnic minorities on a massive scale, forcible evacuations of huge populations, and subjugation of much of the citizenry to exhausting labor in the countryside, leaving dead over 1.5 million of the state's 7.3 million people.

Cambodia represents an ideal case study for three reasons. First, as a historical matter, the events of this horrific period have now proved the subject of significant research by scholars, non-governmental organizations, and governments. The facts have been laid bare for all to see, permitting a more sophisticated and, one hopes, unbiased, application of the law. Secondly, as a subject for analysis under international law, the atrocities of the Khmer Rouge involve nearly every aspect of international criminal law. The regime has been accused of committing the full gamut of human rights abuses, and advocates of accountability have spoken of the need to engage the complete range of mechanisms for bringing Khmer Rouge officials to justice. This case study is thus not merely one application of the law and process, but, because it gives a picture of the whole field of accountability, one that should interest all students of this subject.

Thirdly, despite the passage of significant time, accountability has never been achieved. Global power politics delayed matters at first, and the country's domestic woes and conflicts have prolonged the impunity of the offenders. As one of the worst government-sanctioned slaughters since World War II, it deserves the attention of those concerned with accountability and those with the power to bring it about.

Our study thus proceeds in three parts. Part I provides an introduction to the substantive law that recognizes individual accountability for human rights atrocities and follows with individual chapters on the most recognized and important international crimes—genocide, crimes against humanity, and war crimes. It then considers a set of other abuses for which the international community has, in one way or another, imputed individual criminal responsibility—slavery and forced labor, torture, apartheid, and forced disappearances—as well as related offenses and defenses to criminality.

Part II examines the primary mechanisms for accountability. After a discussion of the ongoing debate over the duties and propriety of accountability, we offer separate chapters on domestic courts (both of the state where the offenses occurred and of other states), international tribunals, and three prominent non-prosecutorial processes—investigatory commissions, civil suits, and immigration measures. Following these is an overview of two critical issues necessary to building an effective case against human rights abusers—the gathering and evaluation of evidence and international judicial assistance.

Part III is the Cambodia case study. After reviewing the historical record, it considers the applicability of the crimes analyzed in Part I to the Khmer Rouge period and the possibilities for engaging the mechanisms addressed in Part II to bring about some form of accountability. The appraisal of the law and mechanisms is designed to parallel the exegeses in Parts I and II of the book.

Our final chapter offers thoughts on the future prospects for individual accountability as a method of enforcing international human rights.

Lastly, a word about our target: this is a book for all those interested in the possibility of individual accountability for human rights atrocities. We assume that some readers will have little exposure to international law and thus reiterate some issues in Chapter 1 with which some more experienced readers may wish to dispense. We hope that human rights advocates, regional specialists, civil servants in governments and international organizations, and others in the human rights community will find this volume a timely contribution to their important task.

PART I

SUBSTANTIVE LAW

1

Individual Accountability for Human Rights Abuses: Historical and Legal Underpinnings

The international legal community is beset today with talk of accountability. Governments, international organizations, non-governmental organizations, and scholars speak of the need to hold individuals responsible for official acts that violate the most cherished of international human rights. Some study the nature of various infractions with an eye toward codification; others seek to create or engage mechanisms for trying or otherwise punishing individuals. Their common mission is based on a shared understanding that international law has a role to play not only in setting standards for governments and their agents, but in prescribing the consequences of a failure to meet those standards.

To understand the promises and limitations of individual accountability as a means to protect human dignity requires treating it as a discrete subject of international law. As such, it demands appraisal of a complex amalgam of law and a wide spectrum of sanctioning processes that transcend orthodox divisions of subjects within international law. Its theory, doctrine, and practice spring from legal sources and events both ancient and modern; and ultimately an appreciation of the topic turns considerably on insights beyond international law, whether political or philosophical in origin. Before any examination of the substantive law and mechanisms can proceed, we begin with the evolution of this concept and the legal threads involved.

A BRIEF HISTORY OF INDIVIDUAL ACCOUNTABILITY

The law is no stranger to the idea of holding individuals responsible for egregious conduct toward their fellow human beings. Domestic criminal law, and part of civil law, evolved precisely to regulate this behavior. But the application of this law when those committing the conduct acted with the authority of the state has followed a far less certain path. For centuries, in tyrannical states, governmental officials could act with impunity; and while the rise of liberal government over the past some 300 years has led to an overall improvement in the human rights records of some states, it has not, until very recently, opened the door to punishment of those officials who might continue to violate fundamental individual rights. Exceptions exist, of course, from older times, such as the prominent trials of British soldiers for the killing in 1770 of five citizens of Boston protesting Britain's quartering of soldiers (and the subsequent acquittal of most of them).[1] But the overall historical pattern was effective immunity from prosecution under domestic law for officials carrying out governmental acts. This pattern applied to those following the policies of Stalin, Hitler, or Mao, each with their millions of victims, or those in other countries—including democracies otherwise committed to the rule of law—who resorted with less intensity to murdering, torturing, or otherwise abusing opponents.

International law, for its part, had little to contribute on this issue for most of its history as well. As defined by the positivist school that dominated the field from the late eighteenth century, it governed principally relations between states (and between their sovereigns), with individuals usually at best third-party beneficiaries. The notion that the law would even govern behavior of governments *vis-à-vis* their own citizens, let alone prescribe accountability for individuals for misconduct, was anathema to the entire exercise. In that respect, internal sovereignty was, until early in the twentieth century, nearly complete and insulated from the law of nations.

The only areas of international law that systematically addressed violations of individual rights by states concerned actions by governments against citizens of *other* states—acts deemed an affront to those states and thus within the ambit of international law.[2] In doctrinal terms, these fell in two areas—the law of state responsibility for injury to aliens, which primarily dealt with disruption of property interests of aliens by foreign states but also included attacks on individual persons; and the laws and customs of war, which recognized certain limitations on the conduct of war that thereby promoted some individual rights in wartime.[3] The latter

[1] *See* 1 Peleg W. Chandler, American Criminal Trials 301–415 (1841, reprinted 1970); Hiller B. Zobel, The Boston Massacre (1970).

[2] *See generally* Karl Josef Partsch, *Individuals in International Law*, *in* 2 Encyclopedia of Public International Law 957, 959–60 (Rudolph Bernhardt ed., 1995). The only notable exception to this general pattern concerned attempts to abolish slavery, which were based on an abhorrence of the practice, rather than its affront to any state. International law addressed another offense against individuals—piracy—but that crime, by definition, involved persons not under the control of any government. In addition, international law regarded attacks on diplomats as a crime as well. *See, e.g.*, U.S. v. Ortega, 24 U.S. (11 Wheat) 467 (1826).

[3] *See generally* Myres S. McDougal, Harold D. Lasswell, and Lung-Chu Chen, Human Rights and World Public Order: The Basic Policies of an International Law of Human Dignity 181–82 (1980).

had ancient origins and applications, dating back at least to the Chinese warrior Sun Tzu in the sixth century B.C.E., its modern incarnation born in the mid-nineteenth century with Jean-Henri Dunant's creation of the International Committee of the Red Cross. By the early part of the twentieth century, the Law of the Hague (so named due to the treaties drafted there) had recognized some constraints on methods of warfare, while the Law of Geneva imposed certain duties toward enemy civilians and soldiers no longer engaged in battle.[4] But even the law of war traditionally was mostly silent in terms of mandating specific consequences for individuals who violated it. The 1899 and 1907 Hague Conventions and the 1929 Geneva Convention on prisoners of war lacked any penal provisions, and the 1929 Geneva Convention on the Wounded and the Sick in Armies had only a weak provision.[5] Nevertheless, some states developed sophisticated domestic codes punishing such violations, and prosecution of soldiers for war crimes dates back at least to the Middle Ages.[6]

The shortcomings of international law regarding personal responsibility for government-sponsored abuses of human rights began to change after World War I, and even more so after World War II. This change in the law flowed directly from the new scale of destruction brought about by these global conflagrations and manifested itself in two ways: first, the beginning of a trend in international law directly mandating some individual criminal accountability for violations of the laws of war; and secondly, the evolution of a corpus of law prescribing limits upon a government's conduct toward its own citizens, in times of peace and war—what is today referred to as international human rights law. These two trends would eventually marry in the Nuremberg trials and their aftermath. (A third constitutive shift in international law, toward the outlawing of war entirely, also transpired during this period.)

[4] *See generally* GEOFFREY BEST, WAR AND LAW SINCE 1945, at 39–59 (1994); Leslie C. Green, *International Regulation of Armed Conflict*, *in* 1 INTERNATIONAL CRIMINAL LAW 355, 365–68 (M. Cherif Bassiouni ed., 2d ed. 1999).

[5] *See* Convention for the Amelioration of the Condition of the Wounded and Sick in Armies in the Field, July 27, 1929, art. 30, 118 LNTS 303, 329 (mandating inquiry and that belligerents 'repress it as promptly as possible').

[6] Timothy L. H. McCormack, *From Sun Tzu to the Sixth Committee: The Evolution of an International Criminal Law Regime*, *in* THE LAW OF WAR CRIMES: NATIONAL AND INTERNATIONAL APPROACHES 31, 32–43 (Timothy L. H. McCormack and Gerry J. Simpson eds., 1997); Yves Sandoz, *Penal Aspects of International Humanitarian Law*, *in* 1 INTERNATIONAL CRIMINAL LAW, *supra* note 4, at 393, 393–401; Leo Gross, *The Punishment of War Criminals: The Nuremberg Trial*, 2 NETH. INT'L L. REV. 356, 358 (1955); James W. Garner, *Punishment of Offenders Against the Laws and Customs of War*, 14 AJIL 70 (1920); *cf.* L. C. Green, *International Crimes and the Legal Process*, 29 INT'L. AND COMP. L.Q. 567, 570 (1980) (noting precursors to individual responsibility among classical writers). Among the most significant was the Lieber Code, promulgated by President Abraham Lincoln in 1863. Instructions for the Government of Armies of the United States in the Field, General Orders No. 100, Apr. 24, 1863, *reprinted in* THE LAWS OF ARMED CONFLICTS: A COLLECTION OF CONVENTIONS, RESOLUTIONS, AND OTHER DOCUMENTS 3 (Dietrich Schindler and Jirí Toman eds., 1973).

With respect to accountability, following World War I, the Allies created a fifteen-member commission to look into the question of war crimes. In its report to the 1919 Preliminary Peace Conference, the majority of the commission found that the Central Powers had committed numerous acts 'in violation of established laws and customs of war and the elementary laws of humanity',[7] and the Allies eventually inserted into the Treaty of Versailles three articles providing for the punishment by Allied military tribunals of persons accused of violating the laws and customs of war.[8] However, the Allies never held any trials, accepting instead a small number of trials at Leipzig by the German government, and developments in the law of war did not substantially move toward individual accountability for violations thereof.[9] As for the development of international human rights law, the inter-war period saw the conclusion of numerous treaties aimed at protecting minorities in the many new or redrawn states of Europe. While hardly effective at—and perhaps counterproductive to—stopping the rise of Nazism and the outbreak of World War II, the League of Nations' system of minorities treaties did prescribe clear legal protections for certain citizens *vis-à-vis* their own government.[10]

Without doubt, however, the watershed for the development of the principle of individual accountability for human rights abuses was the exercise undertaken by the international community following the previously unimaginable atrocities of World War II, particularly the Holocaust. The creation of the International Military Tribunal at Nuremberg and the related war crimes trials evinced a decision by the Allies that individual officials bear personal responsibility for outrageous conduct toward their own citizens and foreigners during wartime and ought to be held accountable. As a result, the IMT Charter provided for individual criminal responsibility for violations of the laws and customs of war, as well as other egregious acts in connection with the war encompassed under the rubric of 'crimes against humanity'. It also criminalized the war itself, and indeed made the initiation of aggressive war the chief crime of the Nazis.[11] The IMT Charter also eliminated the defenses of superior orders,

[7] Commission on the Responsibility of the Authors of the War and on Enforcement of Penalties, *Report Presented to the Preliminary Peace Conference, March 29, 1919*, *reprinted in* 14 AJIL 95, 115 (1920).

[8] Treaty of Peace, June 28, 1919, arts. 228–30, 225 Consol. T. S. 188, 285–86. The Treaty also indicted the Kaiser himself for starting the war and provided for his trial, but the Netherlands refused to hand him over for trial. On crimes against humanity, *see* Ch. 3, *infra*.

[9] Sandoz, *supra* note 6, at 397–98.

[10] *See* Patrick Thornberry, International Law and the Rights of Minorities 38–52 (1991); Francesco Capotorti, Study on the Rights of Persons belonging to Ethnic, Religious and Linguistic Minorities 16–26 (1991), UN Sales No. E.91.XIV.2.

[11] IMT Charter, art. 6(a).

command of law, and act-of-state immunity, thereby subjecting even heads of state to criminal liability. These principles were included in the Charter of the Tokyo Tribunal and in Control Council Law No. 10, the latter of which governed many significant prosecutions of Nazis below the level of those tried before the IMT, and were endorsed by the UN General Assembly in 1946.

Nuremberg had at least three jurisprudential progeny concerning the protection of individuals. First, it paved the way for the International Committee of the Red Cross to lead the effort to codify anew the law of armed conflict, dubbed international humanitarian law, in the 1949 Geneva Conventions and, later, the two 1977 Protocols thereto.

Secondly, although the IMT Charter, strictly speaking, addressed atrocities only in connection with the war, Nuremberg proved a springboard for the development of international human rights law, as much of the international community came to conclude that a government's treatment of its citizens in peacetime was appropriate for general international regulation. The new United Nations took the lead in developing an international 'bill of rights' and other instruments, eventually to include: the Universal Declaration of Human Rights; the Convention on the Prevention and Punishment of the Crime of Genocide; the International Convention on the Elimination of All Forms of Racial Discrimination; the International Covenants on Civil and Political Rights and on Economic, Social, and Cultural Rights; the Convention on the Elimination of All Forms of Discrimination Against Women; the Convention against Torture and Other Cruel, Inhuman or Degrading Treatment or Punishment; and the Convention on the Rights of the Child. Oversight mechanisms grew within both international organizations and non-governmental organizations.[12]

Thirdly, Nuremberg also laid the groundwork for further elaboration of international law on individual criminal responsibility for violations of international humanitarian and human rights law. For violations of the law of armed conflict, the Geneva Conventions and Protocol I include provisions for individual culpability for certain violations and obligate states to prosecute offenders.[13] Beyond war, as stated by the UN War Crimes Commission in 1948, the IMT Charter

> presupposes the existence of a system of international law under which individuals are responsible to the community of nations for violations of rules of international criminal law, and according to which attacks on the fundamental liberties and constitutional rights of peoples and individual[s] . . . constitute international

[12] For excellent studies, *see generally* McDougal et al., *supra* note 3; Human Rights in International Law: Legal and Policy Issues (Theodor Meron ed., 1984); Guide to International Human Rights Practice (Hurst Hannum ed., 3d ed. 1999); International Human Rights in Context: Law, Politics, Morals (Henry J. Steiner and Philip Alston eds., 2d ed 2000).

[13] *See* Ch. 4, *infra*.

crimes not only in time of war, but also, in certain circumstances, in time of peace.[14]

But the process of elaborating such non-war-related crimes after World War II proved more *ad hoc* than concerted. As explained further below, the development of human rights treaties creating obligations for states translated into rules for individual accountability for breach of these obligations in only a handful of cases, most notably genocide, slavery, and torture.

The first significant effort to create a comprehensive regime of individual criminality began in 1947, when the General Assembly asked the International Law Commission to elaborate the principles in the IMT Charter and judgment and draft a Code of Offenses against the Peace and Security of Mankind that would include certain serious violations of human rights. But this process staggered along slowly; after formulating the Nuremberg principles in 1950 and completing a Draft Code in 1954, the ILC suspended work until 1983 because some states insisted that the General Assembly first reach a definition of aggression (the first crime in the Draft Code). From 1983 to 1996, it debated anew the definitions of crimes and the scope of the list, completing a new Draft Code in 1996.

Nevertheless, for most of the post-war period, these processes to make new human rights and humanitarian law were accompanied by very little action by governments to bring to justice individuals committing atrocities (and indeed very little action against states as well). Most governmental officials who abused human rights could count on impunity from their own courts, and the tensions and mistrust of the Cold War stymied any possibility of creating any international mechanisms to bring abusers to justice. With few exceptions, the international regime on individual accountability existed on paper alone.

The most recent *étape* toward promoting individual accountability under international law resulted from two distinct developments beginning in the early 1980s. First, the transition from autocratic rule to some form of democracy in numerous countries, beginning in South America but extending to Eastern Europe and parts of Africa, Central America, and Asia, has caused new governments to devise strategies for coming to terms with the human rights abuses of prior regimes and, in some cases, guerrilla opposition groups. In most cases where societies have decided to seek accountability, they have charted their own course under domestic law, creating mechanisms tailored to their individual circumstances. This pattern has led to criminal trials, truth commissions, and other methods—although impunity through *de jure* or *de facto* amnesties remains the policy in many states. In two cases, El Salvador and Guatemala, the peace

[14] United Nations War Crimes Commission, History of the United Nations War Crimes Commission and the Development of the Laws of War 192–93 (1948).

accords ending the conflict itself provided for an international truth commission. Whether or not these developments suggest the emergence of a duty on states to hold human rights abusers accountable, they clearly highlight the increasing acceptance by states of the need for such a reckoning and the diverse range of mechanisms available.

Secondly, the horrendous atrocities committed in the former Yugoslavia and Rwanda in the early and mid-1990s goaded many governments, prompted by the United States, to seek criminal accountability for them through the creation of two international tribunals. The former situation has concerned primarily violations of international humanitarian law, the latter crimes outside armed conflict. And both have entailed significant atrocities by persons not traditionally regarded as governmental agents. Through carefully drafted statutes passed by the UN Security Council, states have taken to defining acts incurring individual culpability with more precision and devised a judicial mechanism that provides the full range of protections to the accused. Although the Council created these courts as substitutes for robust international action to stop and prevent the atrocities in those two regions, their impact has been significant. By 2000, both had a significant number of defendants in custody and were actively undertaking prosecutions.

These developments, in turn, heightened interest among the UN's members in creating a permanent international criminal court. This process gained significant momentum in the mid-1990s. After nearly four years of contentious negotiations, a diplomatic conference adopted a statute in Rome in July 1998. It contains both detailed definitions of crimes and procedures for prosecutions.

FOUR BODIES OF LAW

The result of this process, born principally in the ashes of World War II, has been a gradual increase in the scope of legal protection afforded to the individual and of the consequences for those who violate that duty of protection. From a time when individuals were barely 'subjects' of international law, governments now have many affirmative obligations toward all persons within and without their territory, during war and peace; and the importance of these obligations has served to raise the violation of some of them to include criminal responsibility of offenders. In a word, the accountability of individuals has grown with the liability of governments.[15]

[15] *See* Steven R. Ratner, *New Democracies, Old Atrocities: An Inquiry in International Law*, 87 Geo. L.J. 707, 714–15 (1999). On whether governments are bound to hold individual officials accountable for human rights abuses, *see* Ch. 7, *infra*.

A study of individual accountability for human rights atrocities as a discrete subject must consider four interrelated bodies of law. To focus on only one or two of these is to miss the full picture of individual accountability. First, *international human rights law* refers to the body of international law aimed at protecting the human dignity of the individual. Developed in largest part since World War II, it principally seeks to guarantee the rights of persons *vis-à-vis* their own government, but also protects them against other actors in the international community that might violate those rights.

Secondly, *international humanitarian law*, a far older concept, is, as noted, synonymous with the law governing the conduct of armed conflict. It addresses both limits on warmaking methods (the Law of the Hague) and protections of certain individuals during wartime (the Law of Geneva).[16]

Thirdly, we must appraise the content of *international criminal law*, a term whose very definition has given rise to much debate.[17] For our purposes, the term refers broadly to the international law assigning criminal responsibility for certain particularly serious violations of international law. This seemingly straightforward definition, however, obscures a core difficulty in clarifying the nature of both international criminal law and an international crime—namely, what does it mean to say that international law assigns criminal responsibility?

A conceptual roadblock would appear to bar the way, one that originates in the hybrid nature of the field—a combination of international law and criminal law. For international criminal law involves the inculpation of individuals, but is developed and enforced by the actions of states. It must address, and reconcile, the dichotomies between its two sets of constituent parts: international law's principal focus upon the obligations of states vs. criminal law's concern with the obligations of individuals; and international law's general lack of vertical prescription and enforcement processes vs. the centrality of both to criminal law.[18] In at least this latter sense, the two fields seem to resemble antipodes more than complements.

Thus, determining the extent to which international law recognizes

[16] For an excellent introduction to the relationship between these first two bodies of law, *see* Louise Doswald-Beck and Sylvain Vité, *International Humanitarian Law and Human Rights Law*, 293 INT'L REV. RED CROSS 94 (1993).

[17] *See, e.g.*, Georg Schwarzenberger, *The Problem of an International Criminal Law*, 3 CURR. LEGAL PROBS. 263 (1950), *reprinted in* INTERNATIONAL CRIMINAL LAW 3 (Gerhard O. W. Muller and Edward M. Wise eds., 1965); M. Cherif Bassiouni, *The Sources and Content of International Criminal Law: A Theoretical Framework*, *in* 1 INTERNATIONAL CRIMINAL LAW, *supra* note 4, at 3.

[18] *See* M. Cherif Bassiouni, *An appraisal of the growth and developing trends of international criminal law*, 45 REV. INT'L DROIT PÉNAL 405, 426–27 (1974).

individual responsibility necessitates an inquiry that takes account of the law's need both to elaborate the crime and to prescribe the role for states. This process requires examining three subsidiary issues that in essence correspond to different strategies for providing international criminal responsibility. First, to what extent does international law *directly provide for individual (or other) culpability*? Secondly, to what extent does international law *obligate* some or all states or the global community at large to try and punish, or otherwise sanction, offenders? And thirdly, to what extent does international law *authorize* these same actors to try and punish, or otherwise sanction, offenders? For example, international law can explicitly provide for individual criminality or require states to make an act a crime under domestic law, or both, as does the Genocide Convention. It can obligate states or an international court to carry out prosecutions or punishment, as with the Genocide Convention or the Geneva Conventions, or to extradite or prosecute offenders, as with the Torture Convention.[19] Or it can simply allow states or international courts to try and punish individuals for certain acts, irrespective of normal jurisdictional limits.[20] These strategies have been combined to a certain extent in the Security Council's Statutes for the Yugoslavia and Rwanda Tribunals and the Statute for the International Criminal Court.[21]

The strategies by which the law provides for individual criminal responsibility can form the basis for various lists of international crimes.[22] The community's reliance on all three strategies suggests that a violation of international law becomes an international crime if the global community intends through any of those strategies (regardless of whether they are implemented through treaty, custom, or other prescriptive method) to hold individuals directly responsible for it.[23] This catholic approach contrasts with methods proffering strict doctrinal criteria that yield a small list of crimes under international law.[24] Yet the debate over the definition of an

19 *See* Ch. 8, A Jurisdictional Primer, *infra*.

20 *See* Yoram Dinstein, *International Criminal Law*, 20 Isr. L. Rev. 206, 222–25 (1985); *cf.* Harvard Research in International Law, Part IV–Piracy, 26 AJIL (Supp.) 739, 757 (1932) (piracy as a crime against the law of nations only in the sense of universal jurisdiction to prosecute).

21 *See, e.g.*, SC Res. 827, para. 2, UN SCOR, 48th Year, Res. and Dec., at 29, 29, UN Doc. S/INF/49 (tribunal's purpose is 'prosecution of persons responsible for serious violations of international humanitarian law'); ICC Statute, arts. 1 ('jurisdiction over persons for the most serious crimes of international concern'), 17 (rules on admissibility).

22 *See, e.g.*, Dinstein, *supra* note 20, at 207–25; Bassiouni, *supra* note 17, at 46–62 (finding twenty-five international crimes).

23 *See Tadic Interlocutory Appeal*, para. 128; Theodor Meron, *International Criminalization of Internal Atrocities*, 89 AJIL 554, 562 (1995); *see also infra* text at notes 43–44 (on possibility of international crimes by states).

24 For examples of such approaches, *see* Hans-Heinrich Jescheck, *International Crimes*, *in* 2 Encyclopedia of Public International Law, *supra* note 2, at 1119, 1120–22 (four international crimes); William T. D'Zurilla, *Individual Responsibility for Torture under International Law*, 56 Tulane L. Rev. 186, 199–202 (1981) (treaty or custom must specify individual criminality under

international crime is ultimately of less importance to the suppression of these acts than the specific strategies and methods chosen by states to provide for individual accountability.[25] The effectiveness of the international law regime will turn on such factors as whether the relevant law mandates or merely authorizes prosecution; and whether it provides for jurisdiction by one state, several states, all states, or an international tribunal.[26]

Although international criminal law shares some of the goals and methods of international human rights and humanitarian law, there is far from a perfect congruence of the first with the other two. Rather, the focus of international human rights law and humanitarian law is upon the prescription of norms for the protection of the individual in peace and war. Those norms are usually formulated as obligations upon states, whether to refrain from certain conduct or to provide remedies in case of their commission. But to the extent that those two bodies of law address accountability of the individual for their violation, they overlap with international criminal law. Geometrically, the three bodies of law might be seen as three circles or rings, each of which overlaps with the other two. For example, certain major human rights treaties, such as the Torture Convention, and humanitarian law treaties, such as the Geneva Conventions, contain penal provisions creating individual responsibility.

International criminal law should thus be viewed as but one of the alternatives along a continuum to enforce international human rights or humanitarianism, with criminality a means of enforcement when other methods prove inadequate.[27] Moreover, international criminal law

international law); Bruno Simma and Andreas L. Paulus, *The Responsibility of Individuals for Human Rights Abuses in Internal Conflicts: A Positivist View*, 93 AJIL 302, 308 (1999) (distinguishing between *delicta juris gentium* and direct international responsibility); *see also* International Responsibility for the Promulgation and Enforcement of Laws in Violation of the Convention, Inter-Am. Ct. Hum. Rts. Advisory Opinion OC-14/94, Dec. 9, 1994, 1994 ANN. REP. INTER-AM. CT. HUM. RTS. 89, 100 (1995) (individual responsibility only for 'violations that are defined in international instruments as crimes under international law') [hereinafter 1994 IACHR Advisory Opinion]. As Hersch Lauterpact wrote many years ago,

> As in the case of international rights so also in the matter of international duties the accurate approach to ascertaining the legal position is to rely not on preconceived notions as to the capacity of individuals to be subjects of international law but, primarily, on the practice of States in both the international and municipal spheres.

HERSCH LAUTERPACHT, INTERNATIONAL LAW AND HUMAN RIGHTS 38 (1950).

[25] *Cf.* RESTATEMENT (THIRD) OF THE FOREIGN RELATIONS LAW OF THE UNITED STATES § 404, Reporter's Note 1, at 255 (1987) ('Whether piracy is an international crime, or is rather a matter of international concern as to which international law accepts the jurisdiction of all states, may not make an important difference.').

[26] *See* Bassiouni, *supra* note 17, at 110–15 (direct vs. indirect enforcement).

[27] *Cf.* Bassiouni, *supra* note 18, at 405–06; W. Michael Reisman, *Institutions and Practices for Restoring and Maintaining Public Order*, 6 DUKE J. COMP. AND INT'L L. 175 (1995).

addresses numerous acts beyond the area of human rights or the conduct of armed conflict, such as hijacking, narcotics offenses, traffic in obscene publications, and, according to some, the initiation of aggressive war.[28]

But under what circumstances will international law hold an individual criminally responsible for violations? As a starting point, states, courts, and others participating in the lawmaking process agree that most violations of international law do not incur individual criminal responsibility.[29] But the question of which violations of international law, including human rights and humanitarian law, do entail such accountability is somewhat unsettled.[30] At the least, the international community must share a consensus on the gravity of these offenses and appropriate means of enforcement.[31] Alas, states do not yet regard many violations of international humanitarian and human rights law, including some truly cruel and heinous conduct, as criminal in nature. International criminal law thus does not 'incorporate' all humanitarian or human rights law.

Instead, international criminal law has adopted a more cautious course, criminalizing only certain acts against the person. In general, those acts—what this volume refers to as 'atrocities'—are characterized by the directness and gravity of their assault upon the human person, both corporeal and spiritual.[32] Most significant in this context are genocide, war crimes, and crimes against humanity. As discussed in the chapters below, they share a special status among acts incurring individual responsibility due to both their extreme seriousness and their historical pedigree, arising from early international humanitarian law (war crimes) or the immediate aftermath of World War II (crimes against humanity and genocide). The disagreements over definitional issues related to them do not shield a consensus on the existence of individual criminal responsibility. A second tier of crimes, not specifically associated with the history of war or World War II, has developed through more *ad hoc* processes—slavery and forced labor, torture, apartheid, and forced disappearances.

28 For a discussion of crimes against peace, *see* Ch. 5, *infra*.

29 *See* SECRETARY-GENERAL OF THE UNITED NATIONS, THE CHARTER AND JUDGMENT OF THE NÜRNBERG TRIBUNAL 45–46 (1949), UN Doc. A/CN.4/5, UN Sales No. 1949.V.7.

30 NGUYEN QUOC DINH, DROIT INTERNATIONAL PUBLIC 621 (Patrick Daillier and Alain Pellet eds., 5th ed. 1994).

31 M. Cherif Bassiouni, *The Proscribing Function of International Criminal Law in the Processes of International Protection of Human Rights*, 9 YALE J. WORLD PUB. ORD. 193, 195–96 (1982); Theodor Meron, *Is International Law Moving towards Criminalization?*, 9 EJIL 18, 24 (1998); Quincy Wright, *The Scope of International Criminal Law: A Conceptual Framework*, 15 VIRG. J. INT'L L. 561, 562–63 (1975).

32 *Cf.* Agnes Heller, *The Limits to Natural Law and the Paradox of Evil*, *in* ON HUMAN RIGHTS: THE OXFORD AMNESTY LECTURES 149, 154–55 (Stephen Shute and Susan Hurley eds., 1993) ('genuinely heinous crimes' and 'manifestations of evil'). Traditionalists might refer to these as serious violations of international human rights and humanitarian law.

This corpus of offenses may also be divided along different lines. A first group might be termed the generic offenses—genocide, crimes against humanity, war crimes, and (more recently and more ambiguously) apartheid. These crimes encompass a broad array of specific acts, such as murder or torture, but are defined in terms of, and limited by, general elements. Thus, in order to be criminal, the particular acts must take place in a certain context, pattern, or setting—e.g., against a particular group with an intent to destroy it (genocide), in a mass or systematic manner (crimes against humanity), or during armed conflict (war crimes). The remainder would be regarded as specific offenses—slavery, forced labor, torture, and forced disappearances. These cover only specified enumerated acts, or at least a fairly narrow range of conduct, but generally (though not always) these acts are criminal regardless of the circumstances (e.g., target, scale, or setting) in which they take place.

Nevertheless, the results of the international legal process of criminalization are far from completely logical. A particular assault on an individual may or may not incur individual responsibility depending upon arguably arbitrary distinctions—whether it takes place during war or peace, in an international conflict or a civil war, or whether it is an isolated act or part of a pattern. As will be discussed later, these schisms leave disturbing gaps in criminality under international law.[33]

Lastly, the *domestic law* of states encountering human rights abuses is pertinent to our study. That law will criminalize many human rights and law of war violations as common crimes. Moreover, states may implement their obligations under international law to suppress certain acts through domestic statutes that criminalize such behavior. They may also promulgate domestic statutes that go beyond their treaty obligations (e.g., a requirement to criminalize only genocide committed on their soil) by criminalizing acts under broad jurisdictional bases permitted under customary international law (e.g., by making genocide a crime under domestic law wherever committed). Domestic and international courts interpreting the material and mental elements of international offenses will often have recourse to domestic law analogies.[34] Domestic law may also provide the legal framework for other methods of accountability, such as investigatory commissions, individual civil liability, and immigration measures.

[33] *See* Steven R. Ratner, *The Schizophrenias of International Criminal Law*, 33 Texas Int'l L.J. 237 (1998).

[34] For a criticism of one supreme court's approach to this question, *see* Irwin Cotler, *International Decisions: Regina v. Finta*, 90 AJIL 460 (1996); *see also Erdemovic Sentencing Appeal*, op. McDonald and Vohrah, paras. 59–66, and *id.*, dissenting op. Cassese, paras. 1–6.

THE NATURE OF LEGAL RESPONSIBILITY

An additional task of clarification involves the lexicon of accountability. The terms 'individual responsibility' (or accountability) and 'criminal responsibility' (or accountability) are often used interchangeably. In fact, the two terms are neither coextensive nor opposite, but address different facets of the law's concern with responsibility for human rights violations. The former concerns a *target* of responsibility for human rights atrocities. Indeed, there would appear to be three such targets, enabling us to speak of individual, group, or state responsibility. The term criminal responsibility, however, addresses the *nature* of the responsibility. In this sense, domestic and international law recognize two broad categories: civil and criminal responsibility.

These targets and forms of accountability, however, interact in less than evident ways. For instance, responsibility for violations of most areas of international law is generally placed under the rubric of state responsibility. It entails only one set of targets—states—because most obligations under international law are placed upon states. And though the term civil is little used to qualify that responsibility, it is indeed civil (as opposed to criminal) in that it entails certain duties of reparation on the part of the state.[35] Thus, *state (civil) responsibility* arises whenever a state fails to comply with applicable human rights or humanitarian law, whether by abusing individuals through domestic law or action or, in some cases, even by failing to provide a remedy for a victim or refusing to prosecute a culprit. International law has recognized *group civil responsibility* (or tort liability) for abuses, in particular for organized non-state actors such as guerrilla or secessionist movements.[36] International law has also accepted determinations by individual states to impose *individual civil responsibility* for human rights abuses through civil liability under domestic law, an issue explored in Chapter 10.

With respect to criminal liability for acts against human dignity, the Nuremberg and other prosecutions of Axis defendants clearly established *individual criminal responsibility* for crimes against peace, crimes against humanity, and war crimes.[37] This concept received global endorsement when the General Assembly affirmed the principles of law from the Nuremberg judgment in 1946 and the ILC formulated these principles in

[35] *See, e.g.*, ROSALYN HIGGINS, PROBLEMS AND PROCESS: INTERNATIONAL LAW AND HOW WE USE IT 162 (1994); Wright, *supra* note 31, at 565–66; DINH, *supra* note 30, at 621.

[36] Such entities may become parties to international agreements and would assume responsibility for violating them. *See, e.g.*, Law of Treaties, Third Report by G. G. Fitzmaurice, Special Rapporteur, UN Doc. A/CN.4/115, *reprinted in* 1958 [II] ILC Y.B. 20, 24.

[37] *See, e.g.*, 22 IMT Trials at 465–66.

1950.[38] In the years that followed, international humanitarian, human rights, and other criminal law instruments including, most recently, the ICC Statute, have all reflected the principle of criminal responsibility. International law today firmly recognizes the principle of individual criminal responsibility for certain violations of international law.[39] Individual responsibility extends beyond governmental officials to private persons, depending upon the definition of the particular crime.[40] As noted earlier, the more difficult issue has turned on determining which violations of human rights and humanitarian law entailing state (civil) responsibility also lead to individual criminal accountability.

With respect to *group criminal responsibility*, Article 9 of the Nuremberg Charter authorized the Tribunal to find any group or organization criminally responsible for offenses under the Charter.[41] It remains unclear, however, whether international law generally imposes criminal responsibility on groups and organizations. For example, the Genocide Convention imposes such responsibility only on individuals, not on political organizations or other non-natural persons, with the possible exception of states. However, international criminal law does recognize notions of conspiracy, complicity, and command responsibility, thereby inculpating individuals who may not have served as the immediate perpetrators of the crimes.[42]

State criminal responsibility for certain violations of international law has proved to be exceptionally controversial. The criminality of violations by a state of certain core norms of international law received support in the ILC's 1980 Draft Articles on State Responsibility, which finds state criminal responsibility for breach of 'an international obligation so essential . . . that its breach is recognized as a crime by that community as a whole', and lists aggression, colonial domination, slavery, genocide, and

[38] GA Res. 95(I), UN Doc. A/64/Add.1, at 188 (1946); Report of the International Law Commission to the General Assembly, UN Doc. A/1316 (1950), *reprinted in* 1950 [II] ILC Y.B. 364, 374.

[39] 1994 IACHR Advisory Opinion, *supra* note 24, at 100; ICC Statute, art. 25; S.C. Res. 1264, Sept. 15, 1999, preamb. para. 13; OPPENHEIM'S INTERNATIONAL LAW 505–08 (Robert Jennings and Arthur Watts eds., 9th ed. 1992); Dietrich Oehler, *Criminal Law, International*, *in* 1 ENCYCLOPEDIA OF PUBLIC INTERNATIONAL LAW, *supra* note 2, at 877, 880–81.

[40] *See* ICTY Statute, art. 7(1) (not limiting culpability to governmental officials); United States v. Flick et al., 6 CCL No. 10 Trials 1187, 1192 ('Acts adjudged criminal when done by an officer of the government are criminal also when done by a private individual.'); Report of the International Law Commission on the work of its forty-third session, UN Doc. A/46/10, *reprinted in* 1991 [II] 2 ILC Y.B. 103–04.

[41] Individuals could be held criminally responsible for membership in an organization found to be criminal, though only if they had knowledge of the organization's criminal purpose or acts. Roger S. Clark, *Apartheid*, *in* 1 INTERNATIONAL CRIMINAL LAW, *supra* note 4, at 643, 646 n.16; Jordan J. Paust, *Superior Orders and Command Responsibility*, *in* 1 INTERNATIONAL CRIMINAL LAW, *supra* note 4, at 223, 223–24.

[42] *See* Ch. 6, Related Crimes, *infra*.

apartheid as examples.[43] This position, however, has been repeatedly challenged, principally by Western states and scholars, for the lack of a clear distinction between crimes and non-criminal violations of international law (delicts), as well as the consequences in terms of permissible responses in the event of a crime of state.[44] Because the focus of this volume remains on individual accountability, we simply note that international criminal law, to the extent it has developed to cover violations of human rights, has centered on individual culpability, on the theory that personal accountability and punishment will serve as the best deterrent.

Thus, this study remains focused upon one core set of targets—individuals, those who actually commit violations of human rights. As for the nature of their liability, it addresses principally criminal responsibility, although it also considers civil liability under domestic law. Moreover, it recognizes that states may choose to punish those responsible for international crimes and other violations of human rights through non-prosecutorial mechanisms.

METHODOLOGY AND SOURCES OF INTERNATIONAL LAW

In determining the relevant norms of international law, we have relied upon the law as a product of a variety of processes among multiple actors making claims in the international arena. The ways in which international law is made, short-handedly referred to as the 'sources' of international law, are numerous, each offering distinct challenges to the analyst and decision-maker to determine the degree of authoritativeness and accompanying mechanisms for compliance of any purported rule. For the benefit of those unaccustomed to these processes of formation, they are reviewed briefly, without any attempt to engage the major debates surrounding this critical subject of international law.

The Traditional Starting Point

For the sake of a common denominator, we note the traditional list of

[43] Report of the International Law Commission to the General Assembly on the work of its thirty-second session, UN Doc. A/35/10, *reprinted in* 1980 [II] 2 ILC Y.B. 32 (article 19 of draft articles); *see generally* Report of the International Law Commission to the General Assembly on the work of its twenty-eighth session, UN Doc. A/31/10, *reprinted in* 1976 [II] 2 ILC Y.B. 95–122.

[44] For a complete account of the varying views, *see* International Crimes of State: A Critical Analysis of the ILC's Draft Article 19 on State Responsibility (Joseph H. H. Weiler et al. eds., 1989). The ILC renewed consideration of Article 19 at its 1995 session, though it remained divided on whether to include the concept of state criminal responsibility. *See* Report of the International Law Commission on the work of its fiftieth session, UN GAOR, 53d Sess., Supp. No. 10, paras. 260–331, UN Doc. A/53/10 (1998).

sources provided in Article 38(1) of the Statute of the International Court of Justice, which identifies the law to be applied by that court:

1. international conventions;
2. international custom as evidence of a general practice accepted as law;
3. general principles of law recognized by civilized nations; and
4. judicial decisions and the teachings of the most highly qualified publicists, as subsidiary means for the determination of rules of law.

With respect to *international conventions*, or treaties, the primary source of guidance for their interpretation is the Vienna Convention on the Law of Treaties.[45] Generally, treaties are to be interpreted in accordance with the ordinary meaning given to their terms in their context and in light of the treaty's object and purpose.[46] Where the general rule leaves the treaty's meaning unclear or leads to an absurd or unreasonable result, decision-makers may resort to certain supplementary means of interpretation, in particular any subsequent agreement or practice between the parties, and, if necessary, its drafting history (*travaux préparatoires*).[47]

Customary international law is, by contrast, a far more unstructured method for prescription of law, and its identification necessitates more careful scrutiny. Legal authorities have formulated numerous approaches and theories to determine whether a norm has achieved the status of customary international law. The most common formulation, one adopted by the International Court itself, stipulates two basic requirements: (1) that the norm be reflected in consistent state practice, and (2) that the practice be adhered to out of a sense of legal obligation (*opinio juris*).[48] Nevertheless, great debate surrounds the degree of consistency required to show state practice and on the necessity of, and requirements to demonstrate, *opinio juris*—especially in the area of human rights law.[49]

General principles of law, as used in the ICJ statute, refers generally to those principles of domestic law common to the world's major legal systems. Yet the International Court of Justice has interpreted this neither

[45] May 23, 1969, 1155 UNTS 331 [hereinafter Vienna Convention]. Although the United States is not a party to the Vienna Convention, it recognizes most of its provisions as binding under customary international law; RESTATEMENT (THIRD) OF THE FOREIGN RELATIONS LAW OF THE UNITED STATES pt. III, Introductory Note (1987).

[46] Vienna Convention, *supra* note 45, art. 31(1), 1155 UNTS at 340.

[47] *Id.* art. 32, 1155 UNTS at 340.

[48] North Sea Continental Shelf (FRG/Den.; FRG/Neth.), 1969 ICJ 3, 45 (Feb. 20).

[49] *See* the excellent discussions in Bruno Simma and Philip Alston, *The Sources of Human Rights Law: Custom, Jus Cogens, and General Principles*, 12 AUSTRALIAN Y.B. INT'L L. 82 (1992); Jordan J. Paust, *The Complex Nature, Sources and Evidences of Customary Human Rights*, 25 GA. J. INT'L AND COMP. L. 147 (1995/96); Arthur M. Weisburd, *The Effect of Treaties and Other Formal International Acts On the Customary Law of Human Rights*, 25 GA. J. INT'L AND COMP. L. 99 (1995/96).

as a mere analogy to national laws nor as generalizations reached through the processes of comparative law, but as something more fundamental—in the words of Shabtai Rosenne, as 'particularizations of a common underlying sense of what is just in the circumstances'.[50] Among the more commonly used general principles are good faith, reliance, and the duty of reparation for damages, although the notion may encompass broader notions from natural law, including certain human rights norms.[51] At the same time, international tribunals tend to examine such principles only if they fail to find an applicable rule of conventional or customary law.[52]

Judicial decisions covers a broad body of case law. While the ICJ relies extensively upon its own previous decisions as well as those of its predecessor (the Permanent Court of International Justice), other decision-makers typically cite other tribunals, whether domestic or international, considered authoritative. While many courts deny any obligation to follow previous decisions strictly, they tend to accord significant weight to precedent and attempt to develop a consistent international case law.[53] The teaching of *publicists* is synonymous with scholarly work, with a correspondingly greater deference to leading authorities in a field. Both of these sources, however, are subsidiary to and of less value than treaties, custom, and general principles of law.

Other Important Conceptual Underpinnings

Article 38's listing of sources offers a formalistic, undynamic, and limited sense of the entire process of law prescription, including the diversity of participants and the difficulties of appraising pretended law from actual law.[54] For instance, it omits one of the most significant methods by which international law has evolved—the practice of *international organizations*. These include resolutions and other decisions of political organs, in particular the UN Security Council and General Assembly. Decisions of the Council represent binding international law, akin to treaties, by virtue of Article 25 of the UN Charter; Assembly resolutions may constitute highly influential or recommended positions, or strong evidence of an

[50] 3 Shabtai Rosenne, The Law and Practice of the International Court, 1920–1996, at 1605 (3d ed. 1997). The reference to 'civilized nations' has been tacitly dropped. *Id.* at 1601–02 n. 81. *See also* Bin Cheng, General Principles of Law as Applied by International Courts and Tribunals (Grotius Pubs. 1987) (1953); Max Sørenson, *Principes de Droit International Public*, 101 Recueil des Cours 1, 16–34 (1960-III).

[51] Oscar Schachter, International Law in Theory and Practice 51–55 (1991).

[52] *Id.* at 52.

[53] 3 Rosenne, *supra* note 50, at 1609–12.

[54] Myres S. McDougal and W. Michael Reisman, *The Prescribing Function in the World Constitutive Process: How International Law is Made*, *in* International Law Essays 355, 362–68 (Myres S. McDougal and W. Michael Reisman eds., 1981).

emergent or emerging custom.[55] In addition, the studies and projects by subsidiary organs, such as the International Law Commission or the Commission on Human Rights, can have significant weight, as do other, less formal indicia of their actions.[56]

Moreover, certain norms have special characteristics in contemporary international law. Obligations *erga omnes* are those norms of international law that a state owes not merely to another state with which it interacts on a certain issue, but to the international community as a whole.[57] Most importantly, international law recognizes certain peremptory norms that override even treaties to the contrary. These norms of *jus cogens* reflect core constitutive values and commitments of the international community. They include the ban on aggression, certain essential human rights principles, and the supremacy of the United Nations Charter over other treaties.[58]

We readily acknowledge the relatively recent development of much of the law considered here and the general unwillingness of governments to prosecute for offenses from the late 1940s to the early 1990s. This dearth of state practice means that treaties often cannot be interpreted in terms of actual subsequent conduct (as required under the Vienna Convention), and customary law proves especially difficult to ascertain. Reliance is thus placed upon the statements of governments as evidence of their belief about the meaning of law where more concrete evidence (such as decisions regarding specific offenders) is lacking.[59] Although this approach may have analytical shortcomings, it seems consistent with the appraisal method of courts and scholars evaluating human rights norms, even if they differ on the exact methodology and the category of the resultant norms (custom vs. general principles).[60] Nevertheless, the talk of governments in favor of a particular customary norm cannot generally override a practice by states contrary to it.

Thus, our linchpin for the determination of the law is, as it must be, whether it 'is viewed as authoritative by those to whom it is addressed and . . . its audience concludes that the prescriber . . . intends to and, indeed,

[55] *See generally* HIGGINS, *supra* note 35, at 22–28.

[56] 1 OPPENHEIM'S INTERNATIONAL LAW, *supra* note 39, at 50.

[57] Barcelona Traction, Light & Power Co. (Second Phase) (Belg. v. Spain), 1970 ICJ 3, 32 (Feb. 5).

[58] *See* IAN BROWNLIE, PRINCIPLES OF PUBLIC INTERNATIONAL LAW 514–17 (5th ed. 1998). On the human rights aspects, *see* MCDOUGAL ET AL., *supra* note 3, at 338–50.

[59] *See Tadic Interlocutory Appeal*, para. 99 ('In appraising the formation of customary rules or general principles [of international humanitarian law] . . . reliance must primarily be placed on such elements as official pronouncements of States, military manuals and judicial decisions.'); Richard Baxter, *Multilateral Treaties as Evidence of Customary International Law*, 41 BRIT. Y.B. INT'L L. 275, 300 (1965–66).

[60] *See* Simma and Alston, *supra* note 49, at 90–106; Pinochet, [1999] All E.R. at 151–52 (Lord Hope).

can make it controlling'.[61] Yet the lack of authoritative jurisprudence on some issues, and competing jurisprudence on others, leads to many areas of ambiguity and uncertainty. Thus, for example, certain crimes may have never been the subject of a court judgment. Others may be defined differently in various domestic and international instruments, interpreted differently by various domestic and international courts, or both. The discussion and analyses that follow note numerous interpretive disputes, and, as seen in the case study in Part III, they suggest that definitive conclusions as to the criminal responsibility of individuals for some violations of law may be impossible or conjectural.[62]

THE PRINCIPLES OF LEGALITY: *NULLUM CRIMEN SINE LEGE* AND RELATED CONCEPTS

A fundamental precept of international criminal law is the prohibition in international and domestic law on assigning guilt for acts not considered as crimes when committed. The maxim *nullum crimen sine lege, nulla poena sine lege*, or 'no crime without law, no punishment without law', captures this notion, which finds different forms in various legal contexts. These include constitutional prohibitions on *ex post facto* laws, judicial rules of construction limiting the use of analogy in interpreting criminal laws, doctrines prohibiting ambiguous criminal laws, and provisions in international human rights instruments barring prosecutions for acts not criminal at the time of their commission.[63] This has a clear methodological impact on those seeking accountability if the law has changed over time. They can appraise conduct only in terms of the law in effect when those crimes occurred, even if later developments have made additional acts criminal.

More importantly, in the context of *international* criminal law, *nullum crimen* has a special dimension. Unlike the domestic criminal law of most countries, much of international criminal law is not codified in treaties or any other agreed code. As a result, the 'law' required for criminality under the *nullum crimen* maxim, at the international level, comes to include not merely conventional (i.e., treaty-based) law but also customary and other

[61] McDougal and Reisman, *supra* note 54, at 377; Carlos S. Nino, *The Duty to Punish Past Abuses of Human Rights Put Into Context: The Case of Argentina*, 100 YALE L.J. 2619, 2621 (1991) ('a necessary criterion for the validity of any norm of ... positive international law is the willingness of...states and international bodies to enforce it.'). *Cf.* Weisburd, *supra* note 49, at 99–111.

[62] *Cf.* Paust, *supra* note 49, at 150 ('If there is a core of settled meaning, measure it. . . . If new *opinio* or practice has torn the core apart, measure this also.')

[63] *See, e.g.*, US CONST. art. I, § 9, cl. 3; M. CHERIF BASSIOUNI, CRIMES AGAINST HUMANITY IN INTERNATIONAL LAW 127–40 (2d ed. 1999) (exhaustively discussing domestic law principles); ICCPR, art. 15, 999 UNTS at 177.

law.[64] This interpretation is, however, fraught with dangers for defendants in criminal cases, who may face judges with different methodologies and approaches to the derivation of custom or other law. Moreover, over-reliance on scholarly writings, where progressive views often seek to move the law forward, could instead lead to prosecutions that run afoul of defendants' rights.[65]

The precise contours of *nullum crimen* received extensive discussion during and after the Nuremberg trials, where the defendants asserted that the charges against them—in particular that of waging a war of aggression—were not crimes as of 1939. The International Military Tribunal took an extremely loose and controversial view of *nullum crimen* in 1946 with regard to the issue of the criminality of aggressive war. The court saw it as 'a principle of justice' and merely stated that it would be unjust to let those who violate treaties go unpunished since 'the attacker must know that he is doing wrong'.[66] It thereby completely evaded the critical distinction between violations of international law and individual criminal culpability for these violations.[67]

The International Covenant on Civil and Political Rights adopts a more ambiguous stance, allowing prosecutions for acts 'criminal according to the general principles of law recognized by the community of nations', which suggests that international criminality might flow directly from widely accepted domestic criminality.[68] In setting up the international tribunal for the former Yugoslavia, the UN took an extremely cautious position, permitting the court to 'apply rules . . . which are beyond any doubt part of customary law';[69] and the Statute of the International Criminal Court resolves any ambiguities in the definition of a crime in

[64] *See, e.g.*, BASSIOUNI, *supra* note 63, at 140–45; STÉFAN GLASER, DROIT INTERNATIONAL PÉNAL CONVENTIONNEL 199–200 and n. 1 (1970) (appropriate term is *nullum crimen sine iure*, i.e., no crime without law in the sense of a norm but not necessarily a code); Fourth Report on the draft Code of Offences Against the Peace and Security of Mankind, by Mr. Doudou Thiam, Special Rapporteur, UN Doc. A/CN.4/398 (1986), *reprinted in* 1986 [I] 1 ILC Y.B. 53, 70–72.

[65] Hans W. Baade, *Individual Responsibility, in* THE FUTURE OF THE INTERNATIONAL LEGAL ORDER 291, 324–25 (Cyril E. Black and Richard A. Falk eds., 1972); *see also* Gerry J. Simpson, *War Crimes: A Critical Introduction, in* THE LAW OF WAR CRIMES, *supra* note 6, at 1, 11–13.

[66] 22 IMT Trials at 462.

[67] For attacks on the judgment, *see, e.g.*, George A. Finch, *The Nuremberg Trial and International Law*, 41 AJIL 20 (1947); for views of some leading scholars defending the trials for crimes against the peace, *see* Quincy Wright, *The Law of the Nuremberg Trial*, 41 AJIL 38, 55–61 (1947); 2 OPPENHEIM'S INTERNATIONAL LAW 190–93 (Hersch Lauterpacht ed., 7th ed. 1952). This approach was not necessary for the criminalization of war crimes and most crimes against humanity.

[68] ICCPR, art. 15(2), 999 UNTS at 177.

[69] Report of the Secretary-General pursuant to paragraph 2 of Security Council Resolution 808 (1993), May 3, 1993, UN Doc. S/25704, at 9. Of course, the existence of rules that are accepted by all states does not imply that all states have accepted that violations thereof incur individual criminal responsibility. The Secretary-General's report seems to address this gap when it suggests that each of the four offenses in the Tribunal's statute was also firmly established in international law as well. *See id.* at 10–13.

favor of the defendant.[70] The judges of the Yugoslavia Tribunal have differed sharply on the extent to which teleological or policy-oriented interpretations of international criminal law are consistent with *nullum crimen*.[71] Some scholars have taken a broader view of *nullum crimen* (though not as broad as the IMT), to suggest it protects defendants only from punishment for acts that they reasonably believed to be lawful when committed.[72]

The approach one adopts to *nullum crimen* directly affects one's legal conclusions regarding the criminality of certain acts, especially in those large areas for which no treaty authoritatively defines the crime. While accepting the Nuremberg Tribunal's strategy for punishing Nazi war criminals for outrageous acts against the peace, we believe its standard of conflating illegality of state action and criminality of individuals no longer reflects the mainstream of expectations of states on *nullum crimen* and cannot be generally sustained. Rather, *nullum crimen* requires an examination of the *criminal* law at the time of the offenses.

At the same time, the analyses in this volume are not limited by the strict standard of the Yugoslavia Tribunal Statute, i.e., 'beyond doubt'. We explore areas of law where doubts remain, and express our views of the state of the law even with such doubts. Indeed, we do not wish to preclude a theory under which persons could be held responsible for particularly outrageous human rights abuses even if the law did not assign criminality to the acts at the time of commission.[73] Ultimately, the mechanism chosen by a state or states for accountability will need to adopt its own interpretation of *nullum crimen* and determine how clear the norm needs to be to inculpate individuals. Domestic courts have already undertaken this exercise in some recent prosecutions of World War II Nazis, offenders from the conflicts in the former Yugoslavia and Rwanda, and others. And the International Criminal Court, whose statute has detailed definitions of crimes, will have its own view as well. Mechanisms that do not have the right to impose a deprivation of liberty on the defendant, such as investigatory commissions, would seem to have more leeway on this question than criminal tribunals.

[70] ICC Statute, art. 22.

[71] *Compare Celebici Judgment*, para. 170, and *Erdemovic Sentencing Appeal*, op. McDonald and Vohrah, para. 78 (need to consider policy) *with id.*, dissenting op. Cassese, para. 11 (rejecting 'policy-oriented approach in the area of criminal law').

[72] *See* Meron, *supra* note 23, at 566; Christopher Greenwood, *International Humanitarian Law and the* Tadic *Case*, 7 EJIL 265, 281 (1996); Jordan J. Paust, *It's No Defense:* Nullum Crimen, *International Crime and the Gingerbread Man*, 60 ALBANY L. REV. 657, 664–79 (1997).

[73] *Cf.* Hans Kelsen, *Will the Judgement in the Nuremberg Trial Constitute a Precedent in International Law?*, 1 INT'L L.Q. 153, 165 (1947) (obligation to punish offenders from World War II 'more important than [compliance] with the rather relative rule against ex post facto laws, open to so many exceptions'); *Eichman*, 36 ILR at 281–3.

Finally, *nullum crimen* does not serve to exculpate all those who committed atrocities under the color of the law or rules in effect at the time. In other words, the promulgation of new rules by a regime violating human rights does not change the international law or criminality of the offenses. This is particularly true with respect to laws that violate those fundamental, peremptory norms (*jus cogens*) at the core of international protection of the individual. The Nuremberg Tribunals definitively rejected this claim with respect to defenses that Nazi law and practice sanctioned various abuses.[74] Those regimes claiming to build a 'new order' through abrogation of law or its replacement by law not meeting minimal human rights standards cannot walk away from international norms. Domestic law that permits or encourages atrocities may, however, relate to the accused's knowledge of the law and provide a possible defense to lower level officials.[75]

A WORD ON CULTURAL RELATIVISM

Much of the law elaborated in this study reflects the strong influence of Western states and scholars on the development of international law over the past several centuries. It may, then, seem odd to seek to invoke these norms in non-Western countries with potentially different views on individual criminal liability, especially for state-sponsored offenses. For example, Eastern cultures have unique normative outlooks on criminal law, whether on the sources of norms, means of compliance, or sanctions.[76] Cultural resistance to the application of these 'Western' norms may be entrenched, and any invocation of them must be sensitive to concerns that foreigners are imposing their values on these states. In one notable example, when the UN Human Rights Commission voted to set up a commission of inquiry to investigate atrocities in East Timor following its 1999 referendum on independence, all Asian states on the Commission opposed or abstained on the resolution.[77]

We nonetheless believe the exercise is ethically appropriate because of the fundamental universality of human rights law. The Universal

[74] *See* 22 IMT Trials at 465–66; United States v. Alstoetter et al. (the '*Justice Case*'), 3 CCL No. 10 Trials 954, 983–84; *see also Eichmann*, 36 ILR at 47–48. *Cf.* CARLOS SANTIAGO NINO, RADICAL EVIL ON TRIAL 163–64 (1996) (resorting to domestic law as solution to retroactivity problem).

[75] *See* Ch. 6, Appraising the Defenses under International Law—Superior Orders and Ignorance of the Law, *infra*.

[76] *See, e.g.*, APIRAT PETCHSIRI, EASTERN IMPORTATION OF WESTERN CRIMINAL LAW: THAILAND AS A CASE STUDY 106–48 (1987).

[77] *See* Comm'n Hum. Rts. Res. 1999/S-4/1, Sept. 27, 1999; *see also* MARK J. OSIEL, OBEYING ORDERS: ATROCITY, MILITARY DISCIPLINE & THE LAW OF WAR 140–43 (1999); José E. Alvarez, *Crimes of States/Crimes of Hate: Lessons from Rwanda*, 24 YALE J. INT'L L. 365, 436–52 (1999).

Declaration of Human Rights affirms the global nature of these rights. The acceptance by states of a right of oversight (*droit de regard*) by international organizations over domestic human rights practices, the signature by non-Western states of numerous human rights and humanitarian law conventions, including the ICC Statute, and UN attempts to expand these norms all testify to the idea that they no longer represent simply Western preferences. In the criminal arena in particular, all states criminalize the most atrocious abuses against the human person, and near-universally accepted treaties single out certain offenses such as genocide and war crimes. States from Southern Africa to Eastern Europe are groping with the need for accountability for the abuses of prior regimes. They will clearly take different paths to that goal, in terms of both detailed elaboration of the law and recourse to different mechanisms (prosecutorial and otherwise), all of which international law may well permit. But the underlying criminality of the abuses can and should be measured to a large degree by an objective standard, which international and domestic law have developed.

2

Genocide and the Imperfections of Codification

Governments and human rights organizations have often termed genocide the most heinous international crime. Emerging from the traumatic barbarism of the Holocaust, genocide has typically been regarded a part of the genus of crimes against humanity. Yet unlike the other crimes against humanity, genocide has been authoritatively codified in a single, widely accepted international instrument—the Genocide Convention of 1948. The Genocide Convention has lent a stability to the definition of genocide that has eluded the other crimes against humanity, but its definition of the crime remains controversial. Moreover, the treaty has clearly not prevented genocide in the post-World War II world, to which tragic events in such varied places as Rwanda, Yugoslavia, and Cambodia attest. Until the late 1990s, there were very few prosecutions for the crime, the Israeli prosecution of Adolf Eichmann being the most famous and authoritative of these. The creation of the UN tribunals for the former Yugoslavia and Rwanda have altered this pattern, with the ICTR offering a series of genocide convictions of high-level officials. As a result, the corpus of legal guidance for interpreting the Genocide Convention's ambiguities and lacunae, so limited for many years, is now slowly expanding. Genocide remains a central conceptual component of international criminal law and international human rights law.

BACKGROUND AND PREPARATION OF THE GENOCIDE CONVENTION

Although human history has witnessed many acts of genocide, the concept of the crime of genocide is relatively new and developed primarily in the aftermath of the Nazi atrocities of World War II. The term 'genocide' finds its origins in the work of the jurist Raphaël Lemkin, a primary proponent of an international convention on the subject. Lemkin's definition of the term centered on the requirement of a coordinated plan to destroy the 'essential foundations' of the life of a group, with the aim of eliminating the group. In his words,

> The objectives of such a plan would be disintegration of the political and social institutions, of culture, language, national feelings, religion, and the economic

existence of national groups, and the destruction of the personal security, liberty, health, dignity, and even the lives of the individuals belonging to such groups. Genocide is directed against the national group as an entity, and the actions involved are directed against individuals, not in their individual capacity, but as members of the national group.[1]

The term 'genocide' received its first formal, legal recognition in the context of the Nuremberg trials. Although the Charter of the Nuremberg Tribunal did not expressly use the term, the definition of crimes against humanity provided in Article 6(c) of the Charter covered many acts today constituting genocide; the indictment of the war criminals tried before the Tribunal expressly charged the defendants with genocide; and the prosecution made reference to the term during the proceedings.[2] Though the term did not appear in the Tribunal's judgment, it discussed in detail acts that would today qualify as genocide, and the term was expressly used in many of the subsequent trials of Nazis.[3]

The UN General Assembly initiated the process of elaborating the Genocide Convention in 1946 with the unanimous passage of Resolution 96(I).[4] The resolution, *inter alia*, affirmed genocide to be a crime under international law carrying individual responsibility, invited member states to take measures to prevent and punish it, and requested the Economic and Social Council to undertake studies of genocide with a view to the preparation of a draft convention on the subject. What followed was a rather circuitous, though by contemporary UN standards a relatively expeditious, process of elaborating such a convention.[5] Following the passage of Resolution 96(I), the Economic and Social Council requested the Secretary-General to prepare a draft convention with the assistance of a group of experts on international and criminal law.[6] The Secretary-General's draft

1 RAPHAËL LEMKIN, AXIS RULE IN OCCUPIED EUROPE 79 (1944).

2 *See* 1 IMT Trials at 43–44; Study of the Question of the Prevention and Punishment of the Crime of Genocide, prepared by Nicodème Ruhashyamiko, July 4, 1978, UN Doc. E/CN.4/ Sub.2/416, at 5–6 [hereinafter 1978 Genocide Study]; LEO KUPER, THE PREVENTION OF GENOCIDE 9, 174 (1985); Matthew Lippman, *The Drafting of the 1948 Convention on the Prevention and Punishment of the Crime of Genocide*, 3 B.U. INT'L L.J. 1, 4 (1985).

3 For several cases where the term 'genocide' was used in connection with Nazi offenders, *see* 1978 Genocide Study, *supra* note 2, at 7, 154–63. *See also* Matthew Lippman, *The 1948 Convention on the Prevention and Punishment of the Crime of Genocide: Forty-Five Years Later*, 8 TEMP. INT'L AND COMP. L.J. 1, 7–9 (1994).

4 GA Res. 96(I), UN Doc. A/64/Add.1, at 188–89 (1946). Resolution 96(I) described genocide as follows: 'Genocide is a denial of the right of existence of entire human groups, as homicide is the denial of the right to live of individual human beings; such denial of the right of existence shocks the conscience of mankind, results in great losses to humanity in the form of cultural and other contributions represented by these human groups, and is contrary to moral law and to the spirit and aims of the United Nations.'

5 For a detailed description of the procedural history of the Convention, *see* 1947–48 UN Y.B. 595–99, UN Sales No. 1949.I.13; 1948–49 UN Y.B. 953–62, UN Sales No. 1950.I.11.

6 ESC Res. 47(IV), UN Doc. E/325, at 33–34 (1947). Among the experts consulted was Raphaël Lemkin.

convention[7] was then submitted to the member states for their comments and subsequently transmitted to the General Assembly. After referring the draft convention and comments to the Sixth Committee, the General Assembly requested ECOSOC to continue work on the draft convention and to submit a revised draft to the Assembly at its 1948 session.[8] ECOSOC created an *Ad hoc* Committee on Genocide composed of seven states to prepare a new draft convention based on the Secretary-General's draft and the comments of the member states.[9] ECOSOC then transmitted the *Ad hoc* Committee's new draft convention[10] to the General Assembly, where the Sixth Committee considered it in detail and submitted it to a drafting sub-committee of thirteen states. The Sixth Committee then adopted the revised draft and, on December 9, 1948, the General Assembly unanimously adopted it as the final version of the Convention.[11] The Convention entered into force on January 12, 1951. One hundred and thirty states have acceded to the Convention.[12]

As the product of a negotiating process, the Genocide Convention represents a political compromise that departs in several important respects from the treatment of genocide in the works of Lemkin, the Nuremberg principles, and Resolution 96(I). Nevertheless, international law now regards the Convention as the authoritative codification of the basic legal principles relating to genocide.

Article I declares genocide to be a crime under international law, whether committed in time of peace or war, thus definitively freeing the crime from the nexus with war crimes or crimes against peace required at Nuremberg (see Chapter 3). Articles II and III, the heart of the Convention, define genocide and enumerate the acts made punishable by the Convention, namely genocide, conspiracy to commit it, direct and public incitement of it, and complicity in it.[13] Article IV, reflecting the Nuremberg principles, provides for individual responsibility, including that of government officials, for genocide. Article V requires parties to enact legislation giving effect to the Convention, while Articles VI and VII stipulate principles on jurisdiction and extradition. Article VIII permits parties recourse to the UN in the case of violations of the Convention, and Article IX provides for dispute resolution by the

[7] Draft Convention on the Crime of Genocide, June 26, 1947, UN Doc. E/447 [hereinafter Report of the Secretary-General].

[8] GA Res. 180(II), UN Doc. A/519, at 129–30 (1947).

[9] ESC Res. 117(VI), UN Doc. E/734, at 19–20 (1948).

[10] Report of the *Ad hoc* Committee on Genocide, UN ESCOR, 7th Sess., Supp. No. 6, UN Doc. E/794/Corr.1 (1948) [hereinafter Report of the *Ad hoc* Committee].

[11] GA Res. 260A(III), UN Doc. A/760, at 9 (1948).

[12] Multilateral Treaties, ch. IV.1; *see also* Genocide Convention, art. XIV, 78 UNTS at 284.

[13] On these related offenses, *see* Ch. 6, *infra*.

International Court of Justice. (The remaining provisions relate to administrative or technical matters.)

That the drafters did not intend the Convention to be a codification of the Nuremberg Charter and judgment is evident from both its terms and its drafting history. Most notably, the Convention covers only a portion of the acts prosecuted at Nuremberg and expressly eliminates any required nexus between those acts and armed conflict. In addition, unlike Nuremberg, the Convention does not address the issue of superior orders. Finally, the framers of the Convention demonstrated their intention to codify a crime distinct from the precedent of Nuremberg by rejecting proposals to refer to Nuremberg and crimes against humanity in the text of the Convention.[14]

DEFINITION OF GENOCIDE

Article II of the Convention defines 'genocide' as:

> [A]ny of the following acts committed with intent to destroy, in whole or in part, a national, ethnical, racial, or religious group, as such:
> (a) Killing members of the group;
> (b) Causing serious bodily or mental harm to members of the group;
> (c) Deliberately inflicting on the group conditions of life calculated to bring about its physical destruction in whole or in part;
> (d) Imposing measures to prevent births within the group;
> (e) Forcibly transferring children of the group to another group.

Thus, genocide is comprised of three main elements: (1) the commission of at least one of the acts enumerated in Article II(a) through (e); (2) the direction of that act at one of the enumerated types of groups; and (3) the intent to destroy the group in whole or in part. It is evident from the language of Article II that it covers the commission of certain acts against specified groups with a specific intent and does not require the complete annihilation of a group.[15] The Convention's definition of genocide is deliberately more limited than many commentators and governments would have preferred, partly as a result of concern that a broader definition would impede the Convention's ratification.[16] Indeed, a preoccupation with securing the widest possible adherence to the Convention was a constant motif throughout the drafting process and explains its relatively conservative approach in a number of areas.

14 *See* NEHEMIAH ROBINSON, THE GENOCIDE CONVENTION: A COMMENTARY 54–55 (1960); Lippman, *supra* note 2, at 38–40.

15 *See, e.g.*, ROBINSON, *supra* note 14, at 57–61; *Akayesu Judgment*, para. 497.

16 *See, e.g.*, Report of the Secretary-General, *supra* note 7, at 16–17 (stressing need to ensure that Convention's definition does not overlap with other areas of law, divert attention from Convention's purpose, or impede ratification).

The Enumerated Acts

The enumeration of genocidal acts in Article II is exhaustive, as opposed to illustrative.[17] While certain of the acts are straightforward enough, others are rather vague. The *travaux* of the Convention suggest the need to focus on an act's potential to cause the physical destruction of a group in determining whether it constitutes a proscribed act.[18]

In the case of Article II(b), nothing in the Convention and little in the *travaux* defines the term 'serious bodily or mental harm'. Some have opined that the provision probably requires that any mental harm be of a serious enough nature that it would tend to lead to the destruction of the target group in order to constitute genocide, though the Convention does not require that such harm be permanent.[19] The *travaux* indicate that some members of the Sixth Committee contemplated the coerced use of drugs as an act falling under that clause.[20] The Israeli trial court that convicted Adolf Eichmann considered the following acts to constitute harm: 'the enslavement, starvation, deportation and persecution of . . . Jews and . . . their detention in ghettos, transit camps and concentration camps in conditions which were designed to cause their degradation, deprivation of their rights as human beings, and to suppress them and cause them inhumane suffering and torture'.[21] The Rwanda Tribunal has stated that the term clearly includes bodily or mental torture, inhuman treatment, and persecution, and found guilt for acts of rape and mutilation.[22]

With respect to the 'conditions of life' contemplated by Article II(c), the *Eichmann* court held that the clause included acts against victims sent to concentration camps as part of the Final Solution and put to hard labor with the intention of ultimately killing them, but who in fact remained

[17] *Akayesu Judgment*, para. 499; 1978 Genocide Study, *supra* note 2, at 13–14. Although several delegations in the Sixth Committee had earlier indicated an intention that the enumeration of acts not be restrictive, the Committee ultimately rejected a Chinese amendment to make the enumeration explicitly non-exhaustive. UN GAOR 6th Comm., 3d Sess., 78th mtg. at 142–45, UN Doc. A/633 (1948). Although the 1954 Draft Code of Offenses against the Peace and Security of Mankind contained an illustrative list of acts, 1954 ILC Report, at 151 (art. 2(10)), more recent texts, including the final version, have contained an exhaustive list, 1996 ILC Report, at 85–87 (art. 17); *see also* ICC Statute, art. 6 (exhaustive list).

[18] *See, e.g.*, John Webb, *Genocide Treaty—Ethnic Cleansing—Substantive and Procedural Hurdles in the Application of the Genocide Convention to Alleged Crimes in the Former Yugoslavia*, 23 Ga. J. Int'l and Comp. L. 377, 392–93 (1993).

[19] *See, e.g.*, Bunyan Bryant, *Part I: Substantive Scope of the Convention, in The United States and the 1948 Genocide Convention*, 16 Harv. Int'l L.J. 683, 686, 693–96 (1975).

[20] *See* Genocide: Draft Convention and Report of the Economic and Social Council, Report of the Sixth Committee, Dec. 3, 1948, UN Doc. A/760, at 3 [hereinafter Report of the Sixth Committee]; Bryant, *supra* note 19, at 694.

[21] *Eichmann*, 36 ILR at 238. The court's judgment was based on an Israeli law which uses the same definition as that found in the Genocide Convention, only applied to the Jewish people.

[22] *Akayesu Judgment*, paras. 502–04, 705–07; *Kayishema and Ruzindana Judgment*, para. 547.

alive.[23] Nehemiah Robinson, one of the leading commentators on the Convention, has emphasized that it is impossible to enumerate in advance such conditions and that determinations can be made only in the context of each case. Nevertheless, he offers as examples placing a group on a subsistence diet, reducing medical services below a certain minimum level, and withholding sufficient living accommodation.[24] The ICTR endorsed these examples, focusing on methods that lead to the slow death of the victims.[25] As for 'measures to prevent births' in Article II(d), Robinson opines that, in addition to clear cases such as sterilization, acts such as separation of the sexes and prohibition of marriage would qualify, and the Rwanda Tribunal has offered other examples.[26]

Both ECOSOC and the General Assembly devoted substantial attention to the subject of 'cultural genocide'. The Secretary-General's and *Ad hoc* Committee's drafts both included it, but the Sixth Committee and the General Assembly plenary rejected it during their deliberations.[27] Generally, 'cultural genocide' refers to acts aimed at the destruction of a group by elimination of its cultural attributes, as opposed to the actual physical destruction of the group. The Secretary-General's and the *Ad hoc* Committee's draft provisions on cultural genocide included such acts as prohibiting the use of a language and destroying or preventing the use of libraries, museums, places of worship, or other cultural institutions or objects. Opposition to the inclusion of cultural genocide focused on the following considerations: that the concept of cultural genocide was not susceptible to adequate definition, thereby potentially giving rise to abusive and illegitimate claims of genocide; that it might interfere with legitimate efforts by states to foster a national community and civilize 'primitive' peoples; that the destruction of a group's cultural attributes did not rise to the level of physical destruction, the main concern of the Convention; that the subject was more appropriately left to the realm of human rights; and that its inclusion might prevent states from joining the Convention.[28]

[23] *Eichmann*, 36 ILR at 235–36.

[24] ROBINSON, *supra* note 14, at 63–64.

[25] *Akayesu Judgment*, paras. 505–06; *Kayishema and Ruzindana Judgment*, paras. 114–17.

[26] ROBINSON, *supra* note 14, at 64; *Akayesu Judgment*, paras. 507–08 (rape where child will bear rapist's group identity); *see also* Report of the Secretary-General, *supra* note 7, at 20–21; Lippman, *supra* note 3, at 34 (includes sterilization and forced abortion).

[27] *See* Report of the Sixth Committee, *supra* note 20, at 3; UN GAOR 6th Comm., 3d Sess., 83d mtg. at 206, UN Doc. A/633 (1948); UN GAOR, 3d Sess., 179th plen. mtg. at 847–48, UN Doc. A/633 (1948). One act originally classified as cultural genocide, forced transfer of children, was retained in the final version of the Convention.

[28] *See, e.g.*, Report of the *Ad hoc* Committee, *supra* note 10, at 7; ROBINSON, *supra* note 14, at 64–65; Lippman, *supra* note 2, at 44–45, 58–59. While they may not constitute genocidal acts in and of themselves, acts aimed at the destruction of cultural attributes would presumably provide strong evidence of genocidal intent. *See* text at note 49, *infra*.

One other notable omission from the Convention has important potential implications for the analysis of forced migrations, such as acts of 'ethnic cleansing' in the former Yugoslavia, under the rubric of genocide. Specifically, during the Convention's preparation the drafters rejected a proposal to include measures intended to force members of a group to abandon their homes in order to escape the threat of ill-treatment.[29] Nevertheless, several sources correctly take the view that mass deportations under inhumane conditions may constitute genocide if accompanied by the requisite intent. The ILC, for example, has opined that deportations carried out with genocidal intent would fall under Article II(c) of the Convention.[30] Likewise, the UN Commission of Experts for the former Yugoslavia found that ethnic cleansing had been carried out through the following acts which it concluded could fall under the Convention: 'murder, torture, arbitrary arrest and detention, extra-judicial executions, rape and sexual assaults, confinement of civilian population in ghetto areas, forcible removal, displacement and deportation of civilian population, deliberate military attacks or threats of attacks on civilians and civilian areas, and wanton destruction of property'.[31] In addition to the sources referred to above, various UN-appointed experts have examined whether acts committed against certain groups qualify as genocide.[32]

The Office of the Prosecutor of the ICTY and ICTR has indicated that it considers genocide to be the most serious offense over which the Tribunals have jurisdiction and that, in determining whether an act is genocidal, it will be guided by the Convention's primary focus on

[29] UN GAOR 6th Comm., 3d Sess., 82d mtg, at 184–86, UN Doc. A/633 (1948); 1978 Genocide Study, *supra* note 2, at 24.

[30] 1996 ILC Report, at 91–92.

[31] Final Report of the Commission of Experts Established Pursuant to Security Council Resolution 780 (1992), May 27, 1994, UN Doc. S/1994/674, at 33 [hereinafter Yugoslavia Commission Final Report]. The commission defined 'ethnic cleansing' as the 'rendering [of] an area ethnically homogenous by using force or intimidation to remove persons of given groups from the area'. *Id.* Unfortunately, the commission merely stated its conclusion on this issue without explaining its reasoning. *See also* Application of the Convention on the Prevention and Punishment of the Crime of Genocide (Bosnia and Herzegovina v. Yugo.), 1993 ICJ 325, 431–32 (Sept. 13) (sep. op. Lauterpacht) (also finding ethnic cleansing in the form of forced migrations to constitute genocide); GA Res. 47/121, UN GAOR, 47th Sess., Supp. No. 49, at 44, UN Doc. A/47/49 (1992) (declaring ethnic cleansing in former Yugoslavia a form of genocide).

[32] *See*, *e.g.*, Report of the Group of Experts for Cambodia established pursuant to General Assembly resolution 52/135, paras. 61–65, *in* Identical Letters dated 15 March 1999 from the Secretary-General to the President of the General Assembly and the President of the Security Council, Mar. 16, 1999, UN Doc. A/53/850-S/1999/321, Annex [hereinafter Cambodia Group of Experts Report]; Revised and updated report on the question of the prevention and punishment of the crime of genocide, prepared by B. Whitaker, July 2, 1985, UN Doc. E/CN.4/Sub.2/1985/6, at 16 [hereinafter 1985 Genocide Study]; Study concerning the question of apartheid from the point of view of international penal law, Feb. 15, 1972, UN Doc. E/CN.4/1075, chap. VI(b). This last report presents a somewhat politicized treatment of the subject and its conclusions are, therefore, of limited authoritative value.

preventing the physical destruction of groups. Accordingly, the Prosecutor has limited charges of genocide to especially heinous acts capable of directly contributing to the physical destruction of a group. As of mid-2000, only a handful of the defendants publicly indicted by the ICTY have been charged with genocide. In light of the more clearly genocidal nature of the violence in Rwanda, the ICTR has charged all its defendants with genocide or genocide-related offenses.

Protected Groups

Article II specifies national, ethnical, racial, and religious groups as those against whom the enumerated acts must be committed in order to constitute genocide. It does not address the attributes that define these groups, and neither the *travaux* nor commentary on the Convention adds much clarification, perhaps on the assumption that such questions tend to be relatively clear-cut. In fact, these issues are very complex, though the social sciences provide useful resources for exploring them.

A 1978 Human Rights Commission study on genocide notes several definitional questions and attempts to shed light on them by quoting various definitions, many of which are inconsistent with each other. The study begins its treatment by quoting from Stéfan Glaser:

> What characterizes a nation is not only a community of political destiny, but, above all, a community marked by distinct historical and cultural links or features. On the other hand, a 'territorial' or 'state' link (with the State) does not appear to me to be essential. 'Race' means a category of persons who are distinguished by common and constant, and therefore hereditary, features. The concept 'ethnic' has a wider meaning; it designates a community of persons linked by the same customs, the same language and the same race (from the Greek *ethnos* = people).[33]

The term 'ethnical group' presents some definitional uncertainties, and the *travaux* indicate a wide divergence in the meanings ascribed by the member states. Among the views delegations expressed were that the term covered groups not specifically included within the concepts of national or religious groups, that an ethnic group is a subgroup of a national group, and that the terms 'ethnic' and 'racial' had the same meaning.[34] Disagreement on the distinction between ethnic and racial groups has continued since the Convention entered into force.[35] One scholar of the

[33] Stéfan Glaser, Droit International Pénal Conventionnel 111–12 (1970), *translated and quoted in* 1978 Genocide Study, *supra* note 2, at 15–16.

[34] *See, e.g.*, UN GAOR 6th Comm., 3d Sess., 75th mtg. at 115–16, UN Doc. A/633 (1948).

[35] 1978 Genocide Study, *supra* note 2, at 19–20; *see also* Myres S. McDougal, Harold D. Lasswell, and Lung-Chu Chen, Human Rights and World Public Order: The Basic Policies of an International Law of Human Dignity 569–71 (1980) (analyzing difficulty in defining 'race');

travaux aptly differentiates 'national' and 'ethnical' groups by characterizing the former as groups whose primary identity rests on affiliation with an established nation-state and the latter as groups that share cultural, linguistic, or similar attributes and that can exist within or outside a state.[36] As for religious groups, the 1978 Study concentrates on the notion of a community united by spiritual ideals or beliefs, whether theistic, non-theistic, or atheistic in nature.[37]

Nevertheless, Article II's exhaustive list of protected groups has engendered far more debate over what it omits than over what it includes. While Lemkin's definition of genocide, Resolution 96(I), and earlier drafts of the Convention included political and certain other groups within the universe of protected groups, it is clear from both the text and the *travaux* of the Convention that it does not include political, economic, or professional groups.[38] The member states' decision to omit political groups, primarily at the insistence of the Soviet bloc, has led to great controversy and was, in part, responsible for the decades-long delay in US ratification of the Convention.[39]

Opposition to the inclusion of political groups during the drafting process focused on several arguments. In particular, opponents asserted that, unlike the other groups covered by the Convention, political groups do not have stable and permanent attributes and that, as voluntary organizations, they are different from the other protected groups. In addition, they argued that the protection of such groups was better addressed under the rubric of human rights and that their inclusion would jeopardize ratification by states who saw it as an intolerable interference in their domestic affairs and an impediment to their national security.[40]

Ch. 5, text at notes 46–51, *infra* (similar concerns in defining 'racial group' for purposes of Apartheid Convention).

[36] *See* Lippman, *supra* note 3, at 28–30 (examining different definitions of protected groups suggested by delegations during drafting of Convention).

[37] 1978 Genocide Study, *supra* note 2, at 20. Reflecting what would now seem an outmoded view, the Soviet delegate in the Sixth Committee indicated that he considered religious groups to be a type of national group. UN GAOR 6th Comm., 3d Sess., 75th mtg. at 116, UN Doc. A/633 (1948).

[38] *See, e.g.*, Report of the Sixth Committee, *supra* note 20, at 7; UN GAOR 6th Comm., 3d Sess., 75th mtg. at 110–21, UN Doc. A/633 (1948); 1978 Genocide Study, *supra* note 2, at 21; M. Cherif Bassiouni, Crimes Against Humanity in International Criminal Law 203–04 (2d ed. 1999); Robinson, *supra* note 14, at 59; Lawrence J. LeBlanc, *The United Nations Genocide Convention and Political Groups: Should the United States Propose an Amendment?*, 13 Yale J. Int'l L. 268, 274–75 (1988).

[39] For criticisms of the omission, *see, e.g.*, 1978 Genocide Study, *supra* note 2, at 21–23 and sources cited therein; Kuper, *supra* note 2, at 15–16, 187; Frank Chalk, *Redefining Genocide, in* Genocide: Conceptual and Historical Dimensions 47, 49–52 (George J. Andreopoulos ed., 1994); LeBlanc, *supra* note 38, at 279–82; Stephen P. Marks, *Forgetting 'The Policies and Practices of the Past': Impunity in Cambodia*, Fletcher F. World Aff., Summer/Fall 1994, at 17, 25.

[40] *See, e.g.*, Report of the *Ad hoc* Committee, *supra* note 10, at 5; UN GAOR 6th Comm., 3d Sess.,

The emerging caselaw of the Rwanda and Yugoslavia Tribunals has supported this view, as both Tribunals have spoken of the Convention's protections of 'stable' rather than 'mobile' groups. At the same time, they have differed significantly on whether certain objective traits of a group render it one of the four protected groups. The ICTR has adopted an objective approach, with the status of group members being determined at birth and continuous, and offered definitions of the four protected groups; the ICTY has said that membership in national, ethnical, or racial (but not necessarily religious) groups must be determined based on the perpetrator's perception of whether the victims are part of such a group.[41] The difficulties in defining race, ethnicity, nationality, and religion make the Yugoslavia Tribunal's approach the more promising.

Aside from the philosophical objections to the exclusion of political groups from the Genocide Convention discussed below, one consequence of this exclusion is the difficulty in determining whether victims are part of one of the protected groups in those cases where political divisions tend to fall along ethnic, racial, or religious lines. In light of the prevailing opinion concerning the irrelevance of motive in determining whether genocide has occurred (see below), it is clear that a protected group does not lose its protected status under the Convention because it happens to include, or even consist entirely of, political opponents.[42] Thus, a target group's status as a protected group takes primacy over its incidental status as a political group. Furthermore, neither the Convention nor the *travaux* requires that the targeted group be separate from the perpetrator's group in order for acts to constitute genocide.[43] And nothing in the Convention requires that a targeted group constitute a minority.[44]

The Intent Requirement

Article II of the Convention also includes an intent requirement—that the act be committed 'with the intent of destroying, in whole or in part, [a protected group], as such'. This element distinguishes genocide most from

74th, 75th, and 128th mtgs. at 98–121, 659–64, UN Doc. A/633 (1948); KUPER, *supra* note 2, at 15–16; ROBINSON, *supra* note 14, at 59; LeBlanc, *supra* note 38, at 274–75; Lippman, *supra* note 2, at 42–43.

[41] *Compare Akayesu Judgment*, paras. 510–16, *with Jelisic Judgment*, paras. 69–72. Both Tribunals found the relevant targets of genocide—Tutsis and Bosnian Muslims—to be protected groups.

[42] ROBINSON, *supra* note 14, at 62 n. 18 ('the destruction of ethnic, racial or religious groups under the guise of "political groups" would be an obvious violation of the Convention').

[43] *See, e.g.*, 1985 Genocide Study, *supra* note 32, at 16; Hurst Hannum, *International Law and Cambodian Genocide: The Sounds of Silence*, 11 HUM. RTS. Q. 82, 105 (1989); David Hawk, *The Cambodian Genocide*, in GENOCIDE, A CRITICAL BIBLIOGRAPHIC REVIEW 137, 141 (Israel W. Charny ed., 1988).

[44] *See, e.g.*, 1985 Genocide Study, *supra* note 32, at 16; Hannum, *supra* note 43, at 104–07.

common crimes, such as murder; and unless this intent element is present, no act, regardless of how atrocious it might be, can constitute genocide. Neither the language nor the drafting history of the Convention provides a definitive interpretation of this requirement and, not surprisingly, this element has given rise to substantial confusion and debate.[45] In light of its intangible nature, the intent requirement presents challenging evidentiary issues in almost any determination of responsibility for genocide. Indeed, intent would seem to be the most difficult element of genocide to prove, and often only indirect or circumstantial evidence will be available.

Authorities have suggested various circumstances that may provide evidence of intent, though some appear to conflate evidentiary issues with the level of culpability required by the intent element.[46] Evidence of written or oral orders, including by way of witness testimony, to eliminate a protected group would obviously establish the requisite intent. The labeling of a protected group as an enemy of the state or a systematic and destructive pattern of behavior with respect to a group would also be highly probative.[47] In the report accompanying the draft convention, the Secretary-General offered the following guidance in connection with acts falling under Article II(c) of the Convention (i.e., conditions of life):

> Obviously, if members of a group of human beings are placed in concentration camps where the annual death rate is thirty per cent to forty per cent, the intention to commit genocide is unquestionable. There may be borderline cases where a relatively high death rate might be ascribed to lack of attention, negligence or inhumanity, which, though highly reprehensible, would not constitute evidence of intention to commit genocide.[48]

Acts of so-called 'cultural genocide' and forced expulsions, though not themselves genocidal, may also prove highly probative of intent.[49]

Trial chambers of the Yugoslavia and Rwanda Tribunals have held that the defendant himself must possess the specific intent to be guilty of genocide; if he merely knew his actions would further the destruction of the

[45] *See, e.g.*, Bryant, *supra* note 19, at 692. For example, debate about whether such events as the Vietnam War and the bombings of Dresden, Hiroshima, and Nagasaki constituted genocide has revolved primarily around the presence or absence of the requisite intent. *See, e.g.*, KUPER, *supra* note 2, at 14 (asserting that Allied bombings of Dresden and Hiroshima constituted genocide); Barry M. Schiller, *Life in a Symbolic Universe: Comments on the Genocide Convention and International Law*, 9 SW. U. L. REV. 47, 61–63 (1977) (noting argument that US government lacked genocidal intent in Vietnam).

[46] *See generally* MODEL PENAL CODE § 2.02 (1985) (distinguishing different levels of culpability).

[47] *See, e.g.*, *Eichmann*, 36 ILR at 228 (finding genocidal intent, *inter alia*, from the defendant's own statements and remarks about the defendant made by another senior Nazi); Cambodia Group of Experts Report, *supra* note 32, para. 64; Gregory H. Stanton, *The Cambodian Genocide and International Law*, *in* GENOCIDE AND DEMOCRACY IN CAMBODIA 141, 141–42 (Ben Kiernan ed., 1993).

[48] Report of the Secretary-General, *supra* note 7, at 25.

[49] *See, e.g.*, Lippman, *supra* note 3, at 35–36, 39.

group but did not have the specific intent to do so, he can only be found guilty of complicity in genocide.[50] This standard somewhat contrasts with earlier cases and opinions that impute intent from the actions and views of others or participation in a genocidal regime (and would thus seem, as a practical matter, to create a lower degree of culpability for the defendant).[51] At the same time, the Tribunals, like earlier authorities, have recognized that the defendant's intent may not only be determined by his own words and deeds, but can be inferred from a variety of contextual factors, including the pattern of the atrocities *vis-à-vis* the victims, the level of planning, and the number of victims.[52] Concerns about determining intent also explain the differences between the two Tribunals in the proportion of indictments that charge defendants with genocide.

Related to the question of intent is the relevance of the actor's motive in committing the enumerated acts, a subject of much debate during the drafting of the Convention. The *Ad hoc* Committee initially included an enumeration of motives in its draft convention, as the Committee considered it indispensable to the definition of genocide.[53] However, delegates in the Sixth Committee disagreed over including a motive requirement in addition to the intent requirement. Debate centered on the meaning of a Venezuelan amendment adopted by the Sixth Committee which replaced the *Ad hoc* Committee's enumeration of motives with the words 'as such'. The amendment's sponsor, the committee chairman, and some delegations considered the amendment implicitly to include motives, albeit in a non-limitative fashion. Other delegations maintained that the amendment did not include the concept of motive at all.[54]

[50] *Akayesu Judgment*, paras. 485, 538–48; *Jelisic Judgment*, para. 86. The specific intent is also required for the other actions incurring direct individual responsibility under the Tribunals' Statutes, e.g., planning, instigating, ordering, and aiding and abetting in genocide.

[51] *See Eichmann*, 36 ILR at 228–35 (dictum) (imputing intent to defendant in light of his awareness of Nazi policies and his extensive activities on their behalf); Paul Starkman, *Genocide and International Law: Is There a Cause of Action?*, 8 ASILS Int'l L.J. 1, 52–53 (1984); 1985 Genocide Study, *supra* note 32, at 19 (intent inferable from 'actions or omissions of such a degree of criminal negligence or recklessness that the defendant must reasonably be assumed to have been aware of the consequences of his conduct'); Kuper, *supra* note 2, at 12 (intent established 'if the foreseeable consequences of an act are, or seem likely to be, the destruction of a group'). Imputation of intent based on organizational affiliation would appear consistent with the Nuremberg Charter and jurisprudence, under which an individual could be held criminally responsible for membership in a criminal organization. *See* Ch. 1, note 41, *supra*.

[52] *Akayesu Judgment*, paras. 523–24, 728–30; *Kayishema and Ruzindana Judgment*, paras. 93–94, 531–40; *Rutaganda Judgment*, paras. 424–28. The ICTY focused on the defendant's own actions e.g., the randomness of his cruelty, to acquit him of genocide. *See Jelisic Judgment*, paras. 99–108.

[53] Report of the *Ad hoc* Committee, *supra* note 10, at 5.

[54] *See, e.g.*, UN GAOR 6th Comm., 3d Sess., 75th–78th mtgs. at 109–48, UN Doc. A/633 (1948); *see also* 1978 Genocide Study, *supra* note 2, at 26–27; Robinson, *supra* note 14, at 59–61; LeBlanc, *supra* note 38, at 288–90; Hurst Hannum and David Hawk, The Case Against the Standing Committee of the Communist Party of Kampuchea, Sept. 15, 1986, at 140–48 (draft ICJ memorial) (on file with authors).

While the *travaux* are not entirely clear, it appears that a majority of the Sixth Committee interpreted the Venezuelan amendment either as eliminating any motive requirement or as implying a non-limitative description of motives. Under either view, the practical effect of the amendment would be to eliminate the need to establish a particular motive as an element of genocide, and most commentators agree that so long as the requisite intent is established, underlying motives are irrelevant.[55] This distinction between intent and motive would suggest that an act does not fail to constitute genocide under the Convention merely because political considerations motivated it.[56]

The inclusion of the words 'as such' would appear to reinforce another aspect of the intent requirement—that the intent to destroy be directed at the group as a protected group.[57] In the words of the ILC,

> The prohibited act must be committed against an individual because of his membership in a particular group and as an incremental step in the overall objective of destroying the group. It is the membership of the individual in a particular group rather than the identity of the individual that is the decisive criterion in determining the immediate victims of the crime of genocide. The group itself is the ultimate target or intended victim of this type of massive criminal conduct.[58]

Thus, for example, even if mass killings result in the death of a large portion of a protected group, such acts would not constitute genocide if they were part of a random campaign of violence or were actually directed at a larger, though unprotected, group.

Numerical Issues

The language and *travaux* of the Convention make clear that an intent to destroy a protected group in its entirety is not required for genocide; the intent need only be to destroy the group 'in part'. The Convention's language does not directly address how large that 'part' of the group must be in order for acts to constitute genocide. Robinson and most other commentators assert that the number of individuals intended to be destroyed must be substantial, in light of the Convention's emphasis on acts against large numbers, rather than individuals.[59] Other sources

[55] *See, e.g.*, Hannum, *supra* note 43, at 108–12; LeBlanc, *supra* note 38, at 289–90; Starkman, *supra* note 51, at 7 n.14.

[56] *See, e.g.*, Final Report of the Commission of Experts established pursuant to Security Council Resolution 935 (1994), Dec. 9, 1994, UN Doc. S/1994/1405, at 31 [hereinafter Rwanda Commission Report]; LeBlanc, *supra* note 38, at 288–90.

[57] Lippman, *supra* note 3, at 22–24.

[58] 1996 ILC Report, at 88 (citing ROBINSON, *supra* note 14, at 58); *see also Akayesu Judgment*, para. 521; *Jelisic Judgment*, para. 79.

[59] *See, e.g.*, ROBINSON, *supra* note 14, at 62–63; Lawrence J. LeBlanc, *The Intent to Destroy Groups in the Genocide Convention: The Proposed U.S. Understanding*, 78 AJIL 369, 370–72 (1984).

support this view and suggest that numerical requirements may vary depending upon the nature of the victims and the proportion of the group's total population they represent. The 1985 Genocide Study, for example, noted that 'in part' seemed to imply a 'reasonably significant number, relative to the total of the group as a whole, or else a significant section of a group such as its leadership'.[60] The UN Commission of Experts for the former Yugoslavia similarly stated that the targeting of a significant section of a group, such as its leadership, may constitute genocide in light of its impact on the rest of the group.[61] And the Yugoslavia and Rwanda Tribunals have endorsed this principle as well.[62] Thus, no precise rule governs the proportion of a group which must be targeted in order for the related acts to constitute genocide, and the number of victims required may vary from case to case.[63] However, as a practical matter, the evidentiary hurdles posed by the intent requirement would seem to preclude prosecutions for acts directed at small numbers of people.

RESERVATIONS TO THE GENOCIDE CONVENTION

Although the Genocide Convention has been widely adhered to, the effect of reservations made by many parties has complicated its application. A substantial portion of these reservations concern the jurisdiction of domestic courts and of the International Court of Justice regarding disputes under Article IX and the creation of the international penal tribunal contemplated under Article VI. These reservations led to objections by a number of parties, soon confronting the UN Secretary-General, as depository for the Convention, with a dilemma as to the effect to be

[60] 1985 Genocide Study, *supra* note 32, at 16; *see also* KUPER, *supra* note 2, at 12.

[61] Yugoslavia Commission Final Report, *supra* note 31, at 25. The report also suggested that, where several groups are targeted, all of them can be regarded as part of a larger whole for purposes of numerical requirements. *Id.*

[62] *See Jelisic Judgment*, para. 82 (substantial part or limited group whose destruction would have major impact on group); *Kayishema and Ruzindana Judgment*, para. 97 ('considerable number of individuals').

[63] As for whether an act committed against a single individual can ever constitute genocide, some delegations involved in drafting the Convention and some commentators have argued that it can constitute genocide if the perpetrator had the requisite intent. Others conclude that, in light of the Convention's concern with protecting large numbers of persons and the use of the plural in the Convention, such an act would constitute a common crime only. *See, e.g.*, UN GAOR 6th Comm., 3d Sess., 69th mtg. at 62, 73d mtg. at 90–95, 81st mtg. at 176, UN Doc. A/633 (1948); 1985 Genocide Study, *supra* note 32, at 16 (more than one victim required); 1978 Genocide Study, *supra* note 2, at 14–15 (refusing to take a position on the issue, though suggesting that Convention should not be subject to a broad interpretation); Lippman, *supra* note 2, at 40–41; *see also* Rwanda Commission Report, *supra* note 56, at 32–33 (determination will depend on person's intent).

accorded them in light of the Convention's silence on the question.[64] As a result, the General Assembly submitted the issue to the ICJ for an advisory opinion under Article 96 of the UN Charter.

Noting the special nature of the Genocide Convention and the General Assembly's intent that it be as widely adhered to as possible, the ICJ's 1951 opinion abandoned the traditional rule under international law requiring that a state's reservations to a multilateral convention be unanimously accepted by the other parties to the convention in order for the reserving state to be considered a party. Instead, the Court adopted a new test, by which the effect of a state's reservation (and of any objection to it) would depend upon the reservation's compatibility with the 'object and purpose' of the Convention. Thus, a state that had made a reservation to which other parties had objected could nevertheless be considered a party to the Convention if its reservation was compatible with the object and purpose of the Convention. However, a party that objected to a reservation incompatible with that object and purpose was under no obligation to regard the reserving state as a party.[65] Thus, each party would determine the effect of another state's reservation on their treaty relationship. The Court expressly noted that states could resolve disputes about the effect of a reservation or objection through a special agreement or submission of the dispute to the ICJ pursuant to Article IX of the Convention.[66] The Vienna Convention on the Law of Treaties codified this rule, which is now accepted as custom in the absence of a different rule in a particular treaty.[67]

The ICJ's rather flexible rule creates the possibility that a reserving state may be a party with respect to some parties to the Convention but not others, depending on which parties objected and whether the reservation is compatible with the object and purpose of the Convention. The matrix of relationships under the Convention is further muddied by the failure of most of the objections made to reservations under the Convention to indicate whether the objection is based on the incompatibility of the reservation with the Convention, as the ICJ's opinion and the Vienna Convention

64 Although the United States signed the Convention in 1948, the Senate delayed its ratification until 1988 and attached several reservations and understandings that have proved highly controversial. *See generally* JASON S. ABRAMS AND STEVEN R. RATNER, STRIVING FOR JUSTICE: ACCOUNTABILITY AND THE CRIMES OF THE KHMER ROUGE 42–43 (1995) (consultants' study prepared for US Department of State).

65 Reservations to the Convention on the Prevention and Punishment of the Crime of Genocide, 1951 ICJ 15, 20–30 (May 28) [hereinafter *Reservations Case*]. The Court went on to note that a state which had not signed the Convention had no right to object to another state's reservation, as a non-signatory generally state has no rights with regard to a treaty. *Id.* at 27, 30.

66 *Id.* at 27.

67 *See* Vienna Convention on the Law of Treaties, May 23, 1969, arts. 20–21, 1155 UNTS 331, 337; *see also* GA Res. 598(VI), UN GAOR, 6th Sess., Supp. No. 20, at 84, UN Doc. A/2119 (1952); Bryant, *supra* note 19, at 690–91.

appear to require. Adding to the confusion, some states, presumably for political reasons, have objected to reservations made by some states but not to similar reservations made by other states.[68] As a result of these and related issues,[69] it is not entirely clear which states are party to the Convention *vis-à-vis* other parties, leaving such cases for further judicial determination.

GENOCIDE UNDER CUSTOMARY INTERNATIONAL LAW

The status of genocide under customary international law is significant because it determines the obligations of all states regarding genocide, whether or not they are party to the Convention. Most important sources conclude that obligations concerning genocide are part of customary international law.[70] In particular, the ICJ recognized genocide's status under customary international law when it remarked in the *Reservations* case that 'the principles underlying the Convention are principles which are recognized by civilized nations as binding on States, even without any conventional obligation'.[71] The ILC's work for many decades has also indicated unquestioning agreement with this view.[72] In addition, the ICJ has recognized that obligations concerning genocide are *erga omnes*, and it has been suggested that the prohibition of genocide has achieved the status of a *jus cogens* norm.[73]

Although international law recognizes genocide's prohibition as a norm under customary international law, the precise contours of that norm are not entirely clear. Those sources addressing the scope of the norm generally agree that, at the least, the Genocide Convention's definition of genocide enjoys the status of custom. This view has been manifested in the positions of states during their preparation of the ICTY, ICTR, and ICC

[68] *See* Lawrence J. LeBlanc, *The ICJ, the Genocide Convention, and the United States*, 6 WISC. INT'L L.J. 43, 58–59 (1987).

[69] For example, the Court's opinion did not address the status of understandings and declarations, as opposed to reservations.

[70] *See, e.g.*, *Reservations Case*, 1951 ICJ at 23; *Eichmann*, 36 ILR at 11; *Akayesu Judgment*, para. 495; RESTATEMENT (THIRD) OF THE FOREIGN RELATIONS LAW OF THE UNITED STATES §§ 404, 702 (1987). Even at the time of the Convention's drafting, several delegations expressed the view that genocide was already a crime under international law. *See also* ROBINSON, *supra* note 14, at 56–57 (acknowledging that genocide might eventually become a customary law crime). *But see Genocide: The Convention, Domestic Laws, and State Responsibility*, 1989 AM. SOC'Y INT'L L. PROC. 314, 326 (remarks of Benjamin Ferencz).

[71] 1951 ICJ at 23.

[72] All versions of the ILC's Draft Code have used a definition of genocide derived from the Convention. *See, e.g.*, 1954 ILC Report, at 151 (art. 2(10)); 1996 ILC Report, at 85–87 (art. 17).

[73] *See, e.g.*, Barcelona Traction, Light & Power Co. (Second Phase) (Belg. v. Spain), 1970 ICJ 3, 32 (Feb. 5); Rwanda Commission Report, *supra* note 56, at 30. *But see* Starkman, *supra* note 51, at 18–21.

Statutes, and in the ILC's 1996 Draft Code, all of which use the Convention's definition; and the *ad hoc* tribunals have endorsed this position.[74]

Some sources suggest that the prohibition on genocide under customary law is even broader than that under the Convention.[75] They note that the definition of genocide under Resolution 96(I) is broader than the definition under the Genocide Convention; the Charters of the Nuremberg and Tokyo Tribunals contained non-exhaustive definitions of crimes against humanity; and many of the prosecutions of Nazi war criminals used the term 'genocide' to encompass acts which, strictly speaking, would not constitute genocide under the Convention.[76] In a surprising piece of dictum, the Rwanda Tribunal's trial chamber has stated that the list of four groups in the Convention is not exclusive insofar as the Convention's drafters sought to protect 'any stable and permanent group'.[77] Nevertheless, the evidence of state practice to date appears insufficient to support the proposition that the definition of genocide under customary international law is broader than that in the Convention, as attested to by the approach of states at the Rome Conference.[78]

THEORETICAL AND PRACTICAL CHALLENGES

Although the crime of genocide has the advantage, as it were, of having been authoritatively codified, the definition adopted in the Genocide Convention represents a least common denominator that emerged out of a political context now over five decades old. The two most prominent aspects of that context were the trauma of the recent Nazi Holocaust and the incipient Cold War. Not surprisingly, the definition adopted in the Convention hewed closely to the paradigm of the Holocaust and omitted protection for certain groups (e.g., political, economic, and social) with whom the states of the Soviet bloc wished to retain a free hand.

The limitations of that definition—particularly the restricted list of protected groups and the intent requirement—impose significant obstacles

[74] *See, e.g.*, ICTY Statute, art. 4; ICTR Statute, art. 2; ICC Statute, art. 6; 1996 ILC Report, at 85–87 (art. 17); *Akayesu Judgment*, para. 495; *Jelisic Judgment*, para. 60.

[75] Until recently, all texts of the ILC's Draft Code had adopted a non-exhaustive enumeration of genocidal acts, though it is not clear whether these texts represented codification of custom or progressive development of international law. *See, e.g.*, note 17, *supra*.

[76] *See, e.g.*, 1978 Genocide Study, *supra* note 2, at 154–63 (quoting excerpts from prosecutions of Nazis).

[77] *Akayesu Judgment*, para. 516; *see also* Johan D. van der Vyver, *Prosecution and Punishment of the Crime of Genocide*, 23 FORDHAM INT'L L.J. 286, 303–06 (1999).

[78] Herman von A.M. Hebel and Darryl Robinson, *Crimes within the Jurisdiction of the Court*, *in* THE INTERNATIONAL CRIMINAL COURT: THE MAKING OF THE ROME STATUTE 79, 89–90 (Roy S. Lee ed., 1999).

to making out a case of genocide in many situations. In many cases, it may be difficult to determine whether victims constitute a cohesive group that the Convention protects. For example, in response to the charge that Saddam Hussein's *Anfal* campaign against the Iraqi Kurds constituted genocide, the defense would undoubtedly argue that the victims were, in fact, a political opposition group whose members happened to be Kurds. The correct characterization would likely depend to a large extent on the arbitrariness of the attacks—i.e., whether they were directed primarily at those Kurds who were political opponents of the regime or were directed more generally at Kurdish populations in the expectation that political opposition would thereby be quelled. In this case, the available evidence strongly suggests a finding of genocide.[79]

The intent requirement likewise presents a challenge. Did US forces, through their bombing and other attacks during the Vietnam War, intend to destroy the Vietnamese nation in part, or was the intent purely to achieve a military objective?[80] Again, the answer will depend on the nature of the bombings and may, in fact, differ depending on the individual actor. To take a more recent case, some controversy has swirled around the question whether rape committed in the Balkan War was genocidal, especially in light of the hope expressed by some Serb attackers that they would make their victims give birth to Serb babies.[81] Here again, the correct characterization will probably vary from case to case. Where an attacker rapes a victim solely as an act of vengeance or hostility toward the victim, the rape is not genocidal, even if the attacker has selected the victim on the basis of her religion or ethnicity. On the other hand, if evidence suggests that the attacker committed the rape as part of an effort to drive the victim or members of her group into mental states that the attacker hopes will lead to the group's destruction, a finding of genocide is justifiable, as the Rwanda Tribunal has found in several cases.[82] The line between intent, a relevant factor, and motive, an irrelevant one, may thus prove thin in practice.

The limitations and requirements of the Genocide Convention have also inevitably precipitated sterile debates over the definition of genocide that run the unfortunate risk of detracting from the enormity of the atrocities

[79] *See, e.g.*, Lori F. Damrosch, Kurdish Genocide Case—Legal Memorandum for Governments, June 4, 1993 (memorandum for Middle East Watch) (on file with authors).

[80] For an account of the debate, *see* Matthew Lippman, *The Convention on the Prevention and Punishment of the Crime of Genocide: Fifty Years Later*, 15 ARIZ. J. INT'L AND COMP. L. 415, 476–80 (1998).

[81] *See, e.g.*, sources cited in Ch. 3, note 155, *infra*.

[82] *See Musema Judgment*, para. 933; *Akayesu Judgment*, paras. 731–33; *see also* Kelly D. Askin, *Sexual Violence in Decisions and Indictments of the Yugoslav and Rwandan Tribunals: Current Status*, 93 AJIL 97, 105–08, 115, 122 (1999); Catharine A. MacKinnon, *Rape, Genocide, and Women's Human Rights*, 17 HARV. WOMEN'S L.J. 5 (1994).

themselves. And an opposite, yet equally disconcerting trend in contemporary discourse on genocide has also resulted—an abuse of the term that robs the concept of genocide of its definitional integrity. Such is the term's emotional and political potency that the label 'genocide' is used today in a more expansive sense than its legal definition might allow to refer to almost any instance of mass killing. In the words of Helen Fein:

> Since genocide is widely conceived of as the most reprehensible of crimes, many people use genocide-labeling both to vent outrage and to describe situations in which they perceive themselves as threatened, regardless of how these situations have come about, the source of threat, the truth of accusation against the putative perpetrator, and so on. Their reasoning seems to be: if this is awful, it must be genocide. . . . At times such labeling verges on the paranoid and incendiary, as when Westerners or Jews are accused of genocide by giving Africans or African-Americans AIDS.[83]

Rescuing genocide from this trend is part of the work which responsible decision-makers and commentators must vigilantly undertake.

At the same time, it is long overdue for the law of genocide to evolve beyond its 1940s roots to more closely reflect the values and political landscape of the twenty-first century. The Convention's limited definition perhaps had some inherent justification in that it attached special opprobrium to attempts to exterminate groups defined by what were traditionally considered immutable traits. However, it is increasingly difficult to justify including within the definition of genocide human collectives based on religion, nationality, and ethnicity, while excluding those based on political views, social status, or economic station.[84] Indeed, the decades since the Genocide Convention's adoption have seen several episodes of mass killing, including Stalin's purges and the Khmer Rouge terror, to name just two, which in large part fall outside the Convention's ambit, yet which from today's perspective are in many respects morally indistinguishable from those that do fall within it. Attributes such as religion and nationality, which in earlier times seemed immutable, are today shed more readily and easily, whereas traits such as political ideology, which in those days were regarded as less stable, are now regarded as an integral a part of human identity as one's theistic views and national allegiance. And, with the end of the Cold War and the nearly universal professed commitment to a core corpus of human rights, the least common denominator that prevailed in 1948 has certainly increased. Accordingly, only when the legal definition of genocide expands to

[83] Helen Fein, *Genocide, Terror, Life Integrity, and War Crimes: The Case for Discrimination, in* GENOCIDE: CONCEPTUAL AND HISTORICAL DIMENSIONS, *supra* note 39, at 95, 95.

[84] *Cf. Kambanda Sentencing Judgment*, para. 14 ('it seems more difficult for the Chamber to rank genocide and crimes against humanity in terms of their respective gravity.').

encompass the mass destruction of any human collective based on any core element of human identity will it fully address the most heinous international offenses.

Indeed these sentiments have spawned a number of proposals for a modified, or entirely new, definition of genocide. While some of these proposals seek only to bring certain unprotected groups within the ambit of genocide, others go further to bring other means of destruction (e.g., ecological genocide) into the definition.[85] Although some of these proposals are worthy of support, those which go beyond the crime's essential focus on the physical destruction of human collectives dilute the concept of genocide and call into question its status as a unique international crime.

In light of the analysis of the Convention presented above, accomplishing the necessary expansion in the Convention's definition through judicial interpretation of its text seems quite challenging (although the *Akayesu* trial court's dictum certainly shows the possibilities). Moreover, the political hurdles to amending the Convention would be daunting. Accordingly, the most promising route for the future evolution of international law on genocide would be through clearer expansion of customary international law. In this connection, states could expand the definition of genocide under their domestic law and press for recognition of a more expansive interpretation of the crime in international fora. International tribunals, such as the Yugoslavia and Rwanda Tribunals and the International Court of Justice, will also have an important impact in clarifying the status of customary international law on genocide and in recognizing any expansion in its scope.

[85] *See, e.g.*, Chalk, *supra* note 39 (examining various definitions proposed by scholars); Israel W. Charny, *Toward a Generic Definition of Genocide, in* GENOCIDE: CONCEPTUAL AND HISTORICAL DIMENSIONS, *supra* note 39, at 64; *see generally* CONTEMPORARY GENOCIDES: CAUSES, CASES, CONSEQUENCES (Albert J. Jongman ed., 1996) (examining the terms 'genocide', 'politicide', and 'democide').

3

Crimes Against Humanity and the Inexactitude of Custom

Although the Genocide Convention represents a historic turning point in the use of the treaty formula to define and proscribe massive human rights abuses, international law has also developed an elaborate body of law outside the treaty process that addresses a broad range of systematic atrocities. This corpus, known as crimes against humanity, emerged primarily as a product of customary international law, and thus its elaboration involves a different intellectual task from that in comprehending the Genocide Convention and other treaties.

EVOLUTION OF THE CONCEPT

Crimes against humanity, in the words of the Swiss jurist Jean Graven, are as old as humanity itself.[1] Since the earliest days of international law, scholars and statesmen have referred to fundamental notions of humanity as governing the conduct of states. States used these concepts in justifying instances of intervention to assist minorities persecuted by their own government in the age before the UN Charter.[2] They also became linked with a state's conduct of war, eventually through incorporation in the first significant modern treaties on *jus in bello*, the Hague Conventions on the Laws and Customs of War.[3]

The first modern attempt to impute individual criminal responsibility for crimes against humanity took place after World War I. In a report to the 1919 Preliminary Peace Conference, the majority of a special fifteen-member Allied commission found that the Central Powers had committed numerous acts 'in violation of the established laws and customs of war

[1] Jean Graven, *Les Crimes Contre l'Humanité*, 76 Recueil des Cours 427, 433 (1950-I).

[2] *See, e.g.*, James T. Brand, *Crimes Against Humanity and the Nürnberg Trials*, 28 Oreg. L. Rev. 93, 108–10 (1949).

[3] *See* Convention Respecting the Laws and Customs of War on Land (Hague, IV), Oct. 18, 1907, 1 Bevans 631, 633 (incorporating so-called Martens Clause in preamble); *see also* the historical review in M. Cherif Bassiouni, Crimes Against Humanity in International Criminal Law 44–68 (2d ed. 1999).

and the elementary laws of humanity'.[4] The Turkish massacre of Armenians received prominent attention. The two American members of the commission, however, dissented from this finding, dismissing the concept of laws of humanity as 'not the object of punishment by a court of justice', but rather a question of 'moral law' lacking any 'fixed and universal standard'.[5] As a result, the Versailles Treaty did not call for any trials for crimes against humanity.

The Charter of the International Military Tribunal marked the birth of the modern notion of crimes against humanity. Article 6(c) of the Charter defines them as follows:

> [N]amely, murder, extermination, enslavement, deportation, and other inhumane acts committed against any civilian population, before or during the war, or persecutions on political, racial or religious grounds in execution of or in connection with any crime within the jurisdiction of the Tribunal, whether or not in violation of the domestic law of the country where perpetrated.[6]

The history of the drafting of the Charter reveals intense discussions among the Allies regarding the appropriateness of prosecuting Axis leaders for acts beyond war crimes.[7] Although the bulk of Nazi and Japanese atrocities clearly constituted war crimes, Article 6(c) also criminalized additional categories of acts that are not war crimes, notably those against a state's own citizens, those arising before the outbreak of war, and acts that, even in wartime against enemy nationals, were not war crimes.[8] At the same time, the Charter incorporates a critical compromise by defining crimes against humanity only 'in connection with' other crimes, i.e., crimes against peace and war crimes. The Charter of the International Military Tribunal for the Far East adopted an identical definition.[9]

Of the eighteen Nazi leaders indicted for crimes against humanity, sixteen were convicted and two (Hess and Fritzsche) were acquitted of those charges. Two (Streicher and von Schirach) were found guilty of crimes against humanity alone. The twenty-five Japanese leaders tried at

[4] Commission on the Responsibility of the Authors of the War and on Enforcement of Penalties, *Report Presented to the Preliminary Peace Conference, March 29, 1919*, *reprinted in* 14 AJIL 95, 115 (1920).

[5] *Id.* at 144; *see also* Lord Wright, *War Crimes Under International Law*, 62 LAW Q. REV. 40, 48–49 (1946) (critique of US position); Graven, *supra* note 1, at 446–51; Egon Schwelb, *Crimes Against Humanity*, 23 BRIT. Y.B. INT'L L. 178, 181–82 (1946).

[6] IMT Charter, art. 6(c).

[7] *See* Roger S. Clark, *Crimes Against Humanity at Nuremberg*, *in* THE NUREMBERG TRIAL AND INTERNATIONAL LAW 177, 180–92 (George Ginsburgs and V.N. Kudriavtsev eds., 1990).

[8] *See* UNITED NATIONS WAR CRIMES COMMISSION, HISTORY OF THE UNITED NATIONS WAR CRIMES COMMISSION AND THE DEVELOPMENT OF THE LAWS OF WAR 193–95 (1948) [hereinafter UNWCC].

[9] Charter of the International Military Tribunal for the Far East, Jan. 19, 1946, *amended* Apr. 26, 1946, art 5(c), 4 Bevans 20, 28.

Tokyo were indicted for conventional war crimes and crimes against humanity, but the judgment addressed only the former.[10]

In addition to the trials of the major criminals, the Allies prosecuted or oversaw German prosecutions of other Nazi leaders in the zones they occupied pursuant to Law No. 10 of the Control Council for Germany. Law No. 10 provided for prosecutions of crimes against humanity, adopting a definition that lacked the nexus to other crimes in the IMT Charter. Trials under this law by American courts in the American zone resulted in the convictions of hundreds of Nazi soldiers and officials for crimes against humanity before and during the war.[11]

Individual states in Europe (including Germany) and the Soviet Union conducted numerous trials under national laws, with charges usually brought for war crimes or common crimes under domestic law, rather than crimes against humanity *per se*.[12] These trials wound down in the 1950s, but never ended, as a trickle of Nazis continued to be hauled before domestic courts. In the most prominent case, Israel tried Adolf Eichmann, the chief organizer of the Final Solution, for crimes against the Jewish people, war crimes, and crimes against humanity.[13] In the 1980s and 1990s, France tried Klaus Barbie, Paul Touvier, and Maurice Papon for crimes against humanity.[14]

The atrocities of the Nazis prompted a sustained effort by the nascent United Nations to enshrine the notion of crimes against humanity into international law on a permanent basis. This process began with the General Assembly's endorsement in 1946 of the principles of international law recognized in the IMT Charter, its request to ECOSOC to draft a convention on genocide, and its request to the ILC to formulate the Nuremberg principles and to draft a Code of Offenses Against the Peace and Security of Mankind.[15] The International Law Commission formulated the

[10] 22 IMT Trials at 524–87; *id.* at 549, 566; International Military Tribunal for the Far East, Judgment, Part C, ch. IX, at 1143–44; Annex A-6, at 48–60 (1948).

[11] *See* UNWCC, *supra* note 8, at 464–66; *see also* HENRI MEYEROWITZ, LA RÉPRESSION PAR LES TRIBUNAUX ALLEMANDS DES CRIMES CONTRE L'HUMANITÉ ET DE L'APPARTENANCE À UNE ORGANISATION CRIMINELLE 120–21 (1960). The American zone cases remain those most frequently cited.

[12] For individual jurisdictional bases, *see, e.g.*, 3 War Crimes Reports 81 (Norway); 3 War Crimes Reports 93 (France). The Netherlands did prosecute for crimes against humanity as defined in the IMT Charter, *see, e.g.*, Trial of Hans Albin Rauter, 14 War Crimes Reports 89 (Special Ct. the Hague and Special Ct. Cass. 1948–49); China prosecuted for crimes against humanity under Chinese law, *see, e.g.*, Trial of Takashi Sakai, 14 War Crimes Reports 1 (Military Tribunal 1946); and Poland prosecuted for genocide, *see, e.g.*, Trial of Rudolf Hoess, 7 War Crimes Reports 11 (Supreme National Tribunal 1947). *See also* UNWCC, *supra* note 8, at 216–19.

[13] Attorney-General of the Government of Israel v. Eichmann, 36 ILR 5 (Dist. Ct. Jerusalem 1961), *aff'd*, 36 ILR 277 (Israel 1962).

[14] Fédération Nationale des Déportés et Internés Résistants et Patriotes and Others v. Barbie, 78 ILR 125 (Fr. Cour de Cassation 1985); Touvier, 100 ILR 338 (Fr. Cour de Cassation 1992).

[15] GA Res. 95(I), UN Doc. A/64/Add.1, at 188 (1946); GA Res. 96(I), UN Doc. A/64/Add.1, at 188, 189 (1946); GA Res. 177(II), UN Doc. A/519, at 111, 112 (1947).

Nuremberg principles by 1950 and adopted a Draft Code in 1954.[16] The inability of states to agree upon a definition of aggression prevented any further progress on the Code, and the ILC did not resume work on it until 1983. Since that time, the ILC revisited the issue extensively, completing consideration of the Draft Code in 1996.[17]

Apart from the ILC, the UN considered the issue during the drafting of the 1968 Convention on the Non-Applicability of Statutory Limitations to War Crimes and Crimes Against Humanity[18] and codified treaties on two subjects that have been grouped with crimes against humanity—torture and apartheid.[19] At the regional level, the Council of Europe adopted its own convention on the non-applicability of statutes of limitations,[20] and the Organization of American States proclaimed 'disappearances' crimes against humanity in 1983.[21]

The most significant recent development has centered around the statutes of the Yugoslavia and Rwanda Tribunals and the International Criminal Court. Each statute gives the respective court subject matter jurisdiction over crimes against humanity, with different definitions adopted for each.[22] The two *ad hoc* tribunals have issued judgments further elaborating the elements of the crime as it is defined in their statutes, as has the preparatory committee of the ICC.

CORE DEFINITIONAL ISSUES: ELEMENTS OF THE INTERNATIONAL CRIME

The term 'crimes against humanity' is used in this chapter in its generally accepted sense to cover a range of crimes much broader than genocide, and indeed where the elements of genocide often prove lacking. In the absence of any authoritative treaty or set of treaties on crimes against humanity, their meaning must be found in customary international law, with reliance as necessary on other processes of prescription. Thus, prior prosecutions, other state practice, and deliberations of international organizations assume greater significance. Instruments such as the ICTY,

[16] Report of the International Law Commission to the General Assembly, UN Doc. A/1316 (1950), *reprinted in* 1950 [II] ILC Y.B. 364, 374–78; 1954 ILC Report, at 149–52.

[17] *See* 1996 ILC Report, at 14–120.

[18] Nov. 26, 1968, 754 UNTS 73.

[19] *See* Ch. 5, *infra.*

[20] European Convention on the Non-Applicability of Statutory Limitation to Crimes Against Humanity and War Crimes, Europ. T.S. No. 82, Jan. 25, 1974, *reprinted in* 13 ILM 540 (1974) [hereinafter European Convention].

[21] AG/Res. 666 (XIII-0/83), OAS General Assembly, 13th Sess., Proceedings Vol. 1, at 68, 69, OAS Doc. OEA/Ser.P.XIII.0.2 (1983); *see also* Velasquez Rodriguez Case, Inter-Am. Ct. Hum. Rts. (Ser. C), No. 4, para. 153, at 146 (1988) (judgment).

[22] ICTY Statute, art. 5; ICTR Statute, art. 3; ICC Statute, art. 7.

ICTR, and ICC Statutes that define crimes against humanity as part of the jurisdiction of specific courts will also shed light on the community's expectations of individual responsibility. The ICC Statute appears especially significant in this regard as much of its definition seems to have largely been viewed as a codification of existing law, rather than progressive development of the law.[23]

The approach adopted here for appraising the scope of criminal responsibility under international law involves two steps—(1) a determination of the distinguishing features that make an act a crime against humanity under *international law*, as opposed to a crime prosecutable only as a matter of domestic criminal law;[24] and (2) a determination of the specific acts that international law regards as so offensive as to impute *criminal responsibility*, as opposed to more typical state responsibility for violations of human rights. This section considers the first of these questions; the following considers the second.

Nexus to Armed Conflict

The first element that various sources of international law have assigned to crimes against humanity concerns the need for a connection between the crimes and armed conflict. This nexus originated in both the IMT Charter and the traditional tendency of states to focus upon human rights abuses during armed conflict.

Nuremberg and the Post-World War II Trials

The IMT Charter defines crimes against humanity as requiring a nexus with the other crimes over which the IMT had jurisdiction, namely crimes against peace (the crime of aggression) and war crimes (violations of *jus in bello*). Disagreement remains, however, over whether the linkage in the definition suggests that international law requires a connection between crimes against humanity and armed conflict, or that the IMT Charter simply limited the jurisdiction of the IMT to a certain set of crimes against humanity, i.e., those connected with crimes against peace and war crimes.

The IMT itself skirted the question whether the Charter represented a complete or incomplete codification of international law, viewing its task as simply one of interpreting and following the Charter. It therefore

[23] *See* Herman von A.M. Hebel and Darryl Robinson, *Crimes within the Jurisdiction of the Court*, *in* THE INTERNATIONAL CRIMINAL COURT: THE MAKING OF THE ROME STATUTE 79, 91 and n. 40 (Roy S. Lee ed., 1999); *cf. Furundzija Judgment*, para. 227 ('[d]epending on the matter at issue, the Rome Statute may be taken to restate, reflect or clarify customary rules or crystallise them, whereas in some areas it creates new law or modifies existing law.').

[24] *See* Ch. 1, text at notes 19–32, *supra*, on the notion of an international crime.

refused to characterize pre-1939 acts as *per se* crimes against humanity.[25] In the portions of the judgment concerning the two defendants convicted only of crimes against humanity, the IMT made specific reference to the required nexus to other crimes.[26] Although the IMT showed some willingness to consider certain pre-war acts as connected with the war (especially those undertaken in Austria) and thus as crimes against humanity, it refused to do so regarding the Nazis' pre-war persecution of Germans.[27] For acts after the beginning of the war that did not constitute war crimes (such as the murder and deportation of German citizens), the court assumed a linkage between the acts and the war crimes or crimes against peace because of the chronological overlap, thereby overcoming any jurisdictional obstacles.[28]

The wording of Control Council Law No. 10 joined the question more fully. It gave the military court jurisdiction over crimes against humanity defined as follows:

> Atrocities and offences, including but not limited to murder, extermination, enslavement, deportation, imprisonment, torture, rape, or other inhumane acts committed against any civilian population, or persecutions on political, racial or religious grounds whether or not in violation of the domestic laws of the country where perpetrated.[29]

The lack of a linkage to armed conflict offers some evidence that the Allies regarded the nexus as legally unnecessary as a matter of custom, yet the preamble to CCL No. 10 states that the law is meant 'to give effect' to the Charter, thus giving rise to confusion.[30] Telford Taylor, the chief American prosecutor of these cases, indicated at the time that he regarded the nexus requirement as eliminated.[31]

Cases under Control Council Law No. 10 do not reveal a consensus position. In *United States* v. *Flick et al.*, the court acquitted the defendant of crimes against humanity for his acquisition of Jewish property before the war, finding itself without jurisdiction.[32] In *United States* v. *von Weizsaecker et al.* (the '*Ministries Case*'), the tribunal dismissed the counts of crimes against humanity against officials in the Nazi foreign

[25] 22 IMT Trials at 498.

[26] 22 IMT Trials at 547–49, 563–66.

[27] Schwelb, *supra* note 5, at 205: *see also* Elisabeth Zoller, *La définition des crimes contre l'humanité*, 120 J. DROIT INT'L 549, 553–55 (1993).

[28] UNWCC, *supra* note 8, at 195; *see also* Beth Van Schaak, *The Definition of Crimes Against Humanity: Resolving the Incoherence*, 37 COLUM. J. TRANSNAT'L L. 787, 803–07 (1999).

[29] CCL No. 10, art. II(1)(c).

[30] *See id.*, preamble.

[31] TELFORD TAYLOR, FINAL REPORT TO THE SECRETARY OF THE ARMY ON THE NUERNBERG WAR CRIMES TRIALS UNDER CONTROL COUNCIL LAW No. 10, at 64–65, 84 and n. 212 (1949).

[32] 6 CCL No. 10 Trials 1187, 1213.

ministry and other bureaucracies, noting that CCL No. 10 was meant to go no further than the IMT itself, which codified international law.[33]

Other cases put forth dicta suggesting that the removal of the nexus requirement allowed for prosecutions for crimes not committed in the war. The military court in *United States* v. *Ohlendorf et al.* (the '*Einsatzgruppen Case*') said as much in convicting the defendants for the large-scale execution of Jews in occupied Europe and the Soviet Union.[34] In *United States* v. *Altstoetter et al.* (the '*Justice Case*'), although the defendants were charged only with crimes committed during the war, the court noted the omission of the nexus language and seemed to suggest in dicta that it was legally unnecessary.[35]

The legacy of the Nuremberg trials is thus one of uncertainty, as the tribunals either found it unnecessary to consider the nexus requirement, or rejected it outright (with the exception of the dicta in the *Einsatzgruppen* and *Justice* cases).[36] As of the end of those trials, one could be certain neither that international law recognized crimes against humanity outside of armed conflict before Nuremberg nor that the Nuremberg instruments newly designated them as international crimes.

National Laws and Prosecutions

The promulgation of domestic laws purporting to penalize acts states regarded as international crimes, as well as prosecutions thereunder, offer some evidence of state practice. Nearly all domestic prosecutions since World War II for crimes against humanity have concerned crimes associated with the war and the Axis powers. The Israeli statute, used for the prosecution of Eichmann and John Demjanjuk, lacks a nexus requirement, although the issue was irrelevant during their prosecutions.[37] France originally tried persons only for collaboration, but in 1964 enacted a statute that defined crimes against humanity based on the IMT Charter.[38] The *Barbie* and *Touvier* decisions skirted the nexus question, as both defendants' actions were clearly linked to other crimes.[39] An official government

[33] 13 CCL No. 10 Trials 112, 112–17; *cf.* United States v. Brandt et al. (the '*Medical Case*'), 2 CCL No. 10 Trials 171, 181; *see also* The Hadamar Trial, 1 War Crimes Reports 46, 52 (1945) (Military Commission at Wiesbaden) (finding lack of jurisdiction).

[34] 4 CCL No. 10 Trials 411, 499.

[35] *See* 3 CCL No. 10 Trials 954, 973–74, 979–82.

[36] *See* Graven, *supra* note 1, at 472–73.

[37] It reads: ' "Crime against humanity" means any of the following acts: murder, extermination, enslavement, starvation or deportation and other inhumane acts committed against any civilian population, and persecution on national, racial, religious or political grounds.' Nazi and Nazi Collaborators (Punishment) Law, 5710/1950, § 1(b), *reprinted in Eichmann*, 36 ILR at 7 [hereinafter Israeli Law]; *see also Eichmann* at 288 (nexus issue irrelevant).

[38] Law No. 64–1326, Dec. 26, 1964, 1965(II) Recueil Dalloz Sirey 41.

[39] *See generally* Leila Sadat Wexler, *The Interpretation of the Nuremberg Principles by the French Court of Cassation: From Touvier to Barbie and Back Again*, 32 COLUM. J. TRANSNAT'L L. 289 (1994).

statement in 1986 accepted only genocide and the crimes defined in the IMT Charter (with the nexus) as crimes against humanity.[40] France enacted a new law in 1992 that lacks the nexus requirement; Belgium's 1999 law is similar in this regard.[41]

Canada's war crimes statute of 1987 is ambiguous on the issue, permitting prosecutions for crimes against humanity if they were regarded at the time of their commission as contravening international law or 'criminal according to the general principles of law recognized by the community of nations'.[42] In *Regina* v. *Finta*, a prosecution of a Hungarian for deporting Jews during the war, neither the Ontario Court of High Justice nor the Supreme Court addressed the nexus question, although they might have assumed a nexus from the purpose of the legislation, i.e., the prosecution of Nazi war criminals in Canada.[43]

Australia enacted a war crimes statute in 1988 to deal specifically with World War II war criminals. It retains the nexus requirement for crimes against humanity.[44] When the High Court of Australia upheld the law in *Polyukhovich* v. *Commonwealth of Australia and Another*, one judge in the majority concluded that today crimes against humanity can be carried out in peacetime, but that as of 1939, the nexus to war crimes was required as a matter of international law.[45]

The United Kingdom enacted its own War Crimes Act in 1991, which also maintains both the temporal nexus to World War II and the general nexus to war crimes.[46] A special commission advising the government on the legality of such a statute concluded that the status of crimes against humanity (with apparent reference to those independent of war crimes) was 'unclear' as of World War II and that enactment of legislation to punish genocide or other crimes against humanity not linked to war crimes would constitute 'retrospective legislation'.[47] Lastly, China's 1946 statute criminalized a variety of acts other than war crimes if committed

[40] Statement of French Foreign Minister to French Senator Moulins, Apr. 25, 1986, *reprinted in* 32 ANNUAIRE FRANÇAIS DROIT INT'L 1019 (1986).

[41] Nouveau Code pénal art. 212–1 (Fr.); Law of 10 February 1999, MONITEUR BELGE, Mar. 23, 1999, at 9286.

[42] R.S.C. 1985, c. C-46, § 3.76.

[43] 69 O.R.2d 557, 573–77 (Ont. High Ct. Just. 1989), *appeal dismissed,* 53 O.A.C. 1 (Ont. Ct. App. 1992), *appeal dismissed,* [1994] 1 S.C.R. 701 (Can.). Finta was acquitted at trial. The Supreme Court did note that war crimes and crimes against humanity 'are usually committed during a time of war'. [1994] 1 S.C.R. at 816. *See generally* Irwin Cotler, *International Decisions: Regina v. Finta,* 90 AJIL 460, 461–64 (1996).

[44] War Crimes Amendment Act, 1989 Austl. Acts No. 3, § 7(3).

[45] 172 C.L.R. 501, 664–77 (Austl. 1991) (Toohey, J., concurring). *But see id.* at 584–91 (Brennan, J., dissenting) (appearing to assert that crimes against humanity did not exist as a separate crime before 1945).

[46] War Crimes Act, 1991, ch. 13, § 1(1) (Eng.).

[47] THOMAS HETHERINGTON AND WILLIAM CHALMERS, WAR CRIMES: REPORT OF THE WAR CRIMES INQUIRY 63–64 (1989).

before or during a 'period of hostilities against the Republic of China'; the mention of 'hostilities' and the qualification that those committing them 'nourish intentions of enslaving, crippling, or annihilating the Chinese Nation' suggest an obvious linkage to the war.[48]

Outside the Axis context, Latvia and Estonia have prosecuted former Soviet secret police officials under domestic law for murder, torture, and deportations; Hungary has prosecuted border guards for the killing of demonstrators during the 1956 uprising; and Ethiopia has begun prosecutions for the leaders of the *Dergue* regime for its many atrocities.[49] It is not readily apparent, however, whether the prosecutors or tribunals considered whether prosecutions for crimes against humanity not linked to armed conflict constituted retroactive application of the law.

Developments at the Global Level

During the debates over the 1968 Convention on Statutory Limitations, the issue of linkage of crimes against humanity to armed conflict arose indirectly. A special working group of the Human Rights Commission first proposed several definitions, the most popular of which deleted the nexus requirement.[50] A joint working group of the Third and Sixth Committees of the General Assembly then defined crimes against humanity without the linkage.[51] Those states opposing the definition seemed to do so based on the inclusion of apartheid and eviction by occupation as crimes, rather than the absence of the nexus requirement, and no government subsequently called for restoring the nexus.[52] In the Third Committee, Western states proposed limiting crimes against humanity to two sets of crimes—the definition in the IMT Charter and genocide. But, significantly, they accepted a non-aligned group proposal that would include those defined in the IMT Charter 'whether committed in time of war or in time of peace'.[53]

[48] Law of 24 October 1946, art. II(3), 14 War Crimes Reports 152, 153.

[49] *See, e.g., Former Latvian KGB official gets 7-year jail term for 'genocide'*, Agence France-Presse, Sept. 27, 1999 (available on LEXIS/NEXIS); *A Look Back At '56: Revolt As Hungary Holds a Trial*, N.Y. Times, Sept. 19, 1999, §1, at 5.

[50] Question of the punishment of war criminals and of persons who have committed crimes against humanity: Note by the Secretary-General, UN GAOR, 22d Sess., Annex, Agenda Item 60, at 1, 6–7, UN Doc. A/6813 (1967) [hereinafter 1967 Note by the Secretary-General]; *see also* Commission on Human Rights, Report on the Twenty-Third Session, UN ESCOR, 42d Sess., Supp. No. 6, at 42–43, UN Doc. E/4322-E/CN.4/940.

[51] 1967 Note by the Secretary-General, *supra* note 50, at 3, 7.

[52] *See* Question of Punishment of War Criminals and of Persons who have committed crimes against humanity: Report of the Secretary-General, Aug. 21, 1968, UN Doc. A/7174.

[53] *See* Report of the Third Committee, UN GAOR, 23d Sess., Annex, Agenda Item 55, at 3, UN Doc. A/7342 (1968); UN GAOR, 3d Comm., 23d Sess., 1563–68th mtgs., UN Doc. A/C.3/SR.1563–68 (1968).

While this definition does not definitively break the connection to war crimes—a crime against humanity could still be linked to war crimes even if it took place in peacetime (*e.g.*, before or after a war)—it shows an agreement among all states, North and South, that crimes against humanity could take place in either peacetime or wartime.[54] The European Convention on the non-applicability of statutory limitations, however, covers only those crimes defined in the Genocide Convention, a more narrow set of crimes against humanity, though one not linked to armed conflict.[55]

The Statutes of the Yugoslavia and Rwanda Tribunals also offer evidence of the international community's understanding of the nexus requirement. The drafters of both statutes intended to include only 'rules of international humanitarian law which are beyond any doubt part of customary law'.[56] The Statute for the Yugoslavia Tribunal maintains the nexus to armed conflict.[57] However, the temporal limitations in the Statute meant that the Council never had to address a broader definition. The Secretary-General's commentary defines the crimes as unrelated to armed conflict, suggesting that the limitation in the Statute is jurisdictional, rather than definitional.[58] The French, Russian, UK, and US permanent representatives all stated after the vote setting up the Tribunal that Article 5 applies during a period of armed conflict, without suggesting whether that limitation is jurisdictional or definitional.[59] However, the US government stated in an amicus brief before the Tribunal that the prohibitions on crimes against humanity apply 'even in times of peace'.[60] The appellate chamber of the Yugoslavia Tribunal has stated in dictum that the nexus to war crimes and crimes against peace was peculiar to the Nuremberg Charter and not required as a matter of custom, although it was slightly less categorical on whether the link to any armed conflict (in particular, civil wars)

[54] The Genocide Convention's use of the same language (*see* art. I, 78 UNTS at 280) to eliminate the nexus to armed conflict is inappòsite as it refers to specific acts defined without reference to armed conflict, whereas the IMT Charter definition itself makes reference to armed conflict. In the end, the majority's insistence on including eviction and apartheid led the Western states to oppose or abstain on the final definition in the Third Committee, and the Assembly's vote split predominantly along ideological lines. *See* Robert H. Miller, *The Convention on the Non-Applicability of Statutory Limitations to War Crimes and Crimes Against Humanity*, 65 AJIL 476, 477–78 n. 6 (1971).

[55] European Convention, *supra* note 20, art. 1(1), 13 ILM at 540.

[56] Report of the Secretary-General pursuant to paragraph 2 of Security Council Resolution 808 (1993), May 3, 1993, UN Doc. S/25704, at 9 [hereinafter Secretary-General's Yugoslavia Report].

[57] ICTY Statute, art. 5.

[58] Secretary-General's Yugoslavia Report, *supra* note 56, at 13; *see also* James C. O'Brien, *The International Tribunal for Violations of International Humanitarian Law in the Former Yugoslavia*, 87 AJIL 639, 649 n. 45 (1993) (noting position letters of various countries not mentioning nexus).

[59] Provisional Verbatim Record of the Three Thousand Two Hundred and Seventeenth Meeting, May 25, 1993, UN Doc. S/PV.3217, at 11 (France), 16 (US), 19 (UK), 45 (Russia).

[60] Prosecutor v. Tadic, Amicus Curiae Brief Presented by the Government of the United States of America, July 25, 1995, at 33 n. 53.

is obsolete.[61] In the case of the Rwanda Statute, the link does not appear at all.[62]

The ICC Statute's definition similarly lacks any requirement of a nexus to armed conflict. During the drafting process, the vast majority of states considered the nexus unnecessary; a small number of delegations, including China, India, Russia, and some Middle Eastern states originally favored retention of the requirement, but acceded to the majority's view at Rome.[63]

Subsidiary Sources

The ILC's work on the Draft Code, while at times controversial among some Western states, serves as evidence of the opinions of legal experts as well as offering subsidiary evidence of the positions of governments (although ILC members do not, in theory, represent governments).[64] The Commission's 1954 Code deleted the nexus requirement from an earlier draft.[65] Although the record is somewhat ambiguous, the members seemed to be assuming during this process that they were engaged in progressive development beyond existing law.[66] After 1983, the ILC's stance seemed much more oriented in the direction of codifying established law than it was in the 1950s.[67] Every member who addressed the issue agreed that the nexus was no longer required.[68] It is absent from the ILC's 1996 Draft Code.[69]

[61] *Tadic Interlocutory Appeal*, paras. 140–41 ('[c]ustomary international law may not require a connection between crimes against humanity and any conflict at all'); *see also Tadic Judgment*, para. 627.

[62] ICTR Statute, art. 3. *But see* Daphna Shraga and Ralph Zacklin, *The International Criminal Tribunal for Rwanda*, 7 EJIL 501, 508 (1994) (omission not expressly intended).

[63] *See* Van Schaak, *supra* note 28, at 844.

[64] *See* Oscar Schachter, *The UN Legal Order: An Overview*, *in* 1 UNITED NATIONS LEGAL ORDER 1, 5–6 (Oscar Schachter and Christopher C. Joyner eds., 1995).

[65] 1954 ILC Report, at 150. The final definition in the 1954 draft code was: 'Inhuman acts such as murder, extermination, enslavement, deportation or persecutions, committed against any civilian population on social, political, racial, religious or cultural grounds by the authorities of a State or by private individuals acting at the instigation or with the toleration of such authorities.' *Id.* at 151–52 (art. 2(11)).

[66] *See* Summary Records of the 269th Meeting, 1954 [I] ILC Y.B. 140, 144 (comments of Mr. Lauterpacht).

[67] *See*, *e.g.*, Second report on the draft Code of Offences against the Peace and Security of Mankind, by Mr. Doudou Thiam, Special Rapporteur, UN Doc. A/CN.4/377 (1984), *reprinted in* 1984 [II] 1 ILC Y.B. 89, 90 ('purpose is to formulate a list of offences today considered as offences'); Summary Record of the 1820th Meeting, 1984 [I] ILC Y.B. 28, 29 (statement of Mr. Sinclair) ('The key element . . . was that the international community . . . recognized the crimes in question as offences.').

[68] *See*, *e.g.*, Summary Records of the 1761st Meeting, 1983 [I] ILC Y.B. 35, 37 (statement of Mr. McCaffrey); Summary Records of the 1958th Meeting, 1986 [I] ILC Y.B. 94, 97 (statements of Messrs. Malek and Flitan); Summary Records of the 1960th Meeting, *id.* at 103, 104 (statement of Mr. Sinclair).

[69] 1996 ILC Report, at 93 (art. 18).

As for commentary, a number of scholars, principally European, long advocated that the nexus requirement is not necessary as a matter of *lex lata*.[70] The 1992 edition of *Oppenheim's International Law* found the link 'somewhat artificial' and the autonomy of crimes against humanity 'now generally regarded'.[71] The Chairmen of the Secretary-General's Commissions of Experts on the Former Yugoslavia and Rwanda have also rejected the link.[72] Today, after the creation of ICTR and the ICC Statutes, it is difficult to find any scholar who argues that the nexus is clearly required as a matter of *lex lata*.

Assessment

The foregoing suggests a gradual evolution of authoritative expectations on the nexus question. The World War II cases do not offer strong evidence on the necessity of the nexus, because the Allies chose to prosecute only crimes connected with the war; and there were few occasions outside the World War II context until the mid-1990s that would shed light on the positions of governments and international organizations. Nonetheless, during the drafting of the Statutory Limitations Convention, Western states came very close to embracing de-linkage by accepting that such crimes could be committed in peacetime. The prosecutions in Latvia, Estonia, and Ethiopia are probative of expectations today, if not perhaps of the time when the offenses were committed, that a linkage is no longer required. And the dicta in the decisions of the Yugoslavia Tribunal and the ILC's deliberations are also persuasive to this effect. The absence of any mention of the nexus in the Rwanda Tribunal Statute, and especially the rejection of such a nexus by the vast majority of states at the Rome Conference, appear very significant as an admission by governments of its obsolescence.

Moreover, behind these specific indicia of expectations has lain a fundamental constitutive change in international law since 1945, namely the elaboration of a comprehensive body of international human rights law to protect persons in times of peace and war, and indeed a general withering away of the traditional division between the international law of

70 *See, e.g.*, Graven, *supra* note 1, at 466–67, 543–44; EUGENE ARONEANU, LE CRIME CONTRE L'HUMANITÉ 48–50 (1961); Vespasien V. Pella, Mémorandum présenté par le Secrétariat, UN Doc. A/CN.4/39, *reprinted in* 1950 [II] ILC Y.B. 278, 347; *see also* Georges Levasseur, *Les crimes contre l'humanité et le problème de leur prescription*, 93 J. DROIT INT'L 259, 270–71 (1966); Resolution of the International Association of Penal Law, 1947, *translated and reprinted in* Joseph Y. Dautricourt, *Crime Against Humanity: European Views on Its Conception and Its Future*, 40 J. CRIM. L. AND CRIMINOLOGY 170, 171–72 (1949) [hereinafter IAPL Resolution].

71 1 OPPENHEIM'S INTERNATIONAL LAW 996 (Robert Jennings and Arthur Watts eds., 9th ed. 1992).

72 Letter dated 24 May 1994 from the Secretary-General to the President of the Security Council, May 27, 1994, UN Doc. S/1994/674, at 21 [hereinafter Yugoslavia Commission Final Report]; Letter dated 9 December 1994 from the Secretary-General Addressed to the President of the Security Council, Dec. 9, 1994, UN Doc. S/1994/1405, at 27 (Rwanda Commission).

peace and law of war.[73] Although this change in the legal landscape cannot alone serve to criminalize human rights violations in peacetime, it provides a context for the developments noted above and suggests an expectation by states that gross human rights violations in peacetime are as criminal as those during armed conflict. Though the question is not entirely free of doubt, the trend of decision since Nuremberg reflects a general acceptance by states of an end to the link between crimes against humanity and war crimes or crimes against the peace, and thus the position that acts may be deemed crimes against humanity without any link to armed conflict, international or internal.

The Mass or Systematic Nature of the Acts

The second distinguishing feature of crimes against humanity has centered on their pattern of occurrence. In its most basic sense, this involves an inquiry into the notion of 'humanity', i.e., does international law require a threshold or certain pattern of violence for a crime to become one against humanity? More specifically, it entails a discussion of the term 'against any civilian population', which appears in numerous definitions of crimes against humanity. The notion that a crime against humanity must be committed 'against a . . . population' has generally been interpreted as qualifying the nature of the atrocities in one of two ways: either in terms of their scale—namely, that they be against a large number of civilians; or alternatively, in terms of their method—namely, that they be committed in a planned, systematic manner insofar as they are directed against a specific 'population' and not merely random individuals.

Nuremberg and the Post-World War II Trials

Crimes against humanity in both the IMT Charter and Control Council Law No. 10 consisted of two separate clauses—murder and other acts 'against any civilian population'; and persecutions on political, racial, or religious grounds.[74] While, strictly speaking, these documents suggest that persecutions against isolated individuals would be covered, in practice the 'civilian population' language applied to both clauses of the definition.[75] In the '*Justice Case*', the American court interpreted this language as requiring systematic governmental action and thus precluded

[73] *See, e.g.*, MYRES S. MCDOUGAL, HAROLD D. LASSWELL, AND LUNG-CHU CHEN, HUMAN RIGHTS AND WORLD PUBLIC ORDER: THE BASIC POLICIES OF AN INTERNATIONAL LAW OF HUMAN DIGNITY 313–32 (1980); W. Michael Reisman, *Sovereignty and Human Rights in Contemporary International Law*, 84 AJIL 866 (1990).

[74] *See supra* text at notes 6 and 29.

[75] *See* Schwelb, *supra* note 5, at 190–91.

prosecutions for any 'isolated crime'.[76] The UN War Crimes Commission spoke of 'systematic mass action' as a necessary element.[77] This concept could refer to the number of victims, or it could simply be a synonym for systematic action, but it does not appear to address isolated acts, however shocking.[78]

National Laws and Prosecutions

Israel's war crimes statute retains the 'any civilian population' language, and the enormity of Eichmann's crimes obviated the need for the court to discuss whether it might cover isolated acts. The French law of 1964, as noted, adopted the IMT's definition, and the Cour de Cassation has equated that language with acts committed 'in a systematic manner'.[79] The 1992 French law also contains a requirement of systematicity, and the 1999 Belgian statute requires 'une attaque généralisée ou systématique'.[80] The Canadian statute uses the term 'against any civilian population or any identifiable group of persons'.[81] Neither the Australian nor Chinese laws mention systematicity or scale.[82]

Developments at the Global Level

The Statutes of the Yugoslavia and Rwanda Tribunals require, respectively, that acts be 'directed against any civilian population', and that they be 'part of a widespread or systematic attack against any civilian population'.[83] The difference in standards is curious, and hard to explain, though it does not seem to have mattered much in practice. The Yugoslavia Tribunal has interpreted crimes against humanity to include a requirement that the acts be part of a widespread *or* systematic attack; it has emphasized that systematicity turns on the existence of a preconceived policy, including the establishment of institutions and devotion of resources to

[76] *See Justice Case*, 3 CCL No. 10 Trials at 973, 985; *see also Einsatzgruppen Case*, 4 CCL No. 10 Trials at 498.

[77] UNWCC, *supra* note 8, at 179; *see also* SECRETARY-GENERAL OF THE UNITED NATIONS, THE CHARTER AND JUDGMENT OF THE NÜRNBERG TRIBUNAL: HISTORY AND ANALYSIS 66–67 (1949), UN Doc. A/CN.4/5, UN Sales No. 1949.V.7 [hereinafter 1949 SECRETARY-GENERAL MEMORANDUM]; Schwelb, *supra* note 5, at 191.

[78] *But see* Levasseur, *supra* note 70, at 270–71 (noting statement of Nuremberg Prosecutor de Menthon that if the authorities arrest and judge a woman for acts of resistance, it is a legitimate act; if they interrogate her under torture, it is a war crime; if they deport her to an extermination camp or use her for medical experiments, it is a crime against humanity).

[79] *Barbie*, 78 ILR at 137; *cf. id.* at 146 (submission by Advocate General).

[80] Nouveau Code pénal, art. 212–1 (Fr.), Law of 10 February 1999, *supra* note 41; *see also* Zoller, *supra* note 27, at 563–67.

[81] R.S.C. 1985, ch. C-46, § 3.76.

[82] War Crimes Amendment Act, 1989 Austl. Acts. No. 3, § 7(3)(a); Law of 24 October 1946, art. II(3), 14 War Crimes Report, at 153. *But see* 14 War Crimes Reports at 155 (commentary that Chinese law 'generally understood' to include acts committed systematically and on mass scale).

[83] ICTY Statute, art. 5; ICTR Statute, art. 3.

implement it. At the same time, the Tribunal has acknowledged that even a single act might qualify as a crime against humanity if it were part of such an attack.[84] The ICTR has interpreted the requirement in its Statute of a widespread or systematic attack as creating a rather high threshold.[85]

Governments at the Rome Conference debated the issue extensively, faced with strong diverging positions on whether the widespread/systematic criterion ought to be conjunctive or disjunctive. In the end, they adopted a disjunctive definition—'when committed as part of a widespread or systematic attack directed against any civilian population'—but then added a separate definition of that term, to wit, 'a course of conduct involving the multiple commission of acts . . . pursuant to or in furtherance of a State or organizational policy to commit such attack.' Whether this definitional solution effectively restores a requirement of both a widespread and systematic nature will depend on the ICC's interpretation of this phrase. Although NGOs lamented the inclusion of the definition, it is certainly possible that the court will interpret the multiple commission and policy elements of the definition as something less than a widespread *and* systematic attack.[86]

Subsidiary Sources

During the ILC's deliberations in the early 1950s, most of its members worked from the presumption that 'civilian population' involved more than individual members.[87] The ILC properly eliminated the awkward bifurcation of the IMT Charter, but maintained the requirement of action against a civilian population without dissent. The issue received significant discussion during the 1980s and 1990s. The 1996 Draft Code uses the term 'when committed in a systematic manner or on a large scale', thus excluding isolated acts not part of an overall policy.[88]

Scholarly opinion remains divided on the question of scale or system-

[84] *See* the detailed discussion in the *Tadic Judgment*, paras. 645–49; *Jelisic Judgment*, para. 53; *see also Tadic Appeal*, para. 248 (citing Prosecutor v. Mile Mrksic et al., Trial Chamber I, Apr. 3, 1996, para. 30). The Tribunal has similarly interpreted the term 'civilian' broadly, to include persons who were formerly combatants. *See Tadic Judgment*, paras. 636–43.

[85] *See Akayesu Judgment*, paras. 579–81 (widespread means 'massive, frequent, large scale action, carried out collectively with considerable seriousness and directed against a multiplicity of victims'; systematic means 'thoroughly organised and following a regular pattern on the basis of a common policy involving substantial public or private resources'); *Musema Judgment*, para. 204. It has also adopted an interpretation of 'civilian' similar to that of the ICTY. *Akayesu Judgment*, para. 582.

[86] ICC Statute, art. 7; *see also* Darryl Robinson, *Defining 'Crimes against Humanity' at the Rome Conference*, 93 AJIL 43, 47–51 (1999); Leila Nadya Sadat and S. Richard Carden, *The New International Criminal Court: An Uneasy Revolution*, 88 Geo. L.J. 381, 429–32 (2000).

[87] *See*, *e.g.*, Summary Records of the 90th Meeting, 1951 [I] ILC Y.B. 63, 68–69; Summary Records of the 91st Meeting, 1951 [I] ILC Y.B. 72, 74 (statement of Mr. Spiropoulos).

[88] 1996 ILC Report, at 93 (art. 18).

aticity.[89] Some have found both these elements unnecessary.[90] Professor Bassiouni, in his capacity as Chairman of the Commission of Experts for Yugoslavia, adopted the ILC's rationale that crimes be either carried out in a systematic way or by means of mass action. At the same time, he noted that 'the number of crimes and perpetrators are characteristically high'.[91]

Assessment

The overwhelming body of authority on this issue suggests that, for acts to be crimes against humanity, they must entail more than isolated instances. In particular, they must be undertaken in the context of a widespread attack or a systematic policy, or perhaps both. In most instances, both will be present, though clearly cases will arise where one is not accompanied by the other.

The law does not require that the defendant commit the act against numerous civilians. Indeed, the total number of direct victims (of the murder, torture, etc.) could be quite small, as long as the defendant nevertheless acted in a preconceived, systematic way; culpability would still appear to arise if the acts would still be, in the words of the IMT Charter, 'against a civilian population'. An example of a crime against humanity in the absence of a large number of direct victims might be the execution by Soviet authorities of Hungarian leader Imre Nagy in 1956; the target 'against' whom the action is committed was more than the victim himself. In such a case, even though the murder itself is not on a widespread or mass scale, because the killing of a political (or religious) leader is systematic insofar as it is meant to intimidate the entire 'civilian population' of his supporters (or coreligionists), it would represent a crime against humanity. Indeed, even if the victims were not leaders, a systematic act against deliberately targeted individuals could well be aimed at intimidating a broader population.[92]

A related interpretive difficulty concerns whether a large number of victims *per se* creates a crime against humanity, for instance in the case of those participating in a widespread or large-scale, but not planned or systematic, killing spree. These acts would seem to be 'against a civilian population' even though they are not truly systematic, simply by virtue of the number of people inherent in a 'population'. An example might entail

[89] *See* the excellent review in Fourth report on the draft Code of Offences against the Peace and Security of Mankind, by Mr. Doudou Thiam, Special Rapporteur, UN Doc. A/CN.4/398 (1986), *reprinted in* 1986 [II] 1 ILC Y.B. 53, 58–60 [hereinafter Fourth Report of the Special Rapporteur].

[90] *See, e.g.*, IAPL Resolution, *supra* note 70, at 172; MEYEROWITZ, *supra* note 11, at 254–55, 275–81; ARONEANU, *supra* note 70, at 56–57.

[91] Yugoslavia Commission Final Report, *supra* note 72, at 23.

[92] *Cf.* Ch. 2, Definition of Genocide, Numerical Issues, *supra*.

a group of Rwandan Hutu under the influence of drugs ransacking a Tutsi town and massacring its inhabitants. If governmental officials tolerated such killings through non-feasance, they might be guilty as well.

A final issue concerns the *mens rea* regarding the attack, i.e., whether the accused must have a certain awareness of the nature of the attack in order to be found guilty. Here the Yugoslavia and Rwanda Tribunals and the ICC Statute, endorsing reasoning of the Canadian Supreme Court in the *Finta* case, have unequivocally answered in the affirmative. This important link between the defendant's state of mind and the overall context of the crime against humanity ensures that acts contemporaneous with, though unrelated to, the attack on the civilian population are not the basis for prosecution.[93]

Grounds for Commission

Closely linked with the notion of systematicity or mass action is the question of the reasons for the attack on the population—namely, whether it must be based on some character trait of the victim. For purposes of discussion, one might also use the term 'discriminatory intent' to describe this element; however, various systems of criminal law use different terms (*e.g.*, specific intent or French phrases such as *mobile*, *intention-mobile*, and *motif*). This element, however, does not strictly speaking concern the precise motives of the perpetrator *vis-à-vis* the victim. That issue instead forms part of the question of the *mens rea*, or degree of consciousness of the perpetrator of his acts as he committed them.[94] Nevertheless, courts and commentators have not always made the distinction clear, often treating this element as part of *mens rea*, rather than as a characterization of the attack.[95]

Nuremberg and the Post-World War II Trials

The IMT Charter and CCL No. 10 list two sets of crimes: (1) murder and a list of other acts committed 'against any civilian population', and (2) 'persecutions on political, racial or religious grounds'. This language indicates the relevance of discriminatory grounds to persecutions, though not to murder and the other enumerated acts.[96] The bifurcation makes sense as an effort to derive notions of humanity. Certain acts are so heinous and

[93] *See Tadic Appeal*, para. 271 (requirement 'that the accused *knew* that his crimes were so related [to the attack on a civilian population]') (emphasis in original)); *Kayishema and Ruzindana Judgment*, paras. 133–34 (actual or constructive knowledge); ICC Statute, art. 7(1) ('with knowledge of the attack'); *see also* Van Schaack, *supra* note 28, at 835–37.

[94] For a detailed discussion, ultimately concluding that the accused's motives are irrelevant to guilt, *see Tadic Appeal*, paras. 238–72.

[95] *See, e.g.*, *Kupreskic Judgment*, paras. 632–66.

[96] 1949 SECRETARY-GENERAL MEMORANDUM, *supra* note 77, at 67–68.

destructive of a person's humanity that they *per se* are crimes. Others are crimes because the assault on the victim is based on political, racial, or religious grounds and thereby attacks humanity through some of the most basic groups into which it is organized.[97] During the post-war trials, the evidence showed overwhelmingly the Nazis' discriminatory basis for all crimes, so the Allies' case would have satisfied even a reading of the Charter that required including this criterion for all acts.

National Laws and Prosecutions

The issue of grounds for commission received extensive attention in several of the key war crime prosecutions. The Israeli law under which Eichmann was prosecuted used the bifurcated strategy of the IMT Charter, listing a series of acts against a civilian population and then adding 'persecution on national, racial, religious or political grounds'.[98] The district court easily found Eichmann guilty of crimes against humanity once it had determined his guilt of the higher threshold offense of crimes against the Jewish people.[99]

In *Barbie*, the Cour de Cassation addressed the issue directly. First, it interpreted the IMT Charter (the basis for the French law) as directed at crimes 'not only against persons by reason of their membership of [sic] a racial or religious community, but also against the opponents of [the government's] policy [of ideological supremacy], whatever the form of their opposition'.[100] It struck down the lower court's dismissal of charges against Barbie on the grounds that that court had mistakenly concluded that crimes against humanity could not occur against members of the Resistance since they did not comprise a racial or religious group. Instead, it found that Barbie could have 'acted with the element of intent [*élément intentionnel*] necessary for the commission of crimes against humanity'.[101] The court thus underlined the importance of grounds for commission and included political factors among them.[102] The 1992 French law lists the grounds for commission as an element of all crimes against humanity other than genocide (which is separately defined).[103]

97 Cf. MEYEROWITZ, *supra* note 11, at 276–77; Graven, *supra* note 1, at 545–48; Pella, *supra* note 70, at 348.

98 *See supra* note 37; *see also* Attorney-General v. Enigster, 18 ILR 540 (Tel Aviv Dist. Ct. 1952); Pal v. Attorney-General, 18 ILR 542 (Isr. Sup. Ct. 1952).

99 *Eichmann*, 36 ILR at 41, 239. This crime was based on the definition of genocide in the 1948 convention.

100 *Barbie*, 78 ILR at 137.

101 *Id.* at 140; *see also* 1986 JCP II No. 20655, paras. 42–43, 60–61 (report of Counsellor Le Gunehec).

102 *See* Wexler, *supra* note 39, at 359–60 (noting that court nonetheless incorrectly applied motive test to all crimes against humanity, when, according to IMT Charter art. 6(c), it applies only to persecutions).

103 Nouveau code pénal, art. 212–1 (Fr.) ('inspired by political, philosophical, racial or religious motives').

The Canadian statute under which Imre Finta was prosecuted lacks any explicit mention of discriminatory intent, although it does use the phrase 'committed against any civilian population or any identifiable group of persons',[104] which may imply a motivation against the 'identifiable group'. The Canadian Supreme Court found that a crime against humanity is distinguishable from an ordinary crime because it is 'undertaken in pursuance of a policy of discrimination or persecution of an identifiable group or race'.[105] The Australian act has two parts—genocidal acts with the specific 'intent to destroy' language of the Genocide Convention; and other crimes against humanity with the requirement that they be committed 'in the course of political, racial or religious persecution'.[106] Two judges in *Polyukhovich* defined a crime against humanity in terms of persecutions, one explicitly noting the grounds for commission.[107] The Chinese law of 1946 has some element of discrimination for all the acts; Belgium's 1999 statute adopts the ICC definition (see below).[108]

Developments at the Global Level

The ICTY Statute makes grounds for commission relevant only in the case of persecutions, and not a factor for murder, extermination, enslavement, deportation, imprisonment, torture, rape, and other inhumane acts; while the ICTR Statute includes grounds for commission for all offenses. For persecution, the Statutes list political, racial, and religious grounds, but not social or cultural grounds.[109] The Security Council thus seems to have assumed that customary international law made discriminatory grounds for the non-persecution offenses irrelevant 'beyond any doubt'[110] as of the adoption of the Yugoslavia Tribunal Statute in 1993. In the *Tadic* appeal, the ICTY reached a similar conclusion based on its view of customary international law, thereby refusing to impose a requirement of discriminatory intent on all crimes against humanity.[111] The inclusion of the discriminatory intent requirement for all crimes against humanity in the ICTR Statute is thus hard to justify, although it does not seem to have made a practical difference in the case of prosecutions.[112] In the case of

[104] *See supra* note 42.

[105] [1994] 1 S.C.R. at 814.

[106] War Crimes Amendment Act, 1989 Austl. Acts No. 3, § 7(3)(a)(i).

[107] 172 C.L.R. 501, 596 (Deane, J., concurring); *id.* at 664 (Toohey, J., concurring).

[108] Law of 24 October 1946, art. II(3), 14 War Crimes Reports at 153 (accused must 'nourish intentions of enslaving, crippling, or annihilating the Chinese Nation'); Law of 10 February 1999, *supra* note 41.

[109] ICTY Statute, art. 5; ICTR Statute, art. 3. The Rwanda Statute article is redundant in including grounds for commission in both the introductory sentence and separately for the persecution offense.

[110] Secretary-General's Yugoslavia Report, *supra* note 56, at 9.

[111] *Tadic Appeal*, paras. 281–305.

[112] *See Akayesu Judgment*, paras. 650, 658; *Rutaganda Judgment*, para. 443. The conviction of the defendants for genocide undoubtedly made the determination of discriminatory intent inevitable.

the ICC Statute, states returned to the more traditional division, requiring proof of discriminatory grounds only for persecutions; they appear, however, to have engaged in at least some progressive development of international law in enlarging the list of grounds substantially to include 'other grounds that are universally recognized as impermissible under international law'.[113]

Subsidiary Sources

The 1954 Draft Code adopted a definition of crimes against humanity in which grounds for commission is highly relevant—an illustrative list of 'inhuman acts' 'committed against any civilian population on social, political, racial, religious or cultural grounds'.[114] By ending the bifurcation in the IMT Charter and CCL No. 10, it sought to attach a discriminatory policy requirement to all crimes against humanity, including murder, torture, and the other enumerated acts.[115] In its discussions in both the 1950s and 1980s, the ILC operated from this premise.[116] The 1996 Draft Code reverts to the bifurcation in the Nuremberg Charter, eliminating the requirement of discriminatory grounds for all crimes against humanity except for 'persecution' and 'institutionalized discrimination'.[117]

Commentators agree upon the importance of grounds of commission to all crimes against humanity, emphasizing that the underlying policy exhibit a particular bias against the victim based on race, religion, politics, or other grouping.[118] The precision of their language regarding this element of the crime leaves something to be desired, with some confusion regarding whether they are concerned with the grounds of the crime—which ultimately turn on the status of the victim—or the state of mind of the perpetrator.[119] Some emphasize that motivation is the central distinguishing feature between a common crime and a crime against humanity.[120]

Assessment

The law thus appears to admit of two interpretations. First, a clear majority position, supported by the IMT Charter and important recent authorities,

113 ICC Statute, art. 7(1)(h); *see also* BASSIOUNI, supra note 3, at 202 (acts prohibited in international law 'though not necessarily criminalized'); Robinson, *supra* note 86, at 54.

114 *See supra* note 65.

115 *See* Sydney L. Goldenberg, *Crimes Against Humanity—1945–1970*, 10 U. W. ONTARIO L. REV. 1, 19 and n. 53 (1971).

116 *See* Summary Records of the 91st Meeting, 1951 [I] ILC Y.B. 72, 74 (statement of Mr. Scelle); Summary Records of the 269th Meeting, 1954 [I] ILC Y.B. 140, 142 (statement of Mr. Lauterpacht); Fourth Report of the Special Rapporteur, *supra* note 89, at 58 ('The only element which seems to be unanimously accepted is the *motive*.') (emphasis in original).

117 1996 ILC Report, at 93–94 (art. 18).

118 *See, e.g.*, Graven, *supra* note 1, at 546–47; ARONEANU, *supra* note 70, at 56–57, 70; BASSIOUNI, *supra* note 3, at 259–63.

119 *See* MEYEROWITZ, *supra* note 11, at 288–91.

120 *See* Pella, *supra* note 70, at 348.

namely the Yugoslavia Tribunal and ICC Statutes, views certain grave acts, such as murder, torture, or deportation, as so horrendous that the grounds for the attack of which they form a part are irrelevant. The discriminatory element of the policy matters only for persecutions, probably because the term suffers from a certain vagueness without such a qualification. A minority position would argue that all crimes against humanity require some underlying discriminatory intent that identifies the victim with a particular racial, religious, political, social, or cultural attribute. As a practical matter, these two positions likely converge in most situations. Gross violators of human rights usually commit their grave acts of terror based on some group affiliation of the victim, usually one based on political beliefs, a very broad category. Nonetheless, the distinction would matter in the case of systematic or widespread acts that are somehow undertaken without apparent discriminatory outlook toward the victims. The case of police officers who decide to demonstrate their authority by randomly selecting citizens for murder or torture would be one such case. Based on the IMT Charter and the Yugoslavia Tribunal and ICC Statutes, the nature of a crime against 'humanity' would justify criminalization even in the absence of special grounds for committing the act.

Second, the differences between the intent element of genocide and the discriminatory intent required for persecutions assumes significance for the gathering of evidence. For genocide, evidence of intent to destroy the group in whole or in part is required, although the precise reasons are irrelevant. For other crimes against humanity, no such intent is required, but for persecutions it must be demonstrated that the attack targeted the victim(s) specifically based on their social, political, racial, religious, or other attributes. A determination of which is more difficult to prove will depend upon the circumstances, although the genocidal intent would generally have a higher threshold.

State or Organizational Action

The final element of crimes against humanity concerns the entity responsible for the attack against the population. The issue here is whether governmental direction is necessary to transform a simple crime into one of interest to the international community rendering it a crime against humanity, or whether direction by some entity other than a state will suffice.[121]

[121] For certain well-recognized international crimes, such as genocide, slavery, and piracy, no link has ever been required. Indeed, piracy was criminal only because it lacked a link to state action. *See generally* NGUYEN QUOC DINH, DROIT INTERNATIONAL PUBLIC 621–24 (Patrick Daillier and Alain Pellet eds., 5th ed. 1994).

Nuremberg and the Post-World War II Trials

The IMT Charter gave the international tribunal the authority to punish persons 'acting in the interests of the European Axis countries, whether as individuals or as members of organizations'.[122] During the trials of the major war criminals, state action was, of course, easily proved. Control Council Law No. 10 is silent on the question of state action, and most of those tried under the law were governmental officials. In the cases of the German industrialists who took advantage of Nazi policies for financial advantage, the American zone courts adopted a looser standard, finding defendants guilty based on the conduct *per se* toward victims and not requiring any connection with state policy.[123]

National Laws and Prosecutions

The Israeli statute makes no reference to governmental conduct, but rather simply requires that the acts have taken place during the period of Nazi rule.[124] In the French prosecutions, the courts interpreted the IMT Charter to imply a linkage to governmental action, indeed that of a government 'practicing a hegemonic political ideology'.[125] The 1992 French law speaks only of a 'common plan'.[126] The Canadian law makes no reference to governmental action, although the Supreme Court of Canada in *Finta* found that the statute implied such a requirement.[127] The Australian law does not require governmental action for its version of crimes against humanity, nor did the Chinese law make any such reference.[128]

Developments at the Global Level

Recent decisions evince a clear move away from a requirement of state action and a recognition that non-state actors can and do commit egregious assaults on human dignity that should incur individual responsibility under international law. Thus, neither the ICTY nor ICTR Statutes makes any such reference,[129] a deliberate decision of the Security Council due to the multiplicity of crimes committed by persons not associated with a recognized state. The ICTY has acknowledged this development,

122 IMT Charter, art. 6; *see also id.* art. 7.

123 *See* United States v. Flick et al., 6 CCL No. 10 Trials at 1201–02 (finding Flick guilty of procurement of slave labor, though not as part of Hitler's program); United States v. Krauch et al. (the '*I.G. Farben Case*'), 8 CCL No. 10 Trials 1081, 1167–92.

124 Israeli Law, *supra* note 37, 36 ILR at 7.

125 *See, e.g., Barbie*, 78 ILR at 137; *Touvier*, 100 ILR at 363; Wexler, *supra* note 39, at 360–61.

126 Nouveau Code pénal, art. 212–1 (Fr.), *see also* the Belgian statute, *supra* note 41, modeled on the ICC definition.

127 R.S.C. 1985, c. C-46, § 3.76; *Finta*, [1994] 1 S.C.R. at 823.

128 War Crimes Amendment Act, 1989 Austl. Acts No. 3, § 7(3); Law of 24 October 1946, art. II(3), 14 War Crimes Reports at 153.

129 *See supra* note 22.

endorsing the view that the attack can emanate from 'entities exercising *de facto* control over a particular territory but without international recognition or formal status of a *de jure* state, or by a terrorist group or organization'.[130] The ICTY and ICTR Prosecutor has not indicted private persons in the sense of those not associated with one of the sides in the conflict.[131] The ICC Statute, for its part, refers in Article 7 to 'a state or organizational policy', a term broad enough to include private entities.

Subsidiary Sources

The ILC's 1954 Draft Code requires that the acts be committed 'by the authorities of a State or by private individuals acting at the instigation or with the toleration of such authorities'.[132] This would ensure that an inhuman act by a private individual would not *per se* constitute an international crime. In the 1980s, the Commission seemed to move in the direction of acknowledging the possibility of crimes against humanity by non-state actors. The 1996 Draft Code speaks of acts 'instigated or directed by a government or by any organization or group', and the ILC's commentary makes clear the desire to cover private groups or criminal gangs committing systematic or mass human rights violations.[133]

Until the 1990s, most commentators have regarded governmental action as required.[134] Most, however, ignored the proliferation of powerful quasi-governmental organizations in civil conflicts, such as those working for a self-proclaimed secessionist state. Recent commentary has taken account of this trend and argued for the recognition of non-state actors as instigators of crimes against humanity.[135]

Assessment

Although the practice of states and other sources were not uniform, the prevailing view until fairly recently remained that crimes against humanity require an element of state action. The IMT Charter, the 1954 Draft Code, and the views of most scholars retained the requirement that crimes

130 *Tadic Judgment*, paras. 654, 655; *Kupreskic Judgment*, paras. 551–52.

131 The Rwanda Tribunal did indict and receive a guilty plea from a Belgian journalist who broadcast anti-Tutsi messages for a government-controlled radio station. *See Ruggiu Sentencing Judgment.*

132 1954 ILC Report, at 140, 150 (art. 2(11)). This language was added to the final definition at the same time that the Commission deleted the nexus to war crimes and crimes against the peace, crimes that typically require state action.

133 1996 ILC Report, at 93 (art. 18), 95.

134 *See, e.g.*, Pella, *supra* note 70, at 348; Jacques-Bernard Herzog, *Contribution à l'étude de la définition de crime contre l'humanité*, 18 Rev. Int'l Droit Pénal 155, 168 (1947); Meyerowitz, *supra* note 11, at 255–57; for alternate views, *see, e.g.*, Graven, *supra* note 1, at 486 n. 3 ('celui qui, sans droit, porte atteinte, pour des motifs'); IAPL Resolution, *supra* note 70, at 171–72.

135 *See* Bassiouni, *supra* note 3, at 273–75; Joseph Rikhof, *Crimes against Humanity, Customary International Law and the International Tribunals for Bosnia and Rwanda*, 6 Nat'l J. Const'l L. 233, 254–61 (1996).

against humanity be instigated or tolerated by governmental authorities, although the sources do not limit the state to the central government. These views, of course, did not take account of the possibility that entities describing themselves as state actors or as powerful as state actors, but not recognized as such, would commit such offenses.[136] The Yugoslavia Tribunal, Rwanda Tribunal, and ICC Statutes recognize this anachronism, as do the French, Canadian, Belgian, and Australian statutes. These developments suggest that a linkage to state action—in the sense of the policy of the recognized government of a state—is now outdated. Non-state entities may perpetrate an attack on civilian populations.

At the same time, the reasoning in the *Tadic* judgment and the focus of prosecutions in the cases of the former Yugoslavia and Rwanda suggests that some sort of 'official' action remains associated with the concept. In particular, those committing the offenses typically are part of an organization seeking political control of or influence over a territory, whether as a *de facto* government, armed insurrection, or otherwise. A more challenging case would concern an attempt to prosecute as crimes against humanity abuses committed by an actor as part of a policy aimed at private gain alone, such as mass killings by a member of an organized crime syndicate or corporation. The German industrialist cases and the ICC Statute would support such an interpretation, based on the teleological view that such private entities are capable of bringing about significant human suffering.

ACTS CONSTITUTING CRIMES AGAINST HUMANITY

As noted in Chapter 1, because international law does not 'incorporate' all human rights law, the acts constituting crimes against humanity will generally be those characterized by the directness and gravity of their assault upon the human person, both corporeal and spiritual. As for the definition of each act, e.g., 'torture' or 'rape', in some instances, states may have agreed upon a definition in an international convention, though their definition of the act as a crime against humanity could be broader or narrower than other international definitions. More commonly, each domestic legal system adopts somewhat differing usages, and international courts or other decision-makers need to derive (and have derived) their own definitions. One method for this exercise entails recourse to general principles of law recognized by the community of nations. Although the criminalization of an act in numerous domestic legal systems does not, *ipso facto*, lead to its international criminalization,

136 *See generally* W. Michael Reisman, *Private Armies in a Global War System: Prologue to Decision*, 14 VIRG. J. INT'L L. 1 (1973).

national definitions prove significant in elaborating the international definition of these acts. In this way, general principles can fill in gaps in international law.[137]

In arriving at a definition, a court will also need to take account of *mens rea*, or the degree of consciousness by the perpetrator required for each act. The United States Model Penal Code identifies four levels—purposely, knowingly, recklessly, and negligently—and defines certain crimes with respect to given levels of *mens rea*.[138] Each system of law may define the requisite *mens rea* differently, however.[139] *Mens rea* becomes more complex with respect to large-scale, orchestrated crimes against humanity. In such cases, each contributor to the crime may have a different awareness of the consequences of his actions. The post-World War II trials dealt with the issue in detail, generally finding guilt for crimes against humanity if the defendant knew the consequences of his actions.[140] The Statute of the International Criminal Court defines a number of the enumerated acts with some precision. Nevertheless, at the insistence of the United States, the Statute contemplates the development of more detailed elements for all the crimes in the Statute (to be adopted by two-thirds of the states parties), and the Preparatory Commission for the Court completed a draft in July 2000.[141]

Murder and Extermination

The deliberate taking of human life represents, of course, the quintessential crime against humanity. Lists of crimes against humanity, beginning with the IMT Charter and up through the ICTY and ICTR Statutes, the ILC's 1996 Draft Code, and the ICC Statute, begin with this crime. Though every legal system outlaws murder, domestic and international

[137] *See* Ian Brownlie, Principles of Public International Law 16 (5th ed. 1998); Bin Cheng, General Principles of Law as Applied by International Courts and Tribunals 389–90 (Grotius Pubs. 1987) (1953); Bassiouni, *supra* note 3, at 284–89; *see also* Ch. 1, note 34, *supra* (disagreement among ICTY judges on this issue).

[138] *See, e.g.*, Model Penal Code, § 2.02 (1985); *id.* § 210.2 (1980) (murder requires homicide done purposely, knowingly, or recklessly manifesting extreme indifference to human life).

[139] *See, e.g.*, Regina v. Finta, [1994] 1 S.C.R. 701, 753–66 (La Forest, J., dissenting) (criticizing trial court for high *mens rea* requirement).

[140] *See* Matthew Lippman, *The Other Nuremberg: American Prosecutions of Nazi War Criminals in Occupied Germany*, 3 Indiana Int'l and Comp. L. Rev. 1, 86–90 (1992). For example, certain German industrialists who shipped Zyklon-B gas and pharmaceuticals to concentration camps were found not guilty based on their defense that the gas could have been used for insecticide purposes and the drugs for legitimate uses. *I.G. Farben Case*, 8 CCL No. 10 Trials at 1167–72. *See also Finta*, [1994] 1 S.C.R. at 819.

[141] *See* ICC Statute, arts. 7(2), 9; *see also* Mahnoush H. Arsanjani, *The Rome Statute of the International Criminal Court*, 93 AJIL 22, 35 (1999); Report of the Preparatory Commission for the International Criminal Court: Addendum: Finalized draft text of the Elements of Crimes, July 6, 2000, UN Doc. PCNICC/2000/INF/3/Add.2.

definitions vary, often with differing *mens rea*.[142] The term starvation appears in the Israeli definition of crimes against humanity as well, and death through this means is tantamount to deliberate killing.[143]

Enslavement and Forced Labor

Enslavement also appears at the beginning of most lists, as it deprives people of their most basic recognition as human beings. Forced labor deprives an individual of control of his body and, typically, the fruits of his labor. The Nuremberg convictions of von Schirach and Sauckel confirmed that, as a general matter, organization of forced labor is a crime against humanity.[144] Both terms have also been defined in numerous conventions.[145] The ICC Statute's definition in Article 7 requires the 'exercise of any or all of the powers attaching to the right of ownership'. States may permit forced labor under limited circumstances (*e.g.*, as part of prison work), suggesting that prohibited forced labor is confined to what the IMT called 'slave labor' or 'the systematic exploitation, by force, of . . . labor resources'.[146] As discussed in Chapter 5 below, slavery incurs individual responsibility under international law apart from its status as a crime against humanity.

Deportation

Deportation, the forced removal of a population from its home state to another state, also formed part of the core list at Nuremberg and has remained on the list of crimes in the ICTY, ICTR, and ICC Statutes and the 1954 and 1996 Draft Codes. In dictum, the lower court in *Eichmann* rejected the notion that a deportation was not a crime against humanity if carried out in a humane manner.[147]

Forced population transfers within a state's borders prove somewhat more controversial.[148] They are not included in the ICTY or ICTR Statutes. Nonetheless, despite disagreements within the ILC, the 1996

[142] *See Akayesu Judgment*, para. 589–92 (distinguishing murder from extermination); *Kupreskic Judgment*, paras. 560–61; *Celebici Judgment*, paras. 422, 439.

[143] Israeli Law, *supra* note 37, 36 ILR at 7.

[144] 22 IMT Trials at 565–68.

[145] *See* Ch. 5, Slavery and Forced Labor, *infra*.

[146] 22 IMT Trials at 567; *see also Ministries Case*, 14 CCL No. 10 Trials 308, 794–800; *cf.* Report of the International Law Commission on the work of its forty-first session, UN Doc. A/44/10 (1989), *reprinted in* 1989 [II] 2 ILC Y.B. 1, 61.

[147] *Eichmann*, 36 ILR at 247–48.

[148] *See generally* Michael P. Roch, *Forced Displacement in the Former Yugoslavia: A Crime Under International Law?*, 14 Dick. J. Int'l L. 1 (1995).

Draft Code adds the term 'forcible transfer of population' to include those movements wholly within the borders of one state; the ICC Statute includes the same term.[149] Commentators have been divided over the inclusion of these acts in crimes against humanity.[150] Their criminality appears to depend upon the purposes for and means by which the state accomplishes the forced transfer.[151] If the state seeks to avoid a humanitarian crisis and accomplishes the transfer with due regard for human welfare, characterization as a crime against humanity seems unlikely. A brutal transfer even for purportedly justifiable reasons (such as claimed lack of food in certain areas) would be a crime.

Imprisonment

Although the IMT Charter did not enumerate imprisonment as a separate offense (but rather incorporated it in the broader notion of 'inhuman acts'[152]), it did appear in the definition in Control Council Law No. 10. The 1954 Draft Code did not list it separately, but it does appear in the ICTY and ICTR Statutes, the 1996 Draft Code, and the ICC Statute. In order to be a crime against humanity, imprisonment must presumably occur without due process.[153]

Torture

Torture was also added to CCL No. 10 from the IMT Charter. While it is not listed in the 1954 Draft Code, it does appear in the Statutes for the Yugoslavia and Rwanda Tribunals, the 1996 Draft Code, and the ICC Statute. Like slavery, torture is also defined separately in international conventions.[154] It clearly constitutes one of the core crimes against humanity.

[149] *Compare* Summary Records of the 2098th Meeting, 1989 [I] ILC Y.B. 16, 17 (statement of Mr. Reuter) *with* Summary Records of the 2100th Meeting, *id.* at 26, 32 (statement of Mr. Tomuschat); *see also* 1996 ILC Report, at 93–94 (art. 18); ICC Statute, arts. 7(1)(d) and 7(2)(d).

[150] *See* Roch, *supra* note 148, at 26; BASSIOUNI, *supra* note 3, at 312; Timothy L.H. McCormack and Gerry J. Simpson, *The International Law Commission's Draft Code of Crimes against the Peace and Security of Mankind: An Appraisal of the Substantive Provisions*, 5 CRIM. L. FORUM 1, 23–24 (1994).

[151] *Cf.* ICC Statute, art. 7(2)(d) ('without grounds permitted under international law'); 1996 ILC Report, at 100; *Eichmann*, 36 ILR at 248.

[152] 1947 ANN. DIG. AND REP. OF PUB. INT'L L. CASES 100–01 (Spruchgericht, Stade 1947) (Germany).

[153] *See* Trial of Willy Zuehlke, 14 War Crimes Reports 139, 145 (Neth. Special Ct. Amsterdam and Special Ct. Cass. 1948); 1996 ILC Report, at 101; ICC Statute, art. 7(1)(e) ('in violation of fundamental rules of international law'); *cf.* Pella, *supra* note 70, at 346 ('la détention illégale').

[154] *See* Ch. 5, Torture, *infra*. The ICTR derived its definition of torture from the 1984 Torture Convention. *Akayesu Judgment*, paras. 593–94; *see also Furundzija Judgment*, paras. 159–64 (definition for purposes of war crime); *Celebici Judgment*, paras. 452–74.

Rape

As with imprisonment and torture, the drafters of CCL No. 10 also added this crime to the list in the IMT Charter. It does not appear in the 1954 ILC Draft Code, but is in the ICTY and ICTR Statutes. The 1996 Draft Code includes enforced prostitution and other forms of sexual abuse, to which the ICC Statute adds sexual slavery, forced pregnancy, and enforced sterilization. Rape has been a feature of the Yugoslavia and Rwanda conflicts, and both Tribunals have offered detailed definitions of rape that encompass a broad range of physical invasions of a sexual nature.[155] Rape and similar acts have clearly come to constitute one of the principal crimes against humanity.[156]

Other Inhumane or Inhuman Acts

This term also owes its origin to the IMT Charter and CCL No. 10, which used the term 'other inhuman acts' (Charter) or 'other inhumane acts' (Law No. 10) to round out the list of the first-tier crimes, i.e., those for which discriminatory intent was not relevant. The term appears in the ICTY, ICTR, and ICC Statutes.

Although the International Military Tribunal never provided a definition of inhuman acts, one CCL No. 10 court adopted a standard that appealed to 'the dictates of public conscience' and thus found medical experimentation to be a crime against humanity.[157] The *Eichmann* court spoke of inhumane acts as those 'causing serious physical and mental harm'.[158] The Australian war crimes statute seems similar, listing a number of acts that would clarify the meaning of inhumane, in particular 'grievous bodily harm'.[159] The Canadian Supreme Court adopted a somewhat different test in *Finta*, noting that inhumane acts have 'that requisite added dimension of cruelty and barbarism'.[160] More recently, the Yugoslavia and Rwanda Tribunals have given further specificity to the terms. The ICTY has determined that other inhumane acts must be as

155 *See Akayesu Judgment*, paras. 596–98; *Furundzija Judgment*, paras. 174–86 (definition for purposes of war crime); *Celebici Judgment*, paras. 475–97 (rape as act of torture); *Musema Judgment*, paras. 220–29; Kelly D. Askin, *Sexual Violence in Decisions and Indictments of the Yugoslav and Rwandan Tribunals: Current Status*, 93 AJIL 97 (1999); *see also* ICC Statute, arts. 7(1)(g) (sexual crimes), 7(2)(f) (definition of forced pregnancy).

156 *Cf.* Patricia Viseur Sellers and Kaoru Okuizumi, *International Prosecution of Sexual Assaults*, 7 TRANSNAT'L L. AND CONTEMP. PROBS. 45 (1997); Theodor Meron, *Rape as a Crime under International Humanitarian Law*, 87 AJIL 424, 427–28 (1993).

157 *Medical Case*, 2 CCL No. 10 Trials at 183.

158 *Eichmann*, 36 ILR at 239; *see also* In re Quispel, 1949 ANN. DIG. AND REP. OF PUB. INT'L L. CASES 395 (Neth. Special Ct. Cass. 1950).

159 War Crimes Amendment Act, 1989 Austl. Acts No. 3, § 6(1)(c).

160 *Finta*, [1994] 1 S.C.R. at 818.

serious as the previously enumerated acts and found two defendants guilty for forcing a family to witness the murder of a family member, expelling them from the house, and burning it down; the ICTR similarly found the forced undressing and parading of women an inhumane act.[161]

The ILC's 1996 Draft Code includes only inhumane acts 'which severely damage physical or mental integrity, health or human dignity', noting mutilation and severe bodily harm as examples; and the ICC Statute adopts a similar view.[162] Writers have similarly emphasized the need for some serious attack on body or health, a characterization that also appears in the grave breaches article of the Geneva Convention Relative to the Protection of Civilian Persons in Time of War.[163] All these characterizations suggest that 'inhuman acts' include numerous horrendous practices that demonstrate the same level of depravity as the listed crimes, such as medical experimentation, mutilations, severe beatings, food deprivation, sterilizations, violations of corpses, forced undressing, forced witnessing of atrocities against loved ones, and other egregious physical and mental assaults.

Persecutions

The term 'persecutions' appears originally in the IMT Charter, and, despite its lack of precision, is on virtually every other list of crimes against humanity. In the IMT Charter and Control Council Law No. 10, only persecutions had the requirement that they be undertaken on racial, religious, or political grounds; this requirement, or a variant of it, remains with the ICTY, ICTR, and ICC Statutes, and the 1996 ILC Draft Code.[164] The Nuremberg trials found that numerous acts committed against Jews and others constituted persecutions, though it remains unclear how the courts would have responded in the absence of the more gross crimes.

The post-war courts did not define persecutions or prosecute for crimes against humanity based solely on that component of the definition. The IMT emphasized the attempted extermination of the Jews, although the American court in the *Ministries Case* listed a series of acts, noting the progressive severity of the Nazi actions. These included deprivations of

[161] *Kupreskic Judgment*, paras. 562–66, 819–22, 830–32; *Akayesu Judgment*, para. 697.

[162] *See* 1996 ILC Report, at 94 (art. 18); ICC Statute, art. 7(1)(k) ('other inhumane acts of a similar character intentionally causing great suffering, or serious injury to body or to mental or physical health').

[163] Geneva Convention IV, art. 147, 75 UNTS at 388; *see* Pella, *supra* note 70, at 346; Graven, *supra* note 1, at 548–54; *Jelisic Judgment*, para. 52 (equating inhumane acts with such treatment under grave breaches provision).

[164] ICTY Statute, art. 5(h); ICTR Statute, art. 3(h); ICC Statute, art. 7(h) ('political, racial, national, ethnic, cultural, religious, gender . . . or other grounds that are universally recognized as impermissible under international law'); 1996 ILC Report, at 94 (art. 18), 98.

the rights to citizenship, to teach, to practice professions, to obtain education, and to marry freely; arrest and confinement; beatings, mutilation, and torture; confiscation of property; deportation to ghettos; slave labor; and extermination.[165]

The most sophisticated modern jurisprudence on the concept of persecution has emanated from the Yugoslavia Tribunal. Trial chambers have carefully reviewed the caselaw and reached similar conclusions on two core issues: (1) persecution includes a broad range of severe acts that violate an individual's basic rights under international law; and (2) persecution requires a discriminatory intent. The court convicted Dusko Tadic of persecution based on his role in numerous attacks on and forced removal of civilians; and convicted others of persecution for the ethnic cleansing of the village of Ahmici.[166] The ICC Statute has adopted a similar notion of persecution.[167] At the same time, however, the ICC Statute requires that the persecution take place in connection with either genocide, war crimes, or the other enumerated acts of crimes against humanity, a compromise reached to respond to the concerns of states that persecution was otherwise too elastic a term. The ICTY found that definition overly strict and not required by customary international law.[168]

These recent developments help remove some of the uncertainty from the notion of persecution. Thus, certain policies clearly detrimental to a person's core humanity are so close to the type of acts for which the Nuremberg courts found guilt that they qualify as crimes against humanity. These would include the acts considered by the Yugoslavia Tribunal, as well as others, such as removal of children from school, forced wearing of distinctive garb, *en masse* disqualification from certain professions, prohibitions on marriage to non-members, closure of religious institutions, and apartheid-like practices.[169] Nevertheless, persecution remains the least precise of the enumerated acts, justifying avoidance of an overly broad interpretation to respect the principle of *nullum crimen sine lege.*

165 22 IMT Trials at 491–96; *Ministries Case*, 14 CCL No. 10 Trials at 471.

166 *See Tadic Judgment*, paras. 694–718 and especially paras. 710 and 717; *Kupreskic Judgment*, paras. 567–636, 770–784 and especially paras. 621 and 627. For commentators favoring this position, *see* Pella, *supra* note 70, at 346; Graven, *supra* note 1, at 554–55; Meyerowitz, *supra* note 11, at 257–59; Bassiouni, *supra* note 3, at 326–30.

167 ICC Statute, para. 7(2)(g) ('intentional and severe deprivation of fundamental rights contrary to international law by reason of the identity of the group or collectivity').

168 *See* ICC Statute, art. 7(1)(h); Robinson, *supra* note 86, at 53–55; *Kupreskic Judgment*, paras. 578–81. The court also found that the other enumerated acts of crimes against humanity could constitute persecution if the requisite discriminatory grounds were present. *Id.* para. 605.

169 In this context, both the ICC Statute and the 1996 ILC Draft Code include apartheid or its equivalent as a crime against humanity. ICC Statute, arts. 7(1)(j), 7(2)(h); 1996 ILC Report, at 94 (art. 18), 99–100.

Property Crimes

The scope of the terms 'persecutions' or 'inhuman' or 'inhumane' acts has also included destruction and plunder of private property. The IMT found Alfred Rosenberg, Minister for the Occupied Eastern Territories, and Walter Funk, the Minister of Economics, Plenipotentiary-General for War Economy, and President of the Reichsbank, guilty of various acts of plunder of Jewish property, including transfer of property of concentration camp victims. However, the court seemed to regard most plunder *per se* as a war crime only.[170]

In *Flick*, the CCL No. 10 court, in dicta, wrote 'the catch-all words "other persecutions" must be deemed to include only such as affect the life and liberty of the oppressed peoples. Compulsory taking of industrial property, however reprehensible, is not in that category.'[171] In the *Ministries Case*, the court found that the imposition of a massive fine on Jews after *Kristallnacht* and confiscation of possessions of inmates or deported Jews were crimes against humanity.[172] In *Eichmann*, the Israeli district court determined that seizure of property could constitute a crime against humanity only if 'committed by pressure of mass terror' or linked with other crimes against humanity.[173]

The Yugoslavia Tribunal has taken a somewhat broader view. Trial courts have noted that property crimes can constitute persecutions if they violate a fundamental right of the victim, e.g., through the destruction of a home or business.[174] Of the handful of commentators who have examined the question, some have noted that the effects of property destruction or the means by which it is accomplished justify including many such acts as crimes against humanity.[175]

Disappearances

A recent addition to the list of acts considered as crimes against humanity is forced disappearance, namely the abduction and clandestine detention of individuals, typically accompanied by violence against them, including murder. The Organization of American States has declared the systematic

[170] 22 IMT Trials at 481–86, 540–41, 551–52.

[171] 6 CCL No. 10 Trials at 1215. The court, however, left open the possibility that seizure of personal assets would merit different treatment. *Id.* at 1214.

[172] 14 CCL No. 10 Trials at 675–78.

[173] 36 ILR at 241.

[174] *Tadic Judgment*, para. 710; *Kupreskic Judgment*, para. 631.

[175] *See* Hersch Lauterpacht, *The Law of Nations and the Punishment of War Crimes*, 21 Brit. Y.B. Int'l L. 58, 79 (1944); Seventh report on the draft code of Crimes against the Peace and Security of Mankind, by Mr. Doudou Thiam, Special Rapporteur, UN Doc. A/CN.4/419 and Add.1 (1989), *reprinted in* 1989 [II] 1 ILC Y.B. 81, 87–88. *But see* Graven, *supra* note 1, at 551–52.

practice of forced disappearances a crime against humanity, as does the 1992 French statute; the ICC Statute also includes the crime.[176] States have also begun to consider disappearance a separate crime as well.[177]

Assessment

As encapsulated by the Yugoslavia Tribunal in one of its first opinions, crimes against humanity are best viewed as 'serious acts of violence which harm human beings by striking what is most essential to them: their life, liberty, physical welfare, health, or dignity'.[178] A review of the above list of crimes leads to the conclusion that the following acts, if they meet the special elements of a crime against humanity, clearly constitute such crimes: murder, extermination, enslavement, forced labor, deportation and unjustified or cruel forced population transfers, imprisonment, torture, rape and other forms of sexual abuse, inhumane acts constituting severe attacks on the human person, persecution that denies basic human rights, and certain severe deprivations of property. Disappearances without proof of murder are now also recognized as crimes against humanity.

THEORETICAL AND PRACTICAL CHALLENGES

Crimes against humanity, as developed from the progeny of Nuremberg, thus remain of central importance to those seeking to bring to justice gross abusers of human rights. The IMT Charter's definition remains, in one sense, the 'common denominator of the conscience of mankind',[179] but its elements and nuances have developed and changed, in particular through the jurisprudence of the Yugoslavia and Rwanda Tribunals and the ICC Statute. Those seeking to apply the law to particular instances, however, face interpretive obstacles with respect to both the general elements and the particular crimes discussed above.

First, although the nexus between crimes against humanity and armed conflict is now severed, those examining older instances need to be aware that customary law usually changes by evolution, not revolution. The state of the law at earlier times may not be as clear on the absence of a required link. Secondly, the systematicity and discriminatory intent elements demand a careful look at the underlying policy of the regime committing

176 *See supra* note 21; Inter-American Convention on the Forced Disappearance of Persons, June 9, 1994, preamb. para. 6, 33 ILM 1529, 1530 (1994); Nouveau Code pénal, art. 212–1 (Fr.); ICC Statute, arts. 7(1)(i), 7(2)(i).

177 *See* Ch. 5, Forced Disappearances, *infra*.

178 *Erdemovic Sentencing Judgment*, para. 28.

179 *Barbie*, 78 ILR at 144 (statement of Advocate General Dontenwille).

the abuses. The lack of precise contours for 'systematic' or 'mass' action suggests that investigators and prosecutors err on the side of proving the existence of both through strong evidence. Thirdly, courts will have to wrestle with the mindset of those actually carrying out the crimes in terms of their awareness of the attack on the civilian population and their particular animus toward the victims' group affiliation.

Fourthly, the official status of the perpetrator can become an issue in a prosecution, especially for those actors not holding themselves out as agents of governments. Many important non-state actors will qualify, typically those seeking control over territory. Private actors committing atrocities for private gain will remain more difficult targets than those connected with a state or political organization. Lastly, the precise definitions of the individual acts will require elaboration from principles of domestic law and other sources of international law. This may not be difficult for many crimes (e.g., rape or deportations), but may require careful line-drawing with respect to less precise terms like 'persecutions'.

Beyond these interpretive difficulties lies the more fundamental question of the normative acceptability of crimes against humanity as currently defined in international law. States and other decision-makers have authoritatively sought to limit the scope of crimes against humanity in two ways: first, by determining that many atrocious acts, such as murder and rape, do not represent crimes against humanity unless they are accompanied by special elements related to an overall attack on a civilian population; and secondly, that many human rights abuses, such as suppression of the press or rigging of elections, will not become crimes against humanity even if they are accompanied by those special elements (unless they could fall under the term 'persecution'). These distinctions are, to say the least, not intuitively obvious.

The notion of confining the scope of crimes against humanity seems desirable at the relatively early stage in the prescriptive and applicative process in which international criminal law finds itself. Just as the International Covenant on Civil and Political Rights does not address all human rights that states should guarantee, or provide the highest level of protection for those recognized, so the concept of crimes against humanity does not include all murders as international offenses. It is important to gain consensus on the most grave crimes, even if that means continued adherence to some of the limitations in crimes against humanity developed at Nuremberg. The change in some expectations since Nuremberg—namely the severing of the nexus to armed conflict and the elimination of the requirement of governmental action—does not mean that all elements of the IMT definition are to be discarded. For the same reason, it appears appropriate to show caution with respect to the list of acts considered as crimes against humanity. The importance of converged expectations on the most grave breaches of human dignity ought not to be sacrificed over disagreements on including acts that, while abusive of human rights, do not create the same impact on the individual. In this sense, the broad acceptance by states of the ICC's definition is most welcome.

At the same time, the elements that confine the scope of crimes against humanity may not always satisfy our normative inclinations. In particular, the requirement of action 'against a civilian population' suggests that even the most atrocious acts are not crimes against humanity if they are truly isolated. Similarly, the discriminatory intent requirement for persecutions suggests that some actions undertaken without regard for specific traits of the victims' identity—*e.g.*, an order by an insane leader to persecute a group picked arbitrarily—is not of international concern. (Indeed, an order to destroy a city for purportedly military reasons alone, without regard to the identity of the inhabitants, might conceivably not qualify presently as a crime against humanity.) The emphasis on some form of official action—though not necessarily that of the recognized government—remains more justifiable because of the focus of human rights and humanitarian law on protecting individuals from those with power over them; yet it is equally clear that profit-driven entities may commit horrendous acts as well.

Despite these shortcomings in the law, it is not immediately apparent that other lines will avoid equally disturbing normative qualms, and the current definitions have the advantage of covering the vast majority of atrocities that governments and non-governmental entities have wreaked upon their populations. Moreover, international law does provide for criminalization of some acts committed without regard to scale or systematicity, such as war crimes, torture, and slavery. At this stage of the international legal process, the priority would appear to lie with sharpening the consensus on those areas of crimes against humanity on which there is general agreement. Through further actions by states, courts, and international organizations, the current shared expectations can be further elaborated into detailed definitions to facilitate future accountability.

4

War Crimes and the Limitations of Accountability for Acts in Armed Conflict

Although states at peace have shown themselves quite capable of committing gross abuses of human rights, the hatred, tension, and upheaval inherent in armed conflicts, and, in particular, civil wars, creates a fertile ground for horrendous attacks on the dignity of the individual. Indeed, as noted in Chapter 1, the protection of non-combatants during wartime through *jus in bello* preceded the development of human rights law and, although influenced by the latter, has in many ways advanced independently of it. Yet, because international humanitarian law provides a base level of protections to persons during times of armed conflict, it clearly has an incidental, if not deliberate, effect on the human rights of those caught up in war.

With respect to criminality, the evolution of international humanitarian law has resulted in the identification of certain acts as crimes—war crimes—even when those acts might not create individual culpability under international law during times of peace. At the same time, of course, the existence of a separate corpus of war crimes in no way diminishes the pertinence of norms concerning genocide, crimes against humanity, and other independent crimes, for they apply both in times of peace and of armed conflict. Consistent with the tenor of this volume, this chapter focuses on those aspects of the law of war relevant to human rights atrocities, rather than the full range of war crimes.

FROM ANCIENT ORIGINS TO MODERN CODES

Jus in bello is one of the oldest subjects of international law.[1] It has a long history in customary law, in sources both Western and Asian.[2] The modern origins spring from the last part of the nineteenth century, during which a

[1] Excellent historical reviews can be found in HILAIRE MCCOUBREY AND NIGEL D. WHITE, INTERNATIONAL LAW AND ARMED CONFLICT 209–24 (1992); L.C. GREEN, THE CONTEMPORARY LAW OF ARMED CONFLICT 18–51 (1993); JAMES E. BOND, THE RULES OF RIOT: INTERNAL CONFLICT AND THE LAW OF WAR 7–31 (1974).

[2] For Asian sources, *see* SUN TZU, THE ART OF WAR 72–76 (Samuel B. Griffith ed., 1963); THE LAWS OF MANU 137–38, 144–50 (Wendy Doniger and Brian K. Smith trans., 1991).

body of law, known as the Law of the Hague, resulted from a series of diplomatic conferences in 1899 and 1907. These treaties covered numerous issues concerning the conduct of war, such as permissible weaponry and targets on land, sea, and air, as well as neutrality.[3] The Hague Law, for instance, prohibits attacks on undefended towns, use of arms designed to cause unnecessary suffering, use of poisonous weapons, collective penalties, and pillage; and includes various protections for hospitals, religious and cultural sites, and family honor.[4] Under the leadership of the International Committee of the Red Cross, states eventually supplemented the Law of the Hague with the so-called Law of Geneva, governing the treatment of non-combatants during war.[5] The most detailed formulations of this law before World War II were the 1929 Geneva Conventions on the Wounded and Sick in Armies in the Field and on the Treatment of Prisoners of War.[6] Nevertheless, these conventions had few, if any, explicit penal provisions.[7]

The Nuremberg process both responded to and fundamentally altered the legal landscape of the law of war. Article 6(b) of the IMT Charter provided for prosecution of war crimes, defined as:

> [N]amely, violations of the laws or customs of war. Such violations shall include, but not be limited to, murder, ill-treatment or deportation to slave labour or for any other purpose of civilian population of or in occupied territory, murder or ill-treatment of prisoners of war or persons on the seas, killing of hostages, plunder of public or private property, wanton destruction of cities, towns or villages, or devastation not justified by military necessity.

Although the Charter relied upon existing law under the Hague and Geneva Conventions, it served the important purpose of affirming individual culpability for violations of the laws or customs of war. Of the eighteen defendants indicted for war crimes, all but two (Hess and Fritzsche) were convicted. The Tokyo Charter defined war crimes similarly, and other post-war trials built upon the trial of the major criminals. These included the trials under Control Council Law No. 10 (with its similar definition of war crimes) as well as those in individual European

[3] *See generally* Documents on the Laws of War 59–153 (Adam Roberts and Richard Guelff eds., 3d ed. 2000).

[4] *See* Convention (IV) Respecting the Laws and Customs of War on Land, Oct. 18, 1907, Annex, arts. 23, 25, 27, 28, 46, 47, 50, 1 Bevans 631, 648–49, 651–52.

[5] The distinction between the two sets of law was never neat, as the Hague Conventions themselves prohibited many acts against non-combatants. *See, e.g., id.* Annex, art. 25, 1 Bevans at 648.

[6] Geneva Convention for the Amelioration of Conditions of the Wounded and Sick in Armies in the Field, July 27, 1929, 118 LNTS 303; Geneva Convention Relative to the Treatment of Prisoners of War, July 27, 1929, 118 LNTS 343.

[7] *See* Yves Sandoz, *Penal Aspects of International Humanitarian Law, in* 1 International Criminal Law 393, 395–99 (M. Cherif Bassiouni ed., 2d ed. 1999).

states. Judges routinely cited Hague and Geneva law to support their views regarding illegal conduct.

The next turning point in the development of war crimes was the drafting of the Geneva Conventions of 1949 under the sponsorship of the ICRC. Three of these conventions—on the wounded and sick armed forces on land; on the wounded, sick, and shipwrecked armed forces at sea; and on prisoners of war—built upon the earlier Geneva and Hague Conventions and Regulations, but the Fourth Convention broke significant ground in providing greater protections to civilians during armed conflict. Among its many protections, it requires humane treatment of protected persons (with special reference to attacks on women), prohibits various inhumane acts against them (including physical suffering, taking of hostages, pillage, and reprisals), and sets up a comprehensive regime for the protection of persons in occupied territories.[8]

All four conventions also reflected the following innovations: (1) applicability in all international armed conflict, regardless of any formal state of war; (2) elaboration of basic principles for non-international armed conflict; and (3) a list of grave breaches for which states were obligated to enact penal legislation and prosecute or extradite individual offenders.[9] The conventions have received near-universal acceptance and have a strong claim to represent customary law.[10]

The Geneva Conventions were supplemented in 1977 by two protocols, one on international armed conflict and one on non-international conflict. Protocol I elaborates, clarifies, and expands on much of the Geneva Conventions. Unlike the Conventions, it uses the term war crimes, defining them as grave breaches of the Conventions or Protocol. Protocol II offers new rules and protections for civil conflicts meeting a certain threshold. Both Protocols today have wide adherence.[11]

Finally, alongside the developments in the ICRC, the United Nations has considered the issue of war crimes in several fora. The International Law Commission's decades-long project on a Draft Code of Offenses Against the Peace and Security of Mankind led to discussions and draft provisions addressing war crimes. In addition, the drafting of the 1968

[8] Geneva Convention IV, arts. 27–82, 75 UNTS at 306–40. Article 4 defines protected persons as civilians who find themselves in the hands of a party to the conflict or occupying power of which they are not nationals. *See* text at notes 35–7, *infra*.

[9] *See* Green, *supra* note 1, at 41–44.

[10] *See* Geneva Conventions of 12 August 1949 and Additional Protocols of 8 June 1977: ratifications, accessions and successions, para. 7 (189 parties), available at www.icrc.org/eng/party_gc#7 [hereinafter ICRC Ratifications]; Report of the Secretary-General pursuant to paragraph 2 of Security Council Resolution 808 (1993), May 3, 1993, UN Doc. S/25704, at 10 [hereinafter Secretary-General's Yugoslavia Report]; Theodor Meron, *The Geneva Conventions as Customary Law*, 81 AJIL 348 (1987).

[11] ICRC Ratifications, *supra* note 10 (157 parties to Protocol I and 150 to Protocol II).

Convention on the Non-Applicability of Statutory Limitations to War Crimes and Crimes Against Humanity offered the opportunity for states to discuss which violations of the laws and customs of war incurred individual criminality. Most recently, the Statutes of the Yugoslavia and Rwanda Tribunals and the ICC Statute have provided for prosecutions of persons accused of war crimes. Each contains different lists of war crimes over which that court will have jurisdiction, with the ICC Statute's list the most detailed.

OFFENSES DURING INTERNATIONAL CONFLICTS

To appraise the crimes under international humanitarian law as they concern abuses against human dignity, it is necessary to examine both the threshold of application of the law as well as those aspects of it that engender individual responsibility.

Threshold of Conflict

Under international humanitarian law prior to the Geneva Conventions, legal protections applied only in the event of war, which had a clear definition in both treaties and custom.[12] The Geneva Conventions, however, apply in the case of (1) 'declared war or of any other armed conflict . . . even if the state of war is not recognized by one of them', as well as (2) 'all cases of partial or total occupation of the territory of a High Contracting Party, even if the said occupation meets with no armed resistance'.[13] The term 'armed conflict' is quite broad compared to the term 'declared war'. Neither party need recognize a state of war or sever diplomatic relations; only *de facto* hostilities are required.[14]

The precise level of hostilities required to trigger the Conventions is subject to some debate. As an initial matter, interstate hostilities typically begin with an invasion, assault, artillery bombardment, or air raid.[15] Beyond this, according to the ICRC's official commentary, they encompass '[a]ny

[12] *See, e.g.*, Convention Relative to the Opening of Hostilities (Hague III), Oct. 18, 1907, art. 1, 1 Bevans 619, 627.

[13] Geneva Convention I, art. 2, 75 UNTS at 32; Geneva Convention II, art. 2, 75 UNTS at 86; Geneva Convention III, art. 2, 75 UNTS at 136; Geneva Convention IV, art. 2, 75 UNTS at 288. Protocol I extends this to conflicts between liberation movements and colonial, alien, or racist regimes. Protocol I, art. 1(4), 1125 UNTS at 7.

[14] GREEN, *supra* note 1, at 69–70, 72; *see also* JEAN S. PICTET, COMMENTARY, IV GENEVA CONVENTION RELATIVE TO THE PROTECTION OF CIVILIAN PERSONS IN TIME OF WAR 21 (1958). On the other hand, the declaration of war without the use of force would meet the threshold of applicability in the Convention.

[15] YORAM DINSTEIN, WAR, AGGRESSION AND SELF-DEFENCE 35 (1988).

difference arising between two States and leading to the intervention of members of the armed forces', regardless of the length of the conflict or the casualties on either side.[16] Others agree, pointing out that the Conventions would apply across a broad spectrum of conflict, including an unauthorized border crossing by troops with damage to persons or property, a minor border incursion with or without force, or the use of one's territory by others against a state.[17] The Yugoslavia Tribunal offered the formulation of 'a resort to armed force between States', noting that humanitarian law applies 'from the initiation' of conflict.[18] The traditional references to armed forces suggest a reluctance by states to consider many types of covert action as triggering the Conventions.[19]

Frits Kalshoven thus correctly notes the lack of any 'exact, objective criterion' defining 'armed conflict'.[20] The applicability of the Conventions will turn upon the perspectives of the belligerents and states observing the situation. States, courts, and commentators agree that it involves the use of armed forces, as opposed to police, and involves the use of force, although that may not involve the actual firing of weapons. Border skirmishes would seem to qualify to invoke the Conventions; even if only sporadic, they ought to trigger the Conventions at least during the period when they are in progress. However, they render a determination as to the termination of armed conflict difficult.[21]

A related important issue concerns the extent to which the Geneva Conventions are triggered in the absence of a classic state-to-state armed conflict, but when one state intervenes in the civil war of another. The Yugoslavia Tribunal Appeals Chamber addressed this matter in considerable detail in its review of the *Tadic* judgment. In determining that the conflict in Bosnia-Herzegovina was international at the time of the acts of the defendant, the court opted for a standard of 'overall control' by the outside state of the armed forces of one side of the internal conflict, in this case, Serbia's control of the Bosnian Serb army. It defined such control as 'going beyond the mere financing and equipping of such forces and involving also participation in the planning and supervision of military operations', but rejected the view that such control extend to the issuance

[16] PICTET, *supra* note 14, at 20.

[17] *See* THE LAW OF WAR 19–20 (Richard I. Miller ed., 1975); *cf.* G.I.A.D. Draper, *The Geneva Conventions of 1949*, 114 RECUEIL DES COURS 59, 73–74 (1965-I).

[18] *Tadic Interlocutory Appeal*, para. 70.

[19] MCCOUBREY AND WHITE, *supra* note 1, at 194–95; *cf.* W. MICHAEL REISMAN AND JAMES E. BAKER, REGULATING COVERT ACTION 72–73 (1992) (noting how Protocol I recognizes covert action in the context of law of armed conflict).

[20] *See* FRITS KALSHOVEN, THE LAW OF WARFARE: A SUMMARY OF ITS RECENT HISTORY AND TRENDS IN DEVELOPMENT 11 (1973).

[21] *See* GREEN, *supra* note 1, at 80; *Tadic Interlocutory Appeal*, paras. 66–70.

of specific orders or instructions relating to individual military actions.[22] Finally, the court stated that if individuals within a civil war became assimilated to foreign state organs based on their behavior, the war will have become internationalized.[23]

Acts Constituting International Crimes

Despite the broad adherence to or endorsement of the Geneva and Hague Conventions, the issue of criminalization for violations of that law raises additional questions, for which a complete international consensus seems lacking.

The Geneva Conventions and Grave Breaches System

The drafters of the Geneva Conventions deliberately abstained from employing the term 'war crimes' or explicitly determining the full scope of violations of the Conventions that would incur individual responsibility.[24] Instead, they adopted a list of 'grave breaches' for each convention. The list of grave breaches, followed by the convention in which they appear, is generally as follows:

- Wilful killing (I, II, III, IV)
- Torture or inhuman treatment (I, II, III, IV)
- Wilfully causing great suffering or serious injury to body or health (I, II, III, IV)
- Extensive destruction and appropriation of property, not justified by military necessity and carried out unlawfully and wantonly (I, II, IV)
- Compelling a prisoner of war or civilian to serve in the forces of the hostile power (III, IV)
- Wilfully depriving a prisoner of war or protected person of the rights of a fair and regular trial (III, IV)
- Unlawful deportation or transfer of a protected person (IV)
- Unlawful confinement of a protected person (IV)
- Taking of hostages (IV).[25]

Although the Convention does not define these terms, the official commentary and scholars have elaborated on the scope of these crimes based on general principles of law among states.[26] The Yugoslavia

22 *Tadic Appeal*, para. 145; *see also Blaskic Judgment*, paras. 75–123 (Croatian intervention in Bosnia).

23 *Tadic Appeal*, paras. 141–44.

24 For background, *see* PICTET, *supra* note 14, at 583–89; Joyce A.C. Gutteridge, *The Geneva Conventions of 1949*, 26 BRIT. Y.B. INT'L L. 294, 304–06 (1949).

25 *See also* ICTY Statute, art. 2 (same list).

26 *See, e.g.*, PICTET, *supra* note 14, at 597–601.

Tribunal has produced significant caselaw defining some of these grave breaches.[27] The list does not, however, include all crimes for which members of the Axis were prosecuted.[28]

Each Convention then contains a common article on the criminality of these breaches. It states in pertinent part:

> The High Contracting Parties undertake to enact any legislation necessary to provide effective penal sanctions for persons committing, or ordering to be committed, any of the grave breaches . . .
>
> Each High Contracting Party shall be under the obligation to search for persons alleged to have committed, or to have ordered to be committed, such grave breaches, and shall bring such persons, regardless of their nationality, before its own courts. It may also, if it prefers, and in accordance with the provisions of its own legislation, hand such persons over for trial to another High Contracting Party concerned.[29]

The grave breaches provisions thus serve to criminalize a core set of violations of the Geneva Conventions by mandating that states enact penal legislation and then extradite or prosecute offenders. In light of the character of the offenses listed as grave breaches, they clearly fall within a definition of war crimes.[30] As for the criminality of violations of the Conventions beyond those listed as grave breaches, the Conventions are less clear. The ICRC's commentary on them suggests both that the list of grave breaches in the Conventions is not exhaustive and that criminality may extend beyond grave breaches in any case.[31]

Protocol I expanded the list of grave breaches substantially. Article 11 identifies certain medical experimentation as a grave breach; Article 85(3) adds certain violations of the Hague Conventions and Regulations concerning battlefield conduct (which are incorporated in Protocol I's prohibitions); and Article 85(4) includes additional violations of the Geneva Conventions and other international law. Article 85(5) characterized these grave breaches, as well as those in the Geneva Conventions, as war crimes.[32] Insofar as some of the grave breaches in Protocol I have

[27] *See, e.g.*, *Celebici Judgment*, paras. 419–583 (wilful killing, torture (including rape, wilfully causing great suffering, inhuman treatment, unlawful confinement)); *Blaskic Judgment*, paras. 151–58 (wilful killing, inhuman treatment, wilfully causing great suffering, destruction of property, taking of hostages).

[28] *See* Waldemar A. Solf and Edward R. Cummings, *A Survey of Penal Sanctions Under Protocol I to the Geneva Conventions of August 12, 1949*, 9 CASE WEST. RES. J. INT'L L. 205, 217 n. 63 (1977).

[29] Geneva Convention I, art. 49, 75 UNTS at 62; Geneva Convention II, art. 50, 75 UNTS at 116; Geneva Convention III, art. 129, 75 UNTS at 236; Geneva Convention IV, art. 146, 75 UNTS at 386.

[30] *See* Gutteridge, *supra* note 24, at 305.

[31] *See* PICTET, *supra* note 14, at 593–94.

[32] Protocol I, arts. 11, 85, 1125 UNTS at 11–12, 41–42. Article 11 added any medical experiments that seriously endanger the physical or mental health or integrity of a protected person. Article 85(3), based on the Law of the Hague, adds the following acts if committed wilfully and causing death or serious injury to body or health: making the civilian population an object of attack; launching an indis-

traditionally been identified as war crimes, in particular those in Articles 11 and 85(3), the Protocol reflects customary international law regarding criminality.[33] In other cases, it creates new law, though of course law binding on the parties to Protocol I.

Several other aspects of the grave breaches provisions of the Geneva Conventions deserve particular mention. First, they apply only in the case of acts against protected persons or property. In Geneva Conventions I and II, these are wounded and sick members of the armed forces, broadly defined; and in Geneva III, they are prisoners of war.[34] Geneva Convention IV generally protects civilians who find themselves in the hands of a party to the conflict or occupying power of which they are not nationals.[35] This covers not only the obvious case of persons in occupied territory, but also nationals of one belligerent state who happen to be residing in the other belligerent state during armed conflict. Thus, an Ecuadorian living in Peru during the 1995 Ecuadorian–Peruvian border war would receive the protections of the Convention, even if he had nothing to do with the conflict. This provides an important shield against abuses or atrocities directed by governments against foreign nationals on their territory. Protocol I does not speak in terms of protected persons; with respect to civilians, its grave breaches apply to all civilians, not merely those under the control of another state. Given the nature of modern warfare, it may be difficult to distinguish civilians from combatants, and Protocol I requires states to resolve all doubts in favor of civilian status.[36]

Moreover, at least according to the Yugoslavia Tribunal, a person may be a protected person under the Conventions even if he has the same legal nationality as the occupier if the occupier treats that person essentially as

criminate attack against the civilian population, civilian objects, or installations, in the knowledge that it will cause excessive loss of life, injury, or damage; attacking demilitarized zones; attacking an individual who is *hors de combat*; and perfidiously using the red cross or other protective insignia. Article 85(4) adds the following if committed wilfully regardless of consequences: settling a state's own population in occupied territory or deporting the population of the occupied territory; delay in repatriating prisoners of war; apartheid; attacking historic, cultural, or religious monuments; and depriving a person of a fair trial. *See also* COMMENTARY ON THE ADDITIONAL PROTOCOLS OF 8 JUNE 1977 TO THE GENEVA CONVENTIONS OF 12 AUGUST 1949, at 150–63, 989–1004 (Yves Sandoz et al. eds., 1987) [hereinafter COMMENTARY ON THE ADDITIONAL PROTOCOLS].

[33] *See* Solf and Cummings, *supra* note 28, at 225–39; *see also* Antonio Cassese, *The Geneva Protocols of 1977 on the Humanitarian Law of Armed Conflict and Customary International Law*, 3 UCLA PAC. BASIN L.J. 55, 101–02 (1984).

[34] Geneva Convention I, art. 13, 75 UNTS at 40; Geneva Convention II, art. 13, 75 UNTS at 94; Geneva Convention III, art. 4, 75 UNTS at 138–39 (adopting same definition of protected persons as Geneva Conventions I and II).

[35] Geneva Convention IV, art. 4, 75 UNTS at 290. Article 4 also protects nationals of neutral states if their state has broken diplomatic relations with the state in whose hands they find themselves.

[36] Protocol I, art. 50(1), 1125 UNTS at 26; *see also* COMMENTARY ON THE ADDITIONAL PROTOCOLS, *supra* note 32, at 610–12.

a non-national on account of his status as a member of a different ethnic group. Because such a person lacks the protection of his legal government, he is entitled to the benefits of the Convention. Thus, at the time during the breakup of Yugoslavia when all Bosnians still had Yugoslav nationality, Bosnian Croats and Muslims could be considered protected persons *vis-à-vis* the occupying Yugoslav (Serbian) army. Bosnian Serbs were protected persons *vis-à-vis* the Bosnian government despite common nationality.[37] This important gloss on nationality promotes the purposes of the Conventions during some situations of civil conflict.

Second, the Conventions and international humanitarian law more generally require some link between the alleged crimes and the armed conflict. The ICTY has required that the crimes be 'closely related to the hostilities'.[38] Nevertheless, as a spatial matter, there need not have been actual fighting occurring in the immediate vicinity of the crimes; as a substantive matter, the acts need not have been part of the policy of one of the parties to the crime.[39] Third, in the case of all war crimes, unlike crimes against humanity, the Conventions and Protocol I do not require any mass or systematic action in order for individuals to be guilty; each act, however isolated, is a crime. The only contextual requirement is the link to the armed conflict.

Crimes Under Customary Law

The Post-World War II Trials: Despite the rather halting acceptance by states prior to World War II of the need for international law to penalize violations of the laws and customs of war,[40] the IMT Charter simply criminalized all such acts and offered only an illustrative list of the worst crimes.[41] The indictment, prosecutions, and judgment concentrated on these enumerated crimes, for which proof of conviction was more than ample. The Tribunal had no difficulty justifying that these violations of the laws of war were international crimes:

> [T]he crimes defined by Article 6, section (b) of the Charter were already recognized as War Crimes under international law. They were covered by Articles 46, 50, 52, and 56 of the Hague Convention of 1907, and Articles 2, 3, 4, 46, and 51

[37] *Tadic Appeal*, paras. 164–66; *Celebici Judgment*, paras. 245–66; *see also Blaskic Judgment*, paras. 125–46 (Bosnian Muslims protected persons *vis-à-vis* Bosnian Croat army); Theodor Meron, *The Humanization of Humanitarian Law*, 94 AJIL 239, 256–60 (2000).

[38] *Tadic Interlocutory Appeal*, para. 70.

[39] *Celebici Judgment*, paras. 193–95; *Tadic Judgment*, para. 573; *Blaskic Judgment*, paras. 69–70; *see also Aleksovski Appeal*, paras. 17–28 (no discriminatory intent required).

[40] For the pre-World War II period, *see* Remigiusz Bierzanek, *The Prosecution of War Crimes*, *in* 1 A Treatise on International Criminal Law 559, 559–71 (M. Cherif Bassiouni and Ved P. Nanda eds., 1973); Green, *supra* note 1, at 276–82.

[41] *See* United Nations War Crimes Commission, History of the United Nations War Crimes Commission and the Development of the Laws of War 221–22 (1948).

of the Geneva Convention of 1929. That violations of these provisions constituted crimes for which the guilty individuals were punishable is too well settled to admit of argument.[42]

This unequivocal position was also accepted in the cases under Control Council Law No. 10.[43]

State Practice: State practice since World War II is not especially probative on this question because of the paucity of prosecutions for violations of the international law of armed conflict. The Israeli statute under which Eichmann was tried defined war crimes more narrowly than did the Nuremberg process, focusing on violations of *jus in bello* with the most severe consequences for persons *hors de combat*.[44] But more generally, when states prosecuted offenders, they did so for common crimes under domestic criminal law; they have furthermore shown an unwillingness to prosecute enemy soldiers as long as a state's own troops are held as prisoners.[45]

US practice is somewhat ambiguous regarding the extent of criminality of violations of the laws of war. The United States has for many years prosecuted violations of the laws of war under American law, particularly the Uniform Code of Military Justice (UCMJ) and its predecessors.[46] The Army's Field Manual regards all violations as war crimes, and the UCMJ gives courts-martial jurisdiction to adjudicate and give any punishment permitted by the law of war.[47] Nevertheless, the United

[42] 22 IMT Trials at 497. The court also found these rules so well recognized that they applied to all World War II belligerents even though some (particularly the USSR) were not parties to the Hague Convention of 1907. It also applied general international law with respect to German treatment of Soviet prisoners of war, as the USSR was not a party to the 1929 convention on prisoners of war. *Id.* at 475.

[43] *See, e.g.*, United States v. Ohlendorf et al. (the '*Einsatzgruppen Case*'), 4 CCL No. 10 Trials 411, 460–62 (citing German legal authorities for proposition of individual criminal responsibility for violations of laws of war).

[44] It defined war crimes as 'murder, ill-treatment or deportation to forced labour or for any other purpose, of civilian population of or in occupied territory; murder or ill-treatment of prisoners of war or persons on the seas; killing of hostages; plunder of public or private property; wanton destruction of cities, towns or villages; and devastation not justified by military necessity'. *Eichmann*, 36 ILR at 7.

[45] G.I.A.D. Draper, *Wars of National Liberation and War Criminality*, *in* RESTRAINTS ON WAR: STUDIES IN THE LIMITATION OF ARMED CONFLICT 135, 153–54 (Michael Howard ed., 1979); *see also* L.C. GREEN, *The Law of Armed Conflict and the Enforcement of International Criminal Law*, *in* ESSAYS ON THE MODERN LAW OF WAR 239, 249–52 (1985).

[46] *See* Jordan J. Paust, *My Lai and Vietnam: Norms, Myths and Leader Responsibility*, 57 MIL. L. REV. 99, 117–18 (1972); for a well-known case, *see* United States v. Calley, 22 U.S.C.M.A. 534, 48 C.M.R. 19 (1973), *habeas corpus granted sub nom.* Calley v. Callaway, 382 F. Supp. 650 (M.D. Ga. 1974), *rev'd*, 519 F.2d 184 (5th Cir. 1975), *cert. denied sub nom.* Calley v. Hoffman, 425 U.S. 911 (1976).

[47] US DEPT. OF THE ARMY, THE LAW OF LAND WARFARE § 499 (Field Manual 27–10, 1956); 10 U.S.C. § 818 (1994); *see also* Ex Parte Quirin, 317 U.S. 1, 11–12 (1942); *cf.* Christopher Greenwood,

States has typically directed its prosecutions at more serious breaches of the law of war.[48]

The Statutory Limitations Convention: During the drafting of the 1968 Convention on the Non-Applicability of Statutory Limitations to War Crimes and Crimes Against Humanity, states again grappled with a definition of war crimes. Both the Secretary-General and the Human Rights Commission's Working Group proposed definitions of war crimes limited to acts 'of a grave nature'.[49] However, the joint working group of the Third and Sixth Committees of the General Assembly eliminated this qualification, making grave breaches only an example of war crimes covered by the draft convention, and defined war crimes in terms of the broad definition in the IMT Charter.[50] Western states objected to this broader term, but a proposal to reintroduce the 'grave breaches' qualification failed in the Third Committee in 1968, leaving the Convention with the broad definition. The vote, however, was close, 27–23–44, suggesting a lack of consensus over the proper scope of war crimes, or at least of those not subject to a statute of limitations.[51]

The Yugoslavia Tribunal: The ICTY Statute[52] provides for the prosecution of war crimes in two provisions—Article 2, for grave breaches listed in the Geneva Conventions of 1949 (but not Protocol I), and Article 3, for '[v]iolations of the laws or customs of war'.[53] According to the Secretary-General, the latter refers to violations of rules concerning methods of engaging in armed conflict stemming from the Hague Convention (IV) Respecting the Laws and Customs of War on Land and its Regulations. He noted that the Nuremberg Tribunal had recognized that violations of these regulations constituted war crimes.[54]

Although Article 2 of the Statute offers a complete list of grave breaches of the Geneva Conventions, Article 3 provides only an illustrative list of

International Humanitarian Law and the Tadic *Case*, 7 EJIL 265, 280 (1996) (British and Canadian military manuals).

48 *Cf.* Jordan J. Paust, *Legal Aspects of the My Lai Incident—A Response to Professor Rubin*, in 3 The Vietnam War and International Law 359, 374 n. 47 (Richard A. Falk ed., 1972).

49 Preliminary draft convention on the non-applicability of statutory limitation to war crimes and crimes against humanity, submitted by the Secretary-General, Jan. 25, 1967, UN Doc. E/CN.4/928, at 8; Commission on Human Rights, Report of the Twenty-Third Session, 20 February–23 March 1967, UN ESCOR, 42d Sess., Supp. No. 6, at 45, UN Doc. E/4322 (1967).

50 Note by the Secretary-General, UN GAOR, 22d Sess., Annex, Agenda item 60, at 5–6, UN Doc. A/6813 (1967).

51 Report of the Third Committee, UN GAOR, 23d Sess., Annex, Agenda item 55, at 2–4, UN Doc. A/7342 (1968).

52 The ICTR Statute is not relevant here, as it concerns a non-international conflict.

53 ICTY Statute, arts. 2–3.

54 Secretary-General's Yugoslavia Report, *supra* note 10, at 11.

violations of the laws or customs of war, mentioning: use of poisonous weapons; wanton destruction of cities, towns, or villages; attacks on undefended towns, villages, dwellings, and buildings; seizure of or damage to religious, charitable, educational, artistic, scientific, or historic works; and plunder of public or private property.

The report of the Commission of Experts notes that, although the Statute does not mention grave breaches of Protocol I, '[m]any' of those grave breaches would fall under the term 'violations of the laws or customs of war'.[55] Indeed, the delegates of France, the United Kingdom, and the United States, in voting for Resolution 827 (creating the Tribunal), implied or stated that the ICTY could, under Article 3, assert jurisdiction over non-grave breaches of the Geneva Conventions as well as breaches of the Protocols.[56] This suggests that these states now believe that criminal responsibility attaches for a wide range of violations of international humanitarian law.

The jurisprudence of the ICTY has elaborated significantly on the scope of customary law war crimes for international conflicts. It held in 1995 that Article 3 criminalized '*any* serious offence against international humanitarian law' other than the grave breaches of the Geneva Conventions, genocide, or crimes against humanity (the other three crimes in the Statute).[57] In two cases where chambers of the Tribunal found the conflict to be international and thus applied humanitarian law applicable to international conflicts, it considered these rules to include the Fourth Hague Convention and common Article 3 of the Geneva Conventions (although the latter on its face only applies to civil conflicts), and it has also offered detailed definitions of various crimes.[58]

ICC Statute: The Rome Statute adopts a very detailed list of 26 violations of the laws and customs of war in international armed conflict. These include various war crimes under Protocol I and the Hague Conventions, as well as acts prohibited, but not necessarily criminalized, under various treaties, such as attacks on UN peacekeepers and conscription of children under fifteen. The list, the product of intense negotiations, received the support of nearly all states (including the United States, which opposed other aspects of the Statute). Nonetheless, because the states drafting the

55 Letter dated 24 May 1994 from the Secretary-General to the President of the Security Council, May 27, 1994, UN Doc. S/1994/674, at 3, 15 [hereinafter Yugoslavia Commission Final Report].

56 Provisional Verbatim Record of the Three Thousand Two Hundred and Seventeenth Meeting, May 25, 1993, UN Doc. S/PV.3217, at 11 (France), 15 (US), 19 (UK); *see also* James C. O'Brien, *The International Tribunal for Violations of International Humanitarian Law in the Former Yugoslavia*, 87 AJIL 639, 646 (1993); Daphna Shraga and Ralph Zacklin, *The International Criminal Tribunal for the Former Yugoslavia*, 5 EJIL 360, 365–66 and n. 20 (1994).

57 *Tadic Interlocutory Appeal*, para. 91; *see also id.* paras. 87–95.

58 *Blaskic Judgment*, paras. 168, 179–87; *Celebici Judgment*, paras. 314, 419–592.

Rome Statute disagreed as to whether the list should reflect only those crimes under customary law or should include others, one cannot simply assume that the full 26 are now crimes under customary law.[59] The Court's jurisdiction is defined to be that of war crimes 'in particular when committed' in a planned or large-scale manner; but the use of 'in particular' ensures that the Court could try individual acts, and, in any case, this limitation is clearly meant to be jurisdictional rather than part of the definition of war crimes.[60]

Subsidiary Sources: The ILC's project on a Draft Code of Crimes Against the Peace and Security of Mankind generated lengthy discussions of the criminality of violations of the laws or customs of war. In the 1954 Draft Code, the Commission simply listed 'acts in violation of the law or customs of war' as one of the crimes, its members apparently concluding that a full elaboration of the list of war crimes was too complex.[61] When the Commission revisited the issue in the 1980s, its members disagreed over the extent to which war crimes should be listed.[62]

With respect to international conflicts, the ILC's 1996 Draft Code adopts a long list of crimes, most of which are recognized as war crimes in the Geneva Conventions, Protocol I, or the ICTY Statute.[63] The Draft Code, however, requires that all the acts listed be committed systematically or on a large scale to be war crimes under the Code. This additional element reflects the ILC's policy that only particularly serious war crimes would qualify as crimes affecting the security of mankind for purposes of the Draft Code.[64] When the ILC drafted a statute in 1994 for an international criminal court, it stated that the list of customary law war crimes overlapped, but was not coextensive with, the list of grave breaches of the Geneva Conventions and Protocol I.[65]

Beyond a clear consensus that grave breaches of the Geneva Conventions are war crimes, scholarly opinion has not clarified the exact extent of criminal conduct under international *jus in bello*. Writers seem to recognize that not all violations of the Conventions and other laws of

[59] *See* Mahnoush H. Arsanjani, *The Rome Statute of the International Criminal Court*, 93 AJIL 22, 32–35 (1999).

[60] ICC Statute, art. 8(1).

[61] 1954 ILC Report, at 152 (art. 2(12)).

[62] *See, e.g.*, Summary Records of the 1820th Meeting, 1984 [I] ILC Y.B. 28, 29 (statement of Mr. Sinclair); Summary Records of the 2100th Meeting, 1989 [I] ILC Y.B. 26, 31 (statements of Mr. Tomuschat); Summary Records of the 2097th Meeting, 1989 [I] ILC Y.B. 9, 15–16 (statement of Mr. Arangio-Ruiz).

[63] 1996 ILC Report, at 110–11 (art. 20).

[64] *See* 1996 ILC Report, at 113–14.

[65] Report of the International Law Commission on the work of its forty-sixth session, UN GAOR, 49th Sess., Supp. No. 10, UN Doc. A/49/10 (1994), *reprinted in* 1994 [II] 2 ILC Y.B. 38–40 (art. 20) [hereinafter 1994 ILC Report].

war are war crimes.[66] They also agree that the grave breaches in the 1949 Conventions are not the only war crimes, and that other offenses against the laws and customs of war are war crimes.[67] Many writers, in line with the Statutes of the ICTY and ICC, focus on violations of international law concerning forbidden methods of warfare, such as core provisions of the 1899 and 1907 Hague Conventions and Regulations, or the use of biological weapons or poisonous gases.[68] Commentators have not stated that all of the grave breaches in Protocol I (that were not already in the Conventions) represented customary international law at the time of their drafting, although most of them do appear to have gained such acceptance at this point.

Assessment

The foregoing suggests the following scheme of violations of *jus in bello* that incur individual responsibility. First, for parties to the Geneva Conventions and Protocol I, the grave breaches provisions therein clearly provide criminal responsibility for those prosecuted under them. Secondly, for all states, customary international law would appear to provide criminality for (a) the grave breaches provisions of the Geneva Conventions; and (b) violations of the laws and customs of war recognized by the IMT or other courts immediately after World War II or universally accepted as crimes today. This latter group would include the list elaborated in the ICTY Statute based on Hague Law (poisonous weapons, wanton destruction of towns, attacks on undefended towns or buildings, damage to special buildings or works, and plunder), and other grave breaches listed in Protocol I long recognized as crimes, including medical experimentation and wilful attacks on persons *hors de combat.* It would also include additional crimes that garnered broad governmental support during the drafting of the ICC Statute and are recognized in it: in particular, rape and sexual crimes (which, while not mentioned *per se* as grave breaches, clearly fall under the definition of several); use of human shields; and intentional starvation of civilians.

Theoretical and Practical Challenges

The most immediate challenge to decision-makers in applying the penal provisions of the law of international armed conflict is to determine when

[66] *See, e.g.*, Bert V. A. Röling, *Aspects of the Criminal Responsibility for Violations of the Laws of War*, *in* The New Humanitarian Law of Armed Conflict 199, 213 (Antonio A. Cassese ed., 1979); Theodor Meron, *International Criminalization of Internal Atrocities*, 89 AJIL 554, 570–71 (1995).

[67] *See, e.g.*, Solf and Cummings, *supra* note 28, at 217 n.63.

[68] *See* Green, *supra* note 1, at 290–92; Röling, *supra* note 66, at 212–13; Sandoz, *supra* note 7, at 406–12; *see also supra* note 32.

a conflict has begun. Although the law seems to favor a broad application, it may prove difficult to know whether a low-level border skirmish triggers the Conventions. At the same time, states must not be able to evade their obligations by pleading beyond reason that they are not engaged in an armed conflict with another state. It would seem that insofar as the protection of persons not engaged in hostilities is an object and purpose of the Conventions specifically, and of international humanitarian law generally, states should err on the side of invoking and applying the Conventions at a low threshold. From the perspective of the protection of human rights and avoidance of atrocities during conflict, the additional obligations imposed on states during armed conflict would also argue for the early application of the Conventions, especially Convention IV. Once the Conventions or Protocol are triggered, they should apply throughout the territories of the parties, not simply in the areas of active hostilities.[69] And, as now recognized by the Yugoslavia Tribunal, they should apply even in conflicts that some outsiders might call internal if the intervention from another state is significant. In the case of state break-ups, protected persons might even be legal co-nationals of the occupier.

As for the crimes themselves, they reflect a decision by states that certain atrocities committed during international armed conflict incur individual responsibility, without prejudice to the duties of *states* to provide a larger range of protections under the Conventions and Protocol I, customary international humanitarian law, and international human rights law. Moreover, the most basic offenses against human dignity do incur individual responsibility, and the inclusion of the Law of the Hague in the laws and customs of war extends individual liability to cover the large-scale atrocities inherent in improper means of warfare.

Yet the choice of war crimes arises from a process of custom-making and codification that is skewed to address those most likely to occur in armed conflict.[70] Thus, some of the crimes under international law may strike students of international human rights law as less 'grave' than others, e.g., compelling a civilian to serve in the forces of a hostile power. Moreover, the laudable absence of any requirement that abuses of human dignity in time of war assume a certain scale or systematicity in order to constitute crimes stands in sharp contrast to the special elements required for crimes against humanity and genocide. It remains wholly unfortunate that, for example, the summary execution of one soldier in wartime is an international crime, while that of a political prisoner in peacetime is not.[71]

[69] *Tadic Interlocutory Appeal*, para. 68.

[70] *See generally* L.C. GREEN, *Human Rights and the Law of Armed Conflict*, *in* ESSAYS ON THE MODERN LAW OF WAR, *supra* note 45, at 83, 92–102.

[71] *See* Steven R. Ratner, *The Schizophrenias of International Criminal Law*, 33 TEX. INT'L L.J. 237 (1998).

Beyond the text of the various instruments, the key impediment to successful invocation of the humanitarian law of international armed conflict is likely to be the attitude of the combatants toward prosecutions. States have proved reluctant to prosecute their own soldiers for war crimes unless they are especially heinous and publicized; they have thus justified impunity, or a small administrative punishment, on the exigencies of warfare. Moreover, they have often hesitated to prosecute the opponent's soldiers if the opponent is still holding some of their prisoners, for fear of retaliation. These problems do not wholly dissipate with the creation of international fora for prosecution, for the same inertia could render states reluctant to hand over suspects to such a tribunal, albeit to a somewhat lesser extent.

OFFENSES DURING NON-INTERNATIONAL CONFLICTS

The more challenging area of appraisal concerns the extent to which international law provides for individual responsibility for violations of *jus in bello* in internal wars.

Nature and Threshold of Conflict

Common Article 3 of the Geneva Conventions

With the drafting of the Geneva Conventions, the law took an important step forward in mandating a minimal level of conduct by states in domestic conflicts.[72] That standard appears in Common Article 3 of the Conventions, which requires parties to any 'armed conflict not of an international character' to apply, 'as a minimum', certain standards to 'persons taking no active part in the hostilities'. In addition to a general requirement of humane treatment and collection and care of the wounded and sick, Common Article 3 prohibits the following 'at any time and in any place whatsoever' with respect to persons not actively involved in hostilities:

(a) violence to life and person, in particular murder of all kinds, mutilation, cruel treatment and torture;
(b) taking of hostages;
(c) outrages upon personal dignity, in particular humiliating and degrading treatment;
(d) the passing of sentences and the carrying out of executions without previous judgment pronounced by a regularly constituted court,

[72] For background, *see* Pictet, *supra* note 14, at 26–34; Geoffrey Best, War and Law Since 1945, at 168–79 (1994).

> affording all the judicial guarantees which are recognized as indispensable by civilized peoples.

Common Article 3 applies to all parties to a conflict in a state party to the Conventions, regardless of their legal status or reciprocity.[73] It offers a minimal level of protection for persons not taking part in hostilities, rather than applying the full set of protections in the four conventions. It is now regarded as customary international law.[74]

The level of conflict necessary to trigger these protections has been a source of uncertainty and contention since the Conventions' drafting. Many delegations were concerned that it might extend beyond civil wars to any insurrection or even routine criminal activity; they believed the government's response to these conflicts ought not to be subject to international humanitarian law. Beyond the obviously low limit of pure banditry or an unorganized riot, the delegations could not agree on the precise level of violence needed to trigger Common Article 3.

The ICRC's official commentary lists some criteria based on the amendments states submitted at the 1949 diplomatic conference that finalized the Conventions. Several approaches would have turned upon the degree of organization of the insurgents. Thus, acts by an organized insurgent military force or a responsible civil authority with the characteristics of a government, control over territory, and the means to ensure respect for the Conventions would render an internal conflict subject to Article 3. Another approach focused on the response of the *de jure* government. If it used regular military forces against the insurgency, recognized the insurgents as belligerents, or submitted the issue to the UN, Common Article 3 would apply.[75] The commentary emphasizes, however, that the article must be applied 'as wide[ly] as possible'. It nonetheless recognizes that the types of armed conflicts involve those 'with armed forces on either side engaged in hostilities . . . which are in many respects similar to an international war'.[76]

Reviews of state practice show a reluctance by governments to invoke Article 3, even in many outright civil or colonial wars.[77] The Rwanda Tribunal has applied the ICRC's criteria to focus on the intensity of the

[73] PICTET, *supra* note 14, at 37.

[74] Military and Paramilitary Activities in and Against Nicaragua (Nicar. v. U.S.), 1986 ICJ 14, 114 (June 27).

[75] PICTET, *supra* note 14, at 35–36.

[76] *Id.* at 36.

[77] *See* BOND, *supra* note 1, at 58–61; Howard J. Taubenfeld, *The Applicability of the Laws of War in Civil War*, *in* LAW AND CIVIL WAR IN THE MODERN WORLD 499, 509–10 and n. 40, 515–17 (John Norton Moore ed., 1974); *see also* Ministère public and Centre pour l'égalité des chances et la lutte contre le racisme v. C and B, Military Ct., Dec. 17, 1997 (Belg.), JOURNAL DES TRIBUNAUX, Apr. 4, 1998, at 286, available at www.icrc.org/ihl-nat.nsf (affirming acquittal of Belgian peacekeepers in Somalia by declaring threshold of Common Article 3 not met).

conflict and the organization of the parties. It found that the events of 1994 triggered the protections of Common Article 3 based on the organization of the two sides and various characterizations of the situation by United Nations officials.[78] The Yugoslavia Tribunal had little difficulty in characterizing the conflict within Bosnia as an armed conflict for purposes of Common Article 3 as well.[79]

Scholars have taken somewhat different positions. In 1962, an ICRC Commission of Experts concluded that Common Article 3 applies 'if the hostile action, directed against a legal government, is of [a] collective character and consists of a minimum amount of organization'.[80] This position seems accepted by several European scholars.[81] Others have concluded that it should apply only in more serious cases of civil strife, emphasizing the resemblance to war. They have stressed that violence must rise to the level of a *bona fide* insurgency to trigger Article 3.[82] Richard Baxter concluded that '[t]here is no consensus as to the application of Article 3 to what are, in comparative terms, the lower levels of violence'.[83]

Additional Protocol II

By the 1960s, states seemed willing to consider a more comprehensive set of protections than those in Common Article 3. In 1968, the General Assembly recognized the 'necessity of applying the basic humanitarian principles in all conflicts' and asked the Secretary-General to work with the ICRC toward new conventions for all conflicts.[84] This process culminated in the drafting of Protocol II, which provides for protections of victims of non-international conflicts. Its article on the scope of application states that it applies to conflicts

[78] *Akayesu Judgment*, paras. 619–21; *Rutaganda Judgment*, para. 91; *Musema Judgment*, paras. 248–51

[79] *Tadic Judgment*, paras. 562–68. The Appeals Chamber's reversal of the trial court on whether the conflict was also international in character, *see supra* note 22, does not affect this issue.

[80] Michel Veuthey, *Non-International Armed Conflict and Guerilla Warfare*, *in* 1 International Criminal Law, *supra* note 7, at 417, 424.

[81] *See, e.g.*, Dietrich Schindler, *The Different Types of Armed Conflicts According to the Geneva Conventions and Protocols*, 163 Recueil des Cours 117, 147 (1979-II); Jean Siotis, Le Droit de la Guerre et les Conflits Armés d'un Caractère Non-International 209 (1958).

[82] *See, e.g.*, Keith Suter, An International Law of Guerrilla Warfare: The Global Politics of Law-Making 16 (1984); Bond, *supra* note 1, at 57–58; Edwin Brown Firmage, *Summary and Interpretation*, in The International Law of Civil War 405, 415 (Richard A. Falk ed., 1971). Even Pictet, in commenting upon the frequent visits of the ICRC to states undergoing domestic strife, contrasted such internal disorder with the 'armed conflict' of Article 3. Jean S. Pictet, Humanitarian Law and the Protection of War Victims 58 (1975).

[83] Richard R. Baxter, *Ius in Bello Interno: The Present and Future Law*, *in* Law and Civil War in the Modern World, *supra* note 77, at 518, 526.

[84] GA Res. 2444, UN GAOR, 23d Sess., Supp. No. 18, at 50, 51, UN Doc. A/7218 (1968).

> which take place in the territory of a High Contracting Party between its armed forces and dissident armed forces or other organized armed troops which, under responsible command, exercise such control over a part of its territory as to enable them to carry out sustained and concerted military operations and to implement this Protocol.

The Protocol then notes that it 'shall not apply to situations of internal disturbances and tensions, such as riots, isolated and sporadic acts of violence and other acts of a similar nature, as not being armed conflicts'.[85]

Despite the similarity to the concepts underlying Common Article 3, Protocol II's definition of non-international armed conflict is not simply an attempt to elaborate upon those situations already covered by Common Article 3. Rather, its threshold is significantly higher.[86] This appears particularly in the requirements of (a) two sets of armed forces, (b) responsible command, and (c) sufficient control over territory to carry out sustained operations, none of which is necessarily required for application of Common Article 3. The Rwanda Tribunal has emphasized the importance of 'continuous and planned' operations by insurgents in finding the 1994 conflict significant enough to trigger Protocol II (violations of which are crimes under the ICTR Statute).[87]

Acts Constituting International Crimes

The criminality of acts violating the laws or customs of war in non-international conflicts has been somewhat obscure until quite recently. Although some international law developed to provide minimal levels of protection, there is little evidence that violations were traditionally regarded as criminal. While the language of the IMT Charter criminalized all violations of the laws and customs of war, presumably including customs for civil wars, the post-World War II prosecutions for war crimes typically involved incidents of a truly international character. Since the early 1990s, however, recognition of individual responsibility for atrocities in internal conflicts has dramatically increased.

The Geneva Conventions and Protocols

As a matter of treaty law, only Common Article 3 of the Geneva Conventions and Protocol II address internal conflicts. Moreover, violations of Common Article 3 are not *per se* grave breaches of the Geneva

85 Protocol II, art. 1(2), 1125 UNTS at 611.

86 COMMENTARY ON THE ADDITIONAL PROTOCOLS, *supra* note 32, at 1350; *Rutaganda Judgment*, para. 92; *see also* Arturo Carrillo-Suárez, *Hors de Logique: Contemporary Issues in International Humanitarian Law as Applied to Internal Armed Conflict*, 15 AM. U. INT'L L. REV. 1, 79–90 (1999) (noting threshold does not require classic civil war).

87 *Akayesu Judgment*, para. 626.

Conventions for which criminal responsibility necessarily lies.[88] The drafters of the Geneva Conventions were not prepared to criminalize this conduct in the context of a domestic conflict. Protocol II contains no provisions on grave breaches or criminal responsibility.[89] Thus the criminality of violations of Common Article 3, Protocol II, or other violations of the law and customs of internal war must turn on customary law alone.

Internal War Crimes Under Customary Law

State Practice: From the drafting of Common Article 3 in the late 1940s until the conclusion of Protocol II in the middle 1970s, states did not appear to assume that international law provided individual criminal responsibility for internal atrocities. As for Common Article 3, while undoubtedly states prosecuted for the acts encompassed in Common Article 3 (e.g., murder) as a matter of domestic criminal law, only a few instances are documented of prosecutions for war crimes as such in the context of internal conflicts until the creation of the Yugoslavia and Rwanda Tribunals in the 1990s.[90] Protocol II did not, as a whole, represent customary international law at the time of its drafting, although parts of it may have represented custom, including those protections already in Common Article 3, as well as those derived from customary human rights law.[91] Many developing world states were unenthusiastic about Protocol II, suggesting again its lack of acceptance as existing custom.[92] Such uncertainty strongly suggests, *a fortiori*, that states would not then have regarded violations of Protocol II as war crimes. At the same time, some states have promulgated domestic statutes on war crimes that cover atrocities in civil

[88] *See, e.g.*, Geneva Convention IV, art. 147, 75 UNTS at 388 (defining grave breaches as those committed 'against persons or property protected by the present Convention', defined in Article 4 as persons who are not nationals of the party under whose control they find themselves). Article 4 could suggest the grave breaches would include acts against non-nationals even in the event of a civil conflict, since those persons are 'protected' under Article 4. However, the overall scope of the Convention defined in Article 2, *i.e.*, conflicts of an international character, militates against this view. *But see* Jordan J. Paust, *Applicability of International Criminal Laws to Events in the Former Yugoslavia*, 9 AM. U. J. INT'L L. AND POL'Y 499, 511–12 and n. 40 (1994).

[89] *See* Denise Plattner, *The Penal Repression of Violations of International Humanitarian Law Applicable in Non-International Armed Conflicts*, 30 INT'L REV. RED CROSS 409, 414–17 (1990) (benefits and complications of criminal liability for violations of Protocol II).

[90] *See Tadic Interlocutory Appeal*, paras. 130–31 (citing Nigerian prosecutions and military manuals of states). The Chamber nonetheless found sufficient evidence of state practice to justify criminalization of internal atrocities for the Yugoslavia conflict. *Id.* paras. 131–34.

[91] *See* Protocol II, preamble, 1125 UNTS at 611 (parties '[e]mphasiz[e] the need to ensure a *better* protection for the victims of those armed conflicts [not of an international character]') (emphasis added); COMMENTARY ON THE ADDITIONAL PROTOCOLS, *supra* note 32, at 1325–26, 1341–42. For scholarly views on Protocol II's status, *compare, e.g.*, GREEN, *supra* note 1, at 306, and Cassese, *supra* note 33, at 109–13 *with* Veuthey, *supra* note 80, at 431.

[92] *See* SUTER, *supra* note 82, at 170, 177; Georges Abi-Saab, *Non-International Armed Conflicts*, *in* INTERNATIONAL DIMENSIONS OF HUMANITARIAN LAW 217, 227 (UNESCO ed., 1988).

wars. This process predates Protocol II and has accelerated since the 1990s, without apparent protest.[93]

The Yugoslavia and Rwanda Tribunals: Article 3 of the Statute of the Yugoslavia Tribunal permits prosecutions for persons 'violating the laws or customs of war', offering only an illustrative list of such violations. On its face, the Statute thus gives the court jurisdiction over any violations of humanitarian law applicable to internal conflict, including Common Article 3 and Protocol II. As noted above, the delegates of France, the United Kingdom, and the United States stated in the Security Council that Article 3 would encompass all humanitarian law in force in the former Yugoslavia.[94] As a product of a Chapter VII decision of the Security Council, the Statute represents international legislation and could thus be interpreted to recognize additional war crimes—those violations of the *jus in bello* of civil wars.

The Commission of Experts, however, adopted a contrasting, conservative interpretation of Article 3 of the Statute. It found the customary law for internal conflicts 'debatable', of uncertain scope, and not incorporating individual criminality.[95] The Secretary-General, in his commentary on the Statute, listed only documents concerning international conflicts as those he regarded as clearly part of customary law.[96]

The Tribunal addressed the question whether defendants could be prosecuted for violations of the law governing the conduct of civil wars in the important *Tadic Interlocutory Appeal* decision of 1995.[97] It upheld such prosecutions under Article 3 of the Statute because (a) the text of and the Security Council debates over Article 3 show an intent to criminalize violations of such law; (b) customary law now had developed specific rules applicable to internal armed conflicts; and (c) customary law recognized

[93] *See* Thomas Graditzky, *Individual criminal responsibility for violations of international humanitarian law committed in non-international armed conflicts*, 322 INT'L REV. RED CROSS 29, 38–44 (1998) (discussing statutes). The Security Council's endorsement of a special independent court in Sierra Leone to try offenders in its civil war, *see* SC Res. 1315, Aug. 14, 2000, is further evidence of support for domestic measures.

[94] *See supra* note 56. The US delegate explicitly mentioned Common Article 3 and the Additional Protocols. *See also* Prosecutor v. Tadic, Amicus Curiae Brief Presented by the Government of the United States of America, July 25, 1995, at 36–37. The United States also argued that Article 2 of the Statute permitted the prosecution of grave breaches of the Geneva Conventions even in situations of internal conflict. *Id.* at 35–36.

[95] Yugoslavia Commission Final Report, *supra* note 55, at 13, 15–16. It did find that Common Article 3 likely reflects customary international law, but not that violations of it were war crimes.

[96] Secretary-General's Yugoslavia Report, *supra* note 10, at 9.

[97] It addressed this question because it had concluded that the conflict in Yugoslavia had both an international and internal character and had refused to find that those acts for which Tadic was indicted involved solely international aspects of the conflict. *Tadic Interlocutory Appeal*, para. 77; *see also* George H. Aldrich, *Jurisdiction of the International Criminal Tribunal for the Former Yugoslavia*, 90 AJIL 64, 67–68 (1996).

individual criminal responsibility for violations of some of these rules.[98] It ultimately found: 'customary international law imposes criminal liability for serious violations of common Article 3, as supplemented by other general principles and rules on the protection of victims of internal armed conflict, and for breaching certain fundamental principles and rules regarding means and methods of combat in civil strife'.[99] The Tribunal's opinion is not without its shortcomings, including the paucity of its reasoning on both individual responsibility[100] and the scope of international humanitarian law whose violation in internal conflicts is to be regarded as criminal.[101] Nevertheless, the entire opinion must be regarded as an important source of law in its own right and significant in influencing, even if not at the time reflecting, the expectations of governments.

The Yugoslavia Tribunal has convicted a number of defendants for violations of the laws and customs of war applicable to internal conflicts. In so doing, it has enumerated and offered detailed definitions of various violations beyond those listed in the Statute, including significant violations of Common Article 3 and Protocol II. These have included rape, torture, murder, cruel treatment, and outrages on personal dignity.[102]

The Rwanda Statute, which concerns an internal conflict, explicitly authorizes prosecutions for 'serious violations' of Common Article 3 and Protocol II.[103] The Commission of Experts did not address the question of criminality that the Yugoslavia Commission had found unrecognized in customary law, but the Secretary-General frankly commented that the Council had thereby criminalized violations of these two documents for the first time.[104] In its first judgment, in the *Akayesu* case, the Tribunal

[98] *Tadic Interlocutory Appeal*, paras. 87–136. The Court rejected the US argument, *see supra* note 94, regarding the coverage of Article 2 of the Statute. *See id.* paras. 80–84; *see also id.*, separate op. Abi-Saab, at 4–6 (justifying application of grave breaches provisions to internal conflict).

[99] *Id.* para. 134.

[100] *See* Theodor Meron, *The Continuing Role of Custom in the Formation of International Humanitarian Law*, 90 AJIL 238, 242 (1996); Marco Sassòli, *La première décision de la chambre d'appel du Tribunal Penal International pour l'ex-Yougoslavie: Tadic (Competence)*, 100 Rev. Gén. Droit Int'l Pub. 101, 129–30 (1996).

[101] *See Tadic Interlocutory Appeal*, dissenting op. Li, para. 13 ('an unwarranted assumption of legislative power'); Meron, *supra* note 100, at 242–44 (under-inclusive and over-inclusive). The Tribunal could have reached the same conclusion on narrower grounds by relying solely on the stated willingness of the Yugoslav parties to apply the law of war to their conflict. *See Tadic Interlocutory Appeal*, paras. 135–36; Sassòli, *supra* note 100, at 129–30.

[102] *Furundzija Judgment*, paras. 134–86 (rape and torture); *Kupreskic Judgment*, paras. 701–05, 712 (murder and cruel treatment); *Aleksovski Judgment*, paras 54–57, 211–29 (outrages on personal dignity); *Tadic Judgment*, paras. 722–26 (cruel treatment); *see also* the excerpts from the *Celebici* and *Blaskic* judgments cited in note 58 *supra*, in which the court offered definitions of crimes under Common Article 3 even though it considered the conflict in Yugoslavia to be international in scope.

[103] ICTR Statute, art. 4. Rwanda became a party to both Protocols in 1984. ICRC Ratifications, *supra* note 10.

[104] *See* Report of the Secretary-General pursuant to paragraph 5 of Security Council Resolution 955 (1994), Feb. 13, 1995, UN Doc. S/1995/134, at 4.

gave its views regarding the criminality of internal war crimes under customary law. It found that the serious violations of Common Article 3 and Protocol II over which it has jurisdiction were precisely those sorts of crimes that the ICTY had found to be customary law crimes in the *Tadic Interlocutory Appeal*. It endorsed that ruling and found that 'the authors of such egregious violations must incur individual criminal responsibility for their deeds'.[105] With regard to Protocol II in particular, it found that serious violations meant violations of Article 4(2) of that instrument, which bans violence to life and health, collective punishments, hostage-taking, terrorism, outrages on personal dignity, slavery, pillage, and threats to commit these acts.[106]

Nonetheless, as of late 2000, no trial chamber of the Rwanda Tribunal had found any defendant guilty of war crimes. In the four judgments it had reached, the ICTR consistently found that the acts of the defendant did not have a sufficient nexus to the armed conflict in the country between the government and rebel Tutsi army (the Rwandan Patriotic Front). The court has required that the Prosecutor demonstrate a 'direct connection' between the alleged crimes and the conflict.[107] It has further determined that a crime is committed only if the perpetrator is engaging in the armed conflict as a member of the armed forces or as a civilian supporting the war effort and if the victims were taking no part in the hostilities.[108]

The ICC Statute and Beyond: The Rome Statute offers the most ambitious and precise list of war crimes in internal conflict thus far, though it is still less extensive than the corresponding list of war crimes in interstate conflicts. It lists in Article 8 two categories of war crimes in civil wars—four 'serious violations' of Common Article 3, and twelve 'other serious violations' of the laws and customs of war applicable to civil conflicts.[109] The latter list of crimes is derived partly from Hague Law on means of combat, with additional provisions taken from the Statute's list of interstate war crimes, such as sexual crimes, conscription of children, physical mutilation, and scientific experimentation. It does not include the full list of prohibited acts from Article 4 of Protocol II, the tactic adopted by the Rwanda Tribunal, by omitting, for instance, collective punishments and terrorism from the list. It nonetheless offers broadly similar criminality for abuses against civilians in internal conflicts as for those against civilians in interstate wars. At the same time, the list of internal war crimes omits

[105] *Akayesu Judgment*, para. 616.
[106] *Id.* paras. 610–16.
[107] *Kayishema and Ruzindana Judgment*, para. 604.
[108] *Id.* paras. 604–24; *Akayesu Judgment*, paras. 640–43; *Rutaganda Judgment*, paras. 94–99.
[109] The two sets have different thresholds of applicability, with the higher standard of Protocol II applying to the second categories. *See* ICC Statute, arts. 8(2)(d) and (f).

certain methods of warfare, such as use of poison weapons, especially harmful bullets, or human shields, that are listed as crimes in interstate conflicts. This evinces a clear decision to provide less individual responsibility for atrocities against insurgent soldiers in a civil war than for acts against foreign soldiers in an interstate war.

As with the ICC Statute's list of customary war crimes for international conflicts, the disagreements among states over some parts of the list of war crimes in civil wars makes it impossible to assume all states regard the entire list as reflecting customary international law. Nonetheless, the overall list was acceptable to nearly all states, suggesting a move toward customary status for all the crimes. Since the conclusion of the Rome Statute, the Security Council called in 1999 and 2000 for individual accountability for atrocities committed in civil conflicts in East Timor, Democratic Republic of the Congo, and Sierra Leone, recognizing the criminal status of such acts.[110]

Subsidiary Sources: The ILC's early work does not support the proposition that internal war crimes merited inclusion in a Code of Offenses Against the Peace and Security of Mankind. The 1954 Draft Code's definition of war crimes applied only 'to all cases of declared war or of any other armed conflict . . . between two or more States'.[111] The 1996 Draft Code does include as war crimes a list of violations of international humanitarian law governing internal conflicts (Common Article 3 and Article 4 of Protocol II) drawn from the Rwanda Tribunal Statute, as well as certain acts intentionally damaging the environment not necessarily regarded previously as war crimes.[112] The commentary to the ILC's 1994 draft statute for an international criminal court makes no mention of violations of Common Article 3 or Protocol II as war crimes.[113]

Some commentators have applauded the recognition as war crimes of

110 *See* Herman von A.M. Hebel and Darryl Robinson, *Crimes within the Jurisdiction of the Court*, *in* The International Criminal Court: The Making of the Rome Statute 79, 104–07 (Roy S. Lee ed., 1999); *see also* SC Res. 1272, Oct. 25, 1999, preamb. para. 14 (noting that persons committing flagrant violations of human rights and humanitarian law in East Timor 'bear individual responsibility'); SC Res. 1304, June 16, 2000, para. 13 (call for 'bringing to justice' those committing massacres in Congo); SC Res. 1315, *supra* note 93, preamb. para. 6 ('persons who commit or authorize serious violations of international humanitarian law are individually responsible and accountable for those violations'); *id.* para. 5 (noting that amnesty will not apply to such crimes). For a similar stance from the Commission on Human Rights, *see, e.g.*, Comm'n Hum. Rts. Res. 2000/20, Apr. 18, 2000, para. 13 (calling on Burundi's government to 'bring[] to trial those responsible for violations of human rights and of international humanitarian law').

111 Report of the International Law Commission to the General Assembly, UN Doc. A/1858, *reprinted in* 1951 [II] ILC Y.B. 123, 126.

112 1996 ILC Report, at 111–12 (art. 20), 118–20; *see also supra* text at note 64 on the requirement of mass or systematic action.

113 1994 ILC Report, *supra* note 65, at 38–40; *see also id.* at 69 (exclusion of Protocol II due to lack of provisions on grave breaches or enforcement).

violations of Common Article 3 by the Yugoslavia Tribunal as well as the inclusion of such violations (along with violations of Protocol II) as crimes in the ICTR Statute, though characterizing it as a recent and incomplete evolution in the law.[114] Others have argued for applying the grave breaches provisions of the Geneva Conventions directly to internal conflicts; or have asserted that Common Article 3 directly creates individual culpability.[115]

Assessment

The extent to which international law provides for individual responsibility for violations of the law governing internal conflicts, consistent with principles of *nullum crimen sine lege*, is perhaps clearer today than it has ever been, but not without room for disagreement. In situations where parties to an internal conflict have signed legal agreements requiring or permitting prosecution for violations of internal *jus in bello*, as was the case in Yugoslavia,[116] individuals would clearly be responsible criminally for such violations. As a matter of custom, if we are willing to assume that the Security Council intended to respect the *nullum crimen* principle in the Yugoslavia and Rwanda Tribunal Statutes, then violations of Common Article 3, certain violations of Protocol II (particularly Article 4), and various parts of the Hague Law on prohibited methods of combat must be regarded today as war crimes. Even if the Council legislated a somewhat new set of crimes at the time, its actions must be viewed alongside the unopposed passage of domestic legislation criminalizing war crimes in internal conflict; the Tribunals' *Tadic Interlocutory Appeal* and *Akayesu* opinions; the actions of states preparing the ICC Statute; and the endorsement by many states of the need for accountability for crimes committed in civil conflicts such as East Timor, Democratic Republic of the Congo, and Sierra Leone. Together, these have surely put on notice those committing such atrocities that the international community now regards these acts as war crimes. It would not, then, run afoul of the *nullum crimen* principle were future courts and decision-makers to inculpate individuals for such violations. Such a list would in fact include those acts listed in the

[114] *See* Meron, *supra* note 66, at 565–68, 577; Bruno Simma and Andreas L. Paulus, *The Responsibility of Individuals for Human Rights Abuses in Internal Conflicts: A Positivist View*, 93 AJIL 302, 312–13 (1999); Sonja Boelaert-Suominen, *Grave Breaches, Universal Jurisdiction and Internal Armed Conflicts: Is Customary Law Moving Towards a Uniform Enforcement Mechanism for all Armed Conflicts?*, 5 J. Conflict and Security L. 63, 101–03 (2000).

[115] *See, e.g.*, Mary Ellen O'Connell, *New International Legal Process*, 93 AJIL 334, 347–49 (1999); Draper, *supra* note 17, at 98; Paust, *supra* note 88, at 511–12 and n. 40. For a debate from seven different perspectives on this question, *see Symposium on Method in International Law*, 93 AJIL 291 (1999).

[116] *See Tadic Interlocutory Appeal*, para. 136 (quoting agreement of May 22, 1992, among Bosnian government, Bosnian Serbs, and Bosnian Croats).

grave breaches provisions of the Geneva Conventions and most of those in the corresponding list of Protocol I. Beyond this list, certain parts of the ICC Statute that garnered strong support, such as sexual crimes and forcible displacement of civilians ('ethnic cleansing'), also have a strong claim to customary status.

Theoretical and Practical Challenges

In determining accountability for internal war crimes, the issue of threshold will obviously play a central role. States facing internal strife, whether in India (Kashmir), the Congo, Colombia, or Russia, are liable to reject applicability of Common Article 3, Protocol II, or customary law because they regard their conflicts as simply matters of internal law enforcement not subject to international norms. They will claim that a rebel group is not sufficiently organized to merit invocation of internal *jus in bello*, preferring to see them as traitors, bandits, or common criminals.[117] Only pressure by outside parties, including international organizations, may succeed in convincing a state to apply international humanitarian law at all.[118] If a state refuses to apply humanitarian law, individuals would remain protected by international human rights law (subject to its exceptions for times of national emergency);[119] but, as noted, most human rights violations do not incur individual responsibility for offenders under international law, although domestic law might apply.

Beyond the threshold of applicability of humanitarian law to internal conflicts, the lack of criminality of internal war crimes as a matter of treaty law (outside the ICC context) may pose obstacles to accountability. Decision-makers, whether domestic legislatures prescribing law for internal war crimes, courts, or investigatory commissions, will have to determine which violations incur individual responsibility. Conceivably, if the state is party to Protocol II or has signed an agreement to apply provisions of the Geneva Conventions beyond Common Article 3 to an internal conflict, it might be more willing to prosecute for violations of the law in force than if it saw itself bound by Common Article 3 alone. If the parties actually agree, as did those in Yugoslavia (however insincerely), to try and punish those responsible for violations of whatever international humanitarian law is in force, then the scope of the law will be clear for any prosecutions.

If accountability is to address abuses that took place before the recent past, more serious obstacles present themselves due to the evolving nature

117 *See* Meron, *supra* note 37, at 260–61.
118 For an excellent case study concerning Colombia, *see* Carrillo-Suárez, *supra* note 86, at 128–41.
119 *See* ICCPR, art. 4.

of custom in this area. While one guesses at one's peril when a norm of customary international law becomes crystallized, it seems safe to say that the criminality of violations of Common Article 3 was not well-established before perhaps the mid to late 1980s; and enough of Protocol II was new law at the time of its conclusion that violations of that Protocol could not *per se* be considered crimes either. Thus, gross abuses of human rights committed during earlier internal rebellions, such as those in Tibet in the 1950s, Biafra in the 1960s, or in Iraqi Kurdistan in the 1970s, would not be regarded as war crimes, although the acts might well qualify as other international crimes.

As to the adequacy of the existing legal framework, the list of war crimes for internal conflicts is extensive and will cover most heinous offenses. Nonetheless, from the perspective of the goals of both international humanitarian law and international human rights law—namely, the protection of individuals—it would seem that there ought to be no distinction between the criminality of offenses committed in civil wars and those committed in interstate wars. The constitutive changes in international law related to human rights, such that states now owe the same duties toward their own citizens as they do toward foreigners—and not lower duties insulated by the *domaine reservé*—would suggest that whatever crimes have developed for international conflicts should apply to domestic situations as well.[120]

It is obvious, however, at least from the scope of Protocol II, that states were not willing to accept this idea in 1977, and remain less than enthusiastic about the broader concept of equating the duties of states during international conflicts with those during civil conflicts. The ICTY and ICTR Statutes and key cases, the 1996 Draft Code, and the Rome Statute move in the direction of recognizing a broad range of internal war crimes; but ultimately *nullum crimen sine lege* demands an appraisal of the full body of international law, which has, even with the ICC Statute, still avoided making the two sets of war crimes identical. It can only be hoped that states working through the ICRC and domestic law codification will further develop the penal aspects of *jus in bello* to eliminate the gap in criminality.

Ultimately, as with interstate war crimes, the prospect of actually achieving individual accountability will depend heavily on the belligerents themselves. Even if they agree, perhaps after pressure by other states and the International Committee of the Red Cross, to apply international humanitarian law to a civil conflict, individual accountability for violations remains a different issue. For instance, it is not at all clear that states have been or will be any more willing to prosecute officials for war crimes

[120] For further reflection, *see* Ratner, *supra* note 71, at 247–51.

committed against their fellow nationals than they have been (or, more aptly, have not been) for crimes against foreign belligerents or civilians. If governmental forces succeed in putting down a rebellion, they would seem prone to prosecute only the losers for violations of domestic law, rather than investigate the actions of both sides for war crimes. If the rebels are successful, they might choose to address only the accountability of the former government and its military forces.

Moreover, the nature of intrastate conflict means that generally only the government at best will have functioning courts. This makes it less likely that opposition forces will be able to try their officials for internal war crimes and perhaps more likely that the government will direct its prosecutions toward opposition figures rather than their own military personnel. In the event an international tribunal is established, it will again depend upon the parties' cooperation in handing over officials, who will doubtless attempt to justify their acts based on military necessity.

AFTERWORD ON DESTRUCTION OF CULTURAL PROPERTY

The international legal process has provided for individual criminal responsibility not only for acts during armed conflict that directly harm the individual physically or mentally, but for a particular set of acts that leave a devastating impact on a community's identity—the destruction of cultural property. Cultural property generally includes movable objects and buildings with a special cultural, religious, or historical significance to a particular state or group; for to destroy a people's unique cultural artifacts is to assault its soul.

The Hague Conventions of 1907 established basic protections during armed conflict for all property.[121] After World War II, the IMT Charter included 'plunder of public and private property' as a war crime; the judgment discussed the issue in some detail, in particular with respect to the role of Alfred Rosenberg and Walter Funk.[122] The Fourth Geneva Convention made extensive destruction and appropriation of property a grave breach.[123]

The most significant development in this realm was the 1954 Hague Convention for the Protection of Cultural Property in the Event of Armed Conflict, which, along with its implementing regulations and protocol, details a series of obligations banning and criminalizing the

121 *See* David A. Meyer, *The 1954 Hague Cultural Property Convention and Its Emergence into Customary International Law*, 11 B. U. INT'L L.J. 349, 354 (1993).
122 *See* Ch. 3, Acts Constituting Crimes Against Humanity—Property Crimes, *supra*.
123 Geneva Convention IV, art. 147, 75 UNTS at 388.

use or targeting of such property.[124] The 1977 Additional Protocols to the Geneva Conventions expand further upon this protection, with Protocol I specifically designating destruction of cultural property a grave breach.[125] The Statute of the Yugoslavia Tribunal also lists as a violation of the laws and customs of war 'seizure of, destruction or wilful damage done to institutions dedicated to religion, charity and education, the arts and sciences, historic monuments and works of art and science'.[126] The 1996 Draft Code proposes criminalizing attacks on cultural property explicitly in the context of war crimes.[127] And the ICC Statute lists as war crimes in both interstate and internal conflicts intentional attacks on 'buildings dedicated to religion, education, art, science or charitable purposes' and historic monuments, as well as pillage.[128] The criminality of wilful destruction or plunder of cultural property during armed conflict unmitigated by some form of military necessity is thus well established under both conventional and customary international law.

The Hague Convention deserves mention for its unique emphasis on cultural property, of which it adopts a rather broad definition.[129] The Convention contains two core obligations for states. They must first refrain from the use of cultural property 'for purposes which are likely to expose it to destruction or damage in the event of armed conflict' and 'from any act of hostility directed against such property', obligations they can waive only 'where military necessity imperatively requires' it. Secondly, they must 'prohibit, prevent and, if necessary, put a stop to any form of theft, pillage or misappropriation of, and any acts of vandalism directed against, cultural property' as well as refrain from 'requisitioning movable cultural property' in another state or committing reprisals against cultural property.[130] These provisions also apply in the

[124] May 14, 1954, 249 UNTS 215 [hereinafter Hague Convention].

[125] Protocol I, arts. 53, 85(4)(d), 1125 UNTS at 27, 42; Protocol II, art. 16, 1125 UNTS at 616. For additional background, *see generally* M. Cherif Bassiouni, *Reflections on Criminal Jurisdiction in International Protection of Cultural Property*, 10 SYRACUSE J. INT'L L. AND COM. 281, 287–97 (1983).

[126] ICTY Statute, art. 3(d).

[127] 1996 ILC Report, at 93, 112 (art. 20), 117.

[128] ICC Statute, arts. 8(b)(ix), 8(b)(xvi), 8(e)(iv), 8(e)(v).

[129] It defines cultural property primarily as 'movable or immovable property of great importance to the cultural heritage of every people, such as monuments of architecture, art or history, whether religious or secular; archaeological sites; groups of buildings which, as a whole, are of historical or artistic interest; works of art; manuscripts, books and other objects of artistic, historical or archaeological interest; as well as scientific collections and important collections of books or archives or of reproductions of the property defined above'. Hague Convention, *supra* note 124, art. 1(a), 249 UNTS at 242. It also includes museums, libraries, and archives for storing such property, as well as centers containing large amounts of such property. *Id.* arts. 1(b), 1(c), 249 UNTS at 242.

[130] *Id.* arts. 4(1)–4(3), 249 UNTS at 242, 244.

event of armed conflict not of an international character.[131] As of late 2000, the Convention had 99 parties.[132]

In 1999, 93 states, including 74 parties to the 1954 Hague Convention, concluded the Second Protocol to that convention, marking a significant advance in both substantive protections and individual responsibility for violations. Its most notable provisions include more detailed requirements for states to protect cultural property before and during armed conflict; a system of 'enhanced protection' for cultural heritage 'of the greatest importance for humanity'; and individual criminal responsibility for certain 'serious violations', for which states must extradite or prosecute any offenders.[133] These offenses are: making property under enhanced protection or otherwise protected under the Convention or Protocol the object of attack; using property under enhanced protection in support of military actions; extensive destruction or appropriation of any property protected under the Convention or Protocol; and theft, pillage, or misappropriation of such property.[134] The Convention also applies in civil wars.[135] As of 2000, 39 states had signed the Protocol, though none had ratified it.[136]

In attempting to punish individuals for this conduct, states will have to decide whether to apply the terms of the 1954 Hague Convention, Geneva Convention IV, Protocol I, and eventually the 1999 Second Protocol, which are not coextensive in their definitions or penal provisions. In any prosecutions under one or the other, the question of military necessity is likely to be the biggest factual issue. For example, Serb forces involved in the destruction of parts of Dubrovnik during the early period of the Balkan war would undoubtedly make such a claim.[137]

Finally, it is worth noting that international law does not appear to penalize individuals for destruction of cultural property outside of armed conflict, with the exception of those acts that meet the elements of crimes against humanity.[138] Although certain obligations in the Hague

[131] *Id.* art. 19, 249 UNTS at 256. This term appears to mean the same as the corresponding language in Common Article 3 of the Geneva Conventions. *See* Sharon A. Williams, The International and National Protection of Movable Cultural Property: A Comparative Study 41–46 (1978).

[132] *See* UNESCO's web site at www.unesco.org/culture/legalprotection.

[133] Second Protocol to the Hague Convention of 1954 for the Protection of Cultural Property in the Event of Armed Conflict, Mar. 26, 1999, chs. 2–4 [hereinafter 1999 Second Protocol], available at www.unesco.org/culture/legalprotection.

[134] *Id.* art. 15(1). States must establish jurisdiction over all these crimes whenever they are committed in their territory or when the offender is a national, and over the first three crimes whenever the alleged offender is present in the country. *Id.* art. 16(1).

[135] *Id.* art. 22.

[136] *See* UNESCO's web site, *supra* note 132.

[137] *See, e.g.*, 1999 Second Protocol, *supra* note 133, arts. 6–8 (military necessity justifications).

[138] The only treaty explicitly dealing with protection of cultural property outside of armed conflict (other then treaties on transfer of stolen property) is the so-called Roerich Pact, adopted under the

Convention and its protocols apply during peacetime,[139] when read as a whole, the treaties are limited to the context of armed conflict, insofar as they generally regulate the use and destruction of such property by military forces during the preparation and the conduct of hostilities.[140] Given the views of states in the 1950s regarding areas of exclusively domestic jurisdiction (especially those of East bloc participants in the negotiations), it seems doubtful that they agreed to criminalize action by governmental officials to seize (or even destroy) cultural property and limited the Convention to the preparation or conduct of armed conflict; the 1999 Protocol does not appear to change this picture.

Beyond the Convention, as noted in Chapter 3, destruction of cultural property has not typically appeared on lists of crimes against humanity, though it could fall within the term 'persecution' that would be outlawed during peacetime. The view among commentators has been to exclude such conduct outside of armed conflict from lists of international crimes.[141]

auspices of the Pan-American Union, which provides simply that historic monuments, museums, and scientific, artistic, educational, and cultural institutions shall receive the same protection in time of peace as in time of war. Treaty on the Protection of Artistic and Scientific Institutions and Historic Monuments, Apr. 15, 1935, 167 LNTS 289. The latter protection is itself vague, as it merely requires belligerents to treat these as neutral and respect and protect them. *Id.* art. I, 167 LNTS at 290.

[139] *See, e.g.*, Hague Convention, *supra* note 124, arts. 3, 7, 249 UNTS at 242, 246; *id.* art. 18, 249 UNTS at 254, 256 ('*Apart from the provisions which shall take effect in time of peace*, the present Convention shall apply' in case of armed conflict between two parties) (emphasis added); 1999 Second Protocol, *supra* note 133, art. 5; *see also* Seventh Report on the draft Code of Crimes Against the Peace and Security of Mankind, by Mr. Doudou Thiam, Special Rapporteur, UN Doc. A/CN.4/419 and Add.1 (1989), *reprinted in* 1989 [II] ILC Y.B. 81, 88.

[140] Apart from the Convention's title referring to armed conflict, its first preambular paragraph states, for instance, '[r]ecognizing that cultural property has suffered grave damage during recent armed conflicts and that . . . it is in increasing danger of destruction'. *See also* Hague Convention, *supra* note 124, arts. 3, 4(1), 5, 7–10, 249 UNTS at 242, 244, 246, 248 (references to armed conflict and military operations); Denise Bindschedler-Robert, *Problems of the Law of Armed Conflicts*, *in* 1 A TREATISE ON INTERNATIONAL CRIMINAL LAW, *supra* note 40, at 295, 296–99; M. Cherif Bassiouni and James A.R. Nafziger, *Protection of Cultural Property*, *in* 1 INTERNATIONAL CRIMINAL LAW, *supra* note 7, at 949, 955–57.

[141] *See, e.g.*, Bassiouni, *supra* note 125, at 304; Bassiouni and Nafziger, *supra* note 140.

5

Other Abuses Incurring Individual Responsibility Under International Law

Although genocide, crimes against humanity, and war crimes form the traditional core of international crimes relevant to atrocities against human dignity, the international legal process has also prescribed norms of individual accountability for acts that may not meet the special criteria of those three categories—namely intent and the type of targeted group for genocide; systematicity or scale for crimes against humanity; and commission during armed conflict for war crimes. Although international criminal law addresses a great many independent offenses,[1] the most significant areas with respect to human rights abuses are slavery and related practices, torture, apartheid, and, most recently, forced disappearances. Other crimes may be relevant in some situations.[2] Although some of these offenses may also be acts of genocide, crimes against humanity, or war crimes, the evidentiary burden for these independent crimes may be easier given the absence of special elements.

Consistent with the approach to international criminal law outlined in Chapter 1, we here consider those delicts for which international law provides for individual criminality, regardless of the particular strategy contemplated for, or obligations upon states regarding, suppression of the act. For instance, this chapter addresses treaties that explicitly recognize individual responsibility as well as those that call on states to make the act criminal under their domestic law. The analysis is not limited to crimes for which all states may or must punish an offender, but includes those allowing only certain states to punish an offender. Clearly, enforcement will depend on the source of the criminality (treaties or custom), the substantive obligations of states, and the jurisdictional limitations of any fora,

[1] *See, e.g.*, M. Cherif Bassiouni, *The Sources and Content of International Criminal Law: A Theoretical Framework, in* 1 INTERNATIONAL CRIMINAL LAW 3, 62–95 (M. Cherif Bassiouni ed., 2d ed. 1999) (listing other offenses).

[2] Atrocities committed against internationally protected persons are made criminal by the Convention on the Prevention and Punishment of Crimes Against Internationally Protected Persons, including Diplomatic Agents, Dec. 14, 1973, 1035 UNTS 167. Hostage-taking is criminalized by the International Convention Against the Taking of Hostages, Dec. 17, 1979, 1316 UNTS 205 (and is covered by various instruments on hijacking as well). As for piracy, international definitions limit it to acts for 'private ends'. *See, e.g.*, Convention on the High Seas, Apr. 29, 1958, art. 15, 450 UNTS 82, 90; Clyde H. Crockett, *Toward A Revision of the International Law of Piracy*, 26 DEPAUL L. REV. 78, 84–87 (1976).

issues discussed further in Part II. This Chapter seeks to elaborate the scope of the offenses under international law; the individual obligations of states are discussed in Chapter 8.

SLAVERY AND FORCED LABOR

Conventional Law

Slavery

International efforts to abolish slavery are more than two centuries old, leading to some eighty conventions and documents on the subject.[3] Slavery in its most traditional sense—the ownership of one person by another—violates international law in all circumstances, its prohibition rising to the level of a *jus cogens* norm.[4] It appears on every list of crimes against humanity, and, in certain circumstances, also represents a war crime when committed against foreign nationals.[5] As for individual responsibility for slavery as a separate crime, while some international instruments do not provide for criminal liability, many important treaties explicitly or implicitly include criminal responsibility and penalties. Most significant among these are the 1926 Slavery Convention[6] and the 1956 Supplementary Convention on the Abolition of Slavery, the Slave Trade, and Institutions and Practices Similar to Slavery,[7] both of which have a large number of states parties.[8] The conventions vary in substance, from mere identification of slavery as a crime, to a duty or right to prosecute, to a duty to extradite or cooperate in law enforcement.[9] In addition, the UN Human Rights Commission has continuously reviewed the question.

[3] *See* A. Yasmine Rassam, *Contemporary Forms of Slavery and the Evolution of the Prohibition of Slavery and the Slave Trade Under Customary International Law*, 39 VIRG. J. INT'L L. 303, 329–42 (1999); M. Cherif Bassiouni, *Enslavement as an International Crime*, 23 N.Y.U. J. INT'L L. AND POL. 445 (1991); *see also* MYRES S. MCDOUGAL, HAROLD D. LASSWELL, AND LUNG-CHU CHEN, HUMAN RIGHTS AND WORLD PUBLIC ORDER: THE BASIC POLICIES OF AN INTERNATIONAL LAW OF HUMAN DIGNITY 473–508 (1980).

[4] *See, e.g.*, IAN BROWNLIE, PRINCIPLES OF PUBLIC INTERNATIONAL LAW 515 (5th ed. 1998).

[5] *See* Geneva Convention IV, art. 147, 75 UNTS at 388 (forced service in the forces of a hostile power as a grave breach).

[6] Sept. 25, 1926, as amended by the Protocol of 7 December 1953, art. 6, 212 UNTS 17, 22 (parties 'whose laws do not at present make adequate provision for the punishment of infractions [under the Convention] . . . undertake to adopt the necessary measures in order that severe penalties may be imposed'.).

[7] Sept. 7, 1956, 266 UNTS 3; *see infra* notes 11–13.

[8] MULTILATERAL TREATIES, ch. XVIII.3–4 (94 parties to 1926 Convention and 118 parties to 1956 Convention).

[9] *See* M. CHERIF BASSIOUNI, 1 INTERNATIONAL CRIMES: DIGEST/INDEX OF INTERNATIONAL INSTRUMENTS 1815–1985, at 499–508 (1986) (categorizing levels of criminality in slavery instruments); *see also* STÉFAN GLASER, DROIT INTERNATIONAL PÉNAL CONVENTIONNEL 121–26 (1970); Ch. 8, text at notes 21–25, *infra*.

Various special rapporteurs and resolutions have affirmed slavery's criminality, explored its contemporary manifestations, and proposed methods of suppression through law enforcement.[10]

The conventions on slavery and related practices cover a broad array of conduct, including the traditional African slave trade, traffic in women and children, and other forms of forced labor. The 1956 Supplementary Convention, for example, defines slavery as 'the status or condition of a person over whom any or all of the powers attaching to the right of ownership are exercised'.[11] It also calls for the elimination of 'institutions and practices similar to slavery', including debt bondage, serfdom, and various types of exploitation of women and children.[12] The precise contours of these definitions remain unclear. They seem to hinge on physical control of the victim or some legal or customary change in status that distinguishes the victim from a free person. This seems inherent in the origins of slavery and the international community's desire to outlaw it.[13]

Criminalization of traffic in women and children and forced prostitution has followed a number of different approaches, some suggesting an analogy to traditional slavery (e.g., conventions on 'white slave traffic') and others distinguishing the two practices.[14] The 1950 Convention for the Suppression of the Traffic in Persons and of the Exploitation of the Prostitution of Others obligates states to punish anyone who '[p]rocures, entices or leads away . . . another person' for prostitution or '[e]xploits the prostitution of another person', regardless of consent, as well as those involved in operating brothels.[15] The touchstone seems to be less one of physical control of the victim (or 'forced prostitution') than the exploitation of a person's body for sexual gratification in exchange for money. Like the slavery conventions, it enjoys fairly wide adherence.[16]

Forced Labor

Forced labor has also been addressed as a broader crime. The first important treaty in this regard was the 1930 Convention Concerning Forced or

[10] *See, e.g.*, Question of Slavery and the Slave Trade in All Their Practices and Manifestations, Including the Slavery-Like Practices of Apartheid and Colonialism, July 16, 1971, UN Doc. E/CN.4/Sub.2/322 (1971); Report of the Working Group on Contemporary Forms of Slavery on its twenty-fourth session, July 20, 1999, UN Doc. E/CN. 4/Sub. 2/1999/17; Comm'n Hum. Rts. Res. 1999/40, Apr. 26, 1999; Rassam, *supra* note 3, at 339–41.

[11] 1956 Slavery Convention, art. 7(a), 266 UNTS at 43.

[12] 1956 Slavery Convention, art. 1, 266 UNTS at 41. This last group includes the delivery of a child by parent(s) or guardian for labor exploitation. *Id.*

[13] *See* Bassiouni, *supra* note 3, at 457–59.

[14] *See* Nora V. Demleitner, *Forced Prostitution: Naming an International Offense*, 18 FORDHAM INT'L L.J. 163, 165–74 (1994); Stephanie Farrior, *The International Law on Trafficking in Women and Children for Prostitution: Making it Live Up to its Potential*, 10 HARV. HUM. RTS. J. 213 (1997).

[15] Mar. 21, 1950, arts. 1–2, 96 UNTS 271, 274.

[16] MULTILATERAL TREATIES, ch. VII.11.a (73 parties).

Compulsory Labor, prepared under the auspices of the International Labor Organization (ILO) and now widely ratified.[17] It defines forced or compulsory labor as 'all work or service which is exacted from any person under the menace of any penalty and for which the said person has not offered himself voluntarily'. It specifically excludes a number of categories, including

- 'any work or service which forms part of the normal civic obligations of the citizens of a fully self-governing entity'; and
- 'any work or service exacted in cases of emergency, that is to say, in the event of war or of a calamity or threatened calamity, such as fire, flood, famine . . . and in general any circumstance that would endanger the existence or the well-being of the whole or part of the population'.[18]

Moreover, forced labor 'for the execution of public works' must be progressively abolished and is permitted only if the work is important, imminently necessary, does not impose 'too heavy a burden' on the population, does not require removal of workers from their residence, and is taken with regard for religion, social life, and agriculture.[19]

Despite these potential loopholes, the Convention includes important restrictions on all forced labor, such as limitation of forced labor to men between 18 and 45, limitation to sixty days per year, a day of rest, working hours equal to those in the regular labor force, non-transfer to areas dangerous to their health, and appropriate medical care. Compulsory cultivation is allowed only as a precaution against famine, and those producing it must be allowed to keep the food cultivated.[20]

Customary Law

As a matter of customary international law, the slave trade itself incurs criminal responsibility insofar as all states would appear to have at least permissive jurisdiction to prescribe domestic law against it when committed anywhere.[21] The wide ratification of the slavery conventions would suggest the same regarding slavery itself. The criminality of forced labor (including forced prostitution) under customary law is not entirely clear.

[17] June 28, 1930, as modified by the Final Articles Revision Convention of the International Labor Organization, 39 UNTS 55. It has 155 parties. *See* the ILO's web site: ilolex.ilo.ch:1567/scripts/ratifce.pl?C29.

[18] *Id.* art. 2, 39 UNTS at 58. It also excludes military service and prison labor.

[19] *Id.* art. 10, 39 UNTS at 62–64.

[20] *Id.* arts. 11–13, 16, 18, 19, 39 UNTS at 64–66, 68, 70–72. For labor apart from that for public works, additional requirements apply, including limitation of the men working to twenty-five percent of the population, and remuneration at the market rate for such labor. *Id.* arts. 11(2), 14, 39 UNTS at 64, 66.

[21] Restatement (Third) of the Foreign Relations Law of the United States § 404 (1987) [hereinafter Restatement]; Kenneth C. Randall, *Universal Jurisdiction Under International Law*, 66 Tex. L. Rev. 785, 798–800 (1981).

Additional authorities provide some further sense of the meaning of forced labor under custom, at least as carried out by governments, but do not criminalize it. The ILO's 1957 Convention Concerning the Abolition of Forced Labor requires states to suppress forced labor in a more limited sense, namely only if it is used for purposes of political coercion, economic development, labor discipline, punishment for participation in strikes, and racial, social, national, or religious discrimination.[22] The International Covenant on Civil and Political Rights and the European Convention on Human Rights, both of which ban, but do not criminalize, forced or compulsory labor, exclude 'any service exacted in case of an emergency or calamity threatening the life or well-being' of the nation or community.[23] Forced labor was not included as a separate offense in the Statutes of the Yugoslavia and Rwanda Tribunals. It was not a significant issue in those contexts, and it is not included as a separate crime in the International Law Commission's 1996 Draft Code of Crimes Against the Peace and Security of Mankind or the ICC Statute.[24]

As a matter of custom, then, an authoritative determination of the scope of criminality beyond archetypal slavery remains difficult. It would seem that any forced labor that involved a *total control* over the person's life such as to resemble slavery would present a strong case for being a crime under international law.[25] In addition, forced labor under *inhuman conditions* would also have close parallels to slavery. The type of forced labor that occurred during World War II and is encompassed in the definition of crimes against humanity met both these criteria of total control and inhuman conditions. Forced prostitution would also appear to meet at least the first criterion, as well as the second in certain situations. Thus, even if total or cruel forced labor took place in the absence of the additional qualifications for crimes against humanity (e.g., systematicity), it still seems close enough to slavery as a matter of customary law to suggest its status as an independent crime.

Theoretical and Practical Challenges

Slavery and forced labor are human rights abuses that are just as likely to

22 June 25, 1957, art. 1, 320 UNTS 291, 294, 296.

23 ICCPR, art. 8(3)(c)(iii), 999 UNTS at 175; European Convention for the Protection of Human Rights and Fundamental Freedoms, Nov. 4, 1950, art. 4(3)(c), 213 UNTS 221, 226; *see also* van der Mussele v. Belgium, Eur. Ct. Hum. Rts. (Ser. A), No. 70 (1983) (judgment), paras. 34–8 (totality of circumstances to determine if labor is forced).

24 1996 ILC Report, at 93–94 (art. 18); ICC Statute, arts. (7)(1)(c), 7(1)(g), 8(2)(b)(xxii), 8(2)(e)(vi) (including enslavement and forced prostitution only as crimes against humanity or war crimes, with accompanying special elements).

25 *Cf.* McDougal et al., *supra* note 3, at 480–81; Bassiouni, *supra* note 3, at 459; Rassam, *supra* note 3, at 341–42.

be carried out by purely private actors as by governments or parastatal entities, and in that respect open the door of international criminal law to the suppression of non-official human rights atrocities. Governments might well find it easier to prosecute private parties than those currently or formerly holding public office. Of course, the economic and political power of those engaging in slavery and other forced labor may dissuade domestic prosecutions as well.

With the law quite clear on the criminalization of slavery, the burden is upon those investigating it in those relatively few states where it remains a practice (primarily in Africa and the Middle East) to prove that the possessor of the person has legal ownership over him or her. Proving legal ownership will vary across national systems, and the trier of fact ought to be able to rely upon customary indicia of ownership in the particular society. To stretch the notion of ownership too far, however, not only would run afoul of *nullum crimen sine lege*, but risks placing slavery on the same level as forced labor which, however horrible, lacks the uniquely heinous aspects of slavery.

In situations short of slavery, the status of a state as a party to the 1930 and 1950 Conventions will obviously be critical insofar as those states parties have an obligation to prosecute. For states not parties to these treaties (as well as states that are parties to them), international law may assist a state in defining the elements of a particular crime either when it drafts legislation or prosecutes individuals under current legislation. The key issues will turn on which types of activities involving attributes of forced labor are in fact criminal. Forced prostitution in Southeast Asia and other areas seems emblematic of the type of offense that states need to address through recourse to international law principles of forced labor (and potentially slavery as well).[26]

But current law also leaves many questions unanswered. For example, at what point does work exacted by one private actor from another in order to settle the latter's financial obligation become criminal? Many employment relationships are onerous on employees, entail appalling conditions, and stem from unacceptable tricks, inducements, or threats from employers—such as those involving agricultural workers or sweatshop employees in many countries. It is not yet apparent how international law would or should treat each case with respect to criminal responsibility. The definition in the 1930 Convention would seem ripe for further elaboration if international criminal law is to have any role in suppressing forced labor. It would appear that much will depend upon the ability of the

[26] *See generally* Janie Chuang, *Redirecting the Debate over Trafficking in Women: Definitions, Paradigms, and Contexts*, 11 HARV. HUM. RTS. J. 65 (1998).

victim to escape his or her fate, and the consequences to the victim and his or her family from abandonment of the labor.

TORTURE

Conventional Law

Like slavery, torture is among those human rights violations whose prohibition is generally regarded as *jus cogens*.[27] As discussed in Chapters 3 and 4, it also appears on lists of crimes against humanity and war crimes. We again focus here on torture as a crime independent of the elements of the other two groups of crimes.

The prospects for individual criminality for acts of torture received their most significant advance in December 1975, when the General Assembly adopted by consensus the Declaration on Protection from Torture. It defines torture and requires each state to ensure that all acts of torture 'are offences under its criminal law' and institute criminal proceedings against alleged offenders.[28] Formal work in the UN on criminalization began in mid-1978, when the Commission on Human Rights, upon the request of the Assembly, began considering a draft convention, leading to the adoption in 1984 of the Convention Against Torture and Other Cruel, Inhuman or Degrading Treatment or Punishment.[29]

The legal sources on torture generally address two separate acts—torture proper; and cruel, inhuman, or degrading treatment or punishment. The most authoritative definition of torture is that found in the Convention.[30] It defines torture as:

> any act by which severe pain or suffering, whether physical or mental, is intentionally inflicted on a person for such purposes as obtaining from him or a third person information or a confession, punishing him for an act he or a third person

[27] *Furundzija Judgment*, para. 153; Siderman de Blake v. Republic of Argentina, 965 F.2d 699, 714–18 (9th Cir. 1992), *cert. denied*, 507 U.S. 1017 (1993); *see also* RESTATEMENT, *supra* note 21, § 702.

[28] GA Res. 3452, Annex, arts. 7, 10, UN GAOR, 30th Sess., Supp. No. 34, at 91, UN Doc. A/10034 (1975) [hereinafter Declaration on Torture].

[29] The Convention had 123 parties as of late 2000. MULTILATERAL TREATIES, ch. IV.9. For a view that the Convention does not render individuals criminally responsible under international law for torture, *see* William T. D'Zurilla, *Individual Responsibility for Torture under International Law*, 56 TULANE L. REV. 186, 210–14 (1981). *But see* Ch. 1, Four Bodies of Law, *supra* (arguing for individual criminality under international law regardless of particular enforcement mechanisms). *See also* Ch. 8, text at notes 26–29, *infra*.

[30] Although slightly narrower than that in the Convention, the definition in the Declaration on Torture is the same in the important respects. Declaration on Torture, *supra* note 28, art. 1, at 91. *See also* Inter-American Convention to Prevent and Punish Torture, Dec. 9, 1985, art. 2, OAS T.S. No. 67, at 13, *reprinted in* 25 ILM 519 (1986) (broader definition).

has committed or is suspected of having committed, or intimidating or coercing him or a third person, or for any reason based on discrimination of any kind, when such pain or suffering is inflicted by or at the instigation of or with the consent or acquiescence of a public official or other person acting in an official capacity. It does not include pain or suffering arising only from, inherent in or incidental to lawful sanctions.[31]

This definition of torture is quite broad, though not without ambiguity.[32] The list of purposes for which the severe pain is inflicted on the victim is illustrative only, thus permitting a wide array of sadistic activity to qualify legally as torture. The perpetrator of the torture need not be a public official, though someone in authority must have authorized or acquiesced in the action. The Convention also rejects any justifications for torture, such as public emergency or state of war.[33] The Convention does not define cruel, inhuman, or degrading treatment or punishment (nor does the Declaration), reflecting the inability of states to agree upon a definition or upon the concomitant criminality.[34]

Customary Law

Like slavery, torture may be said to incur individual responsibility under customary law to the extent that all states may punish acts committed anywhere.[35] The widespread adherence of states to the 1984 Convention, coupled with the importance of the ban on torture to international law, suggests that customary international law is evolving toward a recognition of torture as an international crime. The ILC's draft statute for an international criminal court statute included torture as defined in the Convention in the list of crimes over which the court would have jurisdiction, but it

[31] Torture Convention, art. 1, 1465 UNTS at 113–14.

[32] For background on the Convention's drafting, *see* Ahcene Boulesbaa, *Analysis and Proposals for the Rectification of the Ambiguities Inherent in Article 1 of the U.N. Convention on Torture*, 5 FLA. INT'L L.J. 293 (1990); Matthew Lippman, *The Development and Drafting of the United Nations Convention Against Torture and Other Cruel, Inhuman or Degrading Treatment or Punishment*, 17 B. C. INT'L AND COMP. L. REV. 275 (1994).

[33] Torture Convention, art. 2(2), 1465 UNTS at 114; *see also* Declaration on Torture, *supra* note 28, art. 3, at 91.

[34] *See* Boulesbaa, *supra* note 32, at 296–300; Lippman, *supra* note 32, at 319. On elaboration of the concept in the context of the European Convention on Human Rights, *See* Republic of Ireland v. United Kingdom, 2 EUROP. HUM. RTS. REP. 25, 74–85 (1978); P.J. Duffy, *Article 3 of the European Convention on Human Rights*, 32 INT'L AND COMP. L.Q. 316, 318–22 (1983).

[35] *Furundzija Judgment*, para. 156; *Pinochet*, [1999] 2 All E.R. at 109 (Lord Browne-Wilkinson). The Lords in *Pinochet* nonetheless differed on whether universal jurisdiction sufficed to make extraterritorial torture a crime in the Untied Kingdom prior to the entry into force in 1988 of the U.K. statute that implemented the Torture Convention and specifically criminalized torture abroad. *Compare Pinochet* at 142–44 (negative answer from Lord Hope) with *id.* at 177–78 (affirmative answer from Lord Millett).

was not included in the final ICC Statute as a separate crime.[36] It was not, moreover, included as an independent offense in the Statutes of the Yugoslavia and Rwanda Tribunals.

Theoretical and Practical Challenges

The widespread ratification of the Torture Convention provides a solid legal foundation for enforcement of the criminal law against torture domestically as well as through international institutions. The key issues of application would likely be those already faced by international bodies (*e.g.*, the European Court of Human Rights or the UN's Committee Against Torture established under the Torture Convention) in determining whether states are responsible for acts of torture. These would include the distinction between torture and cruel, inhuman, or degrading punishment; and the need to determine the scope of 'lawful sanctions' that are exempt from the definition of torture.

A further difficulty may arise from the Convention's required nexus to official conduct in those cases where persons not associated with recognized governments participate in torture. On the one hand, the Convention's key phrase—'by or at the instigation of or with the consent or acquiescence of a public official or other person acting in an official capacity'—is broad enough to cover acts where the torturer himself is a private individual (*e.g.*, not part of a police or military apparatus). And even if his acts are only acquiesced in, rather than instigated by, a public official or person in an official capacity, they meet the definition in the Convention. Moreover, it would also seem that this phrase (especially the term 'other person acting in an official capacity') encompasses acts where the person acquiescing is not himself an agent of a recognized government, as long as he is in some sense 'in an official capacity'. This would include officials of organizations seeking or asserting political control over territory and thus cover various groups in the Yugoslavia conflict or guerrilla groups in Latin America.

It would be more difficult to argue that the Convention would address torture undertaken by members of a purely private group, such as a criminal syndicate, against their opponents (even, it would seem, against police officers) to extract information.[37] The spirit of the law on torture might suggest regarding certain individuals as acting in an official capacity within

[36] *See* 1994 [II] 2 ILC Y.B. at 38, 67–68 (art. 20(e) and Annex). It is included in the 1996 Draft Code, but only as a crime against humanity. 1996 ILC Report, at 93 (art. 18).

[37] For a discussion of the *travaux* supporting the nexus to official conduct, *see* J. Herman Burgers and Hans Danelius, The United Nations Convention against Torture: A Handbook on the Convention against Torture and other Cruel, Inhuman or Degrading Treatment or Punishment 45–46 (1988).

whatever organization to which they belong. If such a private actor were found not to have committed torture for purposes of the Convention, the state in which he acted might nonetheless be liable for violating the ICCPR. That treaty does not define torture in such limited terms and obligates states to grant all individuals the rights provided under it.[38]

RACIAL DISCRIMINATION AND APARTHEID

Conventional Law

While racial discrimination violates both customary international law and the 1966 International Convention on the Elimination of All Forms of Racial Discrimination,[39] the individual criminality of racial discrimination *per se* is not yet well established.[40] Rather, certain acts resulting from discrimination have achieved the status of international crimes. The Genocide Convention clearly covers especially egregious forms of racial discrimination, and persecution on racial grounds constitutes a crime against humanity assuming it meets the other elements of that crime.

Apart from these, only one other type of racial discrimination has been regarded by states as incurring individual responsibility—apartheid, which states have singled out for its special invidiousness.[41] Apartheid incurs individual criminal responsibility as a matter of conventional law under the 1973 International Convention on the Suppression and Punishment of the Crime of Apartheid, which entered into force in July 1976. As of late 2000, the Convention had 101 parties.[42]

Although the United Nations developed the Apartheid Convention as part of its long campaign to eliminate the pernicious legal racial discrimination in South Africa, the prohibitions in the Convention are not limited to that country. Rather, the Convention contains a broad definition of apartheid. After characterizing the practice as a crime against humanity, it lists a series of 'inhuman acts committed for the purpose of establishing and maintaining domination by one racial group of persons over any other racial group of persons and systematically oppressing them'. These

[38] *See* ICCPR, arts. 2(2), 7, 999 UNTS at 173, 175.

[39] Mar. 7, 1966, 660 UNTS 195 [hereinafter Racial Discrimination Convention].

[40] *Cf.* M. Cherif Bassiouni, *The Proscribing Function of International Criminal Law in the Processes of International Protection of Human Rights*, 9 YALE J. WORLD PUB. ORD. 193, 202 (1982) (listing apartheid but not racial discrimination as an international crime).

[41] *See generally* MCDOUGAL ET AL., *supra* note 3, at 521–50. The 1966 Racial Discrimination Convention does require states to make dissemination of racist ideas and participation in racist organizations punishable offenses. Racial Discrimination Convention, *supra* note 39, art. 4, 660 UNTS at 218, 220.

[42] MULTILATERAL TREATIES, ch. IV.7.

include denial of the right to life and liberty, imposition of living conditions designed to destroy the group, legislative measures to prevent the group's participation in the life of the country or creation of conditions that prevent its full development, division of the population along racial lines, exploitation of the labor force of the group, and persecution of organizations opposing apartheid.[43] The Convention specifically provides for individual criminal responsibility.[44]

The ambiguities in the Convention have received some scholarly treatment, especially regarding intent and motive.[45] For our purposes, the most significant interpretive question lies in the definition of a 'racial group'. The Convention does not define the term, and the negotiating history sheds no light on this question.[46] As McDougal, Lasswell, and Chen point out, the term 'race' is subject to numerous meanings depending upon the views of the participant or observer of the classification.[47] Since the Convention was principally addressed to South Africa, the term might simply correspond with the South African classifications, which were based primarily upon skin color, though with a component of national origin as well.[48] Thus, a 'racial group' would exclude any group defined (by itself or others) on other terms, such as ethnicity or national origin.[49]

A different interpretation would arise from relying on the definition of racial discrimination in the 1966 Racial Discrimination Convention. It defines racial discrimination broadly, as 'any distinction, exclusion, restriction or preference based on race, colour, descent, or national or ethnic origin' that denies equal enjoyment of human rights.[50] It creates a wide-ranging prohibition on discrimination, whatever particular invidious classification the oppressor chooses.[51] This might suggest that a 'racial group' under the Apartheid Convention is any group that suffers racial discrimination thus broadly defined, including groups identified by themselves or others as 'ethnic groups'.

43 Apartheid Convention, art. II, 1015 UNTS at 245–46; *see also* Roger S. Clark, *Apartheid*, *in* 1 INTERNATIONAL CRIMINAL LAW, *supra* note 1, at 643, 646–50.

44 Apartheid Convention, art. III, 1015 UNTS at 246.

45 *See* Clark, *supra* note 43, at 647–51.

46 46 UN GAOR 3d Comm., 28th Sess., 2002d through 2008th mtgs. at 138–70, UN Docs. A/C.3/SR.2002–08 (1975).

47 MCDOUGAL ET AL., *supra* note 3, at 569–71 (popular categorizations of race 'built upon vague, shifting, and erratic references to . . . skin color, body build, eye cast or color, hair texture, nose shape, blood type, genetic affiliation, and historical or cultural association').

48 *Id.* at 523.

49 *See* Egon Schwelb, *The International Convention on the Elimination of All Forms of Racial Discrimination*, 15 INT'L AND COMP. L.Q. 996, 1001–03, 1006–07 (1966).

50 Racial Discrimination Convention, *supra* note 39, art. 1, 660 UNTS at 216.

51 MCDOUGAL ET AL., *supra* note 3, at 587–90; *cf.* Ch. 2, text at note 41, *supra* (ICTY and ICTR definitions of racial group for purposes of genocide prosecution).

Customary Law

The criminality of apartheid as an independent crime under customary international law is a matter of some conjecture. It has been labeled a crime against humanity in the 1973 Convention,[52] the 1968 Convention on the Non-Applicability of Statutory Limitations to War Crimes and Crimes Against Humanity,[53] and the ICC Statute.[54] The ILC's 1996 Draft Code includes among its list of crimes against humanity 'institutionalized discrimination', meant to resemble a generic version of apartheid, but did not list it as a crime independent of the elements of crimes against humanity.[55] Many, though not all, of the specific acts within the definition of apartheid do resemble the acts generally included on the list of crimes against humanity; and the definition of apartheid seems to incorporate the special elements of crimes against humanity, namely systematicity and discriminatory intent.[56] Thus, much of apartheid as defined in the Convention seems to qualify as *per se* a crime against humanity and incur individual responsibility. The practice of apartheid in South Africa, combining numerous inhuman acts with other forms of systematic persecution, clearly supports this conclusion.[57] Based on this view, the South African Truth and Reconciliation Commission found apartheid 'as a systematic form of racial discrimination and separation' to be a crime against humanity.[58]

Theoretical and Practical Challenges

The prospects for application of the Apartheid Convention in light of the end of apartheid in South Africa are uncertain. The Convention was drafted hastily and was clearly meant to apply to one state alone. For this reason, its definitions may be both too vague and too specific for application beyond South Africa. Moreover, states may feel disinclined to become parties to a treaty that seems to have now served its purpose, even

[52] Art. I, 1015 UNTS at 245.

[53] Art. I(b), 754 UNTS at 75; *see also* Protocol I, art. 85(4)(c), 1125 UNTS at 42 (apartheid a grave breach 'when committed wilfully and in violation of the [Geneva] Conventions or the Protocol').

[54] ICC Statute, art. 7(1)(j) and 7(2)(h).

[55] 1996 ILC Report, at 94 (art. 18), 99–100.

[56] *See* Apartheid Convention, art. II, 1015 UNTS at 245–46 (listing murder, serious bodily harm, imprisonment, and forced labor; chapeau noting that apartheid encompasses 'inhuman acts committed for the purpose of establishing and maintaining domination by one racial group of persons over any other racial group of persons and systematically oppressing them'). Although the systematicity factor is part of the element of motive, rather than a separate criterion, the Convention, read as a whole, addresses acts analogous to those of South Africa, which were clearly systematic policies.

[57] Ronald C. Slye, *Apartheid as a Crime Against Humanity: A Submission to the South African Truth and Reconciliation Commission*, 20 Mich. J. Int'l L. 267 (1999) (views of 21 scholars).

[58] 5 Truth and Reconciliation Commission, Final Report, ch. 6, para. 101 (1998), available at www.mg.co.za/mg/projects/trc.

if—or perhaps because—it might conceivably apply to future instances of systematic racial discrimination. To our knowledge, the ban on apartheid (in treaty or custom) has not been invoked by victims, their advocates, or international bodies in responding to the plight of the Kurds, the Tamils, the South Sudanese, Japanese of Korean descent, or various indigenous peoples, no doubt because that term is still associated with the South African experience. It thus seems best to regard the Apartheid Convention as a potential source of law for imputing criminal responsibility for certain patterns of racial discrimination, but one which states have not yet shown much inclination to apply. Apartheid's inclusion in the ICC Statute nonetheless keeps open the prospect of some individual accountability for the practice as a crime against humanity; but the Court will clearly face interpretive difficulties surrounding the term 'racial group' in the Statute.

FORCED DISAPPEARANCES

A trend toward criminalization is also emerging with respect to forced disappearances. This practice entails the abduction of citizens by police or armed forces, followed by a failure by the authorities to acknowledge the fact of the seizure or the location of the victim and, in most cases, violence against the victim, such as murder, torture, or rape. The technique gained prominence as a method of suppression of dissent in Latin America, particularly Argentina, in the 1970s, and has since become a focus of attention of human rights advocates.[59]

Efforts toward criminalization of forced disappearances have taken place in several fora. In 1992, the General Assembly passed the Declaration on the Protection of All Persons from Enforced Disappearances.[60] Its key provisions declare forced disappearances 'an offence to human dignity', and call for states to take a variety of actions to prevent and punish them.[61] Although non-binding, its passage signifies at least the beginning of a trend toward international criminality, analogous to the passage of the Declaration on Torture in 1975. Binding law has emerged in the inter-American context through the conclusion by the OAS in 1994 of the Inter-American Convention on the Forced Disappearance of Persons.[62] It defines disappearances with some specificity:

59 *See generally* NUNCA MÁS: THE REPORT OF THE ARGENTINE NATIONAL COMMISSION ON THE DISAPPEARED 10–75, 209–34 (Farrar Straus Giroux trans., 1986) (1984).

60 GA Res. 47/133, UN GAOR, 47th Sess., Supp. No. 49, at 207, UN Doc. A/47/49 (1992).

61 *Id.* arts. 1, 3–20, at 207–10; *see also* Ch. 8, text at notes 32–33, *infra*.

62 June 9, 1994, 33 ILM 1529 (1994).

> the act of depriving a person or persons of his or their freedom, in whatever way, perpetrated by agents of the state or by persons or groups of persons acting with the authorization, support, or acquiescence of the state, followed by an absence of information or a refusal to acknowledge that deprivation or freedom or to give information on the whereabouts of that person, thereby impeding his or her recourse to the applicable legal remedies and procedural guarantees.[63]

The importance of criminalizing disappearances globally became clear when the crime appeared as one of the enumerated acts for crimes against humanity in both the 1996 ILC Draft Code and the ICC Statute.[64]

The decision by the Latin American states to address this practice through a regional treaty suggests the possibility of a new method of international criminalization, one in which a region particularly affected by a human rights atrocity starts a process that can lead to criminalization globally. At this point, it seems clear that regional international law imposes individual responsibility on practices within Latin America or by Latin Americans; expectations on criminal culpability under international law generally are most clear regarding those forced disappearances that entail the special elements of crimes against humanity. States have not, however, reached the same level of agreement on the criminality of disappearances *per se* as they have on slavery, torture, and apartheid.

A BRIEF WORD ON CRIMES AGAINST PEACE

Crimes against peace, sometimes known as the crime of aggression, have a controversial pedigree in international law. Although international law has enshrined the illegality of aggression at least since the UN Charter as a matter of *jus cogens*,[65] the criminality of the use of force has not seen an equal degree of shared belief among states and scholars. The IMT Charter offered the following definition of the crime:

> planning, preparation, initiation or waging of a war of aggression, or a war in violation of international treaties, agreements or assurances, or participation in a common plan or conspiracy for the accomplishment of any of the foregoing[66]

The idea of charging the Nazis with the crime of starting World War II was controversial at the time and has remained so ever since. For the Americans, crimes against peace were the chief offense of the Nazis, and the criminality of aggressive war needed to be enshrined in international

[63] *Id.* art. II, 33 ILM at 1530.
[64] 1996 ILC Report, at 94 (art. 18); ICC Statute, art. 7(1)(i) and 7(2)(i).
[65] UN Charter, art. 2(4); *see also* Military and Paramilitary Activities in and Against Nicaragua (Nicar. v. US), 1986 ICJ 14, 100–01 (June 27).
[66] IMT Charter, art. 6(a).

law. But starting a war had not been regarded as criminal up to that time. The Kellogg-Briand Pact of 1928, which outlawed war (not too successfully, to say the least), only rendered aggression an illegal act for states, not a criminal act for which individuals could be tried. The French government resisted the concept for this reason; the Soviets, for their part, were concerned about criminalizing aggressive war given their invasions of Finland and annexation of parts of Eastern Europe. The American view prevailed—though the IMT's jurisdiction was limited to *Axis* aggression—leading to the conviction of leading Nazis for crimes against peace.[67] Afterward, a fierce debate raged as to whether the convictions violated the principle of *nullum crimen sine lege*.[68]

The General Assembly endorsed the IMT's principles in 1946 and in 1950 declared aggression 'the gravest of all crimes against peace and security throughout the world';[69] the International Law Commission listed it first among its crimes against the peace and security of mankind in its 1954 Draft Code.[70] After the ILC resumed its work on the Draft Code following the General Assembly's adoption of a Definition of Aggression, aggression remained first on the Commission's list.

More significant indicia of governmental attitudes, however, are decisions showing hesitation about prosecuting individuals. The 1968 Statutory Limitations Convention did not even address crimes against peace. In addition, in setting up the Yugoslavia Tribunal in 1993, the Security Council did not give it jurisdiction over crimes against peace because its members did not likely wish it to adjudicate the causes of the conflict.[71] And the ICC Statute grants the court jurisdiction over crimes against peace only if states formally amend the treaty to add a definition of the crime and the conditions for the exercise of jurisdiction.[72]

Four factors explain the current state of affairs on crimes against peace. First, the continued debate over the legality of the Nuremberg proceedings with respect to crimes against peace has cast doubt on the authoritativeness of the IMT Charter as a precedent for the notion of

67 *See* TELFORD TAYLOR, THE ANATOMY OF THE NUREMBERG TRIALS 65–67, 76 (1992).

68 For attacks on the judgment, *see* George A. Finch, *The Nuremberg Trial and International Law*, 41 AJIL 20 (1947); Hans Ehard, *The Nuremberg Trial Against the Major War Criminals and International Law*, 43 AJIL 223 (1949). For views of some leading scholars defending the trials for crimes against peace, *see* Quincy Wright, *The Law of the Nuremberg Trial*, 41 AJIL 38, 55–62 (1947); 2 OPPENHEIM'S INTERNATIONAL LAW 190–93 (Hersch Lauterpacht ed., 7th ed. 1952).

69 GA Res. 380(V), UN GAOR, 5th Sess., UN Doc. A/1775, at 13 (1950).

70 1954 ILC Report, at 151 (art. 2(1)). For the ILC's commentary, *see* 1951 [II] ILC Y.B. at 135–36.

71 *See* James C. O'Brien, *The International Tribunal for Violations of International Humanitarian Law in the Former Yugoslavia*, 87 AJIL 639, 645 (1993).

72 ICC Statute, art. 5(1)(c) and 5(2); for background, *see* Herman von A.M. Hebel and Darryl Robinson, *Crimes within the Jurisdiction of the Court*, *in* THE INTERNATIONAL CRIMINAL COURT: THE MAKING OF THE ROME STATUTE 79, 81–85 (Roy S. Lee ed., 1999).

individual criminality.[73] Second, agreement on a definition of aggression specific enough for criminal prosecutions of individuals remains elusive. Third and relatedly, crimes against peace raise especially hard questions regarding the level of involvement of an individual—*actus reus* and *mens rea*—that creates criminality. For instance, how far down the structure of a defense ministry or a military hierarchy should guilt extend?[74] Fourth, authoritative determinations of crimes against peace in many cases encompass complex factual inquiries for which courts may well prove less than fully equipped. While some cases of aggression are as clear as the Nazi invasions in Western Europe or Iraq's invasion of Kuwait, other incidents demand more careful scrutiny.[75] The shortcomings in the handling of the question of aggression by the International Court of Justice in the *Nicaragua* case (which did not even concern implication of criminal conduct) cast some doubt upon the ability of tribunals to handle crimes against peace responsibly, although the Yugoslavia Tribunal has nonetheless handled similarly difficult issues in the context of command responsibility.[76] The result is that states have been reluctant to place legal constraints of a criminal form on their use of force, so that *jus ad bellum* has remained far more immune to criminalization than *jus in bello*.

As for the precise contours of the crime, the only internationally accepted definition remains that in the IMT Charter. It incorporates two notions—direct planning and waging of aggressive wars, as well as conspiracy in a common plan to do so. These became two separate counts of the Nuremberg indictment, with Count One concerning conspiracy and Count Two concerning direct action. In its judgment, the IMT carefully recounted the planning and preparation of Nazi aggression as well as the aggression itself against each victim nation in Europe and the United States. It also reviewed the specific treaties violated.[77] The Court adopted a restrictive view of the concept of 'war of aggression' in characterizing the German takeover of Austria and Czechoslovakia only as *acts* of

[73] Even former US prosecutor Telford Taylor acknowledged that arguments about crimes against the peace, 'if conducted on a plane devoid of political and emotional factors, will be won by the defense.' TAYLOR, *supra* note 67, at 629.

[74] *See* U.S. v. Krauch (the '*I.G. Farben Case*'), 8 CCL No. 10 Trials 1081, 1124–25 (difficulties of assigning guilt for planning of World War II).

[75] *See, e.g.*, TELFORD TAYLOR, FINAL REPORT TO THE SECRETARY OF THE ARMY ON THE NUERNBERG WAR CRIMES TRIALS UNDER CONTROL COUNCIL LAW NO. 10, at 66–67 (1949).

[76] For contrasting views on the ICJ's opinion, *see Appraisals of the ICJ's Decision: Nicaragua v. United States*, 81 AJIL 77 (1987) (views of 16 scholars).

[77] 22 IMT Trials at 428–61. *See also* UNITED NATIONS WAR CRIMES COMMISSION, HISTORY OF THE UNITED NATIONS WAR CRIMES COMMISSION AND THE DEVELOPMENT OF THE LAWS OF WAR 252–53 (1948) [hereinafter UNWCC]; SECRETARY-GENERAL OF THE UNITED NATIONS, THE CHARTER AND JUDGMENT OF THE NÜRNBERG TRIBUNAL: HISTORY AND ANALYSIS 47–50 (1949), UN Doc. A/CN.4/5, UN Sales No. 1949.V.7 [hereinafter 1949 SECRETARY-GENERAL MEMORANDUM].

aggression rather than wars of aggression; and it failed to elaborate on the circumstances under which a war violated treaties.[78]

The Tribunal eventually convicted twelve and acquitted four of crimes against peace. In acquitting the four (Schacht, Sauckel, von Papen, and Speer), the court generally held that acts were not crimes against peace unless done as part of the Nazi policy of waging aggressive war.[79] For example, Speer, who became Hitler's head of armaments in 1942, was acquitted because the production of weapons in support of the war did not form part of a plan to wage aggression.[80] On the conspiracy charge, eight were convicted and fourteen acquitted (including four of the twelve convicted for direct participation). Though the court's reasoning was not the model of clarity, those acquitted were generally found not to have participated actively and early enough in the actual preparation for the war.[81] The Control Council No. 10 trials in the four cases involving crimes against peace further elaborated upon the concept.[82] In the *Ministries Case*, the court explicitly found the conquest of Austria to be such a crime.[83] The American zone tribunals generally mirrored the IMT's views on the high level of responsibility required for guilt.[84]

The ILC's work leading to the 1954 Draft Code developed a long list of crimes beyond those in the IMT Charter. Beyond its many imprecisions and questionable provisions (such as political and economic coercion), the lack of a definition of aggression itself placed the entire Draft Code on hold until the General Assembly adopted a definition in 1974. That elaborate definition, however helpful at identifying various forms of aggression, was developed to assist the UN's political organs in determining aggression, not to determine individual guilt.[85] In its 1996 ILC Draft Code, the ILC did not attempt a definition, other than to refer to aggression.[86]

[78] *See* 1949 SECRETARY-GENERAL MEMORANDUM, *supra* note 77, at 47–50.

[79] 22 IMT Trails at 554 (regarding Schacht); *see also* Wright, *supra* note 68, at 66–67.

[80] 22 IMT Trials at 577.

[81] *See* UNWCC, *supra* note 77, at 249–52; 1949 SECRETARY-GENERAL MEMORANDUM, *supra* note 77, at 51–55; Wright, *supra* note 68, at 67–69.

[82] *See I.G. Farben Case*, 8 CCL No. 10 Trials at 1107–28; U.S. v. Krupp et al. (the '*Krupp Case*'), 9 CCL No 10 Trials 390, 390–401; U.S. v. von Weizsaecker et al. (the '*Ministries Case*'), 14 CCL No. 10 Trials 308, 323–435; U.S. v. von Leeb et al. (the '*High Command Case*'), 11 CCL No. 10 Trials 462, 485–91.

[83] 14 CCL No. 10 Trials at 330–31.

[84] *See, e.g., High Command Case*, 11 CCL No. 10 Trials at 488–91 (finding defendants not guilty because they did not serve at the policy level); *see also* Government Commissioner of the General Tribunal of the Military Government of the French Zone of Occupation in Germany v. Roechling, 14 CCL No. 10 Trials 1097, 1107–10 (Superior Mil. Ct. French Zone Ger. 1949) (finding industrialist not guilty).

[85] GA Res. 3314 (XXIX), UN GAOR, 29th Sess., Supp. No. 31, at 142, 143, UN Doc. A/9631 (1974).

[86] *See* 1996 ILC Report, at 83 (art. 16); M. Cherif Bassiouni and Benjamin B. Ferencz, *The Crime Against Peace*, *in* 1 INTERNATIONAL CRIMINAL LAW, *supra* note 1, at 313, 337–42.

Given the difficulties in finding an acceptable definition of crimes against peace for the Draft Code or the ICC Statute, it is difficult to speak of customary law on this offense. Although the law on the use of force has evolved since the IMT Charter to include many forms of aggression beyond classic invasion, the effect on individual responsibility remains unclear. Nuremberg still exerts a great pull on the law, as it gives notice to potential aggressors of the possibility of prosecution for their actions, and governments seem dedicated to the Nuremberg Principles. But they are unable to agree on a workable definition that would be necessary to bring about real accountability.

6

Expanding and Contracting Culpability: Related Crimes, Defenses, and Other Barriers to Criminality

An understanding of the legal bases for individual responsibility for serious human rights abuses demands more than an elaboration of the elements of the various offenses. For the involvement of individuals in atrocities encompasses countless possibilities—from killer to accomplice, from commander to subordinate, from encourager to unwilling participant. Those in command positions or following orders will typically seek to evade responsibility for their actions. Any methods to achieve accountability must thus reckon with important principles of criminal law, recognized by nearly all states and endorsed in international law, that serve to extend culpability in some instances and limit it in others. These concepts center around the extent to which guilt may be attributed to those not directly committing a crime, as well as defenses and other legal doctrines that may insulate from guilt certain individuals despite their direct role in the offense. Indeed, as much as the definitions of the various crimes, this body of law in many situations proves the linchpin to gauging the responsibility of those accused of atrocities.

RELATED CRIMES

Forms of Complicity

Like domestic criminal law, international law generally recognizes that persons may be held culpable for various acts associated with a recognized crime, even if they did not directly commit it. Notions of *conspiracy* and *complicity* received a clear endorsement in the Nuremberg Charter, Article 6(a) of which criminalized both preparing and conducting aggressive war and 'a common plan or conspiracy' to do so. The International Military Tribunal interpreted the conspiracy charges strictly, limiting the term to acts most closely involved with the planning of the war and thereby acquitting most of the Nazi leaders charged with them.[1] Control Council Law No. 10 took a broader view, singling out accessories, those who took a consenting part, those connected with plans for the crimes, and members of organizations connected with the crime.[2] In addition, Allied military courts convicted numerous defendants based on notions of complicity, including those supplying gas to concentration camps and serving in them.[3]

Article III of the Genocide Convention states that conspiracy to commit, direct and public incitement of, and complicity in genocide also constitute crimes, yet it provides no definitions of these terms.[4] The International Law Commission's elaboration of the Nuremberg principles includes complicity in all three crimes in the IMT Charter (not merely crimes against peace) as an international crime, and the 1954 Draft Code of Offenses Against the Peace and Security of Mankind includes conspiracy, complicity, and direct incitement.[5] The key interpretive problem with all these instruments, however, remains the lack of uniformity among legal systems in defining these terms, rendering the tasks of prosecutors and judges faced with respecting the rights of defendants somewhat complex.[6]

Lawmaking processes beginning in the 1980s have produced greater

[1] 22 IMT Trials at 467–69; *see* United Nations War Crimes Commission, History of the United Nations War Crimes Commission and the Development of the Laws of War 247–52 (1948); Secretary-General of the United Nations, The Charter and Judgment of the Nürnberg Tribunal 51–55 (1949), UN Doc. A/CN.4/5, UN Sales No. 1949.V.7; *see also* 22 IMT Trials at 469 (final sentence of IMT Charter, art. 6, did not create separate crime of conspiracy); *id.* at 498–500.

[2] CCL No. 10, art. II(2); *see* United States v. Pohl et al., 5 CCL No. 10 Trials 958, 989 (knowledge of crime and participation after the fact sufficient for criminality); United States v. Altstoetter et al. (the '*Justice Case*'), 3 CCL No. 10 Trials 954, 1081 (defendants guilty if 'they each consciously participated in the plan or took a consenting part therein').

[3] *See, e.g.*, Trial of Martin Gottfried Weiss and Thirty-Nine Others (*The Dachau Concentration Camp Trial*'), 11 War Crimes Reports 5, 12–16 (US Mil. Ct. Ger. 1945); Trial of Bruno Tesch and Two Others (the '*Zyklon B Case*'), 1 War Crimes Reports 93 (Brit. Mil. Ct. Ger. 1946); Trial of Gustav Becker, Wilhelm Weber and 18 Others, 7 War Crimes Reports 67, 70–72 (Mil. Trib. Lyon 1947).

[4] The drafters also chose not to mention preparatory acts explicitly, as states argued that such acts were difficult to define or too remote from genocide, and that the rest of the Convention punished preparatory acts closely connected with genocide. *See, e.g.*, Nehemiah Robinson, The Genocide Convention: A Commentary 66–70 (1960); Matthew Lippman, *The Drafting of the 1948 Convention on the Prevention and Punishment of the Crime of Genocide*, 3 B.U. Int'l L.J. 1, 31–31 (1985) (on genocidal propaganda).

[5] Report of the International Law Commission to the General Assembly, UN Doc. A/1316 (1950), *reprinted in* 1950 [II] ILC Y.B. 364, 377–78 (principle VII) [hereinafter 1950 ILC Report]; 1954 ILC Report, at 152 (art. 2(13)).

[6] *See* Fourth report on the draft Code of Offences Against the Peace and Security of Mankind, by Mr. Doudou Thiam, Special Rapporteur, UN Doc. A/CN.4/398 (1986), *reprinted in* 1986 [II] 1 ILC Y.B. 53, 66–67 [hereinafter Fourth Report of the Special Rapporteur]; Jacques Francillon, *Crimes de Guerre, Crimes Contre l'Humanité*, Juris–Classeurs, Fasc. 410, at 19 (1983).

specificity, focusing on various forms of accomplice liability. Thus, the Yugoslavia and Rwanda Tribunal Statutes make culpable those who 'planned, instigated, ordered, committed or otherwise aided and abetted in the planning, preparation or execution' of one of the enumerated crimes.[7] The ICC Statute offers the most detailed schema to date, providing for responsibility for a broad range of associated acts, but conditioning guilt for certain of these on completion of various acts or possession of various mental states.[8]

These standards, although helpful, still require elaboration in terms of the degree of involvement of the accomplice in the underlying act and his state of mind. The Yugoslavia and Rwanda Tribunals have attempted to pick up where the post-war tribunals left off. In one lengthy extensive treatment, the trial court in *Tadic* reviewed the earlier caselaw as well as the 1996 ILC Draft Code. Relying extensively on the latter, it concluded that the accomplice is guilty if 'his participation directly and substantially affected the commission of that offence through supporting the actual commission before, during, or after the incident', extending guilt to 'all that naturally results' from the act. Such participation includes words and deeds and does not require the defendant's physical presence at the scene of the underlying act. As for *mens rea*, the court required that the defendant have knowledge of the underlying act.[9] Other trial chambers explicitly adopted the *Tadic* test (which was not challenged on appeal).[10] The Rwanda Tribunal adopted a similar test of knowledge in finding Akayesu and others guilty of numerous killings and inhumane acts.[11]

The current trends in international caselaw thus require a substantial nexus between the defendant's conduct and the alleged crime, although they do not require that the defendant's actions led to or caused the underlying act. Moral encouragement would qualify; indeed, even a bystander would be culpable if he actively provides such support and has the requisite mental state. Furthermore, the *mens rea* need not be the same as that of the immediate perpetrator, but only the knowledge that their actions

[7] ICTY Statute, art. 7(1); ICTR Statute, art. 6(1); *see also* 1996 ILC Report, at 18 (art. 2) (seven categories of participation), 22–27; Torture Convention, art. 4(1), 1465 UNTS at 114.

[8] *See* ICC Statute, art. 25; for the text, *see* Appendix 19.

[9] *Tadic Judgment*, para. 692; *see also id.* paras. 674–77; *id.* paras. 726, 730, 738 (guilty of participation in beatings).

[10] *Aleksovski Judgment*, paras. 61; *see also id.* para. 129 (guilty for aiding and abetting in use of detainees as human shields and trench-digging); *Celebeci Judgment*, paras. 326–29; *see also Furundzija Judgment*, para. 249 (conducting its own review of caselaw and deriving a nearly identical test); *id.* para. 274 (guilty for aiding and abetting rape).

[11] *Akayesu Judgment*, paras. 474–84; *see also id.* paras. 645–71, 676–95 (guilty of ordering deaths, aiding and abetting torture, rape, and other inhumane acts); *Kayeshima and Ruzindana Judgment*, paras. 191–207.

will assist the perpetrator.[12] The scope of liability is thus deliberately very broad, reinforcing a strong deterrence policy.

The ICTR has also considered the Genocide Convention's special list of associated crimes. It has found that complicity under the Convention does not require that the defendant himself have the intent to destroy the group, but only knowledge of the genocide by the principal; and that conspiracy to commit genocide requires the special intent but does not require completion of the act.[13] Equally significant, it has examined the notion of direct and public incitement, defining it as 'directly provoking the perpetrator(s) to commit genocide' through a wide variety of means, whether speeches, publications, inducements, or threats; the accused must have the special intent of genocide, although his incitement need not be successful to incur guilt.[14]

Lastly, *attempt* remains more ambiguous as a matter of international criminal law. It is incorporated in the IMT Charter and Control Council Law No. 10 only insofar as they include the planning of certain crimes. It does appear as a crime in the Genocide Convention, the Torture Convention, and the ILC's 1954 and 1996 Draft Codes.[15] The Yugoslavia and Rwanda Tribunal Statutes do not refer to attempt except in their incorporation of genocide from the Convention.[16] The ICC Statute adopts the position of the 1996 Draft Code that, to be criminal, attempt must include more than mere preparation for the crime.[17]

Superior Responsibility

Apart from the question of complicity in the act, international law recognizes a special and significant form of culpability for acts of *omission* through the doctrine of superior or command responsibility. The doctrine has ancient origins, and has been incorporated in domestic military law as well. At the international level, it received its most significant elaboration during the post-World War II trials, and remains a core question in ongoing

[12] *Furundzija Judgment*, paras. 232–33, 245.

[13] *Akayesu Judgment*, paras. 540–45; *Musema Judgment*, paras. 181–83, 192–93.

[14] *Akayesu Judgment*, paras. 554–62; *see also id.* paras. 672–75 (finding defendant guilty); *Ruggiu Sentencing Judgment* (accepting guilty plea of Belgian journalist for incitement while working for Rwandan radio station).

[15] Genocide Convention, art. III(d); Torture Convention, art. 4(1), 1465 UNTS at 114; 1954 ILC Report, at 152 (art. 2(13)); 1996 ILC Report, at 18 (art. 2); *see also* Summary Records of the 268th Meeting, 1954 [I] ILC Y.B. 137 (7–0–6 vote on retaining the term 'attempt'); Thomas Weigand, *Article 3: Responsibility and Punishment*, *in* COMMENTARIES ON THE INTERNATIONAL LAW COMMISSION'S 1991 DRAFT CODE OF CRIMES AGAINST THE PEACE AND SECURITY OF MANKIND 113, 117–18 (M. Cherif Bassiouni ed., 1993).

[16] *See, e.g.*, ICTY Statute, art. 4(3)(d).

[17] 1996 ILC Report, at 27–28; ICC Statute, art. 25(3)(f).

war crimes prosecutions.[18] The doctrine extends the liability of a commander or other superior for acts of subordinates beyond those covered through the notion of accomplice liability—that is, situations where he orders or assists in the commission of the act—to situations where the superior plays a more passive role by failing to prevent certain actions of subordinates. The theory of such responsibility is that, by virtue of a hierarchical relationship between superior and subordinate, the former should be held criminally liable for failure to exercise his duties as commander when the result is the commission of offenses by subordinates.

In general, the doctrine holds that a commander is responsible for the acts of subordinates if (1) he knew or should have known that the subordinate had committed, or was about to commit, the acts, and (2) he did not take necessary and reasonable measures to prevent the acts or punish the subordinate.[19] The first prong of the test is a compromise between the extreme positions of strict liability for commanders, on the one hand, and non-culpability despite wilful or unjustified ignorance, on the other.[20] This general starting point nonetheless obscures numerous questions regarding the precise scope of the superior's responsibility. Indeed, authoritative sources have posited slightly different tests, making the determination of customary international law on this question a challenge. The Yugoslavia and Rwanda Tribunals have attempted to bring greater clarity to the doctrine.

One area of ambiguity concerns the definition of the superior. On the one hand, the law since World War II has clearly recognized that they need not be military superiors.[21] Yet the degree of authority over the subordinate necessary to assume superior status raises highly case-specific questions. Cases in the ICTY and ICTR emphasize the necessity of *de facto* or

18 For a review of most major World War II trials, *see* 15 War Crimes Reports 62–76; for other key cases, *see* Government Commissioner of the General Tribunal of the Military Government of the French Zone of Occupation in Germany v. Roechling, 14 CCL No. 10 Trials 1097 (Superior Mil. Ct. French Zone Ger. 1949); International Military Tribunal for the Far East, Judgment, ch. X, at 1160–61, 1193–95 (1948) (guilty verdict of Koki Hirota and Mamoru Shigemitsu).

19 For excellent overviews, *see* Ilias Bantekas, *The Contemporary Law of Superior Responsibility*, 93 AJIL 573 (1999); L.C. Green, *Command Responsibility in International Humanitarian Law*, 5 TRANSNAT'L L. AND CONTEMP. PROBS. 319 (1995); William H. Parks, *Command Responsibility for War Crimes*, 62 MIL. L. REV. 1 (1973); for a comparison with US domestic law doctrine, *see* Timothy Wu and Yong-Sung Kang, *Criminal Liability for the Actions of Subordinates—The Doctrine of Command Responsibility and its Analogues in United States Law*, 38 HARV. INT'L L.J. 272 (1997).

20 W. Hays Parks, *A Few Tools in the Prosecution of War Crimes*, 149 MIL. L. REV. 73, 75 (1995); *see also* Bert V. Röling, *Aspects of the Criminal Responsibility for Violations of the Law of War*, *in* THE NEW HUMANITARIAN LAW OF ARMED CONFLICT 199, 213–20 (Antonio Cassese ed., 1979); L.C. Green, *Superior Orders and Command Responsibility*, 27 CANAD. Y.B. INT'L. L. 167, 194–99 (1989).

21 *See, e.g.*, *Roechling Case*, 14 CCL No. 10 Trials at 1111–16.

de jure power of control over subordinates.[22] For civilian superiors, their degree of control must resemble that of military commanders, though civilian authorities clearly will not possess identical powers of sanction as military commanders.[23] Based on these standards, the ICTY found that one defendant's responsibilities during the war in Bosnia did not demonstrate that he had command authority over personnel at the Celebici prison camp, and that another's activities within the camp did not amount to *de facto* control over others.[24]

A second, more important issue concerns the scope of the duty of the superior to be aware of activities by his subordinates, i.e., his responsibility where he lacks actual knowledge of the atrocities. The post-war cases generally emphasize a duty of the commander to know, at least to a reasonable extent, the activities of subordinates.[25] The US military standard suggests a negligence test.[26] Protocol I, the Yugoslavia and Rwanda Tribunal Statutes, the 1996 Draft Code, and the ICC Statute all include the notion, though with variations with regard to the scope of the duty.[27] Protocol I, most notably, could be read to suggest that the commander has little duty to seek out information regarding the activities of his troops, whereas the other standards seem to suggest a higher duty of the commander to remain apprised of these acts. The ICC Statute, for its part, adopts a negligence standard for military commanders and a lower standard for civilian superiors.[28]

[22] *Celebici Judgment*, paras. 370, 377–78, *endorsed in Aleksovski Judgment*, paras. 76–78; *Blaskic Judgment*, paras. 300–01; *Kayishema and Ruzindana Judgment*, paras. 217–23.

[23] *Aleksovski Judgment*, para. 78; *Musema Judgment*, para. 144 ('power of control over persons who *a priori* were not under his authority').

[24] *Celebici Judgment*, paras 644–721, 795–810; *see also Akayesu Judgment*, para. 691 (finding local militia not to be subordinates of defendant). For critique, *see* Bantekas, *supra* note 19, at 581–82.

[25] United States v. List et al. (the '*Hostages Case*'), 11 CCL No. 10 Trials 1230, 1271 (commander of occupied territory 'charged with notice of occurrences taking place within that territory'), 1279–80; United States v. von Leeb et al. (the '*High Command Case*'), 11 CCL No. 10 Trials 462, 543–49; *see also* In re Yamashita, 4 War Crimes Reports 1, 35 (US Mil. Comm'n Manila 1945), *aff'd*, 327 U.S. 1 (1946) (widespread nature of offenses suggests defendant must have known of them and imposing duty to attempt 'to discover and control' them, i.e., near-strict liability). *But see* Final Report of the Commission of Inquiry into the Events at the Refugee Camps in Beirut, 22 ILM 473, 493–99 (1983) (receding from standard through use of 'indirect responsibility').

[26] *See, e.g.*, U.S. DEP'T OF THE ARMY, FIELD MANUAL 27–10, LAW OF LAND WARFARE, para. 501 ('The commander is also responsible if he has actual knowledge, or should have knowledge, through reports received by him or through other means. . . .').

[27] Protocol I, art. 86(2), 1125 UNTS at 43 ('knew, or had information which should have enabled them to conclude in the circumstances at the time'); ICTY Statute, art. 7(3) ('knew or had reason to know'); ICTR Statute, art. 6(3); 1996 ILC Report, at 34 (art. 6) ('knew or had reason to know, in the circumstances at the time'); ICC Statute, art. 28(a)(i) ('either knew or, owing to the circumstances at the time, should have known' for military commanders); *id.* art. 28(b)(i) ('either knew, or consciously disregarded information which clearly indicated' for other superiors). The Geneva Conventions were silent on the issue of command responsibility except for the obvious case of commanders ordering offenses.

[28] For analysis, *see* Greg R. Vetter, *Command Responsibility of Non-Military Superiors in the*

On this question, the ICTY's trial chambers have differed in their interpretations of the standard in their Statute ('knew or had reason to know'). One court adopted a narrow view of customary law, heavily basing its reading on Protocol I—that the defendant is responsible only if 'some specific information was available to him which would provide notice' of the crimes and suggest the need for further inquiry.[29] Another adopted a tougher standard, imputing knowledge to the commander under some circumstances.[30] And a third read it to mean negligence akin to the 'knew or should have known' test; under this view, the commander's duties include a requirement to use reasonable resources to remain aware of the actions of subordinates.[31] The ICTR has also adopted different standards, with one chamber asking whether the defendant's 'negligence was so serious as to be tantamount to acquiescence or even malicious intent' and another adopting a lower standard for non-military superiors based on the ICC Statute.[32] The variety of extant standards in authoritative instruments and of judicial interpretations them suggest a lack of clarity regarding the outer limits of the superior's responsibility.

APPRAISING THE DEFENSES UNDER INTERNATIONAL LAW

In addition to the notion of *nullum crimen sine lege* discussed in Chapter 1, international criminal law has developed a basic doctrine regarding the most common defenses. These are typically raised by defendants to negate *mens rea* (criminal consciousness), the mental element of criminality that must accompany the *actus reus* (criminal act) in order to prove criminal conduct. Other claims are asserted as barriers to guilt regardless of the presence of both a criminal act and consciousness. These general defenses and other claims are in addition to claims defendants may make that a prosecutor or other inquisitor has not proved the particular elements of a crime, e.g., the intent requirement in the Genocide Convention's definition of genocide.[33]

International Criminal Court, 25 YALE J. INT'L L. 89 (2000); on the negotiations, *see* Per Saland, *International Criminal Law Principles*, *in* THE INTERNATIONAL CRIMINAL COURT: THE MAKING OF THE ROME STATUTE 189, 202–04 (Roy S. Lee ed., 1999).

[29] *Celebici Judgment*, para. 393. The court admitted that customary law as of today might hold the commander to a higher standard.

[30] *Aleksovski Judgment*, para. 80 ('an individual's superior position *per se* is a significant indicium that he had knowledge of the crimes committed' depending upon 'geographical and temporal circumstances').

[31] *Blaskic Judgment*, paras. 322, 328–32.

[32] *Akayesu Judgment*, para. 489; *Kayishema and Ruzindana Judgment*, paras. 227, 228, 509.

[33] *See* Yoram Dinstein, *International Criminal Law*, 20 ISR. L. REV. 206, 233 (1985); *see generally* 1996 ILC Report, at 73–80; 15 War Crimes Reports 155–85 (1949); Fourth Report of the Special Rapporteur, *supra* note 6, at 74–81.

Superior Orders and Ignorance of the Law

Perhaps the classic claim asserted by abusers of human rights in their own defense is that they were merely carrying out a superior's orders. The order itself becomes, for the defendant, a justification for any brutality. Yet since Nuremberg, under international law the mere fact that a subordinate followed the orders of a superior is not a defense to an international crime.[34] Rather, an individual is responsible for criminal conduct if he knew or should have known of its illegal nature. By logical implication, if the defendant could not reasonably have known of its illegal nature, his ignorance of the law would provide an excuse. This defense derives from principles of *nullum crimen sine lege*, which protects against unreasonable expectations regarding knowledge of existing law, despite the municipal law maxim that ignorance of the law is no excuse. In the international criminal context, it is accepted that the complexity of certain laws and the inability of some (primarily low-level) defendants to understand them may render it unjust to hold certain persons accountable for their actions.[35]

Successful invocation of the defense necessitates the defendant's showing that he did not know the order was illegal and that it was not, in fact, patently illegal.[36] This standard of manifest illegality clearly places a rather low burden on subordinates regarding knowledge of illegality. Thus, in many situations where orders are not clearly illegal and the defendants lack such knowledge, following orders will be a defense.[37] Various courts and domestic military codes have nonetheless adopted different positions on the standard for a patently illegal order and the corresponding duties of subordinates to ascertain the legality of orders.[38]

[34] IMT Charter, art. 8; CCL No. 10, art. II(4)(b); U.S. DEP'T OF THE ARMY, *supra* note 26, § 509; ICTY Statute, art. 7(4); ICC Statute, art. 33; Torture Convention, art. 2(3), 1465 UNTS at 114.

[35] *See* Trial of Kapitänleutnant Heinz Eck and Four Others (Peleus Trial), 1 War Crimes Reports 1, 12 (British Mil. Ct. Hamburg 1945) (quoting Judge Advocate) ('It is quite obvious that no sailor and no soldier can carry with him a library of international law or have immediate access to a professor . . . who can tell him whether or not a particular command is a lawful one.'). For a careful analysis, *see* YORAM DINSTEIN, THE DEFENSE OF 'OBEDIENCE TO SUPERIOR ORDERS' IN INTERNATIONAL LAW 26–37, 49–57, 76–90 (1965). For a discussion of the relevance of a defense based on mistake of fact, *see id.* at 83–87.

[36] *See, e.g.*, ICC Statute, art. 33(1); Regina v. Finta, [1994] 1 S.C.R. 701, 834. *Cf.* Prosecutor v. Drazen Erdemovic, Sentencing Judgment, ICTY Trial Chamber I, Nov. 29, 1996, para. 18 (duty to disobey manifestly illegal order). Needless to say, those issuing such orders and others in a position to know the illegality of them cannot take advantage of such a defense.

[37] For a broad critique of this notion, *see* MARK J. OSIEL, OBEYING ORDERS: ATROCITY, MILITARY DISCIPLINE, AND THE LAW OF WAR (1999).

[38] *See, e.g.*, U.S. DEP'T OF THE ARMY, *supra* note 26, § 509 (no defense 'unless he did not know and could not reasonably have been expected to know that the act ordered was unlawful'); U.S. v. Griffen, 39 Court Martial Reports 586, 590 (Army Board of Review 1967) (no defense 'when the order is such that a man of ordinary sense and understanding would know it to be illegal'); Chief

With respect to human rights atrocities for which criminal culpability has attached, a great many are so patently atrocious that such ignorance is never an excuse.[39] For some offenses that do not entail a flagrant assault on the human person (most obviously property offenses, but perhaps deportation and other crimes), superior orders might represent a valid defense for some personnel. Moreover, minors might not be able to know of the illegality of some orders under prior national or international law. Beyond this, superior orders are also considered a factor in mitigating punishment and probably also have had a tacit effect on the threshold decision of whether to prosecute.[40]

Although the sharp limitation of the defense of superior orders has arisen predominantly in the context of a military chain of command,[41] this rule is not confined to traditional military hierarchies, or even military relationships at all. Both the IMT Charter as well as more recent elaborations speak of orders 'of a Government or of a superior'.[42] In significant cases after World War II, courts rejected the pleas of civilian defendants that they were merely following the orders of higher administrative authorities.[43] If such pleas have been rejected in the military and civilian context, it would suggest that they are to be dismissed in the case of paramilitary units. Indeed, the absence of a strict chain of military command would further weaken a defendant's claim, as his duty to follow orders generally would be weaker. Furthermore, although in the prior cases the orders emanated from a person in a position of governmental authority, the narrow scope of the following orders defense would not change in the event of orders issued by a non-governmental authority. Because the

Military Prosecutor v. Melinki, *cited in Eichmann*, 36 ILR at 256 ('The distinguishing mark of a "manifestly unlawful order" should fly like a black flag above the order given, as a warning saying "Prohibited!".'); Regina v. Finta, [1994] 1 S.C.R. 701, 834 (order must 'patently and obviously be wrong'). For commentary, *see* DINSTEIN, *supra* note 35, at 121–214; L.C. GREEN, *Superior Orders and the Reasonable Man*, *in* ESSAYS ON THE MODERN LAW OF WAR 43 (1985); Röling, *supra* note 20, at 220–27; HENRI MEYEROWITZ, LA RÉPRESSION PAR LES TRIBUNAUX ALLEMANDS DES CRIMES CONTRE L'HUMANITÉ ET DE L'APPARTENANCE À UNE ORGANISATION CRIMINELLE 408–11 (1960); Irwin Cotler, *International Decisions: Regina v. Finta*, 90 AJIL 460, 473–74 (1996).

39 *See* ICC Statute, art. 33(2) (orders to commit genocide or crimes against humanity *per se* manifestly unlawful).

40 *See, e.g.*, ICTY Statute, art. 7(4); ICTR Statute, art. 6(4); 1996 ILC Report, at 31–34 (art. 5); *see also* Fourth Report of the Special Rapporteur, *supra* note 6, at 77–79; DINSTEIN, *supra* note 35, at 187–88, 205–06.

41 *See, e.g.*, United States v. Ohlendorf et al. (the '*Einsatzgruppen Case*'), 4 CCL No. 10 Trials 411, 470 ('The obedience of a soldier is not the obedience of an automaton.').

42 IMT Charter, art. 8; ICTY Statute, art. 7(4); ICC Statute, art. 33(1).

43 *See* United States v. Krauch et al. (the '*I. G. Farben Case*'), 8 CCL No. 10 Trials 1081, 1137–38; Trial of Alfons Klein and Six Others (Hadamar Trial), 1 War Crimes Reports 46, 54 (US Mil. Comm'n Wiesbaden 1945); *Zyklon B Case*, 1 War Crimes Reports 93, 103 (Brit. Mil. Ct. Hamburg 1946); *cf.* United States v. Flick et al., 6 CCL No. 10 Trials 1187, 1192 ('Acts adjudged criminal when done by an officer of the government are criminal also when done by a private individual.').

theory behind limiting the defense is that *nobody* is authorized to give patently illegal orders,[44] it should not matter whether the orders followed are those of the government or those of a non-governmental movement.

Duress

Even for patently illegal orders, international criminal law, beginning with the Nuremberg Tribunal, has recognized a defense if the accused lacked a 'moral choice' in committing the act.[45] This idea corresponds to defenses under domestic law based upon coercion or other compulsion, although different legal systems adopt varying terminology. The archetypal defense of duress will be accepted only if the defendant can show (1) an immediate threat to his life or physical well-being (or perhaps that of another) if he fails to carry out the crime; (2) no adequate way to avert the threatened evil; (3) that the crime committed was not disproportionate to the threatened evil; and (4) that he did not voluntarily bring about the situation.[46] The ICC Statute includes this defense; and, although it is not specifically mentioned in the ICTY and ICTR Statutes or the 1996 ILC Draft Code, both the Yugoslavia Tribunal and the ILC have recognized it.[47]

One morally and legally difficult aspect of the defense of duress concerns its applicability to large-scale atrocities, such as mass killings of innocent civilians as part of crimes against humanity or genocide. If a defendant is ordered to kill a group of civilians and told that, if he refuses, he will himself be killed, may he assert a defense of duress? Does it matter whether the civilians would clearly be killed by someone else if he were to refuse the order, thus making the sacrifice of his own life serve no purpose? This compelling issue was at the center of the Yugoslavia Tribunal's decision in the *Erdemovic* case, where a Bosnian Serb admitted to participating in the killing of Muslim men and boys at Srebrenica in 1995, but claimed that if he had refused, his fellow Serbs would have killed him along with the Muslim civilians. A three-to-two divided court

[44] *Cf.* 22 IMT Trials at 466 ('He who violates the laws of war cannot obtain immunity while acting in pursuance of the authority of the state if the state in authorizing action moves outside its competence under international law.').

[45] 22 IMT Trials at 466; 1950 ILC Report, *supra* note 5, at 375 (principle IV); *see also Finta*, [1994] 1 S.C.R. at 836–38; Jeanne L. Bakker, *The Defense of Obedience to Superior Orders: The Mens Rea Requirement*, 17 Am. J. Crim. L. 55, 69–75 (1989); Dinstein, *supra* note 35, at 51–57, 76–83.

[46] *Einsatzgruppen Case*, 4 CCL No. 10 Trials at 480–81; United States v. Krupp et al., 9 CCL No. 10 Trials 1327, 1436; 15 War Crimes Reports 170–75 (1949); *Erdemovic Sentencing Appeal*, dissenting op. Cassesse, paras. 20–39 (discussing other World War II cases); Fourth Report of the Special Rapporteur, *supra* note 6, at 75; M. Cherif Bassiouni, Crimes Against Humanity in International Criminal Law 484–91 (2d ed. 1999).

[47] ICC Statute, art. 31(1)(d); *Erdemovic Sentencing Appeal*, paras. 35–36; 1996 ILC Report, at 76–77.

found that duress could not afford a complete defense to the killing of innocent people. Finding no customary international law rule or general principle of law on the issue, the majority adopted an explicitly teleological approach, seeking a rule that would best protect the innocent in times of war.[48] In its view, any duress the defendant experienced should be addressed at the sentencing phase.

At the same time, the powerfully argued dissents found that, in fact, international caselaw and general principles of law had already accepted duress, properly construed, as a defense without exceptions. The dissents held that the proportionality requirement would ensure that the defense was quite limited in its impact, but that, under some circumstances involving the killing of the innocent, duress would and should be a defense. In Erdemovic's case, since the crime committed (the killing of innocent civilians) was not disproportionate to the threatened evil (the death of the innocent civilians as well as of the defendant), he was entitled to assert the defense, not merely receive a reduced sentence.[49]

Necessity, *Force Majeure*, and other Defenses

Claims of state of necessity and *force majeure* arise where the defendant finds himself in circumstances not of his own creation and has to choose between a legal duty not to commit the crime and the need to avoid an imminent harm. It differs from duress or coercion in that the threat to the individual comes not from another person but from the exigencies of a situation. (The classic cases concern lifeboats where the accused killed some passengers to save others.) This defense is also acceptable, provided the value protected is proportional to that lost and the defendant had no other choice.[50] The ICC Statute recognizes this defense to a degree in extending the availability of the duress defense to 'other circumstances beyond [the defendant's] control'.[51] At the same time, while no doubt some scenarios for accepting this defense exist, one may suspect that relatively few of those committing the most serious assaults on the person face these types of pressure; or that the abuses could be

[48] *Erdemovic Sentencing Appeal*, paras. 75–78. The majority found that caselaw had not specifically addressed the issue of the killing of the innocent; and that domestic legal systems were divided, with most civil law systems allowing it as a defense for all crimes and most common law systems rejecting it as a defense to murder.

[49] *Id.*, dissenting op. Cassese, paras. 20–46, and dissenting op. Stephen. On remand, Erdemovic was sentenced to five years in prison, including time served since 1996, due to his remorse and cooperation with the Tribunal.

[50] Bassiouni, *supra* note 46, at 489. An acceptable defense also requires that the defendant did not contribute to the peril. Fourth Report of the Special Rapporteur, *supra* note 6, at 75. It has long been rejected that military necessity alone can justify violations of the laws of war. *Hostages Case*, 11 CCL No. 10 Trials at 1255–56.

[51] ICC Statute, art. 31(d)(ii).

justified according to some balancing test. Rather, history reveals more situations where those who commit such offenses face little or no harm for failure to do so (or at best one that involves a professional setback rather than an overwhelming personal interest), and where no values are protected through the assaults on the victim.[52]

Finally, other defenses have a basis in many domestic systems of criminal law. The ICC Statute listed five for purposes of its jurisdiction, although the formulas chosen often represented a compromise among different systems. First, a defendant can assert a defense of mental disease or defect if it destroys his capacity to distinguish right from wrong or to control his conduct. Second, a defendant can assert intoxication if it destroys these two capacities, but not if he became voluntarily intoxicated and knew or disregarded the risk that he would then commit the crime. Third, a defendant can, under limited circumstances, assert self-defense or defense of property, namely if he responds in a manner proportionate to the danger, which itself involves imminent and unlawful use of force. Fourth, a defendant may assert a mistake of fact if (and only if) it negates *mens rea*. And fifth, a defendant may assert a mistake of law if (and only if) it negates *mens rea*, as for instance, in asserting that he believed an illegal (but not patently illegal) order to be legal. Nonetheless, the questions of voluntary intoxication and defense of property proved controversial at Rome and cannot be considered settled.[53]

Act of State, Sovereign Immunity, and Obedience to National Law

Those suspected or accused of committing human rights atrocities might also claim that their position of authority provides a defense. This position, however, has long been rejected. The IMT Charter and Control Council Law No. 10 explicitly provided that an individual's official position, even as a head of state, could not constitute a defense or mitigate punishment.[54] The ILC's formulation of the Nuremberg principles, the 1954 and 1996 Draft Codes, and the ICTY, ICTR, and ICC Statutes also reject such immunity.[55] The Genocide Convention generally conforms to

[52] *See generally* MEYEROWITZ, *supra* note 38, at 401–08; BASSIOUNI, *supra* note 46, at 490; *see also* Matthew Lippman, *War Crimes Trials of German Industrialists: The 'Other Schindlers'*, 9 TEMPLE INT'L AND COMP. L.J. 173, 256–58 (1995).

[53] ICC Statute, arts. 31(a), (b), (c), 32; *see also* 1996 ILC Report, at 75–76, 79–80; Saland, *supra* note 28, at 207–08, 210; Albin Eser, *'Defences' in War Crime Trials*, *in* WAR CRIMES IN INTERNATIONAL LAW 251, 263, 267–68 (Yoram Dinstein and Mala Tabory eds., 1996).

[54] IMT Charter, art. 7; CCL No. 10, art. II(4)(a); *cf.* Charter of the International Military Tribunal for the Far East, Jan. 19, 1946, *amended* Apr. 26, 1946, art. 6, 4 Bevans 20, 28 (not a defense but could be used to mitigate punishment if justice requires).

[55] 1950 ILC Report, *supra* note 5, at 375 (principle III); 1954 ILC Report, at 152 (art. 3); 1996 ILC Report, at 39–42 (art. 7); ICTY Statute, art. 7(2); ICTR Statute, art. 6(2); ICC Statute, art. 27.

the Nuremberg precedents, providing in Article IV that persons committing genocide shall be punished 'whether they are constitutionally responsible rulers, public officials, or private individuals'.[56] National tribunals have affirmed this principle as well.[57]

Beyond the irrelevance to guilt of the accused's official position, defendants might claim that their position deprives a national court of jurisdiction over them based on notions of sovereign or state or head-of-state immunity—the immunity of governments and their officials from judicial proceedings in other states for their official acts. Although only a relatively small number of states have prosecuted foreign governmental officials, the caselaw has not recognized such jurisdictional immunity. This trend began with the *Eichmann* case and has extended through prosecutions of Bosnian war criminals in Europe in the 1990s.[58] In its 1999 Pinochet decision, the House of Lords found that the Torture Convention's criminalization of torture by official actors, including through universal jurisdiction, would be undermined by recognition of head-of-state immunity for torturers.[59] Courts in the United States have determined in civil suits against former foreign governmental officials that the defendant's once-official status does not give him immunity from US jurisdiction when the suit involves gross violations of human rights; this position is based on the theory that such abuses can never be part of his official activities.[60] Indeed, the decision by states to recognize universal jurisdiction over a particular international crime, by virtue of either a treaty or custom permitting or requiring all states to prosecute, inherently means that state officials do not enjoy immunity.

At the same time, to the extent that the key precedents (in the United States and United Kingdom) concern prosecution of former, rather than current, governmental officials, some states might argue that universal jurisdiction does not deprive current officials of immunities they enjoy under custom and treaty. Their concern has merit with regard to sitting heads of state or ambassadors, where the law seems to have recognized

[56] Genocide Convention, art. IV, 78 UNTS at 280; *see also* ROBINSON, *supra* note 4, at 70–71 (substitution of 'constitutionally responsible rulers' for 'heads of state' to ensure titular leaders not criminally responsible); Study of the Question of the Prevention and Punishment of the Crime of Genocide, prepared by Nicodème Ruhashyamiko, July 4, 1978, UN Doc. E/CN.4/Sub.2/416, at 34, 41.

[57] *Eichmann*, 36 ILR at 308–11.

[58] The Eichmann court did not explicitly address the issue, though it implicitly rejected any jurisdictional immunity, perhaps because Eichmann was the former official of a state that no longer existed. For other cases, *see* Ch. 8, Prosecutions Before National Courts of Other States, *infra*.

[59] [1999] 2 All E.R. 97, 111–15 (Lord Browne-Wilkinson). At the same time, the House of Lords limited its holding to torture (as no other international crimes were charged), and indeed accepted the availability of state immunity for charges of murder and conspiracy to murder.

[60] *See, e.g.*, In re: Estate of Ferdinand Marcos Human Rights Litigation, 25 F.3d 1467, 1470–72 (9th Cir. 1994).

full criminal immunity.[61] The court in *Pinochet* placed significant weight on the general's status as a former, rather than current, head of state, and the corresponding limitation of his immunity.[62] Given the long recognition and importance of head of state and diplomatic immunity in international law, it is hardly clear whether such a claim of immunity would or should fail in a domestic court. States are unlikely to endorse the arrest and domestic prosecution of ambassadors on mission or visiting heads of state, even for horrendous crimes; and, as a normative matter, while such moves would certainly get media attention, their costs to peaceful interstate relations and risk of abuse might well override any benefits to human rights protection. These concerns do not, however, arise in the case of an international court whose jurisdiction is already accepted by the parties to it or which is created under Chapter VII of the UN Charter.[63]

Lastly, such officials—or private actors committing crimes—cannot successfully plead in defense that they were acting in accordance with, or carrying out obligations inscribed in, national law. (This argument is to be distinguished from the following orders defense insofar as it is based on the assumed sanctity of domestic law alone, not any order from a superior.) The Nuremberg Tribunals definitively rejected this argument with respect to claims that Nazi law and practice commanded, condoned, or permitted various abuses.[64] And the Federal Republic of Germany has prosecuted both Nazis and East German border guards despite claims by defendants that those regimes imposed their own legality that trumped other law.[65] Without the supremacy of international law over domestic law, the entire framework of international human rights law would collapse.

[61] *See, e.g.*, Vienna Convention on Diplomatic Relations, Apr. 18, 1961, arts. 29, 31, 500 UNTS 95, 110, 112 (immunity for diplomats); Arthur Watts, *The Legal Position in International Law of Heads of States, Heads of Governments and Foreign Ministers*, 247 RECUEIL DES COURS 9, 54 (1994-III) (though noting, *id.* at 84, that head of state can be 'called to account' for war crimes).

[62] [1999] 2 All E.R. at 111–13; *see also* Jürgen Bröhmer, *Diplomatic Immunity, Head of State Immunity, State Immunity: Misconceptions of a Notorious Human Rights Violator*, 12 LEIDEN J. INT'L L. 361 (1999); Andrea Bianchi, *Immunity versus Human Rights: The* Pinochet *Case*, 10 EJIL 237, 254–62 (1999); *cf.* Watts, *supra* note 61, at 88–96.

[63] *See* ICC Statute, art. 27(2) (immunities attaching to official capacity of person under national or international law do not bar Court from exercising jurisdiction). *See generally* Günther Handl, *The Pinochet Case, Foreign State Immunity and the Changing Constitution of the International Community*, *in* DEVELOPMENT AND DEVELOPING INTERNATIONAL AND EUROPEAN LAW: ESSAYS IN HONOUR OF KONRAD GINTHER ON THE OCCASION OF HIS 65TH BIRTHDAY 59 (W. Benedek ed., 1999).

[64] 22 IMT Trials at 465–66; *Justice Case*, 3 CCL No. 10 Trials at 983–84; *see also Eichmann*, 36 ILR at 47–48; Dinstein, *supra* note 33, at 239, 240.

[65] *See* Border Guards Prosecution Case, 100 ILR 366, 379–86 (Ger. 1992) (relying on international law to strike down defenses under East German law); Kif Augustine Adams, *What is Just?: The Rule of Law and Natural Law in the Trials of Former East German Border Guards*, 29 STAN. J. INT'L L. 271, 295–306 (1993) (use of natural law to find earlier rules incompatible with rule of law).

STATUTES OF LIMITATIONS

The notion of a chronologically fixed endpoint to the possibility of prosecution is common to the world's legal systems, but special issues arise regarding gross offenses against the person. At the level of international law, the 1968 Convention on the Non-Applicability of Statutory Limitations to War Crimes and Crimes Against Humanity prohibits states from imposing statutory limitations for war crimes and crimes against humanity.[66] However, as discussed in Chapters 3 and 4, the definitions of these two terms adopted in the Convention were controversial, and it had only forty-four parties as of late 2000.[67] The domestic laws of many states provide for no statutes of limitations for such crimes, although the drafting history of the UN Convention shows many states do maintain such statutes.[68] In the *Barbie* case, the French Cour de Cassation found the non-applicability of statutory limitations to crimes against humanity to be a part of customary international law.[69] And the Italian Military Court of Rome, in its 1997 conviction of former SS captain Erich Priebke for the murder of 335 people at the Ardeatine caves in 1943, concluded that the non-applicability of statutory limitations for war crimes was part of *jus cogens*.[70] Several commentators have adopted similar positions regarding war crimes and crimes against humanity, including genocide.[71]

However, in light of the UN Convention's limited acceptance and the extensive range of domestic legal approaches on the issue, it is difficult to conclude that *mandatory* non-applicability of statutes of limitations has yet entered the realm of custom.[72] The willingness of many states to eliminate such prescription and the negotiation of the 1968 Convention do, however, support the view that international law at least *permits* states to

[66] The IMT Charter is silent on the issue; Control Council Law No. 10 provides, in poorly drafted language, for either elimination or suspension of the statute of limitations for crimes committed during the Nazi era. CCL No. 10, art. II(5).

[67] MULTILATERAL TREATIES, ch. IV.6.

[68] *See* Robert H. Miller, *The Convention on the Non-applicability of Statutory Limitations to War Crimes and Crimes Against Humanity*, 65 AJIL 476, 478–79, 484 and n. 50 (1971); *see also* 1977 DIGEST US PRAC. IN INT'L L. 927 (1979) (no US statutes of limitations for crimes covered by IMT Charter).

[69] Fédération Nationale des Déportés et Internés Résistants et Patriotes and Others v. Barbie, 78 ILR 125, 135 (Fr. Cour de Cassation 1984).

[70] *See* Sergio Marchisio, *The* Priebke *Case Before the Italian Military Tribunals: A Reaffirmation of the Principle of Non-Applicability of Statutory Limitations to War Crimes and Crimes Against Humanity*, 1 Y.B. INT'L HUMAN. L. 344 (1998).

[71] *See, e.g.*, Hurst Hannum, *International Law and Cambodian Genocide: The Sounds of Silence*, 11 HUM. RTS. Q. 82, 101–02 (1989); Remigiusz Bierzanek, *War Crimes: History and Definition*, *in* 3 INTERNATIONAL CRIMINAL LAW 87, 104 (M. Cherif Bassiouni ed., 2d ed. 1999).

[72] *See* Christine Van Den Wijngaert, *War Crimes, Genocide and Crimes Against Humanity – Are States Taking National Prosecutions Seriously?*, *in* 3 INTERNATIONAL CRIMINAL LAW, *supra* note 71, at 227, 233.

eliminate statutes of limitations for crimes against humanity and war crimes. And states took this step with respect to cases before the International Criminal Court as well.[73]

Because many states have not legislated the non-application of statutory limitations for these crimes, it is possible to imagine situations where the slow pace of investigations or other circumstances will result in the actual or predicted expiry of the statutory limitations period before prosecutions begin. Those concerned with accountability might be able to overcome this obstacle through at least two strategies. First, the legislature might pass new legislation lengthening or eliminating the statute of limitations. This strategy has ample precedents in the actions by Western European states, in particular the Federal Republic of Germany, in the 1960s, when the normal statutory period began to expire for crimes committed by Nazis.[74] The elimination of statutes of limitation, even retroactively, would appear permissible (though not required) under the 1968 Convention, the 1974 Council of Europe Convention on the same subject, and customary law.[75]

As a matter of domestic law, states have adopted different positions on whether the extension or elimination of statutes of limitations for crimes committed in the past (including those for which the statute had already expired) violates domestic law principles of non-retroactivity. The French Cour de Cassation held in *Barbie* that France's 1964 law eliminating the statute of limitations for crimes against humanity could apply retroactively to permit prosecution of Barbie, even though the statute of limitations for murder had expired before the enactment of the 1964 law.[76] The Hungarian Constitutional Court upheld a similar law in 1993 primarily based on Hungary's status as a party to the 1968 Treaty.[77]

Secondly, a court or the legislature could determine that the application of the normal statute of limitations has been suspended during the period in which accountability was impossible. Under this theory, the statute would not begin to run until an independent and effective prosecutor's

[73] *See* ICC Statute, art. 29.

[74] *See* Miller, *supra* note 68, at 478–79 and n. 11; Robert A. Monson, *The West German Statute of Limitations on Murder: A Political, Legal, and Historical Exposition*, 30 AM. J. COMP. L. 605, 609–10 (1982).

[75] Statutory Limitations Convention, art. IV, 754 UNTS at 76; European Convention on the Non-Applicability of Statutory Limitations to War Crimes and Crimes Against Humanity, Jan. 25, 1974, art. 1, Europ. T.S. No. 82, at 2, *reprinted in* 13 ILM 540 (1974); *see also* Miller, *supra* note 68, at 495–97.

[76] 78 ILR at 134–35; *see* Leila Sadat Wexler, *The Interpretation of the Nuremberg Principles by the French Court of Cassation: From Touvier to Barbie and Back Again*, 32 COLUM. J. TRANSNAT'L L. 289, 335–37 (1994); *but see* Miller, *supra* note 68, at 488 and nn.67–68, 495–97 (opposition to retroactive elimination of statutes of limitation).

[77] Constitutional Court Docket No. 288/A/1993, *translated in* HOW DOES LAW PROTECT IN WAR? 746 (Marco Sassòli and Antonio A. Bouvier eds., 1999).

office and court system are again established. One important precedent is French legislation that suspended the application of the statute of limitations on prosecutions due to the absence of an effective judiciary during World War II.[78] This could prove attractive in those many states where the human rights abuses took place in tandem with an assault on the judicial system generally or where the judicial system otherwise lacked the power to prosecute those responsible for abuses.[79]

THEORETICAL AND PRACTICAL CHALLENGES

The extension and limitation of culpability resulting from the above doctrines will prove a cardinal element in any prosecution of human rights offenders, for even if there is a consensus on the scope of the law, individual subjects of investigation or prosecution will assert that they were nonetheless not personally responsible for the crime. Yet the legal framework is far from perfect; three issues in particular merit further elaboration.

First, the scope of superior responsibility remains one of the most important issues in prosecuting human rights atrocities. The law emanating from the *Hostages* and *High Command* cases and their modern progeny has rejected strict liability for superiors by providing for guilt only if the leader knew or had reason to know of the abuses of subordinates. To a certain extent, the difference between the current negligence-type standard and strict liability may be small in practice, if prosecutors or other investigators successfully argue that very little information is in fact needed for a superior to have the ability to know of the existence of abuses. For instance, if the commander knew that many of the persons under his command were poorly trained and disciplined and likely to have scant regard for the dictates of human rights or humanitarian law, he could reasonably be held responsible for their abuses.

But in some cases, a superior may be truly unable to know of particular abuses, and yet it might not be unreasonable to impose strict criminal liability in order to advance the purposes of international human rights

[78] *See* GASTON STEFANI, GEORGES LEVASSEUR, AND BERNARD BOULOC, PROCÉDURE PÉNALE 180 (17th ed. 2000). In 1965, the Federal Republic of Germany suspended the statute of limitations from the end of World War II to the founding date of the FRG for the most serious crimes, presumably based upon the absence of any official FRG legal system during the Allied occupation. As noted in the text, it later eliminated the statute of limitations entirely. *See* Francillon, *supra* note 6, at 24.

[79] *See* GA Res. 47/133, para. 17(2), UN GAOR, 47th Sess., Supp. No. 49, at 207, 209, UN Doc. A/47/49 (permitting suspension when remedies not available); *see also* Naomi Roht-Arriaza, *Special Problems of a Duty to Prosecute: Derogation, Amnesties, Statutes of Limitation, and Superior Orders*, *in* IMPUNITY AND HUMAN RIGHTS IN INTERNATIONAL LAW AND PRACTICE 57, 64–65 (Naomi Roht-Arriaza ed., 1995).

and humanitarian law. That is, it may be reasonable in some instances to elevate the commander's normal responsibility in the chain of command for the acts of subordinates, by which their abuses might justify his demotion for failure to carry out his duties, to criminal responsibility, by which their abuses justify his criminal culpability as well. Protocol I already requires *states* to ensure that their military commanders prevent grave breaches by persons under their control, but does not suggest that a failure by the commanders to do so incurs more than state responsibility.[80]

Any move toward strict liability would need to be balanced against at least two important concerns. First is the potential unfairness of convicting a defendant of a serious moral crime without any *mens rea*. American courts, for instance, have recognized such liability for superiors only in the area of public welfare offenses, e.g., food safety, where conviction does not carry any deprivation of liberty—although they have not suggested that the legislature could not extend such culpability to other crimes.[81] Secondly, from the point of view of the effective functioning of a military or civilian hierarchy, strict liability would need to be limited to avoid suggesting that all superiors are always responsible for all abuses by subordinates. Because international criminal law is often enforced by the very entities that include potential defendants, broad new duties should not be imposed where they do not match expectations of acceptable standards of conduct and are likely to be ignored by all concerned.

One possibility for consideration is a spatial limitation, e.g., camps, prisons, police offices, or other confined areas under the command of a military or civilian superior, where such an affirmative duty might not prove too onerous on the superior.[82] Another way to limit strict liability might entail drawing lines at certain levels of command responsibility, such that, for example, a colonel in charge of a particular occupied area would have strict liability for acts committed there, though the general commanding the entire army would not; or a police commander heading a prison would have responsibility even if the minister of the interior did not. Nevertheless, it may be so difficult in practice to draw such lines as to justify retention of the traditional standard.

Secondly, as a practical matter, the extension of culpability under superior responsibility raises special questions in the context of organizations without rigid military hierarchies. Prosecutors will need to determine the chain of command in the absence of clear rank or even formal decision-making structures. Reliance will need to be placed on witness testimony and other indicia of the customary practices observed within a particular

80 Protocol I, art. 83, 1125 UNTS at 43.
81 *See, e.g.*, United States v. Park, 421 U.S. 658 (1975).
82 *Cf. Aleksovski Judgment*, para. 80.

group. The Yugoslavia and Rwanda Tribunals have already had to confront these evidentiary matters.[83]

A third unsettled issue remains the question of the scope of the duress defense and the consequences of its rejection for the killing of innocent civilians. The ICTY's *Erdemovic* decision clearly represents a major milestone in elaborating the extent of the duress defense. Nonetheless, the closely divided nature of the judgment suggests the case's impact on domestic or other international prosecutions may well be limited. Indeed, the majority's adoption of a teleological approach, especially in the face of caselaw to the contrary, raises serious issues of fairness to a criminal defendant.[84] In addition, the dissent raised a number of scenarios suggesting that, in true situations of duress, the defendant does not have the *mens rea* to be guilty. It does not seem that, in these particularly dire situations, one can regard a person as guilty and merely reduce his sentence.[85]

If, however, domestic and international courts continue to reject duress as a complete defense in these situations, they will nonetheless need to consider the relevance of the duress in sentencing.[86] At this stage, a court's considerations would become similar to those used in determining the effect on punishment of following orders, once that claim has been rejected as a complete defense because of the patent illegality of the orders issued. The key in both situations will be to determine the extent to which the duress or the superior orders in fact lessen the defendant's responsibility in some way so as to justify a reduced sentence.[87] The defendant thus has a less culpable mind, but not one, as it were, enough to justify a defense. In this case, *bona fide* duress should have a greater impact on the sentencing than following orders. The former is true coercion on the defendant; the latter merely pressure to conform. It would not seem unsurprising if, indeed, courts faced with sentencing defendants who had proved *bona fide* duress in killing innocent people in fact imposed only the lightest of sentences.[88]

[83] *See, e.g., Celebici Judgment*, paras. 608–721; *Kayishema and Ruzindana Judgment*, paras. 493–506.

[84] *See* Peter Rowe, *Duress as a Defence to War Crimes after* Erdemovic: *A Laboratory for a Permanent Court?*, 1 Y.B. INT'L HUMAN. L. 210, 225–28 (1998).

[85] *See Erdemovic Sentencing Appeal*, dissenting op. Cassese, paras. 47–48; *id.*, dissenting op. Stephen, paras. 55–58.

[86] *Erdemovic Sentencing Judgment II*, para. 17.

[87] *Erdemovic Sentencing Appeal*, paras. 85–87; 1996 ILC Report, at 33; *see also* DINSTEIN, *supra* note 35, at 156–57, 187–88, 205–06.

[88] *Cf. Erdemovic Sentencing Judgment II*, para. 23 (five-year sentence, with credit for two years served).

PART II

MECHANISMS FOR ACCOUNTABILITY

7

Mechanisms for Accountability: Framing the Issues

The criminal responsibility of individuals for certain gross violations of human rights and humanitarian law is now beyond dispute. But to hold individuals accountable for their abuses in a meaningful sense, rather than merely a theoretical one, requires the creation and engagement of specific mechanisms designed for this purpose. This Part turns to the most important of those fora—national judicial systems; international tribunals, *ad hoc* and permanent; and three principal non-prosecutorial processes, namely investigatory commissions, civil lawsuits, and immigration measures. The method here is to scrutinize the legal structures and practical workings of these processes, with the goal of discovering their promise and limitations under international law. The alternatives are not mutually exclusive, and it may be possible to pursue more than one successively or simultaneously. In light of the importance of evidentiary and international judicial assistance matters, a separate chapter is devoted to those subjects.[1]

The decisions since the early 1980s of societies emerging from periods of gross abuses of human rights to examine their past, as well as the creation by the United Nations of *ad hoc* international tribunals in the 1990s, has kindled a significant dialogue among participants in the international legal and political processes over the importance of accountability. Governments, international organizations, and non-governmental organizations and scholars debate both the duty upon individual states or the community of nations to achieve some form of accountability, and the desirability and practicality of accountability in particular circumstances.

LEGAL REQUIREMENTS OF INDIVIDUAL ACCOUNTABILITY

International law is central to this process insofar as treaties and custom clearly confer obligations and rights upon states to prosecute and punish

[1] The literature on the experiences of individual countries is now vast, and it would be impossible to recount even a small part of it in the legal analyses that follow. For a magisterial collection of materials on accountability mechanisms, *see* Transitional Justice (Neil J. Kritz ed., 1995), and especially the case studies in volumes 2 and 3.

certain acts that incur individual responsibility.[2] But those obligations and rights do not follow inevitably from the law's imputation of individual responsibility; and where they do arise, they may vary from crime to crime. Moreover, alongside these norms for the prosecution of specific offenses is the question of a generalized duty on states to respond in some fashion to abuses of human dignity, and the scope of any such duty in terms of various processes of accountability. Like many debates over emerging norms, this one stems from a vacuum in treaty law—namely the absence of any clear obligations in the key universal human rights accord, the International Covenant on Civil and Political Rights, that a state prosecute and punish all abusers of human rights. Rather, the Covenant contains only less precise obligations, such as those to 'respect and ensure to all individuals within its territory and subject to its jurisdiction the rights recognized [therein]', and to provide 'an effective remedy' for violations thereof, language echoed in the European and American Conventions on Human Rights.[3]

Certain trends in the international legal process suggest these somewhat vaguely worded provisions are evolving into obligations by states to take specific action against offenders. This duty would mean, for instance, that successor governments must prosecute those responsible for serious human rights violations under prior regimes, but the duty would also apply to governments that committed abuses and nonetheless remain in power. Among the most significant developments was a 1988 decision of the Inter-American Court of Human Rights, which interpreted the American Convention on Human Rights to require states to investigate seriously, identify, and punish offenders as well as compensate victims.[4] In addition, the UN Human Rights Committee and the Inter-American Commission on Human Rights have stated that some of the ICCPR's and American Convention's provisions require states to investigate and prosecute offenders and generally preclude the granting of blanket amnesties for violations of international human rights and humanitarian law.[5] And

[2] *See* Ch. 8, A Jurisdictional Primer, *infra*.

[3] ICCPR, arts. 2(2)–(3), 9(5), 14(6), 999 UNTS at 174, 176, 177; American Convention on Human Rights, Nov. 22, 1969, arts. 1(1), 10, 25, 1144 UNTS 123, 145, 148, 151; European Convention for the Protection of Human Rights and Fundamental Freedoms, Nov. 4, 1950, arts. 1, 5(5), 13, 213 UNTS 221, 228, 232.

[4] Velasquez Rodriguez Case, Inter-Am. Ct. Hum. Rts. (Ser. C), No. 4 (1988) (judgment), para. 174. For further elaboration by the Inter-American Commission on Human Rights, *see*, *e.g.*, Report No. 36/96 (Chile), Oct. 15, 1996, para. 111, 1996 ANN. REP. INTER-AM. COMM. ON HUMAN RIGHTS 156, 183 (1997) (calling on Chile to change 1978 self-amnesty law). *See also* McCann and others v. United Kingdom, Eur. Ct. Hum. Rts. (Ser. A), No. 324 (1995) (judgment), para. 161 ('effective official investigation' required after state agents kill individuals).

[5] *See*, *e.g.*, Human Rights Committee Comments on Nigeria, para. 284, *in* Report of the Human Rights Committee, Vol. I, UN GAOR, 51st Sess., Supp. No. 40, at 37, 41, UN Doc. A/51/40 (1996);

the United Nations has endorsed such a duty, through the final declaration of the 1993 World Conference on Human Rights, as well as resolutions of the Security Council, General Assembly, ECOSOC, and the Human Rights Commission calling on states (whether individual states involved in a conflict or states generally) to prosecute human rights abuses.[6] These views have garnered the support of many observers in the academic and non-governmental community.[7]

Nevertheless, the practice of states and international organizations suggests any general duty to prosecute human rights abusers under the ICCPR, the American Convention on Human Rights, or customary law has not yet solidified. Numerous states—including Argentina, Uruguay, Chile, Brazil, Peru, Guatemala, El Salvador, Honduras, Nicaragua, Haiti, Ivory Coast, Angola, and Togo—have passed broad amnesty laws governing past abuses or honored amnesties of prior governments.[8] Others have simply

Human Rights Committee Comments on Argentina, paras. 153, 158, *in* Report of the Human Rights Committee, UN GAOR, 50th Sess., Supp. No. 40, at 31, 32, UN Doc. A/50/40 (1995); Inter-Am Comm'n on Hum. Rts. Report No. 133/99 (Chile), Nov. 15, 1999, paras. 63–107. *See also* Steven R. Ratner, *New Democracies, Old Atrocities: An Inquiry in International Law*, 87 GEO. L. J. 707, 720–21 (1999); Naomi Roht-Arriaza, *Sources in International Treaties of an Obligation to Investigate, Prosecute, and Provide Redress*, *in* IMPUNITY AND HUMAN RIGHTS IN INTERNATIONAL LAW AND PRACTICE 24, 29–30 (Naomi Roht-Arriaza ed., 1995).

[6] *See* Vienna Declaration and Programme of Action, 25 June 1993, para. 60, *in* World Conference on Human Rights: The Vienna Declaration and Programme of Action June 1993, at 61, UN Sales No. DPI/1394-39399-August 1993-20M; SC Res. 1265, Sept. 17, 1999, para. 6 (responsibility of states to 'prosecute those responsible for genocide, crimes against humanity, and other serious violations of international humanitarian law'); GA Res. 54/179, Feb. 24, 2000, para. 4(e) (calling on Democratic Republic of the Congo 'to ensure that those responsible for human rights violations are brought to justice'); ESC Res. 1989/65, Annex, para. 18, UN ESCOR, 1st Sess., Supp. No. 1, at 52–53, UN Doc. E/1989/89 (1989) (containing Principles on the Effective Prevention and Investigation of Extra-legal, Arbitrary and Summary Executions); Comm'n Hum. Rts. Res. 2000/20, Apr. 18, 2000, para. 13 (requesting Burundi to 'bring to trial those responsible for violations of human rights and of international humanitiarian law').

[7] *See, e.g.*, Question of the impunity of perpetrators of human rights violations (civil and political): Revised final report prepared by Mr. Joinet pursuant to subcommission decision 1996/119, Oct. 2, 1997, UN Doc. E/CN.4/Sub. 2/1997/20/Rev. 1, paras. 16–30 (advocating 'right to know' and 'right to justice'); HUMAN RIGHTS WATCH, SPECIAL ISSUE: ACCOUNTABILITY FOR PAST HUMAN RIGHTS ABUSES, no. 4 (1989); Diane F. Orentlicher, *Settling Accounts: The Duty to Prosecute Human Rights Violations of a Prior Regime*, 100 YALE L.J. 2537, 2551–613 (1991); Juan E. Méndez, *Accountability for Past Abuses*, 19 HUM. RTS. Q. 255 (1997).

[8] *See, e.g.*, Decreto Ley No. 2.191, Apr. 18, 1978 (Chile); Lei No. 6.683, Aug. 28, 1979, art. 1 (Brazil); Law. No. 15,848, Dec. 22, 1986 (Uruguay), *reprinted in* 3 TRANSITIONAL JUSTICE, *supra* note 1, at 598; Law No. 23.492, Dec. 23, 1986 (Argentina), *reprinted in* 3 TRANSITIONAL JUSTICE, *supra* note 1, at 505; Law No. 81 on General Amnesty and National Reconciliation, May 9, 1990 (Nicaragua), *reprinted in* 3 TRANSITIONAL JUSTICE, *supra* note 1, at 591; Decreto Numero 87–91, July 23, 1991 (Honduras); *Ivory Coast Parliament Passes Amnesty Law* REUTERS LIBRARY REP., July 29, 1992 (available on LEXIS/NEXIS); Decree No. 486, March 20, 1993 (El Salvador), *reprinted in* 3 TRANSITIONAL JUSTICE, *supra* note 1, at 546; Loi Relative à L'Amnistie, published in Le Moniteur, Journal Officiel de la Republique d'Haiti, Oct. 10, 1994 (Haiti), *reprinted and translated in* Michael P. Scharf, *Swapping Amnesties for Peace: Was There A Duty to Prosecute International Crimes in Haiti?*, 31 TEX. INT'L L.J. 1, 15–16 (1996); Tchidah Banawe, *Togo-Politics: Trying to Heal the*

chosen not to prosecute. With the exception of the human rights monitoring bodies noted above, governments and international organizations have generally tolerated this practice, especially if the state is otherwise making a transition to civil peace or democratic rule and an improved human rights record. Governmental statements do not suggest any strong *opinio juris* either.[9] Yet, in a positive development for an emerging norm requiring prosecutions, some of these amnesties have exempted international crimes or have been narrowed by courts to allow prosecutors to try serious offenses.[10]

Even if a duty to prosecute offenders is not backed by substantial practice or *opinio juris*, a broader duty upon states to undertake some process of individual accountability seems to have more support. Societies seem to be increasingly accepting that they should not completely bury the crimes of the past but should reveal the truth about the role of organizations and of individuals (even if not the names of all the perpetrators), and that at least some of those who committed such crimes should face some form of sanction.[11] This has been evidenced through the decision of many governments—especially in South America, Eastern Europe, and South

Wounds, INTER PRESS SERVICE, Mar. 2, 1995 (available on LEXIS/NEXIS); Ley No. 26479, June 14, 1995, www.congreso.gob.pe/ccd/leyes/cronos/1995/ley26479.htm (Peru); Promotion of National Unity and National Reconciliation Act, Law No. 34 of 1995 (S. Afr.) [hereinafter South Africa Amnesty Law]; *Angola: National Assembly Approves Amnesty Law*, BBC SUMMARY OF WORLD BROADCASTS (Televisao Popular de Angola), May 9, 1996 (available on LEXIS/NEXIS); Ley de Reconciliación Nacional, Decreto No. 145–96, Dec. 18, 1996 [hereinafter Guatemala Amnesty Law]. The Argentine law was repealed in March 1998, *see* Ley No. 24.952, Apr. 15, 1998, though the repeal is not expected to have retroactive effect. *See* Marcela Valente, *Rights-Argentina: Dissatisfaction with Repeal of Amnesty Laws*, INTER PRESS SERVICE, Mar. 25, 1998 (available on LEXIS/NEXIS); *see also infra* note 10 (exceptions from amnesty laws); Kai Ambos, *Impunity and International Criminal Law: A Case Study on Colombia, Peru, Bolivia, Chile, and Argentina*, 18 HUM. RTS. L.J. 1 (1997); US Department of State, *State Practice Regarding Amnesties and Pardons*, available at gopher://gopher.igc.apc.org:70/00/orgs/icc/natldocs/prepcom4/amnesty.us.

[9] *See* Ratner, *supra* note 5, at 722–29. The tensions facing the UN became apparent in 1999, when a UN envoy agreed to witness a peace treaty in Sierra Leone that provided a blanket amnesty to both sides, though with a statement that the UN would not recognize an amnesty for gross human rights abuses. *See* Seventh Report of the Secretary-General on the United Nations Observer Mission in Sierra Leone, July 30, 1999, UN Doc. S/1999/836, paras. 7, 54. *Compare* Human Rights Watch, *UN Role in Sierra Leone Peace Deal Condemned*, July 8, 1999, available at www.hrw.org/press/1999/new-jul.htm *with* Kofi Annan, *Window of African Promise Amid Great Suffering*, INT'L HERALD TRIB., July 31, 1999, at 8 ('the United Nations cannot stand between Sierra Leone's people and their only hope of ending such a long and brutal conflict.').

[10] *See, e.g.*, Guatemala Amnesty Law, *supra* note 8, art. 8; South Africa Amnesty Law, *supra* note 8, § 20 (limited to official acts as determined by Commission); on judicial attempts to limit scope of amnesties, *see* Naomi Roht-Arriaza and Lauren Gibson, *The Developing Jurisprudence on Amnesty*, 20 HUM. RTS. Q. 843 (1998); HUMAN RIGHTS WATCH, CHILE: WHEN TYRANTS TREMBLE: THE PINOCHET CASE (Oct. 1999), § IV.

[11] *See* the comments of Thomas Nagel *in* LAWRENCE WECHSLER, A MIRACLE, A UNIVERSE: SETTLING ACCOUNTS WITH TORTURERS 4 (1990) (need for knowledge and acknowledgment). For views that truth commissions rest upon a right of individuals to know the truth, *see, e.g.*, Jo M. Pasqualucci, *The Whole Truth and Nothing But the Truth: Truth Commissions, Impunity, and the Inter-American Human Rights System*, 12 B.U. INT'L L.J. 321, 323, 330 (1994).

Africa—to conduct some form of inquiry through an investigatory commission, to disqualify certain persons from public office, and administratively to sanction atrocious conduct. State practice is emerging prior to any *opinio juris*, but the normative factors seem clearly at play.[12]

THE BROADER CONTEXT

Although arguments based on legal duties in treaties or custom should and do influence decision-makers, they hardly determine the policies of states and international organizations regarding accountability, criminal or otherwise. Ultimately, their responses to various atrocities will rely principally on independent moral, social, and political considerations. As an initial matter, international actors contemplating holding individuals accountable must explicitly consider the *purpose* behind such a policy. Ideally, accountability following serious violations of international human rights and humanitarian law may serve a number of goals. First, the pursuit of accountability can be highly significant to the victims of atrocities—and their relatives and friends—by giving them a sense of justice and closure. Such closure is neither guaranteed nor complete, but the holding accountable of the perpetrator clearly has significance for victims. Secondly, and relatedly, accountability can, especially in the case of transitional regimes, form a critical element for repairing the damage done to a society traumatized by massive human rights violations and promoting national reconciliation. Such a process may hinge on findings of individual guilt, creation of a historical record, or initiation of a public dialogue over the events of the past and the path to the future.

Thirdly, accountability may deter future violations either by demonstrating to those contemplating such offenses the prospect of punishment or more generally by promoting justice, institutional reform in government, and the rule of law. The empirical evidence on this matter is, however, hardly encouraging.[13] Fourthly, the rehabilitation of the offender is a stated goal of many societies, though it is invoked less prominently than other theories of accountability. Fifthly, beyond these consequentialist arguments, a retributive theory of justice would regard accountability as just punishment for those who do wrong. And finally, accountability may also serve as a righteous expression of moral condemnation of heinous offenses.[14]

12 Ratner, *supra* note 5, at 730–31.

13 *See* David Wippman, *Atrocities, Deterrence, and the Limits of International Justice*, 23 FORDHAM INT'L L.J. 473 (1999); Aryeh Neier, *What Should be Done About the Guilty?*, N.Y. REV. OF BOOKS, Feb. 1, 1990, at 32, 35.

14 For an overview of theories of punishment in the context of human rights abuses, *see* Jaime Malamud-Goti, *Transitional Governments in the Breach: Why Punish State Criminals?*, 12 HUM. RTS. Q. 1, 6–11 (1990); W. Michael Reisman, *Institutions and Practices for Restoring and Maintaining Public Order*, 6 DUKE J. COMP. AND INT'L L. 175 (1995); *see also* the various articles compiled in 1 TRANSITIONAL JUSTICE, *supra* note 1, at 155–221.

These ideals, of course, intersect quickly with the reality of societies facing atrocities. Indeed, the nub of contemporary controversies over accountability concerns two questions about these idealized purposes. First, to what extent should a given society seek to advance one or more of them (or others)? Second, do varying forms of accountability actually promote one or more of these goals (or promote some at the expense of others)? These issues are now the subject of much contemporary political, legal, and philosophical commentary.[15] Thus, for example, in the case of transitional societies, these compelling arguments in favor of accountability must be reconciled with the tensions that some forms of accountability may engender. Attempts to pierce the veil of impunity enjoyed by those associated with a previous regime might in some instances threaten the functioning of the new political system. The larger and more powerful the segment of the population responsible for such abuses, the greater the potential link between any process of accountability and political or social upheaval.[16] Apart from questions of instability, new regimes may seek to use accountability as a weapon to settle old scores and stigmatize large classes of the population, in the process paying scant regard for the rights of the accused.

In answering these two basic questions, decision-makers will be faced with a number of significant choices. We note three here, for they form a thread that links the various forms of accountability we discuss in the ensuing chapters. Each of these questions is a concentric circle within the previous one—and all must be examined within the context of the two questions above.

First, and most basically, governments and non-governmental actors will need to assess the advantages and disadvantages of criminal vs. non-criminal forms of accountability. In this context, various parties will claim, for example, that trials will lead to instability or cannot be undertaken with proper regard for due process, and that nonprosecutorial mechanisms may actually promote human rights more effectively.[17] Claims

[15] For a handful of recent works in this large and growing literature, *see* CARLOS SANTIAGO NINO, RADICAL EVIL ON TRIAL (1996); JAIME MALAMUD-GOTI, GAME WITHOUT END: STATE TERROR AND THE POLITICS OF JUSTICE (1996); MARTHA MINOW, BETWEEN VENGEANCE AND FORGIVENESS: FACING HISTORY AFTER GENOCIDE AND MASS VIOLENCE (1998); Mark J. Osiel, *Ever Again: Legal Remembrance of Administrative Massacre*, 144 U. PA. L. REV. 463 (1995); Stanley Cohen, *State Crimes of Previous Regimes: Knowledge, Accountability, and the Policing of the Past*, 20 LAW AND SOC. INQ. 7 (1995). For older studies, *see, e.g.*, OTTO KIRCHHEIMER, POLITICAL JUSTICE: THE USE OF LEGAL PROCEDURE FOR POLITICAL ENDS (1961); JUDITH SHKLAR, LEGALISM: LAW, MORALS, AND POLITICAL TRIALS (1986).

[16] For example, coup attempts by the Argentine military clearly had a profound impact on the course of accountability in that country. *See* Ch. 8, text at notes 50–51, *infra*.

[17] *See, e.g.*, Carlos S. Nino, *The Duty to Punish Past Abuses of Human Rights Put Into Context: The Case of Argentina*, 100 YALE L.J. 2619 (1991); Diane F. Orentlicher, *A Reply to Professor Nino*, 100 YALE L.J. 2641 (1991); *see also* José Zalaquett, *Confronting Human Rights Violations Committed by Former Governments: Principles Applicable and Political Constraints*, *in* STATE CRIMES: PUNISHMENT OR PARDON 23, 44–48 (Aspen Institute ed., 1989).

that accountability will undermine the political order must always be regarded with some skepticism, as those in power are clearly capable of exaggerating such threats for selfish ends. Claims that trials will be undertaken without regard for due process need to be taken more seriously because of the importance of respecting the human rights of the targets of investigations. Accountability cannot be isolated from a political dynamic in which competing factions within states seek to manipulate the past in order to justify both their prior activities and current programs.[18] Moreover, in the context of ethnic-based strife, criminal trials might provide some closure for victims, but fail to promote any long-term reconciliation for the society if the perpetrators' community believes its concerns were ignored.[19]

Secondly, if trials are determined as useful to advance the relevant goals for the society, decision-makers have increasingly confronted the question of whether these trials should be held through the domestic judiciary or in an international or foreign courtroom. Trials closest to the affected society, victim, perpetrators, and evidence clearly advance the purposes of accountability best. Yet, as the ensuing chapters will reveal, the unwillingness of some governments to prosecute, the inadequacies of domestic judicial systems, and the desire by some powerful states to remove trials from national courts have led to the creation of various international criminal tribunals. The extent to which actors outside an affected society should defer to that society's decisions and standards of justice remains highly problematic.[20]

Thirdly, and intertwined with the other considerations, the affected society, perhaps in conjunction with international actors, will need to make a determination regarding the number of targets involved in any accountability process. For some human rights abuses, the number of perpetrators may be small; for mass atrocities, whether committed over many years (South Africa) or in just a few weeks (Rwanda), the numbers of people may be in the hundreds of thousands. In the latter cases, both the desirability and feasibility of mass criminal trials seems highly questionable. Here, as will be seen, governments have employed other forms of accountability, such as commissions of inquiry, removal from office, or amenability to civil suits. But debate remains strong on whether such mechanisms should be substitutes for, or supplements to, criminal trials.

[18] For a remarkable study of this process in Eastern Europe, *see generally* TINA ROSENBERG, THE HAUNTED LAND: FACING EUROPE'S GHOSTS AFTER COMMUNISM (1995).

[19] *See, e.g.*, MICHAEL IGNATIEFF, THE WARRIOR'S HONOR: ETHNIC WAR AND THE MODERN CONSCIENCE 184 (1997); José E. Alvarez, *Rush to Closure: Lessons of the Tadíc Judgement*, 96 MICH. L. REV. 2031, 2082–112 (1998).

[20] *See, e.g.*, José E. Alvarez, *Crimes of States/Crimes of Hate: Lessons from Rwanda*, 24 YALE J. INT'L L. 365 (1999).

These factors also underlie the ongoing debate over the propriety of amnesties. Although amnesties are highly problematic under international human rights law and indeed violate those treaties that obligate states to punish offenders,[21] their defenders claim they have facilitated or even made possible an abusive regime's surrender of power in the first place. South Africa's innovative confession-for-amnesty scheme represents a thoughtful attempt at balancing these competing considerations.[22]

Although the experiences of other countries may offer some lessons for current decision-makers, there can be no single model for addressing serious violations of international human rights and humanitarian law. Rather, the political, social, and historical conditions in a country will govern the weights of the competing considerations and thus the means for approaching accountability.[23] As Tina Rosenberg has explained in contrasting the experiences of Latin America and Eastern Europe, the nature of the system that produced the abuses, the strength of the successor regime, and the extent and type of abuses endured by the country all exert a powerful influence on the course accountability takes. In Latin America, because successor regimes remain relatively weak and elements of the prior regime retain some power, the methods of accountability have been mild and incomplete; whereas in the latter, because successor regimes have inherited the strong states built up by Communists, accountability has had a tendency to cross the line between justice and revenge without due process. As for the utility of specific forms of accountability, trials have often proved ill-suited for judging abuses that emanated from a 'conspirac[y] of all of society', such as those in Eastern Europe; whereas they have proved more appropriate to bring justice in the aftermath of the acts of a relatively small group of individuals, such as juntas in Latin America.[24]

A final preliminary issue involves the choice of sanction for violations of international human rights and humanitarian law. A formal determina-

[21] *See* Ch. 8, Principles Governing Crimes Under International Law, *infra.*

[22] Promotion of National Unity and National Reconciliation Act, Law No. 34 of 1995 (S. Afr.); Azanian People's Organisation (AZAPO) and Others vs. President of the Republic of South Africa and Others, 1996(4) SA 671 (upholding constitutionality of Act); John Dugard, *Dealing with Crimes of a Past Regime. Is Amnesty Still an Option?*, 12 LEIDEN J. INT'L L. 1001 (1999); *see also* Ch. 8, Precedents for Prosecutions Before National Tribunals: Four Recent Cases—South Africa, *infra.*

[23] *See* Neil J. Kritz, *Coming to Terms with Atrocities: A Review of Accountability Mechanisms for Mass Violations of Human Rights*, 59 LAW AND CONTEMP. PROBS. 127 (1996).

[24] Tina Rosenberg, *Overcoming the Legacies of Dictatorship*, FOREIGN AFF., May/June 1995, at 134, 138; *see also* Luc Huyse, *Justice After Transition: On the Choices Successor Elites Make in Dealing with the Past*, 20 LAW AND SOC. INQUIRY 51, 71–78 (1995); NINO, *supra* note 15, at 107–34 (multivariable approach to prospects for justice during transitions); Samuel P. Huntington, THE THIRD WAVE: DEMOCRATIZATION IN THE LATE TWENTIETH CENTURY 114 (1991) (distinguishing between 'transformations', 'replacements', and 'transplacements'); Zalaquett, *supra* note 17, at 45–47.

tion of individual responsibility, whether by a court verdict or an investigatory commission, constitutes a type of sanction in and of itself. Where a criminal tribunal convicts a perpetrator, a prison sentence will, of course, be an appropriate remedy. Fines and, in a civil context, monetary damages may also be justified. Lustration, or disqualification from public office, has been fairly common in the former communist countries of Eastern Europe. However, lustration programs have raised human rights problems of their own and run the risk of creating large ranks of ostracized opponents who may pose a threat to the new regime.[25] Military demotions for violations of humanitarian law are also possible, though too infrequently employed.

Governments may also provide remedies to victims that do not entail specific actions against those held accountable—or indeed do not even require a finding of accountability of particular individuals. There is strong support in international law, stemming from treaty obligations such as the ICCPR, that states are obligated to compensate victims of human rights violations, whether committed by the current government or a former regime.[26] Remedies can also be symbolic in nature, such as monuments to victims.

The chapters that follow aim to provide a legal overview of the most critical mechanisms of accountability. As others seek to navigate the labyrinth of political and moral factors surrounding the debate over accountability, this section seeks to complement that endeavor on the assumption that a full appreciation of the complexity of accountability demands a careful appraisal of the legal possibilities and constraints upon decision-makers. The challenge for decision-makers will then lie in choosing and combining these mechanisms so as to advance the society's goals for accountability, but to do so in a way that respects international norms.

[25] *See, e.g.*, Mary Albon, Project on Justice in Times of Transition (1992), *reprinted in* 1 Transitional Justice, *supra* note 1, at 42, 50–52; Herman Schwartz, *Lustration in Eastern Europe*, 1 Parker School J. East Europ. L. 141, 141–48 (1994); on the Czech case, *see* Rosenberg, *supra* note 18, at 4–121; Roman Boed, *An Evaluation of the Legality and Efficacy of Lustration as a Tool of Transitional Justice*, 37 Colum. J. Transnat'l L. 357 (1999).

[26] ICCPR, arts. 9(5), 14(6), 999 UNTS at 176–77; Study Concerning the Right to Restitution, Compensation and Rehabilitation for Victims of Gross Violations of Human Rights and Fundamental Freedoms, prepared by Theo van Boven, July 26, 1990, UN Doc. E/CN.4/Sub.2/1990/10, at 4–8.

8

The Forum of First Resort: National Tribunals

Although the international legal process has elaborated a corpus of law providing individual criminal responsibility for various atrocities in peace and war, domestic legal systems remain the primary fora for holding individuals accountable for these acts. National tribunals have the principal responsibility for such trials, as part of a state's duty to uphold the rule of law. Moreover, because such tribunals are closest to the scene, the perpetrators, and the victims of atrocities, they represent the starting point for considering accountability options. The legal processes defining various offenses often specify the role of domestic courts in suppressing crimes. At the same time, governments have also taken to enforcing international norms without reliance upon particular treaties or custom, and of course have prosecuted offenders for many crimes for which international law does not provide individual accountability, e.g., murder.

This analysis of the use of national courts for accountability begins by outlining the international law principles governing the criminal jurisdiction of national courts, for jurisdiction forms the critical legal bridge between international offenses and their suppression by courts. It then turns to review the experiences of four countries that sought to bring to justice individuals responsible for serious human rights violations before their domestic courts, and the difficulties, political and legal, each encountered. It also includes a discussion of the possibilities for trials by domestic courts other than those of the state where the offenses were committed, an option now gaining increasing favor.

A JURISDICTIONAL PRIMER

General Principles: The Five Bases for Jurisdiction

National tribunals cannot exercise jurisdiction over all offenses regardless of where they were committed. Rather, the jurisdiction of national courts is governed by the domestic law of the state concerned and by international law principles of jurisdiction. The jurisdiction of national courts to adjudicate acts of another sovereign is further limited by domestic and international law rules on sovereign immunity and related doctrines.[1]

Generally speaking, international law recognizes five bases for jurisdiction.[2] The primary basis is the territorial principle, which recognizes the right of a state to prescribe and apply its law over acts committed within its territorial boundaries. This basis for jurisdiction has expanded over the years, not without controversy and disagreements among states, to justify jurisdiction not only where the entire offense takes place within a state's territory, but also where a constituent part or immediate effect of the offense occurs in the state.[3] Territoriality has served as the principal legal basis for national trials by states of officials of prior regimes for human rights atrocities under domestic law.

The nationality principle applies where a state exercises jurisdiction over an offender who is one of its nationals, regardless of the situs of the conduct. Under the protective principle, jurisdiction is exercised where extraterritorial conduct would have an actually or potentially harmful effect on important interests of the state, generally relating to national security or some important government function. The passive personality principle, a somewhat less firm basis of jurisdiction, applies where the victim of an offense is a national of the state seeking to exercise jurisdiction, and has on occasion been used to try individuals for crimes under domestic law committed overseas, including human rights violations.[4]

Fifth, and of special importance for serious violations of human rights, the universality principle permits a state to exercise jurisdiction over perpetrators of certain offenses considered particularly heinous or harmful to mankind, regardless of any nexus the state may have with the offense, the offender, or the victim.[5] The notion behind this principle is that the nature of such offenses dictates that all states have an interest in

[1] *See* RESTATEMENT (THIRD) OF THE FOREIGN RELATIONS LAW OF THE UNITED STATES § 451 (1987) [hereinafter Restatement]; Rüdiger Wolfrum, *The Decentralized Prosecution of International Offenses Through National Courts*, *in* WAR CRIMES IN INTERNATIONAL LAW 233, 233–34 (Yoram Dinstein and Mala Tabory eds. 1996).

[2] *See, e.g.*, IAN BROWNLIE, PRINCIPLES OF PUBLIC INTERNATIONAL LAW 303–09 (5th ed. 1998); Kenneth C. Randall, *Universal Jurisdiction Under International Law*, 66 TEX. L. REV. 785, 788–89 n. 2 (1988) and sources cited therein.

[3] *See* Christopher L. Blakesley, *Extraterritorial Jurisdiction*, *in* 2 INTERNATIONAL CRIMINAL LAW 33, 47–54 (M. Cherif Bassiouni ed., 2nd ed. 1999); Randall, *supra* note 2, at 787 n. 8 (distinguishing between objective and subjective territorial principles).

[4] *See* RESTATEMENT, *supra* note 1, § 402 and comments thereto; *see also* Marlise Simons, *Unforgiving Spain Pursues Argentine Killers*, N.Y. TIMES, Oct. 24, 1996, at A3.

[5] *See* Brigitte Stern, *À propos de la compétence universelle*, *in* LIBER AMICORUM JUDGE MOHAMMED BEDJAOUI 735 (Emile Yakpo and Tahar Boumedra eds., 1999); Blakesley, *supra* note 3, at 70–73; Randall, *supra* note 2, at 785, 788–90. For an early elaboration of the principle, *see* EMMERIC DE VATTEL, 1 LE DROIT DES GENS, ch. 19, §§ 232–33 (Charles G. Fenwick trans., Carnegie Institution 1916) (1758).

exercising jurisdiction over them. Though governments, courts, and commentators do not completely concur as to those offenses for which international law confers universal jurisdiction, the list would appear to include at least piracy, slave trade, war crimes, crimes against humanity, torture, aircraft hijacking and sabotage, and genocide.[6] As seen below, however, the legal basis for each—treaty or custom—varies from crime to crime. Where the offense relates to an *erga omnes* obligation or a *jus cogens* norm, the argument that all states have the power to exercise jurisdiction over the offense is even stronger. Nevertheless, when the territorial state is willing and able to carry out a bona fide prosecution, other states should generally defer to it.[7]

Universality may arise under treaty or customary law. Treaties that permit states to apply the law based on universal jurisdiction include the 1949 Geneva Conventions and the 1984 Torture Convention (although in each case the state must extradite to a state willing to prosecute if it fails to prosecute); those that may require states to punish according to universal jurisdiction include the 1956 Slavery Convention and the Apartheid Convention.[8] In the absence of a treaty, customary law regards universal jurisdiction generally as permissive, not mandatory; in these situations states may, but are not required to, prescribe and apply law for offenses committed anywhere and against any victims.[9] Customary law could well evolve, however, to require a state to prescribe law with regard to certain offenses and apply it whenever an offender is located in its territory. Prosecutions based on universality, if accomplished by an absence of protest from other states, will be important indicia of custom in this area.

Principles Governing Crimes Under International Law

Both treaties and customary law have envisaged domestic courts as the primary arena for the trials of those accused of acts incurring individual responsibility under international law. The provisions in treaties and

[6] *See, e.g.*, 1 OPPENHEIM'S INTERNATIONAL LAW 998 (Robert Jennings and Arthur Watts eds., 9th ed. 1992); *Furundzija Judgment*, para. 156 (torture); RESTATEMENT, *supra* note 1, § 404; Blakesley, *supra* note 3, at 70–73; Randall, *supra* note 2, at 788–90. Indeed, it can be argued that individual criminal responsibility arises only where international law provides for universal jurisdiction. *See* Denise Plattner, *The Penal Repression of Violations of International Humanitarian Law Applicable in Non-International Armed Conflicts*, 30 INT'L REV. RED CROSS 409, 417–18 (1990).

[7] Randall, *supra* note 2, at 829–31; Christopher C. Joyner, *Arresting Impunity: The Case for Universal Jurisdiction in Bringing War Criminals to Accountability* 59 LAW AND CONTEMP. PROBS. 153, 165–70 (1997). *Cf.* ICC Statute, art. 17.

[8] *See infra* text at notes 17, 21, 27, and 30. Where universal jurisdiction arises from a treaty provision, the effect of such a provision on non-parties is unclear. *See, e.g.*, Randall, *supra* note 2, at 822–27, 833–34.

[9] *See* RESTATEMENT, *supra* note 1, § 404, comment a; Stern, *supra* note 5, at 737–40.

custom vary widely from crime to crime; they may require a state to prescribe and apply domestic law on the subject under some combination of the accepted bases of jurisdiction (e.g., a requirement to prosecute persons who commit the crime on its territory or against its nationals); or merely permit states to do so. Many international agreements, especially those of more recent origin, impose an obligation on states to extradite or prosecute offenders—*aut dedere aut judicare.*[10]

Genocide

The framers of the Genocide Convention devoted considerable attention to the issue of jurisdiction. Although the Convention expressly contemplates the establishment of an international penal tribunal with jurisdiction over genocide, most member states anticipated that national courts would be the primary fora for the Convention's enforcement. Accordingly, Article VI requires parties to punish acts of genocide committed on their territory, though the Convention is silent as to any rights or obligations concerning extraterritorial jurisdiction.

Although the *travaux* are not entirely clear on the issue, most member states appear to have interpreted the territorial state's jurisdiction as non-exclusive and, in particular, did not regard the Convention as precluding states from exercising jurisdiction based on the nationality and passive personality principles. Indeed, the Sixth Committee's debate culminated in the adoption of an understanding to that effect, and the prevailing view is that the Convention does not limit jurisdictional rights to the territorial state.[11] However, in 1948 the member states were clearly unprepared to recognize the notion of universal jurisdiction over genocide, as the *Ad Hoc* Committee and the Sixth Committee explicitly rejected a provision providing for universal jurisdiction that had appeared in the Secretary-General's draft.[12]

Apart from the Genocide Convention, it is likely that genocide carries

[10] *See* M. Cherif Bassiouni and Edward M. Wise, Aut Dedere Aut Judicare: The Duty to Extradite or Prosecute in International Law 21–25, 51–55 (1995) (arguing this obligation is also customary law and *jus cogens*).

[11] Genocide: Draft Convention and Report of the Economic and Social Council, Report of the Sixth Committee, 3d Sess., UN Doc. A/760 (1948), at 8; UN GAOR Sixth Committee, 3d Sess., 100th, 130th–133d mtgs. (1948); *see* Application of the Convention on the Prevention and Punishment of the Crime of Genocide (Bosnia and Herzegovina v. Yugo.), 1993 ICJ 325, 443 (Sept. 13) (separate op. Lauterpacht); Nehemiah Robinson, The Genocide Convention: A Commentary 82–85 (1960). *But see* Lori Lyman Bruun, *Beyond the 1948 Convention—Emerging Principles of Genocide in Customary International Law*, 17 Md. J. Int'l L and Trade 193, 207 (1993) (jurisdiction solely to territorial state); Robert H. Jones, *Jurisdiction and Extradition Under the Convention, in The United States and the 1948 Genocide Convention*, 16 Harv. Int'l L.J. 683, 696–99 (1975) (nationality jurisdiction unclear).

[12] Report of the *Ad Hoc* Committee on Genocide, UN ESCOR, 7th Sess., Supp. No. 6, at 11–12, UN Doc. E/794/Corr.1, (1948); *see* Robinson, *supra* note 11, at 31–32; Randall, *supra* note 2, at 834–37.

universal jurisdiction under customary international law. Since the Genocide Convention entered into force, authoritative sources such as the *Eichmann* and *Demjanjuk* cases have affirmed the applicability of universal jurisdiction to genocide.[13] Indeed, the *erga omnes* nature of the ban on genocide would also appear to strengthen such a view.[14]

Crimes Against Humanity and War Crimes

The jurisdiction of many of the international tribunals established after World War II to try those accused of war crimes and crimes against humanity, including the Nuremberg and Tokyo Tribunals, was often predicated on the principle of universal jurisdiction, though the courts rarely discussed this issue in their judgments. However, in many cases, jurisdiction also turned on the territorial or nationality principles, and the jurisdiction of the Allied occupation tribunals also derived from Germany's residual jurisdiction.[15]

As with genocide, crimes against humanity today are subject to universal jurisdiction.[16] Regarding war crimes, any state may prosecute grave breaches of the Geneva Conventions and Protocol I; indeed, the Conventions obligate parties to 'provide effective penal sanctions' for anybody committing grave breaches; to search out such persons; and to prosecute or extradite them.[17] Until the 1990s, however, there do not appear to have been any prosecutions for war crimes under these instruments based purely on the universality principle; but the pattern is clearly changing, with prosecutions proceeding without protest from other states.[18] For violations of other parts of the Conventions and Protocols, including of Common Article 3 or Protocol II, the Conventions and Protocols lack any requirements concerning prosecution or extradition, or

[13] *Eichmann*, 36 ILR at 26–57, 279–304 (basing jurisdiction on protective, passive personality, and universality principles); Matter of the Extradition of Demjanjuk, 776 F. 2d. 571, 582–83 (6th Cir. 1985), *cert. denied*, 457 U.S. 1016 (1986); *see also* RESTATEMENT, *supra* note 1, § 404; Johan D. van der Vyver, *Prosecution and Punishment of the Crime of Genocide*, 23 FORDHAM INT'L L.J. 286, 323–35 (1999).

[14] *See* Ch. 2, text at note 73, *supra*.

[15] *See, e.g.*, Randall, *supra* note 2, at 800–10; 15 War Crimes Reports 23–48 (1949).

[16] *See Demjanjuk*, 776 F.2d at 582–83; *Eichmann*, 36 ILR at 299–303; *see also* RESTATEMENT, *supra* note 1, § 404; Letter dated 9 February 1993 from the Secretary-General Addressed to the President of the Security Council, Feb. 10, 1993, UN Doc. S/25274, at 20 [hereinafter Yugoslavia Commission First Interim Report]; Randall, *supra* note 2, at 788–90, 814. The general lack of protest to Canada's and Belgium's legislation and prosecutions for crimes against humanity based on universality is also highly indicative in this regard. *See infra* text at notes 84–85, 91.

[17] *E.g.*, Geneva Convention IV, art. 146, 75 UNTS at 386; Protocol I, art. 85(1), 1125 UNTS at 41; *see also* RESTATEMENT, *supra* note 1, § 404; Yugoslavia Commission First Interim Report, *supra* note 16, at 20; Richard R. Baxter, *The Municipal and International Law Basis of Jurisdiction Over War Crimes*, 28 BRIT. Y.B. INT'L L. 382, 389–91 (1951); Randall, *supra* note 2, at 789–90 (citing US caselaw); Yves Sandoz, *Implementing International Humanitarian Law*, *in* INTERNATIONAL DIMENSIONS OF HUMANITARIAN LAW 259, 277 and n. 27 (Henry Dunant Institute ed. 1988).

[18] *See infra* text at note 88.

any provisions concerning universal jurisdiction. Nevertheless, customary law would seem to recognize universal jurisdiction over a broader range of war crimes than those listed as grave breaches of the Conventions or Protocol I.[19]

The 1954 Hague Convention for the Protection of Cultural Property in the Event of Armed Conflict requires states to take 'all necessary steps to prosecute and impose penal or disciplinary sanctions upon those persons, of whatever nationality, who commit or order to be committed a breach' of the treaty.[20] This appears to provide for mandatory universal jurisdiction, though the treaty contains no other penal provisions.

Other Areas of International Criminal Law

Slavery and Forced Labor: Under the 1956 Slavery Convention, states parties must make slavery and the slave trade a criminal offense, regardless of where it occurs, and make persons convicted liable to 'punishment' in the case of the former and 'very severe penalties' for the latter.[21] Other conventions contain differing penal provisions.[22] It is not clear whether customary international law obligates all states to exercise universal jurisdiction over slavery, although slavery seems to carry at least permissive universal jurisdiction under customary law.[23] As for forced labor, the 1930 Forced Labor Convention requires that states make it 'punishable as a penal offence'.[24] The 1950 Convention on Forced Prostitution obligates states to punish any person who participates in prostitution as defined in the Convention, but contains no obligations regarding extradition.[25]

Torture: The Torture Convention's core provisions on criminal enforcement require states to ensure that torture, the attempt to commit it, and complicity in torture are offenses under their criminal law and to make these offenses 'punishable by appropriate penalties which take into account their grave nature'.[26] They must furthermore prescribe law to

[19] The apparent absence of protest to the war crimes legislation of Belgium, Spain, Sweden, and other states, which are based on universal jurisdiction, *see infra* text at note 83, is significant. *See also* Sonja Boelaert-Suominen, *Grave Breaches, Universal Jurisdiction and Internal Armed Conflicts: Is Customary Law Moving Towards a Uniform Enforcement Mechanism for all Armed Conflicts?*, 5 J. Conflict and Security L. 63 (2000).

[20] May 14, 1954, art. 28, 249 UNTS 215, 260.

[21] 1956 Slavery Convention, arts. 3, 6, 266 UNTS at 42, 43.

[22] *See* 1 M. Cherif Bassiouni, International Crimes: Digest/Index of International Instruments 1815–1985, at 499–508 (1986); Stéfan Glaser, Droit International Pénal Conventionnel 121–26 (1970).

[23] Restatement, *supra* note 1, § 404; Randall, *supra* note 2, at 798–800 and n.79.

[24] Convention Concerning Forced or Compulsory Labor, June 28, 1930, as modified by the Final Articles Revision Convention of the International Labor Organization, art. 25, 39 UNTS 55, 74

[25] Convention for the Suppression of the Traffic in Persons and of the Exploitation of the Prostitution of Others, Mar. 21, 1950, arts. 1–2, 96 UNTS 271, 274; *see also* Ch. 5, text at notes 14–16, *supra*.

[26] Torture Convention, art. 4, 1465 UNTS at 114.

punish torture committed on their territory, by their nationals, and, if appropriate, against their nationals, as well as any other situations where they choose not to extradite offenders. They must also detain any alleged torturer in their territory (regardless of the location of the offense) and either prosecute him or extradite him.[27] As for cruel, inhuman, or degrading treatment or punishment, states need to prevent it through various means and provide victims with the right to complain, but need not criminalize it or even provide a victim with the right to compensation.[28] Beyond the Convention, customary international law would appear to permit states to exercise universal jurisdiction over torture.[29]

Apartheid: The Apartheid Convention permits and indeed requires states parties to prescribe and apply their law for apartheid offenses committed anywhere.[30] It also contemplates trials by an international penal tribunal and requires states to grant extradition of offenders in accordance with their legislation and existing treaties.[31] The scope of jurisdiction and obligations upon states under customary law seems speculative.

Forced Disappearances: Jurisdictional principles concerning forced disappearances (apart from crimes against humanity) are of recent origin. The 1992 General Assembly Resolution calls for states to make such acts serious crimes under domestic law, requires states to extradite or prosecute offenders, and calls for substantially long statutes of limitations.[32] The OAS Convention requires each state to make the practice a crime when committed in its territory; by its nationals; if it sees fit, against its nationals; and in any other case in which it chooses not to extradite an offender. It further contains an extradite or prosecute provision and eliminates any statutes of limitations.[33]

[27] *Id.* arts. 5, 6(1), 7(1), at 198; *see also* Inter-American Convention to Prevent and Punish Torture, Dec. 9, 1985, arts. 6, 12, 14, OAS T.S. No. 67, at 14–16, *reprinted in* 25 ILM 519 (1986).

[28] Torture Convention, art. 16, 1465 UNTS at 116. The lack of a guaranteed remedy is apparent from the omission of the article providing for a remedy for torture (art. 14) from the list of provisions in Article 16 that apply to torture as well as cruel treatment.

[29] *Furundzija Judgment*, para. 156; *Pinochet*, [1999] 2 All E.R. at 109 (Lord Browne-Wilkinson); RESTATEMENT, *supra* note 1, § 404. *But see* Randall, *supra* note 2, at 788–90, 822–23.

[30] Apartheid Convention, arts. IV–V, 1015 UNTS at 246; *see also* Roger S. Clark, *Apartheid, in* 1 INTERNATIONAL CRIMINAL LAW, *supra* note 3, at 643, 653–58 (noting objections to jurisdictional provisions by United States and United Kingdom); Randall, *supra* note 2, at 788–90, 819.

[31] Apartheid Convention, arts. IV–V, XI, 1015 UNTS at 246–47; *see also* Clark, *supra* note 30, at 654, 658–59. The relationship between the requirement to prosecute in Article IV and the requirement to extradite in Article XI is unclear.

[32] GA Res. 47/133, arts. 1, 4, 14, 17(3), UN GAOR, 47th Sess., Supp. No. 49(I), at 207, 207–09, UN Doc. A/47/49(I) (1992).

[33] Inter-American Convention on the Forced Disappearance of Persons, June 9, 1994, arts. 4, 6, 7, 33 ILM 1529, 1530–31 (1994).

Relationship to Domestic Statutes

States parties to treaties obligating them to penalize certain offenses under domestic law must have domestic criminal law statutes implementing this obligation, or a domestic law system that permits prosecution directly under international law; if they do not, they are violating their international legal commitments. Yet because of the variations in these treaty-based duties across different crimes, domestic law implementing international criminal law will likely vary from offense to offense in terms of its coverage. For example, a state's domestic law implementing such treaties might limit one crime to acts committed on the state's soil (e.g., genocide), while extend another crime to acts committed anywhere (e.g., torture). It is also possible that some states will choose to promulgate domestic law that reaches further than their obligations under international law. They might permit prosecutions based on universality when the relevant treaty only requires that they prosecute based on territoriality, or punish acts for which the relevant treaty does not even obligate punishment.[34]

The scope of any obligation or right under international law and the extent to which the state implements any obligation through domestic law—incompletely, fully, or by going further than the obligation—will permit those concerned with accountability to choose a proper forum for prosecution. Thus, the varieties of treaty obligations and domestic law options make it imperative that those considering domestic trials closely review the pertinent corpus of both international and domestic law. Moreover, in domestic law provisions providing for punishment of international offenses, some states will choose simply to adopt international law conceptions and definitions of the crime in toto, while others will seek to define the offense anew for purposes of domestic law.[35]

Finally, and quite crucially, states may simply utilize their existing criminal law on common crimes—such as murder or battery—to prosecute human rights abusers. Regardless of their treaty commitments or implementation of them, states will thus have available a corpus of domestic law for such trials.

[34] *See generally* Stern, *supra* note 5, at 741–46; for examples, *see* the Belgian and Spanish statutes *infra* note 83; *see also* Andrew D. Mitchell, *Genocide, Human Rights Implementation and the Relationship between International and Domestic Law*: Nulyarimma v. Thompson, 24 MELBOURNE U. L. REV. 15 (2000) (on Australia's failure to implement Genocide Convention in domestic law). We do not in this section attempt to survey domestic law statutes that implement treaty obligations or otherwise penalize acts recognized as incurring individual responsibility under international law. However, later in this Chapter we discuss examples of domestic law that permit prosecution of acts not taking place on the territory of the state. For a useful compendium of state practice, *see* 1 Y.B. INT'L HUMAN. LAW 395–527 (1998), and documentation at 529–644.

[35] *Compare* Ex Parte Quirin, 317 U.S. 1, 27–31 (1942) (approving US jurisdiction over violations of the laws of war as defined by the practice of nations) *with* Nouveau Code pénal, art. 212–1 (Fr.) (new definition of crimes against humanity).

PRECEDENTS FOR PROSECUTIONS BEFORE NATIONAL TRIBUNALS: FOUR RECENT CASES

Despite a variety of jurisdictional bases, prosecutions for violations of international human rights and humanitarian law before national tribunals were rare until the 1990s. The prosecutions of Axis war criminals before domestic tribunals after World War II, and in several instances more recently (France, Australia, Canada, United Kingdom, and Croatia), constitute the most notable exceptions. Until the 1980s, the only significant prosecution of state leaders other than agents of the Axis for human rights abuses was the Greek government's successful prosecution of members of the military junta following its demise in 1974.

With respect to genocide, aside from the *Eichmann* case in Israel in the 1960s, only a few prosecutions have been carried out before domestic tribunals since World War II. In Equatorial Guinea, the government tried and executed a former dictator for genocide and other crimes; and in Cambodia, the Vietnamese-installed People's Republic of Kampuchea tried and convicted Khmer Rouge leaders Pol Pot and Ieng Sary *in absentia* on charges of genocide in 1979.[36] However, the highly politicized nature of those prosecutions and the lack of fundamental elements of due process make them poor precedents for examining the prosecution of genocide by individual states. As for violations of the laws of war, domestic trials have occurred with somewhat more frequency (usually under domestic codes of military justice), although the vast majority of war crimes have gone unpunished since the signature of the Geneva Conventions in 1949. Among the more publicized prosecutions have been those by the United States of offenders during the Vietnam War, especially the *Calley* case.[37]

Despite this rather discouraging history from the point of view of accountability, recent years have seen a surge in the use of national courts for the prosecution of wide-scale human rights abuses. Most charges have been brought under domestic rather than international law. This section examines four of the most significant recent precedents. Each demonstrates both the promises and the inherent challenges in bringing former leaders to justice. Although these cases deserve particular attention, they are not alone and represent part of a larger trend. Thus, for example, Latvia has prosecuted Soviet-era officials for genocide, sentencing one to

[36] Israel did not invoke the Genocide Convention in Eichmann's prosecution because it was adopted subsequent to his crimes. Rather, his genocidal acts fell under the Israeli law on crimes against the Jewish people, crimes against humanity, and war crimes. More recent prosecutions in France (*Barbie* and *Touvier*), Canada (*Finta*), and Australia (*Polyukhovich*) against Nazis were not instituted under the Genocide Convention for the same reason.

[37] *See* Ch. 4, note 46, *supra*.

life imprisonment in 1996; and victims of atrocities in Guatemala in the 1980s filed criminal complaints of genocide in 2000 against former military leaders.[38] In the 1990s, Hungary attempted to prosecute various killings committed during the 1956 uprisings.[39] And in 2000, Indonesia's new government tried and convicted 24 soldiers for murdering civilians in Aceh province.[40] In addition, victims groups in several countries, such as Chile and Argentina, have attempted with some success to overcome past amnesties or grants of immunity to military officials.[41]

Argentina

In 1983, following Argentina's humiliating defeat in the Falklands/Malvinas War, the third in a series of military juntas that had ruled the country since 1976 gave way to the democratically elected civilian government of President Raúl Alfonsín. The transition took place peacefully and unconditionally, though the military remained a powerful, albeit discredited, force. The period of military rule had seen widespread human rights violations, including disappearances, arbitrary imprisonment, and torture, in connection with the military's 'dirty war' against left-wing opponents.[42]

In the wake of the transition, victims, their families, and NGOs initiated criminal prosecutions against many of the perpetrators of the abuses. The Argentine truth commission forwarded over 1,000 cases to civilian judicial authorities in 1984, and the release of its report encouraged citizens to bring additional cases.[43] During the presidential campaign,

38 *See Former Latvian KGB official gets 7-year jail term for 'genocide'*, AGENCE FRANCE-PRESSE, Sept. 27, 1999 (available on LEXIS/NEXIS); Mike Lanchin, *Terror on Trial: Guatemala's Indians take their former army tormentors to court,* SAN FRANCISCO CHRONICLE, July 13, 2000, at A12. For an unsuccessful attempt at prosecution of Australian officials for acts against Aboriginal peoples, *see* Nulyarimma and Others v. Thompson, 165 ALR 621 (Fed. Ct. 1999); Mitchell, *supra* note 34.

39 *See* Péter Kovács, *Correspondents Reports*, 1 Y.B. INT'L HUMAN. L. 451–55 (1998).

40 *See* Rajiv Chandrasekaran, *Indonesian Tribunal Convicts Soldiers; Murders in Aceh Prompted Country's First Rights Trial*, WASH. POST, May 18, 2000, at A18. Nonetheless, the soldiers' commanders were not tried.

41 *See generally* IMPUNITY AND HUMAN RIGHTS IN INTERNATIONAL LAW AND PRACTICE (Naomi Roht-Arriaza ed. 1995); TINA ROSENBERG, THE HAUNTED LAND: FACING EUROPE'S GHOSTS AFTER COMMUNISM (1995). On Chile, *see, e.g.*, HUMAN RIGHTS WATCH, CHILE: WHEN TYRANTS TREMBLE: THE PINOCHET CASE (Oct. 1999), available at www.hrw.org; for the August 2000 Chilean Supreme Court decision removing Pinochet's immunity, see www.derechos.org/nizkor/chile/juicio/desafuero2.html.

42 For a description of the military regime's human rights record, *see, e.g.*, NUNCA MÁS: THE REPORT OF THE ARGENTINE NATIONAL COMMISSION ON THE DISAPPEARED (Farrar Straus Giroux trans., 1986) (1984); AMERICAS WATCH, TRUTH AND PARTIAL JUSTICE IN ARGENTINA: AN UPDATE 3–7 (1991).

43 *See, e.g.*, Alejandro M. Garro and Henry Dahl, *Legal Accountability for Human Rights Violations in Argentina: One Step Forward and Two Steps Backward*, 8 HUM. RTS. L.J. 283, 319 (1987). Argentine law permits private citizens to bring criminal complaints, which the courts must investigate. By mid-1984, some 2,000 such complaints had been brought. AMERICAS WATCH, *supra* note 42, at 21; Emilio Fermin Mignone, Cynthia L. Estlund, and Samuel Issacharoff, *Dictatorship on Trial: Prosecution of Human Rights Violations in Argentina*, 10 YALE J. INT'L L. 118, 123, 129 (1984) (Argentine plaintiff-prosecutor system).

Alfonsín had made clear his own intention to prosecute those responsible for the military regime's abuses, a position that enjoyed widespread popular support. Alfonsín identified three levels of responsibility: those who gave orders, those who committed excesses in implementing the orders, and those who simply followed orders. Under the president's plan, only the first two categories would be punished.[44] The implementing legislation provided military courts with original jurisdiction over all prosecutions, subject to mandatory appeal to the civilian federal courts. The federal courts could also assume jurisdiction if the military courts failed to act within a specified period of time. The legislation also afforded certain rights of participation to victims and their families, including the right to appeal an acquittal.[45]

Shortly after taking office, Alfonsín ordered the trial of nine of the junta leaders and a handful of other high-ranking officers, as well as the reputed leaders of the main leftist guerilla organizations.[46] Prosecutors charged the defendants with common crimes under Argentine law, since the country's criminal code did not adequately define certain international crimes, such as crimes against humanity.[47] In response to the military court's refusal to advance the prosecution of the junta leaders, the Federal Appeals Court of Buenos Aires eventually took jurisdiction and, in December 1985, convicted five of the nine defendants.[48] NGOs praised the trials for their scrupulous respect for the rights of the accused. The trials were open to the public, and the defendants enjoyed full rights to defend themselves, including representation of their own choosing. The trials were also marked by riveting and detailed evidence of the junta's human rights abuses provided by victims and other witnesses.[49]

The other prosecutions were consolidated into a smaller number of major cases, and the military courts endeavored to stall these cases as well. In fact, throughout the course of the prosecutions, the armed forces actively sought to impede the judicial process by intimidating witnesses, protecting officers who refused to appear before the courts, and other means. However, intervention by the federal courts and the president achieved progress in some cases, resulting in several arrests and convictions.

As the prosecutions expanded and reached into the ranks of the junior

[44] Mignone et al., *supra* note 43, at 129.

[45] Garro and Dahl, *supra* note 43, at 306–10.

[46] For a first-hand account of the accountability process, *see* Carlos Santiago Nino, Radical Evil on Trial 41–104 (1996).

[47] *Id.* at 302–03, 313–19.

[48] Mignone et al., *supra* note 43, at 138–42; Garro and Dahl, *supra* note 43, at 319–29. The Argentine Supreme Court subsequently confirmed the Appeals Court's ruling. *Id.* at 329–31.

[49] Americas Watch, *supra* note 42, at 21–30; Garro and Dahl, *supra* note 43, at 321–23.

officers, military pressure to halt the trials increased, culminating in a series of revolts that threatened to undermine the civilian government. Beginning in 1987, Alfonsín responded with a series of legal measures designed to limit the prosecutions, and his successor, Carlos Menem, issued sweeping pardons that ultimately put an end to the prosecutions and led to the release of those already convicted.[50] The government's response to the military threat has been criticized as unjustified and harmful to the consolidation of democracy and the rule of law in Argentina.[51] Nevertheless, Argentina remains virtually alone among Latin American countries in attempting to prosecute former regime members, and even some critics acknowledge that its truncated prosecutions still contributed to the goal of accountability.[52] Indeed, despite the pardons granted by President Menem, junta leaders were indicted and arrested in 1999 in connection with the kidnapping of at least 200 babies from 'disappeared' persons.[53]

Post-Communist Germany

In contrast to most other European countries that underwent the transition from communism, Germany embarked on an extensive program to investigate and prosecute officials of the former East German regime following reunification in 1990. While German prosecutors have conducted, and are continuing to conduct, thousands of investigations, legal principles restricting culpability to violations of East German law have significantly limited the number of prosecutions and convictions. The charges brought have been for common crimes under domestic law, as opposed to international law, though the latter has still played a role in the prosecutions. Although prosecutors have already brought several hundred cases, most of those convicted have successfully challenged their convictions on appeal, received light or suspended sentences, or avoided punishment due to illness.[54]

50 *See* AMERICAS WATCH, *supra* note 42, at 49–52; Garro and Dahl, *supra* note 43, at 333–39; Carlos S. Nino, *The Duty to Punish Past Abuses of Human Rights Put Into Context: The Case of Argentina*, 100 YALE L.J. 2619, 2629–30 (1991).

51 *See, e.g.*, Alejandro M. Garro, *Nine Years of Transition to Democracy in Argentina: Partial Failure or Qualified Success?*, 31 COLUM. J. TRANS. L. 1, 16–23 (1993); *contra* Nino, *supra* note 50, at 2637–40 (defending government's policies).

52 *See, e.g.*, Garro, *supra* note 51, at 16–23 (also noting that several defendants served prison time). For a comparison with Chile and Uruguay, *see* LUIS RONIGER AND MARIO SNZAJDER, THE LEGACY OF HUMAN-RIGHTS VIOLATIONS IN THE SOUTHERN CONE: ARGENTINA, CHILE, AND URUGUAY 51–135 (1999).

53 Tim Cornwell, *Junta Bosses Under Arrest 'Stole Babies'*, THE SCOTSMAN, Jan. 10, 2000, at 9.

54 *See, e.g.*, Stephen Kinzer, *Germany Suffers New Setback in Trials of East's Leaders*, N.Y. TIMES, Oct. 19, 1995, at A3.

Among the most noteworthy group of cases are those prosecutors have brought against former East German officials and border guards in connection with the killing of East Germans attempting to flee to the West. The German Supreme Court has ruled that to the extent East German law may have permitted such killings, the law was invalid on the ground that it violated fundamental human rights principles under international law.[55] German authorities have prosecuted some ninety border guards for the killings as well as some generals who oversaw their work, though most of the guards received light or suspended sentences.[56]

Prosecutors have also pursued a number of higher-ranking East German political officials for responsibility for the system that oversaw the border killings. Ten senior East German leaders, including Egon Krenz, the state's last leader, and Defense Minister Heinz Kessler were convicted of manslaughter and attempted manslaughter in 1996 and 1997.[57] Some of the most prominent defendants, however, escaped punishment due to ill health. Former East German leader Erich Honecker, for example, was judged too ill to stand trial in 1992 and left for exile in Chile, where he died in 1994. Former East German Prime Minister Willi Stoph and former Stasi (East German state security service) chief Erich Mielke also avoided punishment on health grounds.[58]

Prosecutors have also obtained convictions against several Stasi officials for espionage activities, including legendary spy chief Markus Wolf. However, in May 1995 the German Supreme Court ruled that East German espionage officers could not be prosecuted for acts committed in East Germany, on the ground that they were acting under the laws of that country. The ruling effectively set aside the convictions of Wolf and other East German officials prosecuted for acts committed in East Germany, though it would still permit espionage prosecutions for acts committed in West Germany.[59]

[55] Border Guards Prosecution Case, 100 ILR 366 (Ger. 1992); for commentary, *see* Manfred J. Gabriel, *Coming to Terms with the East German Border Guards Cases*, 38 COLUM. J. TRANSNAT'L L. 375 (1999); Matthias J. Herdegen, *Unjust Laws, Human Rights, and the German Constitution: Germany's Recent Confrontation with the Past*, 32 COLUM. J. TRANSNAT'L L. 591 (1995) (criticizing court's reasoning). Prosecutors estimate that some 825 people were killed attempting to flee East Germany between 1949 and 1989. Taryn Toro, *German Generals Face Berlin Wall Trial*, UPI, Aug. 17, 1995 (available on LEXIS/NEXIS).

[56] Peter E. Quint, *Judging the Past: The Prosecution of East German Border Guards and the GDR Chain of Command*, 61 REV. POL. 303, 304–07, 323 (1999); Edmund L. Andrews, *Ex-East German Chief Gets 6 Years for Deaths at Wall*, N.Y. TIMES, Aug. 26, 1997, at A6.

[57] Andrews, *supra* note 56; *Last Red jailed for killings at Wall*, THE INDEPENDENT, Aug. 26, 1997, at 10.

[58] *See, e.g.*, Justin Burke, *Retroactive Justice: Applying West German Rules to Ex-Reds*, CHRISTIAN SCIENCE MONITOR, Dec. 21, 1994, at 9. Mielke, however, had already been convicted and served time in prison for the murder of two policemen in 1931. *Id.*

[59] *See, e.g.*, Rick Atkinson, *East German Spy Masters Won't Face Jail; High Court Rules Bonn Cannot Prosecute Most Ex-Agents for Treason*, WASH. POST, May 24, 1995, at A1; Kinzer, *supra* note

Aside from these two categories of cases, prosecutors have also pursued East German political, judicial, and union figures on other charges. For example, former East German Prime Minister Hans Modrow was tried, though acquitted, for vote-rigging; union chief Harry Tisch was convicted of diverting public money to his own use, but was given a suspended sentence; and East German judges were convicted of false imprisonment and perversion of justice for participation in show trials of political dissidents, though appeals courts overturned most of these convictions.[60] Authorities have also pursued several charges against an East German figure who played a prominent role in arranging passage for spies and other individuals between East and West Germany; a Berlin court acquitted him, however, of extortion charges for allegedly helping clients leave the country in return for the right to buy their property at far below fair value.[61]

The prosecution of former East German officials has been a wrenching process for the country. Supporters of the prosecutions have been disappointed by the number of defendants who have escaped punishment. Opponents have challenged the trials on legal grounds and attacked them as hypocritical victor's justice and detrimental to national reconciliation. Egon Krenz summed up some of these sentiments when he wrote in an open letter to prosecutors: 'Courts are not empowered to punish people for carrying out acts that were part of a cold war. A government that once worked so closely with East Germany now presumes to judge and condemn that country.'[62]

Ethiopia

In 1991, a new transitional government under President Meles Zenawi came to power in Ethiopia following the overthrow of the repressive seventeen-year rule of the *Dergue* regime led by Mengitsu Haile-Mariam. The Mengitsu regime had compiled a long record of serious human rights abuses, including arbitrary detention, torture, disappearances, and extra-judicial executions. In addition, the military committed substantial violations of

54. The Supreme Court's ruling is likely to have the anomalous result of subjecting lower-ranking spies to punishment while immunizing higher-ranking officials, since the former were more likely to have carried out their activities outside of East Germany. A Berlin court ruled in 1991 that it could not try Wolf's successor on the ground that it would violate the principle of equality before the law, since West German spies were not being tried. Françoise Kadri, *Former East German Masterspy Sentenced to Six Years for Treason*, AGENCE FRANCE-PRESSE, Dec. 6, 1993 (available on LEXIS/NEXIS).

60 *See, e.g.*, Frank Bajak, *Court Narrows Scope of Prosecutions Against East Germany Judges*, AP WORLDSTREAM, Sept. 15, 1995 (available on LEXIS/NEXIS).

61 *See, e.g.*, Alan Cowell, *Germany Acquits East-West Go-Between of Extortion Charges*, N.Y. TIMES, Nov. 30, 1996, at A6; Kinzer, *supra* note 54.

62 Kinzer, *supra* note 54. For an excellent description of the dilemmas in Germany, *see generally* ROSENBERG, *supra* note 41, at 261–394.

international humanitarian law in connection with the country's internal conflict, and the regime's military and resettlement policies resulted in large numbers of famine-related deaths.[63]

Upon coming to power, the transitional government announced its intention to bring to justice those officials of the former regime responsible for human rights violations between 1974 and 1991.[64] By 2000, the government held over 2,000 officials and soldiers and had charged over 5,000 individuals for offenses including genocide and crimes against humanity.[65] However, the large number of potential defendants and the legal system's limited resources may force the government to consider plea bargaining or granting amnesty to some offenders.[66] The government is trying the detainees in three phases: first, policy- and decision-makers, senior government officials, and senior military commanders; secondly, military and civilian field commanders; and lastly, actual perpetrators of the atrocities. Among the first group is former President Mengitsu who, along with many other defendants, is being tried *in absentia*.

Although the government has held most of the detainees since 1991, the lack of a functioning court system and resources delayed trials of the first group of forty-six defendants until December 1994, and the trials continued through 2000. The charges brought against the first group include both international crimes under international instruments and as codified in Ethiopian law, and common crimes under Ethiopian law. Those convicted will face imprisonment and, in most cases, the death penalty. The government has indicated its intention to seek the death penalty, particularly for the most serious offenders, and the first such sentence was handed down (*in absentia*) in November 1999.[67]

The government has established a special prosecutor's office to conduct the prosecutions.[68] The office also functions as a quasi-truth

[63] *See* AMNESTY INTERNATIONAL, ETHIOPIA, ACCOUNTABILITY PAST AND PRESENT: HUMAN RIGHTS IN TRANSITION 4 (Apr., 1995); ALEXANDER DE WAAL, EVIL DAYS: THIRTY YEARS OF WAR AND FAMINE IN ETHIOPIA (1991); HUMAN RIGHTS WATCH/AFRICA, ETHIOPIA, RECKONING UNDER THE LAW 5–7, 18–23 (Dec., 1994); Alan Zarembo, *In Ethiopia, Time to Settle Accounts*, SAN FRANCISCO CHRON., Apr. 29, 1995, at A1.

[64] *See* AMNESTY INTERNATIONAL, *supra* note 63, at 4–28 (criticizing limitation to former regime officials); John Balzer, *A Day of Reckoning in Ethiopia*, L.A. TIMES, Dec. 13, 1994, at A1.

[65] *See* AMNESTY INTERNATIONAL, *supra* note 63, at 29–30, 32; HUMAN RIGHTS WATCH/AFRICA, *supra* note 63, at 14–15; *Thousands in Ethiopia Accused of Crimes Under Old Regime*, N.Y. TIMES, Feb. 14, 1997, at A6.

[66] HUMAN RIGHTS WATCH/AFRICA, *supra* note 63, at 13, 26–29.

[67] *Id.* at 14, 17, 24; AMNESTY INTERNATIONAL, *supra* note 63, at 30; *see generally* James C. McKinley Jr., *Ethiopia Tries Former Rulers In 70's Deaths*, N.Y. TIMES, Apr. 23, 1996, at A1 (also noting inconsistencies regarding definition of genocide under Ethiopian law); Amnesty International, Ethiopia: First death sentence in Dergue trials, Nov. 12, 1999, available at www.amnesty.org/news/1999/12501099.htm.

[68] *See* Tore Sverdrup Engelschiøn, *Ethiopia: War Crimes and Violations of Human Rights*, 34 REVUE DE DROIT MILITAIRE ET DE DROIT DE LA GUERRE 9 (1995).

commission, as its mandate includes the creation of a historical record of the former regime's human rights abuses. It consists of four teams roughly corresponding to the main categories of crimes being prosecuted, and it has a staff of several hundred, including a handful of foreign advisors. Prosecutors have amassed an enormous record of physical and testimonial evidence, including the regime's own meticulous records, films of torture sessions, and forensic evidence from mass graves. However, the office's lack of experience and resources has hampered and delayed the prosecution's work.[69]

As with many countries emerging from national traumas, Ethiopia's protracted civil conflict and history of repression left its judicial system weak and lacking any tradition of independence. Many experienced judges fled the country during the Mengitsu regime, and many who remained are ineligible to serve due to their connections to the former regime. In 1993, the government created a new independent court system, separated into national and regional systems. As with the prosecutor's office, a severe lack of resources has hindered the new judicial system's development and imposed obstacles to its effectiveness, fairness, and independence.[70]

Foreign entities have closely followed and participated in the government's prosecution program. The prosecutor's office has received technical and personnel assistance from governments and NGOs, and foreign assistance has also funded the provision of defense counsel. Foreign consultants have assisted with the collection and computerized indexing of evidence and advised on matters of international law and trial strategy. Trials are open to international observers, and several NGOs are monitoring the proceedings.[71]

The Ethiopian prosecutions represent a highly ambitious program by a developing country to bring perpetrators of human rights abuses to justice before its domestic judicial system. However, the scope of the offenses, the large number of defendants, and the vast amounts of evidence have placed a heavy burden on the Ethiopian government and challenged its capacity to carry out the prosecutions in a fair and effective manner. Although defendants enjoy the right to defense and appeal, human rights groups have criticized the government's handling of the prosecutions on a number of counts. NGOs have complained about the holding of detainees without charge and accused the government of violating the right of defendants to communicate confidentially with counsel. Serious questions remain about

[69] Human Rights Watch/Africa, *supra* note 63, at 11–12, 15–16; *Ethiopia's State Terror on Trial*, Economist, Dec. 17, 1994, at 43.

[70] Human Rights Watch/Africa, *supra* note 63, at 11–13 (also asserting that division of jurisdiction may cause logistical difficulties).

[71] *Id.* at 12, 15.

the competence and impartiality of the judiciary. Ethiopian criminal procedure does not conform fully with international standards, and not all defendants will have access to adequate counsel and prosecution evidence, due in part to the public defender's office's dearth of resources.[72]

Rwanda

Rwanda's response to the 1994 genocide against the Tutsi population illustrates the perils of attempting to prosecute a huge group of participants in mass atrocities. As is now well known, following several years of civil conflict, Rwanda's Hutu-dominated government and the primarily Tutsi Rwandan Patriotic Front (RPF) insurgency agreed to a comprehensive peace plan in 1993. The downing of a plane carrying the Rwandan president in April 1994, however, scuttled the peace plan and plunged the country into several months of genocidal violence that left between 500,000 and 1,000,000 Rwandans dead. Observers attributed the bulk of the violence to the Hutu-dominated military and Hutu paramilitaries, who had opposed the peace plan and seized the opportunity to eliminate systematically the country's Tutsi minority. By mid-summer 1994, the RPF had defeated the government forces and established a new government. It pledged to bring to justice all those who had participated in the genocidal violence and detained large numbers of suspects. While the Security Council established an international tribunal to try high-ranking offenders,[73] the new Rwandan government maintained its intention to try all other offenders and enacted legislation for this purpose.[74]

However, the destruction from the civil conflict and the flight of the former government left Rwanda without a functioning judicial system. In fact, the Rwandan government did not begin to try its first defendant until the last days of 1996. By 2000, over 2,500 had been tried, with several hundred sentenced to death and 800 sentenced to life imprisonment. Twenty-two were executed in public in April 1998.[75] Meanwhile, the

[72] Amnesty International, *supra* note 67; HUMAN RIGHTS WATCH/AFRICA, *supra* note 63, at 13–14, 33–35; AMNESTY INTERNATIONAL, *supra* note 63, at 31; *see also* Julie V. Mayfield, *The Prosecution of War Crimes and Respect for Human Rights: Ethiopia's Balancing Act*, 9 EMORY INT'L L. REV. 553, 575–92 (1995).

[73] SC Res. 955, UN SCOR, 49th Year, Res. and Dec., at 15, UN Doc. S/INF/50 (1994); *see also* Ch. 9, The International Criminal Tribunal for Rwanda, *infra*.

[74] For a review of the statute, *see* Mark A. Drumbl, *Rule of Law Amid Lawlessness: Counselling the Accused in Rwanda's Domestic Genocide Trials*, 29 COLUM. HUM. RTS. L. REV. 545, 576–601 (1998); Catherine Cissé, *The End of a Culture of Impunity in Rwanda? Prosecution of Genocide and War Crimes before Rwandan Courts and the International Criminal Tribunal for Rwanda*, 1 Y.B. INT'L HUMAN. L. 161, 175–84 (1998); *see also* William A. Schabas, *Justice, Democracy, and Impunity in Post-genocide Rwanda: Searching for Solutions to Impossible Problems*, 7 CRIM. L. F. 523 (1996).

[75] AMNESTY INTERNATIONAL, RWANDA: THE TROUBLED COURSE OF JUSTICE (Apr. 2000), § I.2, available at www.amnesty.org.

government continues to detain suspects without charge in severely overcrowded facilities under appalling conditions. As of late 2000, the government was holding some 125,000 detainees—including minors, the aged, and the infirm—in facilities designed to hold only a small fraction of that number, and the return of refugees continues to fuel additional arrests. Thousands of detainees have died as a result of conditions in the prisons, in particular those organized at the communal level. Beatings and torture have been common, though foreign assistance helped improve conditions somewhat.

Arrests seldom follow any genuine criminal investigations and usually result from mere accusations, often motivated by political rivalry or other illegitimate reasons. Prisoners are detained without due process; few have had their detention reviewed by a judicial officer. Although the government established 'triage commissions' in 1995 to confirm that detentions are supported by adequate evidence, these commissions have been ineffective. The trials thus far suggest that even those who eventually are tried are not receiving the minimal due process to which they are entitled. Statutory provisions for reduced sentences in exchange for confessions have not resulted in speedier justice, and by 2000 the government was considering a plan for transferring many cases to a non-court system of traditional justice known as *gacaca*, involving trials of accused before local tribunals of their peers.[76]

The country's abject poverty, recent violence, and the absence of any tradition of judicial independence meant that the Rwandan judicial system would clearly require substantial international support if it were ever to carry out fair and effective trials. However, international assistance to rebuild the judicial system and relieve prison overcrowding was initially insufficient and slow. Though still inadequate, the scale and pace of foreign aid picked up toward the end of 1995. Foreign governments, the UN, and NGOs have supplied resources, personnel, and training for prosecutors, defense counsel, and judges, but progress remains very slow.[77]

Prospects for fair and effective trials or release of the improperly detained thus remain distant. Though resources are scarce, the main impediments appear to be internal political ones. The government has remained preoccupied with the threat of insurgency from the former regime. In addition, it has proved paralyzed at resolving certain critical issues, including the use of confessions, priorities for prosecution, and

[76] *See, e.g.*, Amnesty International, *supra* note 75; Report on the situation of human rights in Rwanda submitted by the Special Representative, Mr. Michel Moussalli, pursuant to Commission resolution 1999/20, Feb. 25, 2000, UN Doc. E/CN.4/2000/41, paras. 92–168 [hereinafter Rwanda Human Rights Report].

[77] *See* Rwanda Human Rights Report, *supra* note 76, paras. 134–48; Drumbl, *supra* note 74, at 601–22.

appointment of judges. Victim groups and some extremist anti-Hutu elements, motivated by a virulent anti-Hutu ideology and fearful that the judicial process may discredit their claims that all Hutu were responsible for the genocide, have exploited this paralysis to delay the release of detainees and the holding of trials.[78] The adoption of the *gacaca* system would represent a bold new attempt to bring about justice outside the context of a courtroom. It nonetheless faces its own set of obstacles, ranging from logistics, to protection of defendants' rights, to the necessity for witnesses to confront their neighbors. Only its speedy implementation, combined with more releases, will serve to ameliorate the overwhelming problems of pre-trial detention.[79]

PROSECUTIONS BEFORE NATIONAL COURTS OF OTHER STATES

Trials outside the state where atrocities have been committed represent yet another option for the enforcement of criminal law against human rights atrocities. This method permits criminal accountability despite the absence of an effective legal system in the state of commission or of an international court and eliminates a source of refuge for some human rights abusers. Countries seeking to try offenders for crimes committed abroad might be exercising jurisdiction based on the nationality of the offender or the nationality of the victim. If the states have no direct ties to the offenses, it is necessary that the crimes give rise to universal jurisdiction and that the prosecuting state take full advantage of that jurisdiction. In any case, they must have enacted criminal codes permitting prosecutions for extra-territorial acts or allow for prosecution directly under international law. Prosecutions for human rights atrocities committed outside a state by foreigners were rare until the mid-1990s. Since that time, we have witnessed a significant number, though not all reaching the stage of a verdict.

Special Statutes Concerning International Offenses

International offenses committed abroad may be prosecuted under specific statutes states have promulgated to comply with treaty requirements. In some cases, the treaties themselves specify that the state prescribe law to address extraterritorial acts. For example, states meeting

78 *See generally* AMNESTY INTERNATIONAL, *supra* note 75, § III.1.
79 Rwanda Human Rights Report, *supra* note 76, paras. 148–68.

their obligations under the 1984 Torture Convention will have laws in force permitting prosecution for torture committed beyond their borders.[80] Similarly, states fulfilling their duties under the 1949 Geneva Conventions, Protocol I, or both should have legislation necessary to criminalize grave breaches regardless of the place of commission.[81]

Moreover, some states have promulgated legislation that covers extraterritorial conduct even though the relevant treaty that the state is implementing does not require penalization of such acts. For example, both the United States and France have criminal statutes on genocide that go further than the Convention's requirement to penalize genocide based on territoriality alone; US law provides for nationality jurisdiction, while French law provides for nationality and passive personality-based jurisdiction.[82]

Indeed, states have also promulgated domestic laws concerning international offenses apart from those related to specific treaty obligations. For example, the Belgian, Spanish, Swedish, and US war crimes statutes cover acts beyond grave breaches of the Geneva Conventions, including violations of Protocol II.[83] The 1992 French law on genocide also addresses crimes against humanity, and the 1999 Belgian law covers genocide and crimes against humanity; France has also asserted jurisdiction over persons committing crimes defined in the UN's Yugoslavia and Rwanda Statutes.[84] The Canadian law on war crimes and crimes against

[80] *See, e.g.*, Code de procédure pénale, art. 689–2 (Fr.); 18 U.S.C. § 2340A (1994); Crimes (Torture) Act, 1988 Austl. Acts No. 148, § 6; Criminal Justice Act, 1988, ch. 33, § 134 (Eng.).

[81] *See, e.g.*, 18 U.S.C. § 2441 (1998 Supp. IV) (covering broad range of war crimes committed anywhere, but only by or against Americans); Geneva Conventions Act, 1957 Austl. Acts No. 103, § 7, as amended by Geneva Conventions Amendment Act, 1991 Austl. Acts No. 27, § 5.

[82] 18 U.S.C. § 1091 (1994); Nouveau Code pénal, arts. 211–1, 113–6, 113–7 (Fr.). *See also* Lei No. 7.209, July 11, 1984, D.O. de 13.07.1984, arts. 7(I)(d) & 7(II)(a) (Braz.), *reprinted in* 5 Coleção das Leis 38, 39 (1984) (permitting prosecution for genocide committed anywhere by Brazilian citizen or resident).

[83] Law of 16 June 1993, 2 Codes Belges (Bruylant), at 240/5 (62d Supp. 1996); Codigo Penal (1995), arts. 607–14 (Spain), *translated at* 1 Y.B. INT'L HUMAN. LAW 636 (1998); SWEDISH PENAL CODE 1986, ch. 22, § 11 (National Council for Crime Prevention Sweden trans., 1986). The US statute, *supra* note 81, will cover violations of Protocol II when the United States becomes a party to it. *See also* Thomas Graditzky, *Individual criminal responsibility for violations of international humanitarian law committed in non-international armed conflicts*, 322 INT'L REV. RED CROSS 29, 38–44 (1998) (discussing other laws); Kai Ambos, *Aktuelle Probleme der deutschen Verfolgung von 'Kriegsverbrechen' in Bosnien-Herzegowina*, 5 NEUE ZEITSCHRIFT FÜR STRAFRECHT 226 (1999) (on prosecuting civil war crimes in Germany); *see generally* André Andries, *Investigations et Poursuites des Violations du Droit des Conflits Armés, Partie I: Lois et Procédures Nationales*, 37 REVUE DE DROIT MILITAIRE ET DE DROIT DE LA GUERRE 179 (1998).

[84] Nouveau Code pénal, art. 212–1 (Fr.); Law of 10 February 1999, MONITEUR BELGE, Mar. 23, 1999, at 9286; Loi No. 95–1 of 2 January 1995 (Fr.), J.O. 3 Jan. 1995, at 71; Loi No. 96–432 of 22 May 1996 (Fr.), J.O. 23 May 1996, at 7695; *see also* Brigitte Stern, *La compétence universelle en France: le cas des crimes commis en ex-Yougoslavie et au Rwanda*, 40 GER. Y.B. INT'L L. 280, 296–98 (1997).

humanity under which Imre Finta was prosecuted permits prosecution of a foreigner for acts against other foreigners committed abroad if, at the time of the crimes, Canada could exercise jurisdiction over the person based only on his presence in Canada, and the accused is later present in Canada.[85] The United Kingdom and Australia also have war crimes laws concerning acts committed during World War II, in addition to statutes meant to meet their obligations under the Geneva Conventions.[86] The Israeli law under which Adolf Eichmann was prosecuted concerns only crimes during the Nazi period 'in an enemy country'.[87]

Despite the obligation in various treaties to prosecute, or to extradite or prosecute, offenders, state practice until the mid-1990s revealed an unwillingness of states to punish atrocities committed abroad, even more so if the crime was not committed by or against their nationals. Nevertheless, two recent developments suggest a clear move in the direction of further domestic prosecutions outside the states where the atrocities took place. First, after the establishment of the Yugoslavia and Rwanda Tribunals, a number of European states have begun to prosecute offenders found in their territory, relying upon domestic statutes implementing the Geneva Conventions or other treaties. For suspects in the Yugoslavia conflict, these trials have led to convictions (and thus affirmative findings of jurisdiction) in Denmark, Germany, and the Netherlands; acquittals after trial (and affirmative findings of jurisdiction) in Austria and Switzerland; and a disturbing finding of lack of jurisdiction in a 1996 French case.[88] For suspects in the Rwandan genocide, these trials have led to a conviction in Switzerland and ongoing proceedings in France and Belgium.[89]

[85] R.S.C. 1985, ch. C-46, § 7 (3.71)(b); *see generally* Regina v. Finta, [1994] 1 S.C.R. 701.

[86] War Crimes Act, 1991, ch. 13, § 1(1) (Eng.); War Crimes Amendment Act, 1989 Austl. Acts No. 3, § 9(1).

[87] Nazi and Nazi Collaborators (Punishment) Law, 5710/1950, § 1(a), *reprinted in Eichmann*, 36 ILR at 7.

[88] In re Saric (Danish High Court 1994), *summarized and analyzed in* Rafaëlle Maison, *Les premiers cas d'application des dispositions pénales des Conventions de Genève par les jurisdictions internes*, 6 EJIL 260 (1995); Public Prosecutor v. Djajić, 1998 Neue Juristische Wochenscrift 392 (Sup. Ct. of Bavaria), *summarized and analyzed in* Christoph J.M. Safferling, 92 AJIL 528 (1998); In re Knesević, Case No. 3717 (Neth. Sup. Ct. 1997), *translated at* 1 Y.B. INT'L HUMAN. LAW 600 (1998); In re Cvjetkovic (Austria Regional Court at Salzburg 1995), *Bosnian Serb not guilty in war trial*, THE HERALD (Glasgow), June 1, 1995, at 9; In re G (Swiss Military Tribunal, Division I), *translated in* HOW DOES LAW PROTECT IN WAR? 1255 (Marco Sassòli and Antoine A. Bouvier eds., 1999) (acquittal); In re Javor, 1996 Bull. crim., No. 132, at 379 (Fr. Cour de Cassation 1996), *translated in* HOW DOES LAW PROTECT IN WAR?, *supra*, at 1252; *see also* 19 Neue Zeitschrift für Strafrecht 236 (1999) (case in German Federal Court of Justice (Bundesgerichtshof) finding no jurisdiction for prosecution for genocide and war crimes when only the victim, and not the accused, was on German soil). For a critique of the outcome in the French case, *see* Stern, *supra* note 84, at 290–94.

[89] *See, e.g., Rwanda: Former Rwandan Major Gets Life in Swiss Trial*, AFRICA NEWS, May 3, 1999 (available on LEXIS/NEXIS); In re Munyeshyaka, 1998 Bull. crim, No. 2, at 3 (Fr. Cour de Cassation 1998), *translated at* 1 Y.B. INT'L HUMAN. LAW 598 (1998).

Second, and perhaps more significant for the target of the prosecution and the attention they have received, investigating judges in Spain and other states have relied on principles of universal jurisdiction to bring charges against former officials of the Chilean, Argentine, and Guatemalan military regimes of the 1970s and 1980s, most notably General Augusto Pinochet. Spain's highest court has upheld Spanish jurisdiction to investigate and try acts of terrorism and genocide in Chile and Argentina; and at Spain's request, the United Kingdom detained General Pinochet during the course of a private visit to London in 1998, although after protracted legal proceedings, it released him on health grounds in March 2000.[90] In addition, a Belgian court has recognized universal jurisdiction as a basis for prosecuting General Pinochet for crimes against humanity, based on direct incorporation of customary international law, despite the absence of any Belgian statute on the issue at the time of the offenses.[91] In January 2000, a criminal court in Senegal began an investigation into the actions of ex-Chadian dictator Hissene Habre, who has been in exile in Senegal since his ouster in 1990.[92]

Ordinary Criminal Laws of Extraterritorial Application

Beyond statutes addressed specifically to international offenses, the criminal laws of some states envisage general extraterritorial application for common crimes. France permits prosecution of French citizens for acts committed outside France that would be crimes under French law; it also permits prosecution of non-French citizens for crimes against French citizens. For other crimes by non-French citizens, extraterritorial jurisdiction is limited, primarily to crimes against the French state.[93] The United

[90] *See* Richard J. Wilson, *Prosecuting Pinochet: International Crimes in Spanish Domestic Law*, 21 HUM. RTS. Q. 927 (1999); Lanchin, *supra* note 38. The Spanish law providing for such jurisdiction is the Ley Orgánica de Poder Judicial (1985), art. 23(4). For cases in the UK House of Lords (which primarily address extradition and immunity matters, rather than jurisdiction), *see* Regina v. Bow Street Metropolitan Stipendiary Magistrate, Ex Part Pinochet Ugarte, [1998] 4 All E.R. 897 (House of Lords), [1999] 2 All E.R. 97 (House of Lords), *summarized and analyzed in* Christine Chinkin, *International Decisions*, 93 AJIL 703 (1999). *See also* text at note 97, *infra*, on cases based on passive personality principle jurisdiction over ordinary crimes.

[91] Ruling of the Belgian Tribunal of First Instance of Brussels, Nov. 8, 1998, *summarized in* Luc Reydams, *International Decisions*, 93 AJIL 700 (1999). On other Belgian investigations into foreign leaders, *see* Emmanuel Defouloy, *La Belgique genée et isolée dans son application du droit international*, AGENCE FRANCE PRESSE, July 7, 2000 (available on LEXIS/NEXIS); Case Concerning the Arrest Warrant of 11 April 2000 (Dem. Rep. of Congo v. Belg.), Order of Dec. 8, 2000 (refusing to order Belgium to annul arrest warrant of former Congo foreign minister for crimes against humanity).

[92] *See* Norimitsu Onishi, *An African Dictator Faces Trial in His Place of Refuge*, N.Y. TIMES, Mar. 1, 2000, at A3. Senegal's Court of Appeal quashed the indictment in July 2000. Dutch courts are also investigating former Surinamese leader Desi Bouterse for torture and crimes against humanity.

[93] Nouveau Code pénal, art. 113–6, 113–7, 113–10 (Fr.); Code de procédure pénale, art. 689 (Fr.); *see also* GASTON STEFANI, GEORGES LEVASSEUR, AND BERNARD BOULOC, PROCÉDURE PÉNALE 455–63 (17th ed. 2000).

Kingdom permits prosecutions for murder and manslaughter committed by British citizens anywhere.[94]

In other examples, the Swedish Penal Code permits trials of Swedish citizens or aliens domiciled there for crimes committed overseas if the act is punishable under the law of the place where it was committed as well as in other specified cases, including violations of international law.[95] The United States has no such general provisions, but rather confines extraterritorial criminal jurisdiction over non-American defendants to specific areas such as terrorist acts.[96] Extraterritorial criminal law has been invoked in several states to attempt prosecutions of Argentine and Chilean officials for acts against those states' nationals. In 1990, France tried and convicted *in absentia* Alfredo Astiz for the disappearance of two French nuns in Argentina, and a French case against General Pinochet is also proceeding based on the French nationality of the victim. Similar proceedings against other Argentine officers have begun in Italy, France, and Spain.[97]

OPPORTUNITIES AND CHALLENGES

National courts represent the primary forum for prosecuting human rights abuses. Where trials take place in the country where the offenses occurred, the entire process becomes more deeply connected with the society, providing it with the potential to create a strong psychological and deterrent effect on the population. This factor, combined with the greater access to evidence, witnesses, victims, and perpetrators, gives such tribunals a significant potential advantage over international tribunals.[98] Compared to international tribunals, prosecutions before national tribunals are also relatively inexpensive and generally easier to institute.

As an initial matter, the jurisdictional principles described at the beginning of this chapter afford ample authority for states to pursue accountability through their domestic judicial systems. At the very least, the state

[94] Offences against the Person Act, 1861, 24 & 25 Vict., ch. 100, § 9 (Eng.); *see also* BLACKSTONE'S CRIMINAL PRACTICE 916 (Peter Murphy ed., 1994).

[95] SWEDISH PENAL CODE 1986, *supra* note 83, ch. 2, §§ 2, 3(5).

[96] *See, e.g.*, 18 U.S.C. §§ 1203, 2331 (1994).

[97] *See, e.g.*, Laurent Greilsamer, *Pour séquestration et torture de deux religieuses françaises le capitaine argentin Alfredo Astiz est condamné à la reclusion criminelle à perpetuité par contumace*, LE MONDE, Mar. 19, 1990, at 1; Michael A. Meyer, *Liability of Prisoners of War for Offences Committed Prior to Capture: The Astiz Affair*, 32 INT'L AND COMP. L.Q. 948 (1983); Brigitte Stern, *International Decisions*, 93 AJIL 696 (1999); Tim Weiner and Ginger Thompson, *Wide Net in Argentine Torture Case*, N.Y. TIMES, Sept. 11, 2000, at A6; *Italy sentences two Argentinian ex-military chiefs to life*, AGENCE FRANCE-PRESSE, Dec. 6, 2000 (available on LEXIS/NEXIS).

[98] *See* Ch. 9, *infra*, on the difficulties of international criminal prosecutions. For a strong advocacy of the domestic option, *see also* Jose E. Alvarez, *Crimes of States, Crimes of Hate: Lessons from Rwanda*, 24 YALE J. INT'L L. 365, 459–62 (1999).

in whose territory human rights abuses occur, as well as the state of the offender's nationality, will have jurisdiction to prosecute them, and universal jurisdiction applies to a growing corpus of offenses. Yet states have proven very reluctant to exercise even a limited degree of the jurisdiction afforded by international law. In some cases, this may be due to the dysfunctional state of the country's judicial system. However, the most critical reason for the lack of prosecutions, even based on the territoriality or nationality principles, is that serious violations of international human rights or humanitarian law are usually committed on behalf of or with the complicity of the state. Within the context of national systems, aside from the overthrow of the regime, this problem can only be remedied by the development of genuinely independent judiciaries and of political cultures less tolerant of human rights abuses.

National prosecutions will yield benefits only if the judicial system is generally fair and effective. Based on the precedents examined here, a fair and effective judiciary requires four fundamental conditions: a workable legal framework through well-crafted statutes of criminal law and procedure; a trained cadre of judges, prosecutors, defenders, and investigators; adequate infrastructure, such as courtroom facilities, investigative offices, record-keeping capabilities, and detention and prison facilities; and, most important, a culture of respect for the fairness and impartiality of the process and the rights of the accused. In many countries, these conditions are woefully lacking, though, as the Ethiopian case indicates, a concerted program with foreign assistance to prosecute human rights abuses can help develop these conditions.

At the same time, these four conditions must be seen in the context of a state's overall economic and political condition. To demand identical sorts of prosecutions in poor states or those emerging from civil strife as would occur in rich or stable countries would defy reality. Although prosecutions within an inadequate system may have a detrimental impact on both accountability and the rule of law in a country, the standard for justice must acknowledge these factors. International law has developed minimal standards in many areas,[99] and although some must be applied uniformly (e.g., the ban on coerced confessions), others must be viewed in a case-by-case context.

The case studies above present some important general lessons for nations attempting to prosecute human rights violators before their national courts. First, Ethiopia and Rwanda represent important analogues for other desperately poor countries with defunct judicial systems lacking any tradition of independence. In both states, the demands placed on their

[99] *See, e.g.*, the list in GA Res. 48/137, preamb. para. 5, UN GAOR, 48th Sess., Supp. No. 49, at 256, U.N. Doc. A/48/49 (1993).

criminal justice systems have outstripped available resources. Serious backlogs and lapses in procedural safeguards have resulted, yielding criticism from the international community that prosecutions are failing to meet international standards. Their experiences thus underscore the enormous importance of adequate resources and the critical role of foreign assistance in developing a fair and effective domestic judicial process. Where feasible, such governments, perhaps with the assistance of international organizations and NGOs, should explore establishing special judicial processes and programs for conducting trials that make use of resources and expertise from abroad. Such special processes might involve mixed tribunals of domestic and foreign judges or the dispatch of foreign legal experts, as Ethiopia has enjoyed. (The United Nations has considered this option for Cambodia and Sierra Leone as well.) At the same time, the Ethiopian experience also counsels NGOs and foreign governments to avoid interfering too aggressively in the prosecutorial process and to defer appropriately to local officials, lest they alienate them. Finally, the Ethiopian and Rwandan cases caution against overzealous prosecutions, highlighting the need to ensure that the scope of the prosecutions is calibrated to the capacity of the judicial system that will carry them out. Indeed, as Rwanda shows, in the end, states with exceptionally large numbers of targets will have to consider alternatives to Western-style trials, such as traditional justice (consistent with minimal human rights standards) and partial amnesties.

Secondly, Rwanda and Argentina dramatize the political dimensions of prosecuting former regime members where the opponents of accountability have the capacity to derail the process. In Rwanda, the lack of consensus on crucial aspects of the prosecutions and the absence of strong and stable political leadership have paralyzed the prosecutorial process. Rwanda's experience clearly suggests that prosecutions will succeed only if supported by a stable and united government. Indeed, if a nation's leaders allow prosecutions to become a pawn in the competition for power, the trials will lack credibility and damage the foundations of democracy. In Argentina, prosecutions eventually galvanized elements of the discredited, though not impotent, military to challenge the young and insecure civilian government, thereby putting an end to the prosecutorial process. Argentina's experience counsels governments to manage the process carefully and ensure that the scope of prosecutions does not exceed the government's power *vis-à-vis* other elements. At the same time, successor regimes may tend to underestimate their power and maneuvering room, and outside actors—states, international organizations, and NGOs—can often help strengthen regimes seeking accountability and defuse threats from the opponents of prosecutions.

The German prosecutions illustrate some of the legal conundrums and impediments in prosecuting members of a prior regime and the resultant frustrations when a prosecutorial program fails to live up to expectations. The prosecutions have confronted the German legal system with complicated jurisprudential puzzles stemming from the unusual history of relations between the two Germanys and the ostensible legitimacy of the defendants' acts under East German law.[100] In the case of countries with less developed legal systems or which have experienced periods of political upheaval, difficulties in discerning the applicable law may be even more vexing. Germany's experience thus emphasizes the need for governmental authorities to clarify the applicable law and to refrain from raising expectations excessively in the event the government pursues prosecutions. Equally significant, the German trials demonstrate the shortcomings of prosecutions as a form of accountability where, as in the case of ex-communist states, a sizeable portion of the populace has played some role in the former regime's abuses. Those defendants in the dock represent only the tip of the iceberg, and their trial may indeed distract a society from examining its own part in prior events.[101]

Finally, as for states without a territorial or nationality connection to the offenses or offender, they have traditionally chosen not to exercise the full extent of their universal jurisdiction, although the actual or attempted prosecutions of Bosnian war criminals, Rwandan genocide suspects, Augusto Pinochet, Hissene Habre, and others is evidence of an important new trend. No doubt, the impulse not to prosecute often stems from a predisposition to avoid foreign relations tensions that might result when the courts of one state adjudicate matters that transpired elsewhere and to conserve judicial resources. However, the enforcement of human rights remains a duty incumbent on all states, and if prosecutors exercise their discretion prudently, are guided by the evidence, and remain respectful of defendants' rights, these risks can be minimized. Trials by outside states can avoid many of the political tensions of proceedings where the crime occurred; yet they still risk a lesser impact on the relevant population and face logistical obstacles due to the distance from the crimes.[102] Moreover, attempts by outside states may embolden victims, prosecutors, and judges at home to initiate investigations and trials, as appears to have happened with Chile's attempts to prosecute General Pinochet after Spanish prosecutors began proceedings in Spain.

The greatest tensions are likely to arise if a state exercises its jurisdiction against the views of other directly interested states. This could occur

100 *See* Herdegen, *supra* note 55.

101 ROSENBERG, *supra* note 41, at 404–05.

102 A unique iteration on this modality is the trial in a Scottish court sitting in the Netherlands of two Libyans accused of planting a bomb on a Pan Am 747 in 1988. *See* Ch. 11, note 46, *infra*.

through abduction of defendants from a state of refuge—a course of action rarely employed and even more rarely justifiable—or through arrests of travelling former officials (such as General Pinochet) or *in absentia* trials (as in the case of some Italian and Spanish prosecutions). Prosecutions opposed by an ex-official's government clearly help combat a culture of impunity by essentially forcing human rights abusers to remain at home. Yet they nonetheless raise profound moral questions about the degree of deference that states undertaking unilateral prosecutions should afford the decisions of the ex-official's government not to prosecute when these decisions are made as part of a transition to a post-conflict democratic government.

9

The Progeny of Nuremberg: International Criminal Tribunals

The challenges and limitations of prosecuting international crimes through domestic law enforcement institutions have led states, international organizations, and non-governmental organizations periodically to contemplate the creation of international criminal courts that could directly try individuals for such crimes. Yet despite occasional initiatives to establish a permanent international criminal tribunal, such a tribunal did not emerge until the late 1990s. Instead, states have set up *ad hoc* international criminal tribunals, with the Nuremberg Tribunal the most significant historically. These tribunals have been established only in exceptional circumstances, and many states regard them as an extraordinary, and even threatening, law enforcement mechanism.

This Chapter examines the major international criminal tribunals, all of which emerged after World War II. After briefly describing two courts that arose directly from the war and that long ago completed their work—the Nuremberg and Tokyo Tribunals—it turns to two ongoing tribunals that emerged from horrific contemporary conflicts—the tribunals for the former Yugoslavia and Rwanda. In addition, this Chapter examines UN efforts to create a permanent international criminal court and concludes with a brief note on the role of the International Court of Justice and regional human rights courts.

THE NUREMBERG AND RELATED TRIBUNALS

The international military tribunals established after World War II remain the most celebrated international criminal courts in history.[1] Under the Allies' November 1943 Moscow Declaration, minor Nazi war criminals would be judged and punished in the countries where they committed their crimes, while 'the major war criminals, whose offenses have no

[1] The first reported international prosecutions date back several centuries. Plans for the trial of German defendants after World War I proved highly unsuccessful. *See*, *e.g.*, Howard S. Levie, *Criminality in the Law of War*, *in* 1 INTERNATIONAL CRIMINAL LAW 381, 382–83 (M. Cherif Bassiouni ed., 2d ed. 1999); Remigiusz Bierzanek, *War Crimes: History and Definition*, *in* 3 INTERNATIONAL CRIMINAL LAW, *supra*, at 87, 89–95.

particular geographical localization' would be tried and punished 'by joint decision of the Governments of the Allies'.[2] On August 8, 1945, the Allies signed the London Agreement by which they adopted the Charter of the International Military Tribunal.[3] In addition to the Nuremberg Tribunal, several thousand Nazi war criminals were tried before national courts or before tribunals administered by the Allies after the war.[4] In January 1946, the Allies created the International Military Tribunal for the Far East, which, unlike the tribunal at Nuremberg, was established by unilateral proclamation—that of General Douglas MacArthur, Supreme Allied Commander. As in the case of Germany, alongside the Tokyo Tribunal's work, national tribunals tried thousands of Japanese for war crimes.[5]

The Nuremberg Tribunal

The London Agreement and IMT Charter set forth the jurisdiction, substantive law, and procedural principles governing the Nuremberg Tribunal. Article 6 of the Charter granted the Tribunal jurisdiction over individuals who, as individuals or as members of organizations, committed crimes against peace, war crimes, or crimes against humanity. In addition, Article 6 imposed responsibility on leaders, organizers, instigators, and accomplices for all acts performed in execution of a common plan or conspiracy. The Agreement limited the Tribunal's jurisdiction to those war criminals whose crimes had no particular location and stressed that the Tribunal would not prejudice the jurisdiction of any of the national or occupation courts.[6]

The Tribunal had four judges, one appointed by each of the major Allied powers. Governed by its Charter and rules adopted by the Tribunal, procedure before the Nuremberg Tribunal was based on the Anglo-American adversarial system. The Charter afforded defendants certain rights, including the right to counsel, to present evidence, to testify on their own behalf, and to cross-examine witnesses. However, Article 12 of the Charter authorized trials *in absentia*. The Tribunal could order any punishment upon conviction, including restitution of stolen property,

[2] Declaration of German Atrocities, Nov. 1, 1943, *reprinted in* 38 AJIL (Supp.) 3, 7–8 (1944). A defendant's status as a major or minor criminal depended on rank, not on the seriousness of the crime with which they had been charged.

[3] Agreement for the prosecution and punishment of the major war criminals of the European Axis, Aug. 8, 1945, 59 Stat. 1544, 82 UNTS 279. 19 other states subsequently acceded to the Agreement.

[4] National military tribunals also prosecuted some Allied nationals for war crimes and crimes against humanity after the war.

[5] R. John Pritchard, *The International Military Tribunal for the Far East and the Allied National War Crimes Trials in Asia*, *in* 3 International Criminal Law, *supra* note 1, at 109.

[6] Agreement for the prosecution and punishment of the major war criminals of the European Axis, *supra* note 3, arts. 1, 4, 6, 82 UNTS at 282.

imprisonment, and the death penalty. Judgments of the Tribunal were final and not subject to review. The Control Council carried out the sentences and had the power to reduce them.[7] The Tribunal initially indicted twenty-four defendants and ultimately tried twenty-two of them, one *in absentia.* Of the twenty-two tried, the Tribunal convicted nineteen defendants.[8]

Other Post-War International Tribunals

The Allies prosecuted numerous defendants before occupation tribunals pursuant to Control Council Law No. 10, which they had promulgated in order to ensure uniform standards for such prosecutions. Like the IMT Charter, Article II of CCL No. 10 granted the occupation tribunals jurisdiction over crimes against peace, war crimes, and crimes against humanity. It also stipulated that defendants were to be tried in the country or Allied occupation zone where they had committed their crimes. Upon conviction of a defendant, an occupation tribunal could order imprisonment, fines, forfeiture or restitution of property, deprivation of civil rights, or death.[9]

The Tokyo Tribunal consisted of eleven judges, all appointed by General MacArthur.[10] The jurisdiction, powers, and procedures of the Tokyo Tribunal were essentially similar to those of the Nuremberg Tribunal, though MacArthur exerted substantial influence on the trials to ensure that they would not threaten the success of the occupation.[11] For this and other reasons, the Tokyo Tribunal never enjoyed the degree of attention and precedential authority accorded its Nuremberg counterpart. The Tribunal tried twenty-eight Japanese leaders, and of these convicted twenty-five. In addition, Allied tribunals tried over 5,000 other Japanese for war crimes.[12]

The Post-War Tribunals in Retrospect

The post-War tribunals played a critical role in revealing to the world evidence of the brutal atrocities committed by the Axis powers. Moreover, the Nuremberg and Tokyo Tribunals unquestionably represented major steps

[7] IMT Charter, arts. 2, 4(c), 14(e), 16, 26–29.

[8] For more detail on the Nuremberg trials, *see generally* TELFORD TAYLOR, THE ANATOMY OF THE NUREMBERG TRIALS (1992) and ANN TUSA AND JOHN TUSA, THE NUREMBERG TRIAL (1983).

[9] CCL No. 10, arts. II(3), IV; *see also* UNITED NATIONS WAR CRIMES COMMISSION, HISTORY OF THE UNITED NATIONS WAR CRIMES COMMISSION AND THE DEVELOPMENT OF THE LAWS OF WAR 461–74 (1948).

[10] Charter of the International Military Tribunal for the Far East, Jan. 19, 1946, *amended* Apr. 26, 1946, art. 2, 4 Bevans 20, 27.

[11] *See, e.g.*, RICHARD H. MINEAR, VICTOR'S JUSTICE: THE TOKYO WAR CRIMES TRIAL 22–23, 111–13 (1971); B.V.A. RÖLING, THE TOKYO TRIAL AND BEYOND: REFLECTIONS OF A PEACEMONGER 2–3 (Antonio Cassese ed., 1993).

[12] *See, e.g.*, Pritchard, *supra* note 5, at 135–36.

in the elaboration and enforcement of international criminal law. The Nuremberg Tribunal played a particularly prominent role in these respects in light of the greater publicity it received. The Nuremberg trials were remarkably fair and effective, especially in light of the politically and emotionally charged circumstances under which they were held.

Yet both were also marked by significant flaws, many of which resulted from the enormous political interests at stake. As described in Chapter 1, debate has raged over whether the trials violated *nullum crimen sine lege* in light of the novel nature of crimes against peace. The Indian judge on the Tokyo Tribunal, Justice Rahadbinod Pal, issued a voluminous dissent that sharply criticized the legal bases for the majority's opinion, primarily its conclusions on the illegality of aggressive war and the nature of individual responsibility for acts of state.[13] In addition, the tribunals tried only the vanquished, opening them to criticism as victor's justice. As all the judges were Allied nationals, the impartiality of the tribunals is also subject to question.[14] The tribunal charters prohibited the defendants from challenging the tribunals' jurisdiction, and the tribunals did not permit the defendants to invoke Allied practices in their defense.[15] Furthermore, the selection of defendants was often determined more by political considerations than by relative culpability or evidentiary considerations. Finally, the trials themselves suffered some procedural and evidentiary defects.[16]

For many of these reasons, while contributing substantially to the doctrinal and procedural development of international criminal law, and subjecting Nazi crime to some degree of exposure and justice, these trials, even in conjunction with their Control Council Law No. 10 counterparts, could not achieve substantial closure for the societies involved. The ongoing debate over responsibility for and reparation of Nazi atrocities is testimony to this conclusion.

THE INTERNATIONAL CRIMINAL TRIBUNAL FOR THE FORMER YUGOSLAVIA

History: A Tribunal Born of International Impotence

After the post-War prosecutions described above, no prosecutions before international tribunals occurred until the advent of the tribunals for the

[13] *See* Elizabeth S. Kopelman, *Ideology and International Law: The Dissent of the Indian Justice at the Tokyo War Crimes Trial*, 23 N. Y. U. J. INT'L L. AND POL. 373 (1991).

[14] *See, e.g.*, ARNOLD C. BRACKMAN, THE OTHER NUREMBERG: THE UNTOLD STORY OF THE TOKYO WAR CRIMES TRIALS 63–71 (1987) (noting that one Tokyo Tribunal judge had been a prisoner of war of the Japanese); RÖLING, *supra* note 11, at 87 (asserting that Japanese judges should have been included).

[15] IMT Charter, art. 3; *see* RÖLING, *supra* note 11, at 54–55, 59–60, 89.

[16] *See, e.g.*, TAYLOR, *supra* note 8, at 85–94 (though concluding that flaws caused no lasting harm); MINEAR, *supra* note 11, at 86–93, 102–24; RÖLING, *supra* note 11, at 50–55.

former Yugoslavia and Rwanda in the 1990s.[17] The creation of the Yugoslavia Tribunal arose in the aftermath of evidence of horrendous war crimes in that conflict; indeed, it could well be viewed as a substitute for more assertive means to stop that war. The process began in 1991 with several Security Council resolutions that declared the situation in the former Yugoslavia a breach of international peace and security, expressed concern over violations of international law in the region, and affirmed individual responsibility for such violations.[18]

On October 6, 1992, the Council created a commission of experts to examine these violations of international law.[19] The commission concluded in an interim report that serious violations of international humanitarian law were indeed taking place and recommended the creation of an *ad hoc* international tribunal.[20] In the aftermath of the commission's report, on February 11, 1993, the Council declared that the violations of international humanitarian law in the former Yugoslavia constituted a threat to international peace and security, decided to establish an international tribunal to address them, and requested the Secretary-General to prepare a report implementing this decision.[21] The Secretary-General's report set forth a draft statute for an *ad hoc* international tribunal and took the view that the Security Council should establish the tribunal by resolution.[22]

On May 25, 1993, the Security Council unanimously passed Resolution 827, which created the Yugoslavia Tribunal under Chapter VII of the Charter and adopted the draft statute in the Secretary-General's report. Several considerations convinced the Council to establish the Tribunal by

[17] Non-governmental Russell Tribunals periodically convened, one of which found the United States guilty of genocide in Vietnam. Barry M. Schiller, *Life in a Symbolic Universe: Comments on the Genocide Convention and International Law*, 9 Sw. U. L. Rev. 47, 60 (1977).

[18] *See, e.g.*, SC Res. 713, UN SCOR, 46th Year, Res. and Dec., at 42, UN Doc. S/INF/47 (1991). For an excellent collection of information and documentation, *see* Virginia Morris and Michael P. Scharf, An Insider's Guide to the International Criminal Tribunal for the Former Yugoslavia (1995).

[19] SC Res. 780, UN SCOR, 47th Year, Res. and Dec., at 36, UN Doc. S/INF/48 (1992). The commission viewed its mandate as not merely to reach legal conclusions, but also to obtain evidence for prosecution, and created a database of information. *See* Letter dated 9 February 1993 from the Secretary-General Addressed to the President of the Security Council, Feb. 10, 1993, UN Doc. S/25274, at 7–11 [hereinafter Yugoslavia Commission First Interim Report].

[20] Yugoslavia Commission First Interim Report, *supra* note 19. For the commission's second interim and final reports, *see* Letter dated 5 October 1993 from the Secretary-General to the President of the Security Council, Oct. 6, 1993, UN Doc. S/26545; Letter dated 24 May 1994 from the Secretary-General to the President of the Security Council, May 27, 1994, UN Doc. S/1994/674. The Commission on Human Rights' Special Rapporteur coordinated his activities with those of the commission of experts. *See* The Situation of Human Rights in the Territory of the Former Yugoslavia, Sept. 3, 1992, UN Doc. A/47/418-S/24516; The Situation of Human Rights in the Territory of the Former Yugoslavia, Nov. 6, 1992, UN Doc. A/47/635-S/24766.

[21] SC Res. 808, UN SCOR, 48th Year, Res. and Dec., at 28, UN Doc. S/INF/49 (1993).

[22] Report of the Secretary-General pursuant to paragraph 2 of Security Council Resolution 808, May 3, 1993, UN Doc. S/25704 [hereinafter Secretary-General's Yugoslavia Report].

resolution rather than by treaty, which would have been the more traditional route for such an important undertaking. First, the elaboration of a treaty would have been a laborious exercise, whereas a Council resolution would be quicker and simpler. Secondly, unlike a Security Council resolution under Chapter VII which binds all states, a treaty would bind only those states party to it, and certain essential states would probably have refused to join.[23] Nevertheless, some member states in the developing world were uncomfortable with the Security Council approach, considering it an excessive exercise of the Council's power.[24] Despite enthusiastic endorsement by most Council members, several months passed before the Tribunal was set up and a Prosecutor appointed.

Anatomy of the Tribunal

The ICTY is composed of three organs: a prosecutorial organ (the Prosecutor), an adjudicative organ (the Chambers), and a secretariat (the Registry). The Security Council appoints the Prosecutor upon nomination by the Secretary-General. The Prosecutor has established an investigations section staffed by professional investigators, as well as legal advisors who help direct the investigators and prepare indictments. The adjudicative organ consists of trial chambers of three judges (both permanent and temporary) each and an appellate chamber of seven judges. The General Assembly elects the judges from a list of candidates submitted by the Security Council. The Registry provides a vast array of administrative services to the prosecutorial and adjudicative organs, including recordkeeping, security and translation, custody and transfer of defendants, and care and protection for victims and witnesses.[25]

The ICTY sits in The Hague, but it may conduct proceedings elsewhere when in the interests of justice.[26] The Council set no time limit on the Tribunal's existence, and the evolution of the political situation in the region and the extent of its docket will likely guide the Security Council's

[23] *See id.* at 6–8; Paul C. Szasz, *The Proposed War Crimes Tribunal for Ex-Yugoslavia*, 25 N. Y. U. J. Int'l L. and Pol. 405, 411–12 (1993).

[24] Szasz, *supra* note 23, at 414; *see also* James C. O'Brien, *The International Tribunal for Violations of International Humanitarian Law in the Former Yugoslavia*, 87 AJIL 639, 640, 643 (1993) (endorsing Council's Chapter VII findings).

[25] ICTY Statute, arts. 11, 12, 13(2), 16(4), 17(1); *see generally* Report of the International Tribunal for the Prosecution of Persons Responsible for Serious Violations of International Humanitarian Law Committed in the Territory of the Former Yugoslavia Since 1991, Aug. 25, 1999, UN Doc. A/54/187-S/1999/846 [hereinafter 1999 ICTY Report]. The Tribunal's original structure of two trial chambers of three judges each and five appeals judges was augmented due to the escalating workload. *See* SC Res. 1166, May 13, 1998, paras. 1–3; SC Res. 1329, Nov. 30, 2000.

[26] ICTY Statute, art. 31; ICTY Rules, rule 4; *see also* Secretary-General's Yugoslavia Report, *supra* note 22, at 33 (explaining reasons for locating Tribunal at the Hague).

determination as to the Tribunal's duration. The ICTY's expenses are covered by both assessed contributions from UN members and voluntary contributions from states, international organizations, and private entities.

Jurisdiction and Applicable Law

The Statute limits the Yugoslavia Tribunal's jurisdiction to serious violations of international humanitarian law committed in the former Yugoslavia since January 1, 1991.[27] The Statute takes a fairly conservative approach to the corpus of law the ICTY is to apply, granting it jurisdiction over only those aspects of international humanitarian law that the Secretary-General concluded were clearly part of customary law.[28] Articles 2 through 5 set forth the crimes over which the Tribunal has jurisdiction: war crimes, genocide, and other crimes against humanity.[29] The Statute's rules concerning individual responsibility and defenses are generally consistent with the Nuremberg principles and the 1949 Geneva Conventions and Protocol I.[30] The Tribunal's personal jurisdiction extends only to natural persons and is concurrent with that of national courts, although it enjoys primacy and may request a national court to defer to its jurisdiction over a case. [31] The Statute prohibits double jeopardy, except that the Tribunal may try a person who has been tried by a national court where the relevant act was characterized as an ordinary crime or where the national court proceedings were not impartial or independent, were designed to shield the accused from international criminal responsibility, or were not diligently prosecuted.[32]

Procedure

The Tribunal's Statute granted the judges the power to draft and adopt rules of procedure and evidence.[33] In February 1994, the ICTY formally

[27] ICTY Statute, arts. 1, 8.

[28] Secretary-General's Yugoslavia Report, *supra* note 22, at 9; *see also* Provisional Verbatim Record of the Three Thousand Two Hundred and Seventeenth Meeting, May 25, 1993, UN Doc. S/PV.3217, at 11, 15, 16, 19, 37 (emphasis by some Council members that Tribunal should not create new law).

[29] For a detailed discussion of the Statute's definition of these crimes, *see* Chs. 2–4, *supra*.

[30] *See* ICTY Statute, arts. 6, 7; Secretary-General's Yugoslavia Report, *supra* note 22, at 15.

[31] ICTY Statute, art. 9; *see also* ICTY Rules, rules 9–11. As an exception to its primacy, the Tribunal may suspend an indictment where the arresting state is prepared to prosecute the accused and it is appropriate for that state to exercise jurisdiction over the accused. ICTY Rules, rule 11 *bis*. Presumably, this exception was intended to encourage states to arrest offenders.

[32] ICTY Statute, art. 10; *see also* ICTY Rules, rule 13.

[33] ICTY Statute, art. 15; *see also* Helsinki Watch, Procedural and Evidentiary Issues for the Yugoslav War Crimes Tribunal: Resource Allocation, Evidentiary Questions and Protection of Witnesses 4, 6 (Aug., 1993) (lamenting lack of formal provision for input by Security Council or public).

adopted its Rules of Procedure and Evidence, which it later amended on many occasions.[34] These Rules apply to proceedings before both the trial and appellate chambers.[35] Although something of a hybrid, the Tribunal's procedure more closely resembles an adversarial model, rather than the inquisitorial system characteristic of civil law countries. Indeed, the Tribunal's practice has leaned heavily towards the common law model, and decisions tend to cite more common law sources.[36]

The Prosecutor initiates and conducts investigations. She may request a state to arrest a suspect provisionally and to seize evidence, and may also apply to a judge for an order to have such persons provisionally transferred to the Tribunal's detention unit.[37] If the Prosecutor is satisfied that sufficient evidence provides reasonable grounds for believing that the suspect committed a crime, she submits the indictment for confirmation by a trial chamber judge. If the judge agrees that the Prosecutor has established such a case, the judge confirms the indictment and may issue any necessary orders, including orders for the arrest, surrender, and transfer of the accused.[38] To facilitate the arrest of indictees, the ICTY has adopted the practice of issuing sealed indictments in an unknown number of cases.

In 1997, the Tribunal addressed the controversial issue of its powers to order a state to produce documentary evidence, when a trial chamber judge issued a subpoena *duces tecum* to the government of Croatia and a high-ranking Croatian official. Croatia challenged the Tribunal's power to issue a subpoena to a state and its officials. The Appeals Chamber ruled that the Tribunal may order a state, though not its individual officials, to produce documents, though such an order cannot take the form of a subpoena. This holding, now codified in the Tribunal's rules, subjects this power to safeguards intended to protect the state's national security interests.[39]

Upon transfer of the accused to the Tribunal, he is to be brought before

[34] The Tribunal also adopted and amended Rules Governing the Detention of Persons Awaiting Trial or Appeal Before the Tribunal or Otherwise Detained on the Authority of the Tribunal and a Directive on the Assignment of Defence Counsel. UN Docs. IT/38/Rev.8 and IT/73/Rev.7.

[35] ICTY Rules, rule 107.

[36] *The Protection of Human Rights Through International Criminal Law: A Conversation with Madam Justice Louise Arbour, Chief Prosecutor for the International Criminal Tribunals for the Former Yugoslavia and Rwanda*, 57 U. TORONTO FAC. L. REV. 83, 93–94 (1999).

[37] ICTY Statute, art. 18; ICTY Rules, rules 40, 40 *bis*. To carry out investigations and prepare indictments, the Prosecutor has set up an investigative section that works closely with trial attorneys. An intelligence analysis team initially reviews information and channels it to an investigative unit. Once investigators have developed a case, that unit prepares a draft indictment that a trial attorney reviews. The trial attorney then either presents the draft indictment to the Prosecutor or sends it back to the investigative unit for further development. *See generally* Michael J. Keegan, *Prosecuting International Crimes: An Inside View: The Preparation of Cases for the ICTY*, 7 TRANSNAT'L L. AND CONTEMP. PROBS. 119 (1997).

[38] ICTY Statute, arts. 18(4), 19; *see also* ICTY Rules, rules 47, 54, 54 *bis*.

[39] *See Blaskic Interlocutory Appeal*; ICTY Rules, rule 54 *bis*. *See also* Ch. 11, note 38, *infra*.

the Tribunal 'without delay' and asked to enter a plea. Although not originally reflected in the Statute or the rules, the Tribunal has permitted plea bargaining and has now codified the practice in its Rules. The Tribunal may detain defendants in facilities provided either by the host country or another country; in practice all are jailed in a special ICTY unit of a Dutch jail in The Hague. After the initial appearance of the accused, the parties may make preliminary or other motions, including dismissal for lack of jurisdiction and exclusion of evidence. The Trial Chamber may order the accused's provisional release under certain circumstances. Some of these motions are subject to interlocutory appeal.

Trials begin with optional opening statements followed by presentation of the evidence. Witnesses are examined by the parties, though judges may call witnesses and pose questions. In addition to the parties, the Tribunal may invite or permit any state, organization, or person to appear before it and make submissions. After presentation of the evidence, the parties may present closing arguments.[40]

The Statute requires trial chambers to ensure that trials are fair and expeditious and guarantees suspects and the accused internationally recognized rights. These include protections derived from Article 14 of the International Covenant on Civil and Political Rights.[41] Accordingly, among the rights guaranteed to suspects and the accused are the right to presumption of innocence; to be informed promptly and in detail of the charges against him; to have adequate time and facilities for preparation of a defense and to communicate with counsel of his own choosing; to have legal counsel provided if he cannot afford it; to be tried without undue delay; to examine witnesses against him; to remain silent; and to obtain disclosure of certain evidence.[42] Though some observers have pronounced them inadequate, the Statute and Rules also provide for protections for victims and witnesses, including a special unit to provide support and protection for them, the conducting of *in camera* proceedings, and measures to protect identities.[43]

Unlike the Nuremberg Tribunal, the Yugoslavia Tribunal may not

[40] ICTY Statute, art. 20; ICTY Rules, rules 62, 62 *bis*, 64, 65, 72, 73, 74, 84–86. The Appellate Chamber's decision in the *Erdemovic Sentencing Appeal* established the criteria for a valid guilty plea, which are now codified in the Rules. They require that the plea be voluntary, informed, unequivocal, and supported by a sufficient factual basis. ICTY Rules, rule 62 *bis*.

[41] ICCPR, art. 14, 999 UNTS at 176–77.

[42] ICTY Statute, arts. 18(3), 20, 21; ICTY Rules, rules 42, 66–68.

[43] ICTY Statute, art. 22; ICTY Rules, rules 69, 75; *see also* HELSINKI WATCH, *supra* note 33, at 4–5. On protection of victims and witnesses, *see* 1999 ICTY Report, *supra* note 25, paras. 164–68; Y.M.O. Featherstone, *The International Criminal Tribunal for the Former Yugoslavia: Recent Developments in Witness Protection*, 10 LEIDEN J. INT'L L. 179 (1997); Natasha A. Affolder, *Tadic, the Anonymous Witness and the Sources of International Procedural Law*, 19 MICH. J. INT'L L. 445 (1998).

conduct trials *in absentia*.[44] If the Tribunal is unable to obtain custody of the accused, under Rule 61 the prosecution may nevertheless present its case to the trial chamber. On the basis of the evidence so presented, the trial chamber then determines if reasonable grounds exist for believing that the accused committed any of the offenses in the indictment and may then issue an international arrest warrant directed to all states. This procedure could be viewed as similar to a quasi-*in absentia* trial, and the refusal to grant the accused representation through counsel raises questions of fairness that detract from the authority of the procedure's outcome.[45] Nevertheless, the procedure perhaps more closely resembles a quasi-truth commission and is a useful alternative for those cases where the Tribunal cannot obtain custody of the accused. The issuance of an international arrest warrant will stigmatize the accused, effectively preclude his travel abroad, and possibly limit his ability to serve in a leadership position.

Judgments

Judgments require approval by a majority of the chamber. Upon conviction, the Tribunal may sentence a defendant to imprisonment and order restitution, but cannot order the death penalty. Sentences are to take into account aggravating and mitigating circumstances (including cooperation with the Prosecutor) and the general practices of the former Yugoslavia.[46] Consistent with the ICCPR, but unlike Nuremberg, a judgment is subject to appeal in cases of an error of law invalidating a decision or an error of fact occasioning a miscarriage of justice. In contrast to standard common law practice, the Prosecution has a right to appeal a verdict. The appellate chamber may affirm, reverse, or revise a trial chamber's decision, and its decision is final. The defense or, if within one year of the judgment, the Prosecutor, may also make a motion to a chamber to review a judgment if a new fact is discovered that could not have been uncovered through due diligence. The chamber will review the judgment if a majority agrees that the new fact, if proved, could have been a decisive factor in the decision.[47]

The ICTY designates the state in which a convict will serve his sentence from a list of states that have notified the Security Council of their willingness to incarcerate the convict, though the Secretary-General

[44] ICTY Statute, art. 21(4)(d). Although some legal systems permit *in absentia* trials, many states oppose them as violations of due process principles, particularly Article 14 of the ICCPR. *See, e.g.*, James S. Robbins, *War Crimes: The Case of Iraq*, FLETCHER F. WORLD AFF., Summer/Fall 1994, at 45, 60.

[45] *See* Prosecutor v. Karadzic and Mladic, Review of the Indictment Pursuant to Rule 61 of the Rules of Procedure and Evidence, ICTY Trial Chamber I, July 11, 1996.

[46] ICTY Statute, arts. 23(2), 24; ICTY Rules, rules 101, 105 (restitution).

[47] ICTY Statute, arts. 24(1), 26; ICTY Rules, rules 119, 120; Secretary-General's Yugoslavia Report, *supra* note 22, at 29–30.

has indicated that convicts should be incarcerated outside the former Yugoslavia. Imprisonment is carried out according to the laws of the state of incarceration, subject to the Tribunal's supervision. Convicts are subject to the laws of pardon and commutation of sentence of the state of incarceration, though the President of the Tribunal makes decisions in respect of these matters.[48]

Status as of Late 2000

The Tribunal's first few years were devoted to building its institutional capabilities and infrastructure—arranging offices and courtrooms, establishing agreements with governments to provide assistance, selection of judges, and establishing the Rules of Procedure and Evidence. Although these circumstances led the ICTY to get off to a slow start, its judicial activity picked up substantially, requiring the Security Council to expand its resources, including the addition of a third trial chamber and three judges. By 1999, the Tribunal was a fully functioning judicial institution, with a budget of nearly $100 million and over 700 staff members, representing 63 nationalities. Nevertheless, the complexity of the cases, the novelty of the legal principles involved, and the Tribunal's commitment to respecting contemporary human rights norms, have resulted in disturbingly long durations for proceedings, leading the Tribunal to modify its Rules of Procedure and Evidence in an attempt to render them more efficient.[49]

The ICTY has had three Prosecutors since its inception—Richard Goldstone of South Africa (1993–96), Louise Arbour of Canada (1996–99), and Carla Ponte of Switzerland (1999–). As of mid-2000, the ICTY had openly confirmed indictments of some 65 individuals (an unknown additional number of sealed indictments also exists), and held 34 in custody.[50] Most of the indictees have been Serbs, including Radovan Karadzic, the former Bosnian Serb political leader; Ratko Mladic, the former Bosnian Serb military leader; and Slobodan Milosevic, former president of the Federal Republic of Yugoslavia.

On April 26, 1995, Dusko Tadic, the first defendant over whom the Tribunal obtained custody, pleaded not guilty to the charges brought against him. The defense filed several preliminary motions, including challenges to the ICTY's legitimacy and jurisdiction, which the Tribunal

[48] ICTY Statute, arts. 27, 28; ICTY Rules, rules 103(A), 104, 124; Secretary-General's Yugoslavia Report, *supra* note 22, at 30–31. Rule 125 stipulates standards for pardons or commutations.

[49] 1999 ICTY Report, *supra* note 25, paras. 2, 12–14, 175; GA Res. 53/212, UN GAOR, 53d Sess., Supp. No. 49, at 337, UN Doc. A/53/49 (1999). On the totals of voluntary contributions, *see* 1999 ICTY Report, *supra* note 25, paras. 197–98.

[50] For updates on developments at the Yugoslavia Tribunal, *see* its web site, www.un.org/icty.

rejected in a landmark opinion in 1995. In May 1997, the ICTY found Tadic guilty of 11 of 31 counts and sentenced him to 20 years. However, in July 1999, the Appeals Chamber overruled Tadic's acquittal on certain counts; after further consideration at the trial and appellate levels, the Tribunal revised the sentence to ten to twenty years.[51]

In May 1995, the ICTY commenced its first proceedings under Rule 61 in the case of an indicted prison camp guard believed to be in Serb-controlled Bosnia. A little more than a year later, the Tribunal subjected Karadzic and Mladic to the same procedures and issued international warrants for their arrest.[52] In November 1996, the Tribunal handed down its first sentence (ten years' imprisonment) in the case of Drazen Erdemovic, an ethnic Croat who had admitted participating in the mass execution of some 1,200 Muslim civilians at Srebrenica while serving in the Bosnian Serb forces. After the Appeals Chamber determined that the defendant's guilty plea had not been informed or unequivocal and allowed him an opportunity to replead, the trial chamber reduced the sentence to five years.[53] In addition, other trials are at various stages, and the Tribunal has numerous ongoing investigations.

In the aftermath of the 1995 Dayton–Paris Accords, prosecutors agreed with representatives of the Office of the High Representative (the entity responsible for overall implementation of the agreement) on a set of 'Rules of the Road' designed to prevent national courts in Bosnia from engaging in unjustified retaliatory prosecutions and thereby to encourage the return of refugees to the region. Under these rules, no Bosnian court may pursue a prosecution over which the Tribunal would have jurisdiction, unless the ICTY Prosecutor issues an opinion that there is a *prima facie* case against the individual. This scheme has, at the same time, imposed a significant burden on the Tribunal.[54]

As violence began to flare in the Yugoslav province of Kosovo in 1998, the Prosecution turned its attention there. Although Yugoslav authorities initially hampered these efforts, the outflow of refugees from Kosovo

[51] *See Tadic Interlocutory Appeal*; *Tadic Appeal*; *Tadic Sentencing Appeal*. For analyses of the Tribunal's judgments on Tadic's challenges, *see* George H. Aldrich, *Jurisdiction of the International Criminal Tribunal for the Former Yugoslavia*, 90 AJIL 64 (1996); Jose E. Alvarez, *Rush to Closure: Lessons of the Tadic Judgment*, 96 MICH. L. REV. 2031 (1998); Theodor Meron, *The Continuing Role of Custom in the Formation of International Humanitarian Law*, 90 AJIL 238, 238–44 (1996); Marco Sassòli, *La première décision de la chambre d'appel du Tribunal Penal International pour l'ex-Yougoslavie: Tadic (Competence)*, 100 REV. GÉN. DROIT INT'L PUB. 101 (1996).

[52] Marlise Simons, *Broader Warrants Issued for 2 Bosnian Serbs*, N. Y. TIMES, July 12, 1996, at A10.

[53] *See Erdemovic Sentencing Appeal*. For the Appeals Chamber's critical ruling on duress, *see* Ch. 6, Defenses, *supra*; *see also* David Turns, *The International Criminal Tribunal for the Former Yugoslavia: The Erdemovic Case*, 47 INT'L AND COMP. L.Q. 461 (1998).

[54] 1999 ICTY Report, *supra* note 25, paras. 135–37; *The Protection of Human Rights Through International Criminal Law*, *supra* note 36, at 95.

after the start of NATO's 1999 campaign provided the Prosecutor with access to witnesses for her investigations. In May 1999, while the war was still continuing, the Tribunal issued its most dramatic indictments to date—those of President Slobodan Milosevic and four other high-ranking Yugoslav officials for crimes against humanity and violations of the laws and customs of war arising out of the hostilities in Kosovo. The ICTY subsequently issued international arrest warrants and orders seeking to freeze the assets of the accused individuals.[55]

With respect to prosecutorial strategy, the ICTY has neither the time nor the resources to pursue every perpetrator of offenses within its jurisdiction, and the Security Council never intended it to do so. Rather, it focuses on those primarily responsible for the atrocities—i.e., those in leadership positions—and those committing exceptionally serious abuses. However, as the early prosecutions make clear, prosecutors have not always adhered to this policy. Indeed, initially the Tribunal avoided indicting certain high-profile subjects; the Prosecutor may, understandably, have been requiring a higher standard of evidence for indictments in politically sensitive cases, thus targeting lower-ranking offenders to acquire evidence against superiors. Nonetheless, the indictments of Milosevic and others for atrocities in Kosovo suggests a clear readiness on the part of the Prosecutor to indict the most senior officials without indicting junior officials first. Indeed, as more suspects were apprehended after 1997, the Prosecutor even dismissed indictments against lower-level defendants in order to concentrate resources on key defendants. As for the question of equal treatment of all sides in the conflict, the Prosecutor has explained that the ICTY has brought charges primarily against Serbs due to the nature of the sources from which it receives cooperation. Prosecutors have asserted that political considerations do not influence prosecutorial strategy and that it does not consult with any other entities in making decisions.[56]

Among the Tribunal's more controversial practices has been the granting of anonymity to witnesses providing testimony, a measure necessitated by the dangerous security circumstances in the Balkans and the cruel nature of the crimes, particularly sexual offenses. Of course, such a measure must only be used in the most exceptional cases and with the utmost awareness of the potential prejudice to the accused individual's

[55] 1999 ICTY Report, *supra* note 25, paras. 4, 87, 124, 126, 132; *see also* Sonja Boelaert-Suominen, *The International Criminal Tribunal for the former Yugoslavia and the Kosovo Conflict*, 82 Int'l Rev. Red Cross 217 (2000). On plans for a UN-sponsored court in UN-administered Kosovo, *see* Carlotta Gall, *U.N. Mission in Kosovo Proposes to Set Up a War Crimes Court*, N.Y. Times, June 23, 2000, at A3.

[56] Statement by the Prosecutor Following the Withdrawal of the Charges Against 14 Accused, May 8, 1998, ICTY Press Release CC/PIU/314-E (explaining strategy); Judge Richard Goldstone, Remarks at press conference, The Hague, Apr. 24, 1995.

right to a fair trial. At the same time, violations of anonymity orders suggest the difficulty in making such protective measures effective.[57]

The ICTY's fate depends a great deal, of course, on its relationship with the parties, both inside and outside the region, with access to defendants and evidence. Although none of the groups in the former Yugoslavia has an unblemished record of cooperation with the Tribunal, Serb authorities, both in the Federal Republic and in Bosnia, have been especially recalcitrant. Yugoslav authorities have failed to arrest and transfer accused individuals or respect requests for primacy, and have refused to produce evidence. Although the Tribunal has reported these actions to the Security Council repeatedly, in accordance with Article 29 of the Tribunal Statute, these reports have not yielded any change in attitude. Authorities in Republika Srpska, where most indictees still at large are believed to be located, have also consistently refused to exercise arrest warrants. Croatia has improved its cooperation with the ICTY due to political pressure by some Western states and a changeover in governments in 2000, but room for improvement remains. In addition, several governments outside the Balkans have rendered valuable assistance to the Tribunal. And, in a reciprocal twist, the ICTY has been cooperating with national authorities pursuing prosecutions of cases for which it has not requested deferral.[58]

Hopes that the international peacekeeping force installed in Bosnia at the end of 1995 under the Dayton–Paris Accords would play a significant role in supporting the Tribunal's work were initially disappointing. Despite the recognition of the ICTY's work in the agreement and implementing Security Council resolutions,[59] the troop contributors steadfastly refused to give it a mandate to seek out suspects or guard mass grave sites. Instead, the international force only arrested suspects whom it encountered in the normal course of its duties, and only if circumstances permitted, and provided security for ICTY investigators. In fact, it failed to arrest suspects whose whereabouts were clearly known and who could be easily apprehended.[60] The use of sealed indictments and a more robust posture

[57] *Compare, e.g.*, Vincent M. Creta, *The Search for Justice in the Former Yugoslavia and Beyond: Analyzing the Rights of the Accused Under the Statute and the Rules of Procedure and Evidence of the International Criminal Tribunal for the Former Yugoslavia*, 20 Hous. J. Int'l L. 381, 395–96 (1998) *with The Protection of Human Rights Through International Criminal Law*, *supra* note 36, at 89. In one case, the violation of an anonymity order revealed that a prosecution witness had lied, forcing the related charges to be dropped. Creta, *supra*, at 399–400.

[58] *See, e.g.*, 1999 ICTY Report, *supra* note 25, paras. 5–6, 90–106; Sean D. Murphy, *Progress and Jurisprudence of the International Criminal Tribunal for the Former Yugoslavia*, 93 AJIL 57, 64–65 (1999); *The Protection of Human Rights Through International Criminal Law*, *supra* note 36, at 85.

[59] General Framework Agreement for Peace in Bosnia and Herzegovina, Dec. 14, 1995, Bosnia-Croatia-Serbia, art. IX, 35 ILM 75, 90 (1996); SC Res. 1031, UN SCOR, 50th Year, Res. and Dec., at 18, UN Doc. S/INF/51 (1995).

[60] Philip Shenon, *G.I.'s in Bosnia Shun Hunt for War Crime Suspects*, N. Y. Times, March 2, 1996,

by NATO troops beginning in 1997 led to a significant increase in arrests and more extensive execution of search warrants. Nevertheless, scores of indictees remain at large.[61]

Even in its brief lifespan, the Tribunal has produced some significant advancements in the substance and implementation of international criminal law. For example, the indictments and jurisprudence have highlighted the role of sexual violence in the Balkan conflict and more clearly defined the status of such offenses in international criminal law. In the *Celibici* case, for example, the ICTY found that rape may constitute a form of torture. Additional holdings on the scope of command responsibility and the defense of duress are quite significant.[62]

Nevertheless, for all its accomplishments, the ICTY remains far too remote from the population, whose need for justice and healing was the primary reason for its creation. Many elements in the region view the Tribunal as biased or ineffective and have exploited its work for their own political and propaganda purposes. The Tribunal hopes to counteract this problem with an active outreach program.[63]

INTERNATIONAL CRIMINAL TRIBUNAL FOR RWANDA

History: The Yugoslavia Process Revisited

The history of the Rwanda Tribunal mirrors that of the Yugoslavia Tribunal in many respects, as the UN's member states took action after a tragedy had already unfolded. In the aftermath of the violence that devastated Rwanda starting in April 1994, the Security Council passed a series of resolutions expressing its alarm at violations of international law and determining that the conflict represented a threat to international peace and security.[64] Though taking remarkably little action to halt the massive atrocities, in May 1994, the Security Council requested the Secretary-General to prepare a report on violations of international humanitarian law during the conflict and in July passed Resolution 935, which authorized

at A3; Stacy Sullivan, *Bosnia's Most Wanted Mostly Accessible; War Crimes Suspects Maintain High Profile in Croat-Run Town, but Police Pay No Mind*, WASH. POST, Nov. 27, 1996, at A21.

61 *See* Payam Akhavan, *Justice in The Hague, Peace in the Former Yugoslavia?: A Commentary on the United Nations War Crimes Tribunal*, 20 HUM. RTS. Q. 737, 795–813 (1998); *see also* Ch. 11, Judicial Assistance and the Limits of International Cooperation, *infra*.

62 *See, e.g.*, *Celebici Judgment*, paras. 475–96; Kelly D. Askin, *Sexual Violence in Decisions and Indictments of the Yugoslav and Rwandan Tribunals: Current Status*, 93 AJIL 97, 98, 114 (1999); on command responsibility and defenses, *see* Ch. 6, *supra*.

63 1999 ICTY Report, *supra* note 25, paras. 148–53.

64 *See, e.g.*, SC Res. 912, 918, 925, UN SCOR, 49th Year, Res. and Dec., at 4, 6, 8, UN Doc. S/INF/50 (1994).

the creation of a commission of experts to examine the evidence.[65] The commission's December 1994 report concluded that Hutu elements had committed planned and systematic genocide against the Tutsi ethnic group. It also found that individuals on both sides had committed crimes against humanity and other offenses, though it was unable to establish whether Tutsi elements had committed acts against the Hutu population with genocidal intent.[66] On November 8, 1994, the Security Council, acting under Chapter VII of the Charter, established the Rwanda Tribunal.[67] Unlike the resolution creating the Yugoslavia Tribunal, which passed unanimously, the November 1994 resolution passed with Rwanda voting against and China abstaining. The Rwandan government initially objected to the ICTR principally because of its inability to order the death penalty, its limited temporal jurisdiction, and concerns that its seat would be far from Rwanda. The decision to locate the trial chambers' seat in Arusha, Tanzania, and the Tribunal's intended focus allayed some of these concerns.

Anatomy of the Tribunal

The Council did not create the ICTR as an entirely separate entity, but rather appended it to the Yugoslavia Tribunal, and based its Statute closely on the latter's. Like the Yugoslavia Tribunal, it is technically a subsidiary, though independent, organ of the Security Council. Its organization is identical to that of the Yugoslavia Tribunal, with separate prosecutorial, adjudicative, and administrative organs. As with the ICTY, the adjudicative organ is comprised of trial chambers and an appellate chamber. While its trial chambers are separate from those of the ICTY, the organization and procedure of the trial chambers are basically identical, and the two tribunals share a common appellate chamber, as well as a common Prosecutor and some common prosecutorial staff.[68]

65 SC Res. 918, 935, UN SCOR, 49th Year, Res. and Dec., at 6, 11, UN Doc. S/INF/50 (1994). The Secretary-General concluded that the atrocities constituted genocide. *See* Report of the Secretary-General on the Situation in Rwanda, May 31, 1994, UN Doc. S/1994/640, at 11.

66 Final Report of the Commission of Experts established pursuant to Security Council resolution 935 (1994), Dec. 9, 1994, UN Doc. S/1994/1405, at 1, 6–25, 35–36. The Commission on Human Rights had embarked on a parallel initiative. *See* Report on the Situation of Human Rights in Rwanda Submitted by Mr. René Degni-Ségui, Special Rapporteur of the Commission on Human Rights, under Paragraph 20 of Commission Resolution E/CN.4/S-3/1 of May 28, 1994, June 28, 1994, UN Doc. E/CN.4/1995/7, at 7, 11–13 (finding massacres planned, systematic, and genocidal).

67 SC Res. 955, UN SCOR, 49th Year, Res. and Dec., at 15, UN Doc. S/INF/50 (1994); *see also* Report of the Secretary-General Pursuant to Paragraph 5 of Security Council Resolution 955 (1994), Feb. 13, 1995, UN Doc. S/1995/134, at 2 (reasons for creating Tribunal under Chapter VII) [hereinafter 1995 Secretary-General Report].

68 ICTR Statute, arts. 10, 11, 12(2), 15(3), 16(3). As with the ICTY, the ICTR originally had only

Several considerations motivated the decision to link the ICTR so closely to its Yugoslavia counterpart. The sharing of common institutions and rules is aimed at promoting consistency in the law and practice of the two tribunals, as well as efficiency. In addition, reliance on the model provided by the ICTY allowed for fairly quick creation of the ICTR. Unlike the Yugoslavia Tribunal, however, the Rwanda Tribunal carries out its operations in several different locations. The Prosecutor and appeals chamber are located in The Hague, the investigatory and prosecutorial unit operate out of Kigali, and the trial chambers sit in Arusha.[69]

Jurisdiction and Applicable Law

The ICTR's jurisdiction is limited to serious violations of international humanitarian law committed in Rwanda or committed by Rwandan nationals in neighboring states between January 1, 1994, and December 31, 1994.[70] As with the Yugoslavia Tribunal, the Rwanda Tribunal's jurisdiction extends to genocide, crimes against humanity, and war crimes, with adjustments to reflect the conflict's particular circumstances, such as its internal character.[71] Like the ICTY, the ICTR's personal jurisdiction extends only to natural persons. In addition, its jurisdiction is concurrent with national courts, with the Tribunal enjoying primacy. The Statute's provisions on individual responsibility, defenses, immunities, and double jeopardy are identical to those in the ICTY Statute.[72]

Procedure and Judgments

In accordance with the Tribunal's Statute, the ICTR's judges adopted the Rules of Procedure and Evidence of the ICTY, with only minor changes, and, like the ICTY Rules, the ICTR Rules have been revised on several occasions to enhance efficiency and reflect Tribunal practice. The provisions of the Statute concerning judgments, penalties, sentences, appeals, and review are also virtually identical to those of the Yugoslavia Tribunal. Thus, the Rwanda Tribunal will determine sentences by reference to the

two trials chambers, but its expanding workload and complaints over a lack of alacrity in its work led the Security Council to expand it. *See* SC Res. 1165, Apr. 30, 1998; SC Res. 1329, Nov. 30, 2000.

69 *See* 1995 Secretary-General Report, *supra* note 67, at 10 (explaining reasons for selection of Arusha).

70 ICTR Statute, arts. 1, 7. In extending the Tribunal's territorial jurisdiction to neighboring countries, the Council had primarily in mind the refugee camps in then-Zaire and other countries where crimes took place. The Tribunal's temporal jurisdiction commences on January 1, 1994, several months in advance of the events of primary concern, to include the planning stage of the crimes. *See* 1995 Secretary-General Report, *supra* note 67, at 4.

71 For a detailed discussion of the Statute's definition of these crimes, *see* Chs. 2–4, *supra*.

72 ICTR Statute, arts. 5, 6, 8, 9.

general practice of Rwanda, subject to consideration of aggravating and mitigating factors. Convicts will serve their sentences in Rwanda or another willing state (as designated by the Tribunal).[73]

Status as of Late 2000

From its inception, bureaucratic delays, financial problems, serious mismanagement, and a lack of qualified personnel have impeded the progress of the Rwanda Tribunal, leading to vociferous criticism that it was carrying out its mandate too slowly and inefficiently. The Security Council did not elect the Tribunal's judges until May 1995; the ICTR was slow at filling staff positions; and although prosecutors had identified some 400 suspects by mid-1995, it did not confirm its first indictment until November 1995.[74] Despite these daunting problems, by 1997 and 1998, the Tribunal had begun processing its growing caseload, due largely to managerial changes, budgetary increases, and voluntary contributions. By late 2000, the ICTR had indicted some 50 suspects, 40 of whom are in custody in Arusha, though several others are being held in other countries pending transfer to Arusha.[75] The Tribunal's targets have come from a relatively wide range of social and professional groups, including political, media, and business leaders. In light of the ICTR's mandate to examine the genocide against the Tutsis in 1994 and its reliance on the current Tutsi-led government in Rwanda, it has not engaged in any significant examination of the role played by Tutsi elements in Rwanda's violent politics.

In January 1997, the ICTR commenced its first trial, against Jean-Paul Akayesu, the bourgmestre of Taba commune, and launched several other trials over the ensuing months. In September 1998, a trial chamber convicted Akayesu of genocide and crimes against humanity—the first genocide verdict ever issued by an international court—and sentenced him to life in prison. Significantly, the Akayesu verdict also recognized rape as an act of genocide and featured the appearance of a UN force commander as a witness. In May 1998, the Tribunal accepted its first guilty plea, from Jean Kambanda, the prime minister of the interim

[73] *Id.* arts. 22–27; ICTR Rules, rules 101, 103.

[74] In February 1997, the United Nations issued a blistering report criticizing the Tribunal, resulting in the resignations of the Registrar and the Deputy Prosecutor and the implementation of other reforms. *See* Report of the Secretary-General on the Activities of the Office of Internal Oversight Services, Feb. 6, 1997, UN Doc. A/51/789.

[75] *See* Report of the International Criminal Tribunal for the Prosecution of Persons Responsible for Genocide and Other Serious Violations of International Humanitarian Law Committed in the Territory of Rwanda and Rwandan Citizens Responsible for Genocide and Other Such Violations Committed in the Territory of Neighbouring States between 1 January and 31 December 1994, Sept. 7, 1999, UN Doc. A/54/315-S/1999/943, Annex [hereinafter 1999 ICTR Report]; for updates on the Tribunal's work, *see* its web site at www.ictr.org.

government that took power after the plane crash that initiated the genocidal frenzy, and sentenced him to life in prison. Significantly, this outcome resulted from a plea bargain with the Prosecutor, mirroring the ICTY's practice of negotiating pleas in return for the defendant's acknowledgment of the allegations and cooperation with other prosecutions. The Tribunal has since convicted several other significant figures, some following guilty pleas, with sentences of anywhere from fifteen years to life imprisonment.[76] While the pace of trials has picked up considerably since the days of the ICTR's creation, its lack of resources has caused some defendants to remain in custody for extended periods of time without trial.[77]

The Tribunal has focused on those individuals most responsible for the violations of international humanitarian law, leaving the Rwandan courts to address the tens of thousands of lower-level abusers.[78] Therefore, like the Nuremberg and Yugoslavia Tribunals, it has focused on those in leadership positions, particularly those who conspired to commit genocide, while the Rwandan courts have concentrated on lower-ranking defendants. One anomaly of this arrangement, however, is that lower-ranking offenders tried by Rwandan courts have received heavier sentences, including the death penalty, than the higher-ranking offenders tried before the Tribunal.[79]

Like its Yugoslavia counterpart, the ICTR has made extensive use of its powers to protect victims and witnesses, including the use of pseudonyms and non-disclosure of identities to the public. In view of the substantial number of sexual offenses and the special sensitivities and needs for supporting witnesses these offenses present, the Registrar has also established a Unit for Gender Issues and Assistance to Victims.[80]

Concerted efforts to cooperate with the Rwandan authorities and extensive cooperation by a number of African and European states in arresting and transferring accused individuals have allowed the ICTR to gain relatively rapid custody over the substantial number of accused individuals noted above, including many who had fled Rwanda. At the same time, despite the ICTR's and Rwandan government's shared interest in bringing

[76] *See, e.g., Akayesu Judgment; Kambanda Judgment; Rutaganda Judgment; Kayishema and Ruzindana Judgment; Musema Judgment.* For commentary on ICTR and ICTY sentencing practices, *see* Mary Margaret Penrose, *Lest We Fail: The Importance of Enforcement in International Criminal Law*, 15 Am. U. Int'l L. Rev. 321, 371–87 (2000).

[77] 1999 ICTR Report, *supra* note 75, paras. 14–46.

[78] *See* Ch. 8, Precedents for Prosecutions Before National Tribunals: Four Recent Cases—Rwanda, *supra*.

[79] 1999 ICTR Report, *supra* note 75, para. 47; United States Institute of Peace, Rwanda: Accountability for War Crimes and Genocide 8–9, 13 (1994).

[80] 1999 ICTR Report, *supra* note 75, para. 82.

perpetrators to justice, the concurrent jurisdiction between the ICTR and national authorities has led to more friction between them than in the case of the former Yugoslavia, where no court able and willing to prosecute offenders was likely to obtain custody over a substantial number of defendants.[81] In one serious episode for ICTR–Rwandan relations, the Appeals Chamber ordered the release of and dismissal of charges against a genocide suspect, Jean-Bosco Barayagwiza, due to long delays in bringing him to trial. Rwanda responded by threatening to cut off its cooperation with the Tribunal; this result was avoided only after the Appeals Chamber, in a highly unusual move, found that new facts demonstrated that the Prosecutor was not at fault for much of the delays and that any delays that were her fault should be addressed through a reduced sentence (if convicted) or damages (if acquitted).[82] The Tribunal has also benefited by slowly forging close ties with its Yugoslavia counterpart, allowing the tribunals to learn from each other's experiences and, where appropriate, harmonize their practices.[83]

One continuing difficulty for the Tribunal is its geographical, and related psychological, distance from the victims of the crimes it is examining. Although the ICTR has begun to address this problem through greater outreach intended to promote more awareness of its work among the Rwandan people, alienation from the Tribunal's activities continues to be a problem. Cases where the Tribunal has taken decisions that Rwandan elements perceive as excessively lenient, such as that in *Barayagwiza*, or that are otherwise unpopular in Rwanda have fueled this alienation.[84]

TOWARD THE PERMANENT INTERNATIONAL CRIMINAL COURT

A Long and Frustrating History

The first major effort to create an international criminal court was the 1937 Convention for the Creation of an International Criminal Court, an

[81] *See* Madeline H. Morris, *The Trials of Concurrent Jurisdiction: The Case of Rwanda*, 7 DUKE J. COMP. AND INT'L L. 349 (1997).

[82] *See* Jean-Bosco Barayagwiza v. The Prosecutor, Decision on Prosecutor's Request for Review or Reconsideration, ICTR Appeals Chamber, Mar. 31, 2000.

[83] *See, e.g.*, Report of the International Criminal Tribunal for the Prosecution of Persons Responsible for Genocide and Other Serious Violations of International Humanitarian Law Committed in the Territory of Rwanda and Rwandan Citizens Responsible for Genocide and Other Such Violations Committed in the Territory of Neighbouring States between 1 January and 31 December 1994, Sept. 23, 1998, UN Doc. A/53/429/-S/1998/857, paras. 135–44.

[84] *See, e.g.*, Karl Vick, *Rwandan Genocide Case Puts U.N. Court on Trial,* WASHINGTON POST, Mar. 10, 2000, at A15; William A. Schabas, *International Decisions:* Barayagwiza v. Prosecutor, 94 AJIL 563 (2000).

initiative of the League of Nations; but only a single state ratified the convention and it never entered into force.[85] UN efforts to create an international court accompanied the preparation of the Genocide Convention (which contemplates such a court), with the Secretariat preparing two draft statutes in 1947.[86] The General Assembly also adopted a resolution asking the International Law Commission to examine the establishment of an international criminal court with jurisdiction over genocide and other crimes.[87] In the early 1950s, the organization pursued further efforts to create an international criminal court, including the preparation of a draft statute, but these initiatives became tied up in Cold War politics and never proved successful.[88] Thus, although both the Genocide and Apartheid Conventions envision an international criminal tribunal,[89] and despite years of effort, no permanent tribunal with jurisdiction over those or any other offenses was created until several decades later.

In 1989, the UN took up the issue again when Trinidad and Tobago raised it before the Sixth Committee, primarily to combat narcotics trafficking and terrorism.[90] The anxieties of some member states forced caution on the General Assembly, which first requested the ILC's views and only then asked the ILC to commence work on a draft statute.[91] As the conflict in the former Yugoslavia reached more horrendous proportions and states began considering an international tribunal for it, the UN's members, especially the United States, accorded the initiative greater

[85] *See* M. Cherif Bassiouni, *Historical Survey: 1919–1998*, in 3 INTERNATIONAL CRIMINAL LAW, *supra* note 1, at 597, 607–08; *see also* M. CHERIF BASSIOUNI, THE STATUTE OF THE INTERNATIONAL CRIMINAL COURT: A DOCUMENTARY HISTORY 1–35 (1998).

[86] *See* Draft Convention on the Crime of Genocide, June 26, 1947, UN Doc. E/447, at 66. The reference to an international criminal tribunal in the Genocide Convention was a source of extensive debate during its drafting. Ultimately, the drafters adopted a provision giving a future international penal tribunal jurisdiction over genocide with respect to those parties who accepted its jurisdiction. *See, e.g.*, UN ESCOR, 7th Sess., 219th mtg. (1948); UN GAOR, 3d Sess., 179th plen. mtg. (1948).

[87] GA Res. 260B(III), UN Doc. A/760, at 12–13 (1948).

[88] The UN put these early projects on hold pending the elaboration of a draft code of offenses, which was itself postponed until after agreement on a definition of aggression. Although the General Assembly agreed on a definition in 1974, the initiative to create an international criminal court remained dormant until the late 1980s. *See* M. Cherif Bassiouni, *The Prosecution of International Crimes and the Establishment of an International Criminal Court*, *in* 3 INTERNATIONAL CRIMINAL LAW, *supra* note 1, at 3.

[89] Genocide Convention, art. VI, 78 UNTS at 280, 282; Apartheid Convention, art. V, 1015 UNTS at 246.

[90] For information on other proposals for an international penal tribunal, *see* the UN records relating to the initiatives mentioned in the previous paragraph.

[91] *See* GA Res. 44/39, para. 1, UN GAOR, 44th Sess., Supp. No. 49, at 311, UN Doc. A/44/49 (1990); GA Res. 45/41, para. 3, UN GAOR, 45th Sess., Supp. No. 49A, at 363, 364, UN Doc. A/45/49 (1991); GA Res. 46/54, para. 3, UN GAOR, 46th Sess., Supp. No. 49, at 286, UN Doc. A/46/49 (1992); GA Res. 47/33, para. 6, UN GAOR, 47th Sess., Supp. No. 49, at 287, UN Doc. A/47/49 (1993); *see also* Robert Rosenstock, *The Forty-Fourth Session of the International Law Commission*, 87 AJIL 138, 138 (1993).

attention and oriented it more toward the offenses implicated in the Yugoslav conflict.[92]

The ILC Draft Statute

During the early 1990s, pursuant to General Assembly mandates, the ILC first produced a set of principles for a court and subsequently adopted a draft statute in 1994.[93] Heavily influenced by the Yugoslavia Tribunal model, the ILC's Draft Statute was primarily directed at the suppression of war crimes, genocide, and other crimes against humanity, though it did not jettison the notion of jurisdiction over narcotics trafficking and terrorism. The Draft Statute extended the Court's personal jurisdiction to natural persons and granted it subject matter jurisdiction over the following crimes: (a) genocide, (b) aggression, (c) serious violations of the laws and customs applicable in armed conflict, (d) crimes against humanity, and (e) crimes under certain treaties set out in an annex. At the same time, it showed greater deference to states and the Security Council than did its predecessors. Notably, the Court would only be a complement to national criminal justice systems where they were not effective or available.[94] In addition, the Court's jurisdiction over a case could be triggered only by the bringing of a complaint by a state party to the statute or by the referral of a matter by the Security Council; the Prosecutor would not have had any powers to bring cases on his or her own. The Draft Statute further restricted the Court's jurisdiction by requiring the consent of the custodial state, the territorial state, and any state that requested the offender's extradition to any prosecution other than for genocide. The Security Council would have enjoyed extensive prerogatives under the Draft Statute, which permitted it to refer matters to the Court without the consent of any state, required a determination by the Council that aggression had occurred before any prosecution for that crime, and precluded prosecutions arising from a situation that the Council was addressing under Chapter VII.[95]

Before turning the project over to a diplomatic conference to

[92] *See* Szasz, *supra* note 23, at 405–06 n. 5.

[93] Report of the International Law Commission on the work of its forty-fourth session, UN Doc. A/47/10 (1992), *reprinted in* 1992 [II] 2 ILC Y.B. 59–78; GA Res. 47/33, *supra* note 91, para. 6; Report of the International Law Commission on the work of its forty-fifth session, UN Doc. A/48/10 (1993), *reprinted in* 1993 [II] 2 ILC Y.B. 100–32; Report of the International Law Commission on the work of its forty-sixth session, UN Doc. A/49/10 (1994), *reprinted in* 1994 [II] 2 ILC Y.B. 18–87 [hereinafter 1994 ILC Report].

[94] 1994 ILC Report, *supra* note 93, at 27.

[95] 1994 ILC Report, *supra* note 93, at 38–46 (arts. 20, 21, 23, 25). These arrangements would potentially have given the Council an extensive veto power over the Court's jurisdiction.

conclude a convention as the ILC had recommended, the General Assembly established special committees to negotiate a draft statute that would command broad political acceptance.[96] From March 1996 to April 1998, a preparatory committee met to consider the ILC's Draft Statute and revisions proposed by the UN's members. In April 1998, the committee completed work on a new text and transmitted it to a diplomatic conference that the General Assembly had convened to finalize and adopt the Court's Statute during the summer of 1998 in Rome. As a result of the gaping differences of opinion among states that characterized the deliberations preceding the Rome conference, the draft text transmitted to the Conference, was, rather than a unified text, more of a working document setting forth various proposed alternatives, leaving it for the Rome delegates to resolve these issues.[97]

The Rome Statute

On July 17, 1998, after a month of intensive negotiations, the UN diplomatic conference meeting in Rome adopted the statute for a permanent international criminal court (ICC) by a vote of 120 in favor, seven against, and 21 abstentions.[98] In view of the contentious and complex nature of the negotiations that preceded the Statute's adoption and the aggressive determination of the Rome conference delegates to complete a statute within the conference's time limits, the ICC Statute is, not surprisingly, a complex pastiche of compromises and an intricate blending of different legal systems. Our discussion below seeks to highlight its principal areas of significance.

The ICC, which will come into existence once 60 states have ratified the Statute, will be an independent body with jurisdiction over the most serious international crimes. Unlike the ICTY and ICTR, which have primacy over national tribunals, a central attribute of the ICC is that, like

[96] GA Res. 49/53, UN GAOR, 49th Sess., Supp. No. 49, at 293–94, UN Doc. A/49/49 (1995); GA Res. 50/46, UN GAOR, 50th Sess., Supp. No. 49, at 307–08, UN Doc. A/50/49 (1996).

[97] GA Res. 51/207, UN GAOR, 51st Sess., Supp. No. 49, at 342, UN Doc. A/51/49 (1996); GA Res. 52/160, UN GAOR, 52d Sess., Supp. No. 49, at 384, UN Doc. A/52/49 (1997); Report of the Preparatory Committee on the Establishment of an International Criminal Court, Apr. 14, 1998, UN Doc. A/CONF.183/2/Add.1.

[98] For a detailed history of the Rome Conference's deliberations, *see* THE INTERNATIONAL CRIMINAL COURT: THE MAKING OF THE ROME STATUTE (Roy S. Lee ed., 1999); M. Cherif Bassiouni, *Negotiating the Treaty of Rome on the Establishment of an International Criminal Court*, 32 CORNELL INT'L L.J. 443 (1999); Mahnoush H. Arsanjani, *The Rome Statute of the International Criminal Court*, 93 AJIL 22 (1999); Fanny Benedetti and John L. Washburn, *Drafting the International Criminal Court Treaty: Two Years to Rome and an Afterword on the Rome Diplomatic Conference*, 5 GLOBAL GOVERNANCE 1 (1999). Some 160 states, 33 international organizations, and 236 NGOs participated in the Rome Conference. The United States was among the states voting against adoption of the Statute.

the court devised by the ILC, it will be complementary to national criminal jurisdictions. Thus, national tribunals will continue to have primary jurisdiction over criminal offenses falling under the Statute, and the ICC will hear cases only where national tribunals are unable or unwilling to do so.[99]

Anatomy of the ICC

The Court will have a prosecutorial organ (the Prosecutor), an adjudicative organ (the Pre-Trial, Trial, and Appeals Divisions), and an administrative organ (the Registry).[100] The Office of the Prosecutor is responsible for receiving and examining information relating to crimes within the Court's jurisdiction and for investigating and prosecuting cases. The Prosecutor and Deputy Prosecutors are elected by the states parties, hold office for nine-year terms, and are not eligible for re-election.[101]

As for the adjudicative organ, the Court will have 18 judges, a number that may be increased by the states parties. They are elected by the states parties from among candidates nominated by any party, taking into account representation of the principal legal systems of the world, equitable geographical representation, fair gender representation, and the need for specialized legal expertise (e.g., violence against women or children). A judge must be a national of a state party, and no two judges may be of the same nationality. A set minimum portion of the judges must have established competence and experience in criminal law and procedure, while another set minimum portion must have established competence and experience in relevant areas of international law. These requirements will help ensure that the Court has a sufficient pool of judges on which to draw with expertise in the main areas relevant to the Court's work. Except at the first election, all judges will serve for nine-year terms and will not be eligible for re-election. They will serve on a full-time basis, unless the workload of the Court does not so require.[102]

The Court is organized into Pre-Trial, Trial, and Appellate Divisions.

[99] ICC Statute, preamble, arts. 1, 126(1). The Court will be brought into relationship with the United Nations through a separate agreement, thus avoiding the need to amend the UN Charter and limiting potential political encroachments on the ICC's independence by other UN organs. *See* Jelena Pejic, *Creating a Permanent International Criminal Court: The Obstacles to Independence and Effectiveness*, 29 COLUM. HUM. RTS. L. REV. 291, 299–302 (1998).

[100] ICC Statute, art. 34. The Statute also provides for a Presidency (selected from among the judges) to exercise certain administrative functions of a judicial nature. *Id.* art. 38.

[101] *Id.* art. 42. The Prosecutor may be removed on grounds of serious misconduct or incapacity by an absolute majority of the states parties. *Id.* art. 46(1), (2)(b).

[102] *Id.* art. 36; *see also id.* arts. 35 (service of judges), 37 (judicial vacancies), 40 (independence of judges), 41 (excusing and disqualification of judges). *See* Leila Nadya Sadat and Richard Carden, *The New International Criminal Court: An Uneasy Revolution*, 88 GEO. L. J. 381, 397–98 (2000) (arguing that term limits for judges will hamper continuity). Judges may be removed on grounds of serious misconduct or incapacity by a vote of two-thirds of the states parties upon a recommendation adopted by a two-thirds majority of the other judges. ICC Statute, art. 46(1), (2)(a).

The Pre-Trial and Trial Divisions each have no fewer than six judges, while the Appeals Division consists of the President and four other judges. Assignment of judges is to be based on the functions performed by each division, with the Trial and Pre-Trial Divisions composed predominantly of judges with criminal trial experience. Each division will work in chambers composed of a set number of judges.[103]

The Registry is responsible for the non-judicial aspects of the ICC's administration. Elected by the judges taking into account the recommendations of the states parties, the Registrar holds office for a five-year term and is eligible for re-election once. The Registry will include a Victims and Witnesses Unit responsible for providing security, counseling, and other services for victims and witnesses at risk.[104]

The Court's seat will be at The Hague, though it may sit elsewhere if needed. It may exercise its powers in any state party to the Statute and, by special agreement, in any other state.[105]

Jurisdiction, Admissibility, and Applicable Law

The provisions on jurisdiction, admissibility, and applicable law proved the most contentious during the Statute's negotiation.[106] The ICC will have the power to try only natural persons over the age of 18 at the time the crime is committed.[107] Like its Yugoslavia and Rwanda predecessors, the Statute grants the ICC jurisdiction only over so-called 'core' crimes: genocide, crimes against humanity, and war crimes. (A controversial transitional provision in the Statute allows states to opt out of the Court's jurisdiction over war crimes with respect to its nationals for a period of seven years after the Statute's entry into force for that state.) Thus, in ironic counterpoint to the 1989 Trinidad and Tobago initiative that had launched the enterprise, the Statute abandons jurisdiction over crimes such as terrorism and narcotics trafficking, though the Statute's amendment provisions would allow for these crimes to be added at a later point. In addition, while the crime of aggression appears in the Statute, due to a lack of consensus among the negotiators over the crime's definition and the proper role of the Security Council in connection with prosecutions for it, the Court will not have jurisdiction over aggression until the states parties adopt a definition of the crime and conditions for the Court's jurisdiction with respect to it.[108]

[103] ICC Statute, art. 39(1), (2).

[104] *Id.* art. 43.

[105] *Id.* arts. 3(1), 3(3), 4(2).

[106] For a thorough discusssion, *see* Timothy L.H. McCormack and Sue Robertson, *Jurisdictional Aspects of the Rome Statute for the New International Criminal Court*, 23 MELBOURNE U. L. REV. 635 (1999).

[107] ICC Statute, arts. 25(1), 26.

[108] *Id.* arts. 5–8, 124; *see also id.* art. 30 (mental element).

The decision to limit the Statute to the core crimes stemmed from a recognition by the states at Rome that those crimes are of greatest concern and enjoy a clear status under customary international law, as well as from their view that inclusion of other crimes would impede acceptance of the Statute. The Statute's definitions of the crimes are broadly consistent with those elaborated by international law, though the Statute also reflects some significant progressive development in defining some crimes, notably gender-related offenses, and in expanding the list of offenses constituting war crimes. To assist the Court in applying the definitions, the Statute envisages the adoption of Elements of Crimes by the states party; in July 2000, the Court's Preparatory Commission completed a draft of the Elements.[109] The Statute also addresses command responsibility and the full range of possible defenses.[110]

The ICC will have jurisdiction only over crimes committed after the Statute's entry into force, and in the case of states which become party after that point, only for crimes committed after the Statute's entry into force for that state, unless the state declares otherwise.[111] Except where the Security Council has referred a situation to the ICC under Chapter VII of the UN Charter, the Court may only exercise jurisdiction if (a) the state on whose territory the offense occurred, or (b) the state of which the accused is a national is a party to the Statute or has accepted the Court's jurisdiction with respect to the crime. This disjunctive approach, giving the Court jurisdiction over nationals of non-party states if the territorial state has consented, constitutes one of the most controversial aspects of the ICC and was among the core reasons for the US rejection of it. In addition, the Court may only exercise its jurisdiction where (a) a state party has referred a case, (b) the Security Council, acting under Chapter VII, has referred a 'situation' to the Prosecutor, or (c) the Prosecutor has initiated an investigation on his or her own (*proprio motu*). The Prosecutor's power to initiate cases *proprio motu*—a power provided for in the ICTY and ICTR Statutes, but absent from the ILC Draft Statute—was a highly contentious issue for the negotiators. However, a consensus gradually emerged that an independent prosecutor was necessary, since decisions by states or the Security Council as to whether to refer a case might be influ-

[109] *See* Pejic, *supra* note 99, at 311; Arsanjani, *supra* note 98, at 29–30. For a discussion of the Statute's definitions of crimes, *see* Chs. 2–6, *supra*; *see also* Sadat and Carden, *supra* note 102, at 421–36; Herman von A.M. Hebel and Darryl Robinson, *Crimes within the Jurisdiction of the Court*, *in* THE INTERNATIONAL CRIMINAL COURT, *supra* note 98, at 79. The Statute expressly provides that its definitions will not limit existing or developing rules of international law for purposes other than the Statute. ICC Statute, art. 10. On the elements, *see* ICC Statute, art. 9; Report of the Preparatory Commission for the International Criminal Court: Finalized draft text of the Elements of Crimes, July 6, 2000, UN Doc. PCNICC/2000/INF/3/Add.2.

[110] ICC Statute, arts. 26–29, 31–33.

[111] *Id.* art. 11; *see also id.* art. 24(1).

enced by political motives, leaving the Court powerless to address serious offenses.[112] In order to prevent the ICC from interfering with efforts by the Security Council to address a conflict, no investigation or prosecution may be pursued if the Council, acting under Chapter VII, requests the Court to refrain from doing so.[113]

In keeping with the principle of complementarity, a case will be inadmissible before the Court where a state having jurisdiction over the crime is investigating or prosecuting the case or has declined to prosecute, unless the state is unwilling or unable genuinely to carry out the investigation or prosecution. In this connection, except in cases of referral by the Security Council, Article 18 requires the Prosecutor to notify states of investigations and, unless the Pre-Trial Chamber decides otherwise, to defer action where a state so requests on the grounds that the state is investigating or has investigated the case. This requirement may potentially give states opposed to an investigation an opportunity to subvert it, at least temporarily. In addition, a case will be inadmissible if it would constitute double jeopardy or if the case 'is not of sufficient gravity' to justify prosecution before the Court.[114] This gravity requirement, along with other elements of the Statute, suggests that the framers intended the ICC to be a forum for trying major offenders, rather than for pursuing perpetrators of isolated acts falling under the Court's jurisdiction.[115]

Article 20, regarding double jeopardy, prohibits the ICC from trying a person for a crime for which the ICC or another court has previously tried that person, unless the proceedings before the other court sought to shield the person from criminal responsibility or were not independent or impartial and were inconsistent with an intent to bring the person to justice. In addition, no other court may try a person for a crime for which that person has already been convicted or acquitted by the ICC.[116]

Article 21 sets forth the applicable substantive law. First, it will apply the Statute, the Elements of Crimes, and the Rules of Procedure and

[112] *Id.* arts. 12–15; *see also* Silvia A. Fernández de Gurmendi, *The Role of the International Prosecutor, in* The International Criminal Court, *supra* note 98, at 175, 176–80.

[113] ICC Statute, art. 16. In order to prevent a deferral request by the Security Council from blocking the ICC's involvement indefinitely, the Council must renew such requests every 12 months. *Id.*

[114] *Id.* arts. 17, 18; *see generally* John T. Holmes, *The Principle of Complementarity, in* The International Criminal Court, *supra* note 98, at 41. In determining whether a state is unwilling to carry out an investigation or prosecution, the Court will look to whether the state is shielding the person from criminal responsibility or whether the circumstances (e.g., an unjustified delay) are inconsistent with an intent to bring him to justice. In determining inability to investigate or prosecute, the Court will examine whether the collapse or unavailability of a national judicial system has prevented access to the accused or evidence or otherwise impeded the proceedings. ICC Statute, arts. 17(2), (3).

[115] *See* Sadat and Carden, *supra* note 102, at 419; David J. Scheffer, *The United States and the International Criminal Court*, 93 AJIL 12, 16 (1999).

[116] *See* Holmes, *supra* note 114, at 56–60.

Evidence; second, applicable treaties and principles and rules of international law; and third, general principles of law derived from national legal systems. In addition, the Court may apply its previous interpretations of the law. The Court's application and interpretation of the law must be consistent with internationally recognized human rights. Articles 22 and 23 incorporate the principles of *nullum crimen sine lege* and *nulla poena sine lege*, and Article 24 provides that the accused will be entitled to the benefits of any favorable changes in the law that occur prior to final judgment.

Procedure and Judgments

In contrast to the ILC Draft Statute, the ICC Statute sets forth detailed procedural and evidentiary principles in the Statute itself and retains for the states party the power to adopt the Court's Rules of Procedure and Evidence.[117] After evaluating the available information on a case, the Prosecutor initiates an investigation, unless he or she determines that there is 'no reasonable basis to proceed under [the] Statute'. In making this determination, the Prosecutor is to consider whether there is a reasonable basis to believe that a crime within the ICC's jurisdiction has been or is being committed, the admissibility of the case, and whether, taking account of the gravity of the crime and the interests of the victims, there are 'substantial reasons' to believe that an investigation 'would not serve the interests of justice'. If the Prosecutor determines that there is not a sufficient basis to pursue a prosecution, the Pre-Trial Chamber may request the Prosecutor to reconsider the decision or even require the Prosecutor to proceed. Before the Prosecutor may pursue an investigation *proprio motu*, the Pre-Trial Chamber must find that there is 'a reasonable basis to proceed with an investigation' and that the case appears to fall within the Court's jurisdiction.[118]

In carrying out an investigation, the Prosecutor may collect evidence, question suspects and witnesses, seek the cooperation of any state or intergovernmental organization, take measures to protect persons or evidence, and receive, solely for the purpose of generating new evidence, documents or information on a confidential basis. Among its other functions, the Pre-Trial Chamber issues orders and warrants for the conduct of an investigation; protects victims, witnesses, persons who have been arrested, and evidence; authorizes the Prosecutor to conduct investigations within a state party that is unable to execute requests for cooperation; and seeks the cooperation of states in obtaining forfeiture for the

[117] ICC Statute, art. 51(1); *see also* Report of the Preparatory Commission for the International Criminal Court: Addendum: Finalized draft text of the Rules of Procedure and Evidence, July 12, 2000, UN Doc. PCNICC/2000/INF/3/Add.1.

[118] ICC Statute, arts. 15, 53.

benefit of victims. After the initiation of an investigation, the Pre-Trial Chamber also issues warrants of arrest or summonses, provided there are reasonable grounds to believe the person has committed a crime within the Court's jurisdiction.[119]

After receipt of a request for arrest, a state party must immediately take steps to arrest the person in accordance with its laws and the Statute. In this connection, after promptly confirming before the competent judicial authority that the warrant applies to the individual and that proper procedures and the individual's rights have been respected, the state party must then deliver the individual to the Court.[120]

Upon a person's surrender to the Court, the Pre-Trial Chamber must satisfy itself that the person has been informed of the charges against him and of his rights under the Statute. The Chamber must then hold a hearing within 'a reasonable time' thereafter to determine whether there 'is sufficient evidence to establish substantial grounds' to believe that the person committed the crime charged. If the Pre-Trial Chamber confirms the charge, a Trial Chamber is constituted and the case proceeds to trial.[121]

The Statute affords individuals certain rights during investigations and prosecutions that are broadly reflective of the ICCPR, including the right to remain silent and not to incriminate oneself, freedom from cruel, inhuman or degrading treatment, the right to counsel, the presumption of innocence, and the right to be tried fairly and without undue delay. In addition, the Prosecutor must disclose to the defense evidence helpful to the accused's case.[122] The accused must be present at the trial, which is held in public unless otherwise necessary to protect victims, witnesses, or confidential information. The Trial Chamber is responsible for ensuring a fair and expeditious trial, with full respect for the rights of the accused and the protection of victims and witnesses. The Chamber can require the attendance of witnesses and the production of evidence and provide for the protection of confidential information, the accused, witnesses, and victims. In addition, the Trial Chamber has broad authority to issue directions necessary for the fair and impartial conduct of the trial.[123]

At the beginning of the trial, the accused may enter a plea. If the accused pleads guilty, the Court must still determine that the plea is informed, voluntary, and supported by the evidence before accepting it. In addition, if the Court believes that a more complete presentation of the facts is required in the interests of justice, in particular the interests of the

119 *Id.* arts. 54(3), 57, 58.

120 *Id.* art. 59. The state party may, under appropriate circumstances, grant the individual interim release pending surrender. *Id.* art. 59(3)–(6).

121 *Id.* arts. 60, 61. The confirmation hearing may be held without the presence of the accused, if he has waived his right, fled, or cannot be located. *Id.* art. 61(2).

122 *Id.* arts. 55, 66(1), 67; *see also* ICCPR, art. 14.

123 *Id.* arts. 63, 64, 67(1).

victims, it may request the Prosecutor to present additional evidence or may set aside the guilty plea and remit the case for trial. This will enable the Court to serve as a forum not only to try offenders, but also to expose the crimes and allow witnesses to tell their stories. Plea agreements between the prosecution and defense are not binding on the Court.[124]

The Statute requires the Court to protect the safety, physical and psychological well-being, dignity, and privacy of victims and witnesses, in particular where the crime involves sexual or gender violence or violence against children. Any such measures must be consistent with the accused's rights and the fairness of the proceedings. In this connection, the Statute authorizes *in camera* proceedings and the presentation of evidence by electronic or other special means, in particular where a victim of sexual violence or a child is involved. In addition, the Statute provides for the presentation and consideration of the views of victims where their personal interests are affected.[125]

In addition to the evidence submitted by the parties, the Court may request any evidence necessary for the determination of the truth. Evidence obtained in violation of the Statute or internationally recognized human rights is not admissible if the violation casts substantial doubt on the reliability of the evidence or if its admission would seriously damage the integrity of the proceedings. The Statute also stipulates detailed provisions for the protection of information which, in the opinion of a state, would prejudice its national security interests, including consultation obligations with the state concerned and the use of *in camera* or *ex parte* proceedings.[126]

In order for the accused to be convicted, the prosecution must prove guilt 'beyond reasonable doubt'. The Statute expressly calls for the judges to reach decisions by unanimity, but authorizes decisions by majority where the judges cannot reach a unanimous decision. In the event of conviction, the Trial Chamber determines the appropriate sentence, and its decision may include reparations for victims, though any such order will be without prejudice to the rights of the victims under national or international law.[127]

Assessment

The ICC Statute unquestionably represents an immensely important development for international human rights, humanitarian, and criminal

[124] *Id.* arts. 64(8)(a), 65.

[125] *Id.* art. 68. Article 68 also permits the Prosecutor to submit a summary of any information which may lead to the grave endangerment of a witness or his or her family and allows states to apply to the Court for protection of their officials and of confidential or sensitive information. *Id.* art. 68(5), (6).

[126] *Id.* arts. 69(3), (7), 72; *see also id.* art. 73 (information or documents).

[127] *Id.* arts. 66(3), 74(3), 75, 76.

law, in terms of both its institutional contribution to the law's implementation and its codification and progressive development of the substantive law. The Court's constitution reflects a unique and promising blend of the civil and common law systems. Thus, for example, while trial proceedings are largely akin to the more adversarial procedure of the common law, the judges will exercise a degree of supervision over the pre-trial phase similar to that found in civil law countries. Much of the Statute also represents an effort to address deficiencies in the Yugoslavia and Rwanda Tribunal models or to develop attributes of those courts that responded to the special nature of the crimes they adjudicate. Among the noteworthy features of the Statute in this regard are the heightened attention to gender issues, more extensive protection for victims and witnesses, as well as for sensitive information provided by states, and the Court's power to proceed with a trial even where the accused has entered a guilty plea.[128]

While bestowing important supranational elements on the ICC, the Statute also reflects substantial deference to state prerogatives, the complementarity principle being, of course, the central element in this regard. The Statute's admissibility and consent requirements and the rights accorded to interested states to intervene before a prosecution proceeds also represent important concessions to state control of the process. As noted above, the Prosecutor's power to initiate cases was a difficult feature for some states to accept. Accordingly, the Statute includes a number of checks on this power to prevent its abuse or arbitrary use. Thus, for example, the Prosecutor must present any such case to the Pre-Trial Chamber before it goes forward, and interested states have the right to intervene. In addition, the provisions on selection of the Prosecutor and the ability of the states party to remove the Prosecutor from office should limit the potential for abusive conduct.[129]

As noted above, some states have criticized the ICC's potential jurisdiction over nationals of non-parties. However, because the crimes covered by the Statute are subject to universal jurisdiction, this aspect of the Court's jurisdiction is not overreaching from a legal perspective and is consistent with the precedent set by the Yugoslavia Tribunal, which is trying nationals of states that did not consent to its establishment. While legally sound, the assertion of universal jurisdiction on the scale contemplated by the ICC Statute is certainly unusually bold.[130]

128 *See* Arsanjani, *supra* note 98, at 25; *see also* Association of American Law Schools, *Panel on the International Criminal Court*, 36 AM. CRIM. L. REV. 223, 251–52, 254–56 (1999) (remarks of Prof. Blakesley) (ICC leans more heavily to the civil law model and in some ways may be unfair to defendants) [hereinafter AALS Panel].

129 *See* Fernández, *supra* note 112, at 182–88.

130 *See* Roy S. Lee, *Introduction, in* THE INTERNATIONAL CRIMINAL COURT, *supra* note 98, at 1, 29; Sadat and Carden, *supra* note 102, at 412–13; for less friendly critiques, *see* John R. Bolton, *Courting Danger: What's Wrong with the International Criminal Court*, THE NATIONAL INTEREST, Winter

Although participating vigorously in the Statute's drafting, the United States was among the handful of states that voted against its adoption, though eventually signing it at the end of 2000. In particular, the United States considered the ICC's jurisdiction over nationals of non-parties unacceptable in light of the United States military's extensive activities around the globe and was dissatisfied with the degree of Prosecutorial independence. The United States also criticized the Statute for anomalously allowing parties to immunize their nationals from ICC jurisdiction for new crimes added to the Statute by opting out under Article 121(5), while nationals of non-parties would be subject to ICC's jurisdiction for such new crimes. In addition, the US delegation opposed the inclusion of the crime of aggression in light of the inability of the negotiators to agree on a definition and objected to the absence of any requirement for a decision by the Security Council before a prosecution for the crime can take place.[131]

Certainly, the United States is correct in drawing attention to those elements of the Statute which accord the Court greater jurisdiction over nationals of non-parties than over nationals of parties—aspects of the Statute which were undoubtedly added to encourage states to become parties. And, especially in light of the United States' extensive military presence around the world, its anxiety over the Prosecutor's independence and the inclusion of the crime of aggression is not surprising. However, other objections inconsistent with principles recognized by the United States in other contexts or assume the Court will not respect the complementarity regime.[132]

Despite the undeniable accomplishment that the Statute represents, the ability of the Court to address cases of serious human rights abuses will confront a variety of challenges. To begin with, unless the Security Council refers the situation or there is a subsequent change in a state's government, the consent requirements will prevent the ICC from taking jurisdiction over abuses by state-sponsored actors against their own nationals on their own soil—the type of situation most commonly associated with widespread atrocities. This outcome would presumably prevail even if the perpetrator were to travel to another state willing to turn him over to the Court for prosecution. This jurisdictional formula could prevent a tyrant who commits atrocities against his own people from facing justice before the Court, while subjecting to possible prosecution foreign military personnel intervening to halt the atrocities.[133]

Secondly, even with the Statute's extensive detail, significant aspects

1998/99, at 60, 65–66 (criticizing ICC for lacking political accountability); Alfred P. Rubin, *A Critical View of the Proposed International Criminal Court*, 23 FLETCHER F. WORLD AFF. 139 (1999).

131 *See* Scheffer, *supra* note 115, at 17–21. US signature thus hardly suggests ratification.

132 *See* Sadat and Carden, *supra* note 102, at 447–57 (addressing US objections).

133 *See* AALS Panel, *supra* note 128, at 230–31, 257–59.

are articulated only in general terms, leaving it to the prosecution and the judges to define them through the exercise of their discretion and the development of practice and jurisprudence. The Court will thus face a number of thorny questions in interpreting its Statute. One significant issue that the Rome Conference failed to resolve is the effect that amnesties or pardons will have on the Court's jurisdiction. Although prosecution by the ICC in light of amnesties or pardons is not specifically precluded in the Statute, the lawfulness of such trials might well turn on the legality of the underlying amnesty.[134] In this connection, the discretion that the Statute accords the Prosecutor to decline to pursue a case where it would not be in the interests of justice may play a central role. The Prosecutor will need to consider carefully the seriousness of the offenses and, in the case of amnesties or pardons issued after conviction, whether the prosecution by national authorities was, in fact, genuine.[135]

Beyond amnesties, other determinations by the Prosecutor and judges will inevitably call for difficult and subjective inquiries, the outcome of which may produce significant political shockwaves for the countries involved. These include the Prosecutor's ability to decline to pursue a case where prosecution would not be in the interests of justice; the requirement that the Court refuse to admit cases that are not sufficiently serious; and the complementarity provisions that permit the Court's involvement only if it has decided that national tribunals are unable or unwilling to prosecute a case.

Even with its complexities, ambiguities, and anomalies, the Statute birthed by the participants in the Rome Conference represents a generally solid and coherent constitutional foundation for the ICC. Accordingly, its success will ultimately depend on the adequacy of its resources, the integrity and skill of the individuals selected by the states party to staff the Court, and the support accorded its work both by the states party and other states whose cooperation the Court will need to carry out its work.

OPPORTUNITIES AND CHALLENGES

The performance of the UN's *ad hoc* tribunals and the clear prospect of a permanent court shift the debate over the merits of such courts from the speculative to the very real. These tribunals clearly present some merits for trying perpetrators of human rights atrocities. First and most obviously, where national tribunals are truly ineffective or unavailable, international

134 *See* Ch. 7, *supra*; *see also* Steven R. Ratner, *New Democracies, Old Atrocities: An Inquiry in International Law*, 87 GEO. L. J. 707, 720–31 (1999).

135 *See* Holmes, *supra* note 114, at 76–77 (suggesting that if a national prosecution were genuine, *non bis in idem* would preclude prosecution by the ICC); Michael P. Scharf, *The Amnesty Exception to the Jurisdiction of the International Criminal Court*, 32 CORNELL INT'L L.J. 507 (1999).

tribunals may represent the only available judicial option for addressing atrocities, and their international character provides them with some credibility that can aid the transitional process in a fractured society.

Beyond this, like other adjudicative models, an international tribunal can promote the development and clarification of international criminal law. Indeed, the Statutes of the ICTY, ICTR, and ICC have proven important slates on which to advance the codification of international law, and their elaboration has provided invaluable opportunities for states to contribute to the codification process. Moreover, the early decisions of the ICTY and ICTR demonstrate that they will play an authoritative and dynamic role in helping to clarify and advance international law; each *ad hoc* tribunal is influencing the jurisprudence and practice of the other, national courts, the incipient ICC, and even the ICJ.[136] Once the ICC is operational, its broader geographical jurisdiction should allow it to play an even more potent role in advancing the implementation and elaboration of international law. Moving beyond tribunals limited to Yugoslavia and Rwanda also represents an important response to those critics of the *ad hoc* tribunals who complain that the international community has unfairly and hypocritically targeted those conflicts while ignoring others.

As for the prospects for *ad hoc* tribunals, the ICTY and ICTR have so far proven to be models generally acceptable to states. Although any comprehensive assessment of their fairness and effectiveness remains premature, they appear to have addressed many of the problems associated with their Nuremberg and Tokyo predecessors. The substantive crimes over which they have jurisdiction are better established and more clearly defined than five decades ago. The charges of bias and victor's justice leveled at the post-war trials have been addressed in several ways, including by ensuring that the composition of the Tribunals is not limited to any group of states or system and, in the case of the Yugoslavia Tribunal, by making concerted efforts to prosecute offenders from all sides of the conflict. The selection of defendants appears, for the most part, to have remained insulated from direct political pressure, though the Prosecutor's strategy clearly reflects her assessment of political realities. The Tribunals' procedural and evidentiary rules and practice afford greater protection to defendants than did the post-World War II trials and generally comport with contemporary international standards of due process.[137] While one may question particular practices of the Yugoslavia and Rwanda Tribunals, few would argue with the conclusion that the Tribunals are generally dispensing fair justice to their defendants.

136 *See* Murphy, *supra* note 58, at 95–96.

137 *But see* Alvarez, *supra* note 51, at 2039–40, 2061–68 (asserting mixed success of ICTY in overcoming Nuremberg's shortcomings).

Accordingly, if human rights atrocities in other situations are to be pursued through *ad hoc* tribunals, one obvious alternative would be to follow the Rwandan precedent and graft a court onto the existing UN tribunals. This would promote efficiency and ensure uniformity in the interpretation and application of the relevant law. The trial chamber should sit in the country where the atrocities occurred or in a nearby state, with prosecutorial and investigatory staff working there, while the tribunal would share a common appellate chamber and prosecutor with the ICTY and ICTR at The Hague. Jurists from the region should be represented on the court. Alternatively, such a tribunal could be independent of the existing international courts, though this would sacrifice some advantages of efficiency and uniformity.

Nonetheless, the *ad hoc* tribunal model presents a number of daunting issues. First, if the Yugoslavia and Rwanda models are to be followed, the circumstances must support a finding that the requirements for action under Chapter VII (i.e., a 'threat to the peace, breach of the peace, or act of aggression') are met and galvanize the necessary political will for its use. Although the Security Council probably enjoys the prerogative to interpret the meaning of a threat to the peace,[138] some situations may be too remote from the necessary threshold or too politically charged to allow the Council to make the necessary finding. The General Assembly, another UN organ or international organization, a group of interested states, or perhaps even the state where the offenses occurred itself could sponsor a tribunal. However, this method would lack the authority and legally binding effect of a Chapter VII resolution.

Furthermore, some states with their own dubious human rights records are already anxious about the precedent set by the Yugoslavia and Rwanda Tribunals. Although many of these states may have voiced support for creation of the ICC, such easy political gestures do not translate into genuine support for *ad hoc* tribunals, or even the ICC. China and Brazil were particularly wary in the Security Council and only acquiesced to the creation of the Yugoslavia and Rwanda Tribunals because of the extreme and immediate need presented by the respective conflicts.[139] The UN is already said to be suffering from 'tribunal fatigue', especially now that the blueprint for a permanent court has been agreed to; overcoming it, even to address serious offenses, will be no easy task. One response to this concern has been the UN's consideration for Sierra Leone and Cambodia

[138] *Cf.* Interpretation and Application of the 1971 Montreal Convention Arising from the Aerial Incident at Lockerbie (Libya v. U.S.), 1992 ICJ 114, 126 (Apr. 14); *but see Tadic Interlocutory Appeal*, paras. 28–30 (reviewing Council's decision, though finding it justified).

[139] *See* Provisional Verbatim Record of the Three Thousand Two Hundred and Seventeenth Meeting, May 25, 1993, UN Doc. S/PV.3217, at 33–37.

of hybrid tribunals established under domestic law but international in composition, funding, and other aspects.

The existing *ad hoc* tribunals have not been without their flaws, and the problems they have encountered suggest some of the difficulties that any future bodies would inevitably confront. To begin with, although the definitions of the crimes over which the tribunals have jurisdiction, as well as their procedural and evidentiary rules, are substantially more developed than at Nuremberg and Tokyo, the Yugoslavia and Rwanda Tribunals have nevertheless heard cases and issued opinions at a slow pace. Moreover, the tribunals have regrettably failed to attract the same degree of attention around the globe as did the Nuremberg and Tokyo Tribunals. The media coverage of the trials, while increasing, remains sporadic and disappointing; and the courts have not reached out adequately to the populations most affected by their rulings.

Of course, once the ICC comes into existence, an *ad hoc* tribunal to adjudicate human rights abuses falling within the ICC's jurisdiction would be unnecessary. However, as noted above, the ICC's Statute contains various novel or controversial elements, the effect of which remains to be seen. The ICC's prospective jurisdiction will obviously make it useless for addressing atrocities committed before its creation.

The number of states that actually become party to the Court's Statute will be a key determinant of the Court's efficacy and remains a point of speculation. This consideration is significant, because the obligation to cooperate with the Court and to recognize its judgments will extend only to states party to its Statute. Recognizing that acceptance by only a small number of states would impede the Court and detract from its influence and legitimacy, the framers of the Rome Statute required a relatively large number of parties to bring the Court into existence. And, even if a substantial number of states do join the Rome Statute, whether they include those states over whom the Court's jurisdiction will be most needed (i.e., those with troubled human rights situations) will be an important factor in the Court's impact. The Court must also prove itself an effective, efficient, and impartial judicial forum.

Thus, prosecutions before any international tribunal, *ad hoc* or permanent, demand the cooperation of many states, especially the state where the atrocities took place and other states with custody of potential defendants and evidence. Where the offenders have been defeated unconditionally, as in Nazi Germany, this consideration may not pose a problem. However, where the offenders retain some degree of power or remain outside the government's reach, prosecutions before an international tribunal, as with domestic trials, become considerably more problematic. A tribunal unable to enforce its orders and judgments becomes at best an academic exercise and at worst a cynical set-back for international law and justice. The existing *ad hoc* tribunals have found themselves almost entirely dependent on the engagement of interested powers to overcome cases of serious recalcitrance, with pleas to the Security Council virtually useless on their own. There is little reason to expect that the ICC will fare much better in this regard, despite its creation by a larger number of states and its more global character.

Resources are also key to any tribunal's efficacy, and they have been a recurrent problem for both existing tribunals, limiting their ability to obtain needed equipment, conduct investigations, and protect witnesses, and even threatening the tribunals' very survival on occasion. The sense of accomplishment that accompanied the tribunals' creation has at times given way to complacency by much of the international community, throwing into question states' commitment to the missions of these courts. Although certain economies of scale will be achieved with the ICC or by grafting future *ad hoc* tribunals onto the existing UN courts, all require significant additional resources. Criminal investigations and prosecutions require years to run their course. No doubt, many developing countries would likely insist that wealthy nations carry a disproportionate share of the cost of any future *ad hoc* tribunal; and the provisions of the Rome Statute on the ICC's financing present ambiguities that may give rise to knotty disagreements among the states parties.[140] In addition to resource problems, various administrative problems have hampered the ICTY and ICTR and are likely to impede future bodies; these include the difficulties posed by bringing together personnel reared in different legal systems and, if the UN creates the tribunal, frustrations with the UN bureaucracy.

Many of the challenges encountered by the Yugoslavia Tribunal stem from its operation in the context of an ongoing conflict. The disadvantages confronting the defense, which has fewer resources at its disposal than the prosecution, are magnified when trials take place in another country and evidence is located in a land shattered by war. Ongoing conflict greatly hampers the work of the prosecutors and chambers as well. In the former Yugoslavia, the international peacekeeping force initially perceived its goals and those of the ICTY as inconsistent. Although this tension has declined in the former Yugoslavia, similar tensions may very well arise in future contexts.

On a more fundamental level, although an international tribunal can advance the goal of bringing perpetrators of human rights abuses to justice, one must not overemphasize the extent to which even a well-functioning international tribunal can bring about closure to an episode of

[140] *See* ICC Statute, arts. 113–18. For example, while the ICC Statute provides for contributors to be assessed on the basis of the UN scale of assessment, it does not explain how that assessment will take account of the fact that not all UN members will be parties to the ICC or whether Security Council referrals should be assessed in a different manner.

violence and oppression and reconciliation to a society. As discussed in Chapter 7, adversarial proceedings before a criminal tribunal are designed primarily to determine the guilt of individuals, not to produce a comprehensive and balanced analysis of a conflict's historical, political, social, or moral context. In view of such limitations, it should come as little surprise that Serb elements challenge the legitimacy of the Yugoslavia Tribunal.[141] On the other hand, although trials before international tribunals may not generate the emotional closure that many assume, they may still have a profound effect on the way in which the core conflicts are addressed by a society. Such trials at least prompt public discussion and direct it along reasoned and respectful lines.[142]

Finally, on the political plane, the relationship between international courts and conflict resolution has been a subject of concern. As one ILC member succinctly put it, 'When you create an *ad hoc* tribunal, the tribunal itself becomes part of the dispute.'[143] The involvement of tribunals in an ongoing conflict may impede a diplomatic resolution of the conflict, as many of the court's targets will be the very same people with whom the peacemakers must negotiate.[144] Indeed, such concerns gave rise to substantial debate during the negotiation of the Rome Statute over the appropriate relationship between the Security Council and the ICC. As Anthony D'Amato explains:

> [H]owever desirable the idea of war crimes accountability might appear in the abstract, pursuing the goal of a war crimes tribunal may simply result in prolonging a war of civilian atrocities. This would surely be a paradoxical result, for the idea of war crimes accountability is to deter the commission of war crimes and not to serve as a barrier to discontinuing them.[145]

However, D'Amato further suggests that even if a tribunal were bargained away as part of a diplomatic settlement, the court would still have served a useful purpose as a bargaining chip to elicit greater concessions for the more victimized party.[146] The bargaining away of tribunals raises similar considerations as the question of amnesties in the case of national prosecutions, and the international community should tolerate it only under exceptional circumstances. The creation of the ICC in theory mitigates such concerns by making prosecution a clear option rather than merely a

[141] *See* Alvarez, *supra* note 51.

[142] *See id.* at 2084 (quoting Osiel in part) (trials as 'discursive phenomena that, if conducted as "effective public spectacle, stimulate public discussion in ways that foster the liberal virtues of toleration, moderation, and civil respect"').

[143] *The Internationalization of Criminal Law*, 1995 AM. SOC'Y INT'L L. PROC. 297, 303 (remarks of James Crawford).

[144] Anthony D'Amato, *Peace vs. Accountability in Bosnia*, 88 AJIL 500 (1994); David P. Forsythe, *Politics and the International Tribunal for the Former Yugoslavia*, 5 CRIM. L. F. 401, 415–17 (1994).

[145] D'Amato, *supra* note 144, at 502.

[146] *Id.* at 503–05.

bargaining chip; yet some abusers of human rights might seek to demand non-cooperation with the ICC in exchange for giving up an armed struggle or surrendering power.

AFTERWORD ON THE INTERNATIONAL COURT OF JUSTICE AND REGIONAL HUMAN RIGHTS COURTS

In addition to international criminal tribunals, several other international courts can adjudicate cases relating to international criminal law and human rights. Three of these, the Inter-American Court of Human Rights, the European Court of Human Rights, and the recently created African Court of Human Rights are, as their names suggest, geographically limited as to both composition and jurisdiction, while the International Court of Justice is a global institution.[147] These courts are not, however, fora for determining individual accountability for international crimes, as they enjoy neither jurisdiction over individuals nor criminal nor penal jurisdiction in the traditional sense. Instead, they possess jurisdiction only over states and adjudicate state (civil) responsibility for violations of international law.

The courts may nonetheless address issues of international criminal law. For example, petitions by states or individuals may call upon these courts to determine whether a state is violating its international obligations regarding human rights and humanitarian law and, if so, to declare what measures that state must take to remedy the violation. In the most significant case of this type before one of these courts, Bosnia and Herzegovina asked the ICJ in 1993 to find the Federal Republic of Yugoslavia (Serbia-Montenegro) responsible for genocide and to order remedial measures. The ICJ decided that it has jurisdiction over the case and is proceeding to the merits portion of the case.[148] At the end of December 1994, the Inter-American Court of Human Rights issued a

[147] For background on the regional human rights courts, *see generally* THE EUROPEAN SYSTEM FOR THE PROTECTION OF HUMAN RIGHTS (R. St. J. MacDonald et al. eds., 1993); SCOTT DAVIDSON, THE INTER-AMERICAN COURT OF HUMAN RIGHTS (1992). For background on the ICJ, *see generally* THE INTERNATIONAL COURT OF JUSTICE AT A CROSSROADS (Lori F. Damrosch ed., 1987); FIFTY YEARS OF THE INTERNATIONAL COURT OF JUSTICE (Vaughan Lowe and Malgosia Fitzmaurice eds., 1996); SHABTAI ROSENNE, THE LAW AND PRACTICE OF THE INTERNATIONAL COURT, 1920–1996 (3d ed. 1997).

[148] Application of the Convention on the Prevention and Punishment of the Crime of Genocide (Bosnia and Herzegovina v. Yugo.), 1993 ICJ 3 (Apr. 8), 1993 ICJ 325 (Sept. 13). Two of the opinions on provisional measures have already tentatively addressed the question whether Yugoslavia had committed genocide. 1993 ICJ at 431–32 (sep. op. Lauterpacht) (concluding Serbian actions in Bosnia constitute genocide under Convention); *id.* at 449 (dissenting op. Tarassov) (opining that neither genocidal character of alleged acts nor Serbia's responsibility for them had been established).

significant advisory opinion affirming that enforcement of domestic law by governmental officials in a manner that violates certain human rights may give rise to individual criminal responsibility under international law.[149]

Although these courts cannot actually prosecute perpetrators of human rights violations, their involvement in cases relating to them can serve important goals. First, their judgments can put pressure on governments to comply with their international obligations (including duties to prosecute offenders) and to co-operate with efforts to bring perpetrators to justice. They can also establish an authoritative factual record and adjudicate state responsibility for violations of international law, which may provide psychological support to victims and their loved ones. Their decisions have also served the cause of developing human rights and humanitarian law by interpreting unsettled legal issues. Finally, as these courts are established institutions, parties can initiate cases relatively quickly and inexpensively, and their work does not require apprehension of offenders.

Yet beyond their inability to prosecute offenders, use of these courts presents a number of disadvantages for the goal of accountability. Their physical distance from the victims and the abstract and convoluted nature of their judgments dilute the psychological impact of their work. The extensive time required for them to render their decisions compounds this problem. Moreover, because international adjudication tends to be conservative, its results may disappoint a party that seeks a broader and more activist interpretation of the law. There can also be no guarantee that states will comply with decisions; states have resisted the authority of the ICJ on a number of occasions, notably Iran during the 1979–81 hostage crisis and the United States during the conflict in Nicaragua. Finally, although the jurisdiction of the regional courts is sufficient to cover most serious violations of international human rights law occurring in their region, the ICJ's jurisdictional rules are complex and its jurisdiction more difficult to invoke.

Furthermore, where atrocities were committed by a prior regime and a new regime has condemned the practices of its predecessor, such courts would seem an inappropriate forum for such cases, which would perhaps even be barred by requirements that they hear only actual and ongoing disputes. And, while it might conceivably be possible to fashion cases involving the adjudication of individual accountability, the willingness of these courts to act as quasi-criminal tribunals is highly questionable, and

[149] International Responsibility for the Promulgation and Enforcement of Laws in Violation of the Convention, Inter-Am. Ct. Hum. Rts. Advisory Op. OC-14/94, Dec. 9, 1994, 1994 ANN. REP. INTER-AM. CT. HUM. RTS. 89, 100 (1995); *see also* Velasquez Rodriguez Case, Inter-Am. Ct. Hum. Rts. (Ser. C), No. 4, para. 166, at 152 (1988) (judgment) (duty of states to investigate and prosecute serious human rights abuses).

their evidentiary practices and capabilities are ill-suited to the task. Finally, a respondent state is likely to perceive a case brought by another state as an unfriendly act, perhaps hampering prospects for co-operation by the former in bringing perpetrators to justice and yielding undesirable political consequences for a young democracy's political system. Thus, finding a state that is both willing and able to bring a case will often be difficult, if not impossible.[150] Even if the court's intervention is sought through advisory proceedings, building the necessary political support in an international organ to request an advisory opinion can be difficult, often resulting in a confusing or tepid request.[151] In the case of the regional courts, however, the availability of individual petition procedures alleviates many of these difficulties and provides an important mechanism for the advancement of human rights.

In light of the above, cases before the ICJ or regional human rights courts may serve their most useful purpose as an adjunct to other mechanisms of individual accountability. Such a suit might seek to clarify international obligations concerning arrest, prosecution, extradition, or judicial assistance and encourage recalcitrant states to comply with them. For example, if a state were known to have custody of a defendant and refused requests for extradition to a national or international tribunal with jurisdiction over that defendant, a case might be brought to induce that state to extradite the defendant. In addition, were a state to refuse to investigate abuses or grant an amnesty to offenders in violation of its international law duties to prosecute them, a suit might be brought against that state to stop it from doing so.

150 For a discussion of the political impediments to interstate enforcement mechanisms concerning human rights, *see* Payam Akhavan, *Enforcement of the Genocide Convention Through the Advisory Opinion Jurisdiction of the International Court of Justice*, 12 HUM. RTS. L.J. 285, 287–88 (1991) and sources cited therein.

151 *See* 1 ROSENNE, *supra* note 147, at 351–61.

10

Non-Prosecutorial Options: Investigatory Commissions, Civil Suits, and Immigration Measures

Despite the appeal of criminal prosecutions as the most direct way of pursuing justice for gross violations of international human rights and humanitarian law, the political and practical challenges to employing prosecutorial mechanisms have led to the dramatic development in the 1980s and 1990s of alternative processes. These mechanisms may not provide as rigorous a determination of, or as serious a punishment for, an individual's culpability as do prosecutions. Yet in many cases they represent the best or only alternative to criminal trials, valuable precursors or complements to criminal trials, or even, under some theories of justice, the optimal form of accountability in certain situations. We here examine three such processes: investigatory commissions, civil suits, and revocation of immigration status.[1]

INVESTIGATORY COMMISSIONS: ACCOUNTABILITY THROUGH TRUTH AND ACKNOWLEDGMENT

Many nations that have endured serious human rights violations have pursued accountability by establishing an investigatory commission, often referred to as a truth commission or a commission of inquiry.[2] Speaking generally, these panels investigate a past period of human rights abuses (or, in fewer cases, humanitarian law-based crimes) in a particular country, in the end producing an official report. Priscilla Hayner enumerates four criteria that generally characterize a commission:

1. it focuses on the past;
2. it does not concentrate on any one specific event, 'but attempts to paint

[1] In the case of the last two mechanisms, we focus on civil suits and immigration status under US law.

[2] In offering an overview of this ever more utilized mechanism, we recognize the many permutations possible as well as the prospect of new forms in the future. *See generally* Truth Commissions: A Comparative Assessment (Harvard Law School Human Rights Program ed., 1997).

the overall picture of certain human rights abuses, or violations of international humanitarian law, over a period of time';

3. it 'usually exists temporarily and for a pre-defined period of time, ceasing to exist with the submission of a report of its findings'; and
4. it gains some sort of authority from its sponsor 'that allows it greater access to information, greater security or greater protection to dig into sensitive issues, and a greater impact with its report'.[3]

Aside from these common threads, panels have varied widely; and many of a commission's attributes will depend on its historical, political, and security context.

Investigatory commissions are a relatively young, though increasingly common, form of accountability. The panels established for Argentina, Chile, El Salvador, and South Africa are probably the most widely known examples, though numerous other commissions have been created in such varied places as Uganda, Germany, and Zimbabwe.[4] Several panels formed in the late 1990s are also of particular interest, including the Guatemalan Commission for Historical Clarification and UN commissions of inquiry concerning massacres in Burundi in 1993 and East Timor in 1999.[5]

Commissions are usually created at a transition point in a society 'to demonstrate or underscore a break with a past record of human rights abuses, to promote national reconciliation, and/or to obtain or sustain political legitimacy'.[6] Reflecting one common pattern, the civilian governments that replaced repressive regimes in Argentina and Chile created panels to

[3] Priscilla Hayner, *Fifteen Truth Commissions—1974 to 1994: A Comparative Study*, 16 HUM. RTS. Q. 597, 599, 604 (1994). Hayner's comprehensive study considers commissions in: Uganda (1974 and 1986), Bolivia (1982), Argentina (1983), Uruguay (1985), Zimbabwe (1985), Philippines (1986), Chile (1990), Chad (1991), African National Congress (1992 and 1993), Germany (1992), El Salvador (1992), Rwanda (1993), and Ethiopia (1993).

[4] For detailed examinations of the Argentine and Salvadoran commissions, *see, respectively*, AMERICAS WATCH, TRUTH AND PARTIAL JUSTICE IN ARGENTINA: AN UPDATE (1991); Thomas Buergenthal, *The United Nations Truth Commission for El Salvador*, 27 VAND. J. TRANSNAT'L L. 498 (1994); for some of the numerous commentary on South Africa's Truth and Reconciliation Commission, *see* MARTHA MINOW, BETWEEN VENGEANCE AND FORGIVENESS: FACING HISTORY AFTER GENOCIDE AND MASS VIOLENCE 52–90 (1998); John Dugard, *Reconciliation and Justice: The South African Experience*, 8 TRANSNAT'L L. AND CONTEMP. PROBS. 277 (1998); Albie Sachs, *Truth and Reconciliation*, 52 SMU L. REV. 1563 (1999); Jennifer J. Llewellyn and Robert Howse, *Institutions for Restorative Justice: The South African Truth and Reconciliation Commission*, 49 U. TORONTO L.J. 355 (1999); LOOKING BACK, REACHING FORWARD: REFLECTIONS ON THE TRUTH AND RECONCILIATION COMMISSION OF SOUTH AFRICA (Charles Villa-Vicencio and Wilhelm Verwoerd eds., 2000).

[5] GUATEMALA: MEMORIA DEL SILENCIO (1999), available at http://hrdata.aaas.org/ceh [hereinafter MEMORIA DEL SILENCIO]; Letter dated 25 July 1996 from the Secretary-General Addressed to the President of the Security Council, Aug. 22, 1996, UN Doc. S/1996/682 (transmitting Burundi Report); Identical Letters dated 31 January from the Secretary-General Addressed to the President of the General Assembly, the President of the Security Council and the Chairperson of the Commission on Human Rights, Jan. 31, 2000, UN Doc. A/54/726-S/2000/59 (transmitting East Timor Report).

[6] Hayner, *supra* note 3, at 604.

investigate human rights abuses of prior regimes. In yet another pattern, best exemplified by the experience of El Salvador, South Africa, and Guatemala, commissions have emerged from a political agreement aimed at resolving a civil conflict.[7] Not surprisingly, commissions have also differed in their success and impact, depending upon the underlying political will of a variety of actors, the state of a country's transition, and the available resources.

Sponsors and Staffing

Investigatory commissions are usually established by the executive branch of a national government, though national legislatures, international organizations, non-governmental organizations, and other entities have also organized them. Thus, for example, the UN sponsored El Salvador's highly regarded panel and the commissions for Burundi and East Timor; a group of human rights NGOs sponsored a panel for Rwanda; and the African National Congress created two commissions to investigate abuses by its own officials. International sponsorship, particularly by the UN, can bring many benefits, including greater neutrality, financial and other support, security, and international attention. UN sponsorship of the Salvadoran commission encouraged witnesses to come forward and enhanced the commission's credibility among certain elements of Salvadoran society. Guatemala's commission was an independent entity established under the 1994 peace accord, but enjoyed financial support from the EU, Japan, the United States, other governments, and the UN.[8] However, international sponsorship may sometimes be infeasible, for example where domestic opposition to foreign involvement in the country's affairs is powerful and inflexible.[9] Nevertheless, the emerging trend suggests that most future panels will continue to be government-sponsored, although it should be added, they must not be government-controlled.[10]

[7] *See generally* Americas Watch, Human Rights and the 'Politics of Agreements' (1991); The Healing of a Nation? 38–65 (Alex Boraine and Janet Levy eds., 1995) (essays by Patricio Aylwin, José Zalaquett, and Catalina Smulovitz); Sachs, *supra* note 4; Christian Tomuschat, *Between National and International Law: Guatemala's Historical Clarification Commission*, *in* Liber Amicorum Günther Jaenicke – Zum 85. Geburtstag 991, 992–96 (Christiane Philipp ed., 1998).

[8] 1 Memoria del Silencio, *supra* note 5, paras. 21–23.

[9] Hayner, *supra* note 3, at 599, 604, 641–43; *see also* Margaret Popkin and Naomi Roht-Arriaza, *Truth as Justice: Investigatory Commissions in Latin America*, 20 Law and Social Inquiry 79, 94 (1995).

[10] José Zalaquett, a member of the Chilean commission, stresses that establishing public approval for a government's human rights policy, either through legislative approval or referendum, is crucial to the policy's legitimacy. José Zalaquett, *Confronting Human Rights Violations Committed by Former Governments: Principles Applicable and Political Constraints*, 13 Hamline L. Rev. 623, 628, 632 (1990). South Africa encouraged extensive public debate and input in constructing the mandate of its truth commission.

A commission's composition profoundly influences its functioning and ultimate impact. A broad range of individuals have served on panels, including judges, lawyers, human rights activists, military and police officers, labor union representatives, legislators, forensic experts, academics, and social workers. Most commissions have consisted heavily or entirely of citizens of the particular country, though some have been exclusively foreign. Foreign personnel present a number of trade-offs. In many cases, the foreign origin of commissioners may be necessary to impart a sense of confidence and security among witnesses, to bring expertise or a broader perspective, to encourage impartiality, and to enhance the weight of the commission's work. Neutrality concerns were so strong in El Salvador that even the commission's staff was entirely foreign. This foreign composition allowed the commission access to information that would have been unobtainable by Salvadorans and proved crucial to its success. The Guatemalan Commission, however, had one foreign member and a mixed staff. In some cases, security concerns may preclude the inclusion of the subject country's nationals. In Chad and Uganda, domestic commissioners faced threats and reprisals, causing some members to flee, and the Argentine panel's members became targets of attacks by right-wing paramilitary groups.[11]

On the other hand, domestic commissioners may offer a better understanding of their country's social and political context, and their presence following completion of the commission's work can encourage compliance with its recommendations and promote national confidence. Moreover, where a commission relies on foreign personnel, its opponents may exploit sovereignty sensitivities to discredit its work.[12] In asking the Secretary-General to set up the commission on East Timor, the UN Human Rights Commission apparently was addressing this issue in specifically requesting 'adequate representation of Asian experts'.[13] While there can be no blanket rule for the optimal composition of a commission, past experience reveals that a commission's success will depend heavily on the independence, stature, and moral authority of its members. The nature and history of the abuses that the commission will be examining may also make diversity in its composition—whether as to ethnicity, politics, profession, or other attributes—critical to establishing credibility.[14]

[11] Popkin and Roht-Arriaza, *supra* note 9, at 94–95; Buergenthal, *supra* note 4, at 517, 542–43; Roberto Canas, *Acknowledgement, Truth & Justice, El Salvador*, *in* DEALING WITH THE PAST: TRUTH AND RECONCILIATION IN SOUTH AFRICA 54 (Alex Boraine et al. eds., 1994); AMNESTY INTERNATIONAL, ARGENTINA: THE MILITARY JUNTA AND HUMAN RIGHTS: REPORT OF THE TRIAL OF THE FORMER JUNTA MEMBERS 9 (1987); Tomuschat, *supra* note 7, at 1000–01.

[12] *See, e.g.*, Hayner, *supra* note 3, at 612, 624, 631, 643, 654; Popkin and Roht-Arriaza, *supra* note 9, at 94–95.

[13] Comm'n Hum. Rts. Res. 1999/S-4/1, Sept. 27, 1999.

[14] TRUTH COMMISSIONS, *supra* note 2, at 21–22, 42–43 (need for diversity among national commis-

Mandate and Scope of Activities

At the time of a commission's establishment, the sponsoring entity provides it with a mandate usually setting forth its goals, powers, and procedures. Commissions in Latin America have generally pursued four goals: creating an authoritative record, providing redress and a platform for victims, making recommendations for reform, and establishing accountability of perpetrators.[15] In some cases, the mandates have confined the activities of the commission to particular types of abuses, preventing it from investigating other significant human rights abuses. For example, the mandates of the Bolivian and Uruguayan panels limited their inquiries to disappearances, precluding investigations into torture and other major abuses.[16] The statute creating the South African Truth and Reconciliation Commission (TRC) limited its mandate to killing, abduction, torture, and severe ill-treatment, rather than all the abuses of the apartheid years.[17]

In addition to its official mandate, the scope of activities will also depend on such factors as the commission's resource and time constraints, political conditions in the country, and the scale of the abuses it examines. El Salvador's commission concentrated on a limited number of the most serious cases—specifically, those that were especially heinous or representative of a pattern of outrageous conduct. The Chilean panel reported on every case resulting in the death or disappearance of the victim where it was able to reach a conclusion. Argentina's commission documented almost 9,000 disappearances, though its report took a more general approach and did not report on individual cases. While Uganda's 1986 commission was broadly mandated to investigate all aspects of human rights violations, breaches of the rule of law, and excessive abuses of power during a twenty-four-year period, in practice it examined only certain representative cases. And the Guatemalan panel, faced with an impossible mandate of investigating all human rights abuses during the 32-year civil conflict (within six months), focused on particularly egregious

sioners); Paul Lansing and Julie C. King, *South Africa's Truth and Reconciliation Commission: The Conflict between Individual Justice and National Healing in the Post-Apartheid Age*, 15 ARIZ. J. INT'L AND COMP. L. 753, 762–64 (1998); Buergenthal, *supra* note 4, at 541–43 (noting also the importance of good rapport among commissioners); David Weissbrodt and Paul W. Fraser, *Book Review: Report of the Chilean National Commission on Truth and Reconciliation*, 14 HUM. RTS. Q. 601, 603–04 (1992) (Chilean president selected representatives from non-governmental sector and individuals with ties to Pinochet regime).

[15] Popkin and Roht-Arriaza, *supra* note 9, at 80.

[16] Hayner, *supra* note 3, at 613–14, 616, 636–38 (arguing for broad mandates with commission left to limit scope of its activities).

[17] *See* 1 TRUTH AND RECONCILIATION COMMISSION: FINAL REPORT, ch. 4, paras. 42–59 (1998), available at www.mg.co.za/mg/projects/trc [hereinafter TRC REPORT].

situations (e.g., genocide against indigenous peoples) and registered other cases that concerned violations of Common Article 3, without inquiring into the fate of the estimated 200,000 victims.[18]

Although some panels have focused solely on governmental abuses (usually those of a prior regime), many have also addressed abuses by other elements, such as rebel groups, for example, the URNG in Guatemala or the ANC in South Africa. In light of international law's recognition of duties on non-state actors, serious human rights abuses by opposition forces must face similar scrutiny, whatever the justice of their cause.[19] Most commissions have not examined the role of foreign governments in the country's human rights abuses, though some, such as those in Chad, Chile, Honduras, and Guatemala, have done so.[20]

Commission Recommendations

Commissions need not only focus on the past, and some have also had the authority to make recommendations for the future. These recommendations include legal, institutional, and judicial reforms to promote compliance with human rights norms and measures concerning compensation. The Salvadoran panel went even further, advising the dismissal and disqualification from office of those responsible for certain abuses, including the resignation of the Supreme Court. The Rwandan commission's report included recommendations concerning foreign assistance directed at the international community. The Honduran panel called for the creation of a human rights education program, as well as an official apology and monument to the victims. Unfortunately, although commission recommendations sometimes enjoy a legally binding status, the entrenched interests of those responsible for abuses have led to a disappointing record of compliance.[21]

Identifying Perpetrators

Whether a commission should identify perpetrators by name has proved an extremely sensitive issue, both politically among elites and emotionally among victims and abusers. Commission mandates have generally

18 Hayner, *supra* note 3, at 615, 621–22, 636–37; Popkin and Roht-Arriaza, *supra* note 9, at 96–97; Buergenthal, *supra* note 4, at 502–04; Jorge Correa S., *Dealing with Past Human Rights Violations: The Chilean Case After Dictatorship*, 67 NOTRE DAME L. REV. 1455, 1464 (1992); Remarks by Justice Arthur H. Oder, Chairman, Commission of Inquiry into Violations of Human Rights, Feb. 14–17, 1990, *reprinted in* 2 TRANSITIONAL JUSTICE 515–16 (Neil J. Kritz ed., 1995); 1 MEMORIA DEL SILENCIO, *supra* note 5, paras. 75–78.

19 For an intelligent discussion of the question of moral equivalence and impartiality, *see* 1 TRC REPORT, *supra* note 17, ch. 4, paras. 60–81.

20 Hayner, *supra* note 3, at 637–39; *see also* Popkin and Roht-Arriaza, *supra* note 9, at 96–98 (merits and risks of examining abuses by all parties to a conflict).

21 Hayner, *supra* note 3, at 609, 622–23, 638; Popkin and Roht-Arriaza, *supra* note 9, at 85–86; 5 TRC REPORT, *supra* note 17, ch. 8; 5 MEMORIA DEL SILENCIO, *supra* note 5.

not addressed the question, though the Guatemalan commission's mandate specifically precluded it and the South African TRC's required publication of the names of those receiving amnesty.[22] Until 1992, no commission had published names. Identifying perpetrators seems important to the goals of a commission and does not itself result in loss of liberty for a named perpetrator. Where the country does not have a judicial system capable of carrying out fair and effective prosecutions, this consideration is particularly salient. Yet, insofar as the naming of names exposes the accused to public condemnation, perception of guilt, and possibly even security risks, it raises due process concerns and may prove politically infeasible.[23] Thus, for example, the Salvadoran commission named names, because it considered it necessary to put an end to impunity and because the judicial system was corrupt and incapable of rendering impartial judgments. In contrast, the Chilean panel determined that its mandate prohibited naming perpetrators, likely out of fear of the military's reaction; instead, it indicated the perpetrators' organizational affiliations. Although the Argentine commission did not name names, it submitted a list of perpetrators to the president, which was soon leaked to the press.[24]

Relationship to Judicial Proceedings

Commissions need not act as the sole mechanism of accountability. Some have, either by mandate or by choice, forwarded their findings to judicial authorities. The Argentine commission submitted more than 8,000 cases to authorities for possible prosecution, though victims and NGOs initiated most of the prosecutions after the release of the commission's report. Both the Chilean and Ugandan commissions also handed over information to judicial authorities. In contrast, information derived by the South African panel is not admissible in subsequent criminal or civil proceedings against an individual who has been denied amnesty. However, commission findings have only rarely become the subject of later criminal prosecutions, due to the fragility of the political or judicial system. Indeed, such weakness likely motivated resort to a commission in the first place as a substitute for prosecutions.[25]

[22] *See* Agreement on the establishment of the Commission to clarify past human rights violations and acts of violence that have caused the Guatemalan population to suffer, June 23, 1994, 36 ILM 283 (1997); Promotion of National Unity and Reconciliation Act, Law No. 34 of 1995, § 20(6) (S. Afr.). On the TRC's approach to naming others, *see* 1 TRC REPORT, *supra* note 17, ch. 4, paras. 152–57.

[23] *Compare* Mark Ensalaco, *Truth Commissions for Chile and El Salvador: A Report and Assessment*, 16 HUM. RTS. Q. 656, 662–63 (1994) with Hayner, *supra* note 3, at 648. *See also* 1 TRC REPORT, *supra* note 17, ch. 4, paras. 152–57.

[24] Hayner, *supra* note 3, at 647–50; Popkin and Roht-Arriaza, *supra* note 9, at 105–07; Correa, *supra* note 18, at 1472; *see also* Buergenthal, *supra* note 4, at 519–22.

[25] Weissbrodt and Fraser, *supra* note 14, at 605–06; Oder, *supra* note 18, at 515–16; Peter Parker,

Amnesties or pardons granted before, after, or even during the commission's investigations have sometimes prevented prosecutions. Chile's 1978 amnesty law precluded prosecution of the vast majority of cases examined by the commission. In Argentina, although several major prosecutions preceded the commission's report, amnesties and pardons granted after the report's release effectively halted judicial proceedings. In a creative and potentially far-reaching variation on this approach, South Africa's amnesty plan shields only individuals who acknowledge their offenses and acted for political motives, providing some closure for victims without a full-fledged trial.[26] This has elicited some dramatic admissions concerning the apartheid regime's abuses, but has also ignited a wrenching national debate over whether such confessions are worth the price of individual impunity for some unbearably awful deeds.[27] Although an amnesty might assist a commission in obtaining cooperation from targets and officials, amnesties can contravene a state's obligations under international law.[28]

Resources

Adequate resources prove a determining factor in the success of commissions. The Bolivian panel was not afforded sufficient resources by the government, while South Africa's commission had a very large budget (though its task was enormous). El Salvador's UN-sponsored commission enjoyed ample funding of about $2.5 million, and the international source of its resources helped to protect the panel's independence, credibility, and authority. Many other commissions have relied on substantial assistance, both in cash and in kind, from foreign sources, including governments, international organizations, NGOs, foundations, and even private companies.[29]

The Politics of Indemnities, Truth Telling and Reconciliation in South Africa, 17 HUM. RTS. L.J. 1, 8 (1996). On Latin American experiences concerning the relationship between investigatory commissions and judicial proceedings, *see* Popkin and Roht-Arriaza, *supra* note 9, at 107–13.

[26] *See* Law No. 34, *supra* note 22, § 20 (1).

[27] *See, e.g.*, Ronald C. Slye, *Amnesty, Truth, and Reconciliation*, *in* TRUTH V. JUSTICE: THE MORAL EFFICACY OF TRUTH COMMISSIONS IN SOUTH AFRICA AND BEYOND (Robert I. Rotberg and Dennis Thompson eds., 2000); Sachs, *supra* note 4, at 1573–77; Timothy Garton Ash, *True Confessions*, N.Y. REV. BOOKS, July 17, 1997, at 33.

[28] *See* Ch. 7, *supra*.

[29] Douglass W. Cassel, Jr., *International Truth Commissions and Justice*, 5 ASPEN INST. Q. 77 (1993); Hayner, *supra* note 3, at 614, 619–20, 623–24, 628, 644; Oder, *supra* note 18, at 521–22. Staff sizes of commissions have ranged from the minimal levels of commissions in Honduras, Chad, and the Philippines, to the higher levels of the Argentine and Chilean commissions, which each had staffs of approximately 60 full-time personnel, to the Guatemala and South Africa commissions, which employed over 250 people. Hayner *supra* note 3, at 644; Popkin and Roht-Arriaza, *supra* note 9, at 85; 1 MEMORIA DEL SILENCIO, *supra* note 5, para. 27; *South Africa: TRC Monthly Wage Bill Totals 2.7M Rands—Minister*, BBC MONITORING AFRICA, May 22, 1998 (available on LEXIS/NEXIS).

Duration

The duration of commission mandates ranges considerably, though in most cases they operate for less than a year. Duration and quality are not, however, necessarily correlated. While time limits have constrained the work of some panels, others that are highly regarded, such as the Chilean and Argentine commissions, had relatively brief durations. In contrast, Brazil's unofficial commission, whose work also garnered respect, conducted its clandestine research for over five years; South Africa's commission submitted its report after three years (although amnesty ruling and reparations processing continued); and the Guatemalan commission operated for eighteen months. Other panels without time limits, such as Uganda's in 1984, have broken up without producing a report or taken so long that the public lost confidence in the process.[30] Ideally, the scope of the abuses under study should determine the appropriate duration. However, where resources are especially constrained, salaries and other time-dependent expenses may require the commission to operate for a more limited period.

Procedures and Dissemination of Findings

A commission's mandate or the panel itself determines the nature of its procedures.[31] The rigor of a commission's methodology is important to its credibility, and, certainly, the greater the potential impact of its work on the rights of suspected perpetrators, the higher the procedural standards required. With regard to transparency, closed proceedings may lead to accusations of partiality and abuse; yet, public proceedings may pose risks to the security of commissioners and witnesses. In the end, the country's political and security situation will determine the best balance between public and non-public proceedings. While Uganda's 1974 commission operated very publicly, broadcasting some testimony on live radio and television, security concerns led El Salvador's commission to operate more confidentially.[32] Consistent with the South African TRC's victim-centered approach, its hearings were quite deliberately public, unless the panel determined that the interests of justice or safety required otherwise.[33]

[30] Hayner, *supra* note 3, at 619–20, 640–41.

[31] The procedures and methodologies employed by a commission are usually described in its report. *See, e.g.*, NUNCA MÁS: THE REPORT OF THE ARGENTINE NATIONAL COMMISSION ON THE DISAPPEARED 428–41(Farrar Straus Giroux trans., 1986) (1984); 1 CHILEAN NATIONAL COMMISSION ON TRUTH AND RECONCILIATION, REPORT OF THE CHILEAN NATIONAL COMMISSION ON TRUTH AND RECONCILIATION 13–25 (Phillip E. Berryman trans., 1993); 1 TRC REPORT, *supra* note 17, ch. 6; 1 MEMORIA DEL SILENCIO, *supra* note 5, paras. 86–208.

[32] Hayner, *supra* note 3, at 611–13, 627–29, 647; Buergenthal, *supra* note 4, at 513–16.

[33] Law No. 34, *supra* note 22, § 33; 1 TRC REPORT, *supra* note 17, ch. 5, paras. 5–6 and ch. 6, paras. 32–41, 60–62; *see generally* Tina Rosenberg, *Recovering from Apartheid*, THE NEW YORKER, Nov. 18, 1996, at 86; Ash, *supra* note 27.

A panel's resources and mandate, as well as the political and security conditions in the country, will also dictate its methodologies. Usually, commissions rely on testimony from individuals and information from governmental and non-governmental sources. Chile's commission, for example, received information from over 4,000 witnesses and scores of organizations. In contrast, Brazil's unofficial panel, which had to operate secretly, relied almost exclusively on clandestine use of the military government's own records.[34] Often, security conditions will require reliance on confidential information, though this may undermine due process for targets of inquiry as well as the commission's credibility. A commission operating during civil conflict may be unable to obtain access to parts of the country.

Commissions generally do not enjoy the power to subpoena witnesses or evidence, though in a rare and dramatic exception, South Africa's TRC was given search and seizure powers, as well as the authority to compel witnesses to testify.[35] Many panels, such as those of Argentina, El Salvador, and Guatemala, and the UN commissions for Burundi and East Timor, encountered serious difficulties in obtaining cooperation and information from certain elements—usually the armed forces and security services—that felt threatened by their work. The Salvadoran commission also found that lingering fear and suspicion prevented many witnesses from coming forward, especially in the early months of its work, a problem exacerbated by the continued presence of many of its expected targets in positions of power.[36]

The extent to which a panel's inquiry resembles judicial proceedings assumes great importance where the commission intends to identify perpetrators. Some commissions have tried to address the due process concerns engendered in identifying perpetrators by employing quasi-judicial procedures. The African National Congress' 1992 commission, the TRC, and the Ugandan panel allowed or provided the accused legal representation and permitted them to question witnesses. The Salvadoran commission interviewed the accused, explained the accusations against them, and gave them an opportunity to defend themselves. However, the continuing potential of some elements for violence even after the formal end of the civil war prevented it from informing the accused of the identities of witnesses against them and from affording them an opportunity to cross-examine.[37]

The dissemination of commission reports correlates closely with their

[34] Weissbrodt and Fraser, *supra* note 14, at 607–08; LAWRENCE WESCHLER, A MIRACLE, A UNIVERSE: SETTLING ACCOUNTS WITH TORTURERS 9–11 (1990); TORTURE IN BRAZIL: A REPORT BY THE ARCHDIOCESE OF SÃO PAULO (Joan Dassin ed., 1986).

[35] Law No. 34, *supra* note 22, §§ 29–32.

[36] AMNESTY INTERNATIONAL, *supra* note 11, at 9; Buergenthal, *supra* note 4, at 513–19.

[37] Hayner, *supra* note 3, at 632–33, 649–50; Oder, *supra* note 18, at 513–14.

impact, as wide dissemination allows a larger audience to benefit from the commission's work. In addition, broad distribution indicates that the country's political climate is respectful of the commission and its work, increasing the likelihood that those in positions of power will accord its findings authority and implement its conclusions. The Argentine commission's report, *Nunca Mas*, was widely circulated and became a quick best-seller. The Chilean president presented the report of Chile's panel on national television, publicly apologized to victims on behalf of the state, and sent a copy of the report to each victim's family with a letter indicating on what page information on the victim could be found. In contrast, opponents of accountability succeeded in significantly limiting circulation of the Uruguayan commission's report and in preventing any release of the Zimbabwean commission's 1985 report. The tense security situation in Burundi prompted that panel's sponsor, the UN Security Council, to delay release of its findings, out of concern that they could further inflame the country's ethnic strife. And, as Uganda's experience demonstrated, where illiteracy is relatively high and media penetration limited, adequate dissemination of a commission's work will be most difficult.[38]

Opportunities and Challenges

Investigatory commissions are now a firmly entrenched mechanism of accountability, to which they can make a significant contribution in a number of ways. First, an effective panel can establish an official, authoritative record of abuses in a country, thereby helping to educate the public, possibly deter future abuses, and strengthen the rule of law. Indeed, by examining the full scope of abuses in historical context, these panels are likely to paint a more complete picture of abuses—a more useful truth, as it were—than a trial court focusing on the guilt or innocence of a limited set of defendants. Secondly, by acknowledging the suffering of victims and their families, helping to resolve uncertain cases, and involving ordinary citizens in its work, a commission can act as a cathartic and healing psychological balm for the victims of human rights abuses and their families. This helps impart to the citizenry a sense of dignity and empowerment that can help them move beyond the pain of the past. Truth-telling by victims and perpetrators advances the restorative component of justice in a most direct way.[39]

[38] Hayner, *supra* note 3, at 615–18; José Zalaquett, *Acknowledgement, Truth & Justice, Chile, in* DEALING WITH THE PAST, *supra* note 11, at 47, 52; Oder, *supra* note 18, at 520, 521–22.

[39] *See* 1 TRC REPORT, *supra* note 17, ch. 5, paras. 29–52, 80–100. For a philosophical defense of the TRC from this perspective, *see* Jonathan Allen, *Balancing Justice and Social Unity: Political Theory and the Idea of a Truth and Reconciliation Commission*, 49 U. TORONTO L.J. 315 (1999). In the words of one commentator on the TRC: 'Truth telling is a form of accountability. An arena in

Thirdly, a commission can promote justice by imposing moral condemnation and possibly laying the groundwork for other sanctions, especially if it assigns responsibility for abuses. Fourthly, it can demonstrate that human rights are a priority for a successor government and further discredit the perpetrators of abuses. In so doing, the commission can attempt to lay the basis for the rule of law as meaningfully as do trials.[40] Fifthly, while a judicial model is limited to the establishment of guilt or innocence, an investigatory panel can more readily go beyond such confines to make recommendations to deal with past abuses and prevent future ones. Indeed, its most important role may lie in these advisory functions. Even in cases where panel recommendations are ignored, they may still 'provide pressure points around which civilian society or the international community can lobby for change in the future'.[41]

Although some of the goals described above can be achieved through adjudicative models, an investigatory commission is especially suited for achieving them in countries where limited resources, the absence of a strong and impartial legal system, and other circumstances make a judicial approach infeasible.[42] In addition, in comparison to most of the other mechanisms examined in this volume, an investigatory commission can be created and carry out its functions relatively quickly and easily. Truth commissions thus cannot be criticized uniformly as a second-best form of accountability and justice. Their utility depends upon the purposes of holding individuals responsible for human rights abuses.[43]

Nevertheless, investigatory commissions are not substitutes for criminal trials. They do not make a true judicial determination of responsibility and cannot directly punish perpetrators. In addition, their activities usually lack the solemnity and authority of judicial proceedings.[44] Identification of a perpetrator and his offense seems a paltry substitute for trial and punishment where he is personally responsible for atrocities of the severest magnitude. Moreover, where a society is unable to pursue a genuine process for reconciliation or a commission is not properly designed and administered, a panel runs the risk of aggravating matters. Their activities may become little more than political fodder for manipulation by competing elements, create unrealistic expectations of further

which the powerful must account for their past misdeeds and in which the violator and accuser stand as equals is one of empowerment, in which the aura of inviolability is removed.' Parker, *supra* note 25, at 13. *See generally* TRUTH V. JUSTICE, *supra* note 27.

40 *See* Allen, *supra* note 39, at 335–38 (on 'justice as ethos').

41 Hayner, *supra* note 3, at 609; *see also* Ensalaco, *supra* note 23, at 666, 673.

42 *See* Ensalaco, *supra* note 23, at 671. Such was the case in Chile, El Salvador, and Guatemala.

43 *See* Ch. 7, *supra*.

44 *See* Naomi Roht-Arriaza, *Conclusion: Combating Impunity*, *in* IMPUNITY AND HUMAN RIGHTS IN INTERNATIONAL LAW AND PRACTICE 281, 286 (Naomi Roht-Arriaza ed., 1995).

accountability, or, perhaps worst of all, whet a hunger for vengeance and exacerbate a society's already seething divisions. For these reasons, proponents of accountability must carefully examine the political and social context in which the commission would operate and tailor the commission's attributes to that environment.[45] Likewise, the panel itself must manage its activities with the utmost sensitivity to such constraints.

The task of investigatory commissions is further complicated by their lack of the institutional history and credibility from which well-functioning judicial mechanisms benefit. Although their architects now have a variety of precedents from which to learn, commissions remain *ad hoc* institutions that must build their acceptability and *modus operandi* almost from the ground up, and are likely to be greeted with a combination of hope and distrust. Compounding these challenges, the states most in need of an investigatory panel are often the ones least able to provide the resources necessary for it to conduct its work. States emerging from an episode of massive human rights violations may be desperately poor, devastated by violence, and depleted of their most talented and uncorrupted citizens. Such shattered states are unlikely to have the economic or human resources necessary to create a commission, making engagement by the international community imperative.

CIVIL SUITS: AN ALTERNATIVE DAY IN COURT FOR VICTIMS

The legal systems of some countries offer victims of human rights abuses opportunities to seek civil redress against the perpetrators for international law violations. This section briefly examines special laws applicable to such actions in the United States, which has proved the source of nearly all such litigation. Other states are now beginning to see victims institute cases as well, although these have involved the filing of criminal complaints demanding prosecution rather than true civil suits.[46]

Statutory Framework

US federal courts have relied on different sources of authority to adjudicate

[45] *See* Priscilla B. Hayner, *International Guidelines for the Creation and Operation of Truth Commissions: A Preliminary Proposal*, 59 LAW AND CONTEMP. PROBS. 173, 178–80 (1996).

[46] *See, e.g.*, Luc Reydams, *Universal Jurisdiction over Atrocities in Rwanda: Theory and Practice*, 4 EUR J. CRIME, CRIM. L. AND CRIM. JUSTICE 18, 35–47 (1996); *Who's Next? Asks French Press as Kabila Feels Heat of Ruling*, BIRMINGHAM POST, Nov. 28, 1998, at 7.

civil claims arising out of human rights and humanitarian law violations committed abroad.[47]

Alien Tort Claims Act

Enacted in 1789, the Alien Tort Claims Act provides that '[t]he district courts shall have original jurisdiction of any civil action by an alien for a tort only, committed in violation of the law of nations or a treaty of the United States'.[48] Thus, the ATCA provides federal courts with *subject matter jurisdiction* if three basic requirements are met: (1) the plaintiff is an alien, (2) the defendant is responsible for a tort, and (3) the tort violates the law of nations or a treaty to which the United States is party.[49]

The ATCA remained an obscure basis for US federal court jurisdiction until the 1980 landmark case *Filartiga* v. *Peña-Irala*.[50] In that case, the family of a Paraguayan man who had been tortured to death brought a civil action against the alleged perpetrator while he was physically present in the United States. The Second Circuit Court of Appeals held that the ATCA provided it with subject matter jurisdiction over the case. Since *Filartiga*, plaintiffs have brought several other cases under the ATCA against perpetrators of human rights violations committed abroad. Many have been brought against very high-ranking former or current foreign government officials, including presidents and cabinet ministers. For the most part, the courts have followed the *Filartiga* court's interpretation of the ATCA, the most glaring exception being Judge Robert Bork's opinion concurring in a decision of the Court of Appeals for the District of Columbia Circuit in *Tel-Oren* v. *Libyan Arab Republic*.[51]

Due to the high incidence of default by defendants in ATCA cases owing to their non-appearance in court, and the variety of approaches taken by courts, several aspects of the ATCA remain unsettled. The principal issue usually involves the interpretation of the term 'in violation of the law of nations'. In *Filartiga*, the Second Circuit held that the phrase referred to 'international law not as it was in 1789, but as it has evolved and exists among the nations of the world today'.[52] In *Forti* v. *Suarez-*

[47] Civil suits against perpetrators of human rights abuses might also be brought in US state courts under state law.

[48] 28 U.S.C. § 1350 (1994).

[49] The ATCA does not require that the defendant have personally committed the offense, and principles of command responsibility would apply. *See, e.g.*, Forti v. Suarez-Mason, 672 F. Supp. 1531, 1537–38 (N.D. Cal. 1987). The place of commission and defendant's nationality are irrelevant under the ATCA, and, as noted, the plaintiff must be a non-US national. These aspects appear to make the ATCA (and TVPA) unique worldwide.

[50] 630 F.2d 876 (2d Cir. 1980); *see also, e.g.*, Jean-Marie Simon, *The Alien Tort Claims Act: Justice or Show Trials?*, 11 B. U. INT'L L.J. 1, 11–28 (1993).

[51] 726 F.2d 774, 798–823 (D.C. Cir. 1984).

[52] 630 F.2d at 881. Further refining its interpretation, the court stated that: 'It is only where the nations of the world have demonstrated that the wrong is of mutual, and not merely several, concern,

Mason, a California district court described the acts falling under the statute as those that violate 'universal, definable, and obligatory international norms'.[53] Among the acts courts have found to constitute violations of the law of nations for purposes of the ATCA are torture, extrajudicial killings, disappearances, unpaid forced labor, and prolonged arbitrary detention.[54] Future litigation under the ATCA is likely to expand further the universe of human rights violations falling under the statute.[55]

In order to sue successfully in a US court, a plaintiff must not only establish the court's subject matter jurisdiction, but also the existence of a *cause of action*, or right to sue, for the violation complained of. Most courts have held that the ATCA provides a federal cause of action for violations of international law falling under it.[56] However, the courts have not demonstrated uniformity on this question.[57]

Although most courts have applied international law as the *substantive law* in suits under the ATCA, either directly or by virtue of its incorporation into federal law,[58] the choice of substantive law can be complicated, and courts have not always automatically looked to international law. Rather, the court's choice of substantive law will depend to a large extent on its determination as to which jurisdiction's law gives rise to the cause of action, sometimes leading to the application of state or foreign tort law to the merits portion of the case.[59]

by means of express international accords, that a wrong generally recognized becomes an international violation within the meaning of the statute.' *Id.* at 888.

[53] 672 F. Supp. at 1540. The court further explained that the international consensus on the norm must have existed at the time of the alleged violations. *Id.* at 1540 n. 5; *see also, e.g.*, In re: Estate of Ferdinand Marcos Human Rights Litigation, 25 F.3d 1467, 1474–76 (9th Cir. 1994); Xuncax v. Gramajo, 886 F. Supp. 162, 184 (D. Mass. 1995) (endorsing *Forti*).

[54] *See, e.g.*, Kadic v. Karadzic, 70 F.3d 232, 241–44 (2d Cir. 1995), *cert. denied*, 518 U.S. 1005 (1996) (genocide, war crimes, torture, summary execution); *Marcos*, 25 F.3d 1467 (torture, summary execution, disappearances); Trajano v. Marcos, 978 F.2d 493 (9th Cir. 1992), *cert. denied*, 508 U.S. 972 (1993) (torture); *Filartiga*, 630 F.2d 876 (torture); *Xuncax*, 886 F. Supp. 162 (torture, summary execution, prolonged arbitrary detention, disappearances); *Forti*, 672 F. Supp. 1531 (torture, extrajudicial killings, prolonged arbitrary detention); Doe v. Unocal Corp., 963 F. Supp. 880, 892 (C.D. Cal. 1997) (forced labor); Iwanowa v. Ford Motor Company, 67 F. Supp.2d 424, 440–42 (D.N.J. 1999) (forced labor and enslavement) (dictum).

[55] *See* Beth Stephens and Michael Ratner, International Human Rights Litigation in U.S. Courts 79–94 (1996); *Tel-Oren*, 726 F.2d at 782 (Edwards, J., concurring) (suggesting that a crime carrying universal jurisdiction would give rise to jurisdiction under ATCA). *But see, e.g., Xuncax*, 886 F. Supp. at 186–92; Forti v. Suarez-Mason, 694 F. Supp. 707, 709–12 (N.D. Cal. 1988) (norm against cruel, inhuman, and degrading treatment not sufficiently defined to give rise to jurisdiction).

[56] *See, e.g.*, Abebe-Jira v. Negewo, 72 F.3d 844, 846–48 (11th Cir. 1996), *cert. denied*, 519 U.S. 830; *Marcos*, 25 F.3d at 1475; *Filartiga*, 630 F.2d at 887; *Xuncax*, 886 F. Supp. at 179; Jama v. United States Immigration and Naturalization Service, 22 F. Supp.2d 353, 362–63 (D.N.J. 1998).

[57] *See Tel-Oren*, 726 F.2d at 801, 804–19 (Bork, J., concurring) (concluding that ATCA does not provide cause of action); *see also Tel-Oren*, 726 F.2d at 775–88 (Edwards, J., concurring) (concluding that domestic tort law may also provide cause of action); *Trajano*, 978 F.2d at 500–03.

[58] *See, e.g.*, Filartiga v. Peña-Irala, 577 F. Supp. 860, 863–65 (E.D.N.Y. 1984).

[59] *See* Jeffrey M. Blum and Ralph G. Steinhardt, *Federal Jurisdiction Over International Human Rights Claims: The Alien Tort Claims Act after Filartiga v. Peña-Irala*, 22 Harv. Int'l L.J. 53, 102 (1981).

Torture Victim Protection Act

In 1992, the United States enacted the Torture Victim Protection Act, which authorizes civil suits against individuals who, under the color of law of any foreign nation, torture or summarily execute another person.[60] The TVPA requires four basic elements: (1) the defendant must have committed torture or an extrajudicial killing; (2) the defendant must have acted under actual or apparent authority, or color of law, of a foreign nation; (3) the plaintiff must be a victim, their legal representative, or a person who may be a claimant in a wrongful death action; and (4) the plaintiff must have exhausted remedies in the country where the conduct giving rise to the claim occurred. The TVPA bolsters the ATCA by extending the right to sue to US citizen plaintiffs. In addition, it was intended to codify the *Filartiga* court's interpretation of the ATCA, thereby explicitly granting the basis for a cause of action which Judge Bork had found lacking in *Tel-Oren*. Unlike the ATCA, however, the TVPA covers only torture and summary execution claims.

Other Sources

Pursuant to their federal question jurisdiction, federal courts possess jurisdiction over any case 'arising under' the Constitution or laws of the United States.[61] US courts have long held, at least in theory, that international law forms part of US federal law,[62] and a few courts have found that violations of specific and universal norms of international law are actionable under US federal question jurisdiction.[63] However, the courts have not been uniform on this issue.[64] A US federal court may also enjoy jurisdiction under the 'diversity' statute if the litigants are from different countries or states.[65] Finally, litigants may also be able to bring claims before state courts under applicable state law and, if related to a federal court claim, a federal court may also be able to hear a claim under state law pursuant to its pendant jurisdiction.[66]

60 28 U.S.C. § 1350 note (1994). It is unclear whether the TVPA is jurisdictional or merely provides a cause of action which gives rise to federal jurisdiction under the ATCA or federal question jurisdiction. *See, e.g., Kadic*, 70 F.3d at 246 (adopting latter view).

61 28 U.S.C. § 1331 (1994).

62 *See, e.g.,* The Paquete Habana, 175 U.S. 677, 700 (1900); Banco Nacional de Cuba v. Sabbatino, 376 U.S. 398 (1964).

63 *See, e.g., Forti*, 672 F. Supp. at 1543–44; *Filartiga*, 630 F.2d at 887 n. 22 (dictum); White v. Paulsen, 997 F. Supp. 1380, 1383–84 (E.D. Wa. 1998) (dictum).

64 *See, e.g., Tel-Oren*, 726 F.2d at 810–16 (Bork, J., concurring); *Xuncax*, 886 F. Supp. at 193–94.

65 28 U.S.C. § 1332 (1994). *See, e.g.,* Linder v. Portocarrero, 963 F.2d 332, 336–37 (11th Cir. 1992) (diversity jurisdiction in action by US plaintiffs against aliens who had allegedly murdered US citizen in Nicaragua).

66 *See, e.g., Xuncax*, 886 F. Supp. at 194–97. For this reason, claims for international human rights law violations brought before federal courts usually include corresponding state law claims. STEPHENS AND RATNER, *supra* note 55, at 167.

Parties and Personal Jurisdiction

As indicated above, the identity of a plaintiff or a defendant in international human rights law claims before US courts will depend on the basis for the court's jurisdiction. Plaintiffs in past cases have included victims, their families, and legal representatives of their estates. Plaintiffs may also be able to bring claims as class actions.[67] Although plaintiffs need not be physically present in the United States, their absence may pose logistical difficulties (e.g., communication and evidentiary problems) and legal hurdles (e.g., increased risk of dismissal for *forum non conveniens*). Where plaintiffs face security risks, they may be able to bring their claims anonymously.[68]

As for defendants, cases have successfully been brought only against individuals, as foreign governments have usually enjoyed sovereign immunity, and the TVPA only authorizes claims against individuals.[69] The TVPA also expressly requires that the defendant have acted under authority or color of law of a foreign nation. Some courts have interpreted the ATCA implicitly to include a similar requirement on the erroneous assumption that international law never applies to private actors.[70] Usually, the defendant's official position has been sufficient to satisfy this requirement. At the same time, courts are increasingly recognizing that non-state actors may violate the law of nations, giving rise to a cause of action under the ATCA.[71] Victims are also suing multinational corporations under the ATCA, alleging complicity in human rights abuses.[72] US courts also need to satisfy due process requirements under the US Constitution in exercising personal jurisdiction over a defendant, which require that the defendant have certain minimum contacts with the jurisdiction.[73] However, service of process over a person physically present within the state where the court sits, even if only transiently, will satisfy constitutional requirements.[74]

[67] *See, e.g.*, *Marcos* and *Kadic*, in which classes included all those who suffered certain human rights abuses by the defendant's agents.

[68] STEPHENS AND RATNER, *supra* note 55, at 41, 44–45.

[69] 28 U.S.C. §§ 1604–05 (1994); 28 U.S.C. § 1350 note (1994); *see also* Antiterrorism and Effective Death Penalty Act of 1996, Pub. L. No. 104–132, § 221, 110 Stat. 1214, 1241 (1996) (eliminating immunity for certain cases of torture and killing).

[70] *See, e.g.*, *Tel-Oren*, 726 F.2d at 791–95; *Forti*, 672 F. Supp. at 1541.

[71] *See Kadic*, 70 F.3d at 239–44 (genocide and war crimes by private actor); *Unocal*, 963 F. Supp. at 892 (forced labor).

[72] *See generally* Doe v. Unocal Corp., 110 F.Supp. 2d 1294 (C.D. Cal 2000) (summary judgment for defendant); Beanal v. Freeport-McMoran, 969 F.Supp. 362 (E.D. La. 1997), *aff'd*, 197 F.3d 161 (5th Cir. 1999) (dismissing claims for failure to plead sufficient facts).

[73] *See* International Shoe Co. v. Washington, 326 U.S. 310, 316–17 (1945).

[74] Burnham v. Superior Court of California, 495 U.S. 604, 612–16 (1990).

Defenses

Statutes of limitations may pose a hurdle to suits in US federal courts arising from relatively old human rights abuses. The TVPA limits actions to those commenced within ten years of the relevant events, although the legislative history indicates that equitable tolling principles may apply. Thus, for example, the statutory period would stop running during any period of time the defendant was outside the United States, enjoyed immunity, or concealed his whereabouts, or the judicial system of the foreign country made filing a suit futile.[75] The ATCA contains no specific statute of limitations, and a court will, therefore, look to other sources of law on this issue. The cases do not demonstrate uniformity, with courts looking to analogous federal law (especially the TVPA), international law, forum state law, and the law of the state where the acts occurred.[76] The TVPA was enacted only in 1992, and the question of its retroactive application is thus sometimes crucial, though the issue is not entirely settled. Although statutes are generally presumed not to have retroactive effect, those courts which have considered the issue have applied the TVPA retroactively.[77]

As noted above, the TVPA requires the plaintiff to have exhausted domestic remedies in the country where the acts occurred. Although not explicit in the ATCA, this requirement also applies to suits under that statute, but it will not bar a suit where domestic remedies would be ineffective, futile, or unduly prolonged.[78] While *forum non conveniens* rules are often at issue in suits for acts committed abroad, they have never successfully been raised in ATCA or TVPA suits. Generally, courts accord deference to the plaintiff's choice of forum; in order for a court to dismiss a case, the defendant must establish that an adequate alternative forum exists and that the private and public interest weigh heavily in favor of

[75] Pub. L. No. 102–256, § 2(c), 106 Stat. 73, 73 (1992), *codified at* 28 U.S.C. § 1350 note (1994); H.R. Rep. No. 367, 102d Cong., 2d Sess. 5 (1991), reprinted in 1992[4] U.S.C.C.A.N. 84, 88; Stephens and Ratner, *supra* note 55, at 147–48.

[76] The law governing tolling principles may be different from that governing the statute of limitations. Thus, for example, while the *Forti* court applied the forum state's statute of limitations, it applied federal tolling principles. The court went on to hold that these principles toll the statutory period where the defendant's wrongful conduct or extraordinary circumstances, such as a war, prevented timely assertion of the claim. 672 F. Supp. at 1547–51. *See also* Hilao v. Estate of Marcos, 103 F.3d 767, 773–74 (9th Cir. 1996); *Iwanowa*, 67 F. Supp.2d at 461–68.

[77] *See Marcos*, 25 F.3d at 1475–76; Cabiri v. Assasie-Gyimah, 921 F. Supp. 1189, 1194–97 (S.D.N.Y. 1996); *Xuncax*, 886 F. Supp. at 176–78.

[78] *See, e.g.*, *Xuncax*, 886 F. Supp. at 178; Mushikiwabo v. Barayagwiza, 1996 WL 164496 (S.D.N.Y. 1996) (finding that plaintiffs had fulfilled exhaustion requirements of TVPA by demonstrating that Rwandan judicial system is virtually inoperative and unable to deal with civil claims in the near future).

trial in that forum.[79] Where the foreign country lacks a reasonably effective and independent judicial system, where obtaining personal jurisdiction over the perpetrator before another forum would be difficult, or where it would be dangerous for the plaintiff to return to the foreign country, a court is unlikely to find that an adequate alternative forum exists.[80]

While sovereign immunity would preclude most civil suits against a foreign government,[81] US courts have recognized immunity for individuals only when they acted within the scope of their authority and have refused to consider gross violations of human rights as meeting that test.[82] Diplomatic immunity would also preclude suits against individuals who are accredited diplomats at the time of suit. In any event, the foreign state can always waive any immunity which might apply to an individual.[83] Likewise, the act of state doctrine is unlikely to preclude claims arising from serious human rights abuses, since the doctrine applies only to public acts committed by a government recognized by the United States at the time of suit, and a US court would likely refuse to consider gross human rights violations to be legitimate public acts.[84] Finally, the courts have generally held that the political question doctrine does not preclude consideration of an ATCA or TVPA case.[85]

Remedies

Both compensatory and punitive damage awards are generally available to victorious plaintiffs in ATCA and TVPA cases, and many awards have been quite large.[86] Damages in the Marcos litigation, which involves

[79] Piper v. Reyno, 454 U.S. 235, 250–52, 257–61 (1981). Dismissal on grounds of *forum non conveniens* is waived by the defendant's default. *Id.* *See also* Wiwa v. Royal Dutch Petroleum Company, 226 F.3d 88 (2d Cir. 2000).

[80] *See, e.g., Cabiri*, 921 F. Supp. at 1198–99.

[81] *See, e.g.*, Argentine Republic v. Amerada Hess, 488 U.S. 428, 434–39 (1989); *Tel-Oren*, 726 F.2d at 775 (Edwards, J., concurring), 804 (Bork, J., concurring); *Unocal*, 963 F.Supp. at 886–88; *see also supra* note 69 (1996 amendment to FSIA).

[82] *See, e.g., Marcos*, 25 F.3d at 1470–72 (no immunity for acts violating Philippine and international law); Chuidian v. Philippine National Bank, 912 F.2d 1095, 1106 (9th Cir. 1990); *Xuncax*, 886 F. Supp. at 174–76.

[83] *See, e.g.*, In re Doe, 860 F.2d 40 (2d Cir. 1988); Paul v. Avril, 812 F. Supp. 207, 210–11 (S.D. Fla. 1993).

[84] *See, e.g., Marcos*, 25 F.3d at 1470–72; *Filartiga*, 630 F.2d at 889–90; *Filartiga*, 577 F. Supp. at 862; *Unocal*, 963 F. Supp. at 893–95. *But see Forti*, 672 F. Supp. at 1544–47, 1551 (doctrine might apply if defendant acted pursuant to direct orders). Head of state immunity should also not preclude suits in similar circumstances.

[85] *See, e.g., Kadic*, 70 F.3d at 248–50; *Marcos*, 25 F.3d at 1470–72; STEPHENS AND RATNER, *supra* note 55, at 141–43. *But see Tel-Oren*, 726 F.2d at 801–04 (Bork, J., concurring), 823 (Robb, J., concurring); *Iwanowa*, 67 F. Supp.2d at 483–89.

[86] *See, e.g., Filartiga*, 577 F. Supp. at 863–65; *Mushikiwabo*, 1996 WL164496 at 3; *US jury orders Radovan Karadzic to pay 745 million [dollars] in damages to women*, AGENCE FRANCE PRESSE, Aug. 10, 2000 (available on LEXIS/NEXIS).

nearly 10,000 class action plaintiffs, amount to some $2 billion.[87] However, virtually no judgments under the ATCA or TVPA have been collected, and many defendants have chosen to flee the United States during the course of the litigation.[88] Plaintiffs may be able to minimize this problem by obtaining pre-judgment attachment of the defendant's assets and pursuing enforcement of any judgment against assets located abroad.[89]

Opportunities and Challenges

The US legal system clearly provides unique avenues for victims of human rights abuses to pursue civil redress against perpetrators present in the United States, and the legal systems of other countries may also provide victims with some opportunities. While civil suits do not lead to the same degree of accountability as a criminal process, they do offer a way of seeking justice and represent one form of authoritative adjudication of legal issues relating to human rights violations. Monetary reparations, even if less satisfying to many victims than criminal convictions, do demonstrate the perpetrator's harm to, and duty to, the victim.[90] Even if defendants flee the jurisdiction, such suits still bring attention to past atrocities, provide victims with a forum to present their claims, and deprive the defendants of foreign refuge in the countries where the cases are brought.[91] Moreover, obtaining a judgment against the defendant affords the plaintiff an opportunity to pursue any of the defendant's assets uncovered in jurisdictions willing to enforce the judgment.

Certainly, such suits can face a number of legal and practical hurdles. As noted above, some courts have adopted relatively restrictive interpretations of the relevant law. While evidentiary standards in civil suits are lower than in criminal cases, many of the same evidentiary problems confronting prosecutions also impede civil suits, and long distances between the forum and the places where the abuses occurred surely exacerbate them. On the other hand, if civil suits could proceed in the territorial state, some of these problems could be avoided.

87 In re: Estate of Ferdinand Marcos Human Rights Litigation, 910 F. Supp. 1460 (D. Ha. 1995), *aff'd sub nom Hilao*, 103 F.3d 767.

88 Stephens and Ratner, *supra* note 55, at 216–18 (also noting that, while theoretically available, US courts are unlikely to grant injunctive relief). Attorneys' fees may also be available, depending on which law the court believes governs the issue. *Id.*; *see, e.g.*, *Filartiga*, 577 F. Supp. at 865 (ordering payment on grounds that Paraguayan law so provides).

89 Stephens and Ratner, *supra* note 55, at 218–24.

90 *Cf.* ICC Statute, arts. 77, 79 (empowering court to fine convicted persons and place proceeds in trust fund for victims).

91 For further thoughts, *see* Beth Stephens, *Conceptualizing Violence Under International Law: Do Tort Remedies Fit the Crime?* 60 Alb. L. Rev. 579, 603–06 (1997).

Of course, the option of civil suits will not be available in all countries and under all circumstances. The ATCA's and TVPA's reliance on universal jurisdiction, to permit suits based on acts with which the United States has little or no connection, appears to be unique. Even in those countries where the courts would be able to entertain purely domestic cases, the judicial branch may not be independent enough to withstand pressure from political leaders bent on closing their courts to politically sensitive lawsuits.

IMMIGRATION MEASURES: DENYING REFUGE TO OFFENDERS

The penchant of gross violators of human rights for escaping justice has led many to flee the site of their atrocities. This tendency became most apparent after World War II, when many Nazis moved to other countries where they hoped to begin new lives in relative obscurity. More recently, perpetrators of the Rwandan genocide have sought to avoid retribution at home or prosecution before the international tribunal in Arusha by seeking refuge in other African countries, Europe, Canada, and the United States. They have joined other potential human rights abusers in seeking refuge.[92] In such cases, the immigration law of their country of refuge may permit the denaturalization and deportation of such individuals. This section briefly examines US immigration law on this issue.[93]

Denaturalization

Naturalization as a US citizen may be challenged only by a denaturalization proceeding brought by the government. Denaturalization not only deprives an individual of his US citizenship, but also renders him amenable to deportation if he otherwise falls within one of the classes of deportable aliens. It must be premised on some impropriety in the original naturalization, usually some form of misrepresentation or concealment. The law authorizes denaturalization: (1) where the naturalization was 'illegally procured', or (2) where it was 'procured by concealment of a material fact or by wilful misrepresentation'.[94]

The contours of the illegal procurement ground are particularly unclear,

[92] *See* Chitra Ragavan, *A safe haven, but for whom?*, U.S. News and World Rep., Nov. 15, 1999, at 22.

[93] For a key Canadian case ordering the expulsion of a Rwandan, *see* Mugesera v. Minister of Citizenship and Immigration, Immigration and Refugee Board Appeal Division, Nov. 6, 1998, *discussed in* William A. Schabas, *International Decisions*, 93 AJIL 529 (1999).

[94] 8 U.S.C. § 1451(a) (1994).

though the government seldom brings proceedings on this ground alone.[95] Deliberately giving false testimony in naturalization proceedings, however, would justify denaturalization on this ground.[96] As for the second ground for denaturalization, it applies only to material misrepresentations and concealment. The Supreme Court has defined materiality to refer to cases where disclosure of the truth would have justified denial of citizenship or might have led to the discovery of other facts that would have justified denial of citizenship.[97] However, later court opinions attempting to refine this standard have actually confused its interpretation and left it unclear.[98] Among the types of misrepresentations and concealment that have given rise to denaturalization under this ground are those concerning prior criminal records, subversive activities and associations (mainly former Nazis), and identity.[99] Denaturalization is a civil, rather than criminal, proceeding. No time limits apply to denaturalization; proceedings may be brought at any time after an alien has been naturalized.[100]

Deportation

Deportation is the primary means by which a state removes undesirable individuals from its territory. US law only permits deportation of aliens,[101] thus requiring that any US citizen first be denaturalized before being deported. Human rights offenders could potentially fall within four of the classes of deportable aliens defined under US law by virtue of their human rights abuses or their affiliation with certain organizations—namely, aliens who have engaged in certain criminal activities; aliens whose presence may have adverse foreign policy consequences; aliens affiliated with certain proscribed organizations; and aliens who have engaged in fraud or misrepresentation.[102]

As for aliens who have committed crimes, US law generally permits

95 4 Charles Gordon and Stanley Mailman, Immigration Law and Procedure § 11.02[3][c] (2000).

96 Kungys v. United States, 485 U.S. 759, 779–80 (1988).

97 *See* Chaunt v. United States, 364 U.S. 350 (1960).

98 *See, e.g.*, *Kungys*, 485 U.S. 759 (five separate opinions on issue); Gordon and Mailman, *supra* note 95, § 100.02[3][b].

99 *See, e.g.*, Federenko v. United States, 449 U.S. 490 (1981) (failure to disclose service as Nazi death camp guard); Gordon and Mailman, *supra* note 95, § 100.02[3][b][iv].

100 *See, e.g.*, Costello v. United States, 365 U.S. 265 (1961) (denaturalization after 27 years). For more detail on denaturalization procedure, *see* Gordon and Mailman, *supra* note 95, § 100.02[4].

101 Bilokumsky v. Tod, 263 U.S. 149 (1923).

102 8 U.S.C. § 1227 enumerates the classes of aliens deportable from the United States. 8 U.S.C. § 1227(a)(1)(A) broadly provides for the deportability of any alien who, at the time of entry or adjustment of immigration status, was within one or more of the classes of excludable aliens under the law at such time.

the deportation of any alien who has been convicted of a crime involving 'moral turpitude', an aggravated felony, or multiple crimes; who has engaged in any criminal activity that 'endangers public safety or national security'; who has engaged in terrorist activity; or who has engaged in genocide as defined by the Genocide Convention.[103] Secondly, any alien may be deported if his presence or activities in the United States would, as determined by the Secretary of State, have 'potentially serious adverse foreign policy consequences'; however, if the foreign policy consequences arise from beliefs, statements, or associations which would be lawful within the United States, then the Secretary of State must determine that the alien's presence or activities would 'compromise a compelling United States foreign policy interest'.[104] This is a relatively broad ground for exclusion that rests solely in the reasonable discretion of the Secretary of State.

Thirdly, any alien who is or has been a member of, or affiliated with, the Communist or any other totalitarian party is deportable. However, exceptions apply where the membership or affiliation was involuntary or necessary to obtain certain essentials of living, occurred solely when the alien was under sixteen years of age, or has been terminated for a certain period of time.[105] Lastly, US law authorizes the deportation of an alien who has committed fraud or misrepresentation of a material fact in procuring a visa, other documentation, entry into the United States, or any other benefit under US immigration law.[106] As in the denaturalization context, the courts have not clearly defined the contours of the materiality standard. Misrepresentation of a fact that would have been grounds for exclusion will clearly qualify.[107] Thus, concealing one's identity or untruthfully responding to questions on immigration forms concerning prior commission of crimes will often justify deportation.

Like denaturalization, deportation is a civil proceeding,[108] and no statute of limitations generally applies to it.[109] If found deportable, the deportee designates the country of deportation, provided that country is willing to accept him and the Attorney General does not conclude that it would be prejudicial to the United States to deport him there. The deportee

[103] 8 U.S.C. §§ 1227(a)(2)(A), (a)(4)(A), (a)(4)(B), (a)(4)(D), 1182(a)(2)(A), (a)(3)(A), (a)(3)(B), (a)(3)(C), (a)(3)(E) (1994 and 1998 Supp. IV). A conviction *in absentia* does not constitute a conviction for these purposes. 22 C.F.R. § 40.21(a)(4) (2000).

[104] 8 U.S.C. §§ 1227(a)(4)(C), 1182(a)(3)(C) (1998 Supp. IV).

[105] 8 U.S.C. §§ 1227(a)(1)(A), 1182(a)(3)(D) (1998 Supp. IV). Service in the armed forces does not in and of itself constitute membership or affiliation with a proscribed organization for immigration law purposes. 22 C.F.R. § 40.34(b) (2000).

[106] 8 U.S.C. §§ 1227(a)(1)(A), 1182(a)(6)(C) (1998 Supp. IV).

[107] GORDON AND MAILMAN, *supra* note 95, § 71.04[2][a].

[108] *See, e.g.*, Harisiades v. Shaughnessy, 342 U.S. 580 (1952). For more detail on deportation procedures, *see* GORDON AND MAILMAN, *supra* note 95, chap. 72.

[109] GORDON AND MAILMAN, *supra* note 95, §§ 71.01[2][c], 71.01[4].

may make only one such determination, and if that designation fails, the Attorney General then designates the country of deportation. The Attorney General must give first priority to the country of which the deportee is a national; failing that, the Attorney General may select from among a broad variety of alternatives.[110]

Opportunities and Challenges

Although not a criminal prosecution, immigration sanctions, whether in the United States or other countries, nevertheless present an opportunity for bringing some justice to bear on those responsible for human rights abuses. Immigration proceedings can provide a forum for exposing an individual's involvement in past abuses and, as civil proceedings, procedural and evidentiary requirements are considerably less burdensome than in a criminal context. If successful, such proceedings can deprive perpetrators of havens from which they can escape justice. And deportation may also provide a means for bringing such individuals into the custody of tribunals with jurisdiction to try them.

The greatest hurdles to engaging this mechanism lie in tracking down perpetrators and convincing governments to invoke the requisite procedures. Many human rights violators attempting to escape justice will have carefully covered their tracks and, in some cases, they may have benefited from the clandestine assistance of the government or other elements in the country in which they have sought refuge. Of course, where the foreign government has provided the perpetrator refuge, the political barriers to engaging immigration sanctions are especially formidable. A transition in governments within the state of refuge can offer an opportunity for deportation, as was the case with the deportation of Nazi fugitive Klaus Barbie from Bolivia. And, even though the standard of proof is lower in immigration proceedings, the gathering of adequate evidence can still present serious obstacles, especially where a long period of time has elapsed since the abuses or the country where they occurred does not wish to cooperate.

Finally, there is the question of where to send the perpetrator after the engagement of immigration measures. Obviously, the best result entails sending the individual back to his home state (or possibly a third country) where he will be fairly prosecuted. If deportation merely transfers a perpetrator to a new refuge where he can enjoy continued impunity, the effort to bring immigration sanctions to bear will likely have been in vain, and perhaps even counter-productive. Furthermore, the deporting country will face a serious moral, political, and even legal dilemma where the only countries willing to accept a deported perpetrator are prepared to prosecute the

110 8 U.S.C. § 1231(b)(2) (1998 Supp. IV).

individual, but are unlikely to afford him due process. One last possibility is that no country will be willing to accept the individual, in which case the deporting state may have no choice but to tolerate his continued presence or consider trying him under principles of universal jurisdiction.

For all these reasons, immigration measures will be most successful if they are the product of careful planning, coordination, and execution within and among governments and human rights NGOs. This may call for formal consultations and institutions to achieve these goals. In 1979, the US government initiated a program to denaturalize former Nazis in the United States; Canada began such a program in 1995 but extended it to contemporary abusers of human rights.[111] In light of the dwindling number of targets of the US program, its mandate also merits expansion to target other human rights violators residing in the United States.

[111] For a discussion of the Canadian initiative, *see* DEPARTMENT OF JUSTICE, CANADA'S WAR CRIMES PROGRAM ANNUAL REPORT 1998–1999 (1999), available at canada.justice.gc.ca/en/dept/pub/cca/cwcp.html

11

Developing the Case: Comments on Evidence and Judicial Assistance

Any analysis of the process of accountability would be incomplete without a brief review of two issues critical to building a case against those committing atrocities—access to evidence and custody of suspected abusers. Although a full exploration of evidentiary principles, extradition, and judicial assistance (already the subject of extensive bodies of literature) is beyond the scope of this book, this chapter seeks to introduce readers to the issues most relevant to accountability mechanisms.

EVIDENCE: A DEARTH OF UNIFORM STANDARDS

Those overseeing accountability face a legal landscape devoid of any uniform rules of evidence and characterized by different approaches across various fora. International law provides no clear evidentiary standards for international tribunals, nor are there many uniform principles across national legal systems. As a result, international tribunals have taken an *ad hoc* and fairly liberal approach to evidentiary matters, and national legal systems vary significantly. The goal here is to sketch out general principles concerning the admissibility and weight of evidence and standards of proof before international tribunals, national courts, and investigatory commissions.[1]

Admissibility, Weight, and Standards of Proof

The practice of international tribunals reveals some general observations concerning their treatment of evidence. Most precedent comes from international commercial tribunals due to the rarity of criminal courts.[2] To begin with, in contrast to domestic tribunals based on the Anglo-American

[1] *See generally* DURWARD V. SANDIFER, EVIDENCE BEFORE INTERNATIONAL TRIBUNALS 8–12, 22–29 (1975); *see also* Charles N. Brower, *Evidence Before International Tribunals: The Need for Some Standard Rules*, 28 INT'L LAW. 47, 47–48 (1994).

[2] For a useful review of trends in international criminal courts, *see* Richard May and Marieke Wierda, *Trends in International Criminal Evidence: Nuremberg, Tokyo, The Hague, and Arusha*, 37 COLUM. J. TRANSNAT'L L. 725 (1999).

tradition, international tribunals tend to eschew strict rules of evidence. As a result, they generally admit virtually any evidence presented and impose few restrictions on its form. In light of the lack of any precise evidentiary standards, the weight given varies from judge (or arbitrator) to judge and is heavily influenced by the judge's own legal background. As for the form of evidence, written evidence tends to be much more prevalent than live testimony.[3]

Neither the Statute nor the Rules of the Yugoslavia or Rwanda Tribunals impose any significant limits on admissibility.[4] A chamber may admit any relevant evidence, though it may exclude evidence if the need to ensure a fair trial substantially outweighs its probative value.[5] This notably includes hearsay evidence and even uncorroborated evidence, which both tribunals have admitted.[6] The rules of evidence for the two tribunals' trial chambers also apply to proceedings before the appellate chamber, although that chamber is generally limited to the evidentiary record presented to the trial chamber.[7] The tribunals' Statutes require a *prima facie* standard for indictment of a suspect; the standard for conviction is 'beyond reasonable doubt'.[8] The Statutes and Rules are silent on the standard of review on appeal. Nonetheless, the ICTY Appeals Chamber has determined that it may overturn factual determinations only if they are unreasonable; legal determinations, however, appear subject to *de novo* review.[9]

National evidentiary rules vary considerably, though the French and Anglo-American systems have been particularly influential on other

[3] *See* SANDIFER, *supra* note 1, at 3–13, 197; *see also* Brower, *supra* note 1, at 47–48, 50–53.

[4] For an overview of the Tribunals' application of their generally similar rules of evidence, *see* JOHN R.W.D. JONES, THE PRACTICE OF THE INTERNATIONAL CRIMINAL TRIBUNALS FOR THE FORMER YUGOSLAVIA AND RWANDA 409–31, 621–30 (2d ed. 2000); May and Wierda, *supra* note 2. For the draft set of Rules of Procedure and Evidence for the ICC, *see* Report of the Preparatory Commission for the International Criminal Court: Addendum: Finalized draft text of the Rules of Procedure and Evidence, July 12, 2000, UN Doc. PCNICC/2000/INF/3/Add.1. For a discussion of evidence in ICJ cases, *see* 3 SHABTAI ROSENNE, THE LAW AND PRACTICE OF THE INTERNATIONAL COURT, 1920–1996, at 1083–92 (3d ed. 1997).

[5] ICTY Rules, rules 89(C), (D); ICTR Rules, rule 89(C); *see also* ICC Statute, art. 69(4). ICTY and ICTR Rule 95 bars admission of evidence obtained by methods 'which cast substantial doubt on its reliability or if its admission is antithetical to, and would seriously damage, the integrity of the proceedings.' *See also* Prosecutor v. Tadic, Decision on Appellant's Motion for the Extension of the Time Limit and Admission of Additional Evidence, ICTY Appeals Chamber, Oct. 15, 1998, paras. 33–45, 60–74; ICC Statute, art. 69(7).

[6] On hearsay, *see, e.g.*, Prosecutor v. Aleksovski, Decision on Prosecutor's Appeal on Admissibility of Evidence, ICTY Appeals Chamber, Feb. 16, 1999, para. 15; *Akayesu Judgment*, para. 136; on the testimony of a single witness, *see Tadic Judgment*, paras. 535–39; *Akayesu Judgment*, paras. 132–35.

[7] ICTY and ICTR Rules, rules 107, 115 (allowing additional evidence only if 'the interests of justice so require').

[8] ICTY Statute, art. 19(1); ICTR Statute, art. 18(1); ICTY Rules and ICTR Rules, rules 47, 87.

[9] *See Tadic Appeal*, para. 64; the *de novo* standard for legal findings is apparent from the discussion in *id.* paras. 115, 149.

national systems. The French criminal law system is generally governed by the system of *la liberté des preuves*, under which courts admit a wide variety of types of evidence. The judge evaluates all the evidence based on his *intime conviction*, whereby he decides according to his conscience without any obligation to state his reasons.[10] Evidence before US federal courts is governed by the Federal Rules of Evidence. In civil cases, such as those under the Alien Tort Claims Act, a plaintiff must prove his case by 'a preponderance of the evidence'.[11] In criminal cases, the prosecution must establish the defendant's guilt 'beyond a reasonable doubt'.[12]

Similarly, investigatory commissions evince no uniformity of practice with respect to evidentiary principles. Rather, their more informal nature allows them to operate with even less strict rules concerning the admissibility and weight of evidence than those of international tribunals. Standards of proof have varied across commissions, and in some cases their mandates and reports have been completely silent on the issue. By way of example, the Israeli Kahan commission required a preponderance of the evidence to establish general factual conclusions, but demanded proof beyond a reasonable doubt for establishing individual responsibility.[13] The El Salvador commission imposed similar, multi-tiered standards; the South African commission made findings on the identities of individual perpetrators based on 'the balance of probability'.[14]

Opportunities and Challenges

To the extent that any mechanism seeks to establish the responsibility of individuals for international crimes, investigators will need to develop sufficient evidence establishing each element of the offense with respect to each target. The legal ambiguities surrounding the definition of many offenses, the difficult circumstances under which investigators must often conduct their evidence-gathering, and the long lapses of time between the offense and the investigation only exacerbate this challenge.

Certain principles must guide any investigations concerning serious human rights violations, regardless of fora. At the outset, it is desirable not

[10] Code de procédure pénale, arts. 353, 427 (Fr.); *see also* Gaston Stefani, Georges Levasseur, and Bernard Bouloc, Procédure pénale 105–18 (17th ed. 2000).

[11] *See generally* 9 John H. Wigmore, Evidence in Trials at Common Law § 2498 (1981).

[12] *Id.* § 2497.

[13] The Kahan commission was created by the Israeli Government to investigate the responsibility of Israeli officials for massacres at two Lebanese refugee camps in 1982. Final Report of the Commission of Inquiry into the Events at the Refugee Camps in Beirut, 22 ILM 473 (1983).

[14] Report of the Commission on the Truth for El Salvador, *in* Letter dated 29 March 1993 from the Secretary-General addressed to the President of the Security Council, Apr. 1, 1993, UN Doc. S/25500, at 24–25; 1 Truth and Reconciliation Commission: Final Report, ch. 4, paras. 155–57 (1998), available at www.mg.co.za/mg/projects/trc [hereinafter TRC Report].

to put the proverbial cart before the horse. That is, decision-makers should ideally determine the purposes for the information and the forum in which it is to be used (e.g., criminal trial vs. investigatory commission) *before* investigators are given the task of developing evidence. Investigators need to have a focus for their activities, and sending them out without defined objectives can be detrimental to the development of sound cases if their methods result in inadmissible, unreliable, or contradictory evidence. Investigations will be most effective if investigators have an idea of the suspects' identities and a thorough understanding of the elements of the relevant offenses and the standards of proof. In the case of criminal trials, prosecutors can also rely upon plea-bargaining and exploit evidence obtained in prosecuting lower-ranking defendants to move up the chain of command. For example, Drazen Erdemovic, the first defendant convicted by the ICTY, provided prosecutors with invaluable evidence concerning previously unknown massacres of Bosnian Muslims and served as the prosecution's chief witness in the Rule 61 proceedings concerning Karadzic and Mladic. In return, the prosecution sought a relatively lenient sentence for Erdemovic.[15]

The dearth of uniform rules of evidence across legal systems presents both an obstacle and an opportunity for those invoking processes of accountability. Precedents and clear guidelines may be lacking, but this may result in a more flexible approach by various fora. For criminal tribunals, rather strict standards for proof are to be expected. Evidence normally gathered by journalists, academics, and NGOs for historical or reporting purposes is typically different from that needed before such courts. The experience of the Yugoslavia and Rwanda Tribunals underscores this observation. Investigators working on cases for the tribunals have found much of the evidence uncovered by the respective commissions of experts that preceded the tribunals to be less useful than it might have been, since it often contained inconsistencies and was not in the form required for criminal prosecutions. Moreover, while the work of journalists and NGOs helps identify potential witnesses and provides a general understanding of particular situations, their activities have at times interfered with the work of the tribunals' investigatory staff. The tribunals have, in fact, requested NGOs to stop taking statements from witnesses.

Furthermore, certain basic investigatory principles are especially important if the evidence is to be used in a prosecutorial forum. First, investigators and prosecutors should always remain cognizant of the standards of proof. As for the types of evidence gathered, while direct evidence is preferable,

15 *Erdemovic Sentencing Judgment II*, paras. 16(iv), 18–19. Although neither the Statute nor Rules addresses the issue, the Prosecutor has claimed the authority to grant immunity to witnesses in return for testimony. *See The Internationalization of Criminal Law*, 1995 Am. Soc'y Int'l L. Proc. 297, 311 (statement of Mr. Blewitt).

circumstantial evidence may also be useful. Investigators for the Yugoslavia and Rwanda Tribunals have found that while cases against lower-level defendants have tended to rely on witness testimony, in cases against those in leadership positions investigators must rely more heavily on documentary evidence, particularly with respect to the key issue of chain of command. Forensic evidence also plays an important role in prosecutions, particularly in the identification of victims. As for witness testimony, once witnesses are located, investigators and prosecutors should exercise care in confining the witness' testimony to facts within his or her direct knowledge. They should avoid reliance on hearsay and remain cognizant of potential challenges to the witness' credibility that may arise from their motives or other factors. Any statements from witnesses should be signed, preferably under penalty of perjury. Investigators should also be alert to using witnesses as leads to other witnesses and evidence.

In light of the above, investigators must receive proper training and support. In addition to basic principles of international human rights and humanitarian law and of evidence, they must be trained in proper investigative techniques. These include establishing a chain of custody for physical evidence, the taking of statements, and concepts of basic fairness.[16] Investigatory teams should include experienced investigators and forensic experts; legal experts must also be integrated into the process. Investigators must also be supported by personnel who can analyze any evidence and by databases and storage facilities to ensure that any information is properly stored and retrievable. A criminal database differs from an academic one, and the establishment and operation of an effective criminal database will demand appropriately experienced personnel.

Many of these observations and recommendations also apply to non-prosecutorial mechanisms. However, the less stringent evidentiary requirements of these processes inevitably render the evidence-gathering task somewhat easier, though their credibility and success will still depend on careful and prudent investigatory techniques. The major challenge in evidence-gathering for non-prosecutorial processes is to ensure that investigators carry it out with sufficient regard for the possibility of subsequent prosecutions, so that their activities do not taint important evidence and jeopardize the success of those prosecutions.

[16] Training curricula must be carefully designed since, as one prosecutor on the staff of the ICTY pointed out, defense counsel may be able to use such curricula as evidence against the prosecution in a case. *See also* HUMAN RIGHTS WATCH/AFRICA, ETHIOPIA: RECKONING UNDER THE LAW 15–16 (1994) (investigatory process followed by Ethiopia in connection with prosecution of members of Mengitsu regime); *cf.* 1 TRC REPORT, *supra* note 14, ch. 6 (discussing methodology).

JUDICIAL ASSISTANCE AND THE LIMITS OF INTERNATIONAL CO-OPERATION

A second critical issue inherent in pursuing accountability, especially through criminal prosecutions for violations of international law, is the need for access to defendants and evidence located in another jurisdiction. Extradition remains the most formalized international mechanism by which a tribunal obtains custody of offenders located outside its jurisdiction. It has developed, in part, because many legal systems prohibit trials *in absentia*, and a strong current of opinion maintains that international law principles of due process require the presence of the accused.[17] Yet, extradition is not obligatory under international law in the absence of a treaty, and many states, including the United States, do not permit extradition absent a treaty or statute.[18] Although some states will grant extradition based on reciprocity and comity alone, the modern international extradition system relies primarily on an intricate system of bilateral and, to a lesser extent, multilateral treaties. Likewise, customary international law does not obligate states to make evidence available to foreign or international tribunals.[19] However, here, too, mechanisms have developed for obtaining access to evidence located in another jurisdiction. In all cases of requests for extradition and other forms of judicial assistance, states carry out such requests through their domestic legal rules and procedures.

Proceedings Before National Tribunals

The intricate latticework of bilateral and multilateral treaties that provide national courts with custody of defendants located abroad is riddled with conditions and exceptions. Bilateral treaties generally limit extradition to offenses listed in the treaty and constituting crimes in both the requesting and requested states (double criminality). In addition, many states will not extradite their own nationals. Under the Rule of Speciality incorporated in treaties, the requesting state may try a defendant only for the crimes with respect to which the requested state extradited him. The political offense exception in treaties, which exempts politically related offenses from the obligation to extradite, imposes a further limitation under bilateral

[17] *See* Ch. 9, note 44, *supra*. *But see* Louis René Beres, *Iraqi Crimes and International Law: The Imperative to Punish*, 21 DENV. J. INT'L L. AND POL'Y 335, 353 (1993) (if accused has right to counsel of his own choosing, international law does not require his physical presence).

[18] Torsten Stein, *Extradition*, *in* 2 ENCYCLOPEDIA OF PUBLIC INTERNATIONAL LAW 327, 328–29 (Rudolph Bernhardt ed., 1995); Valentine v. United States, 299 U.S. 5, 9 (1936).

[19] *See* RESTATEMENT (THIRD) OF THE FOREIGN RELATIONS LAW OF THE UNITED STATES pt. IV, ch. 7, subch. A, Intro. Note (1987); Heinrich Grützner, *International Judicial Assistance in Criminal Matters*, in 2 A TREATISE ON INTERNATIONAL CRIMINAL LAW 189, 189 (M. Cherif Bassiouni and Ved P. Nanda eds., 1973).

treaties, though the scope of the exception for serious crimes of violence is narrowing.[20] However, where the lack of an extradition treaty or other factors preclude extradition, an accused can still be brought into a state's jurisdiction through deportation to the requesting state or a third state acting as intermediary.

Most international criminal law treaties contain provisions on extradition. Reflecting a common approach, the Torture Convention and the Geneva Conventions require parties to extradite or prosecute offenders.[21] However, the Genocide and Apartheid Conventions do not go as far, only requiring parties to grant extradition in accordance with laws and treaties in force. They thus do not automatically make offenses extraditable under existing extradition agreements or require parties to enact laws or enter into agreements to that effect, though they bar application of the political offense exception to those offenses.[22] Article III of the Convention on the Non-Applicability of Statutory Limitations to War Crimes and Crimes Against Humanity obligates parties to 'undertake to adopt all necessary domestic measures, legislative or otherwise, with a view to making possible the extradition, in accordance with international law', of perpetrators of offenses covered by that Convention.[23] However, that convention has not garnered wide adherence.

Once a defendant is physically present before a court, the means by which he was brought before the court, even if extra-judicial, have generally been regarded by domestic courts as irrelevant for challenging the court's jurisdiction.[24] Indeed, states have, on occasion, resorted to abduction without the consent of the state of refuge to obtain custody of defendants where extradition was not a viable option, even though such seizures violate international law and give rise to serious political repercussions. The most famous such case remains Israel's abduction of Adolf Eichmann from Argentina in 1960. Such measures might be tolerable in exceptional circumstances. Certainly, however, in cases where especially

[20] *See generally* M. CHERIF BASSIOUNI, INTERNATIONAL EXTRADITION: UNITED STATES LAW AND PRACTICE 515–88 (3d ed. 1996).

[21] Torture Convention, art. 7, 1465 UNTS at 115 (also expressly making torture an extraditable offense under existing extradition treaties); Geneva Convention IV, art. 146, 75 UNTS at 386.

[22] Genocide Convention, art. VII, 78 UNTS at 282; Apartheid Convention, art. XI, 1015 UNTS at 247; *see also* UN GAOR 6th Comm., 3d Sess., 94th, 95th mtgs., UN Doc. A/633 (1948); NEHEMIAH ROBINSON, THE GENOCIDE CONVENTION: A COMMENTARY 86–89 (1960). The prevailing opinion expressed in the Sixth Committee during its consideration of Article VII of the Genocide Convention was that it did not impose any obligation on parties to extradite their nationals if their laws did not permit it. The limited nature of the Genocide Convention's provisions on extradition is problematic, as many extradition treaties do not include it as an extraditable offense and exclude nationals of the requested state from extradition.

[23] Statutory Limitations Convention, art. III, 754 UNTS at 76.

[24] *See, e.g.*, *Eichmann*, 36 ILR at 57–76, 304–08; United States v. Alvarez-Machain, 504 U.S. 655, 661–62 (1992); Anthony D'Amato, *National Prosecution for International Crimes*, *in* 3 INTERNATIONAL CRIMINAL LAW 217, 219 (M. Cherif Bassiouni ed., 2d ed. 1999).

brutal methods of abduction are employed, courts are unlikely to overlook such circumstances, and kidnapping would be entirely unjustifiable between countries enjoying normal extradition relations.

Legal obligations to provide evidence and other assistance to foreign authorities are weaker and even more diffuse than extradition obligations. Requests for such assistance usually take the form of letters rogatory (formal requests to a foreign court) or are made pursuant to a mutual legal assistance treaty. In addition, some treaties contain special provisions on these matters, albeit in general terms. Thus, the 1926 and 1956 Slavery Conventions, the Torture Convention, and Protocol I to the Geneva Conventions all obligate parties to cooperate with and assist each other.[25]

Proceedings Before International Tribunals

The legal instruments establishing an international tribunal typically set out the obligations of states to respond to requests for judicial assistance. In addition, the tribunal may enter into treaties with states relating to these matters. The Yugoslavia Tribunal has entered into a number of such treaties, which eliminate many of the exceptions typically found in bilateral extradition treaties, including the political offense exception and defenses based on the nationality of the accused.[26]

The Yugoslavia and Rwanda Tribunals have essentially the same powers to obtain custody of defendants and evidence. Security Council Resolution 827, which established the ICTY, states that 'all states shall cooperate fully with the Tribunal and shall take any measures necessary under their domestic law to implement the provisions' of the Statute and comply with 'requests for assistance or orders issued by a trial chamber'.[27] The ICTY and ICTR Statutes also require all states to comply with any request for assistance, including for the arrest, detention, and transfer of the accused.[28]

Where a crime within the Tribunals' jurisdiction is or has been the subject of investigations or proceedings before a national court, the Prosecutor may request information from that state. In conducting investigations, the

[25] Slavery Convention, Sept. 25, 1926, as amended by the Protocol of 7 December 1953, art. 4, 212 UNTS 17, 20; 1956 Slavery Convention, art. 8, 266 UNTS at 43–44; Torture Convention, art. 9, 1465 UNTS at 115; Protocol I, art. 88, 1125 UNTS at 43; *see also* GA Res. 3074 (XXVIII), UN GAOR, 28th Sess., Supp. No. 30, at 78, 79, UN Doc. A/9030 (1973) (declaring that states shall cooperate in halting and preventing war crimes and crimes against humanity and cooperate in extraditing offenders and providing information to facilitate prosecution in the state where the offense was committed).

[26] *See* Robert Kushen and Kenneth J. Harris, *Surrender of Fugitives by the United States to the War Crimes Tribunals for Yugoslavia and Rwanda*, 90 AJIL 510 (1996).

[27] SC Res. 827, para. 4, UN SCOR, 48th Year, Res. and Dec., at 29, UN Doc. S/INF/49 (1993); *see also* SC Res. 955, para. 2, UN SCOR, 49th Year, Res. and Dec., at 15, UN Doc. S/INF/50 (1994).

[28] ICTY Statute, art. 29; ICTR Statute, art. 28.

Prosecutor may summon suspects, victims, and witnesses, collect evidence, conduct on-site investigations, undertake other necessary matters, and seek the assistance of any state or international body. She can also request the Tribunal to issue orders needed to carry out these functions. In case of urgency, the Prosecutor may request any state provisionally to arrest a suspect, seize evidence, or take measures to prevent the escape of a suspect, injury to or intimidation of a witness, or the destruction of evidence.[29] If the Tribunal confirms an indictment, a judge may issue orders for the arrest, detention, surrender, and transfer of persons or any other necessary orders. The Registrar transmits arrest warrants to the relevant national authorities and, upon arrest of the individual, the arresting authorities are to transfer the individual to the Tribunal. If an arrest warrant is not executed, the Tribunal can issue an international arrest warrant directed at all states.[30]

As the Security Council established both tribunals under Chapter VII of the UN Charter, Article 25 of the Charter mandates compliance by all states, obligations that prevail over a state's extradition laws or treaties.[31] The Dayton–Paris Accords and the Security Council resolution endorsing them reaffirm the duty of states to cooperate with the ICTY.[32] Transfer of accused persons to the Tribunals is, in principle, more straightforward than in the state-to-state context because, as noted, many of the conditions and exceptions to interstate extradition do not apply. Yet some states may still confront legal difficulties in conforming their domestic laws to their obligations to the Tribunals, as the former were not designed to effect transfers to international institutions.[33] In an embarrassing episode for the United States, in 1997 a federal magistrate, based on a mistaken interpretation of US law concerning cooperation with the Tribunals, prevented the

[29] ICTY Rules and ICTR Rules, rules 8, 39, 40.

[30] ICTY Statute, art. 19(2); ICTR Statute, art. 18(2); ICTY Rules and ICTR Rules, rules 54, 55, 57, 61.

[31] UN CHARTER, arts. 25, 103; ICTY Statute, art. 29; ICTR Statute, art. 18. *See also* ICTY Rules and ICTR Rules, rule 58. In many cases, states will need to enact implementing legislation to authorize their compliance with these obligations. For examples, *see* 1996 Y.B. ICTY, ch. V, Annex A, available at www.un.org/icty/publication/yearbook/1996/year0.htm; *see also* Ivo Josipović, *Implementing Legislation for the Application of the Law on the International Criminal Tribunal for the Former Yugoslavia and Criteria for its Evaluation*, 1 Y.B. INT'L HUMAN. L. 35 (1998); Göran Sluiter, *Obtaining Evidence for the International Criminal Tribunal for the Former Yugoslavia: An Overview and Assessment of Domestic Implementing Legislation*, 45 NETH. INT'L L. REV. 87 (1998).

[32] General Framework Agreement for Peace in Bosnia and Herzegovina, Dec. 14, 1995, Bosnia-Croatia-Serbia, art. IX, 35 ILM 75, 90 (1996); SC Res. 1031, para. 4, UN SCOR, 50th Year, Res. and Dec., at 18, UN Doc. S/INF/51 (1995).

[33] *See* Karin Oellers-Frahm, *Cooperation: The Indispensable Prerequisite to the Efficiency of International Criminal Tribunals*, 1995 AM. SOC'Y INT'L L. PROC. 304, 306–08 (discussing experience of Germany); Kenneth J. Harris and Robert Kushen, *Prosecuting International Crime: Surrender of Fugitives to the War Crimes Tribunals for Yugoslavia and Rwanda: Squaring International Legal Obligations with the United States Constitution*, 7 CRIM. L.F. 561 (1996).

transfer to the ICTR of an indictee arrested in Texas, leading to two more years of litigation and the transfer of the accused only in March of 2000.[34]

More significantly for the functioning of the *ad hoc* tribunals, and a foretaste of challenges facing the ICC, has been the refusal by states to cooperate with the ICTY's request for assistance despite clear international obligations to do so. (This issue has proved less of a problem for the ICTR, where state cooperation has proved impressive.[35]) Lack of cooperation by the states and other entities in the former Yugoslavia, including Serbia, Croatia, and Republika Srpska has been endemic with respect to apprehension of indictees, provision of evidence and other witnesses, and access to crime scenes (although Croatia's stance improved following the electoral defeat in 2000 of the Croatian Democratic Union). At least thirty publicly indicted individuals are suspected of residing in those three entities, whose authorities (some of them themselves indicted) have refused to turn them over, despite Tribunal and Security Council demands to do so.[36] As a result, the Tribunal has come to rely upon the assistance of the NATO-led Stabilization Force overseeing the implementation of the Bosnian peace agreement. Although that force has assumed an overall passive stance with respect to searching for indicted war criminals in Bosnia, it detained indictees with some frequency beginning in 1997, arresting some 20 (many the subject of sealed indictments) as of late 2000.[37] With respect to furnishing of evidence, the Tribunal's Appeals Chamber held during the course of the Blaskic trial that, although the Tribunal cannot issue a subpoena to states for the production of witnesses and evidence, it can issue 'binding orders' to that effect.[38] Nevertheless,

[34] *See* Ntakirutimana v. Reno, 184 F.3d 419, *cert. denied,* 120 S. Ct. 977 (2000); for commentary, *see* Mary Coombs, *International Decisions*, 94 AJIL 171 (2000).

[35] *See* Report of the International Criminal Tribunal for the Prosecution of Persons Responsible for Genocide and Other Serious Violations of International Humanitarian Law Committed in the Territory of Rwanda and Rwandan Citizens Responsible for Genocide and Other Such Violations Committed in the Territory of Neighbouring States between 1 January and 31 December 1994, Sept. 7, 1999, UN Doc. A/54/315-S/1999/943, para. 112; Catherine Cissé, *The End of a Culture of Impunity in Rwanda? Prosecution of Genocide and War Crimes before Rwandan Courts and the International Criminal Tribunal for Rwanda*, 1 Y.B. INT'L HUMAN. L. 161, 169–70 (1998).

[36] Report of the International Tribunal for the Prosecution of Persons Responsible for Serious Violations of International Humanitarian Law Committed in the Territory of the Former Yugoslavia Since 1991, Aug. 25, 1999, UN Doc. A/54/187-S/1999/846, paras. 90–106 and Annex III.

[37] Latest list of Detainees and Former Detainees, available at www.un.org/icty/glance/detain.htm. On NATO's legal powers, *see* Paola Gaeta, *Is NATO Authorized or Obliged to Arrest Persons Indicted by the International Criminal Tribunal for the Former Yugoslavia?*, 9 EJIL 174 (1998); *see also* Payam Akhavan, *Justice in The Hague, Peace in the Former Yugoslavia?: A Commentary on the United Nations War Crimes Tribunal*, 20 HUM. RTS. Q. 737, 795–813 (1998). On the luring of one suspect into ICTY custody, *see* Michael P. Scharf, The Prosecutor v. Slavko Dokmanović: *Irregular Rendition and the ICTY*, 11 LEIDEN J. INT'L L. 369 (1998).

[38] *Blaskic Interlocutory Appeal*, for commentary, *see* Jacob Katz Cogan, *The Problem of Obtaining Evidence for International Criminal Courts*, 22 HUM. RTS. Q. 404 (2000); Yves Nouvel, *Précisions sur le pouvoir du Tribunal pour l'ex-Yougoslavie d'ordonner la production des preuves et la comparu-*

the subject of such orders, Croatia, refused to comply with them in time for the use of the evidence sought therein in Blaskic's trial.[39]

The Rome Statute's detailed provisions regarding judicial assistance reflect the hesitancy of states to infuse the ICC with broad powers in this area. The Court has the authority to issue 'requests' for cooperation on arrests, evidence, and other matters. As a general matter, states must comply with such requests, but these obligations are subject to various procedural steps and some significant exceptions.[40] These include the ability to withhold evidence that relates to national security or refuse cooperation if it would be prohibited 'on the basis of an existing fundamental legal principle of general application'.[41] The Court's only power in the face of noncooperation is to refer the issue to the Assembly of States Parties or the Security Council if the latter has referred the matter to the Court; but resolutions or statements by these two bodies are unlikely to sway recalcitrant states absent pressure from influential actors.[42]

Opportunities and Challenges

Although the architecture of international law enforcement cooperation is far from complete, the most significant barrier to accountability for gross abuses of human rights is not a lack of law. Rather, even with many legal obligations to render judicial assistance, the failure of states to cooperate, whether because of a lack of political will or of the capacity to do so, will continue to hinder many methods of accountability. The most notable examples emanate from the former Yugoslavia, where resistance from forces in control of areas where atrocities have occurred has impeded investigations by the Tribunal, and many key defendants still remain at large. If a state fails to cooperate with a national or international tribunal, the international community could impose sanctions on that state through the Security Council or through unilateral or multilateral action.[43]

tion des témoins: L'Arrêt de la Chambre d'appel du 29 octobre 1997 dans L'affaire Blaskic, 102 REV. GÉN. DROIT INT'L PUB. 157 (1998); Ruth Wedgwood, *International Criminal Tribunals and State Sources of Proof: The Case of Tihomir Blaškić*, 11 LEIDEN J. INT'L L. 635 (1998). The Appeals Chamber found that such orders were distinguishable from subpoenas because only the Security Council, rather than the Tribunal, could impose sanctions for noncompliance with the orders.

[39] Sean Murphy, *Progress and Jurisprudence of the International Criminal Tribunal for the Former Yugoslavia*, 93 AJIL 57, 81–82 (1999).

[40] ICC Statute, arts. 86–101; for background, *see* Phakiso Mochochoko, *International Cooperation and Judicial Assistance*, *in* THE INTERNATIONAL CRIMINAL COURT: THE MAKING OF THE ROME STATUTE 305 (Roy S. Lee ed., 1999).

[41] ICC Statute, art. 93(3)–(4).

[42] *See* Cogan, *supra* note 38, at 423–27.

[43] *See* ICTY Rules, rule 61(E) (notification to Security Council of cases where failure to effect personal service of an indictment is due to failure or refusal of a state to cooperate with Tribunal); Christopher Joyner, *Strengthening Enforcement of Humanitarian Law: Reflections on the*

But action against recalcitrant parties requires yet another amalgam of political will, as is amply illustrated by the efforts of the United States, Britain, and France to obtain access to Libyan suspects implicated in the 1988 and 1989 bombings of Pan Am 103 and UTA 772. Faced with Libyan recalcitrance, the three governments brought the issue before the Security Council, which imposed sanctions against Libya.[44] However, some governments viewed these sanctions as an abuse of the Council's power, many ignored them, and Libya challenged them before the International Court of Justice (though it lost the case at the provisional measures phase).[45] Only in 1999 did a combination of Libyan frustration with the sanctions, flexibility by the United States and Britain, and diplomacy by intermediaries lead to a solution involving the trial of the suspects before a special Scottish court sitting in the Netherlands.[46]

Finally, a frustrating tension arises in those situations where governments or international organizations seek to persuade a human rights violator to surrender power in return for sanctuary abroad coupled with some form of impunity. Foreign governments have granted such refuge to former dictators from the Philippines, Haiti, Uganda, Ethiopia, Paraguay, and elsewhere, claiming that such action will help effect a peaceful transfer of power and an improvement in the human rights situation. In some cases, the successor regime may have approved of the deal in advance, while in others it may grudgingly accept it or even oppose it. Whatever the attitude of the successor regime, the troubling price of these arrangements is that they shield human rights abusers from accountability in the form of prosecution. Yet, were sanctuary states to renege on their pledges to the former dictators and thereby hand them over for prosecution, abusers of human rights who hold power might possibly choose to cling to office even longer. At the same time, a more principled refusal by governments to harbor former leaders who have committed atrocities would clearly send a signal to incumbent leaders to refrain from such practices in the first place.

International Criminal Tribunal for the Former Yugoslavia, 6 DUKE J. COMP. AND INT'L L. 79, 92–93 (1995).

44 SC Res. 748, UN SCOR, 47th Year, Res. and Dec., at 52, UN Doc. S/INF/48 (1992).

45 Interpretation and Application of the 1971 Montreal Convention Arising from the Aerial Incident at Lockerbie (Libya v. U.S.), 1992 ICJ 114 (Apr. 14).

46 *See* Report of the Secretary-General submitted pursuant to Paragraph 16 of Security Council Resolution 883 (1993) and Paragraph 8 of Resolution 1192 (1998), June 30, 1999, UN Doc. S/1999/726.

PART III

A CASE STUDY: THE ATROCITIES OF THE KHMER ROUGE

12

The Khmer Rouge Rule over Cambodia: A Historical Overview

April 17, 1975 marked a horrific turning point in the history of Cambodia. On that day, Phnom Penh fell to the forces of the Communist Party of Kampuchea, or the Khmer Rouge (red Khmer). The Khmer Rouge victory marked the end of a decade-long struggle for power in Cambodia. That effort had begun during the reign of Prince Norodom Sihanouk, the hereditary monarch who governed the country as the Kingdom of Cambodia from independence in 1953 until 1970. During those years, Sihanouk succeeded in marginalizing the movement politically, but it remained a powerful force in the country, largely due to support from the communist leaders in Vietnam.[1]

On March 17, 1970, while on a visit to the Soviet Union and China, Sihanouk was overthrown in a bloodless coup led by Prime Minister Lon Nol and Prince Sisowath Sirik Matak, a cousin of Sihanouk. The installation of the new government, under the name of the Khmer Republic, and its alliance with the United States in the Vietnam War, gave new impetus to the Khmer Rouge's movement. Sihanouk, who shortly thereafter set up an opposition government, allied himself with the Khmer communists. With the support of North Vietnam and China (and recruitment aided by the US bombing campaign), and through a combination of strict discipline and terror tactics toward the civilian population, the Khmer Rouge began to seize large amounts of territory. Despite vast quantities of US aid, the poorly trained republican army and ineffective, corrupt civilian leadership proved no match for the Khmer Rouge. With the withdrawal, and eventual elimination in 1975, of US assistance to the Khmer Republic, the Khmer Rouge became assured of victory.[2]

The Khmer Rouge victory marked an important break in modern Cambodian history. Sihanouk had governed as both a popular sovereign

[1] Among the best works on this period are David P. Chandler, The Tragedy of Cambodian History: Politics, War, and Revolution since 1945 (1991); Ben Kiernan, How Pol Pot Came to Power: A History of Communism in Kampuchea (1985); and Library of Congress, Federal Research Division, Cambodia: A Country Study (Russell R. Ross ed., 1990).

[2] In addition to the sources above, *see* William Shawcross, Sideshow: Kissinger, Nixon and the Destruction of Cambodia (rev. ed. 1987); Timothy Carney, *The Unexpected Victory*, *in* Cambodia 1975–1978: Rendezvous with Death 13 (Karl D. Jackson ed., 1989).

and a sly autocrat, under the banner of a political movement called the Sangkum Reastr Niyum (People's Socialist Community). By the late 1950s, he completely controlled Cambodian politics, stifling all dissent. Yet the country prospered somewhat in the 1960s, developing the basic infrastructure of a newly independent state, often with foreign assistance. Educational institutions were especially impressive for a country its size.[3] Lon Nol did not fundamentally alter the social structure; his regime simply proved extraordinarily corrupt, uninterested in the future of the country, and ultimately unable to resist the forces of both the Khmer Rouge and the Vietnamese communists. During their conquest of the countryside, the Khmer Rouge showed that they intended to tolerate none of the influences that they believed had brought disgrace upon Cambodia.

THE PHILOSOPHY AND STRUCTURE OF THE KHMER ROUGE

The atrocities committed during the reign of Democratic Kampuchea were not isolated acts of individual elements of the new regime. Rather, they reflected a deliberate strategy of the Khmer Rouge leadership, which was committed to a political philosophy developed years earlier. That philosophy transcended the asserted commitment to a dictatorship of the proletariat proclaimed by communists since the days of Marx. It was marked by a desire for a pure Khmer nation, one completely sovereign and self-reliant, free of subjugation by foreign and class enemies.[4] That ideology fed upon the long-held fears among Cambodians of all socio-economic levels that Cambodia's neighbors, in particular Vietnam, sought to envelop and take over the country. The Khmer Rouge, like Sihanouk, pointed to the loss of territory since the historical days of Angkor (eleventh to thirteenth centuries). They directed particular vitriol at the loss of the parts of the Mekong River Delta ('Kampuchea Kraom', or lower Cambodia) to Vietnam before the period of French rule.

To achieve their goal of a sovereign, self-reliant, and pure Khmer nation, the Khmer Rouge called for a total revolution. For example, in a radio address shortly after their victory, the government stated:

> A clean social system is flourishing throughout new Cambodia. Since 17 April, Cambodia has been totally and permanently emancipated. The sound, clean social

[3] CHANDLER, *supra* note 1, at 82–83, 199–200.

[4] *See* Karl D. Jackson, *The Ideology of Total Revolution*, Kenneth M. Quinn, *Explaining the Terror*, and Karl D. Jackson, *Intellectual Origins of the Khmer Rouge*, *in* CAMBODIA 1975–1978, *supra* note 2, at 37, 215, 241.

system formerly prevailing in the liberated zone has now been expanded to Phnom Penh, a number of provincial capitals and throughout the country.[5]

That 'clean social system' would be produced in primarily two ways: the massive reorganization of the economic and social structure of the country; and the persecution and physical elimination of those elements of Cambodian society regarded as enemies of the new system.

Supervising this total revolution was the Communist Party of Kampuchea, which called itself the *Angkar Padevat*, or 'revolutionary organization'. The Khmer Rouge thus saw themselves as not merely a political party or a government, but an entire movement to supervise the restructuring of society. Party and government were thus closely intertwined. Indeed, the Khmer Rouge did not formally proclaim the establishment of Democratic Kampuchea, promulgate their constitution, and form their government until April 1976, and the identity of its leaders remained a mystery during much of that year.

For most of the Khmer Rouge years, the party's leadership consisted of a standing committee composed of the following members:

—Pol Pot (born Saloth Sar): Secretary
—Nuon Chea: Deputy Secretary
—Mok: Second Deputy Secretary
—Ieng Sary: Member
—Vorn Vet: Member
—Son Sen: Candidate Member
—Keu: Candidate Member[6]

The government established in 1976 comprised the following leadership:[7]

—Khieu Samphan: Chairman, State Presidium (*de facto* head of state in three-man State Presidium[8])
—Pol Pot: Prime Minister
—Ieng Sary: Deputy Prime Minister (foreign affairs)
—Vorn Vet: Deputy Prime Minister (economy)
—Son Sen: Deputy Prime Minister (national defense; also Chief of the General Staff of the Revolutionary Armed Forces of Kampuchea)
—Hu Nim: Minister of Information and Propaganda

5 Foreign Broadcast Information Service, May 9, 1975, at H1, *quoted in* Jackson, *The Ideology of Total Revolution*, *supra* note 4, at 67.

6 This list is taken from Timothy Carney, *The Organization of Power*, *in* CAMBODIA 1975–1978, *supra* note 2, at 79, 102 (table 3).

7 *See id.* at 101 (table 2).

8 Prince Sihanouk resigned as head of state in April 1976, three months after signing the constitution proclaiming the establishment of Democratic Kampuchea. After resigning, he remained under house arrest in his palace in Phnom Penh, although he was occasionally used for propaganda purposes by the new government.

—Thiounn Thioeunn: Minister of Health
—Ieng Thirith: Minister of Social Affairs
—Toch Phoeun: Minister of Public Works
—Yun Yat: Minister of Culture, Education, and Instruction

To exercise control over the country, the Khmer Rouge eventually divided it into zones, of which there were seven by 1978 (north, northwest, northeast, central, west, southwest, and east). These were further divided into thirty-two administrative regions, with party officials controlling all aspects of life down to the village level. The local population was organized into cooperatives, each overseen by a committee led by party members.

The center in Phnom Penh set policy through numerous directives to regional and local officials. Most notably, these directives set the country's basic economic policies and dictated the various purges of elements deemed anti-revolutionary that characterized Democratic Kampuchea. At the same time, the center did not directly control the workings of many cooperatives, and historians differ regarding the amount of effective central control.[9] When Phnom Penh learned that local cadres were not implementing its directives, or that those policies were failing to remedy the country's problems (most notably in terms of food production), it responded with purges of many thousands of its own officials.

THE PATTERN OF ABUSES

The years of Democratic Kampuchea were marked by abuses of individual and group human rights on an immense and brutal scale. For purposes of this study, we group them into four categories, as well as consider their *modus operandi* and the resulting death toll.[10]

The Evacuation of the Cities and Towns

The first priority of the new leadership upon taking power was the forced evacuation of the cities and towns of Cambodia. In a week following the victory, the government forced two to three million people out of these areas and into the countryside.[11] Although the Khmer Rouge claimed at the time that the evacuation was necessary due to threats of American

[9] *See* Ben Kiernan, *The Cambodian Genocide: Issues and Responses*, *in* GENOCIDE: CONCEPTUAL AND HISTORICAL DIMENSIONS 191, 205–06 (George J. Andreopoulos ed., 1994).

[10] In addition to the sources cited in the previous notes, *see generally* Kenneth M. Quinn, *The Pattern and Scope of Violence*, *in* CAMBODIA 1975–1978, *supra* note 2, at 179; David Hawk, *International Human Rights Law and Democratic Kampuchea*, 16 INT'L J. OF POL. 3 (1986).

[11] CHANDLER, *supra* note 1, at 246–47.

bombing or insufficient food supplies, Pol Pot and the leadership actually planned it in advance.[12] The leadership saw the cities as the breeding grounds of those who threatened their vision of Cambodia—civil and military personnel of the Khmer Republic, foreign (especially Western) sympathizers, the middle class, intellectuals and teachers, other professionals, religious leaders, and ethnic minorities. The emptying of the cities (whose populations were referred to as 'new people') would serve both to dilute the power of those viewed as counter-revolutionaries and further the government's plan for a society based primarily on communal agriculture. Only the 'old people'—the peasants who lived in the Khmer Rouge zones of control prior to April 17—were regarded as true Khmer.

The evacuation of Phnom Penh serves as an example. The capital, which had swelled to some 2,000,000 people due to the influx of refugees during the war, was quickly emptied by the soldiers of the Khmer Rouge. Many thousands, especially among the aged and the young, died on forced marches to the countryside from lack of food, water, and medical assistance. Witnesses reported numerous instances of hospital patients dragged from their beds and dying on roads out of the city. Disease was rampant, with bodies accumulating without burial. By the end of the evacuation, the capital had as few as 20,000 residents. The evacuation was clearly intended to move the 'new people' out into the countryside, while letting the weakest of them fall prey to exhaustion.[13]

Forced Labor and Inhumane Living Conditions

Once the government had moved the urban population into the countryside, it organized huge communal farms from hundreds to thousands of persons in size. Cambodians were forced onto work teams, under the constant oversight of armed Khmer Rouge cadres or soldiers, and made to grow rice and other crops, or construct large-scale irrigation projects or roads. Work hours were long, seven days a week (often beginning before dawn and continuing into the night); food rations proved meager as the country suffered vast food shortages and its leaders refused to accept outside humanitarian assistance. The labor proved especially traumatic for those millions of city-dwellers who had never been exposed to agrarian life. Private property and money virtually disappeared as institutions.[14]

[12] Carney, *supra* note 2, at 33 n. 21.

[13] On the population of Phnom Penh, *see* LIBRARY OF CONGRESS, *supra* note 1, at 152; ELIZABETH BECKER, WHEN THE WAR WAS OVER: THE VOICES OF CAMBODIA'S REVOLUTION AND ITS PEOPLE 183 (1986); correspondence from Professor Ben Kiernan, Yale University, to the authors, Sept. 15, 1995. For among the most vivid descriptions of the evacuation, *see* FRANÇOIS PONCHAUD, CAMBODIA: YEAR ZERO (Nancy Amphoux trans., 1978).

[14] For descriptions, *see* CHANDLER, *supra* note 1, at 258–61, 265–70; Charles H. Twining, *The Economy*, *in* CAMBODIA 1975–1978, *supra* note 2, at 109, 119–37.

The Khmer Rouge organized communal life in a manner designed to obliterate traditional family structures. It separated children from families and encouraged them to report on any 'unreliable' relatives. Marriages required approval of party authorities; clandestine sexual relations often met with death for both parties.

The misery caused by the Khmer Rouge's policy of transforming the Cambodian economy constituted the single largest source of deaths during the Khmer Rouge period. Starvation, disease, and physical exhaustion, caused by inadequate food, medicine, and sanitation, and oppressive work requirements, killed hundreds of thousands from 1975 to 1978. Witnesses reported that the Khmer Rouge overseers routinely killed many thousands who refused or could no longer work, often murdering their family members as well.[15]

Attacks on Enemies of the Revolution

Beyond the many deaths attributable to Democratic Kampuchea's population transfers and forced communalization, the regime also targeted certain identifiable groups for extermination. The regime regarded the existence of these groups as inconsistent with the goals of the regime for a pure Khmer nation. Through racist discourse, the Khmer Rouge identified many of their victims as surrogate Vietnamese and thereby sought to dehumanize them. Virtually every unit of the regime appears to have had the duty to detain and execute these enemies. While not as organized as the killing machines of Stalin or Hitler, the regime embarked on a similar path.

Officials of the Prior Regime: Former government leaders, military officers, and bureaucrats were immediately targeted for elimination. During the first few months of the regime, it committed thousands of summary executions, either individually or in large round-ups. Many were killed out of public view, clubbed or shot in isolated fields; others were deliberately murdered in front of their families, who were often killed as well. By 1977, this purge had extended to the lowest officials of the Lon Nol army as well as their relatives and friends. The systematicity of this campaign is well documented.[16]

Ethnic Minorities: The Khmer Rouge targeted several ethnic minorities for discrimination, forcible assimilation, or worse, although the regime's

15 *See generally* BECKER, *supra* note 13, at 237–53; HAING NGOR, A CAMBODIAN ODYSSEY (1987).
16 *See, e.g.*, BECKER, *supra* note 13, at 205–07.

exact motives remain a subject of scholarly disagreement.[17] The Cham, a Muslim sect present in Cambodia for 500 years, faced forced assimilation as the regime broke up their families, banned their language and customs, and eventually killed their leaders and others resisting governmental policies. Ethnic Vietnamese, long a backbone of the Cambodian economy (especially as fishermen on the Tonle Sap lake), were expelled in 1975, with only a small number (mostly relatives of other Cambodians) staying behind. By 1977, the regime began killing those remaining in the country. Ethnic Chinese, who occupied prominent business positions in the cities, joined the march to the countryside, where they faced special discrimination. Ethnic Thai in western Cambodia also suffered.[18]

Teachers, Students, and Other Educated Elements: The regime saw the educated sectors of the population as part of the corrupt class that had made Cambodia a puppet of outside influences and had exploited the peasants, and thus as potential counter-revolutionaries. While many thousands perished in the communes alongside the rest of the population, others were deliberately targeted for execution. Troops raided schools or tricked teachers and students into identifying themselves, whereupon they were rounded up and killed. The government saw Cambodians with foreign language proficiencies as spies for mysterious enemy forces and killed hundreds. Thousands were accused of ties with foreign intelligence agencies and forced, under torture, to confess to false connections. Whatever cosmopolitanism had existed in Cambodia's cities disappeared over the next three years, as the intelligentsia were exterminated or fled to Thailand.

Religious Leaders and Institutions: In overturning the structures of Khmer society, the government also aimed its sights at organized religion, especially Buddhism, the religion of most Khmers. The regime forced monks to leave the priesthood for agricultural work or the army, killing those who refused. It destroyed numerous temples and converted others into storage areas, obliterating many sacred objects and texts in the process. As a result, the entire organized priesthood in the country was disbanded. The government also destroyed hundreds of mosques and many churches.[19]

[17] *Compare* David Hawk, *The Photographic Record, in* CAMBODIA: 1975–1978, *supra* note 2, at 209, 212–13; Kiernan, *supra* note 9, at 198–201; BECKER, *supra* note 13, at 253–64 (three authors asserting the regime targeted minorities *qua* minorities) *with* CHANDLER, *supra* note 1, at 285 (claiming regime targeted political enemies rather than specific ethnic groups).

[18] *See* Hurst Hannum, *International Law and Cambodian Genocide: The Sounds of Silence*, 11 HUM. RTS Q. 82, 86–87 (1989); Hawk, *supra* note 10, at 15–19; BECKER, *supra* note 13, at 253–70.

[19] *See* Hawk, *supra* note 10, at 19–23; François Ponchaud, *Social Change in the Vortex of Revolution, in* CAMBODIA: 1975–1978, *supra* note 2, at 151, 170–76; BECKER, *supra* note 13, at 264–65.

Purges within the Party

The paranoia of the Khmer Rouge regime showed itself most clearly regarding its own cadres. For this reason, the Khmer Rouge, almost from the inception of Democratic Kampuchea, searched for enemies within the party, many of whom it accused of serving as secret agents of the Central Intelligence Agency, the KGB, or Vietnam. An apparent attempt to poison Pol Pot in mid-1976 led to massive killings of longtime Khmer Rouge loyalists, including some senior leaders. A rebellion in the Northern Zone in early 1977 led to the execution of party officials in Siem Reap and Kompong Thom provinces.

May 1978 marked the beginning of a large but regionally confined insurrection in Democratic Kampuchea, as military elements in the Eastern Zone rebelled against the capital. When Pol Pot responded by sending armored troops against the rebels, the Eastern Zone became a battlefield between government and rebel troops from June through September 1978. The battle was characterized by horrific human rights abuses by government forces, who may have systematically killed at least 100,000 people in the region.[20] The government killed not only rebel soldiers, but countless civilians in the Eastern Zone whom it regarded as 'Khmer bodies with Vietnamese minds'.[21] Party members, their families, and villagers were systematically exterminated. Hundreds of thousands of others were evacuated to points north and west, where they died of starvation and disease or were later murdered.

No discussion of these purges, as well as other persecutions, would be complete without mention of the network of official torture and interrogation centers that the leadership set up. Its Phnom Penh hub, known as S–21 and established at the former girls school at Tuol Sleng, offers one of the most macabre chapters of the Khmer Rouge years. From 1976 to 1978, approximately 20,000 suspected enemies, mostly party members and their families, passed through Tuol Sleng. After photographing the prisoners on arrival, the center's officials subjected them to constant torture to force confessions of crimes against the revolution or involvement with foreign intelligence services.[22] The Khmer Rouge maintained meticulous records of the torture sessions, conducted according to an official manual of torture procedures. Those who did not die as a result of the

[20] Ben Kiernan, Cambodia: The Eastern Zone Massacres 7 (1986); Becker, *supra* note 13, at 320–23.

[21] *Quoted in* Nayan Chanda, Brother Enemy: The War After the War 254 (1986).

[22] For a Tuol Sleng document that combines the confessions extracted through torture into a grand conspiracy theory, *see* Appendix D of Cambodia 1975–1978, *supra* note 2, at 299; *see also* Becker, *supra* note 13, at 294–96 (methods of torture).

torture were dispatched to the nearby town of Choeng Ek, where they were killed.[23] Only six of the 20,000 people sent to S–21 survived.[24]

The Khmer Rouge's *Modus Operandi*

Several general observations can be made regarding the methods by which the Khmer Rouge committed their acts. First, the government utilized direct executions against certain specified targets, e.g., Lon Nol officials, ethnic Vietnamese, Buddhist leaders, party officials suspected of being traitors, and certain people in the intelligentsia. Some were taken by surprise, as their home was raided or they were removed from a work site surreptitiously, often during the night. Others were lured to their death, either through assurances that they were merely going to be questioned or through other ruses. Some were murdered after torture sessions or detention.

Secondly, the regime instigated or tolerated massive abuses that led to the deaths of the majority of those who perished during these years. These stemmed from the forced marches, long work hours, and insufficient food and medicine inflicted upon Cambodians, particularly upon the 'new people'. Other abuses may have been beyond the leadership's actual knowledge, although the turmoil in the country makes it difficult to determine the extent to which the central authorities knew or could have known of them.

Thirdly, some abuses appear to have occurred without any clearly identifiable pattern. Local cadres, especially children given authority over people's life and death, often committed atrocities out of irrational hatred or fear. Fourthly, not all Cambodians suffered to the same degree. As noted below, ethnic minorities suffered most, while certain rural populations suffered less. Despite the appalling number of dead (see below), the vast majority of Cambodians survived this period, although the long-term impact on the country remains incalculable because the educated and skilled were especially targeted and because of the physical and psychological scars on the survivors.

Finally, identification of the full scope of participants and victims in the terror seems impossible. Apart from the meticulous confessions kept in some of the torture centers, the Khmer Rouge did not compile records of most of their actions. They did not operate with the Nazi penchant for efficiency and detail, but rather perpetrated and were swept up in a complete

[23] The records of Tuol Sleng were collected and translated by the Cambodia Documentation Center, a non-profit organization in New York City. For photographs of Tuol Sleng collected by the Center's director, *see* Hawk, *supra* note 17, at 214.

[24] CHANDLER *supra* note 1, at 285 (*citing* Anthony Barnett et al., *Bureaucracy of Death: Documents from Inside Pol Pot's Torture Machine*, NEW STATESMAN, May 2, 1980, at 668–76).

social turmoil. The names of all the perpetrators and victims will never be known. As for the leaders of Democratic Kampuchea, although Cambodians and historians know well the result of their policies and practices, the lack of record-keeping means that assignment of criminal responsibility raises difficult evidentiary questions.

The Tally of the Dead

Scholars and governments have offered differing totals for the number of Cambodians killed by the Khmer Rouge. The Vietnamese and PRK governments, as well as some popular accounts, refer to two to three million killed, although historians of Cambodia have rejected this figure. Karl Jackson and Ben Kiernan arrive separately at a figure of 1.5 million; Stephen Heder posits a figure of nearly 1.7 million. Each adopts somewhat differing estimates of the pre- and post-Khmer Rouge populations and the demography of the dead (e.g., urban compared to rural).[25] One careful extrapolation of data shows the sharp disparity among victim groups, from a 100 per cent death rate for rural and urban ethnic Vietnamese, to 25 per cent for urban and rural Khmer 'new people', to 15 per cent for rural Khmer 'base people'.[26] Overall, the various estimates point to a death rate of approximately 20 per cent of the April 1975 population of 7.3 to 7.9 million people.

Despite this toll, the international community exercised virtually no scrutiny of the Khmer Rouge during its reign. Lack of information due to the regime's autarkic nature, the West's exhaustion with Indochina, and the developing world's penchant for state sovereignty (and reluctance to question any regime that had defeated the Americans) all kept Cambodia away from the spotlight. The UN Human Rights Commission finally considered the issue in 1978, when a group of Western states brought reports from fleeing refugees to the attention of its Sub-Commission on the Prevention of Discrimination and Protection of Minorities. This led to the only official UN report on the period, by the Sub-Commission's Chairman.[27] The Commission never considered the report in light of the Vietnamese invasion.

[25] *See* Karl D. Jackson, *Introduction: The Khmer Rouge in Context, in* CAMBODIA 1975–1978, *supra* note 2, at 3, 3; Kiernan, *supra* note 9, at 191–92 (including his and others' estimates); *see also* Judith Banister and Paige Johnson, *After the Nightmare: The Population of Cambodia, in* GENOCIDE AND DEMOCRACY IN CAMBODIA 65, 90 (Ben Kiernan ed., 1993) (deaths of 1.05 million, plus an additional dearth of 570,000 births and emigration of 218,000).

[26] *See* Kiernan, *supra* note 9, at 193 (table 5). Kiernan relies on data of Stephen Heder. The data also show a death rate of 50 per cent for the Chinese minority, 36 per cent for the Cham, and 40 per cent for ethnic Thai.

[27] *See* Analysis prepared on behalf of the Sub-Commission by its Chairman of materials submitted to it and the Commission on Human Rights under decision 9 (XXXIV) of the Commission on Human Rights, Jan. 30, 1979, UN Doc. E/CN.4/1335.

HOSTILITIES WITH VIETNAM

Despite the unimaginable horror of the Democratic Kampuchea regime after 1975, it was Cambodia's relations with its key neighbor, Vietnam, that eventually led to the overthrow of the regime.[28] The alliance of convenience between the Khmer and Vietnamese communists began to wither shortly after their respective victories in the spring of 1975, replaced by the ancient animosity more typical of Khmer–Vietnamese relations. Democratic Kampuchea became obsessed with the longstanding border dispute between the two countries, overtly claiming the need to regain Kampuchea Kraom and other territory in southern Vietnam.

From 1975 to 1977, Democratic Kampuchea and Vietnam engaged in a low-intensity border war. By 1977, Cambodia had escalated the conflict to include vicious raids in which it massacred hundreds of Vietnamese in border villages (this in addition to the many Vietnamese and Khmer in Cambodia killed as part of the same policy). Vietnam eventually responded by sending troops into Cambodia in December 1977, launching the Third Indochina War. Vietnam's occupation of parts of the Eastern Zone prompted the purges of the zone's leaders by the center, leading eventually to the uprising by Eastern Zone officials in May 1978. By the summer and fall of 1978, a group of Eastern Zone leaders fled to Vietnam, where they became the core of an opposition group. Vietnam built up its forces along the Cambodian border, and on December 24, 1978, launched a full-scale invasion of Cambodia. On January 6, 1979, its army reached Phnom Penh and installed the opposition group in power. Later declaring itself the People's Republic of Kampuchea (after 1989, the State of Cambodia or SOC), it ruled Cambodia for over a decade with the support of the Vietnamese army. In August 1979, it held a show trial of Pol Pot and Ieng Sary *in absentia*, convicting both and sentencing them to death.

THE KHMER ROUGE SINCE 1979

The Khmer Rouge fled power quickly, establishing themselves along both sides of the Cambodian–Thai border. Their ruthless methods against those in their zones of control continued, although they also enjoyed some credibility in the region and elsewhere as the most powerful opposition to the Vietnamese army. Significant military support from China and the states of the Association of Southeast Asian Nations (ASEAN), which harbored fears of Vietnamese hegemony, maintained the Khmer Rouge as an active

[28] The authoritative source for this subject remains CHANDA, *supra* note 21.

fighting force. Democratic Kampuchea retained Cambodia's seat in the United Nations during the 1980s, even as word of its atrocities became known internationally. This sad development resulted from an effective anti-Vietnam coalition led by China and ASEAN, and supported by the United States (due to the Cold War), as well as many Third World nations who placed a premium on the need to condemn aggression against small states.

In 1982, as refugees and human rights groups disseminated more information about life in Democratic Kampuchea, China and ASEAN pressured the Khmer Rouge to join with two non-communist resistance forces to form a coalition government-in-exile. Despite the presence of Sihanouk's United National Front for an Independent, Neutral, Prosperous, and Cooperative Cambodia (FUNCINPEC), and the Khmer People's National Liberation Front (KPNLF, led by Son Sann, a prime minister under Sihanouk) in the Coalition Government of Democratic Kampuchea (CGDK), the Khmer Rouge remained the dominant member. Equally important, the China–ASEAN–US front against Vietnam prevented any legal or diplomatic action against the Khmer Rouge during this period.

The Khmer Rouge battled the Vietnamese throughout the 1980s, but the PRK and Vietnam managed to maintain control of about 90 per cent of the countryside. Diplomatic efforts to end the conflict bore no fruit during most of the 1980s. In 1987, Indonesia initiated a regional peace process known as the Jakarta Informal Meetings, to include all the regional players, which made modest progress on the elements of a solution. Vietnam's announcement in early 1989 that it would withdraw its combat forces from Cambodia by September 1989 prompted a diplomatic scramble among ASEAN and the West to avoid a solution that would ratify PRK control over the country. This led to the convening in the summer of 1989 of the Paris Conference on Cambodia, which included all the regional actors, the five permanent members of the Security Council, and other interested states. The Khmer Rouge served as one of four delegations (along with the SOC, FUNCINPEC, and KPNLF) representing Cambodia. Those delegations proved unable, however, to agree upon any formula for sharing power, and the conference adjourned in August 1989.

As fighting between the resistance and the SOC resumed in late 1989, the Permanent Five pursued a plan for peace authored by US Congressman Stephen Solarz and promoted by Australian Foreign Minister Gareth Evans for an enhanced UN role in Cambodia. After nearly two years of negotiations, the result was achieved in the signature of the Paris Agreements of October 23, 1991. All four Khmer factions, which, at the urging of the Permanent Five, had formed a symbolic Supreme National Council, signed on behalf of Cambodia. The Khmer

Rouge were included as a full party to the peace plan due to both their effective power on the ground and the unrelenting diplomatic support of China.

The peace agreements called for the UN Transitional Authority in Cambodia (UNTAC) to organize and conduct elections in an atmosphere of peace and political neutrality. The former was to be achieved by the demobilization and disarmament of the factions; the latter by the insertion of UNTAC personnel into the factions' governmental administrations (principally the SOC's) to ensure their neutrality. UNTAC had no power to try or punish the group's leadership for their atrocities in the 1970s. The accords did not specifically require trials of Khmer Rouge leaders by a future Cambodian government, although some provisions recognized the need for Cambodia to avoid a repeat of those abuses and live up to its international human rights commitments, which include such trials.[29]

In June 1992, the Khmer Rouge refused to participate in the demobilization process, and ceased its cooperation with the United Nations for the remainder of the mission (with the exception of the refugee repatriation process). It boycotted the electoral process and later resorted to massacres of Vietnamese in Cambodia, as well as limited attacks on UNTAC itself. The Khmer Rouge did not, however, disrupt the polling, which was held in a calm atmosphere in late May 1993. FUNCINPEC garnered 45.5 per cent of the votes, and the SOC's party 38.2 per cent.[30] In November 1993, the constituent assembly elected by the people adopted a new constitution for the country. Once again known as the Kingdom of Cambodia, with Norodom Sihanouk as King, Cambodia was first led by a coalition government with Norodom Ranariddh, the chief of FUNCINPEC and a son of the King, as First Prime Minister, and Hun Sen, the former Prime Minister of the SOC, as the Second Prime Minister.

The new government, with an army consisting of the former SOC military as well as former non-communist soldiers and defectors from the Khmer Rouge, continued to conduct campaigns against the Khmer Rouge, which controlled small stretches of territory in the west of the country. The government used the threat of a Khmer Rouge takeover as a justification for an enormous military and security budget, as well as for various restrictions on democratic freedoms, such as freedom of the press and political expression. On July 7, 1994, the national legislature passed a law outlawing the Khmer Rouge.

Yet simultaneously, the government engaged in a campaign to obtain the defection of Khmer Rouge guerrillas through offers of amnesty and

29 *See* Steven R. Ratner, *The Cambodia Settlement Agreements*, 87 AJIL 1, 25–26 (1993).

30 For a review of UNTAC's performance, *see* STEVEN R. RATNER, THE NEW UN PEACEKEEPING: BUILDING PEACE IN LANDS OF CONFLICT AFTER THE COLD WAR 157–206 (1995).

integration into the Royal Cambodian Armed Forces. This policy resulted in the surrender and defection of a number of Khmer Rouge commanders as well as thousands of soldiers. A significant development in this area took place in September 1996, when the Cambodian government provided an amnesty to Ieng Sary, the number two leader in Democratic Kampuchea. The government decree may not legally amount to a complete immunity from all prosecution, although the surrender of Ieng Sary and his forces appeared to be in form only.[31] Perhaps as a result of the government's overtures, the movement splintered into rival factions. By the mid-1990s, the Khmer Rouge had effectively ceased operations, with its soldiers returning to civilian life or joining the national army.

The late 1990s brought some prospect of accountability for the members of the Khmer Rouge. As a result of successful persuasion by the Secretary-General's Special Representative for Human Rights in Cambodia, Thomas Hammarberg of Sweden, Cambodia's government formally asked the United Nations in June 1997 to assist it in bringing to justice members of the Khmer Rouge for their atrocities from 1975–79.[32] Hammarberg saw an inextricable link between the impunity of Cambodia's current government officials for significant human rights abuses and the impunity enjoyed by the Khmer Rouge for its far more extensive atrocities. The United States, for its part, began to consider the possibility of apprehending Pol Pot in Cambodia and sending him for trial in another state (one whose criminal law, based on universal jurisdiction, covered Pol Pot's actions) or before a UN tribunal; however, no states proved willing to conduct such a trial.[33] Following the Cambodian government's request, states interested in the issue managed to insert into the next General Assembly resolution on Cambodia a paragraph asking the Secretary-General to examine the request, 'including the possibility of the appointment, by the Secretary-General, of a group of experts . . .'[34] Meanwhile, however, Hun Sen staged a coup in July 1997 that left him in unrivalled control and called into question the government's position on its request for UN assistance.

[31] *See* Seth Mydans, *An Amnesty in Cambodia*, N.Y. TIMES, Sept. 18, 1996, at A13; *see also* Seth Mydans, *Cambodia's 2 Premiers Fight Over Ex-Rebels' Loyalty*, N.Y. TIMES, Dec. 27, 1996, at A3.

[32] Letter dated 21 June 1997 from the First and Second Prime Ministers of Cambodia addressed to the Secretary-General, *in* Identical letters dated 23 June 1997 from the Secretary-General addressed to the President of the General Assembly and to the President of the Security Council, June 24, 1997, UN Doc. A/51/930-S/1997/488.

[33] *See, e.g.*, Elizabeth Becker, *U.S. Spearheading Effort to Bring Pol Pot to Trial*, N.Y. TIMES, June 23, 1997, at A1; Craig Turner, *U.N. Examines How to Bring Pol Pot to Trial*, L.A. TIMES, June 24, 1997, at A4; Seth Mydans, *Cambodia Victors Kill Off Losers, Raising the Specter of a Civil War*, N.Y. TIMES, July 9, 1997, at A1.

[34] GA Res. 52/135, para. 16, UN GAOR, 52d Sess., Supp. No. 49, at 288, 289, UN Doc. A/52/49 (1997).

In the spring of 1998, Secretary-General Kofi Annan appointed such a group with a mandate to evaluate the existing evidence and determine the nature of the crimes committed, assess the feasibility of bringing Khmer Rouge leaders to justice, and explore options for trials before international or domestic courts. (A staged denunciation of Pol Pot by Khmer Rouge cadre in the jungle of western Cambodia in July 1997 and his death in April 1998 brought renewed public attention to the issue.) The Group consisted of Ninian Stephen, a former Governor-General of Australia and judge of the International Criminal Tribunal for the former Yugoslavia; Rajsoomer Lallah, a long-time member of the UN Human Rights Committee; and one of the authors of this book (Ratner). While not formally a 'commission' of experts, the Secretary-General saw the Group as serving the same purpose, by allowing independent experts to examine the evidence, the law, and the various options and make proposals that would, it was hoped, advance the prospects of accountability. The Group, which represented the first formal UN response to the Khmer Rouge years since the aborted efforts of the Human Rights Commission in 1978, carried out its work from July of 1998 until February 1999. Its main conclusion regarding criminal accountability was that the neglected and corrupt nature of the Cambodian court system rendered it unable, even with international assistance, to conduct fair trials; as a consequence, it recommended the creation of a new UN *ad hoc* criminal tribunal to try leaders of the Khmer Rouge.[35]

Hun Sen's government (now elected following a tainted electoral process in July 1998) almost immediately rejected the proposal for a UN tribunal; instead, it captured Ta Mok, who had long eluded apprehension, and stated that it would try him in a domestic court. The government justified its action by claiming that an international tribunal could never work because China would veto it.[36] (In fact, the Chinese government had told the Group of Experts that it would not oppose any tribunal requested by the Cambodian government, only one imposed on Cambodia.) The initial opposition of the Cambodian government greatly weakened prospects for the UN tribunal option. When the Secretary-General submitted the report to the Security Council and the General Assembly, he endorsed the thrust of the report in stating that 'if the international standards of justice, fairness

[35] Report of the Group of Experts for Cambodia established pursuant to General Assembly resolution 52/135, *in* Identical letters dated 15 March 1999 from the Secretary-General to the President of the General Assembly and the President of the Security Council, Mar. 16, 1999, UN Doc. A/53/850-S/1999/231 [hereinafter Secretary-General's Letter], Annex [hereinafter Group of Experts Report]; for a summary and assessment, *see* Steven R. Ratner, *The United Nations Group of Experts for Cambodia*, 93 AJIL 948 (1999). *See also* Ch. 14, *infra*.

[36] *See* Elizabeth Becker, *Cambodia Spurns U.N. Plan for Khmer Rouge Tribunal*, N.Y. TIMES, Mar. 13, 1999, at A4; *Hun Sen Moves Ahead*, ASIAWEEK (internet ed.), May 21, 1999, available at www.cnn.com/asianow/asiaweek/99/0521/nat2.html.

and the process of law are to be met . . . , the tribunal in question must be international in character';[37] but based on the Cambodian government's reaction and the lack of any immediate groundswell of support among member states for the Group's proposal, he did not specifically endorse its recommendation for a new UN tribunal. In addition, those states (principally Western) that had supported the principle of an international tribunal became preoccupied with Kosovo during the spring and summer of 1999 and did not attempt to persuade Cambodia to accept such a court.

Nonetheless, the Group of Experts report focused attention in Phnom Penh, in foreign capitals, and at UN Headquarters on the accountability issue, in particular by highlighting the importance of international control of the proceedings. As a result, in the summer of 1999, the UN Secretariat began developing plans for a Cambodian court with significant UN participation—a majority of foreign judges and a foreign prosecutor picked by the UN—which it presented to the Cambodian government in August 1999.[38] Negotiations between the United Nations legal staff and Cambodia continued on this proposal into 2000. A handful of Western states seem to support this process, but most UN members remained silent on the issue.

The events since 1997 have highlighted the real obstacles for advocates of human rights to persuade governments opposed to individual accountability to initiate such a process, even when the abuses rise to the scale of the Khmer Rouge's crimes. Many governments refuse to shatter various myths about the prior regime or themselves that they have used to justify their own grip on power, or to show to their people that governmental officials can and should be held responsible for abusing citizens' rights. In Cambodia's case, accountability would challenge the official party line since 1979 that only a handful of Khmer Rouge officials are responsible for the atrocities of 1975–79 and that members of the current government are blameless for events in that period; it would also demonstrate that the law does apply to governmental officials, thereby threatening the impunity these officials enjoy in Cambodia. Moreover, other states unfortunately remain reluctant to urge governments like Cambodia's to initiate such a process or to condemn them for failing to do so, either because human rights are not central to their foreign policy or because they regard accountability issues as tangential to protection of human rights.

As for Cambodia today, while neither a model democracy nor an economic dynamo even during its most peaceful and prosperous years, it remains a shadow of its former self due to a generation of war, revolution, and systematic abuses. The lack of a significant educated class continues

[37] Secretary-General's Letter, *supra* note 35, at 3.

[38] *See* Philip Shenon, *U.N. Plans Joint War Crimes Tribunal for Khmer Rouge*, N.Y. TIMES, Aug. 12, 1999, at A8.

to have profound repercussions throughout society as Cambodia attempts to rebuild. The Khmer Rouge also left a society so traumatized and unprepared for governance that unscrupulous and corrupt forces—whether allied with the former SOC, FUNCINPEC, or foreign business interests—continue to thrive.[39] These have stifled efforts to build a culture of respect for human rights and permit the country to join its neighbors on the path to development.

[39] *See, e.g.*, William Shawcross, *Tragedy in Cambodia*, N.Y. REV. BOOKS, Nov. 14, 1996, at 41, 45.

13

Applying the Law

The appraisal in Part I of the various acts incurring individual responsibility under international law portrays a legal landscape marked by areas of clarity as well as uncertainty. To demonstrate most directly the promises and limitations of ascribing criminal accountability for violations of human rights and humanitarian law, this Chapter applies the norms of international criminal law to the Cambodia tragedy. Here the complex definitional issues inherent in that law become most apparent. Yet because accountability also arises under domestic law, it is also necessary to evaluate the events of the Khmer Rouge period under Cambodian criminal law. While obviously the law of only one small state, an examination of the coverage of Cambodian law is, in two senses, indicative of the process needed for application of the law in other cases—because of the similarity of the basic substance of the written code (borrowed from the French criminal code) to those of other states; and because it highlights the constraints on invoking the law when a state's tumultuous history leaves the choice of applicable law, as well as its interpretation, subject to significant uncertainty.

Two preliminary points deserve mention. First, with respect to both international law and domestic law, the strictures of *nullum crimen sine lege* dictate application of the international and domestic law in force in 1975, at the start of the atrocities, rather than that in effect today.[1] Secondly, any application of the law in a volume such as this can reach only *prima facie* conclusions based on the historical record. Definitive findings concerning the guilt of individuals require an examination of detailed evidence deemed admissible by a particular forum regarding precise events and the role of individual actors in them.

GENOCIDE

Cambodia has been a party to the Genocide Convention, without reservation, since the Convention's entry into force in 1951.[2] The Khmer Rouge never, it appears, denounced the Convention when they were in power. As discussed in Chapter 12, the Khmer Rouge subjected the people of

[1] *See* Ch. 1, The Principles of Legality, *supra*.
[2] MULTILATERAL TREATIES, ch. IV.1.

Cambodia to almost all of the acts enumerated in Article II(a) through (e) of the Genocide Convention during their rule. The more difficult task is determining whether the Khmer Rouge carried out these acts with the requisite intent and against groups protected by the Convention.

The existing literature presents a strong *prima facie* case that the Khmer Rouge committed acts of genocide against the Cham minority group, the ethnic Vietnamese, Chinese, and Thai minority groups, and the Buddhist monkhood. While some commentators suggest otherwise,[3] virtually every author on the subject has reached this conclusion.[4] The Khmer Rouge subjected these groups to an especially harsh and extensive measure of the acts enumerated in the Genocide Convention. The requisite intent appears demonstrated by both direct and indirect evidence, including Khmer Rouge records and statements, eyewitness accounts, and the nature and number of victims in each group, both in absolute terms and in proportion to each group's total population.[5]

More specifically, in the case of the Buddhist monkhood, their intent seems established by the Khmer Rouge's intensely hostile statements toward religion, and the monkhood in particular; the Khmer Rouge's policies to eradicate the physical and ritualistic aspects of the Buddhist religion; the disrobing of monks and abolition of the monkhood; the number of victims; and the executions of Buddhist leaders and recalcitrant monks. Likewise, in addition to the number of victims, the intent to destroy the Cham and other ethnic minorities appears evidenced by such Khmer Rouge actions as their announced policy of homogenization, the total prohibition of these groups' distinctive cultural traits, their dispersal among the general population, and the execution of their leadership.[6]

These groups clearly qualify as protected groups under the

[3] *See, e.g.*, DAVID P. CHANDLER, A HISTORY OF CAMBODIA 218–19 (1992).

[4] *See, e.g.*, Hurst Hannum, *International Law and Cambodian Genocide: The Sounds of Silence*, 11 HUM. RTS. Q. 82, 110–12 (1989); Ben Kiernan, *The Cambodian Genocide: Issues and Responses*, *in* GENOCIDE: CONCEPTUAL AND HISTORICAL DIMENSIONS 191, 191–93 (George J. Andreopoulos ed., 1994); Revised and updated report on the question of the prevention and punishment of the crime of genocide, prepared by B. Whitaker, July 2, 1985, UN Doc. E/CN.4/Sub.2/1985/6, at 10; *see also Issues Affecting the Question of United States Relations with Vietnam: Hearing Before the Subcomms. on Asian and Pacific Affairs and on International Economic Policy and Trade of the House Comm. on Foreign Affairs*, 101st Cong., 1st Sess. 120, 139 (1990) (US government view to this effect). Some literature includes Cambodian Christians among the victims of genocide. *See* Gregory H. Stanton, *The Cambodian Genocide and International Law*, *in* GENOCIDE AND DEMOCRACY IN CAMBODIA 141, 141 (Ben Kiernan ed., 1993).

[5] *See, e.g.*, Kiernan, *supra* note 4, at 191–93 (estimates of each group who perished); Hannum, *supra* note 4, at 110–12; Stanton, *supra* note 4, at 142; Kathryn Railsback, *A Genocide Convention Action Against the Khmer Rouge: Preventing a Resurgence of the Killing Fields*, 5 CONN. J. INT'L L. 457, 465 (1990). *But see* CHANDLER, *supra* note 3, at 219.

[6] *See, e.g.*, Hurst Hannum and David Hawk, The Case Against the Standing Committee of the Communist Party of Kampuchea, Sept. 15, 1986, at 147–49 (draft ICJ memorial) (on file with authors) [hereinafter Draft Memorial].

Convention:[7] the Cham as an ethnic and religious group; the Vietnamese, Chinese, and Thai communities as ethnic and, perhaps, racial groups; and the Buddhist monkhood as a religious group. That the Khmer Rouge targeted the ethnic Chinese as an ethnic group, rather than merely as part of an economic class, is supported by reports that their mistreatment continued well after the Khmer Rouge had confiscated their property and had forced them to live as Khmer peasants.[8]

A more complicated issue, however, is the characterization of atrocities committed against the general Cambodian population. Several observers have asserted that the Khmer Rouge committed genocide against the Khmer national group, though they recognize that the Khmer Rouge obviously did not intend to destroy the Khmer nation as a whole.[9] These arguments take various forms. For example, one line maintains that the Khmer Rouge committed genocide against that portion of the Khmer national group that did not conform to their notions of social and ideological purity. This portion transcended characterization as a political or economic group, neither of which is protected by the Convention, since it represented a far broader segment of the society—basically, that segment that did not fit into the vision of the Khmer nation that the Khmer Rouge sought to impose.[10] Some have contended that the Khmer Rouge committed genocide against the urban Khmer population, the Khmer in the Eastern Zone (who were subjected to brutal treatment in connection with the hostilities with Vietnam and the rebellion in the zone), or both.[11]

The Khmer people of Cambodia clearly constitute a national group within the meaning of the Convention.[12] However, the question whether the Khmer Rouge committed genocide with respect to part of the Khmer national group turns on certain difficult interpretive issues, especially concerning the Khmer Rouge's intent with respect to its non-minority-group victims. While the drafters of the Convention eliminated any specific motive test, the requirement that intent be directed at a protected group 'as such' suggests that victims must have been targeted by virtue of their membership in a protected group.[13] Accordingly, if the Khmer Rouge targeted these victims solely as members of political, professional, or economic groups, or they were victims of random violence or harsh conditions imposed on society at large, it would be difficult to conclude

[7] *See, e.g.*, Railsback, *supra* note 5, at 464.

[8] *See* Draft Memorial, *supra* note 6, at 148–49.

[9] *See* David Hawk, *The Cambodian Genocide, in* Genocide: A Critical Bibliographic Review 137, 139–40 (Israel W. Charny ed., 1988); Kiernan, *supra* note 4, at 201–02; Hannum, *supra* note 4, at 111–12.

[10] Hannum, *supra* note 4, at 111–12.

[11] *See, e.g.*, Kiernan, *supra* note 4, at 201–02.

[12] *See* Draft Memorial, *supra* note 6, at 133–40.

[13] Genocide Convention, art. II, 78 UNTS at 280. *See* Ch. 2, text at notes 57–58, *supra*.

that acts committed against them constituted genocide under the Convention.[14] On the other hand, if the Khmer Rouge targeted these non-minority elements as members of the Khmer nation, then an argument that the Khmer Rouge committed genocide with respect to the Khmer nation becomes more plausible.

The Convention's failure to address the type of situation that prevailed in Cambodia stems largely from the mindset that dominated its elaboration; the drafters did not appear to have contemplated the mass killing of one segment of a group by another segment of that same group. The paradigms that guided the drafting, primarily the Nazi genocide against the Jews, involved attempts to destroy groups that were distinct from the perpetrators, as opposed to the bulk of the atrocities committed by the Khmer Rouge. Thus, although arguments can be advanced that the Convention ought to be interpreted in light of its spirit and purpose to cover the mass killing of Cambodians by the Khmer Rouge, it is uncertain how a court would decide the issue. This question turns in part on whether the Convention is to be accorded a relatively broad or more limited interpretation.[15]

The argument that the Khmer Rouge committed genocide with respect to the Khmer national group appears to be relatively weak in light of the facts. Most of the literature suggests that the Khmer Rouge did not target their non-minority victims as members of the Khmer nation 'as such'. Rather, it indicates either that the regime targeted them as economic, social, or political elements whom the Khmer Rouge sought to eradicate but whom the Convention does not protect; or that they were victims of arbitrary violence and harsh conditions that the government imposed on virtually the entire country. Adoption of the alternative legal interpretation, though morally appealing, would, as a practical matter, enlarge the deliberately limited scope of the Convention's list of protected groups, insofar as almost any political, social, or economic element of a population can be viewed as a part of a larger national group. As the definition of genocide under customary international law likely coincides with that under the Convention, arguments based on custom would also appear problematic.

It bears mention that the use of the term 'genocide' in the context of Cambodia may cause Cambodians and others to view the above conclusion regarding atrocities committed against the general population with some

[14] *See, e.g.*, Stephen P. Marks, *Forgetting 'The Policies and Practices of the Past': Impunity in Cambodia*, FLETCHER F. WORLD AFF., Summer/Fall 1994, at 17, 25 (arguing Khmer victims were victims of 'political genocide').

[15] *Compare* Draft Memorial, *supra* note 6, at 153–56, *with* Study of the Question of the Prevention and Punishment of the Crime of Genocide, prepared by Nicodème Ruhashyamiko, July 4, 1978, UN Doc. E/CN.4/Sub.2/416, at 5, 185.

anxiety. Indeed, for many years the Cambodian government has used the term as a blanket label for the full gamut of the Khmer Rouge's atrocities. Taxonomical debates such as this should, however, in no way detract from the gravity of the Khmer Rouge's abuses or diminish efforts to address them.

CRIMES AGAINST HUMANITY

As developed from the progeny of Nuremberg, crimes against humanity remain of central importance to those seeking to bring the Khmer Rouge to justice. As for the state of the law as of 1975, the most difficult issue to determine is whether the nexus to armed conflict was still required at that time. If one adopts a conservative view, requiring a linkage, the result is the exclusion of the vast majority of the Khmer Rouge's atrocities, because the Khmer Rouge did not commit most of their offenses in connection with war crimes *vis-à-vis* Vietnam or the rebels in the Eastern Zone.

In theory, of course, prosecutors and judges could, like the Nuremberg Tribunal, assume that all crimes against humanity were in connection with war crimes simply because they took place contemporaneously with them.[16] As a matter of history, however, the facts do not easily support such a legal theory. Historians have not linked the bulk of the atrocities of the Khmer Rouge to the armed conflicts in which it engaged, except to point out that the Khmer Rouge leadership's concept of self-reliance included an overall hatred of foreign and Vietnamese elements that they manifested in numerous ways.[17] But this hatred does not mean that the preponderance of their crimes committed at an earlier time than, or in a different place from, the armed conflict were, as a legal matter, 'in connection with' it. Irony abounds here, as the Khmer Rouge themselves might well have regarded all their policies as related to the struggle with Vietnam or an internal war against enemies; but we doubt whether any principles of international or domestic law would stop them from denying the linkage of their acts to armed conflict. A continued linkage to armed conflict would thus insulate many Khmer Rouge acts from international culpability.

At the same time, the analysis of developments since Nuremberg discussed in Chapter 3 suggests that, while the issue is certainly open to debate, on balance, the bond between crimes against humanity and war

[16] *See* Ch. 3, text at and note 28, *supra*.

[17] *See* Karl D. Jackson, *The Ideology of Total Revolution*, *in* CAMBODIA: 1975–1978: RENDEZVOUS WITH DEATH 37, 39–49 (Karl D. Jackson ed., 1989); BEN KIERNAN, THE POL POT REGIME 65–125 (1996).

crimes or crimes against the peace appears to have been severed by 1975. The views of states during the drafting of the 1968 Statutory Limitations Convention and the position of the International Law Commission in its 1954 Draft Code seem especially relevant in this context. The trends that have now solidified were well in place at that period, so that a prosecution of Khmer Rouge leaders for such violations would not violate a reasonable reading of the *nullum crimen* principle.

If the linkage to war crimes is dropped, those gathering evidence must focus on the other core elements historically part of crimes against humanity: the systematic or mass nature, the discriminatory intent, and state action. The literature by historians and other scholars suggests that a significant, even predominant, part of Khmer Rouge atrocities exhibited these features as a general matter, with different acts showing differing levels of conformity.

A far greater scope of atrocities are subject to individual culpability as crimes against humanity than as genocide defined in the Genocide Convention. Most importantly, the former includes atrocities against the hundreds of thousands of people, if not more, regarded as political enemies by the regime. As for the acts against the Cham, Buddhists, Chinese, and other minorities, they qualify as crimes against humanity even without proof that the Khmer Rouge intended to destroy them (the touchstone of genocide); and the sufficiency of political grounds as a basis for discrimination (to the extent any discriminatory intent is required at all) means that it is not necessary to prove that the Khmer Rouge acted against them based on their religion or ethnicity.

Nevertheless, further research would be needed, especially regarding the systematicity behind the terror, as some have argued that many atrocities, especially those in outlying areas, lacked direction and amounted effectively to random cruelty.[18] If governmental non-feasance in the face of such acts were motivated by animosity toward the victims' political or other status, it would seem equivalent to systematicity. Such an inquiry would also need to determine whether Khmer Rouge cadres who simply killed those whose work habits or demeanor they disliked, or on even more arbitrary grounds, as well as their superiors who tolerated such acts, may be guilty only of crimes under Cambodian law or also of crimes against humanity.

As for state action, assuming governmental action was still required as of 1975, it would seem to follow from evidence of systematicity, since only the government of Democratic Kampuchea had the control of the country needed to engage in these acts. Actions by regional authorities would also qualify, as would the implementation of policies through party

[18] *See* the contrasting views described in Kiernan, *supra* note 4, at 205–06.

channels, rather than formal state agencies, since the party controlled the state.

As for the individual crimes, the historical record discussed in Chapter 12 suggests clear *prima facie* cases of murder (rising to the level of extermination of political opposition), forced labor, torture, imprisonment, and other inhumane acts. Regarding forcible transfers of population, the evidence shows a cruel and unlawful means of accomplishing the plan, as well as an unjustifiable purpose aimed against the city-dwellers. The records of Tuol Sleng and other torture and interrogation centers offer immediate sources of evidence for some of these crimes, and eyewitness accounts would presumably fill in the details on the many acts for which written records prove lacking.

Regarding other persecutions, there is ample evidence of Khmer Rouge action in closing religious institutions and defrocking monks, removing children from school, and forcing some enemies to wear distinctive garb.[19] The resemblance of these crimes to those of the Nazis makes criminality compelling. Nevertheless, the inexactitude of the term 'persecutions', at least as of 1975, suggests that any organ determining culpability should follow the strategy of the Nuremberg prosecutors and focus on particular acts defined elsewhere (murder, etc.), rather than introduce a broad definition for which individual culpability does not clearly lie. The Khmer Rouge also destroyed public and private property in connection with the above crimes. Under the standard in *Eichmann*, this would also create *prima facie* culpability for a crime against humanity.[20]

WAR CRIMES

This area of law remains pertinent because certain Khmer Rouge atrocities took place in the course of warfare with other states, especially Vietnam, as well as perhaps with certain domestic resistance forces, primarily during their last year in power. At the same time, this aspect of Khmer Rouge activity constituted at best a small portion of their human rights abuses.

Law of International Armed Conflict

Cambodia, Laos, Thailand, and Vietnam were parties to all four Geneva Conventions during the period at issue, although none became a party to

[19] *See* David Hawk, *International Human Rights Law and Democratic Kampuchea*, 16 INT'L J. POL. 3, 19–23 (1986); Ben Kiernan, *Genocidal Targeting: Two Groups of Victims in Pol Pot's Cambodia, in* STATE ORGANIZED TERROR: THE CASE OF VIOLENT INTERNAL REPRESSION 207, 212–17 (P. Timothy Bushnell et al. eds., 1991).

[20] *See Eichmann*, 36 ILR at 241.

the Protocols before 1980.[21] The grave breaches provisions thus apply, although criminality might have extended beyond these grave breaches under the customary law of the time. Because Democratic Kampuchea's hostilities with Vietnam varied over time in scope and intensity, special attention must be devoted to the threshold of armed conflict.

As for the initiation of hostilities, Cambodian and Vietnamese forces engaged in border skirmishes as early as May 1975, when the Khmer Rouge attempted to seize the Vietnamese islands of Phu Quoc and Tho Chu as well as border provinces. According to Nayan Chanda, the Khmer Rouge evacuated 500 Vietnamese civilians who were never seen again.[22] Despite a few outward signs of friendship, efforts to solve the crisis and demarcate the border proved fruitless, and incidents continued along Cambodia's northeastern border. After a lessening of tensions in 1976, the Khmer Rouge began attacking villages in its three neighbors' border areas in the spring of 1977, and in September attacked villages in Vietnam's Tay Ninh Province, killing hundreds of civilians. That year also marked the beginning of systematic deportations and executions of Vietnamese in Cambodia, which worsened in 1978 as the government sought to eliminate what it called a Vietnamese-inspired threat from Khmer Rouge loyalists in the Eastern Zone. Vietnam responded with an attack by a force of 20,000 on Cambodia in October 1977, and in late December sent 58,000 reinforcements to Cambodia's Eastern Zone, penetrating up to twenty-five miles and prompting Cambodia to sever diplomatic relations. Vietnam's troops began withdrawing in January 1978, but in March, Cambodia launched another raid on Vietnam, killing hundreds or more civilians in the village of Ha Tien. After spending much of 1978 organizing a Cambodian resistance force, Vietnam launched its massive invasion of Cambodia on December 25, 1978.[23]

This factual pattern suggests that, for purposes of the Geneva Conventions, armed conflict between Vietnam and Cambodia clearly began by September 1977, and most likely earlier. Indeed, the border skirmishes in May 1975 and the continuation of incidents make a strong case

[21] Geneva Conventions of 12 August 1949 and Additional Protocols of 8 June 1977: ratifications, accessions, and successions, available at www.icrc.org/eng/party_gc#7. The Provisional Revolutionary Government of the Republic of Vietnam (the Vietcong) became a party in 1974; the Socialist Republic of Vietnam confirmed the continued adherence of Vietnam to the Conventions on July 4, 1976. *See also infra* note 26.

[22] Nayan Chanda, Brother Enemy: The War after the War 13 (1986); *see also id.* at 11–13, 192–225; David P. Chandler, The Tragedy of Cambodian History: Politics, War and Revolution since 1945, at 256–57, 271–72 (1991); Library of Congress, Federal Research Division, Cambodia: A Country Study 66–68 (Russell R. Ross ed., 1990); Ben Kiernan, *New Light on the Origins of the Vietnam-Kampuchea Conflict*, 12 Bull. of Concerned Asian Scholars 61 (1980).

[23] Chanda, *supra* note 22, at 86–87, 192–96, 206–13, 223–25, 333–43.

for the applicability of the Conventions in relations between Cambodia and Vietnam during nearly the entirety of Democratic Kampuchea's rule. Certainly Cambodia's attacks on Vietnam, Thailand, and Laos in 1977 would trigger the Conventions with regard to the non-Cambodians killed or injured and the targets attacked.

With respect to the crimes committed, the grave breaches provisions of the Geneva Conventions apply only in the cases of acts taken against 'protected persons or property'. In Geneva Conventions I and II, these are wounded and sick members of the armed forces, broadly defined;[24] and in Geneva III, they are prisoners of war.[25] The exact nature of Khmer Rouge acts against members of the armed forces is not, however, well documented and requires further investigation.[26]

Geneva Convention IV protects civilians who find themselves in the hands of a party to the conflict or occupying power of which they are not nationals.[27] This would clearly include Vietnamese in Vietnam as well as in Cambodia during the armed conflict. As most ethnic Vietnamese in Cambodia were regarded as residents rather than Cambodian citizens, the Conventions would protect them.[28] The acts against Vietnamese in Vietnam and Cambodia seem to meet the standard of *prima facie* grave breaches under Article 147 of Geneva Convention IV. In particular, the Cambodian army committed wilful killing, torture or inhuman treatment, wilful causing of great suffering, unlawful deportation or confinement, and extensive destruction of property. Beyond the Geneva Conventions, the record also suggests commission of other crimes that violate the laws or customs of war emanating from the Hague Conventions: wanton destruction of towns or villages; attack of undefended towns or villages;

[24] Geneva Convention I, art. 13, 75 UNTS at 40.

[25] Geneva Convention III, arts. 4–5, 75 UNTS at 138–42 (adopting same definition of protected persons as Conventions I and II).

[26] Vietnam became a party to the Geneva Conventions subject to various conditions, including a reservation to Article 85 of the Convention (III) on Prisoners of War, which protects prisoners prosecuted under the laws of the detaining power for acts committed prior to capture. Vietnam stated that 'prisoners of war prosecuted and convicted for war crimes or for crimes against humanity, in accordance with the principles laid down by the Nuremberg Court of Justice shall not benefit from the present Convention'. Reservations of the Democratic Republic of Vietnam, June 5, 1957 (copy from US Department of State Office of Treaty Affairs) (on file with authors). This could mean that Vietnam and Cambodia need not afford some of each other's prisoners of war the protections of the Third Convention regarding prosecutions (unless these provisions have become customary law).

[27] Geneva Convention IV, art. 4, 75 UNTS at 290.

[28] Under Cambodia's citizenship law, to be a citizen, a person generally had to have been born in Cambodia to parents born in Cambodia, or the child (wherever born) of such a person. Kram No. 913-NS, art. 22, Journal Officiel du Cambodge, Dec. 2, 1954. The definition of protected persons in Article 4 of Geneva Convention IV covers persons who are stateless as well as nationals of states other than Cambodia. JEAN S. PICTET, COMMENTARY, IV GENEVA CONVENTION RELATIVE TO THE PROTECTION OF CIVILIAN PERSONS IN TIME OF WAR 47 (1958); *see also* Steven R. Ratner, *The Cambodia Settlement Agreements*, 87 AJIL 1, 20 and nn. 118–19 (1993). The authors thank Ben Kiernan for information on this issue.

and plunder of public or private property. Additional crimes may well come to light after full investigation.

Law of Internal Armed Conflict

As Cambodia was not during this period a party to Protocol II of the Geneva Conventions concerning non-international conflicts (and since Protocol II did not codify existing custom), an appraisal of Khmer Rouge activities regarding internal armed conflict must begin with Common Article 3 of the Geneva Conventions. Yet, it appears that no international consensus prevailed in 1975 that would criminalize individuals for violations of Common Article 3 *per se*.[29] This was two years before the ICRC completed its first detailed elaboration of the laws of war in internal conflicts (i.e., Protocol II), and the fairly recent development of the law on this issue suggests criminality was not accepted at that time.

It remains possible that individual culpability could lie for certain violations of the laws and customs of war in internal conflicts. Yet our conclusion that the Yugoslavia and Rwanda Tribunal Statutes legislate a relatively new set of war crimes with respect to internal conflicts (though not too recent, as the Yugoslavia Tribunal indicates in the *Tadic* case) provokes hesitancy in finding any individual criminality under customary law either.[30] Rather, the underdeveloped state of international criminal law as of 1975 means that the acts of the Khmer Rouge against their Eastern Zone opponents were not likely then regarded as war crimes.

If, however, it were assumed that the law did impute such individual criminal responsibility, an inquiry into the internal conflict in Cambodia would reveal it to be quite limited in scope, though nonetheless brutal. Disagreements over policy between the center and officials in the northwest led to massive purges in that area in mid-1977, but not any armed conflict that would meet the standards of Common Article 3. The rebellion in the Eastern Zone from May through July 1978 likely did cross the threshold of insurrection inherent in Common Article 3.[31] Kiernan and Chanda describe organized forces of the Eastern Zone engaging in battles or hit-and-run attacks for several months with troops from the center.[32] The forces from the center, led by Mok, conducted a severe suppression campaign against the zone, whose inhabitants it referred to as 'Khmer bodies with Vietnamese minds'. In a systematic, government-organized

[29] *See* Ch. 4, text at and notes 88–93, *supra*.

[30] *See* Ch. 4, text at notes 88–90, *supra*; *Tadic Interlocutory Appeal*, paras. 128–36.

[31] For excellent background, *see* CHANDA, *supra* note 22, at 247–55.

[32] Ben Kiernan, *Wild Chickens, Farm Chickens, and Cormorants: Kampuchea's Eastern Zone Under Pol Pot*, *in* REVOLUTION AND ITS AFTERMATH IN KAMPUCHEA: EIGHT ESSAYS 136, 192–94 (David P. Chandler and Ben Kiernan eds., 1983); CHANDA, *supra* note 22, at 252–55.

killing spree, perhaps a hundred thousand or more perished, with many more exiled to other parts of the country or Vietnam.[33] The evidence gathered to date of the acts of Democratic Kampuchea in the Eastern Zone in 1978 thus suggests numerous *prima facie* violations of Common Article 3.

Destruction of Cultural Property

The Khmer Rouge's destruction of cultural property is well documented. As part of their systematic attack upon Buddhism, the Khmer Rouge desecrated or destroyed most of the country's 3,000 pagodas, inflicting irreparable damage on statues, sacred literature, and other religious items.[34] Similar damage was inflicted on Moslem mosques of the Cham people. The regime also attacked Christian places of worship, even disassembling the Catholic cathedral of Phnom Penh stone by stone until only a vacant lot remained.[35]

Although Cambodia has since 1962 been a party to the Hague Convention for the Protection of Cultural Property in the Event of Armed Conflict,[36] the Convention's nexus to armed conflict, together with the absence of criminality under customary law for peacetime destruction, means that only desecrations in connection with Cambodia's conflict with Vietnam or an internal conflict would trigger any criminal responsibility. Regarding interstate war, additional evidence would need to be gathered, though the usefulness of such an exercise is questionable due to the insignificance of this issue compared to other atrocities committed by Democratic Kampuchea. As for the internal conflict, assuming that the 1978 rebellion in the Eastern Zone meets the definition of non-international armed conflict from the Hague Convention, evidence would also need to be assembled regarding destruction of cultural property during these massacres.

OTHER ACTS INCURRING INDIVIDUAL CRIMINAL RESPONSIBILITY

Slavery and Forced Labor

Cambodia is a party to the 1956 Supplementary Convention on Slavery

[33] Kiernan, *supra* note 32, at 197; CHANDA, *supra* note 22, at 254.

[34] *See, e.g.*, ELIZABETH BECKER, WHEN THE WAR WAS OVER: THE VOICES OF CAMBODIA'S REVOLUTION AND ITS PEOPLE 264–65 (1986); LIBRARY OF CONGRESS, *supra* note 22, at 118–19.

[35] The Khmer Rouge did not harm the monuments at Angkor, regarding them as a critical symbol of past Cambodian accomplishments. David Chandler, *Seeing Red: Perceptions of Cambodian History in Democratic Kampuchea*, *in* REVOLUTION AND ITS AFTERMATH IN KAMPUCHEA, *supra* note 32, at 34, 34–35, 45–46.

[36] May 14, 1954, 249 UNTS 215; BOWMAN AND HARRIS, *supra* note 21, at 192, 193.

and to the 1930 Convention on Forced Labor, and was so during the Khmer Rouge period.[37] Regarding slavery, it is difficult to endorse a finding that the Khmer Rouge committed slavery as that term is narrowly defined in international conventions. Evidence showing some sort of ownership of persons during the period under consideration would be legally probative. As for forced labor beyond that encompassed in crimes against humanity, the 1930 Convention criminalizes certain forced labor not carried out in conformity with the treaty. Khmer Rouge conduct does not *prima facie* fall within the exceptions built into the Convention's definition of forced labor; in particular, the type of virtual enslavement of the population does not represent service as part of the 'normal civic obligations' of citizens except under the most twisted meaning of that term.[38]

Their acts also do not fall under the exception for work 'exacted in cases of emergency'.[39] The Khmer Rouge leadership at least asserted, and may have believed, that the food shortages necessitated forced labor, although scholars have refuted this.[40] Yet even assuming, contrary to the evidence, a worst case scenario of massive food shortages throughout the country, this would not justify the forced labor of the bulk of the population in the countryside. This is particularly true in light of the regime's refusal to accept much foreign food and medical aid.[41]

Having used forced labor as defined in the 1930 Convention, the regime *prima facie* routinely flouted virtually all the conditions in the Convention. These include the limitations on age, number of days of work, working hours, non-transfer to areas dangerous to health, and access to medical care. In addition, even assuming compulsory cultivation was necessary against famine, the regime did not allow those producing the food to keep it. The regime also disregarded the special requirements for forced labor in connection with public works, such as the ban on removal from the place of residence and due regard for religion and social life. These violations of the Convention all incur individual responsibility.

As a matter of customary law, the type of forced labor undertaken by the Khmer Rouge so resembles slavery in its totality and cruelty that a strong argument can be made for individual responsibility. The long working hours, meager rations, primitive living conditions, great distance from normal place of habitation, and constant surveillance by Khmer Rouge cadres distinguish the Khmer Rouge's acts from any possible justifiable

37 MULTILATERAL TREATIES, ch. XVIII.4; ilolex.ilo.ch:1567/scripts/ratifice.pl?C29.

38 Convention Concerning Forced or Compulsory Labor, June 28, 1930, as modified by the Final Articles Revision Convention of the International Labor Organization, art. 2(b), 39 UNTS 55, 58.

39 *Id.* art. 2(d), 39 UNTS at 58.

40 *See, e.g.*, CHANDLER, *supra* note 3, at 214–15; Charles H. Twining, *The Economy*, *in* CAMBODIA: 1975–1978, *supra* note 17, at 109, 115.

41 *See* Jackson, *supra* note 17, at 48–49.

forced labor. Whatever crisis may have prevailed in the country at the time would not justify the type of totalistic or cruel labor imposed by the regime.

Torture

Because the UN Convention on Torture was not concluded until 1984, the principle of *nullum crimen sine lege* renders it necessary to examine the criminality of torture under customary international law. The legal effect of UN General Assembly resolutions purporting to declare the law, in this case the Declaration on Protection from Torture,[42] even those passed by consensus, is a subject of much controversy in international law.[43] At the least, it would seem that the resolution's adoption by consensus offers strong evidence of an emerging norm of international criminality at the time. Given the general recognition of torture as a crime against humanity and a war crime,[44] the question is whether custom had also recognized it as an independent crime by, for instance, accepting universal jurisdiction to prosecute torture.

Apart from the Declaration, the evidence, including scholarly commentary, regrettably remains scant on independent criminality, instead focusing on the unlawfulness of torture and the prohibition as a *jus cogens* norm.[45] It thus cannot readily be assumed that international law recognized torture as an independent crime by 1975, although such a conclusion can be justified. A court would face a difficult determination, and, if it adopted a high standard of proof of custom and *nullum crimen sine lege*, might find no criminality in customary law at the time.

If a court decided in favor of criminality, then the historical record leaves little doubt regarding culpability. As the archives of Tuol Sleng bear witness, Democratic Kampuchea employed torture systematically against tens of thousands of enemies of the regime. The evidence of individual guilt is stronger for these acts than for any other crimes. Although nearly every victim of Khmer Rouge torture died from it, the documentary record is depressingly complete. Among the evidence are a Khmer Rouge manual for torturers and detailed records of the torture sessions and the confessions of the prisoners.[46]

[42] GA Res. 3452, Annex, arts. 7, 10, UN GAOR, 30th Sess., Supp. No. 34, at 91, UN Doc. A/10034 (1975).

[43] *See, e.g.*, ROSALYN HIGGINS, PROBLEMS AND PROCESS: INTERNATIONAL LAW AND HOW WE USE IT 25–28 (1994).

[44] *See* Ch. 3, text at note 154, *supra*; Geneva Convention IV, art. 147, 75 UNTS at 388.

[45] *See, e.g.*, Yoram Dinstein, *The Right to Life, Physical Integrity, and Liberty*, *in* THE INTERNATIONAL BILL OF RIGHTS: THE COVENANT ON CIVIL AND POLITICAL RIGHTS 114, 122–23 (Louis Henkin ed., 1981); *see also* Daniel Derby, *Torture*, *in* 1 INTERNATIONAL CRIMINAL LAW 705, 714–27 (M. Cherif Bassiouni ed., 2d ed. 1999).

[46] The Cambodia Documentation Commission has compiled and translated many of these records. For an excerpt, *see* BECKER, *supra* note 34, at 465–72.

Racial Discrimination and Apartheid

Cambodia became a party to the Apartheid Convention in 1981, when the exiled government of Democratic Kampuchea holding Cambodia's UN seat acceded to the Convention.[47] Thus, criminal responsibility for apartheid would apply only if it incurred individual responsibility as a matter of custom during the Khmer Rouge period. As for its criminality—in particular, universal jurisdiction to prosecute—under customary law at the time, there is little evidence to this effect. The Convention represented progressive development of international law, rather than mere codification of existing custom.[48] Only a handful of the current parties to the Convention joined it before the Khmer Rouge took power. The refusal of many states to join the Convention and the lack of any attempts at enforcement suggest the absence of individual criminality as a matter of customary law in 1975.[49]

An additional barrier to prosecution lies in the uncertainty over the term 'racial group'. If the term covers any group with common physical features, it could include non-Khmer minorities in Cambodia, including Vietnamese and Chinese. Such an argument has ample basis,[50] although a court could determine that fairness to defendants dictates a narrow interpretation of an imprecise term, which might well exclude some ethnic minorities in Cambodia.

If individual culpability did exist as a matter of custom in 1975 and the definition of racial group were broad enough to encompass these minorities, then the historical record would seem to present a *prima facie* case of apartheid. In particular, the leaders and cadres in Democratic Kampuchea committed murders of Vietnamese, Cham, and Chinese; infliction upon them of mental harm, arbitrary arrest, and imprisonment; imposition upon them of inhumane living conditions; and other measures to prevent their full development and deny them basic human rights. Indeed, the regime spoke in racial terms and of the need for racial purity.[51]

47 MULTILATERAL TREATIES, ch. IV.7; *see also id.* (protests to Cambodian accession from PRK supporters). Cambodia also signed the Racial Discrimination Convention in 1966 but became a party only in 1983 by the accession of the exiled government of Democratic Kampuchea, which held Cambodia's UN seat throughout the 1980s. *See* MULTILATERAL TREATIES, ch. IV.2 (protests to accession from PRK supporters and France).

48 *See, e.g.*, Roger S. Clark, *Apartheid, in* 1 INTERNATIONAL CRIMINAL LAW, *supra* note 45, at 643, 654–58; MYRES S. MCDOUGAL, HAROLD D. LASSWELL, AND LUNG-CHU CHEN, HUMAN RIGHTS AND WORLD PUBLIC ORDER: THE BASIC POLICIES OF AN INTERNATIONAL LAW OF HUMAN DIGNITY 542 (1980) (Convention seeks to make apartheid a crime against humanity).

49 *See* Clark, *supra* note 48, at 312–15.

50 *See* Ch. 5, text at note 51, *supra*.

51 *See, e.g.*, BECKER, *supra* note 34, at 253–64. If, however, the Khmer Rouge targeted enemies based on political, rather than purely racial, grounds, *see supra* note 3, the case for apartheid becomes

Other Crimes

It bears brief mention that the Khmer Rouge leaders and cadres appear to have committed at least one other crime on a far smaller scale—namely crimes against internationally protected persons. In April 1975, the regime detained personnel in the French embassy and then removed and murdered Cambodian husbands of foreign diplomatic personnel.[52] As for hostage-taking, because the International Convention Against the Taking of Hostages was concluded after the acts in question and covers only seizure of foreign individuals to compel third parties to undertake specific action, it would not address detention by the Khmer Rouge of either Cambodians or foreign citizens in Cambodia.[53] It would, however, appear to address Khmer Rouge activities after 1979, such as their detention of UN personnel and the kidnapping and murder of several groups of foreign tourists beginning in 1992. Finally, the limited definition of piracy to acts for 'private ends'[54] would appear to preclude characterization of the 1975 seizure of the *Mayaguez* or of an Australian yacht (and the subsequent murder of its crew in Tuol Sleng) as piracy.

DEFENSES

Although following orders *per se* would be an unacceptable defense in any prosecutions of Khmer Rouge officials or subordinates, many low-ranking Khmer Rouge actors, especially minors, presumably could not have known of the illegality of some of their orders under prior Cambodian law or international law (especially as the Democratic Kampuchea regime emphasized the new beginning for the country).[55] Although some crimes are so patently atrocious that such ignorance is never an excuse, many such cadres committing lesser offenses ought not to be held to an unreasonable standard of knowledge and would seem to have a valid defense. In other situations, where lack of knowledge of the law is not a defense, following orders might be used to mitigate punish-

more speculative. The Convention speaks of 'inhuman acts committed *for the purpose of* establishing and maintaining domination *by one racial group* of persons over any other racial group of persons and systematically oppressing them', Apartheid Convention, art. II, 1015 UNTS at 245–46 (emphasis added), and might not address oppression organized with race merely an incidental factor.

[52] *See* William Shawcross, Sideshow: Kissinger, Nixon and the Destruction of Cambodia 366–67 (rev. ed. 1987).

[53] Dec. 17, 1979, art. 13, 1316 UNTS 205, 210.

[54] *See, e.g.*, Convention on the High Seas, Apr. 29, 1958, art. 15, 450 UNTS 82, 90; *see also* Clyde H. Crockett, *Toward A Revision of the International Law of Piracy*, 26 DePaul L. Rev. 78, 84–87 (1976); Jacob W.F. Sundberg, *Piracy*, *in* 1 International Criminal Law, *supra* note 45, at 803, 805–06.

[55] *See* Ch. 6, text at notes 35–39, *supra*.

ment. As affirmed at Nuremberg, leaders would be held to have known of the criminality of their acts *vis-à-vis* earlier Cambodian law or international law.

Many Khmer Rouge offenders, especially those at lower levels facing threats from other cadres, might also benefit from a defense of coercion. Evidence regarding such compulsion would, however, be quite difficult to gather and evaluate given the length of time since the events and the traumatic atmosphere of the period. As for the defenses of necessity or *force majeure*, it seems difficult to imagine how they would excuse most Khmer Rouge crimes; in order for these defenses to apply, the atrocities of the acccused would have had to preserve more lives than they cost.

CAMBODIAN LAW

As the territorial state of the acts at issue, Cambodia clearly has jurisdiction to prescribe criminal law addressing Khmer Rouge atrocities, as well as jurisdiction to apply that law through criminal trials. Equally important, crimes under Cambodian law—or any domestic law—will generally lack the special elements of many international crimes and thus be far easier to prove.

A review of domestic law involves a somewhat different exercise from that in determining the international crimes relevant to Khmer Rouge activities. As an initial matter, certain similarities in the content of the law emerge, as international criminal law derives much of its substance from the legal systems of the world, and the Cambodian system developed from one of them—the French civil law system. Difficulties in appraising customary international law are attenuated in the case of domestic law, where codes define crimes more clearly.

However, two obstacles make the task complex for those invoking or applying domestic law. First, as with many less developed countries, the sources on Cambodian law are extremely scarce. The primary source of criminal law prior to the Khmer Rouge period is the 1956 volume *Code Pénal et Lois Pénales*, published by the Ministry of Justice of the Kingdom of Cambodia, though it appears that no sources reliably and comprehensively update this law through 1975.[56] As for subsequent law that might govern the Khmer Rouge years, Democratic Kampuchea, not

[56] Although Cambodia developed during its years of relative peace a fairly impressive body of statutory law and other decrees for a poor country, no available caselaw appears to elaborate the codes. The 1956 Code is not published in a form that shows amendments and other changes since its original publication. Although a review of all Cambodian laws for this 19-year period might reveal amendments to the criminal code, the authors' research in Cambodia found none of our Cambodian interlocutors aware of any.

surprisingly, appears to have published none.[57] No secondary sources on Cambodian criminal law appear extant.[58] Secondly, because Cambodia has seen at least six legal regimes since independence,[59] the extent to which the law of the prior regimes has remained in force is simply undetermined in many cases.[60]

At a minimum, then, this analysis assumes that, based on the principle of *nullum crimen sine lege*, pre-1975 Cambodian criminal law represents the primary source of law concerning the culpability of the Khmer Rouge for acts from 1975 to 1979.[61] While Cambodian law might recognize the possibility that a later statute can simply codify a domestic offense already recognized at the time of its commission even if not explicitly outlawed in the code, this interpretation of *nullum crimen* is far more problematic in the sphere of domestic law.[62] Even though Cambodian courts have not applied the 1956 law for a generation, and its use could lead to confusion by judges and attorneys, it remains the primary source of law for domestic prosecutions.

Implicit in this assumption is that the major crimes in the 1956 criminal code remained crimes during the subsequent years. This seems the case during the later years of the Kingdom of Cambodia and the Khmer Republic. As for the effect of the Khmer Rouge period, no evidence

[57] As for law since the Khmer Rouge fled power, the People's Republic of Kampuchea issued a decree on May 15, 1980, on 'Treason Against the Revolution and Other Crimes' that punishes a broad category of self-styled counter-revolutionary offenses. During the UNTAC period, the Supreme National Council promulgated an UNTAC-drafted code of criminal law and procedure on September 10, 1992. *See infra* note 60.

[58] The authors benefited from a legal memorandum of Mr. Douc Rasy, a former dean of the University of Phnom Penh Law School. *See* Douc Rasy, Remarks on the Punishment of Genocide in Cambodia, June 23, 1995 (on file with authors) [hereinafter Douc Rasy Memorandum].

[59] These are the Kingdom of Cambodia (1953–70), the Khmer Republic (1970–75), Democratic Kampuchea (1975–79), the PRK/SOC (1979–91), the Supreme National Council/UNTAC (1991–93), and again the Kingdom of Cambodia (1993–present).

[60] As a starting point, the 1956 Code should remain in force unless denounced or overridden by later law. The 1992 UNTAC Law has provisions on a variety of crimes, including homicide, rape, assault, unlawful detention, and theft. Provisions Relating to the Judiciary and Criminal Law and Procedure Applicable in Cambodia during the Transitional Period, Decision of 10 September 1992, arts. 31–65. It also claims to abolish any prior inconsistent laws, *id.* art. 73, meaning that provisions of the 1956 Code not overridden should remain in force. Although the UNTAC law is facially limited to the period prior to the May 1993 elections, it remains in force until a new criminal code is promulgated. *See* CAMBODIAN CONST. (1993), art. 139 ('laws and standard documents . . . that safeguard State properties, rights, freedom[s] and legal private properties' remain applicable if consistent with Constitution).

[61] Cambodian criminal law, based on French law, also recognizes the principle of non-retroactivity, clearly prohibiting application of penalties for any infraction not included in the code when committed. Code Pénal, art. 6, *citing* CAMBODIA CONST. (1947), art. 19(2).

[62] *See generally* GASTON STEFANI, GEORGES LEVASSEUR, AND BERNARD BOULOC, DROIT PÉNAL GÉNÉRAL 95–98, 114–25 (16th ed. 1997) (noting French strict view on *nullum crimen*). International law has recognized the possibility of international crimes without statutes precisely because of the importance of customary law and the absence of an international criminal code, considerations generally inapplicable in the context of a domestic criminal code. *See* Ch. 1, text at note 64, *supra*.

suggests that Democratic Kampuchea formally repealed or denounced the criminal law in effect at the time it took power.[63] Although Democratic Kampuchea clearly intended to create a new beginning ('Year Zero') in Cambodia, it cannot be assumed, absent clear proof, that the regime eliminated the criminality of egregious acts regarded as crimes by nearly all states. Moreover, even an explicit denunciation would not *per se* insulate the Khmer Rouge's acts from criminality under earlier Cambodian law, especially if the regime sought to justify violations of the most basic protections of human dignity.[64]

Principal Crimes under Pre-1975 Cambodian Law

The 1956 Penal Code covers the primary crimes recognized by most states. According to French practice, the code classifies offenses by severity into *crimes* (akin to felonies); *délits* (misdemeanors); and *contraventions* (police violations or minor offenses). Felonies and misdemeanors are further qualified as first, second, or third degree in increasing order of severity according to their corresponding degree of punishment.[65] Felonies were punishable by *peines criminelles*: those of the third degree were punishable by death; second-degree felonies were punishable by life at forced labor; and first-degree felonies were punishable by forced labor for a limited period. Misdemeanors were punishable by *peines correctionnelles*, namely imprisonment, fines, or both, each increasing based on the degree of the misdemeanor. Police infractions were punishable by *peines de simple police*, namely police detention, police fines, or both.[66]

The primary crimes and corresponding punishment may be summarized as follows:

Homicide (Articles 501–08): Voluntary homicide committed with the intention of causing death is murder, a second-degree felony; premeditated murder qualifies as assassination, a third-degree felony. Involuntary homicide includes manslaughter through negligence and other types of recklessness and is punishable in varying degrees of severity.[67]

Torture (Article 500): Torture is a third-degree felony. The definition resembles the internationally accepted definition of torture, involving

[63] *Accord* Douc Rasy Memorandum, *supra* note 58, at 1.

[64] *See* Ch. 6, text at notes 64–65, *supra*; *see also* this Chapter, Defenses, *supra*.

[65] Code Pénal, art. 5.

[66] *Id.* arts. 4, 21–23. The court may decrease or increase the penalty based on attenuating or aggravating circumstances, the latter of which include those stemming from the method of the crime, the situation of the victim, and the offender's criminal record. *Id.* arts. 115–69.

[67] Article 505 states that intent to cause death is presumed from the use of a lethal weapon and can also be presumed based on the severity, multiplicity, or location of the blows to the victim. *See also* Code Pénal, arts. 455, 460 (forced abortions and infanticide).

infliction of pain in order to extract information or punish the victim; however, it lacks any required nexus to official conduct.

Rape (Articles 443–46): Article 443 defines rape as the introduction or attempted introduction of the perpetrator's sexual organ into another person by force or threats without the other's consent.[68] For victims of thirteen years of age and above, it is a third degree misdemeanor; for those under thirteen, it is a first degree felony.

Other physical assaults (Articles 495–99): A voluntary act of violence that leaves traces on the victim is a second-degree misdemeanor if done without the use of an armed object and a third-degree misdemeanor if done with an armed object. If it results in a permanent infirmity, mutilation, loss of a limb or senses, mental problems, or abortion, it is a first-degree felony.[69]

Arbitrary arrest or detention (Articles 482–86): Anyone who arrests or detains another, except under legitimate authority or in the case of a crime, is liable for a second-degree misdemeanor if the detention lasts ten days or less; otherwise, it is a third-degree misdemeanor. The maximum penalty is to be applied if the victim is subjected to violence, maltreatment, or deprivation of food or care.[70] In addition, articles 249–51 make unlawful detention by a public official, whether a policeman, jailer, or judge, a second-degree misdemeanor.

Attacks on religion (Articles 209–18): An attack on the life of any monk practicing a religion recognized by the Cambodian government during the exercise of his profession is a third-degree felony; other attacks on his person are second-degree felonies.[71] Other second-degree felonies include preventing or stopping religious practices and desecration of religious places or objects.

Other abuses of governmental authority (Articles 240–44): The Code punishes arbitrary use of power by governmental officials or public

[68] The law also recognizes statutory rape for any sex with girls under 13. *Id.* art. 444.

[69] *See also id.* art. 487 (first-degree misdemeanor is any act of negligence or recklessness that causes wounds, sickness, or temporary incapacity to work; second-degree misdemeanor results if victim incurs permanent infirmity, mutilation, or loss of limb or senses).

[70] *See also* Code Pénal arts. 418–19 (traffic in persons); 420–22 (kidnapping).

[71] Articles 209 and 210 speak of any monk practicing a religion recognized by the Cambodian government, which need not only be Buddhism, the official religion under the Constitution. Nevertheless, its application to Buddhist monks alone seems to flow from a note to these two articles that refers the reader to other Code provisions (the general provisions on murder and assault) for attacks on any '*religieux non bouddhiste*' (non-Buddhist monk).

authorities as a second-degree misdemeanor. Arbitrary acts are defined as deprivations of the political, civil, or family rights or liberties of people without legal justification.

Related crimes (Articles 77–88): Article 77 punishes attempts at felonies like the crimes themselves if they failed to achieve their goal solely due to actions independent of the offender. Attempts at misdemeanors are punishable only if specifically provided for; attempts at *contraventions* are not punishable. As for participation, Article 82 states that all persons participating voluntarily, either directly or indirectly, in a felony or misdemeanor are susceptible to the same punishment as the principal. Indirect participation is limited by Article 83 to incitement, training, furnishing of means, and assistance.

In addition to the above offenses, the Code of Military Justice, published along with the Penal Code, provides for a number of additional crimes when committed by military personnel. The crimes and punishments are generally defined along the same lines as those in the Penal Code.[72]

Finally, the 1956 Code does not explicitly criminalize international offenses such as genocide, crimes against humanity, or war crimes *per se*. Whether Cambodian law permits direct prosecution of individuals for international crimes absent codification of those crimes in the penal code remains unresolved. French constitutional law appears to allow prosecution under at least treaty-based criminal law, since treaties become applicable domestically subject only to some official publication.[73] If Cambodia were to follow the French approach, retroactive application of such decrees might nonetheless be viewed as an *ex post facto* criminal statute.[74]

Principal Defenses and Other Exculpatory Provisions

The Penal Code provides the typical listing of defenses. First, any person found by a court to be insane is not criminally responsible for his actions

[72] Code de Justice Militaire, art. 155 (Penal Code applicable to offenses except for imposition of fines). The major part of the Code concerns simply military-type offenses. It does, however, make a second-degree felony any pillage by a group of military personnel if committed with arms, force, or other violence; if the group is led by officers, the other perpetrators are guilty of only a first-degree felony. *Id.* art. 214.

[73] *See* Pierre Michel Eisemann and Catherine Kessedjian, *National Treaty Law and Practice: France, in* NATIONAL TREATY LAW AND PRACTICE 1, 11–12 (Monroe Leigh and Merritt R. Blakeslee eds., 1995); NGUYEN QUOC DINH, DROIT INTERNATIONAL PUBLIC 228–29, 632–33 (Patrick Daillier and Alain Pellet eds., 5th ed. 1994); Elisabeth Zoller, *La définition des crimes contre l'humanité*, 120 J. DROIT INT'L 549, 550–51 (1993).

[74] If Cambodia had decreed the Genocide Convention or other international criminal law conventions as applicable domestically before 1975, the retroactivity problem would not arise for those crimes.

and instead faces a separate penal regime.[75] Secondly, an offender under the age of eighteen at the time of the offense can be found guilty only after a determination of his ability to discern his crime when committed. If he did have such an ability to judge, the penalties are nevertheless reduced due to his minor status.[76] Thirdly, an offender can plead *force majeure*, defined as a state of absolute necessity where the offender faced an imminent and inevitable danger not of his own creation that he could stop only by committing the offense.[77]

Fourthly, no guilt arises if the action was ordered by law and commanded by legitimate authority; in the case of illegal orders given by legitimate authorities, the judge will determine the accused's degree of responsibility.[78] Fifthly, self-defense is a permitted defense only if it arises out of an unjust attack, is based on actual necessity, and is limited in scope to that needed to repel the attack.[79] Finally, the Penal Code provides for clear statutes of limitations—ten years for felonies, five years for misdemeanors, and one year for police infractions. These run from the date of the commission and are interrupted by any judicially ordered investigation.[80]

Prima Facie Conclusions

Although authoritative determinations demand an analysis of the entire corpus of domestic criminal law and consideration of other prudential and precedential factors, certain *prima facie* conclusions seem nonetheless possible. As for the basic offenses, the Khmer Rouge's atrocities meet the general definitions of the various crimes in the Cambodian Penal Code of 1956. These include murder, torture, rape, unlawful detention, other physical assaults, attacks on religion, and other abuses of governmental authority.[81] Because these are crimes under Cambodian law, prosecutors would not need to prove the additional elements for various international offenses, such as an intent to destroy groups (genocide), systematicity or scale (crimes against humanity), or link to armed conflict (war crimes).

The defenses recognized in domestic law, however, raise a number of important considerations that would be relevant in situations beyond

[75] Code Pénal, arts. 89–90 and implementing rules.

[76] If he lacked such a capacity, he must be returned to his parents or placed in a special prison until the age of majority. *Id.* arts. 91–95, 117–22.

[77] *Id.* arts. 96–98.

[78] *Id.* arts. 99–100; *see also id.* art. 329 (definition of legal orders).

[79] *Id.* arts. 101–04.

[80] *Id.* arts. 109–14; *see generally* Gaston Stefani, Georges Levasseur, and Bernard Bouloc, Procédure Pénale 162–77 (17th ed. 2000).

[81] An exhaustive review of the criminal code would reveal other crimes, including many property crimes and other infringements on civil rights and property rights.

Cambodia. First, youthful offenders may well be exempt from any culpability, especially given the totalistic control and atmosphere of terror and siege that gripped the country during that period. Secondly, the precise status of the *force majeure* defense will require elaboration, although the code seems to suggest that an offender would have to prove that he faced a virtual 'kill or be killed' scenario. This might limit the number of persons who could rely on such a defense to a small number. Similarly, a self-defense claim would seem inapplicable in many situations given the helplessness of most victims.

Thirdly, the scope of the following-orders defense under Cambodian law requires definition. Were the Khmer Rouge's orders lawful for purposes of this defense? If not, to what degree are subordinates liable for carrying out illegal orders? The precedents arising out of World War II and other situations may help answer these questions.[82] Nevertheless, those in a position of national leadership or others with sufficient discretion to issue orders clearly cannot invoke such a defense.

Finally, as for statutes of limitations, one interpretation would simply take the law's provision at face value and bar any prosecutions for atrocities committed during 1975–79 after January 1989, ten years from the Khmer Rouge's loss of governmental power. Indeed, crimes committed before 1979 would have had to be investigated or prosecuted before 1989. However, other options discussed in Chapter 6 remain available to the National Assembly and domestic courts, namely the elimination of statutes of limitations legislatively (even retroactively), and the judicial or legislative suspension of the operation of the statute due to the lack of a functioning criminal justice system.[83] These choices seem particularly justified in light of the destruction of the judiciary by the Khmer Rouge itself and the resultant primitive and disorganized state of that system.[84]

The application of international and domestic criminal law to the human rights abuses of the Khmer Rouge thus reveals a wide variety of offenses for which a *prima facie* case of guilt for many cadres can be made. The majority of international law offenses qualify as crimes against humanity rather than genocide, although the regime also undertook the latter against specifically targeted groups. Khmer Rouge soldiers also committed war crimes during the conflict with Vietnam, even if those acts remain beyond the limelight of most accounts of the period. Forced labor as made criminal in the 1930 Convention appears to have been rampant, as was torture. The range of offenses under Cambodian law is, not surprisingly, much

[82] *See* Ch. 6, Appraising the Defenses under International Law—Superior Orders and Ignorance of the Law, *supra*.

[83] *See* Ch. 6, text at notes 74–79, *supra*.

[84] *See generally* Ch. 14, National Tribunals—The Functioning of the Judicial System, *infra*.

wider, covering many areas of its criminal code. Yet under both sets of law, certain defendants, particularly youthful offenders, might be able to take advantage of various defenses, whether the narrow defense of coercion under international law or potentially broader defenses under domestic law.

14

Engaging the Mechanisms

Any *prima facie* conclusion that the Khmer Rouge committed serious offenses under international and domestic law remains a largely academic exercise unless measures are taken to make those responsible accountable in some way. This process requires a re-examination of the various accountability mechanisms explored in the second part of this volume. As the balance between the strengths and weaknesses of each mechanism will vary depending on the context in which it may be used, acute attention must be directed to a constellation of factors, including public attitudes, domestic politics, the state of the country's judiciary, its resources, the seriousness of the abuses, the availability of defendants and evidence, and international political currents. Indeed, since 1997, the United Nations, Cambodia, and other states have finally begun to scrutinize these factors in a series of steps attempting to bring about some form of accountability.[1]

As an initial matter, legal obligations regarding past human rights violations are quite explicit in the case of Cambodia. In the 1991 Paris Accords, it undertook 'to take effective measures to ensure that the policies and practices of the past shall never be allowed to return', to 'ensure respect for and observance of human rights and fundamental freedoms in Cambodia', and 'to adhere to relevant international human rights instruments'.[2] This last duty would include, for example, fulfillment of its obligation to punish genocide on its territory under the Genocide Convention.[3] The other signatories to the accords assumed obligations to promote and encourage respect for human rights in Cambodia and to prevent the recurrence of human rights abuses, clearly implying a duty to support efforts by Cambodia to bring Khmer Rouge offenders to justice and even to take measures to ensure that the Cambodian government fulfils its obligations in this regard.[4]

[1] *See* Ch. 12, The Khmer Rouge Since 1979, *supra*.

[2] Agreement Concerning the Sovereignty, Independence, Territorial Integrity and Inviolability, Neutrality and National Unity of Cambodia, Oct. 23, 1991, art. 3(2), 31 ILM 200, 202 (1992) [hereinafter Paris Agreement].

[3] Genocide Convention, art. VI, 78 UNTS at 282; Steven R. Ratner, *The Cambodia Settlement Agreements*, 87 AJIL 1, 26 (1993).

[4] Paris Agreement, *supra* note 2, art. 3(2), at 202; *see, e.g.*, Stephen P. Marks, *Forgetting 'The Policies and Practices of the Past': Impunity in Cambodia*, FLETCHER F. WORLD AFF., Spring/Summer 1994, at 17, 36, 39–40. Cambodia's new constitution is silent on accountability for past crimes.

Yet beyond these legal duties, Cambodia is different from most other transitional countries that have confronted the issue of accountability for past human rights abuses. To begin with, Cambodia's transition has not taken one of the more familiar forms and, in many respects, is still evolving. The targets of accountability did not negotiate a transfer of power, nor were they completely vanquished. Although the movement is no longer a military threat to the government, some members negotiated a truce with the regime in return for amnesty and some of the trappings of sovereignty, including control over territory. Others have quietly merged into the general populace, are hiding abroad, or, in some cases, may even be serving in the Royal Government.[5] In addition, the abuses in Cambodia were among the worst endured by any society since the atrocities of World War II.

The Cambodian context thus clearly presents impediments to accountability. The difficulty of gaining access to evidence, the government's ambivalence and shortcomings, lack of resources, and the shortage of Cambodians with the necessary expertise and untainted by the past are all themes that run through the discussions of the available mechanisms that follow. In addition, one can fairly ask whether these mechanisms, Western in origin, have much relevance for Cambodian society and its non-Western approach to concepts of justice. On the international plane, certain foreign governments have resisted efforts to pursue accountability in Cambodia, even though recent developments, such as the tribunals for Yugoslavia and Rwanda, have highlighted the available options.

The prospects for efforts to pursue accountability depend most of all upon the support of the Cambodian people and government. These sentiments are somewhat difficult to determine in the absence of valid polling data, but our research leads us to identify several strands of general sentiment.[6] First, some elements of the Cambodian polity are clearly concerned that the pursuit of accountability may further destabilize Cambodia, divert resources from social and economic reconstruction, and run counter to Cambodia's spiritual principles. Indeed, the primary concern among Cambodians appears to be toward the present and future, not the past.

Secondly, Cambodians, or at least their leaders, do not appear eager to bring to justice all persons who committed atrocities during the Khmer

[5] On the status of the Khmer Rouge, *see* Report of the Group of Experts for Cambodia established pursuant to General Assembly resolution 52/135, paras. 95–121, *in* Identical letters dated 15 March 1999 from the Secretary-General to the President of the General Assembly and the President of the Security Council, Mar. 16, 1999, UN Doc. A/53/850-S/1999/321, Annex [hereinafter Group of Experts Report].

[6] *See* the acknowledgements to this volume for the authors' sources in this regard; *see also* Group of Experts Report, *supra* note 5, paras. 93–94.

Rouge period. They recognize the extent of involvement of vast elements of the population, including many who acted under some form of duress or in a climate of terror and confusion. The emphasis seems to be on national reconciliation. King Sihanouk has emphasized such reconciliation in public statements, and the government's leadership has demonstrated its willingness to strike a deal with even the highest ranking Khmer Rouge.[7]

Finally, however, most Cambodians would appear to like to see those persons most responsible for the crimes brought to justice. The 1979 show trials in Cambodia focused only on Pol Pot and Ieng Sary and left them and the other worst abusers of human rights unpunished and beyond the reach of the law. The passage of anti-Khmer Rouge legislation in 1994 also indicates some domestic pressures for accountability, though the 1996 amnesty to Ieng Sary and non-prosecution of other former leaders of Democratic Kampuchea suggests that those behind the law viewed it as more of a political maneuver than a genuine step toward accountability. The heightened attention devoted to accountability for human rights abuses today, as exemplified by the tribunals for Rwanda and Yugoslavia, seems to have further emboldened proponents of accountability for the Khmer Rouge.

Beyond these general public attitudes, any decision to pursue accountability requires a high-level political commitment. On the one hand, the Royal Government should have a strong interest in taking some dramatic action to mark the country's transition from the horrors and isolation of the past. However, there is ample reason to believe some of its members have other motives. As discussed in Chapter 12, accountability could prove embarrassing for certain officials due to their ties with, or membership in, the Khmer Rouge during the period of Democratic Kampuchea and thereafter. It would also interfere with the government's policy of granting *de facto* amnesties to the Khmer Rouge's members. And accountability of Khmer Rouge officials would threaten the general culture of impunity from which Cambodia's current governmental officials benefit significantly. The government's commitment to accountability, let alone to a fair process for achieving it, is thus questionable, even if Cambodia's leaders have endorsed the concept of trials of senior Khmer Rouge leaders and asked the United Nations to assist in the process.[8]

If Cambodia's political leadership continues to show less than a firm

[7] *See, e.g., Sihanouk calls on Khmer Rouge to join mainstream*, BBC Summary of World Broadcasts, Jan. 25, 1995; William Shawcross, *Tragedy in Cambodia*, N.Y. REV. BOOKS, Nov. 14, 1996, at 41, 45; Group of Experts Report, *supra* note 5, paras. 44–45.

[8] *See, e.g.*, Letter dated 21 June 1997 from the First and Second Prime Ministers of Cambodia addressed to the Secretary-General, *in* Identical letters dated 23 June 1997 from the Secretary-General addressed to the President of the General Assembly and to the President of the Security Council, June 24, 1997, UN Doc. A/51/930-S/1997/488 (Cambodian government request).

desire to pursue accountability, then any mechanism faces tremendous obstacles. The international community, which has its own interest in bringing to justice those accused of crimes against humanity, will have to convince the Cambodian government of the need for such accountability. If the government cannot be convinced, then the only feasible options will be those that do not absolutely require its cooperation. And as a practical matter, they will likely prove fruitless without Cambodia's help.

The Cambodian case study thus presents a challenging, though not entirely unique, combination of circumstances. The country has experienced the most serious of atrocities, and its resources are severely limited. Its political system is unstable and riddled with corruption and division, while its criminal justice system is dysfunctional at best. The attitudes of its leaders are dominated by shifting political priorities. Gathering of evidence is a problem. And the passage of time since the atrocities and the international political dynamics of Cambodia's history may well diminish the motivation of foreign states for accountability.

NATIONAL TRIBUNALS

Because the primary onus of accountability for the acts of the Khmer Rouge rests with the Cambodian government, domestic trials must be considered as an important potential mechanism for accountability. Indeed, beyond the moral and political obligations upon the Cambodian government are legal obligations as well, most notably the requirement under the Genocide Convention to punish genocide committed on its territory (even if the bulk of the terror did not qualify as genocide).[9] That the present Cambodian government has not prosecuted or punished any Khmer Rouge for genocide, and in fact granted an amnesty to defecting Khmer Rouge, presents a strong case of a violation of this obligation.[10] Any state that fails to comply with requests for extradition of perpetrators of genocide to Cambodia in accordance with its laws would also be in violation of the Convention.

Legal Framework for Trials

The principle of *nullum crimen sine lege* requires that the crimes at issue be judged solely from the perspective of the law in force in 1975, presumably the Code Pénal of 1956. No principle of either international law or

[9] *See supra* note 3.

[10] The precise scope of the amnesty granted by the government in 1996 to Ieng Sary, the Khmer Rouge's second-in-command, is unclear. It may cover only the crimes for which he was tried *in absentia* in 1979. *See* Seth Mydans, *An Amnesty in Cambodia*, N.Y. TIMES, Sept. 18, 1996, at A13.

domestic law would appear to bar the application of the 1956 law to prospective trials, regardless of the criminal law in force in Cambodia at the time of trials. To make the application of such law explicit, the National Assembly could pass a special statute recognizing the applicability of such law for crimes committed during the 1975–79 period (as well as after that period, if it so chose). Provisions incompatible with the Constitution, notably the death penalty for certain crimes, would not remain in force.[11] Nevertheless, the lack of familiarity of Cambodian judges with that old code could render its use in trials quite difficult.

Criminal procedure in Cambodia is in a state of flux. It is governed in theory by the 1993 Constitution and several prior and subsequent laws. First, the Constitution provides that the arrest, indictment, or detention of any person must be done in accordance with law, and bans coercion or physical mistreatment as well as confessions obtained through force. It also includes the right to counsel and the presumption of innocence, adding that '[a]ny case of doubt shall be resolved in favor of the accused'.[12] The judiciary is to be independent and impartial, and is composed of a Supreme Court and lower courts.[13]

Secondly, the 1992 Supreme National Council Decree on Criminal Law and Procedure, drafted by UN officials during the UNTAC period, provides a 75-article basic framework of criminal justice. This law appears to remain in force by virtue of Article 139 of the 1993 Constitution, under which '[l]aws and standard documents . . . that safeguard State properties, rights, freedom[s] and legal private properties' remain applicable if consistent with the Constitution. According to the law, judges 'must decide in complete impartiality, on the basis of facts which are presented to them, and in accordance with law, refusing any pressure, threat or intimidation, direct or indirect, from any of the parties to a proceeding or any other person'.[14] A simplified system of criminal procedure includes basic provisions on the right to counsel, prohibition of cruel and inhuman punishment, arrest and detention, searches, evidence, the presumption of innocence, and statutes of limitation.[15]

Thirdly, the National Assembly of the SOC adopted a Law on Criminal

[11] *See* CAMBODIA CONST. (1993), art. 32.

[12] *Id.* art. 38.

[13] Judges are to be appointed by the King upon the recommendation of the Supreme Council of Magistracy. The King is to guarantee the independence of the judiciary; judges cannot be dismissed, although the Supreme Council of Magistracy may take disciplinary action against delinquent judges. *Id.* arts. 109–15; *see also* Stephen P. Marks, *The New Cambodian Constitution: From Civil War to a Fragile Democracy*, 26 COLUM. HUM. RTS. L. REV. 45, 79–81, 86–91 (1994).

[14] Provisions Relating to the Judiciary and Criminal Law and Procedure Applicable in Cambodia during the Transitional Period, Decision of 10 September 1992, art. 1.

[15] *Id.* arts. 10–30. The statute of limitations for crimes defined under the law is ten years. *Id.* art. 30.

Procedure on January 28, 1993, which the Council of State promulgated on March 8, 1993. This 238-article law, which remains in force as well by virtue of Article 139 of the Constitution (to the extent not inconsistent with it), contains detailed provisions on all aspects of criminal procedure. In accordance with continental practice, it provides for both public and private (i.e., victim-initiated) prosecutions. Although poorly drafted, it does offer certain basic rights to the accused, such as the right to counsel, some provisions aimed at ensuring an impartial court, and the right to appeal.[16] Courts in Cambodia have relied upon this law for their proceedings, ignoring the greater protections afforded defendants in the 1992 law.[17]

Fourthly, the National Assembly of the Kingdom of Cambodia passed on December 22, 1994, the Law on the Organization and Functioning of the Supreme Council of Magistracy. The Council recommends the appointment of, and can take disciplinary action against, judges and prosecutors. It is composed of the King as Chairman, as well as the Minister of Justice, the Chief of the Supreme Court, the General Prosecutor to the Supreme Court, the Chief of the Appeal Court, the General Prosecutor to the Appeal Court, and three judges.[18]

Beyond the supremacy of the Constitution—at least as a matter of principle—the relationship among the laws of criminal procedure continues to be vague and the system subject to abuse by those in power. The courts do not follow consistent procedures concerning the conduct of trials and appeals.

The Functioning of the Judicial System

The Cambodian judiciary presently meets none of the key criteria for a fair and effective judiciary—a workable legal framework; a trained cadre of legal advocates, decision-makers, and investigators; adequate infrastructure; and a culture of respect for due process.[19] Instead, like those of many countries emerging from national traumas, it is a disorganized, ineffective, and unfair system, currently failing to mete out criminal justice, notwithstanding the laudable aid programs of NGOs, the UN, and foreign governments.[20]

16 Law on Criminal Procedure, arts. 76, 97–98, 161.

17 Group of Experts Report, *supra* note 5, para. 125.

18 Law on the Organization and Functioning of the Supreme Council of Magistracy, Dec. 22, 1994, arts. 2, 9, 12.

19 *See* Ch. 8, Opportunities and Challenges, *supra*.

20 These conclusions are based on the Reports of the Special Representative of the Secretary-General for human rights in Cambodia from 1994–2000, UN Docs. A/49/635, E/CN.4/1995/87 and Add.1, E/CN.4/1996/93, E/CN.4/1997/85, E/CN.4/1998/95, E/CN.4/1999/101, and E/CN.4/2000/109; Human Rights Watch, Cambodia at War 75–78 (1995); various articles in periodicals

First, the inadequacies of the legal framework remain. Although officials in the Ministry of Justice, with some foreign assistance, have begun work on new codes of criminal law and procedure, these were not yet promulgated as of 2000. Moreover, it is not evident that that they will be either well drafted or consistent with the standards of the Cambodian Constitution or international human rights instruments concerning the rights of defendants.

Secondly, one of the many sad legacies of Cambodia's decades of civil conflict is the lack of a qualified legal profession in Cambodia. Most attorneys and scholars fled during the 1960s and 1970s or were killed by the Khmer Rouge; those who entered the profession during the years of the People's Republic of Kampuchea or the SOC received their training under a system in which courts were not independent.[21] Lack of experience with evidentiary issues has often led courts to use shoddy police reports as the sole basis for convictions. Thirdly, the infrastructure of the Cambodian legal system is pitiful. Courts lack law books (including the basic codes), typewriters, and other basic necessities, especially in the provinces. The buildings are, like most governmental offices, run down. Jails are marked by deplorable conditions.

Finally, and most importantly, Cambodia lacks—and perhaps has never had—a culture of respect for an impartial criminal justice system. Criminal justice receives only a fraction of a per cent of the national budget, with judges paid as little as US $20 per month.[22] As a result, judges can often be bribed by defendants or victims. Powerful elements in the government, such as important political figures, the security apparatus, and the Ministry of Justice, exert overt and covert influence over the decisions of investigating judges and trial courts. These include threats and attacks on judges, or simply the realization among judges that their tenure and often their prospect of future livelihood depend upon the approval of political elements, thus undermining the essence of an impartial judiciary. The placement of the Minister of Justice on the Council of Magistracy encourages that interference and bodes poorly for the future of judicial independence.

Moreover, criminal defense attorneys, even if trained properly, are impeded in their work. Judges pay little attention to their legal arguments,

(especially THE NEW YORK TIMES and THE FAR EASTERN ECONOMIC REVIEW); meetings and interviews conducted by the authors with Cambodians and representatives of foreign non-governmental organizations in Phnom Penh, Aug. 21–24, 1995; and the 1999 Group of Experts Report, *supra* note 5, paras. 126–38.

21 Instead, the June 1995 Law on the Bar provides for a complex system of admission to the bar that allows persons to practice law without ample legal training. Law on the Bar, June 23, 1995, arts. 31–37, 79–83.

22 Group of Experts Report, *supra* note 5, para. 129.

even in routine cases. The courts and police restrict their contact with clients, even during court sessions. Defenders can also face threats from victims' families or friends. Treatment of those jailed pending trial or those in prison remains far below international standards. Officials fail to inform the accused of the progress of his case or his legal options, and family members often remain uninformed of the status of the accused. Convicted prisoners have little ability to complain about the conditions of their confinement, and the beating of prisoners remains common.

Options for Cambodian Trials

Until systemic improvement is achieved, the only option for trials that might overcome the fundamental shortcomings of the judicial system in Cambodia or other similar states would involve a special judicial process. This solution would demand significant international effort to achieve credibility inside and outside Cambodia. To implement such a plan, a number of steps would need to be taken:

- Cambodia would need to clarify the law and procedure to apply in such trials, e.g., through special legislation prepared with the assistance of foreign legal experts. It could make clear the application of the 1956 Code Pénal and, perhaps international law as well, as a matter of substantive law and set forth procedures for trials.
- Trained jurists and investigators would need to conduct the process. In the absence of more qualified Cambodians, international experts seconded from governments, international organizations, and NGOs would have to work alongside Cambodian prosecutors, investigators, and defenders to produce effective trials.
- A functioning set of facilities would need to be established for this purpose, including a courtroom, prison, and other facilities. Security for defendants and the court would require special attention.
- Most importantly, some mechanism would be required to ensure a fair and independent set of judges and prosecutors, free from political control or pressure. This could entail the creation of a special Cambodian court with foreign judges and prosecutors alongside, or instead of, local officials, as these jurists would offer the prospect of impartiality in a way that a purely Cambodian court might not.[23]

The benefits of such an approach would include a trial under Cambodian law in a domestic court, under the sponsorship of the

[23] Foreign officials might be picked by the King or by the UN (perhaps by the UN's Special Representative for human rights in Cambodia). They could come from countries not associated with foreign involvement in Cambodia's past. Assuming these officials apply Cambodian law and not exclusively international law, they would need to educate themselves in the Cambodian legal system.

Cambodian government. Such trials place the responsibility for accountability on the polity most concerned. Ordinary citizens could observe—even attend—the proceedings, which would become part of their history. Equally important, the trials could have long-term benefits for the Cambodian legal and political culture. Citizens would witness how public officials can be held accountable in their own courts for their misdeeds, thereby helping in a small way to break the cycle of impunity that still pervades the country.[24] And if Cambodian jurists observed the importance of judicial impartiality and protection of the rights of even the most vilified defendants, they may be inclined to show more respect for the rule of law. On the other hand, the trials could have no long-term effect upon the Cambodian legal system and may divert international attention and resources from remedying its systemic problems.

Nonetheless, significant obstacles loom over such a plan. Foreign states and organizations might prove unwilling to make the necessary investment even in a Cambodian trial, although the costs of such assistance would be far less than those of an international tribunal. Most important, even with foreign assistance and involvement, domestic trials would demand a significant political commitment from Cambodia's leaders because of the need for a serious undertaking to rectify abuses within the current judicial system. Domestic trials could easily be manipulated and impeded by the government, as it sought to use the trials against its enemies and to shield its allies. This concern caused the UN's Group of Experts to recommend against domestic trials in 1999.[25] The United Nations has been negotiating with the Cambodian government since 1999 over the details of a Cambodian tribunal with significant UN involvement, e.g., through its selection of some judges and a foreign co-prosecutor, that might insulate the process from Cambodian politics. These talks have highlighted the government's interest in controlling the trials by limiting UN authority over them.[26]

Prosecutions before Courts of Other States

The review of foreign law provisions covering extraterritorial acts reveals few possibilities for prosecution of the Khmer Rouge outside Cambodia, especially in those countries where they are most likely to be located. US law would not apply because of the territorial link generally required in US criminal statutes. As for criminal code provisions on genocide, war

24 *See* Group of Experts Report, *supra* note 5, para. 2.

25 *See id.* paras. 131–38.

26 *See, e.g.*, Barbara Crossette, *U.N. Allows Cambodians to Take Part in Trial of Khmer Rouge*, N.Y. Times, May 25, 2000, at A9.

crimes, and torture, they were enacted after the acts in question.[27] French law seems a possible source of prosecutions, though several immediate hurdles appear. The 1992 French law on crimes against humanity does not apply to crimes committed before its entry into force.[28] France's general extraterritorial provisions would allow for prosecution of those Khmer Rouge who were then also French citizens (or for acts against French citizens), as would British law for those accused murderers who might conceivably also be British citizens.[29]

As for earlier French law, the only law in force during the Khmer Rouge period was whatever international law had been incorporated domestically. This included the Charter of the International Military Tribunal and the Genocide Convention.[30] The former is confined to events during World War II, while the latter, as incorporated in French law prior to the 1992 statute, might permit prosecutions for genocide.[31] Other domestic laws, such as Canada's or Belgium's, might permit prosecutions as well. Moreover, if more states followed the Geneva Conventions' obligations to prosecute grave breaches, prosecutions outside Cambodia of Khmer Rouge for war crimes could be possible, although this would exclude the vast majority of the regime's offenses.

More important, however, as a practical matter, states whose domestic laws might permit trials of Khmer Rouge leaders have shown no interest in doing so. This state of affairs became most apparent in 1997, when the United States government broached with a number of states a plan under which Pol Pot would be captured and sent to trial abroad for his acts during the 1970s. No state expressed a desire to hold such trials.[32]

INTERNATIONAL CRIMINAL TRIBUNALS

An international criminal tribunal for Cambodia would also satisfy the

[27] *See* 18 U.S.C. §§ 1091, 2340, 2441 (1994 and 1998 Supp. IV). Moreover, the first two provisions would not cover acts abroad by non-Americans or persons not in the US military.

[28] Nouveau Code pénal, arts. 211–1, 212–1 (Fr.); Frédéric Desportes and Francis Le Gunehec, *Présentation des dispositions du nouveau Code Pénal*, 1992 JCP I G, No. 3615, at 423.

[29] *See* Ch. 8, text at notes 93–94, *supra*.

[30] Elisabeth Zoller, *La définition des crimes contre l'humanité*, 120 J. DROIT INT'L 549, 550–51 (1993).

[31] *Barbie* and *Touvier* are inapposite as they were not brought under the Genocide Convention and the crimes did occur in French territory. France's strict view of *nullum crimen sine lege* would bode poorly for prosecutions based on crimes against humanity outside of the IMT Charter or the Genocide Convention. *See generally* GASTON STEFANI, GEORGES LEVASSEUR, AND BERNARD BOULOC, DROIT PÉNAL GÉNÉRAL 95–98, 114–25 (16th ed. 1975).

[32] *See, e.g.*, Anthony DePalma, *Canadians Surprised by Proposal to Extradite Pol Pot*, N.Y. TIMES, June 24, 1997, at A10. This contrasts with the practice of European states in prosecuting persons involved in the conflict in the former Yugoslavia. *See* Ch. 8, Prosecutions Before National Courts of Other States, *supra*.

goals of accountability in their fullest sense by prosecuting Khmer Rouge offenders. Certainly, the *prima facie* case of guilt for severe violations of international criminal law is manifest enough to justify use of this mechanism. More importantly, we believe the severe difficulties of domestic trials, in particular the clear prospect of their manipulation by domestic political forces, justify an international tribunal as the best forum for achieving fair and effective justice in this case. These factors thus override both our general preference for domestic courts (including those aided by foreign donors) and concerns about the costs of UN tribunals. Nonetheless, events since 1999 have significantly dimmed the prospects for such a tribunal. We thus discuss this important option as a forum for accountability while also addressing the factors that have caused a lack of significant state support for it.

Following the Rwandan model, the Security Council could graft an *ad hoc* tribunal for Cambodia onto the existing UN tribunals by acting under Chapter VII of the Charter. Alternatively, the Council, acting under Chapter VI, another UN organ such as the General Assembly, or another international organization could create an *ad hoc* tribunal, though these options would lack the legally binding effect of a Chapter VII resolution.[33] Regional states could attempt to create a court by treaty, but this plan would prove difficult and time-consuming. Creation of a tribunal by the Cambodian government is also legally possible, but would face most of the obstacles of domestic prosecutions. The International Criminal Court, even when created, is not an option, as its jurisdiction is prospective only.[34]

Use of the *ad hoc* Chapter VII tribunal model for Cambodia is more problematic than in Yugoslavia and Rwanda, where the circumstances supported a colorable legal argument for invocation of Chapter VII and the necessary political support for its use. The connection between impunity of Khmer Rouge offenders for acts committed over two decades ago and international peace and security today is somewhat more tenuous. Arguably, of course, accountability for these offenses is linked to a resolution of the Cambodian conflict, a subject the Security Council has already addressed; and impunity for atrocities on this scale threatens international peace and security generally.[35] However, the Council would be on somewhat new ground were it to find the current situation in Cambodia a threat to the peace or determine that prosecutions would alleviate the threat.

33 For further details, *see* Group of Experts Report, *supra* note 5, paras. 140–48.

34 ICC Statute, arts. 11(1), 24.

35 *Cf.* UN GAOR 6th Comm., 3d Sess., 100th, 101st mtgs., UN Doc. A/633 (1948) (suggestions by some drafters of Genocide Convention that all cases of genocide inherently threaten international peace); Payam Akhavan, *Enforcement of the Genocide Convention: A Challenge to Civilization*, 8 Harv. Hum. Rts. J. 229, 253–54 (1995).

Aside from questions of authority, creation of an *ad hoc* tribunal would require the active support of Cambodia's government along with a substantial investment of political effort by states. The centrality of such domestic and international support is amply demonstrated by the fate of the 1999 recommendation of the Secretary-General's Group of Experts that the Security Council create a new *ad hoc* tribunal under Chapter VII. The Group had determined that only such a tribunal would prove insulated from the pressures of Cambodian politics and thereby provide impartial justice. Indeed, the Group went so far as to recommend that, following the model of the existing tribunals, the trials themselves take place outside Cambodia.[36] As discussed in Chapter 12, Cambodia's government quickly rejected the proposal.[37] The rejection highlights the difficulties of gaining a state's support for an international tribunal when its targets may well constitute members of the government and other powerful figures. The very factors that necessitate an alternative to domestic trials and make an international court the best option for criminal accountability in this case triggered the government's opposition to it.

In the ensuing months, those states that had supported the idea of an international court became so preoccupied with the situation in Kosovo that they did not try to persuade Cambodia to accept such a tribunal. None of the regional states indicated any interest in such an endeavor. States with an interest in keeping the spotlight off the Khmer Rouge because of their previous or current ties with them (e.g., China, Thailand, and other ASEAN states) were reticent about such a plan. They also seem opposed to revisiting the Khmer Rouge era, at least without a review of the Vietnamese occupation, to which Vietnam would surely object. The unease of other states over the creation of *ad hoc* tribunals and the 'tribunal fatigue' afflicting the UN further diluted support for a tribunal, even for atrocities as serious as these. As a result, the Secretary-General did not press the Cambodians toward this option, instead proposing to Cambodia in August 1999 the concept of trials in a special Cambodian domestic court with significant UN involvement.[38]

INVESTIGATORY COMMISSIONS

Investigatory commissions do not, of course, result in judicial determinations of guilt, and many of the Khmer Rouge's crimes are so atrocious that nothing short of prosecution serves our sense of justice and account-

[36] *See* Group of Experts Report, *supra* note 5, paras. 139–84.

[37] *See* Elizabeth Becker, *Cambodia Spurns U.N. Plan for Khmer Rouge Tribunal*, N.Y. Times, Mar. 13, 1999, at A4.

[38] *See* Philip Shenon, *U.N. Plans Joint War Crimes Tribunal for Khmer Rouge*, N.Y. Times, Aug. 12, 1999, at A8.

ability.[39] Thus, ideally, a commission would not serve as a substitute for prosecutions, but as one component in an array of mechanisms for accountability against Khmer Rouge offenders and a precursor to prosecutions.

Even without other mechanisms, an effective investigatory commission could serve important interests. It would contribute to achieving in Cambodia virtually all of the educational, psychological, political, and justice goals of such commissions. It would make a powerful contribution to the healing needed in Cambodia, and, by acknowledging the victims, would provide a form of spiritual reparation for them. The advisory and recommendatory role of some panels also seems especially important in Cambodia, which is in the process of promulgating new laws in nearly every area and where the commitment of key political elements to human rights is subject to serious question.[40] Cambodia's poverty and dysfunctional criminal justice system argue for pursuing these goals through an investigatory commission. A panel could be an important first step to other actions by the Cambodian government, including future trials or non-penal sanctions, such as disqualification from public office. It would also dilute further the attractiveness of the Khmer Rouge as an alternative to the constitutional system.

The wide knowledge of the Khmer Rouge's atrocities would not detract from the useful role of a commission.[41] Although the general pattern of crimes is well known, a detailed, authoritative, and unbiased accounting, including identification of specific perpetrators and victims, has not been assembled in a single source.[42] The PRK's *in absentia* trials from 1979 lack credibility due to their tainted circumstances. The UN has never produced any detailed study of the atrocities, the 1978 Human Rights Commission report being merely a compilation of information from governments and NGOs. Scholars have either written with a broader brush or addressed particular aspects in separate articles. Disagreement continues on many aspects of the Khmer Rouge period, including discrepancies over the number of people killed. Indeed, in light of reports of Khmer Rouge disinformation concerning their brutal record, as well as the Cambodian government's use of its own version of history, an authoritative examination seems especially important.[43]

39 *See* Diane F. Orentlicher, *Settling Accounts: The Duty to Prosecute Human Rights Violations of a Prior Regime*, 100 YALE L.J. 2537, 2546 n. 32 (1991).

40 *See* sources cited in note 20, *supra*.

41 Nevertheless, in light of the widespread knowledge of much of the 'truth' concerning the Khmer Rouge's abuses, any panel should avoid the label 'truth commission'.

42 The largest depository of potentially useful written evidence is held by the Documentation Center of Cambodia (DCC), a Phnom Penh-based NGO supported by foreign grants.

43 *See, e.g.*, Ben Kiernan, *The Cambodian Genocide: Issues and Responses*, in GENOCIDE: CONCEPTUAL AND HISTORICAL DIMENSIONS 191, 191–94 (George J. Andreopoulos ed., 1994) (estimates of number of victims); Ashley Dunn, *Cambodians in U.S. Say the Dark Shadow of the Khmer Rouge is Back*, N.Y. TIMES, Aug. 14, 1995, at A11 (Khmer Rouge disinformation).

Moreover, an investigatory commission would allow Cambodia to accomplish these goals in a relatively expeditious and uncomplicated manner, which has an important independent value. While trials of perpetrators of atrocities are an imperative, the impediments to swift justice, including the elusiveness of most of the prime targets and the reluctance of the government to confront the Khmer Rouge, are daunting. Rather than simply using the immediate future as some type of preparation for trials, the Cambodian government and the international community, by creating a commission, could concretely demonstrate their resolve and highlight Cambodia's transition from its haunted past to perhaps a brighter future.

Nonetheless, three factors suggest the need for some circumspection in creating such a commission.[44] First, Cambodians do not appear to understand the purpose of these panels and would need some education about their role in bringing about individual accountability and national reconciliation. Secondly, some Cambodians might not cooperate in its activities, either by refusing to testify or by failing to tell the truth out of fear of retaliation. A lack of witness testimony undermines some of the closure-related purposes of commissions and, perhaps, the credibility of the final report. Thirdly, and most significant, previous panels have proved most successful where the process of transition toward democracy was advanced enough that the government and people believed that the panel would further national reconciliation and were committed in advance to respect its findings. In Cambodia, an authoritarian government still rules (under the guise of democratic elections); and national reconciliation is not far advanced. Thus, various factions in Cambodian politics, in particular former Khmer Rouge who later served in the PRK and SOC, might well oppose even non-prosecutorial inquiries into the past, reject the findings of a commission, and thereby severely undermine its effectiveness. However, such opposition is unlikely to be as daunting an impediment as in the case of prosecutions.

Were such a commission nonetheless deemed useful, the universe of entities that could sponsor a panel is quite broad and would include the Cambodian government, a group of interested states, NGOs, or the UN. Although the Cambodian government is probably the easiest candidate, the UN would seem the most desirable due to the current divisions and policies of the Cambodian government. In any case, due to the lack of resources and expertise in Cambodia, the international community would need to play an active role in the commission. An optimal formula would be a mixed commission, composed of both Cambodian and foreign commissioners and staff, chaired by a Cambodian. The Cambodian

[44] For further thoughts on these issues, *see* Group of Experts Report, *supra* note 5, paras. 202–09.

commissioners would need to have stature and respect across the political spectrum. While this could be obtained through the presence of panelists appealing to different interest groups, ideally each Cambodian expert should have independent stature. Alumni of previous commissions represent a logical pool for foreign commissioners, but other respected international figures could well qualify. The panel would need significant resources from the UN and states (although not as much as domestic or international trials), primarily investigators and legal experts.

The commission could have a number of different mandates. Cambodia's circumstances would suggest giving it the power to investigate and report fully on serious violations of international and Cambodian criminal law by the Khmer Rouge. The panel could either name offenders or refrain from doing so, although the former would best fulfil the goals of accountability. Former friends of the Khmer Rouge might insist that the mandate extend to offenses by Vietnam and the PRK after the Pol Pot era, and some political effort would be necessary to overcome this diversion.

The commission would also need to lay the groundwork for future prosecutions, but without jeopardizing their success. This would require a significant level of detailed investigation, but ideally avoid probing witnesses in ways that might cause inconsistent statements later. The Argentine commission, with its preparation of *Nunca Más* and subsequent turning over of evidence to prosecutors, would represent a model. Experienced prosecutors must be included on the staff to help guide the panel through the legal and evidentiary terrain so that its work would help, and not hinder, later prosecutions. Subpoena authority, like that granted to the South African commission, would also be enormously helpful. As for the panel's duration, the wide scale of the atrocities, the length of time since the acts, and the limited infrastructure for gathering evidence suggest that it would need to operate longer than many of those previously undertaken. A term of from two to three years, depending on political and resource constraints, would seem advisable.

CIVIL SUITS

In light of the seriousness of the Khmer Rouge's atrocities and the lack of alternative fora, individuals who suffered especially grievous harm under the Khmer Rouge could institute civil actions against Khmer Rouge officials under the US Alien Tort Claims Act, other US law, or any foreign equivalents. While not a completely satisfying substitute for prosecutions and geographically removed from most of the victims, such suits do offer an opportunity for some adjudication of Khmer Rouge abuses. If, for example, a Cambodian victim or NGO could identify an individual

Khmer Rouge cadre who committed torture or other inhumane acts, a successful lawsuit would offer both a form of punishment as well as the prospect of some monetary and psychological compensation for the victim. Although such suits would face a number of legal and evidentiary difficulties, they could well meet with favorable court judgments.

The legal impediments to suits under US law seem rather limited. Presumably, the requirement for suits under the ATCA and the TVPA that the defendant have acted under authority of law of a foreign nation would not pose a problem if defendants were servants of the Khmer Rouge government. In light of the current state of the Cambodian legal system and the difficulty in obtaining jurisdiction over a Khmer Rouge defendant before another forum, a court is also unlikely to find that an adequate alternative forum exists to justify dismissing a suit based on *forum non conveniens* or failure to exhaust local remedies. While sovereign immunity would preclude suits against the Cambodian government, it should not prevent suits against Khmer Rouge individuals, as US courts have applied immunity to individuals only when they acted within the scope of their authority and have refused to recognize gross violations of human rights as meeting that test. Likewise, the act of state doctrine is unlikely to preclude claims against Khmer Rouge individuals, since the doctrine applies only to public acts committed by a government recognized by the United States at the time of suit. A US court would almost certainly refuse to consider the Khmer Rouge's abuses to be legitimate public acts, and the Khmer Rouge government was never recognized by the United States.

This approach has limits, however. Appropriate litigants must be identified,[45] and courts typically need to have jurisdiction over the defendant for such a suit to proceed. Accordingly, lawyers, NGOs, and governments would need to cooperate in identifying potential defendants and to assist plaintiffs in bringing suits. Some aspects of US law remain unsettled, while experience with these cases outside the United States is limited.[46] A defendant may very well follow the practice seen in past cases and escape execution of judgments by fleeing the jurisdiction. However, even if he were to flee, a civil suit would still draw attention to his acts, provide victims with a forum in which to tell their stories, and deprive the offender of at least one refuge outside Cambodia.

[45] A substantial number of individuals affiliated with the Khmer Rouge are believed to be residing among the Cambodian refugee communities in the United States and other countries. *See infra* text at notes 47–49.

[46] For one attempt under French law, *see Cambodge: Une plainte contre les dirigeants khmers rouges a été deposée*, LE MONDE, Apr. 4–5, 1999, at 6 (plaintiff-prosecutor complaint).

IMMIGRATION MEASURES

The turmoil of the Khmer Rouge period and the following years led large numbers of Cambodians to flee their homeland, creating sizeable expatriate communities in other countries, notably the United States, Canada, France, Australia, and Thailand. These communities may include as many as several thousand individuals formerly or currently affiliated with the Khmer Rouge.[47] In the summer of 1995, press reports focused attention on one individual, Thiounn Prasith, a former Khmer Rouge representative to the UN residing in the United States.[48] Many may be subject to immigration sanctions, particularly denaturalization and deportation from the countries where they now reside. Deportation both removes offenders and can support prosecutions and other legal action by Cambodia, other states, and international institutions.

US immigration law would appear to provide several potential bases for denaturalizing and deporting Khmer Rouge offenders residing in the United States.[49] Khmer Rouge responsible for any of the offenses described in Part I of this book would, presumably, fall under one or more of the criminal activities categories. In light of current US policy toward the Khmer Rouge, the presence of a former Khmer Rouge official in the United States would, presumably, meet the required standard for deportation on foreign policy grounds. If the Khmer Rouge qualifies as a proscribed organization and none of the exceptions applies, this ground would also potentially permit deportation. And, in order to conceal their pasts, many former Khmer Rouge likely committed fraud or misrepresentation in obtaining entry, rendering them vulnerable to deportation on these grounds as well.

Optimal use of denaturalization and deportation, however, will require careful thought and planning. Governments and NGOs would need to undertake investigations to identify former or current Khmer Rouge members outside Cambodia; and interested governments would need to coordinate immigration sanctions to ensure that they serve not only to punish Khmer Rouge offenders, but to bring them to a jurisdiction able to prosecute them. Use of these measures would be counterproductive if prosecutorial efforts were under way and deportation merely drove suspects to countries unwilling to cooperate. They would

[47] Telephone interview with Craig Etcheson, Program Manager, Cambodian Genocide Program, Yale University (Oct. 10, 1995).

[48] Barbara Crossette, *Ex-Official's Life in U.S. Evokes Fear*, N.Y. TIMES, Aug. 14, 1995, at A11.

[49] The discussion of deportation in Chapter 10 was based on the law governing exclusions as of 2000, which differs in some respects from the law governing exclusions at the time most Cambodian expatriates entered the United States. However, the differences do not significantly affect the conclusions set forth in this section.

also be detrimental if they flooded Cambodia with Khmer Rouge offenders before the government were able and willing to prosecute them fairly and effectively.[50]

INTERNATIONAL COURT OF JUSTICE

Until the 1990s, the most widely discussed proposal for addressing the regime's crimes involved action in the ICJ against Cambodia as a state, rather than against individual Khmer Rouge officials.[51] In theory, the ICJ may provide a forum in which to pursue some of the goals of accountability for Khmer Rouge atrocities.[52] Yet, under current circumstances, ICJ adjudication is unlikely to represent an effective primary mechanism for pursuing accountability. At best, ICJ adjudication might serve to support other processes.

Although a contentious case could seek to pressure Cambodia to comply with its international obligations regarding the prosecution of Khmer Rouge offenders, this approach might prove excessively confrontational and thus a counterproductive way to encourage prosecutions; it is also extremely doubtful that any state would initiate such a suit.[53] A contentious suit might conceivably seek to persuade other governments to support other accountability mechanisms, such as a demand for an offender from an international or Cambodian court. Nevertheless, jurisdictional bases for suits against the most likely respondent states are extremely limited, and most governments favor non-adjudicative solutions to such issues. The meager benefits an advisory opinion might yield would not seem worth the formidable political obstacles that option would confront.

[50] Immigration measures often entail hardships for family members, and any initiative to target Khmer Rouge officials should accord due concern to the interests of innocent family members.

[51] For examples of literature supporting the use of ICJ adjudication, *see* Hurst Hannum, *International Law and Cambodian Genocide: The Sounds of Silence*, 11 HUM. RTS. Q. 82 (1989); Marks, *supra* note 4, at 41–42; Gregory H. Stanton, *The Khmer Rouge Genocide and International Law*, *in* GENOCIDE AND DEMOCRACY IN CAMBODIA 141, 161 (Ben Kiernan ed., 1993).

[52] *See* Ch. 9, Afterword, *supra*. Cambodia recognized the Court's compulsory jurisdiction under Article 36(2) of the ICJ Statute, subject to reciprocity and certain reservations, by its declaration of September 9, 1957. Other states with a particular interest in Cambodia that have accepted the Court's compulsory jurisdiction include Australia and Canada. MULTILATERAL TREATIES, ch. I.4.

[53] In 1986, the Cambodian Documentation Commission and Cambodian Genocide Project prepared a draft Memorial for use in bringing a case against Cambodia before the ICJ under Article IX of the Genocide Convention and under the Court's compulsory jurisdiction, charging Cambodia with crimes against humanity. No government stepped forward to bring a case. *See* Hurst Hannum and David Hawk, The Case Against the Standing Committee of the Communist Party of Kampuchea, Sept. 15, 1986 (on file with authors); *see also* Marks, *supra* note 4, at 23; Stanton, *supra* note 51, at 147.

EVIDENCE AND JUDICIAL ASSISTANCE

Evidence

Researchers, NGOs, and journalists have already uncovered significant evidence concerning Khmer Rouge atrocities. This includes hundreds of hours of interviews with witnesses and Khmer Rouge records from Tuol Sleng and other prison and extermination sites. These establish the identities of some officials responsible for some atrocities and the knowledge of Khmer Rouge officials at the highest levels. Nonetheless, documentary evidence that directly implicates governmental officials for many atrocities appears lacking, necessitating heavy reliance on witness testimony. This has proved the case with the Yugoslavia and Rwanda tribunal caseload as well.[54]

For some non-prosecutorial mechanisms, such as an investigatory commission or the ICJ, adequate evidence may already exist with respect to some offenders. For criminal tribunals, requirements of due process will impose high standards of credibility, placing heavy burdens on the prosecution. As an initial matter, some elements of the international offenses and the nature of evidence needed to establish them are far from clear. Moreover, the length of time since the events and the relative paucity of records maintained by the regime seriously hamper the development and credibility of evidence. Memories will have faded; appearances will have changed; much physical evidence will no longer be available; and many witnesses are likely to be dead, difficult to locate, or afraid to provide information.[55]

Certainly, the caveats concerning evidence-gathering identified in Chapter 11 would suggest caution in proceeding with investigations of Khmer Rouge. These include the importance of knowing in advance the evidentiary rules of the forum in which the evidence will be used and a thorough understanding of the elements of offenses. On the other hand, strict adherence to this policy would carry some drawbacks in the Cambodian context. No mechanism for accountability has yet been selected, and delaying investigations will mean the loss of evidence.

Until the purposes of investigations and the forum for the information are determined, any investigatory work carried out in Cambodia would

[54] *See, e.g.*, Group of Experts Report, *supra* note 5, paras. 46–58; David Hawk, *The Cambodian Genocide*, *in* GENOCIDE: A CRITICAL BIBLIOGRAPHIC REVIEW 137, 142 (Israel W. Charny ed., 1988); Kiernan, *supra* note 43, at 191.

[55] The proceedings in the United States and Israel concerning John Demjanjuk, who was accused of being a sadistic concentration camp guard during World War II, dramatically demonstrate the impediments that the passage of time can impose on a prosecution. *See* Alex Kozinski, *Sanhedrin II: The Case of Ivan Demjanjuk*, NEW REPUBLIC, Sept. 13, 1993, at 16.

need to be conducted with the utmost care and should focus on background fact-gathering. This would entail, for example, obtaining information on the general conditions and chain of command in an area and identifying witnesses, documents, and other potential sources of evidence.[56] Investigators would need to refrain from taking formal or detailed statements from witnesses until particular cases are ready for development. Such activities can pollute later evidence-gathering by annoying and confusing witnesses and eliciting contradictions that can prejudice cases. However, where there is a genuine risk that evidence may not be available later, for example because a witness is elderly or physical evidence is likely to deteriorate, investigators would have to pursue it carefully.

Once a mechanism for accountability is chosen, the investigatory principles described in Chapter 11 would need to be applied. Thus, for example, the investigations will need to be carried out and supported by experienced personnel and adequate resources. It may even be desirable to have experts of Cambodian or other nationality accompany the investigators into the field, especially in the early stages. Clearly, much of the personnel and resources needed to conduct and support investigations in Cambodia will be available only from outside the country.

Judicial Assistance

Treaty-based obligations on states to extradite Khmer Rouge offenders and provide other forms of judicial assistance to Cambodia are fairly limited. Some international criminal law agreements to which Cambodia is party, such as the Torture Convention, contain obligations on these matters. However, at present, Cambodia lacks extradition treaties with some states where Khmer Rouge may be present, such as the United States, Thailand, or China.[57] Extradition obligations with respect to an international tribunal created by treaty or under Chapter VII would, of course, confront fewer legal obstacles than do those in the bilateral context.

As for the possibility of locating offenders, the identities and locations of many potential Khmer Rouge defendants are known. Most are in Cambodia, in areas formally under the administration of the Cambodian government, although some reside in areas near the Thai border effectively controlled by former Khmer Rouge. They are capable of capture and not physically protected from arrest.[58] Bringing them to justice will

[56] The DCC has undertaken work along these lines since the late 1990s.
[57] A May 6, 1998, agreement with Thailand has not yet entered into force.
[58] Group of Experts Report, *supra* note 5, paras. 112–14.

thus depend principally on the work of authorities in Cambodia. Although the Cambodian government has officially professed an intention to bring the Khmer Rouge to justice, the amnesty for Ieng Sary, the non-prosecution of many others, and the official welcome by the government of three leaders of the Democratic Kampuchea regime in December 1998 all suggest a lack of commitment to it. The Cambodian government has also publicly expressed an expectation that Thailand and other neighboring countries will arrest and extradite Khmer Rouge who enter their territory,[59] though there is no reason to believe the government in fact assumes that such cooperation will occur or even desires such an outcome.

Although Thai leaders claim that they do not officially support or work with the Khmer Rouge and have promised to cooperate with Cambodia,[60] they have shown little inclination to control military and commercial elements in the border area who have forged close ties with the Khmer Rouge.[61] These elements have served as a valuable conduit for materials and financing for former members of the Khmer Rouge. Meaningful Thai assistance seems possible only with a concerted governmental policy that will require enormous political will against entrenched business and military interests. As for other states, in light of Vietnam's hostility toward the Khmer Rouge, it would likely comply with requests for judicial assistance, and there is reason to believe it has access to Khmer Rouge records seized during the 1978–79 invasion.[62] Even though both China and Laos are parties to the Genocide Convention, prospects for the former's assistance are slim due to its long history of support for the Khmer Rouge.

Governments could, of course, encourage cooperation by recalcitrant states through UN resolutions or even sanctions. Such measures may provide cooperative elements within target states with useful political support to overcome resistance from elements opposing cooperation, although they could also encourage intransigence by inflaming nationalist sentiments. However, unlike the case of the Libyan suspects in the Pan Am 103 and UTA 772 cases, the commitment to compel states to apprehend and surrender Khmer Rouge offenders seems woefully lacking. China's veto power in the Security Council makes any action by that body highly unlikely.[63]

In conclusion, although the human rights abuses inflicted on Cambodia by the Khmer Rouge merit the strongest forms of accountability, a variety

59 *See Thai Security Council's Stance on Khmer Rouge Praised*, Foreign Broadcast Information Service, Daily Report, East Asia, July 20, 1994, at 48, 49.

60 *See* Group of Experts Report, *supra* note 5, para. 116.

61 HUMAN RIGHTS WATCH, *supra* note 20, at 106–28.

62 *See* Group of Experts Report, *supra* note 5, para. 53.

63 Although China was formerly the Khmer Rouge's foremost patron, it has claimed since the mid-1990s that it no longer maintains contacts with the group and supports national reconciliation. HUMAN RIGHTS WATCH, *supra* note 20, at 106.

of factors combine to continue to render that an elusive goal. The pathetic state of Cambodia's judiciary and the country's meager resources demand significant international involvement in any domestic proceedings. But the government has resisted UN demands that it accept a fair process insulated from governmental control in exchange for UN support. The *ad hoc* UN tribunal option enjoys little support domestically and internationally. And political impediments, the passage of time, and other factors make access to offenders and evidence highly problematic. The more feasible options are those that require the fewest resources and the least political will—an investigatory commission, civil suits in other countries, and immigration measures. These avenues can, at least, chip away at some of the impunity the Khmer Rouge has enjoyed. But the criminal process remains an imperative in order for Cambodians and their government to reckon with their nation's tragic past.

PART IV

CONCLUSIONS

15

Striving for Justice: The Prospects for Individual Accountability

In September 1946, the International Military Tribunal at Nuremberg offered the following words as both an explanation of its own place in history and a summons to future generations:

> Crimes against international law are committed by men, not by abstract entities, and only by punishing individuals who commit such crimes can the provisions of international law be enforced.[1]

More than a half-century later, the response of the world's governments to this cardinal challenge seems lukewarm. International law has only haltingly and incompletely recognized individual responsibility for human rights abuses in peace and war, and states have only established or engaged domestic or international fora to hold persons accountable sporadically and often with reluctance. This volume thus reveals a legal environment resembling more a patchwork than a coherent, let alone complete, regime—criminal liability under treaty law overlapping with some criminality under customary law; general rules common to most systems of law that expand or contract the culpability of an offender; a variety of rights and obligations upon states to prosecute offenders; domestic courts with jurisdiction to prosecute, but often with no will or ability to do so; a few *ad hoc* international tribunals and an emerging permanent court with limited jurisdiction; and special procedures that states have legislated or invoked to provide a non-prosecutorial form of accountability.

THE STATE OF THE LAW

For the foreseeable future, international criminal law seems destined to remain the product of an *ad hoc* process of prescription, rather than the subject of a widely accepted international criminal code. This fate for the enterprise is the result of the decision made by governments to avoid a single, authoritative code in favor of penalizing a limited number of acts

1 22 IMT Trials at 466.

in various ways. The observer thus confronts treaties on individual crimes or a set of crimes, and lawmaking processes addressed to a confined group of offenses, such as the Yugoslavia and Rwanda Tribunal Statutes. Even exercises such as the International Law Commission's Draft Code of Crimes Against the Peace and Security of Mankind, or the Statute of the International Criminal Court, have tended to be relatively conservative in declaring acts criminal.

The inability to promulgate a comprehensive code, and indeed the glacial pace on preparing even the more modest statutes, seems an inevitable product of the lack of consensus among states on which acts create—or should create—individual responsibility under international law. The elaboration of human rights through binding treaties has itself proved a somewhat slow process, and experience has shown states unable to reach as much agreement on determining crimes inculpating individuals as they have on defining basic norms whose violations engender state responsibility.

But the lack of a centralized process or product should not be equated with an absence of norms, and indeed these norms have their own logic. As a general matter, international law clearly makes individuals responsible for certain gross violations of human dignity during peace and war. This study identifies those crimes as genocide, crimes against humanity, war crimes, slavery and forced labor, torture, apartheid, and forced disappearances. The *methods*, *strategies*, *scope*, and *consequences* of that responsibility may vary from crime to crime, but not so haphazardly as to defy analysis.

As for the *methods* of proscription, international law relies principally on treaties and customary law to identify crimes. With the conclusion of the Rome Statute, all are defined and criminalized in some form in treaties; genocide, crimes against humanity, war crimes, slavery, some forced labor, torture, and aspects of apartheid constitute crimes under customary law as well. Various details in the law can be filled in through recourse to general principles of law common to most states. These include the definitions of certain acts involved in the generic crimes (e.g., murder as an act of genocide or a crime against humanity); or extensions and contractions of criminality through notions of complicity, command responsibility, mistake, or duress. Treaties and custom have, moreover, adopted various *strategies* for imputing individual responsibility, most notably by declaring an act to be an international crime or by obligating states to extradite offenders or punish them under different jurisdictional bases.

The *scope* of these crimes suggests that the current list, however *ad hoc* in terms of its formation, nevertheless covers a broad array of human rights abuses. These crimes address both systematic atrocities as well as certain isolated gross abuses; they cover conduct in times of peace and of armed conflict; and they include acts by agents of governments and, depending upon the crime, by agents of non-governmental groups seeking official control or even wholly private actors. They form an adequate, if nevertheless unfinished, framework of binding legal norms for holding individuals accountable for serious violations of human dignity under many circumstances and situations. Although many acts remain at this time beyond the scope of the criminal law, the existing corpus would address most of the serious atrocities since World War II, whether in Cambodia, Rwanda, Ethiopia, Uganda, the Central African Empire, Sudan, Sri Lanka, South Africa, Equatorial Guinea, Central and South America, Bosnia-Herzegovina, China, Indonesia, or Iraq, to name the most obvious.

Genocide and crimes against humanity, with their special elements of criminality, encompass the most atrocious of acts—those, respectively, committed with an intent to destroy specific ethnic, religious, racial, or national groups; or carried out in a systematic or mass manner based on the victims' political or other identification. Genocide remains the clearer of the two offenses in terms of the specificity and certainty of its definition under the Genocide Convention, but it addresses a narrower set of crimes. Crimes against humanity covers a broader range of acts, though its evolution through customary law leaves certain of its elements and constituent acts the subject of some debate (even with the inclusion of a definition in the Rome Statute).

The criminality of certain violations of the laws of war ensures that not even the dictates of military necessity can insulate individuals from responsibility for serious abuses of one's fellow man. Though by its nature culpability for war crimes offers protection only to those trapped in an armed conflict, many atrocities today are connected with war, particularly civil strife. The criminality of offenses during internal conflicts remains uncodified under the Red Cross conventions, but the recent actions of the Security Council, the ICTY, the states negotiating the Rome Statute, and some individual states have helped to clarify the nature of internal war crimes. *Jus in bello* has perhaps the longest pedigree of all international law, and thus criminalization of atrocities during civil wars works from a solid doctrinal basis.

War crimes, as well as the more specific crimes, such as slavery and torture, also permit prosecution of the violator who commits the isolated atrocity, with its seeming cloak of impunity, rather than the more systematic abuses inherent in genocide and crimes against humanity. Slavery and torture are clearly defined by treaty, so as to place all on notice of their criminality. The ambiguities inherent in the definition of forced labor would render reliance on that offense alone for assigning individual accountability somewhat less than reassuring. Similarly, the criminal law of apartheid is underdeveloped, with no instances of application on which to rely, a somewhat inartfully drafted treaty, and uncertainty surrounding its customary status. Yet future instances of apartheid might well qualify as crimes against humanity. The criminalization process for forced disappearances is clearly emerging, with its advancement outside Latin America demonstrated by its inclusion as a crime against humanity in the ICC Statute.

Yet the irrational elements of the current regime of criminality should not be overlooked. Three seemingly arbitrary schisms remain: (1) between criminality for abuses in wartime and those in peacetime; (2) among wartime abuses between the criminality of those committed in interstate conflicts and the criminality of those in civil wars; and (3) among peacetime abuses between the criminality of seemingly equally egregious acts (e.g., torture vs. murder). Thus, for example, a single murder by a soldier against a civilian in wartime constitutes a war crime (under the Geneva Conventions or customary law); a single murder by a governmental official in peacetime against a political prisoner would most likely not (due to the special elements required of genocide and crimes against humanity); but a single act of torture by that same official against the same victim does (under the Torture Convention). On the one hand, these distinctions might be dismissed as minor insofar as the law has clearly made significant strides toward criminalizing the worst acts and, as noted, would regard as criminal the horrendous government-led campaigns against the innocent that have characterized the last century. Yet, the inconsistencies reveal a disturbing unwillingness of governments to adopt a victim-centered approach to international criminality.[2]

Although the acceptance in international law of individual responsibility for a broad array of atrocities gives some solace that international law has begun to heed the advice of the Nuremberg Tribunal, it is the *consequences* of criminality under international law that are of most relevance for those seeking to achieve the Tribunal's goal of punishing the responsible parties. These consequences emerge not from an understanding of the content of treaties or custom alone. Rather, they must take account of the fundamental dichotomy of international criminal law—that individuals commit the crimes, but states and international organizations (and occasionally domestic organizations) implement forms of accountability. Although international criminal law has not yet developed clear doctrine on these questions, the following general principles can be derived:

[2] For further thoughts, *see* Steven R. Ratner, *The Schizophrenias of International Criminal Law,* 33 Texas Int'l L.J. 237 (1998).

- First, treaties with penal provisions can place various obligations on states to take certain actions against offenders—whether to criminalize the conduct under domestic law, prosecute it, or extradite offenders, or some combination of these.
- Secondly, treaties, custom, and judicial opinions have had the effect of authorizing states—either all states, or states party to particular treaties, depending upon the crime—to assert universal jurisdiction over these crimes. Where such jurisdiction lies, a state may prosecute any offender in its midst for these acts regardless of the location of the crime or nationality of the offender or the victims. Yet most governments have not prosecuted such offenses. Domestic law typically requires that crimes be defined in the national criminal code, although some states may be unwilling to prescribe criminal law based on universal jurisdiction; other states may recognize the right to prosecute crimes arising under treaties but not under customary international law. More significantly, whether for treaty or custom-based crimes, governments have chosen not to prosecute a particular offender or class of offenders due to political considerations or the practical capacity of their judicial system. But an offender is on notice that he may be prosecuted anywhere.
- Thirdly, violations of widely ratified treaties or of customary international law that incur individual responsibility are more likely than other offenses to form the subject-matter jurisdiction of any future *ad hoc* international criminal tribunals. While it is always possible that the Security Council or a future treaty may seek to codify new crimes (as the Security Council may have done in criminalizing violations of Common Article 3 and Protocol II in the Rwanda Tribunal Statute), the caution states have generally exhibited suggests any new courts will tend to have jurisdiction only over well-accepted crimes. The limited subject matter jurisdiction of the ICC is strong evidence of this trend. Indeed, even widely accepted crimes like torture, disappearances, and slavery have not been included in the jurisdiction of these courts except if they meet the special elements of genocide, crimes against humanity, or war crimes.
- Fourthly, if an individual commits a treaty-based crime in a state party to one of the treaties once it is in force for the state, he should not be able to plead successfully before any mechanism responsible for accountability (whether prosecutorial or not), domestic or international, that international law did not recognize his offense as a crime for purposes of *nullum crimen sine lege.*
- Fifthly, if an individual commits a crime for which customary law provides for universal jurisdiction in any state, regardless of its status as a party to any particular treaty, he should not be able to plead successfully

before a decision-maker that his action was not an international crime for purposes of *nullum crimen sine lege.*

- Finally, as the product of a decidedly political process among many diverse actors, international criminal law will seldom match perfectly with one state's or community's sense of what the law ought to be or with the comprehensiveness of domestic criminal law.

THE PROCESS FOR PURSUING JUSTICE

A Global Responsibility: Whatever individual responsibility the law establishes, it must be coupled with yet another form of responsibility—that of states and the rest of the international community. But here we mean not state responsibility in the international law sense of liability for the violations themselves, but rather in terms of a duty to achieve justice for the victims through accountability of the offenders. For although individuals commit crimes, only other actors on the international stage can ensure that they are properly punished or otherwise assessed for their abuses.

This responsibility upon states and other relevant participants follows from moral, political, and, in many instances, legal considerations. As for the particular state that has endured the abuses, a continued failure to address the crimes of the past through some mechanism leaves open the wounds in a society. Morally, victims, their loved ones, and the citizenry at large have a right to know the details regarding the perpetrators, victims, and circumstances of atrocities. Politically, accountability could help build a culture of respect for human rights and highlight the dangers of individuals and groups espousing philosophies of hatred.

Moreover, accountability serves goals for the international community as a whole. International crimes violate the most central norms of humanity, and all states have a moral and political interest in seeing an effective remedy. Accountability, whether through prosecutions or otherwise, also serves a preventive purpose. It can signal to future violators of human rights that their actions will not simply be forgotten in some political compromise. The exact form of accountability is less important than the existence of some process for stigmatizing the offender, aiding the victim, informing the society, and ensuring that political settlements and transitions take account of human rights abuses. We recognize, of course, that accountability alone is no deterrent to future atrocities.

Lastly, as discussed in Chapter 7, international law imposes duties on states to address various atrocities—duties that have arisen from the very moral and political concerns noted above. The treaty-based obligations in international criminal law are the most central, and various human rights treaties also contain provisions regarding accountability. In addition, recent actions by states suggest that a general norm requiring investigation and punishment of gross abusers is gradually emerging. We are not overly sanguine as to whether this in fact reflects the actual expectations of most states today, or whether most states that choose accountability do so out of any sense of legal obligation. Indeed, governments and international organizations have thus far proved quite deferential to the choices by individual states in this area. But at the very least, the actions of states and international organizations in recent years—from the creation of diverse commissions of inquiry, to trials based on universal jurisdiction, to the preparatory work for the permanent international criminal court—suggest that the international legal process is now encouraging the creation of mechanisms of accountability.

Yet many states still remain reluctant to apply these lofty principles to their own abuses. In some instances, those who have committed the abuses still retain power in the country; in others, the new government may fear that accountability of a prior regime will eventually lead to a reckoning for its own actions against that prior regime. Outside governments may oppose accountability as revealing their role in the atrocities, or as creating a precedent for bringing their own officials to justice for domestic abuses. Those in foreign governments, international organizations, and NGOs who declare accountability a moral or political imperative have had difficulty convincing both targets and other foreign governments to support such a seemingly ethereal cause. Ironically, if they make the link between impunity for past abuses and an ongoing culture of impunity explicit, as may have happened with Cambodia, they risk scaring the government off entirely. (This, of course, is the case with all attempts to convince reluctant governments to protect human rights.) Individual accountability has thus far proved most successful where domestic constituencies clearly want it and the government heeds their call. But these outside supporters of human rights can nonetheless play an important role where popular support for accountability has not yet materialized into governmental action.

The Issue of Selectivity: The perpetrators of human rights abuses can range from one rogue policeman to an entire bureaucracy of governmental officials supported by numerous private citizens. In the extreme, it can reach the level of a whirlwind of atrocities, committed by many thousands of people across an entire country trapped in a frenzy—a scenario witnessed in Cambodia in the late 1970s and Rwanda in 1994. Clearly, no single rule of selectivity can apply to this vast spectrum of atrocities.

In situations involving a small number of abusers, nothing less than full accountability is required, principally through prosecution by a domestic court, or, if it could not mete out impartial justice, through international proceedings or public naming by an investigatory commission. But as the numbers of human rights abusers become larger, full accountability becomes more complex both in principle and in practice, though in many situations no less morally imperative. As appealing in the abstract as a notion of 'full accountability' may seem, in many countries, a complete accounting of all those responsible is ill-advised for several reasons.

First, although accountability has a premium in and of itself, it is not the only value. The divisiveness of calling forth all those who committed atrocities may be more than a country emerging from a horrid past can handle, as the number of lives disrupted would be enormous. The possibility of massive political unrest or violent reactions by perpetrators and victims cannot go entirely ignored, although governments routinely overstate this danger. Secondly, the rights of suspects, especially in criminal trials, must be respected. Thus, the defenses to criminal responsibility inherent in the notions of duress, or the inability to know right from wrong, have their own intrinsic value, even if they impose enormous obstacles to inculpating, through prosecutions or otherwise, the full gamut of participants in many forms of terror. Thirdly, financial, evidentiary, and other practical limitations, such as access to accused offenders and the state of the judiciary, may make full accountability impossible.

In the case of mass abuses, then, a more nuanced form of accountability is required. This would entail that prosecutorial mechanisms limit their focus to those leaders with a policy-making responsibility over the crimes of the period, as well as those individuals who played important roles in the most heinous of the offenses, such as large-scale massacres or operation of torture and extermination centers. While this line may not always be easy to draw, focusing on those leaders who directed the terror, as well as a select group of participants in particularly atrocious acts, will give these societies a sense of the identity of those most guilty of the crimes. Various UN institutions have indeed adopted this strategy for pursuing abusers in certain countries.[3] At the same time, non-prosecutorial mechanisms, notably truth commissions, can and generally should scrutinize a far broader range of actors and actions.

[3] *See, e.g.*, Statement by the Prosecutor Following the Withdrawal of the Charges Against 14 Accused, May 8, 1998, ICTY Press Release CC/PIU/314-E, available at www.un.org/icty/pressreal/p314-e.htm ('maintaining an investigative focus on persons holding higher levels of responsibility, or on those who have been personally responsible for the exceptionally brutal or otherwise extremely serious offences'); Report of the Group of Experts for Cambodia established pursuant to General Assembly resolution 52/135, para. 110, *in* Identical letters dated 15 March 1999 from the Secretary-General to the President of the General Assembly and the President of the Security Council, Mar. 16, 1999, UN Doc. A/53/850-S/1999/321, Annex; SC Res. 1315, Aug. 14, 2000, para. 3 (endorsement of special court for prosecuting atrocities in Sierra Leone); SC Res. 1329, Nov. 30, 2000, preamb. para. 7; *see also* Diane F. Orentlicher, *Settling Accounts: The Duty to Prosecute Human Rights Violations of a Prior Regime*, 100 YALE L.J. 2537, 2602–03 (1991).

These starting points do not, however, address the many cases in the middle, where full accountability will be costly to a country, in many senses, but perhaps well worth it. Moreover, any decision will need to take into account the extent to which those involved in abuses may still wield some levers of power. As much as new governments or outside actors should seek to bring such criminals to justice, if their reaction is a takeover and their return to power, it would not have proved a wise decision. But assertions of such threats must be viewed with great caution and with the recognition that to err too far in this direction will prove short-sighted. These individuals may be discredited, and the government may have more power than it chooses to admit.

Choice of Mechanisms: The fora for holding individuals accountable for gross human rights abuses represent an amalgam of the old, the new, and the speculative, each with its promise and drawbacks.

National tribunals have become an arena in which some states can prosecute former officials and attempt to bring closure for the victims, thereby creating some national reconciliation. They remain the optimal venue for criminal forms of accountability due to their proximity—politically, psychologically, and logistically—to the events and people involved in atrocities. But they can also remain hostages to political forces and decisions contracting their jurisdiction or prove a low priority for those states seeking to rebuild themselves after a national catastrophe; they can be incapable of dispensing fair and effective justice; and they can become tools for political vendettas and intimidation. Tribunals outside the state of the crimes can hear cases only if the authorities in those states take the initiative to prosecute crimes committed abroad and states where defendants and evidence are located cooperate.

A shift to an international system of accountability is no panacea either. The *ad hoc* courts for Yugoslavia and Rwanda required a decision of the Security Council that those situations represented a threat to the peace under Chapter VII of the Charter; and the inconsistent cooperation from governments harboring fugitives and those disinclined to fund these projects suggests that any future tribunals will require heavy investments of political capital to be successful. The International Criminal Court, when it is operational, represents a somewhat promising avenue for accountability. But the Rome Statute will need widespread ratification, and the layers of consent give great power to individual states. Most important, its success will still turn on the cooperation of governments in gaining custody over defendants, providing evidence, and giving it adequate financial support. Its prospective jurisdiction means that it can only prosecute abuses that have not yet occurred. The International Court of Justice, as well as the regional human rights courts, can clarify legal obligations of states and perhaps place some facts on the record, but they cannot adjudicate the responsibility of individuals.

As for truth commissions, they represent ongoing experiments in accountability, which have helped reveal the pattern of and participants in abuses in some important instances and have the virtue of not requiring extensive investment of resources. A panel can offer the state and the international community a detailed, authoritative, and unbiased accounting, including identification of specific perpetrators and victims. Its work, in particular if it includes public testimony, can foster the healing of the current generation through a form of spiritual reparation; support future trials or non-penal sanctions (such as disqualification from public office); put the atrocities in historical, political, and social context and thereby set the record clear for future generations; and make recommendations for reforms, compensation, or other corrective measures. It permits a state or interested outside entities to take immediate, dramatic action to highlight the former's transition from its traumatic past. Yet for many victims they remain poor substitutes for criminal accountability and punishment. Civil remedies and immigration measures remain a promising avenue of limited accountability, but require states often far from the site of abuses to devote governmental resources to the cause.

Each of these fora also serves differing goals. Criminal proceedings best accomplish punishment and deterrence, with the accused facing a tribunal in public and the guilty imprisoned for their conduct. All the mechanisms, but especially investigatory commissions, serve to acknowledge the plight of the victims and promote transitions from times of trauma. As the most flexible mechanism, these panels are also in the best position to encourage specific reforms. Criminal or civil proceedings could conceivably result in financial reparation. The issues of selectivity noted earlier clearly affect and are affected by the relative weight states will assign to achieving each goal.

In choosing the means by which to advance these goals, societies must balance the legal, ethical, and social imperatives served by each approach against its social and political risks and other costs. Moreover, and significantly, they must differentiate between legal obstacles, on the one hand, and practical and political barriers, on the other. The legal impediments to all of the options considered are, relatively speaking, quite limited. Most choices will be dictated by concerns of practicality and a hefty dose of political realism.

With this in mind, some general principles for consideration can be elaborated.

- National tribunals are most likely to be successful in situations where a country's judicial system possesses the four critical prerequisites to the administration of justice outlined in Chapter 8—a legal framework of criminal law and procedure; a trained cadre of judges, lawyers, and other experts; adequate infrastructure; and a culture of respect for the fairness and impartiality of the process. This has meant some successful trials in Germany, Argentina, and South Korea. Where that system is dysfunctional or non-functional, local trials risk becoming a forum for settling personal and political vendettas, or may become mired in endless delays without regard for the human rights of the accused. In those situations, significant international assistance should be deployed to lay the groundwork for prosecutions meeting some minimal standards of fairness. This can rise to the level of dispatching foreign judges and prosecutors, thereby creating a quasi-international tribunal under domestic law.

- Where defendants are located outside the state of the atrocities and for some reason cannot face justice at home, national trials by other states represent an appealing method of accountability. Success depends upon the extent to which the state is prepared to assert its prescriptive jurisdiction over crimes under international law, as well as its willingness to try a particular defendant. Many states will find the circumstances giving rise to the offenses too distant to justify prosecutions; but atrocities committed in states with a special connection to the forum states, e.g., a neighbor or former colony, may merit the attention of authorities. Nonetheless, the distance from the scene creates clear drawbacks both in terms of access to evidence and the impact of the trial on the society.
- Trials before an international criminal tribunal will prove possible only if it is established by a resolution of an international organization, most likely the United Nations, or when the ICC becomes operational. A tribunal established under Chapter VII of the UN Charter will require members of the Security Council to be convinced of the existence of a threat to the peace and that prosecutions would alleviate the threat. It remains unclear whether governments will move from their current willingness to consider a serious interstate or internal conflict as a threat to the peace (Yugoslavia and Rwanda) to considering the mere existence of atrocities by a government against its people as such a threat. Any new tribunal will clearly demand substantial investment of political effort by members who deem such prosecutions worthwhile. As for the ICC, its great utility lies in its mere availability in the event individual states cannot or do not wish to prosecute offenders. States with offenders will be able to hand them over to the Court, and those concerned with combating impunity will be well advised to put pressure on them to do so; those refusing to transfer defendants may face binding orders to comply.
- Although a suit or advisory opinion in the International Court of Justice or before a regional human rights court cannot directly assess individual responsibility, it might support other methods of accountability

under limited circumstances, by pressuring a state to fulfil obligations to prosecute individuals or supporting a demand from an international or domestic court for the surrender of an offender. But the option may also prove a confrontational way to encourage a successor government to pursue prosecutions.

- An investigatory commission can represent a highly effective method of accountability, preferably as a predecessor or complement to criminal trials. Where criminal trials are not feasible for the foreseeable future, such a process would appear indispensable. The key to their success will be in the mandate, resources, and time they are given. A thinly stretched staff, or an inability to name names, can easily undermine the restorative purposes of these panels. The political elites involved in setting up these bodies must allow them to work independently and agree to honor their findings and recommendations.
- Victims living in states that offer civil remedies can consider institution of civil actions both as a form of punishment as well as a possible source of some small compensation for the victim. The prime model here remains the US Alien Tort Claims Act. In order to prevail, a victim would need to identify a particular abuser. However, courts typically need to have jurisdiction over the defendant; there are few analogues outside the United States; US law is somewhat unsettled; and monetary damages remain extraordinarily difficult to collect.
- If offenders have traveled overseas since the time of the abuses, other states can bring immigration measures to bear to deprive them of safe havens. Deportation both removes offenders and can support prosecutions and other legal action.
- If former human rights abusers have stowed assets overseas, governments can consider instituting legal proceedings to retrieve them. This may prove extremely onerous given bank secrecy laws and the requirements for international cooperation, as the government of the Philippines has discovered in its search for, and attempt to retrieve, the assets of Ferdinand and Imelda Marcos. It will also require substantial assistance from experts on money laundering.
- The success of domestic or international tribunals depends critically upon gaining custody over the defendants. If they have fled the country (in the case of national tribunals) or remain in havens within the country, their apprehension becomes the critical issue for the forum, as seen with the impunity enjoyed by Idi Amin and key suspects indicted by the Yugoslavia Tribunal. International law enforcement cooperation is required to arrest these fugitives. In the absence of the defendant, under an approach similar to the ICTY's and ICTR's Rule 61 procedure, a court could issue a warrant that effectively prevents the accused's international travel.

- All the mechanisms depend upon access to usable evidence. It is a truism, though an important one, that those attempting accountability must obtain control of physical evidence as speedily as possible and ensure its preservation, and locate witnesses and ensure their protection from retaliation for their testimony.
- The feasibility of any option will hinge on the amount of resources devoted to it. Any mechanism will also have to set priorities for the crimes it chooses to investigate. Efforts to bring people to justice face diminishing returns after a certain point. Investigations of sporadic or otherwise less important violations thus seem an inefficient use of resources.
- Once decision-makers choose one or more mechanisms, they will often have to manage the process in a highly volatile political environment. They will have to ensure that accountability measures do not turn into a free-for-all or excuse for vengeance against political enemies. To ensure impartiality, political leaders must keep their rhetoric in check and refrain from interfering in the proceedings. Outside participants, in particular NGOs, will have to be sensitive to the constraints on a polity to undertake any form of accountability.
- Any mechanism can only work with the support of the people of the particular state. Although the crimes concern all mankind, it is ultimately the people of a state—past, present, and future—who remain most affected. If they have a democratically elected government, it must be their primary voice on this question. If that government rejects accountability in favor of a compromise with former abusers, amnesty, or other forms of impunity, or seeks to use accountability as a weapon against political enemies, almost any effort at accountability seems crippled, if not still-born. Although international law imposes some duties on states to refrain from such policies, proponents of accountability may end up bearing the burden of persuading a government to foreswear impunity.
- If the state asks for international support for its own efforts, the global community can offer significant assistance at relatively low cost. Loans of law enforcement officials, forensic experts, legal advisors, and other specialists represent an immediate and tangible contribution to the state's efforts.

THE FATE OF INDIVIDUAL ACCOUNTABILITY: A WORD OF CAUTION

The global community's attempt to erect an architecture of individual accountability from the ashes of World War II presents an opportunity to enforce human rights in the most direct way possible—by assigning responsibility to those who abuse human rights in the belief that they do so with impunity. The duty of states, international organizations, and non-governmental organizations in this regard is thus clear.

The enterprise of such accountability remains at a fairly early stage in treaties, state practice, judicial opinion, and doctrine. Neither the ILC's 1996 Draft Code nor the ICC Statute offers a true codification of international criminal law concerning human rights abuses. The existing fora for enforcement, notably domestic courts, international tribunals, and investigatory commissions, have created a basic caselaw to elaborate the substantive norms of accountability, but much work remains to determine both the culpability of individuals and the duties of states. These implementation mechanisms, while greater in variety and more active than ever before, do not operate with full vigor and regularity, leaving individual accountability inconsistent and, in many ways, exceptional.

To accelerate the clarification of the law and the operation of mechanisms of accountability requires national and global decision-makers to take action grounded in the precedents dating back to Nuremberg but imaginative in its possible scope. Because the burden of enforcing international criminal law and promoting accountability remains and should remain on governments, they must seek to codify crimes and develop strategies for enforcement. At the domestic level, penal statutes that implement international norms—including universal jurisdiction—are critical, as they allow global offenses to assume their place in national law; but the political will to undertake trials or other meaningful sanctioning processes against offenders is even more important. At the international level, treaties on additional crimes, such as crimes against humanity or forced prostitution, that permit universal jurisdiction and require states to extradite or prosecute offenders represent a promising avenue for further lawmaking, as would additional work by governments and the International Committee of the Red Cross on criminalization of internal war crimes. The preparatory work of establishing a permanent international institution must continue, and, in the interim, *ad hoc* tribunals must remain an option to respond to gross abuses in war and peace.

But however significant further progress on the regime of individual accountability for human rights atrocities will be, it cannot substitute for other forms of action; and it would indeed be a serious error for the international human rights and humanitarian community to focus all its attention on this enterprise. Governments should be goaded into expanding the law and building the mechanisms; and NGOs can play an important part in this regard. But the decision to try offenders domestically, hand them over to an international tribunal, or achieve some other form of accountability eventually rests with the elites of nation-states, many of whose commitment to human rights does not now, and may not in the foreseeable future, extend to seeing themselves or their colleagues placed in the dock. Though the law can be pushed in steps, it ultimately will expand through consensus-building. Attempts to create criminal law and mechanisms that will be ignored by those responsible for applying them result only in pretended law, not an improvement in human rights enforcement. Judicial romanticism has serious systemic costs in a global community with sharply differing notions about the best way to mete out justice to individuals.

Thus the traditional strategies to secure compliance with international human rights and humanitarian law remain highly pertinent as states and international organizations continue the experiment with individual accountability. These means turn on making the state or non-state entity overseeing abuses the target of opprobrium for the actions of its agents—through the glare of publicity thrown on abuses by international organizations and NGOs, through diplomatic isolation, through economic sanctions and suspension of foreign aid, and, in exceptional cases, through military intervention to prevent or bring a halt to large-scale atrocities. Alongside these strategies to respond to abuses, governments, international organizations, and NGOs must also deploy preventive processes to keep political differences from turning into atrocities. It was, after all, not the threat of individual culpability that brought an end to apartheid in South Africa, military rule in Haiti, and the end of civil wars in Latin America, but concerted and united, if too often delayed, action against states and other authorities. Given the state of enforcement mechanisms for international criminal law, those contemplating or committing human rights abuses may not yet fear individual accountability; but they should know that outside actors remain prepared to make robust use of other sanctioning devices. Until individuals can be caught, tried, and otherwise uncovered, their sponsors must feel the heat of the abuses they commit.

Appendices

List of Excerpted Documents
(in chronological order)

TREATIES AND OTHER INTERNATIONAL INSTRUMENTS

1. Charter of the International Military Tribunal at Nuremberg, August 8, 1945

2. Allied Control Council Law No. 10, December 20, 1945

3. Convention on the Prevention and Punishment of the Crime of Genocide, December 9, 1948

4. Geneva Convention (I) for the Amelioration of the Condition of the Wounded and Sick in Armed Forces in the Field, August 12, 1949

5. Geneva Convention (II) for the Amelioration of the Condition of Wounded, Sick and Shipwrecked Members of Armed Forces at Sea, August 12, 1949

6. Geneva Convention (III) Relative to the Treatment of Prisoners of War, August 12, 1949

7. Geneva Convention (IV) Relative to the Protection of Civilian Persons in Time of War, August 12, 1949

8. Convention for the Suppression of the Traffic in Persons and of the Exploitation of the Prostitution of Others, March 21, 1950

9. Supplementary Convention on the Abolition of Slavery, the Slave Trade, and Institutions and Practices Similar to Slavery, September 7, 1956

10. International Covenant on Civil and Political Rights, December 16, 1966

11. Convention on the Non-Applicability of Statutory Limitations to War Crimes and Crimes Against Humanity, November 26, 1968

12. International Convention on the Suppression and Punishment of the Crime of *Apartheid*, November 30, 1973

13. Protocol Additional to the Geneva Conventions of 12 August 1949, and Relating to the Protection of Victims of International Armed Conflicts (Protocol I), December 12, 1977

14. Protocol Additional to the Geneva Conventions of 12 August 1949, and Relating to the Protection of Victims of Non-International Armed Conflicts (Protocol II), December 12, 1977

15. Convention against Torture and Other Cruel, Inhuman or Degrading Treatment or Punishment, December 19, 1984

OTHER DOCUMENTS

1. Charter of the International Military Tribunal at Nuremberg, August 8, 1945

I
Constitution of the International Military Tribunal

Article 1. In pursuance of the Agreement signed on the 8th day of August 1945, by the Government of the United States of America, the Provisional Government for the French Republic, the Government of the United Kingdom and Northern Ireland and the Government of the Union of Soviet Socialist Republics, there shall be established an International Military Tribunal (hereinafter called 'the Tribunal') for the just and prompt trial and punishment of the major war criminals of the European Axis.

Article 2. The Tribunal shall consist of four members, each with an alternate. One member and one alternate shall be appointed by each of the Signatories. The alternates shall, so far as they are able, be present at all sessions of the Tribunal. In case of illness of any member of the Tribunal or his incapacity for some other reason to fulfil his functions, his alternate shall take his place.

Article 3. Neither the Tribunal, its members nor their alternates can be challenged by the prosecution, or by the Defendants or their Counsel. Each Signatory may replace its member of the Tribunal or his alternate for reasons of health or for other good reasons, except that no replacement may take place during a Trial, other than by an alternate.

Article 4

(a) The presence of all four members of the Tribunal or the alternate for any absent member shall be necessary to constitute the quorum.

(b) The members of the Tribunal shall, before any trial begins, agree among themselves upon the selection from their number of a President, and the President shall hold office during that trial, or as may otherwise be agreed by a vote of not less than three members. The principle of rotation of presidency for successive trials is agreed. If, however, a session of the Tribunal takes place on the territory of one of the four Signatories, the representative of that Signatory on the Tribunal shall preside.

(c) Save as aforesaid the Tribunal shall take decisions by a majority vote and in case the votes are evenly divided, the vote of the President shall be decisive: provided always that convictions and sentences shall only be imposed by affirmative votes of at least three members of the Tribunal.

Article 5. In case of need and depending on the numbers of the matters to be tried, other Tribunals may be set up; and the establishment, functions and procedure of each Tribunal shall be identical, and shall be governed by this Charter.

II
Jurisdiction and General Principles

Article 6. The Tribunal established by the Agreement referred to in Article I hereof for the trial and punishment of the major war criminals of the European Axis countries shall have the power to try and punish persons who, acting in the interests of the European Axis countries, whether as individuals or as members of organizations, committed any of the following crimes.

The following acts, or any of them, are crimes coming within the jurisdiction of the Tribunal for which there shall be individual responsibility:

(a) *Crimes against peace*: namely, planning, preparation, initiation or waging of a war of aggression, or a war in violation of international treaties, agreements or assurances, or participation in a common plan or conspiracy for the accomplishment of any of the foregoing;

(b) *War crimes*: namely, violations of the laws or customs of war. Such violations shall include, but not be limited to, murder, ill-treatment or deportation to slave labour or for any other purpose of civilian population of or in occupied territory, murder or ill-treatment of prisoners of war or persons on the seas, killing of hostages, plunder of public or private property, wanton destruction of cities, towns or villages, or devastation not justified by military necessity;

(c) *Crimes against humanity*: namely, murder, extermination, enslavement, deportation, and other inhumane acts committed against any civilian population, before or during the war, or persecutions on political, racial or religious grounds in execution of or in connection with any crime within the jurisdiction of the Tribunal, whether or not in violation of the domestic law of the country where perpetrated.

Leaders, organizers, instigators and accomplices participating in the formulation or execution of a common plan or conspiracy to commit any of the foregoing crimes are responsible for all acts performed by any persons in execution of such plan.

Article 7. The official position of defendants whether as Heads of State or responsible officials in Government Departments, shall not be considered as freeing them from responsibility or mitigating punishment.

Article 8. The fact that the Defendant acted pursuant to order of his Government or of a superior shall not free him from responsibility, but may be considered in mitigation of punishment if the Tribunal determines that justice so requires.

Article 9. At the trial of any individual member of any group or organization the Tribunal may declare (in connection with any act of which the individual may be convicted) that the group or organization of which the individual was a member was a criminal organization.

After receipt of the Indictment the Tribunal shall give such notice as it thinks fit that the prosecution intends to ask the Tribunal to make such declaration and any member of the organization will be entitled to apply to the Tribunal for leave to be heard by the Tribunal upon the question of the criminal character of the organization. The Tribunal shall have power to allow or reject the application. If the application is allowed, the Tribunal may direct in what manner the applicants shall be represented and heard.

Article 10. In cases where a group or organization is declared criminal by the Tribunal, the competent national authority of any Signatory shall have the right to bring individuals to trial for membership therein before national, military or occupation courts. In any such case the criminal nature of the group or organization is considered proved and shall not be questioned.

Article 11. Any person convicted by the Tribunal may be charged before a national, military or occupation court, referred to in Article 10 of this Charter, with a crime other than of membership in a criminal group or organization and such court may, after convicting him, impose upon him punishment independent of and additional to the punishment imposed by the Tribunal for participation in the criminal activities of such group or organization.

2. Allied Control Council Law No. 10, December 20, 1945

Article I

The Moscow Declaration of 30 October 1943 'Concerning Responsibility of Hitlerites for Committed Atrocities' and the London Agreement of 8 August 1945 'Concerning Prosecution and Punishment of Major War Criminals of the European Axis' are made integral parts of this Law. Adherence to the provisions of the London Agreement by any of the United Nations, as provided for in Article V of that Agreement, shall not entitle such Nation to participate or interfere in the operation of this Law within the Control Council area of authority in Germany.

Article II

1. Each of the following acts is recognized as a crime:

(a) *Crimes against Peace*. Initiation of invasions of other countries and wars of aggression in violation of international laws and treaties, including but not limited to planning, preparation, initiation or waging a war of aggression, or a war of violation of [*sic*] international treaties, agreements or assurances, or participation in a common plan or conspiracy for the accomplishment of any of the foregoing.

(b) *War Crimes*. Atrocities or offences against persons or property constituting violations of the laws or customs of war, including, but not limited to, murder, ill treatment or deportation to slave labour or any other purpose, of civilian population from occupied territory, murder or ill treatment of prisoners of war or persons on the seas, killing of hostages, plunder of public or private property, wanton destruction of cities, towns or villages, or devastation not justified by military necessity.

(c) *Crimes against Humanity*. Atrocities and offences, including but not limited to murder, extermination, enslavement, deportation, imprisonment, torture, rape, or other inhumane acts committed against any civilian population, or persecutions on political, racial or religious grounds whether or not in violation of the domestic laws of the country where perpetrated.

(d) Membership in categories of a criminal group or organization declared criminal by the International Military Tribunal.

2. Any person without regard to nationality or the capacity in which he acted, is deemed to have committed a crime as defined in paragraph 1 of this Article, if he was (a) a principal or (b) was [*sic*] an accessory to the commission of any such crime or ordered or abetted the same or (c) took a consenting part therein or (d) was connected with plans or enterprises involving its commission or (e) was a member of any organization or group connected with the commission of any such crime or (f) with reference to paragraph 1(a), if he held a high political, civil or military (including General Staff) position in Germany or in one of its Allies, co-belligerents or satellites or held high position in the financial, industrial or economic life of any such country.

3. Any person found guilty of any of the Crimes above mentioned may upon conviction be punished as shall be determined by the tribunal to be just. Such punishment may consist of one or more of the following:

(a) Death.
(b) Imprisonment for life or a term of years, with or without hard labour.
(c) Fine, and imprisonment with or without hard labour, in lieu thereof.
(d) Forfeiture of property.
(e) Restitution of property wrongfully acquired.
(f) Deprivation of some or all civil rights.

Any property declared to be forfeited or the restitution of which is ordered by the Tribunal shall be delivered to the Control Council for Germany, which shall decide on its disposal.

4. (a) The official position of any person, whether as Head of State or as a

responsible official in a Government Department, does not free him from responsibility for a crime or entitle him to mitigation of punishment.

(b) The fact that any person acted pursuant to the order of his Government or of a superior does not free him from responsibility for a crime, but may be considered in mitigation.

5. In any trial or prosecution for a crime herein referred to, the accused shall not be entitled to the benefits of any statute of limitation in respect of the period from 30 January 1933 to 1 July 1945, nor shall any immunity, pardon or amnesty granted under the Nazi regime be admitted as a bar to trial or punishment.

3. Convention on the Prevention and Punishment of the Crime of Genocide, December 9, 1948

Article I

The Contracting Parties confirm that genocide, whether committed in time of peace or in time of war, is a crime under international law which they undertake to prevent and to punish.

Article II

In the present Convention, genocide means any of the following acts committed with intent to destroy, in whole or in part, a national, ethnical, racial or religious group, as such:

(a) Killing members of the group;
(b) Causing serious bodily or mental harm to members of the group;
(c) Deliberately inflicting on the group conditions of life calculated to bring about its physical destruction in whole or in part;
(d) Imposing measures intended to prevent births within the group;
(e) Forcibly transferring children of the group to another group.

Article III

The following acts shall be punishable:

(a) Genocide;
(b) Conspiracy to commit genocide;
(c) Direct and public incitement to commit genocide;
(d) Attempt to commit genocide;
(e) Complicity in genocide.

Article IV

Persons committing genocide or any of the other acts enumerated in article III shall be punished, whether they are constitutionally responsible rulers, public officials or private individuals.

Article V

The Contracting Parties undertake to enact, in accordance with their respective

Constitutions, the necessary legislation to give effect to the provisions of the present Convention and, in particular, to provide effective penalties for persons guilty of genocide or any of the other acts enumerated in article III.

Article VI

Persons charged with genocide or any of the other acts enumerated in article III shall be tried by a competent tribunal of the State in the territory of which the act was committed, or by such international penal tribunal as may have jurisdiction with respect to those Contracting Parties which shall have accepted its jurisdiction.

Article VII

Genocide and the other acts enumerated in article III shall not be considered as political crimes for the purpose of extradition.

The Contracting Parties pledge themselves in such cases to grant extradition in accordance with their laws and treaties in force.

Article VIII

Any Contracting Party may call upon the competent organs of the United Nations to take such action under the Charter of the United Nations as they consider appropriate for the prevention and suppression of acts of genocide or any of the other acts enumerated in article III.

Article IX

Disputes between the Contracting Parties relating to the interpretation, application or fulfilment of the present Convention, including those relating to the responsibility of a State for genocide or for any of the other acts enumerated in article III, shall be submitted to the International Court of Justice at the request of any of the parties to the dispute.

4. Geneva Convention (I) for the Amelioration of the Condition of the Wounded and Sick in Armed Forces in the Field, August 12, 1949

Article 2

In addition to the provisions which shall be implemented in peacetime, the present Convention shall apply to all cases of declared war or any other armed conflict which may arise between two or more of the High Contracting Parties, even if the state of war is not recognized by one of them.

The Convention shall also apply to all cases of partial or total occupation of the territory of a High Contracting Party, even if the said occupation meets with no armed resistance.

Although one of the Powers in conflict may not be a party to the present Convention, the Powers who are parties thereto shall remain bound by it in their mutual relations. They shall furthermore be bound by the Convention in relation to the said Power, if the latter accepts and applies the provisions thereof.

Article 3

In the case of armed conflict not of an international character occurring in the territory of one of the High Contracting Parties, each Party to the conflict shall be bound to apply, as a minimum, the following provisions:

1. Persons taking no active part in the hostilities, including members of armed forces who have laid down their arms and those placed *hors de combat* by sickness, wounds, detention, or any other cause, shall in all circumstances be treated humanely, without any adverse distinction founded on race, colour, religion or faith, sex, birth or wealth, or any other similar criteria. To this end, the following acts are and shall remain prohibited at any time and in any place whatsoever with respect to the above-mentioned persons:

(a) violence to life and person, in particular murder of all kinds, mutilation, cruel treatment and torture;

(b) taking of hostages;

(c) outrages upon personal dignity, in particular humiliating and degrading treatment;

(d) the passing of sentences and the carrying out of executions without previous judgment pronounced by a regularly constituted court, affording all the judicial guarantees which are recognized as indispensable by civilized peoples.

2. The wounded and sick shall be collected and cared for.

An impartial humanitarian body, such as the International Committee of the Red Cross, may offer its services to the Parties to the conflict.

The Parties to the conflict should further endeavour to bring into force, by means of special agreements, all or part of the other provisions of the present Convention.

The application of the preceding provisions shall not affect the legal status of the Parties to the conflict.

Article 49

The High Contracting Parties undertake to enact any legislation necessary to provide effective penal sanctions for persons committing, or ordering to be committed, any of the grave breaches of the present Convention defined in the following Article.

Each High Contracting Party shall be under the obligation to search for persons alleged to have committed, or to have ordered to be committed, such grave breaches, and shall bring such persons, regardless of their nationality, before its own courts. It may also, if it prefers, and in accordance with the provisions of its own legislation, hand such persons over for trial to another High Contracting Party concerned, provided such High Contracting Party has made out a *prima facie* case.

Each High Contracting party shall take measures necessary for the suppression of all acts contrary to the provisions of the present Convention other than the grave breaches defined in the following Article.

In all circumstances, the accused persons shall benefit by safeguards of proper trial and defence, which shall not be less favourable than those provided by Article 105 and those following of the Geneva Convention relative to the Treatment of Prisoners of War of August 12, 1949.

Article 50

Grave breaches to which the preceding Article relates shall be those involving any of the following acts, if committed against persons or property protected by the Convention: wilful killing, torture or inhuman treatment, including biological experiments, wilfully causing great suffering or serious injury to body or health, and extensive destruction and appropriation of property not justified by military necessity and carried out unlawfully and wantonly.

5. Geneva Convention (II) for the Amelioration of the Condition of Wounded, Sick and Shipwrecked Members of Armed Forces at Sea, August 12, 1949

Article 51

Grave breaches to which the preceding Article relates shall be those involving any of the following acts, if committed against persons or property protected by the Convention: wilful killing, torture or inhuman treatment, including biological experiments, wilfully causing great suffering or serious injury to body or health, and extensive destruction and appropriation of property, not justified by military necessity and carried out unlawfully and wantonly.

6. Geneva Convention (III) Relative to the Treatment of Prisoners of War, August 12, 1949

Article 130

Grave breaches to which the preceding Article relates shall be those involving any of the following acts, if committed against persons or property protected by the Convention: wilful killing, torture or inhuman treatment, including biological experiments, wilfully causing great suffering or serious injury to body or health, compelling a prisoner of war to serve in the forces of the hostile Power, or wilfully depriving a prisoner of war of the rights of fair and regular trial prescribed in this Convention.

7. Geneva Convention (IV) Relative to the Protection of Civilian Persons in Time of War, August 12, 1949

Article 147

Grave breaches to which the preceding Article relates shall be those involving any of the following acts, if committed against persons or property protected by the present Convention: wilful killing, torture or inhuman treatment, including biological experiments, wilfully causing great suffering or serious injury to body or health, unlawful deportation or transfer or unlawful confinement of a protected person, compelling a protected person to serve in the forces of a hostile Power, or wilfully depriving a protected person of the rights of fair and regular trial prescribed in the present Convention, taking of hostages and extensive destruction and appropriation of property, not justified by military necessity and carried out unlawfully and wantonly.

8. Convention for the Suppression of the Traffic in Persons and of the Exploitation of the Prostitution of Others, March 21, 1950

Article 1

The Parties to the present Convention agree to punish any person who, to gratify the passions of another:

1. Procures, entices or leads away, for purposes of prostitution, another person, even with the consent of that person;

2. Exploits the prostitution of another person, even with the consent of that person.

Article 2

The Parties to the present Convention further agree to punish any person who:

1. Keeps or manages, or knowingly finances or takes part in the financing of a brothel;

2. Knowingly lets or rents a building or other place or any part thereof for the purpose of the prostitution of others.

Article 3

To the extent permitted by domestic law, attempts to commit any of the offences referred to in articles 1 and 2, and acts preparatory to the commission thereof, shall also be punished.

Article 4

To the extent permitted by domestic law, intentional participation in the acts referred to in articles 1 and 2 above shall also be punishable. To the extent permitted by domestic law, acts of participation shall be treated as separate offences whenever this is necessary to prevent impunity.

9. Supplementary Convention on the Abolition of Slavery, the Slave Trade, and Institutions and Practices Similar to Slavery, September 7, 1956

Article 1

Each of the States Parties to this Convention shall take all practicable and necessary legislative and other measures to bring about progressively and as soon as possible the complete abolition or abandonment of the following institutions and practices, where they still exist and whether or not they are covered by the definition of slavery contained in article 1 of the Slavery Convention signed at Geneva on 25 September 1926:

(*a*) Debt bondage, that is to say, the status or condition arising from a pledge by a debtor of his personal services or of those of a person under his control as security for a debt, if the value of those services as reasonably assessed is not applied towards the liquidation of the debt or the length and nature of those services are not respectively limited and defined;

(*b*) Serfdom, that is to say, the condition or status of a tenant who is by law, custom or agreement bound to live and labour on land belonging to another person and to render some determinate service to such other person, whether for reward or not, and is not free to change his status;

(*c*) Any institutions or practice whereby:

(i) A woman, without the right to refuse, is promised or given in a marriage on payment of a consideration in money or in kind to her parents, guardian, family or any other person or group; or

(ii) The husband of a woman, his family, or his clan, has the right to transfer her to another person for value received or otherwise; or

(iii) A woman on the death of her husband is liable to be inherited by another person;

(*d*) Any institution or practice whereby a child or young person under the age of 18 years is delivered by either or both of his natural parents or by his guardian to another person, whether for reward or not, with a view to the exploitation of the child or young person or of his labour.

Article 6

1. The act of enslaving another person or of inducing another person to give himself or a person dependent upon him into slavery, or of attempting these acts, or being accessory thereto, or being a party to a conspiracy to accomplish any such acts, shall be a criminal offence under the laws of the States Parties to this Convention and persons convicted thereof shall be liable to punishment.

2. Subject to the provisions of the introductory paragraph of article 1 of this Convention, the provisions of paragraph 1 of the present article shall also apply to the act of inducing another person to place himself or a person dependent upon him into the servile status resulting from any of the institutions or practices mentioned in article 1, to any attempt to perform such acts, to being accessory thereto, and to being a party to a conspiracy to accomplish any such acts.

10. International Covenant on Civil and Political Rights, December 16, 1966

Article 14

1. All persons shall be equal before the courts and tribunals. In the determination of any criminal charge against him, or of his rights and obligations in a suit at law,

everyone shall be entitled to a fair and public hearing by a competent, independent and impartial tribunal established by law. The Press and the public may be excluded from all or part of a trial for reasons of morals, public order (*ordre public*) or national security in a democratic society, or when the interest of the private lives of the parties so requires, or to the extent strictly necessary in the opinion of the court in special circumstances where publicity would prejudice the interests of justice; but any judgement rendered in a criminal case or in a suit at law shall be made public except where the interest of juvenile persons otherwise requires or the proceedings concern matrimonial disputes or the guardianship of children.

2. Everyone charged with a criminal offence shall have the right to be presumed innocent until proved guilty according to law.

3. In the determination of any criminal charge against him, everyone shall be entitled to the following minimum guarantees, in full equality:

(*a*) To be informed promptly and in detail in a language which he understands of the nature and cause of the charge against him;

(*b*) To have adequate time and facilities for the preparation of his defence and to communicate with counsel of his own choosing;

(*c*) To be tried without undue delay;

(*d*) To be tried in his presence, and to defend himself in person or through legal assistance of his own choosing; to be informed, if he does not have legal assistance, of this right; and to have legal assistance assigned to him, in any case where the interests of justice so require, and without payment by him in any such case if he does not have sufficient means to pay for it;

(*e*) To examine, or have examined, the witnesses against him and to obtain the attendance and examination of witnesses on his behalf under the same conditions as witnesses against him;

(*f*) To have the free assistance of an interpreter if he cannot understand or speak the language used in court;

(*g*) Not to be compelled to testify against himself or to confess guilt.

4. In the case of juvenile persons, the procedure shall be such as will take account of their age and the desirability of promoting their rehabilitation.

5. Everyone convicted of a crime shall have the right to his conviction and sentence being reviewed by a higher tribunal according to law.

6. When a person has by a final decision been convicted of a criminal offence and when subsequently his conviction has been reversed or he has been pardoned on the ground that a new or newly discovered fact shows conclusively that there has been a miscarriage of justice, the person who has suffered punishment as a result of such conviction shall be compensated according to law, unless it is proved that the non-disclosure of the unknown fact in time is wholly or partly attributable to him.

7. No one shall be liable to be tried or punished again for an offence for which he has already been finally convicted or acquitted in accordance with the law and penal procedure of each country.

11. Convention on the Non-Applicability of Statutory Limitations to War Crimes and Crimes Against Humanity, November 26, 1968

Article I

No statutory limitation shall apply to the following crimes, irrespective of the date of their commission:

(*a*) War crimes as they are defined in the Charter of the International Military Tribunal, Nürnburg, of 8 August 1945 and confirmed by resolutions 3(I) of 13 February 1946 and 95(I) of 11 December 1946 of the General Assembly of the United Nations, particularly the 'grave breaches' enumerated in the Geneva Conventions of 12 August 1949 for the protection of war victims;

(*b*) Crimes against humanity whether committed in time of war or in time of peace as they are defined in the Charter of the International Military Tribunal, Nürnberg, of 8 August 1945 and confirmed by resolutions 3(I) of 13 February 1946 and 95(I) of 11 December 1946 of the General Assembly of the United Nations, eviction by armed attack or occupation and inhuman acts resulting from the policy of *apartheid*, and the crime of genocide as defined in the 1948 Convention on the Prevention and Punishment of the Crime of Genocide, even if such acts do not constitute a violation of the domestic law of the country in which they were committed.

Article II

If any of the crimes mentioned in article I is committed, the provisions of this Convention shall apply to representatives of the State authority and private individuals who, as principals or accomplices, participate in or who directly incite others to the commission of any of those crimes, or who conspire to commit them, irrespective of the degree of completion, and to representatives of the State authority who tolerate their commission.

12. International Convention on the Suppression and Punishment of the Crime of *Apartheid*, November 30, 1973

Article I

1. The States Parties to the present Convention declare that *apartheid* is a crime against humanity and that inhuman acts resulting from the policies and practices of *apartheid* and similar policies and practices of racial segregation and discrimination, as defined in article II of the Convention, are crimes violating the principles of international law, in particular the purposes and principles of the Charter of the United Nations, and constituting a serious threat to international peace and security.

2. The States Parties to the present Convention declare criminal those organizations, institutions and individuals committing the crime of *apartheid*.

Article II

For the purpose of the present Convention, the term 'the crime of apartheid', which shall include similar policies and practices of racial segregation and discrimination as practised in southern Africa, shall apply to the following inhuman acts committed for the purpose of establishing and maintaining domination by one racial group of persons over any other racial group of persons and systematically oppressing them:

(*a*) Denial to a member or members of a racial group or groups of the right to life and liberty of person:

- (i) By murder of members of a racial group or groups;
- (ii) By the infliction upon the members of a racial group or groups of serious bodily or mental harm, by the infringement of their freedom or dignity, or by subjecting them to torture or to cruel, inhuman or degrading treatment or punishment;
- (iii) By arbitrary arrest and illegal imprisonment of the members of a racial group or groups.

(*b*) Deliberate imposition on a racial group or groups of living conditions calculated to cause its or their physical destruction in whole or in part;

(*c*) Any legislative measures and other measures calculated to prevent a racial group or groups from participation in the political, social, economic and cultural life of the country and the deliberate creation of conditions preventing the full development of such a group or groups, in particular by denying to members of a racial group or groups basic human rights and freedoms, including the right to work, the right to form recognized trade unions, the right to education, the right to leave and to return to their country, the right to a nationality, the right to freedom of movement and residence, the right to freedom of opinion and expression, and the right to freedom of peaceful assembly and association;

(*d*) Any measures, including legislative measures, designed to divide the population along racial lines by the creation of separate reserves and ghettos for the members of a racial group or groups, the prohibition of mixed marriages among members of various racial groups, the expropriation of landed property belonging to a racial group or groups or to members thereof;

(*e*) Exploitation of the labour of the members of a racial group or groups, in particular by submitting them to forced labour;

(*f*) Persecution of organizations and persons, by depriving them of fundamental rights and freedoms, because they oppose *apartheid*.

Article III

International criminal responsibility shall apply, irrespective of the motive involved, to individuals, members of organizations and institutions and representatives of the State, whether residing in the territory of the State in which the acts are perpetrated or in some other State, whenever they:

(*a*) Commit, participate in, directly incite or conspire in the commission of the acts mentioned in article II of the present Convention.

(*b*) Directly abet, encourage or co-operate in the commission of the crime of *apartheid*.

Article IV

The States Parties to the present Convention undertake:

(*a*) To adopt any legislative or other measures necessary to suppress as well as to prevent any encouragement of the crime of *apartheid* and similar segregationist policies or their manifestations and to punish persons guilty of that crime;

(*b*) To adopt legislative, judicial and administrative measures to prosecute, bring to trial and punish in accordance with their jurisdiction persons responsible for, or accused of, the acts defined in article II of the present Convention, whether or not such persons reside in the territory of the State in which the acts are committed or are nationals of that State or of some other State or are stateless persons.

Article V

Persons charged with the acts enumerated in article II of the present Convention may be tried by a competent tribunal of any State Party to the Convention which may acquire jurisdiction over the person of the accused or by an international penal tribunal having jurisdiction with respect to those States Parties which shall have accepted its jurisdiction.

13. Protocol Additional to the Geneva Conventions of 12 August 1949, and Relating to the Protection of Victims of International Armed Conflicts (Protocol I), December 12, 1977

Article 85.—Repression of Breaches of this Protocol

1. The provisions of the Conventions relating to the repression of breaches and grave breaches, supplemented by this Section, shall apply to the repression of breaches and grave breaches of this Protocol.

2. Acts described as grave breaches in the Convention are grave breaches of this Protocol if committed against persons in the power of an adverse Party protected by Articles 44, 45 and 73 of this Protocol, or against the wounded, sick and shipwrecked of the adverse Party who are protected by this Protocol, or against those medical or religious personnel, medical units or medical transports which are under the control of the adverse Party and are protected by this Protocol.

3. In addition to the grave breaches defined in Article 11 [concerning prohibited medical experimentation], the following acts shall be regarded as grave breaches of this Protocol, when committed wilfully, in violation of the relevant provisions of this Protocol, and causing death or serious injury to body or health:

(a) Making the civilian population or individual civilians the object of attack;

(b) Launching an indiscriminate attack affecting the civilian population or civilian objects in the knowledge that such attacks will cause excessive loss of life, injury to civilians or damage to civilian objects, as defined in Article 57, paragraph 2(a)(iii);

(c) Launching an attack against works or installations containing dangerous forces in the knowledge that such attack will cause excessive loss of life, injury to civilians or damage to civilian objects, as defined in Article 57, paragraph 2(a)(iii);

(d) Making non-defended localities and demilitarized zones the objects of attack;

(e) Making a person the object of attack in the knowledge that he is *hors de combat*;

(f) The perfidious use, in violation of Article 37, of the distinctive emblem of the red cross, red crescent or red lion and sun or of other protective signs recognized by the Conventions or this Protocol.

4. In addition to the grave breaches defined in the preceding paragraphs and in the Conventions, the following shall be regarded as grave breaches of this Protocol, when committed wilfully and in violation of the Conventions or the Protocol;

(a) The transfer by the Occupying Power of parts of its own civilian population into the territory it occupies, or the deportation or transfer of all or parts of the population of the occupied territory within or outside this territory, in violation of Article 49 of the Fourth Convention;

(b) Unjustifiable delay in the repatriation of prisoners of war or civilians;

(c) Practices of *apartheid* and other inhuman and degrading practices involving outrages upon personal dignity, based on racial discrimination;

(d) Making the clearly recognized historic monuments, works of art or places of worship which constitute the cultural or spiritual heritage of peoples and to which special protection has been given by special arrangement, for example, within the framework of a competent international organization, the object of attack, causing as a result extensive destruction thereof, where there is no evidence of the violation by the adverse Party of Article 53, sub-paragraph (b), and when such historic monuments, works of art and places of worship are not located in the immediate proximity of military objectives;

(e) Depriving a person protected by the Conventions or referred to in paragraph 2 of this Article of the rights of fair and regular trial.

5. Without prejudice to the application of the Conventions and of this Protocol, grave breaches of these instruments shall be regarded as war crimes.

Article 86.—Failure to Act

1. The High Contracting Parties and the Parties to the conflict shall repress grave breaches, and take measures necessary to suppress all other breaches, of the Conventions or of this Protocol which result from a failure to act when under a duty to do so.

2. The fact that a breach of the Conventions or of this Protocol was committed by a subordinate does not absolve his superiors from penal or disciplinary responsibility, as the case may be, if they knew, or had information which should have enabled them to conclude in the circumstances at the time, that he was committing or was going to commit such a breach and if they did not take all feasible measures within their power to prevent or repress the breach.

Article 87.—Duty of Commanders

1. The High Contracting Parties and the Parties to the conflict shall require

military commanders, with respect to members of the armed forces under their command and other persons under their control, to prevent and, where necessary, to suppress and to report to competent authorities breaches of the Convention and of this Protocol.

2. In order to prevent and suppress breaches, High Contracting Parties and Parties to the conflict shall require that, commensurate with their level of responsibility, commanders ensure that members of the armed forces under their command are aware of their obligations under the Conventions and this Protocol.

3. The High Contracting Parties and Parties to the conflict shall require any commander who is aware that subordinates or other persons under his control are going to commit or have committed a breach of the Conventions or of this Protocol, to initiate such steps as are necessary to prevent such violations of the Conventions or this Protocol, and, where appropriate, to initiate disciplinary or penal action against violators thereof.

14. Protocol Additional to the Geneva Conventions of 12 August 1949, and Relating to the Protection of Victims of Non-International Armed Conflicts (Protocol II), December 12, 1977

Article 1.—Material field of application

1. This Protocol, which develops and supplements Article 3 common to the Geneva Conventions of 12 August 1949 without modifying its existing conditions of application, shall apply to all armed conflicts which are not covered by Article I of the Protocol Additional to the Geneva Conventions of 12 August 1949, and relating to the Protection of Victims of International Armed Conflicts (Protocol I) and which take place in the territory of a High Contracting party between its armed forces and dissident armed forces or other organized armed groups which, under responsible command, exercise such control over a part of its territory as to enable them to carry out sustained and concerted military operations and to implement this Protocol.

2. This Protocol shall not apply to situations of internal disturbances and tensions, such as riots, isolated and sporadic acts of violence and other acts of a similar nature, as not being armed conflicts.

Article 4.— Fundamental guarantees

1. All persons who do not take a direct part or who have ceased to take part in hostilities, whether or not their liberty has been restricted, are entitled to respect for their person, honour and convictions and religious practices. They shall in all circumstances be treated humanely, without any adverse distinction. It is prohibited to order that there shall be no survivors.

2. Without prejudice to the generality of the foregoing, the following acts against the persons referred to in paragraph I are and shall remain prohibited at any time and in any place whatsoever:

(a) violence to the life, health and physical or mental well-being of persons, in particular murder as well as cruel treatment such as torture, mutilation or any form of corporal punishment;

(b collective punishments;

(c) taking of hostages;

(d) acts of terrorism;

(e outrages upon personal dignity, in particular humiliating and degrading treatment, rape, enforced prostitution and any form of indecent assault;

(f) slavery and the slave trade in all their forms;

(g pillage;

(h) threats to commit any of the foregoing acts.

15. Convention against Torture and Other Cruel, Inhuman or Degrading Treatment or Punishment, December 10, 1984

Article 1

1. For the purposes of this Convention, the term 'torture' means any act by which severe pain or suffering, whether physical or mental, is intentionally inflicted on a person for such purposes as obtaining from him or a third person information or a confession, punishing him for an act he or a third person has committed or is suspected of having committed, or intimidating or coercing him or a third person, or for any reason based on discrimination of any kind, when such pain or suffering is inflicted by or at the instigation of or with the consent or acquiescence of a public official or other person acting in an official capacity. It does not include pain or suffering arising only from, inherent in or incidental to lawful sanctions.

2. This article is without prejudice to any international instrument or national legislation which does or may contain provisions of wider application.

Article 2

1. Each State Party shall take effective legislative, administrative, judicial or other measures to prevent acts of torture in any territory under its jurisdiction.

2. No exceptional circumstances whatsoever, whether a state of war or a threat of war, internal political instability or any other public emergency, may be invoked as a justification of torture.

3. An order from a superior officer or a public authority may not be invoked as a justification of torture.

Article 4

1. Each State Party shall ensure that all acts of torture are offences under its criminal law. The same shall apply to an attempt to commit torture and to an act by any person which constitutes complicity or participation in torture.

2. Each State Party shall make these offences punishable by appropriate penalties which take into account their grave nature.

Article 5

1. Each State Party shall take such measures as may be necessary to establish its jurisdiction over the offences referred to in article 4 in the following cases:

(*a*) When the offences are committed in any territory under its jurisdiction or on board a ship or aircraft registered in that State;

(*b*) When the alleged offender is a national of that State;

(*c*) When the victim is a national of that State if that State considers it appropriate.

2. Each State Party shall likewise take such measures as may be necessary to establish its jurisdiction over such offences in cases where the alleged offender is present in any territory under its jurisdiction and it does not extradite him pursuant to article 8 to any of the States mentioned in paragraph 1 of this article.

3. This Convention does not exclude any criminal jurisdiction exercised in accordance with internal law.

Article 7

1. The State Party in the territory under whose jurisdiction a person alleged to have committed any offence referred to in article 4 is found shall in the cases contemplated in article 5, if it does not extradite him, submit the case to its competent authorities for the purpose of prosecution.

16. Statute of the International Tribunal for the Prosecution of Persons Responsible for Serious Violations of International Humanitarian Law Committed in the Territory of the Former Yugoslavia Since 1991, May 25, 1993, as amended

Article 1

Competence of the International Tribunal

The International Tribunal shall have the power to prosecute persons responsible for serious violations of international humanitarian law committed in the territory of the former Yugoslavia since 1991 in accordance with the provisions of the present Statute.

Article 2

Grave breaches of the Geneva Conventions of 1949

The International Tribunal shall have the power to prosecute persons committing or ordering to be committed grave breaches of the Geneva Conventions of 12 August 1949, namely the following acts against persons or property protected under the provisions of the relevant Geneva Convention:

(a) wilful killing;

(b) torture or inhuman treatment, including biological experiments;

(c) wilfully causing great suffering or serious injury to body or health;

(d) extensive destruction and appropriation of property, not justified by military necessity and carried out unlawfully and wantonly;

(e) compelling a prisoner of war or a civilian to serve in the forces of a hostile power;

(f) wilfully depriving a prisoner of war or a civilian of the rights of fair and regular trial;

(g) unlawful deportation or transfer or unlawful confinement of a civilian;

(h) taking civilians as hostages.

Article 3

Violations of the laws or customs of war

The International Tribunal shall have the power to prosecute persons violating the laws or customs of war. Such violations shall include, but not be limited to:

(a) employment of poisonous weapons or other weapons calculated to cause unnecessary suffering;

(b) wanton destruction of cities, towns or villages, or devastation not justified by military necessity;

(c) attack, or bombardment, by whatever means of undefended towns, villages, dwellings, or buildings;

(d) seizure of, destruction or wilful damage done to institutions dedicated to religion, charity and education, the arts and sciences, historic monuments and works of art and science;

(e) plunder of public or private property.

Article 4

Genocide

1. The International Tribunal shall have the power to prosecute persons committing genocide as defined in paragraph 2 of this article or of committing any of the other acts enumerated in paragraph 3 of this article.

2. Genocide means any of the following acts committed with intent to destroy, in whole or in part, a national, ethnical, racial or religious group, as such:

(a) killing members of the group;

(b) causing serious bodily or mental harm to members of the group;

(c) deliberately inflicting on the group conditions of life calculated to bring about its physical destruction in whole or in part;

(d) imposing measures intended to prevent births within the group;

(e) forcibly transferring children of the group to another group.

3. The following acts shall be punishable:

(a) genocide;

(b) conspiracy to commit genocide;

(c) direct and public incitement to commit genocide;

(d) attempt to commit genocide;

(e) complicity in genocide.

Article 5
Crimes against humanity

The International Tribunal shall have the power to prosecute persons responsible for the following crimes when committed in armed conflict, whether international or internal in character, and directed against any civilian population:

(a) murder;
(b) extermination;
(c) enslavement;
(d) deportation;
(e) imprisonment;
(f) torture;
(g) rape;
(h) persecutions on political, racial and religious grounds;
(i) other inhumane acts.

Article 6
Personal jurisdiction

The International Tribunal shall have jurisdiction over natural persons pursuant to the provisions of the present Statute.

Article 7
Individual criminal responsibility

1. A person who planned, instigated, ordered, committed or otherwise aided and abetted in the planning, preparation or execution of a crime referred to in articles 2 to 5 of the present Statute, shall be individually responsible for the crime.

2. The official position of any accused person, whether as Head of State or Government or as a responsible Government official, shall not relieve such person of criminal responsibility nor mitigate punishment.

3. The fact that any of the acts referred to in articles 2 to 5 of the present Statute was committed by a subordinate does not relieve his superior of criminal responsibility if he knew or had reason to know that the subordinate was about to commit such acts or had done so and the superior failed to take the necessary and reasonable measures to prevent such acts or to punish the perpetrators thereof.

4. The fact that an accused person acted pursuant to an order of a Government or of a superior shall not relieve him of criminal responsibility, but may be considered in mitigation of punishment if the International Tribunal determines that justice so requires.

Article 8
Territorial and temporal jurisdiction

The territorial jurisdiction of the International Tribunal shall extend to the territory of the former Socialist Federal Republic of Yugoslavia, including its land surface, airspace and territorial waters. The temporal jurisdiction of the International Tribunal shall extend to a period beginning on 1 January 1991.

Article 9
Concurrent jurisdiction

1. The International Tribunal and national courts shall have concurrent jurisdiction to prosecute persons for serious violations of international humanitarian law committed in the territory of the former Yugoslavia since 1 January 1991.

2. The International Tribunal shall have primacy over national courts. At any stage of the procedure, the International Tribunal may formally request national courts to defer to the competence of the International Tribunal in accordance with the present Statute and the Rules of Procedure and Evidence of the International Tribunal.

Article 10
Non-bis-in-idem

1. No person shall be tried before a national court for acts constituting serious violations of international humanitarian law under the present Statute, for which he or she has already been tried by the International Tribunal.

2. A person who has been tried by a national court for acts constituting serious violations of international humanitarian law may be subsequently tried by the International Tribunal only if:

(a) the act for which he or she was tried was characterized as an ordinary crime; or

(b) the national court proceedings were not impartial or independent, were designed to shield the accused from international criminal responsibility, or the case was not diligently prosecuted.

3. In considering the penalty to be imposed on a person convicted of a crime under the present Statute, the International Tribunal shall take into account the extent to which any penalty imposed by a national court on the same person for the same act has already been served.

Article 11
Organization of the International Tribunal

The International Tribunal shall consist of the following organs:

(a) The Chambers, comprising three Trial Chambers and an Appeals Chamber;
(b) The Prosecutor, and
(c) A Registry, servicing both the Chambers and the Prosecutor.

Article 21
Rights of the accused

1. All persons shall be equal before the International Tribunal.

2. In the determination of charges against him, the accused shall be entitled to a fair and public hearing, subject to article 22 of the Statute.

3. The accused shall be presumed innocent until proved guilty according to the provisions of the present Statute.

4. In the determination of any charge against the accused pursuant to the present Statute, the accused shall be entitled to the following minimum guarantees, in full equality:

(a) to be informed promptly and in detail in a language which he understands of the nature and cause of the charge against him;

(b) to have adequate time and facilities for the preparation of his defence and to communicate with counsel of his own choosing;

(c) to be tried without undue delay;

(d) to be tried in his presence, and to defend himself in person or through legal assistance of his own choosing; to be informed, if he does not have legal assistance, of this right; and to have legal assistance assigned to him, in any case where the interests of justice so require, and without payment by him in any such case if he does not have sufficient means to pay for it;

(e) to examine, or have examined, the witnesses against him and to obtain the attendance and examination of witnesses on his behalf under the same conditions as witnesses against him;

(f) to have the free assistance of an interpreter if he cannot understand or speak the language used in the International Tribunal;

(g) not to be compelled to testify against himself or to confess guilt.

Article 22
Protection of victims and witnesses

The International Tribunal shall provide in its rules of procedure and evidence for the protection of victims and witnesses. Such protection measures shall include, but shall not be limited to, the conduct of in camera proceedings and the protection of the victim's identity.

Article 23
Judgement

1. The Trial Chambers shall pronounce judgements and impose sentences and penalties on persons convicted of serious violations of international humanitarian law.

2. The judgement shall be rendered by a majority of the judges of the Trial Chamber, and shall be delivered by the Trial Chamber in public. It shall be accompanied by a reasoned opinion in writing, to which separate or dissenting opinions may be appended.

Article 24
Penalties

1. The penalty imposed by the Trial Chamber shall be limited to imprisonment. In determining the terms of imprisonment, the Trial Chambers shall have recourse to the general practice regarding prison sentences in the courts of the former Yugoslavia.

2. In imposing the sentences, the Trial Chambers should take into account such factors as the gravity of the offence and the individual circumstances of the convicted person.

3. In addition to imprisonment, the Trial Chambers may order the return of any property and proceeds acquired by criminal conduct, including by means of duress, to their rightful owners.

Article 25
Appellate proceedings

1. The Appeals Chamber shall hear appeals from persons convicted by the Trial Chambers or from the Prosecutor on the following grounds:

(a) an error on a question of law invalidating the decision; or
(b) an error of fact which has occasioned a miscarriage of justice.

2. The Appeals Chamber may affirm, reverse or revise the decisions taken by the Trial Chambers.

Article 26
Review proceedings

Where a new fact has been discovered which was not known at the time of the proceedings before the Trial Chambers or the Appeals Chamber and which could have been a decisive factor in reaching the decision, the convicted person or the Prosecutor may submit to the International Tribunal an application for review of the judgement.

Article 27
Enforcement of sentences

Imprisonment shall be served in a State designated by the International Tribunal from a list of States which have indicated to the Security Council their willingness to accept convicted persons. Such imprisonment shall be in accordance with the applicable law of the State concerned, subject to the supervision of the International Tribunal.

Article 29
Cooperation and judicial assistance

1. States shall cooperate with the International Tribunal in the investigation and prosecution of persons accused of committing serious violations of international humanitarian law.

2. States shall comply without undue delay with any request for assistance or an order issued by a Trial Chamber, including, but not limited to:

(a) the identification and location of persons;
(b) the taking of testimony and the production of evidence;
(c) the service of documents;
(d) the arrest or detention of persons;
(e) the surrender or the transfer of the accused to the International Tribunal.

17. Statute of the International Criminal Tribunal for Rwanda, November 8, 1994

Article 3
Crimes against humanity

The International Tribunal for Rwanda shall have the power to prosecute persons responsible for the following crimes when committed as part of a widespread or systematic attack against any civilian population on national, political, ethnic, racial or religious grounds:

(a) Murder;
(b) Extermination;
(c) Enslavement;
(d) Deportation;
(e) Imprisonment;
(f) Torture;
(g) Rape;
(h) Persecutions on political, racial and religious grounds;
(i) Other inhumane acts.

Article 4
Violations of Article 3 common to the Geneva Conventions and of Additional Protocol II

The International Tribunal for Rwanda shall have the power to prosecute persons committing or ordering to be committed serious violations of Article 3 common to the Geneva Conventions of 12 August 1949 for the Protection of War Victims, and of Additional Protocol II thereto of 8 June 1977. These violations shall include, but shall not be limited to:

(a) Violence to life, health and physical or mental well-being of persons, in particular murder as well as cruel treatment such as torture, mutilation or any form of corporal punishment;

(b) Collective punishments;

(c) Taking of hostages;

(d) Acts of terrorism;

(e) Outrages upon personal dignity, in particular humiliating and degrading treatment, rape, enforced prostitution and any form of indecent assault;

(f) Pillage;

(g) The passing of sentences and the carrying out of executions without previous judgement pronounced by a regularly constituted court, affording all the judicial guarantees which are recognized as indispensable by civilized peoples;

(h) Threats to commit any of the foregoing acts.

18. International Law Commission Draft Code of Crimes Against the Peace and Security of Mankind, 1996

Article 1
Scope and application of the present Code

1. The present Code applies to the crimes against the peace and security of mankind set out in Part II.

2. Crimes against the peace and security of mankind are crimes under international law and punishable as such, whether or not they are punishable under national law.

Article 2
Individual responsibility

1. A crime against the peace and security of mankind entails individual responsibility.

2. An individual shall be responsible for the crime of aggression in accordance with article 16.

3. An individual shall be responsible for a crime set out in article 17, 18, 19 or 20 if that individual:

(a) intentionally commits such a crime;

(b) orders the commission of such a crime which in fact occurs or is attempted;

(c) fails to prevent or repress the commission of such a crime in the circumstances set out in article 6;

(d) knowingly aids, abets or otherwise assists, directly and substantially, in the commission of such a crime, including providing the means for its commission;

(e) directly participates in planning or conspiring to commit such a crime which in fact occurs;

(f) directly and publicly incites another individual to commit such a crime which in fact occurs;

(g) attempts to commit such a crime by taking action commencing the execution of a crime which does not in fact occur because of circumstances independent of his intentions.

Article 3
Punishment

An individual who is responsible for a crime against the peace and security of mankind shall be liable to punishment. The punishment shall be commensurate with the character and gravity of the crime.

Article 5
Order of a Government or a superior

The fact that an individual charged with a crime against the peace and security of mankind acted pursuant to an order of a Government or a superior does not relieve him of criminal responsibility, but may be considered in mitigation of punishment if justice so requires.

Article 6
Responsibility of the superior

The fact that a crime against the peace and security of mankind was committed by a subordinate does not relieve his superiors of criminal responsibility, if they knew or had reason to know, in the circumstances at the time, that the subordinate was committing or was going to commit such a crime and if they did not take all necessary measures within their power to prevent or repress the crime.

Article 7
Official position and responsibility

The official position of an individual who commits a crime against the peace and security of mankind, even if he acted as head of State or Government, does not relieve him of criminal responsibility or mitigate punishment.

Article 16
Crime of aggression

An individual who, as leader or organizer, actively participates in or orders the planning, preparation, initiation or waging of aggression committed by a State shall be responsible for a crime of aggression.

Article 17
Crime of genocide

A crime of genocide means any of the following acts committed with intent to destroy, in whole or in part, a national, ethnic, racial or religious group, as such:

(a) killing members of the group;

(b) causing serious bodily or mental harm to members of the group;

(c) deliberately inflicting on the group conditions of life calculated to bring about its physical destruction in whole or in part;

(d) imposing measures intended to prevent births within the group;

(e) forcibly transferring children of the group to another group.

Article 18
Crimes against humanity

A crime against humanity means any of the following acts, when committed in a systematic manner or on a large scale and instigated or directed by a Government or by any organization or group:

(a) murder;

(b) extermination;

(c) torture;

(d) enslavement;

(e) persecution on political, racial, religious or ethnic grounds;

(f) institutionalized discrimination on racial, ethnic or religious grounds involving the violation of fundamental human rights and freedoms and resulting in seriously disadvantaging a part of the population;

(g) arbitrary deportation or forcible transfer of population;

(h) arbitrary imprisonment;

(i) forced disappearance of persons;

(j) rape, enforced prostitution and other forms of sexual abuse;

(k) other inhumane acts which severely damage physical or mental integrity, health or human dignity, such as mutilation and severe bodily harm.

Article 20
War Crimes

Any of the following war crimes constitutes a crime against the peace and security of mankind when committed in a systematic manner or on a large scale:

(a) any of the following acts committed in violation of international humanitarian law:

(i) wilful killing;

(ii) torture or inhuman treatment, including biological experiments;

(iii) wilfully causing great suffering or serious injury to body or health;

(iv) extensive destruction and appropriation of property, not justified by military necessity and carried out unlawfully and wantonly;

(v) compelling a prisoner of war or other protected person to serve in the forces of a hostile Power;

(vi) wilfully depriving a prisoner of war or other protected person of the rights of fair and regular trial;

(vii) unlawful deportation or transfer or unlawful confinement of protected persons;

(viii) taking of hostages;

(b) any of the following acts committed wilfully in violation of international humanitarian law and causing death or serious injury to body or health:

(i) making the civilian population or individual civilians the object of attack;

(ii) launching an indiscriminate attack affecting the civilian population or civilian objects in the knowledge that such attack will cause excessive loss of life, injury to civilians or damage to civilian objects;

(iii) launching an attack against works or installations containing dangerous forces in the knowledge that such attack will cause excessive loss of life, injury to civilians or damage to civilian objects;

(iv) making a person the object of attack in the knowledge that he is *hors de combat*;

(v) the perfidious use of the distinctive emblem of the red cross, red crescent or red lion and sun or of other recognized protective signs;

(c) any of the following acts committed wilfully in violation of international humanitarian law:

(i) the transfer by the Occupying Power of parts of its own civilian population into the territory it occupies;

(ii) unjustifiable delay in the repatriation of prisoners of war or civilians;

(d) outrages upon personal dignity in violation of international humanitarian law, in particular humiliating and degrading treatment, rape, enforced prostitution and any form of indecent assault;

(e) any of the following acts committed in violation of the laws or customs or war:

(i) employment of poisonous weapons or other weapons calculated to cause unnecessary suffering;

(ii) wanton destruction of cities, towns or villages, or devastation not justified by military necessity;

(iii) attack, or bombardment, by whatever means, of undefended towns, villages, dwellings or buildings or of demilitarized zones;

(iv) seizure of, destruction of or wilful damage done to institutions dedicated to religion, charity and education, the arts and sciences, historic monuments and works of art and science;

(v) plunder of public or private property;

(f) any of the following acts committed in violation of international humanitarian law applicable in armed conflict not of an international character:

- (i) violence to the life, health and physical or mental well-being of persons, in particular murder as well as cruel treatment such as torture, mutilation or any form of corporal punishment;
- (ii) collective punishments;
- (iii) taking of hostages;
- (iv) acts of terrorism;
- (v) outrages upon personal dignity, in particular humiliating and degrading treatment, rape, enforced prostitution and any form of indecent assault;
- (vi) pillage;
- (vii) the passing of sentences and the carrying out of the executions without previous judgement pronounced by a regularly constituted court, affording all the judicial guarantees which are generally recognized as indispensable;

(g) in the case of armed conflict, using methods or means of warfare not justified by military necessity with the intent to cause widespread, long-term and severe damage to the natural environment and thereby gravely prejudice the health or survival of the population and such damage occurs.

19. Statute of the International Criminal Court, July 17, 1998

Article 1
The Court

An International Criminal Court ('the Court') is hereby established. It shall be a permanent institution and shall have the power to exercise its jurisdiction over persons for the most serious crimes of international concern, as referred to in this Statute, and shall be complementary to national criminal jurisdictions. The jurisdiction and functioning of the Court shall be governed by the provisions of this Statute.

Article 3
Seat of the Court

1. The seat of the Court shall be established at The Hague in the Netherlands ('the host State').

3. The Court may sit elsewhere, whenever it considers it desirable, as provided in this Statute.

Article 5
Crimes within the jurisdiction of the Court

1. The jurisdiction of the Court shall be limited to the most serious crimes of concern to the international community as a whole. The Court has jurisdiction in accordance with this Statute with respect to the following crimes:

- (a) The crime of genocide;
- (b) Crimes against humanity;
- (c) War crimes;
- (d) The crime of aggression.

2. The Court shall exercise jurisdiction over the crime of aggression once a provision is adopted in accordance with articles 121 and 123 defining the crime and setting out the conditions under which the Court shall exercise jurisdiction with respect to this crime. Such a provision shall be consistent with the relevant provisions of the Charter of the United Nations.

Article 6
Genocide

For the purpose of this Statute, 'genocide' means any of the following acts committed with intent to destroy, in whole or in part, a national, ethnical, racial or religious group, as such:

(a) Killing members of the group;

(b) Causing serious bodily or mental harm to members of the group;

(c) Deliberately inflicting on the group conditions of life calculated to bring about its physical destruction in whole or in part;

(d) Imposing measures intended to prevent births within the group;

(e) Forcibly transferring children of the group to another group.

Article 7
Crimes against humanity

1. For the purpose of this Statute, 'crime against humanity' means any of the following acts when committed as part of a widespread or systematic attack directed against any civilian population, with knowledge of the attack:

(a) Murder;

(b) Extermination;

(c) Enslavement;

(d) Deportation or forcible transfer of population;

(e) Imprisonment or other severe deprivation of physical liberty in violation of fundamental rules of international law;

(f) Torture;

(g) Rape, sexual slavery, enforced prostitution, forced pregnancy, enforced sterilization, or any other form of sexual violence of comparable gravity;

(h) Persecution against any identifiable group or collectivity on political, racial, national, ethnic, cultural, religious, gender as defined in paragraph 3, or other grounds that are universally recognized as impermissible under international law, in connection with any act referred to in this paragraph or any crime within the jurisdiction of the Court;

(i) Enforced disappearance of persons;

(j) The crime of apartheid;

(k) Other inhumane acts of a similar character intentionally causing great suffering, or serious injury to body or to mental or physical health.

2. For the purpose of paragraph 1:

(a) 'Attack directed against any civilian population' means a course of conduct involving the multiple commission of acts referred to in paragraph 1 against any civilian population, pursuant to or in furtherance of a State or organizational policy to commit such attack;

(b) 'Extermination' includes the intentional infliction of conditions of life, *inter alia* the deprivation of access to food and medicine, calculated to bring about the destruction of part of a population;

(c) 'Enslavement' means the exercise of any or all of the powers attaching to the right of ownership over a person and includes the exercise of such power in the course of trafficking in persons, in particular women and children;

(d) 'Deportation or forcible transfer of population' means forced displacement of the persons concerned by expulsion or other coercive acts from the area in which they are lawfully present, without grounds permitted under international law;

(e) 'Torture' means the intentional infliction of severe pain or suffering, whether physical or mental, upon a person in the custody or under the control of the accused; except that torture shall not include pain or suffering arising only from, inherent in or incidental to, lawful sanctions;

(f) 'Forced pregnancy' means the unlawful confinement of a woman forcibly made pregnant, with the intent of affecting the ethnic composition of any population or carrying out other grave violations of international law. This definition shall not in any way be interpreted as affecting national laws relating to pregnancy;

(g) 'Persecution' means the intentional and severe deprivation of fundamental rights contrary to international law by reason of the identity of the group or collectivity;

(h) 'The crime of apartheid' means inhumane acts of a character similar to those referred to in paragraph 1, committed in the context of an institutionalized regime of systematic oppression and domination by one racial group over any other racial group or groups and committed with the intention of maintaining that regime;

(i) 'Enforced disappearance of persons' means the arrest, detention or abduction of persons by, or with the authorization, support or acquiescence of, a State or a political organization, followed by a refusal to acknowledge that deprivation of freedom or to give information on the fate or whereabouts of those persons, with the intention of removing them from the protection of the law for a prolonged period of time.

3. For the purpose of this Statute, it is understood that the term 'gender' refers to the two sexes, male and female, within the context of society. The term 'gender' does not indicate any meaning different from the above.

Article 8
War crimes

1. The Court shall have jurisdiction in respect of war crimes in particular when committed as part of a plan or policy or as part of a large-scale commission of such crimes.

2. For the purpose of this Statute, 'war crimes' means:

(a) Grave breaches of the Geneva Conventions of 12 August 1949, namely, any of the following acts against persons or property protected under the provisions of the relevant Geneva Convention:

(i) Wilful killing;
(ii) Torture or inhuman treatment, including biological experiments;

(iii) Wilfully causing great suffering, or serious injury to body or health;

(iv) Extensive destruction and appropriation of property, not justified by military necessity and carried out unlawfully and wantonly;

(v) Compelling a prisoner of war or other protected person to serve in the forces of a hostile Power;

(vi) Wilfully depriving a prisoner of war or other protected person of the rights of fair and regular trial;

(vii) Unlawful deportation or transfer or unlawful confinement;

(viii) Taking of hostages.

(b) Other serious violations of the laws and customs applicable in international armed conflict, within the established framework of international law, namely, any of the following acts:

(i) Intentionally directing attacks against the civilian population as such or against individual civilians not taking direct part in hostilities;

(ii) Intentionally directing attacks against civilian objects, that is, objects which are not military objectives;

(iii) Intentionally directing attacks against personnel, installations, material, units or vehicles involved in a humanitarian assistance or peacekeeping mission in accordance with the Charter of the United Nations, as long as they are entitled to the protection given to civilians or civilian objects under the international law of armed conflict;

(iv) Intentionally launching an attack in the knowledge that such attack will cause incidental loss of life or injury to civilians or damage to civilian objects or widespread, long-term and severe damage to the natural environment which would be clearly excessive in relation to the concrete and direct overall military advantage anticipated;

(v) Attacking or bombarding, by whatever means, towns, villages, dwellings or buildings which are undefended and which are not military objectives;

(vi) Killing or wounding a combatant who, having laid down his arms or having no longer means of defence, has surrendered at discretion;

(vii) Making improper use of a flag of truce, of the flag or of the military insignia and uniform of the enemy or of the United Nations, as well as of the distinctive emblems of the Geneva Conventions, resulting in death or serious personal injury;

(viii) The transfer, directly or indirectly, by the Occupying Power of parts of its own civilian population into the territory it occupies, or the deportation or transfer of all or parts of the population of the occupied territory within or outside this territory;

(ix) Intentionally directing attacks against buildings dedicated to religion, education, art, science or charitable purposes, historic monuments, hospitals and places where the sick and wounded are collected, provided they are not military objectives;

(x) Subjecting persons who are in the power of an adverse party to physical mutilation or to medical or scientific experiments of any kind which are neither justified by the medical, dental or hospital treatment of the person concerned nor carried out in his or her interest, and which cause death to or seriously endanger the health of such person or persons;

(xi) Killing or wounding treacherously individuals belonging to the hostile nation or army;

(xii) Declaring that no quarter will be given;

(xiii) Destroying or seizing the enemy's property unless such destruction or seizure be imperatively demanded by the necessities of war;

(xiv) Declaring abolished, suspended or inadmissible in a court of law the rights and actions of the nationals of the hostile party;

(xv) Compelling the nationals of the hostile party to take part in the operations of war directed against their own country, even if they were in the belligerent's service before the commencement of the war;

(xvi) Pillaging a town or place, even when taken by assault;

(xvii) Employing poison or poisoned weapons;

(xviii) Employing asphyxiating, poisonous or other gases, and all analogous liquids, materials or devices;

(xix) Employing bullets which expand or flatten easily in the human body, such as bullets with a hard envelope which does not entirely cover the core or is pierced with incisions;

(xx) Employing weapons, projectiles and material and methods of warfare which are of a nature to cause superfluous injury or unnecessary suffering or which are inherently indiscriminate in violation of the international law of armed conflict, provided that such weapons, projectiles and material and methods of warfare are the subject of a comprehensive prohibition and are included in an annex to this Statute, by an amendment in accordance with the relevant provisions set forth in articles 121 and 123;

(xxi) Committing outrages upon personal dignity, in particular humiliating and degrading treatment;

(xxii) Committing rape, sexual slavery, enforced prostitution, forced pregnancy, as defined in article 7, paragraph 2(f), enforced sterilization, or any other form of sexual violence also constituting a grave breach of the Geneva Conventions;

(xxiii) Utilizing the presence of a civilian or other protected person to render certain points, areas or military forces immune from military operations;

(xxiv) Intentionally directing attacks against buildings, material, medical units and transport, and personnel using the distinctive emblems of the Geneva Conventions in conformity with international law;

(xxv) Intentionally using starvation of civilians as a method of warfare by depriving them of objects indispensable to their survival, including wilfully impeding relief supplies as provided for under the Geneva Conventions;

(xxvi) Conscripting or enlisting children under the age of fifteen years into the national armed forces or using them to participate actively in hostilities.

(c) In the case of an armed conflict not of an international character, serious violations of article 3 common to the four Geneva Conventions of 12 August 1949, namely, any of the following acts committed against persons taking no active part in the hostilities, including members of armed forces who have laid down their arms and those placed *hors de combat* by sickness, wounds, detention or any other cause:

(i) Violence to life and person, in particular murder of all kinds, mutilation, cruel treatment and torture;

(ii) Committing outrages upon personal dignity, in particular humiliating and degrading treatment;

(iii) Taking of hostages;

(iv) The passing of sentences and the carrying out of executions without previous judgement pronounced by a regularly constituted court, affording all judicial guarantees which are generally recognized as indispensable.

(d) Paragraph 2(c) applies to armed conflicts not of an international character and thus does not apply to situations of internal disturbances and tensions, such as riots, isolated and sporadic acts of violence or other acts of a similar nature.

(e) Other serious violations of the laws and customs applicable in armed conflicts not of an international character, within the established framework of international law, namely, any of the following acts:

(i) Intentionally directing attacks against the civilian population as such or against individual civilians not taking direct part in hostilities;

(ii) Intentionally directing attacks against buildings, material, medical units and transport, and personnel using the distinctive emblems of the Geneva Conventions in conformity with international law;

(iii) Intentionally directing attacks against personnel, installations, material, units or vehicles involved in a humanitarian assistance or peacekeeping mission in accordance with the Charter of the United Nations, as long as they are entitled to the protection given to civilians or civilian objects under the international law of armed conflict;

(iv) Intentionally directing attacks against buildings dedicated to religion, education, art, science or charitable purposes, historic monuments, hospitals and places where the sick and wounded are collected, provided they are not military objectives;

(v) Pillaging a town or place, even when taken by assault;

(vi) Committing rape, sexual slavery, enforced prostitution, forced pregnancy, as defined in article 7, paragraph 2(f), enforced sterilization, and any other form of sexual violence also constituting a serious violation of article 3 common to the four Geneva Conventions;

(vii) Conscripting or enlisting children under the age of fifteen years into armed forces or groups or using them to participate actively in hostilities;

(viii) Ordering the displacement of the civilian population for reasons related to the conflict, unless the security of the civilians involved or imperative military reasons so demand;

(ix) Killing or wounding treacherously a combatant adversary;

(x) Declaring that no quarter will be given;

(xi) Subjecting persons who are in the power of another party to the conflict to physical mutilation or to medical or scientific experiments of any kind which are neither justified by the medical, dental or hospital treatment of the person concerned nor carried out in his or her interest, and which cause death to or seriously endanger the health of such person or persons;

(xii) Destroying or seizing the property of an adversary unless such destruction or seizure be imperatively demanded by the necessities of the conflict;

(f) Paragraph 2(e) applies to armed conflicts not of an international character and thus does not apply to situations of internal disturbances and tensions, such as riots, isolated and sporadic acts of violence or other acts of a similar nature. It applies to armed conflicts that take place in the territory of a State when there is protracted armed conflict between governmental authorities and organized armed groups or between such groups.

3. Nothing in paragraph 2(c) and (e) shall affect the responsibility of a Government to maintain or re-establish law and order in the State or to defend the unity and territorial integrity of the State, by all legitimate means.

Article 9
Elements of Crimes

1. Elements of Crimes shall assist the Court in the interpretation and application of articles 6, 7 and 8. They shall be adopted by a two-thirds majority of the members of the Assembly of States Parties.

Article 10

Nothing in this Part shall be interpreted as limiting or prejudicing in any way existing or developing rules of international law for purposes other than this Statute.

Article 11
Jurisdiction ratione temporis

1. The Court has jurisdiction only with respect to crimes committed after the entry into force of this Statute.

2. If a State becomes a Party to this Statute after its entry into force, the Court may exercise its jurisdiction only with respect to crimes committed after the entry into force of this Statute for that State, unless that State has made a declaration under article 12, paragraph 3.

Article 12
Preconditions to the exercise of jurisdiction

1. A State which becomes a Party to this Statute thereby accepts the jurisdiction of the Court with respect to the crimes referred to in article 5.

2. In the case of article 13, paragraph (a) or (c), the Court may exercise its jurisdiction if one or more of the following States are Parties to this Statute or have accepted the jurisdiction of the Court in accordance with paragraph 3:

(a) The State on the territory of which the conduct in question occurred or, if the crime was committed on board a vessel or aircraft, the State of registration of that vessel or aircraft;

(b) The State of which the person accused of the crime is a national.

3. If the acceptance of a State which is not a Party to this Statute is required under paragraph 2, that State may, by declaration lodged with the Registrar, accept the exercise of jurisdiction by the Court with respect to the crime in question. The accepting State shall cooperate with the Court without any delay or exception in accordance with Part 9 [International Cooperation and Judicial Assistance].

Article 13
Exercise of jurisdiction

The Court may exercise its jurisdiction with respect to a crime referred to in article 5 in accordance with the provisions of this Statute if:

(a) A situation in which one or more of such crimes appears to have been committed is referred to the Prosecutor by a State Party in accordance with article 14;

(b) A situation in which one or more of such crimes appears to have been committed is referred to the Prosecutor by the Security Council acting under Chapter VII of the Charter of the United Nations; or

(c) The Prosecutor has initiated an investigation in respect of such a crime in accordance with article 15.

Article 14
Referral of a situation by a State Party

1. A State Party may refer to the Prosecutor a situation in which one or more crimes within the jurisdiction of the Court appear to have been committed requesting the Prosecutor to investigate the situation for the purpose of determining whether one or more specific persons should be charged with the commission of such crimes.

Article 15
Prosecutor

1. The Prosecutor may initiate investigations *proprio motu* on the basis of information on crimes within the jurisdiction of the Court.

2. The Prosecutor shall analyse the seriousness of the information received. For this purpose, he or she may seek additional information from States, organs of the United Nations, intergovernmental or non-governmental organizations, or other reliable sources that he or she deems appropriate, and may receive written or oral testimony at the seat of the Court.

3. If the Prosecutor concludes that there is a reasonable basis to proceed with an investigation, he or she shall submit to the Pre-Trial Chamber a request for authorization of an investigation, together with any supporting material collected.

Victims may make representations to the Pre-Trial Chamber, in accordance with the Rules of Procedure and Evidence.

4. If the Pre-Trial Chamber, upon examination of the request and the supporting material, considers that there is a reasonable basis to proceed with an investigation, and that the case appears to fall within the jurisdiction of the Court, it shall authorize the commencement of the investigation, without prejudice to subsequent determinations by the Court with regard to the jurisdiction and admissibility of a case.

Article 16
Deferral of investigation or prosecution

No investigation or prosecution may be commenced or proceeded with under this Statute for a period of 12 months after the Security Council, in a resolution adopted under Chapter VII of the Charter of the United Nations, has requested the Court to that effect; that request may be renewed by the Council under the same conditions.

Article 17
Issues of admissibility

1. Having regard to paragraph 10 of the Preamble and article 1, the Court shall determine that a case is inadmissible where:

(a) The case is being investigated or prosecuted by a State which has jurisdiction over it, unless the State is unwilling or unable genuinely to carry out the investigation or prosecution;

(b) The case has been investigated by a State which has jurisdiction over it and the State has decided not to prosecute the person concerned, unless the decision resulted from the unwillingness or inability of the State genuinely to prosecute;

(c) The person concerned has already been tried for conduct which is the subject of the complaint, and a trial by the Court is not permitted under article 20, paragraph 3;

(d) The case is not of sufficient gravity to justify further action by the Court.

2. In order to determine unwillingness in a particular case, the Court shall consider, having regard to the principles of due process recognized by international law, whether one or more of the following exist, as applicable:

(a) The proceedings were or are being undertaken or the national decision was made for the purpose of shielding the person concerned from criminal responsibility for crimes within the jurisdiction of the Court referred to in article 5;

(b) There has been an unjustified delay in the proceedings which in the circumstances is inconsistent with an intent to bring the person concerned to justice;

(c) The proceedings were not or are not being conducted independently or impartially, and they were or are being conducted in a manner which, in the circumstances, is inconsistent with an intent to bring the person concerned to justice.

3. In order to determine inability in a particular case, the Court shall consider

whether, due to a total or substantial collapse or unavailability of its national judicial system, the State is unable to obtain the accused or the necessary evidence and testimony or otherwise unable to carry out its proceedings.

Article 18
Preliminary rulings regarding admissibility

1. When a situation has been referred to the Court pursuant to article 13(a) and the Prosecutor has determined that there would be a reasonable basis to commence an investigation, or the Prosecutor initiates an investigation pursuant to articles 13(c) and 15, the Prosecutor shall notify all States Parties and those States which, taking into account the information available, would normally exercise jurisdiction over the crimes concerned. The Prosecutor may notify such States on a confidential basis and, where the Prosecutor believes it necessary to protect persons, prevent destruction of evidence or prevent the absconding of persons, may limit the scope of the information provided to States.

2. Within one month of receipt of that notification, a State may inform the Court that it is investigating or has investigated its nationals or others within its jurisdiction with respect to criminal acts which may constitute crimes referred to in article 5 and which relate to the information provided in the notification to States. At the request of that State, the Prosecutor shall defer to the State's investigation of those persons unless the Pre-Trial Chamber, on the application of the Prosecutor, decides to authorize the investigation.

3. The Prosecutor's deferral to a State's investigation shall be open to review by the Prosecutor six months after the date of deferral or at any time when there has been a significant change of circumstances based on the State's unwillingness or inability genuinely to carry out the investigation.

4. The State concerned or the Prosecutor may appeal to the Appeals Chamber against a ruling of the Pre-Trial Chamber, in accordance with article 82. The appeal may be heard on an expedited basis.

5. When the Prosecutor has deferred an investigation in accordance with paragraph 2, the Prosecutor may request that the State concerned periodically inform the Prosecutor of the progress of its investigations and any subsequent prosecutions. States Parties shall respond to such requests without undue delay.

6. Pending a ruling by the Pre-Trial Chamber, or at any time when the Prosecutor has deferred an investigation under this article, the Prosecutor may, on an exceptional basis, seek authority from the Pre-Trial Chamber to pursue necessary investigative steps for the purpose of preserving evidence where there is a unique opportunity to obtain important evidence or there is a significant risk that such evidence may not be subsequently available.

7. A State which has challenged a ruling of the Pre-Trial Chamber under this article may challenge the admissibility of a case under article 19 on the grounds of additional significant facts or significant change of circumstances.

Article 20
Ne bis in idem

1. Except as provided in this Statute, no person shall be tried before the Court

with respect to conduct which formed the basis of crimes for which the person has been convicted or acquitted by the Court.

2. No person shall be tried by another court for a crime referred to in article 5 for which that person has already been convicted or acquitted by the Court.

3. No person who has been tried by another court for conduct also proscribed under article 6, 7 or 8 shall be tried by the Court with respect to the same conduct unless the proceedings in the other court:

(a) Were for the purpose of shielding the person concerned from criminal responsibility for crimes within the jurisdiction of the Court; or

(b) Otherwise were not conducted independently or impartially in accordance with the norms of due process recognized by international law and were conducted in a manner which, in the circumstances, was inconsistent with an intent to bring the person concerned to justice.

Article 22
Nullum crimen sine lege

1. A person shall not be criminally responsible under this Statute unless the conduct in question constitutes, at the time it takes place, a crime within the jurisdiction of the Court.

2. The definition of a crime shall be strictly construed and shall not be extended by analogy. In case of ambiguity, the definition shall be interpreted in favour of the person being investigated, prosecuted or convicted.

Article 25
Individual criminal responsibility

1. The Court shall have jurisdiction over natural persons pursuant to this Statute.

2. A person who commits a crime within the jurisdiction of the Court shall be individually responsible and liable for punishment in accordance with this Statute.

3. In accordance with this Statute, a person shall be criminally responsible and liable for punishment for a crime within the jurisdiction of the Court if that person:

(a) Commits such a crime, whether as an individual, jointly with another or through another person, regardless of whether that other person is criminally responsible;

(b) Orders, solicits or induces the commission of such a crime which in fact occurs or is attempted;

(c) For the purpose of facilitating the commission of such a crime, aids, abets or otherwise assists in its commission or its attempted commission, including providing the means for its commission;

(d) In any other way contributes to the commission or attempted commission of such a crime by a group of persons acting with a common purpose. Such contribution shall be intentional and shall either:

(i) Be made with the aim of furthering the criminal activity or criminal purpose of the group, where such activity or purpose involves the commission of a crime within the jurisdiction of the Court; or

(ii) Be made in the knowledge of the intention of the group to commit the crime;

(e) In respect of the crime of genocide, directly and publicly incites others to commit genocide;

(f) Attempts to commit such a crime by taking action that commences its execution by means of a substantial step, but the crime does not occur because of circumstances independent of the person's intentions. However, a person who abandons the effort to commit the crime or otherwise prevents the completion of the crime shall not be liable for punishment under this Statute for the attempt to commit that crime if that person completely and voluntarily gave up the criminal purpose.

Article 27
Irrelevance of official capacity

1. This Statute shall apply equally to all persons without any distinction based on official capacity. In particular, official capacity as a Head of State or Government, a member of a Government or parliament, an elected representative or a government official shall in no case exempt a person from criminal responsibility under this Statute, nor shall it, in and of itself, constitute a ground for reduction of sentence.

2. Immunities or special procedural rules which may attach to the official capacity of a person, whether under national or international law, shall not bar the Court from exercising its jurisdiction over such a person.

Article 28
Responsibility of commanders and other superiors

In addition to other grounds of criminal responsibility under this Statute for crimes within the jurisdiction of the Court:

(a) A military commander or person effectively acting as a military commander shall be criminally responsible for crimes within the jurisdiction of the Court committed by forces under his or her effective command and control, or effective authority and control as the case may be, as a result of his or her failure to exercise control properly over such forces, where:

(i) That military commander or person either knew or, owing to the circumstances at the time, should have known that the forces were committing or about to commit such crimes; and

(ii) That military commander or person failed to take all necessary and reasonable measures within his or her power to prevent or repress their commission or to submit the matter to the competent authorities for investigation and prosecution.

(b) With respect to superior and subordinate relationships not described in paragraph (a), a superior shall be criminally responsible for crimes within the jurisdiction of the Court committed by subordinates under his or her effective authority and control, as a result of his or her failure to exercise control properly over such subordinates, where:

(i) The superior either knew, or consciously disregarded information which clearly indicated, that the subordinates were committing or about to commit such crimes;

(ii) The crimes concerned activities that were within the effective responsibility and control of the superior; and

(iii) The superior failed to take all necessary and reasonable measures within his or her power to prevent or repress their commission or to submit the matter to the competent authorities for investigation and prosecution.

Article 29
Non-applicability of statute of limitations

The crimes within the jurisdiction of the Court shall not be subject to any statute of limitations.

Article 30
Mental element

1. Unless otherwise provided, a person shall be criminally responsible and liable for punishment for a crime within the jurisdiction of the Court only if the material elements are committed with intent and knowledge.

2. For the purposes of this article, a person has intent where:

(a) In relation to conduct, that person means to engage in the conduct;

(b) In relation to a consequence, that person means to cause that consequence or is aware that it will occur in the ordinary course of events.

3. For the purposes of this article, 'knowledge' means awareness that a circumstance exists or a consequence will occur in the ordinary course of events. 'Know' and 'knowingly' shall be construed accordingly.

Article 31
Grounds for excluding criminal responsibility

1. In addition to other grounds for excluding criminal responsibility provided for in this Statute, a person shall not be criminally responsible if, at the time of that person's conduct:

(a) The person suffers from a mental disease or defect that destroys that person's capacity to appreciate the unlawfulness or nature of his or her conduct, or capacity to control his or her conduct to conform to the requirements of law;

(b) The person is in a state of intoxication that destroys that person's capacity to appreciate the unlawfulness or nature of his or her conduct, or capacity to control his or her conduct to conform to the requirements of law, unless the person has become voluntarily intoxicated under such circumstances that the person knew, or disregarded the risk, that, as a result of the intoxication, he or she was likely to engage in conduct constituting a crime within the jurisdiction of the Court;

(c) The person acts reasonably to defend himself or herself or another person or, in the case of war crimes, property which is essential for the survival of the person or another person or property which is essential for accomplishing a military mission, against an imminent and unlawful use of force in a manner proportionate to the degree of danger to the person or the other person or property protected. The fact that the person was involved in a defensive operation conducted by forces shall not in itself constitute a ground for excluding criminal responsibility under this subparagraph;

(d) The conduct which is alleged to constitute a crime within the jurisdiction of the Court has been caused by duress resulting from a threat of imminent death or of continuing or imminent serious bodily harm against that person or another person, and the person acts necessarily and reasonably to avoid this threat, provided that the person does not intend to cause a greater harm than the one sought to be avoided. Such a threat may either be:

(i) Made by other persons; or

(ii) Constituted by other circumstances beyond that person's control.

Article 32

Mistake of fact or mistake of law

1. A mistake of fact shall be a ground for excluding criminal responsibility only if it negates the mental element required by the crime.

2. A mistake of law as to whether a particular type of conduct is a crime within the jurisdiction of the Court shall not be a ground for excluding criminal responsibility. A mistake of law may, however, be a ground for excluding criminal responsibility if it negates the mental element required by such a crime, or as provided for in article 33.

Article 33

Superior orders and prescription of law

1. The fact that a crime within the jurisdiction of the Court has been committed by a person pursuant to an order of a Government or of a superior, whether military or civilian, shall not relieve that person of criminal responsibility unless:

(a) The person was under a legal obligation to obey orders of the Government or the superior in question;

(b) The person did not know that the order was unlawful; and

(c) The order was not manifestly unlawful.

2. For the purposes of this article, orders to commit genocide or crimes against humanity are manifestly unlawful.

Article 53

Initiation of an investigation

1. The Prosecutor shall, having evaluated the information made available to him or her, initiate an investigation unless he or she determines that there is no reasonable basis to proceed under this Statute. In deciding whether to initiate an investigation, the Prosecutor shall consider whether:

(a) The information available to the Prosecutor provides a reasonable basis to believe that a crime within the jurisdiction of the Court has been or is being committed;

(b) The case is or would be admissible under article 17; and

(c) Taking into account the gravity of the crime and the interests of victims, there are nonetheless substantial reasons to believe that an investigation would not serve the interests of justice.

If the Prosecutor determines that there is no reasonable basis to proceed and his or her determination is based solely on subparagraph (c) above, he or she shall inform the Pre-Trial Chamber.

2. If, upon investigation, the Prosecutor concludes that there is not a sufficient basis for a prosecution because:

(a) There is not a sufficient legal or factual basis to seek a warrant or summons under article 58;

(b) The case is inadmissible under article 17; or

(c) A prosecution is not in the interests of justice, taking into account all the circumstances, including the gravity of the crime, the interests of victims and the age or infirmity of the alleged perpetrator, and his or her role in the alleged crime;

the Prosecutor shall inform the Pre-Trial Chamber and the State making a referral under article 14 or the Security Council in a case under article 13, paragraph (b), of his or her conclusion and the reasons for the conclusion.

Article 54
Duties and powers of the Prosecutor with respect to investigations

1. The Prosecutor shall:

(a) In order to establish the truth, extend the investigation to cover all facts and evidence relevant to an assessment of whether there is criminal responsibility under this Statute, and, in doing so, investigate incriminating and exonerating circumstances equally;

3. The Prosecutor may:

(a) Collect and examine evidence;

(b) Request the presence of and question persons being investigated, victims and witnesses;

(c) Seek the cooperation of any State or intergovernmental organization or arrangement in accordance with its respective competence and/or mandate;

(e) Agree not to disclose, at any stage of the proceedings, documents or information that the Prosecutor obtains on the condition of confidentiality and solely for the purpose of generating new evidence, unless the provider of the information consents; and

(f) Take necessary measures, or request that necessary measures be taken, to ensure the confidentiality of information, the protection of any person or the preservation of evidence.

Article 58
Issuance by the Pre-Trial Chamber of a warrant of arrest or a summons to appear

1. At any time after the initiation of an investigation, the Pre-Trial Chamber shall, on the application of the Prosecutor, issue a warrant of arrest of a person if, having examined the application and the evidence or other information submitted by the Prosecutor, it is satisfied that:

(a) There are reasonable grounds to believe that the person has committed a crime within the jurisdiction of the Court; and

(b) The arrest of the person appears necessary:

(i) To ensure the person's appearance at trial,

(ii) To ensure that the person does not obstruct or endanger the investigation or the court proceedings, or

(iii) Where applicable, to prevent the person from continuing with the commission of that crime or a related crime which is within the jurisdiction of the Court and which arises out of the same circumstances.

Article 59
Arrest proceedings in the custodial State

1. A State Party which has received a request for provisional arrest or for arrest and surrender shall immediately take steps to arrest the person in question in accordance with its laws and the provisions of Part 9 [International Cooperation and Judicial Assistance].

2. A person arrested shall be brought promptly before the competent judicial authority in the custodial State which shall determine, in accordance with the law of that State, that:

(a) The warrant applies to that person;
(b) The person has been arrested in accordance with the proper process; and
(c) The person's rights have been respected.

Article 63
Trial in the presence of the accused

1. The accused shall be present during the trial.

Article 64
Functions and powers of the Trial Chamber

2. The Trial Chamber shall ensure that a trial is fair and expeditious and is conducted with full respect for the rights of the accused and due regard for the protection of victims and witnesses.

6. In performing its functions prior to trial or during the course of a trial, the Trial Chamber may, as necessary:

(b) Require the attendance and testimony of witnesses and production of documents and other evidence by obtaining, if necessary, the assistance of States as provided in this Statute;

(c) Provide for the protection of confidential information;

(d) Order the production of evidence in addition to that already collected prior to the trial or presented during the trial by the parties;

(e) Provide for the protection of the accused, witnesses and victims; and

(f) Rule on any other relevant matters.

7. The trial shall be held in public. The Trial Chamber may, however, determine that special circumstances require that certain proceedings be in closed session for the purposes set forth in article 68, or to protect confidential or sensitive information to be given in evidence.

Article 66
Presumption of innocence

1. Everyone shall be presumed innocent until proved guilty before the Court in accordance with the applicable law.

2. The onus is on the Prosecutor to prove the guilt of the accused.

3. In order to convict the accused, the Court must be convinced of the guilt of the accused beyond reasonable doubt.

Article 67
Rights of the accused

1. In the determination of any charge, the accused shall be entitled to a public hearing, having regard to the provisions of this Statute, to a fair hearing conducted impartially, and to the following minimum guarantees, in full equality:

(a) To be informed promptly and in detail of the nature, cause and content of the charge, in a language which the accused fully understands and speaks;

(b) To have adequate time and facilities for the preparation of the defence and to communicate freely with counsel of the accused's choosing in confidence;

(c) To be tried without undue delay;

(d) Subject to article 63, paragraph 2, to be present at the trial, to conduct the defence in person or through legal assistance of the accused's choosing, to be informed, if the accused does not have legal assistance, of this right and to have legal assistance assigned by the Court in any case where the interests of justice so require, and without payment if the accused lacks sufficient means to pay for it;

(e) To examine, or have examined, the witnesses against him or her and to obtain the attendance and examination of witnesses on his or her behalf under the same conditions as witnesses against him or her. The accused shall also be entitled to raise defences and to present other evidence admissible under this Statute;

(f) To have, free of any cost, the assistance of a competent interpreter and such translations as are necessary to meet the requirements of fairness, if any of the proceedings of or documents presented to the Court are not in a language which the accused fully understands and speaks;

(g) Not to be compelled to testify or to confess guilt and to remain silent, without such silence being a consideration in the determination of guilt or innocence;

(h) To make an unsworn oral or written statement in his or her defence; and

(i) Not to have imposed on him or her any reversal of the burden of proof or any onus of rebuttal.

2. In addition to any other disclosure provided for in this Statute, the Prosecutor shall, as soon as practicable, disclose to the defence evidence in the Prosecutor's possession or control which he or she believes shows or tends to show the innocence of the accused, or to mitigate the guilt of the accused, or which may affect the credibility of prosecution evidence. In case of doubt as to the application of this paragraph, the Court shall decide.

Article 68
Protection of the victims and witnesses and their participation in the proceedings

1. The Court shall take appropriate measures to protect the safety, physical and psychological well-being, dignity and privacy of victims and witnesses. In so doing, the Court shall have regard to all relevant factors, including age, gender as defined in article 7, paragraph 3, and health, and the nature of the crime, in particular, but not limited to, where the crime involves sexual or gender violence or violence against children. The Prosecutor shall take such measures particularly during the investigation and prosecution of such crimes. These measures shall not be prejudicial to or inconsistent with the rights of the accused and a fair and impartial trial.

2. As an exception to the principle of public hearings provided for in article 67, the Chambers of the Court may, to protect victims and witnesses or an accused, conduct any part of the proceedings *in camera* or allow the presentation of evidence by electronic or other special means. In particular, such measures shall be implemented in the case of a victim of sexual violence or a child who is a victim or a witness, unless otherwise ordered by the Court, having regard to all the circumstances, particularly the views of the victim or witness.

3. Where the personal interests of the victims are affected, the Court shall permit their views and concerns to be presented and considered at stages of the proceedings determined to be appropriate by the Court and in a manner which is not prejudicial to or inconsistent with the rights of the accused and a fair and impartial trial. Such views and concerns may be presented by the legal representatives of the victims where the Court considers it appropriate, in accordance with the Rules of Procedure and Evidence.

Article 69
Evidence

4. The Court may rule on the relevance or admissibility of any evidence, taking into account, *inter alia*, the probative value of the evidence and any prejudice that such evidence may cause to a fair trial or to a fair evaluation of the testimony of a witness, in accordance with the Rules of Procedure and Evidence.

7. Evidence obtained by means of a violation of this Statute or internationally recognized human rights shall not be admissible if:

(a) The violation casts substantial doubt on the reliability of the evidence; or

(b) The admission of the evidence would be antithetical to and would seriously damage the integrity of the proceedings.

Article 72
Protection of national security information

5. If, in the opinion of a State, disclosure of information would prejudice its national security interests, all reasonable steps will be taken by the State, acting in conjunction with the Prosecutor, the defence or the Pre-Trial Chamber or Trial Chamber, as the case may be, to seek to resolve the matter by cooperative means. Such steps may include:

(a) Modification or clarification of the request;

(b) A determination by the Court regarding the relevance of the information or evidence sought, or a determination as to whether the evidence, though relevant, could be or has been obtained from a source other than the requested State;

(c) Obtaining the information or evidence from a different source or in a different form; or

(d) Agreement on conditions under which the assistance could be provided including, among other things, providing summaries or redactions, limitations on disclosure, use of *in camera* or *ex parte* proceedings, or other protective measures permissible under the Statute and the Rules of Procedure and Evidence.

6. Once all reasonable steps have been taken to resolve the matter through cooperative means, and if the State considers that there are no means or condi-

tions under which the information or documents could be provided or disclosed without prejudice to its national security interests, it shall so notify the Prosecutor or the Court of the specific reasons for its decision, unless a specific description of the reasons would itself necessarily result in such prejudice to the State's national security interests.

7. Thereafter, if the Court determines that the evidence is relevant and necessary for the establishment of the guilt or innocence of the accused, the Court may undertake the following actions:

(a) Where disclosure of the information or document is sought pursuant to a request for cooperation under Part 9 [International Cooperation and Judicial Assistance] or the circumstances described in paragraph 2, and the State has invoked the ground for refusal referred to in article 93, paragraph 4:

(ii) If the Court concludes that, by invoking the ground for refusal under article 93, paragraph 4, in the circumstances of the case, the requested State is not acting in accordance with its obligations under this Statute, the Court may refer the matter in accordance with article 87, paragraph 7, specifying the reasons for its conclusion; and

(iii) The Court may make such inference in the trial of the accused as to the existence or non-existence of a fact, as may be appropriate in the circumstances; or

(b) In all other circumstances:

(i) Order disclosure; or

(ii) To the extent it does not order disclosure, make such inference in the trial of the accused as to the existence or non-existence of a fact, as may be appropriate in the circumstances.

Article 74
Requirements for the decision

3. The judges shall attempt to achieve unanimity in their decision, failing which the decision shall be taken by a majority of the judges.

Article 75
Reparations to victims

2. The Court may make an order directly against a convicted person specifying appropriate reparations to, or in respect of, victims, including restitution, compensation and rehabilitation.

Article 77
Applicable penalties

1. Subject to article 110, the Court may impose one of the following penalties on a person convicted of a crime referred to in article 5 of this Statute:

(a) Imprisonment for a specified number of years, which may not exceed a maximum of 30 years; or

(b) A term of life imprisonment when justified by the extreme gravity of the crime and the individual circumstances of the convicted person.

2. In addition to imprisonment, the Court may order:

(a) A fine under the criteria provided for in the Rules of Procedure and Evidence;

(b) A forfeiture of proceeds, property and assets derived directly or indirectly from that crime, without prejudice to the rights of bona fide third parties.

Article 81

Appeal against decision of acquittal or conviction or against sentence

1. A decision under article 74 may be appealed in accordance with the Rules of Procedure and Evidence as follows:

(a) The Prosecutor may make an appeal on any of the following grounds:
- (i) Procedural error,
- (ii) Error of fact, or
- (iii) Error of law;

(b) The convicted person, or the Prosecutor on that person's behalf, may make an appeal on any of the following grounds:
- (i) Procedural error,
- (ii) Error of fact,
- (iii) Error of law, or
- (iv) Any other ground that affects the fairness or reliability of the proceedings or decision.

Article 83

Proceedings on appeal

2. If the Appeals Chamber finds that the proceedings appealed from were unfair in a way that affected the reliability of the decision or sentence, or that the decision or sentence appealed from was materially affected by error of fact or law or procedural error, it may:

(a) Reverse or amend the decision or sentence; or

(b) Order a new trial before a different Trial Chamber.

Article 86

General obligation to cooperate

States Parties shall, in accordance with the provisions of this Statute, cooperate fully with the Court in its investigation and prosecution of crimes within the jurisdiction of the Court.

Article 87

Requests for cooperation: general provisions

1. (a) The Court shall have the authority to make requests to States Parties for cooperation. The requests shall be transmitted through the diplomatic channel or any other appropriate channel as may be designated by each State Party upon ratification, acceptance, approval or accession.

7. Where a State Party fails to comply with a request to cooperate by the Court contrary to the provisions of this Statute, thereby preventing the Court from exercising its functions and powers under this Statute, the Court may make a finding to that effect and refer the matter to the Assembly of States Parties or, where the Security Council referred the matter to the Court, to the Security Council.

Article 89
Surrender of persons to the Court

1. The Court may transmit a request for the arrest and surrender of a person, together with the material supporting the request outlined in article 91, to any State on the territory of which that person may be found and shall request the cooperation of that State in the arrest and surrender of such a person. States Parties shall, in accordance with the provisions of this Part and the procedure under their national law, comply with requests for arrest and surrender.

Article 101
Rule of speciality

1. A person surrendered to the Court under this Statute shall not be proceeded against, punished or detained for any conduct committed prior to surrender, other than the conduct or course of conduct which forms the basis of the crimes for which that person has been surrendered.

2. The Court may request a waiver of the requirements of paragraph 1 from the State which surrendered the person to the Court and, if necessary, the Court shall provide additional information in accordance with article 91. States Parties shall have the authority to provide a waiver to the Court and should endeavour to do so.

Article 105
Enforcement of the sentence

2. The Court alone shall have the right to decide any application for appeal and revision. The State of enforcement shall not impede the making of any such application by a sentenced person.

Article 124
Transitional Provision

Notwithstanding article 12, paragraphs 1 and 2, a State, on becoming a party to this Statute, may declare that, for a period of seven years after the entry into force of this Statute for the State concerned, it does not accept the jurisdiction of the Court with respect to the category of crimes referred to in article 8 when a crime is alleged to have been committed by its nationals or on its territory. A declaration under this article may be withdrawn at any time. The provisions of this article shall be reviewed at the Review Conference convened in accordance with article 123, paragraph 1.

20. United States Alien Tort Claims Act, 1789

The district courts shall have original jurisdiction of any civil action by an alien for a tort only, committed in violation of the law of nations or a treaty of the United States.

21. United States Torture Victim Protection Act, 1991

Sec. 2. Establishment of civil action.

(a) Liability.—An individual who, under actual or apparent authority, or color of law, of any foreign nation—

(1) subjects an individual to torture shall, in a civil action, be liable for damages to that individual; or

(2) subjects an individual to extrajudicial killing shall, in a civil action, be liable for damages to the individual's legal representative, or to any person who may be a claimant in an action for wrongful death.

(b) Exhaustion of remedies.—A court shall decline to hear a claim under this section if the claimant has not exhausted adequate and available remedies in the place in which the conduct giving rise to the claim occurred.

(c) Statute of limitations.—No action shall be maintained under this section unless it is commenced within 10 years after the cause of action arose.

Bibliography

The following bibliography lists the secondary sources used in the research for this volume, as well as a core group of United Nations and other official reports. The list of secondary sources is divided into four categories: general international law, offenses under international law, mechanisms for accountability, and Cambodia and the Khmer Rouge. Where a source straddles more than one category, it is listed based upon the subject matter for which the authors principally used the source in their research. Where several sources appear in one edited work or symposium issue of a journal, only that work is cited. The list does not include newspaper articles, short magazine articles, or wire service reports. Beyond the intergovernmental and governmental reports listed at the end of this bibliography, information on all other primary sources—such as treaties, cases, statutes, UN resolutions, and other documents—may be found in the relevant footnotes as well as, in some cases, the list of abbreviations used in the notes located on page xvi.

General International Law (including Human Rights)

Baxter, Richard, *Multilateral Treaties as Evidence of Customary International Law*, 41 British Year Book of International Law 275 (1965–66)

Bernhardt, Rudolph (ed.), Encyclopedia of Public International Law (2 vols.), Amsterdam: North Holland Publishing Co., 1992, 1995

Brownlie, Ian, Principles of Public International Law (5th edn.), Oxford: Clarendon Press, 1998

Cheng, Bin, General Principles of Law as Applied by International Courts and Tribunals (1953), Cambridge: Grotius Publications, 1987

de Vattel, Emmeric, Le Droit des Gens (Vol. 1, 1758, Charles G. Fenwick (trans.)), Washington, DC: Carnegie Institution, 1916

Dinh, Nguyen Quoc, Droit International Public (Patrick Daillier and Alain Pellet (eds.), 5th edn.), Paris: Librairie Générale de Droit et de Jurisprudence, 1994

Hannum, Hurst (ed.), Guide to International Human Rights Practice (3d edn.), Philadelphia, Penn.: University of Pennsylvania Press, 1999

Heller, Agnes, *The Limits to Natural Law and the Paradox of Evil, in* On Human Rights: The Oxford Amnesty Lectures 149 (Stephen Shute and Susan Hurley (eds.)), New York: Basic Books, 1993

Higgins, Rosalyn, Problems and Process: International Law and How We Use It, Oxford: Clarendon Press, 1994

Jennings, Robert, and Watts, Arthur (eds.), Oppenheim's International Law (2 vols., 9th edn.), Harlow: Longman, 1992

Lansing, Robert, *Notes on World Sovereignty*, 15 American Journal of International Law 13 (1921)

LAUTERPACHT, HERSCH, INTERNATIONAL LAW AND HUMAN RIGHTS, New York: F.A. Praeger, 1950

—— (ED.), OPPENHEIM'S INTERNATIONAL LAW (2 vols., 7th edn.), London: Longmans Green, 1952

MCDOUGAL, MYRES S., and REISMAN, W. MICHAEL (EDS.), INTERNATIONAL LAW ESSAYS, Mineola, NY: Foundation Press, 1981

—— LASSWELL, HAROLD D., and CHEN, LUNG-CHU, HUMAN RIGHTS AND WORLD PUBLIC ORDER: THE BASIC POLICIES OF AN INTERNATIONAL LAW OF HUMAN DIGNITY, New Haven, Conn.: Yale University Press, 1980

MERON, THEODOR (ED.), HUMAN RIGHTS IN INTERNATIONAL LAW: LEGAL AND POLICY ISSUES, Oxford: Clarendon Press, 1984

Paust, Jordan J., *The Complex Nature, Sources and Evidences of Customary Human Rights*, 25 GEORGIA JOURNAL OF INTERNATIONAL AND COMPARATIVE LAW 147 (1995/96)

Reisman, W. Michael, *Private Armies in a Global War System: Prologue to Decision*, 14 VIRGINIA JOURNAL OF INTERNATIONAL LAW 1 (1973)

—— *Sovereignty and Human Rights in Contemporary International Law*, 84 AMERICAN JOURNAL OF INTERNATIONAL LAW 866 (1990)

ROBERTSON, GEOFFREY, CRIMES AGAINST HUMANITY, London: Allen Lane, 1999

SASSÒLI, MARCO, and BOUVIER, ANTONIO A. (EDS.), HOW DOES LAW PROTECT IN WAR?, Geneva: International Committee of the Red Cross, 1999

SCHACHTER, OSCAR, INTERNATIONAL LAW IN THEORY AND PRACTICE, Dordrecht: Martinus Nijhoff Publishers, 1991

—— *The UN Legal Order: An Overview, in* UNITED NATIONS LEGAL ORDER (Vol. 1) 1 (Oscar Schachter and Christopher C. Joyner (eds.)), Washington, DC: American Society of International Law, 1995

Simma, Bruno, and Alston, Philip, *The Sources of Human Rights Law: Custom, Jus Cogens, and General Principles*, 12 AUSTRALIAN YEAR BOOK OF INTERNATIONAL LAW 82 (1992)

Sørenson, Max, *Principes de Droit International Public*, 101 RECUEIL DES COURS 1 (1960–III)

STEINER, HENRY J., and ALSTON, PHILIP (EDS.), INTERNATIONAL HUMAN RIGHTS IN CONTEXT: LAW, POLITICS, MORALS (2d edn.), Oxford: Clarendon Press, 2000

THORNBERRY, PATRICK, INTERNATIONAL LAW AND THE RIGHTS OF MINORITIES, Oxford: Clarendon Press, 1991

Weisburd, Arthur M., *The Effect of Treaties and Other Formal International Acts On the Customary Law of Human Rights*, 25 GEORGIA JOURNAL OF INTERNATIONAL AND COMPARATIVE LAW 99 (1995/96)

Offenses under International Law

Ackerman, Steven, *Torture and Other Forms of Cruel and Unusual Punishment in International Law*, 11 VANDERBILT JOURNAL OF TRANSNATIONAL Law 653 (1978)

Adams, Kif Augustine, *What is Just?: The Rule of Law and Natural Law in the Trials of Former East German Border Guards*, 29 STANFORD JOURNAL OF INTERNATIONAL LAW 271 (1993)

Akhavan, Payam, Memorandum on Crimes Against Humanity and Genocide, June 14, 1994 (prepared for the International Criminal Tribunal for the former Yugoslavia) (on file with authors)

ALLEN, BEVERLY, RAPE WARFARE: THE HIDDEN GENOCIDE IN BOSNIA-HERZEGOVINA AND CROATIA, Minneapolis, Minn.: University of Minnesota Press, 1996

AMERICAN LAW INSTITUTE, MODEL PENAL CODE AND COMMENTARIES, Philadelphia, Penn.: American Law Institute, 1985

ANDREOPOULOS, GEORGE J. (ED.), GENOCIDE: CONCEPTUAL AND HISTORICAL DIMENSIONS, Philadelphia, Penn.: University of Pennsylvania Press, 1994

APPLEMAN, JOHN ALAN, MILITARY TRIBUNALS AND INTERNATIONAL CRIMES, Indianapolis, Ind.: Bobbs-Merrill, 1954

Appraisals of the ICJ's Decision: Nicaragua v. United States, 81 AMERICAN JOURNAL OF INTERNATIONAL LAW 77 (1987)

ARONEANU, EUGENE, LE CRIME CONTRE L'HUMANITÉ, Paris: Dalloz, 1961

Arsanjani, Mahnoush H., *The Rome Statute of the International Criminal Court*, 93 AMERICAN JOURNAL OF INTERNATIONAL LAW 22 (1999)

ASIA WATCH and THE WOMEN'S RIGHTS PROJECT, A MODERN FORM OF SLAVERY: TRAFFICKING OF BURMESE WOMEN AND GIRLS INTO BROTHELS IN THAILAND, New York: Human Rights Watch, 1993

Askin, Kelly D., *Sexual Violence in Decisions and Indictments of the Yugoslav and Rwandan Tribunals: Current Status*, 93 AMERICAN JOURNAL OF INTERNATIONAL LAW 97 (1999)

Baade, Hans W., *The Eichmann Trial: Some Legal Aspects*, 1961 DUKE LAW JOURNAL 400 (1961)

—— *Individual Responsibility, in* THE FUTURE OF THE INTERNATIONAL LEGAL ORDER 291 (Cyril E. Black and Richard A. Falk (eds.)), Princeton, NJ: Princeton University Press, 1972

Bakker, Jeanne L., *The Defense of Obedience to Superior Orders: The Mens Rea Requirement*, 17 AMERICAN JOURNAL OF CRIMINAL LAW 55 (1989)

Bantekas, Ilias, *The Contemporary Law of Superior Responsibility*, 93 AMERICAN JOURNAL OF INTERNATIONAL LAW 573 (1999)

Bassiouni, M. Cherif, *An Appraisal of the Growth and Developing Trends of International Criminal Law*, 45 REVUE INTERNATIONALE DE DROIT PÉNAL 405 (1974)

—— *International Law and the Holocaust*, 9 CALIFORNIA WESTERN INTERNATIONAL LAW JOURNAL 201 (1979)

—— *The Proscribing Function of International Criminal Law in the Processes of International Protection of Human Rights*, 9 YALE JOURNAL OF WORLD PUBLIC ORDER 193 (1982)

—— *Reflections on Criminal Jurisdiction in International Protection of Cultural Property*, 10 SYRACUSE JOURNAL OF INTERNATIONAL LAW AND COMMERCE 281 (1983)

—— INTERNATIONAL CRIMES: DIGEST/INDEX OF INTERNATIONAL INSTRUMENTS 1815- 1985 (2 vols.), New York: Oceana, 1986

—— A DRAFT INTERNATIONAL CRIMINAL CODE AND DRAFT STATUTE FOR AN

INTERNATIONAL CRIMINAL TRIBUNAL, Dordrecht: Martinus Nijhoff Publishers, 1987

Bassiouni, M. Cherif, *Enslavement as an International Crime*, 23 NEW YORK UNIVERSITY JOURNAL OF INTERNATIONAL LAW AND POLITICS 445 (1991)

—— (ED.), COMMENTARIES ON THE INTERNATIONAL LAW COMMISSION'S 1991 DRAFT CODE OF CRIMES AGAINST THE PEACE AND SECURITY OF MANKIND, Toulouse: Erès, 1993

—— *Crimes Against Humanity: The Need for a Specialized Convention*, 31 COLUMBIA JOURNAL OF TRANSNATIONAL LAW 457 (1994)

—— CRIMES AGAINST HUMANITY IN INTERNATIONAL CRIMINAL LAW (2d edn.), The Hague: Kluwer Law International, 1999

—— (ED.), INTERNATIONAL CRIMINAL LAW (3 vols, 2d edn.), Ardsley, NY: Transnational Publishers, 1999

—— and NANDA, VED P. (EDS.), A TREATISE ON INTERNATIONAL CRIMINAL LAW (2 vols.), Springfield, Ill.: C. Thomas Publishers, 1973

Beres, Louis René, *Genocide, Law and Power Politics*, 10 WHITTIER LAW REVIEW 329 (1988)

—— *Genocide, State and Self*, 18 DENVER JOURNAL OF INTERNATIONAL LAW AND POLICY 37 (1989)

BEST, GEOFFREY, WAR AND LAW SINCE 1945, Oxford: Clarendon Press, 1994

Bianchi, Andrea, *Immunity versus Human Rights: The* Pinochet *Case*, 10 EUROPEAN JOURNAL OF INTERNATIONAL LAW 237 (1999)

BOND, JAMES E., THE RULES OF RIOT: INTERNAL CONFLICT AND THE LAW OF WAR, Princeton, NJ: Princeton University Press, 1974

BOSSUYT, MARC J., GUIDE TO THE 'TRAVAUX PRÉPARĀTOIRES' OF THE INTERNATIONAL COVENANT ON CIVIL AND POLITICAL RIGHTS, Dordrecht: Martinus Nijhoff Publishers, 1987

BOTHE, MICHAEL, PARTSCH, KARL JOSEF, and SOLF, WALDEMAR A., NEW RULES FOR VICTIMS OF ARMED CONFLICTS: COMMENTARY ON THE TWO 1977 PROTOCOLS ADDITIONAL TO THE GENEVA CONVENTIONS OF 1949, The Hague: Martinus Nijhoff Publishers, 1982

Boulesbaa, Ahcene, *An Analysis of the 1984 Draft Convention Against Torture and Other Cruel, Inhuman or Degrading Treatment or Punishment*, 4 DICKINSON JOURNAL OF INTERNATIONAL LAW 185 (1986)

—— *Analysis and Proposals for the Rectification of the Ambiguities Inherent in Article 1 of the U.N. Convention on Torture*, 5 FLORIDA INTERNATIONAL LAW JOURNAL 293 (1990)

BOWMAN, M.J., and HARRIS, D. J., MULTILATERAL TREATIES: INDEX AND CURRENT STATUS, London: Butterworths, 1984, 1995

Brand, James T., *Crimes Against Humanity and the Nürnberg Trials*, 28 OREGON LAW REVIEW 93 (1949)

Bröhmer, Jürgen, *Diplomatic Immunity, Head of State Immunity, State Immunity: Misconceptions of a Notorious Human Rights Violator*, 12 LEIDEN JOURNAL OF INTERNATIONAL LAW 361 (1999)

—— *Immunity of a Former Head of State: General Pinochet and the House of Lords: Part 3*, 13 LEIDEN JOURNAL OF INTERNATIONAL LAW 229 (2000)

Bruun, Lori Lyman, *Beyond the 1948 Convention—Emerging Principles of*

Genocide in Customary International Law, 17 MARYLAND JOURNAL OF INTERNATIONAL LAW AND TRADE 193 (1993)

Bryant, Bunyan, *Part I: Substantive Scope of the Convention, in The United States and the 1948 Genocide Convention*, 16 HARVARD INTERNATIONAL LAW JOURNAL 683 (1975)

BURGERS, J. HERMAN, and DANELIUS, HANS, THE UNITED NATIONS CONVENTION AGAINST TORTURE: A HANDBOOK ON THE CONVENTION AGAINST TORTURE AND OTHER CRUEL, INHUMAN OR DEGRADING TREATMENT OR PUNISHMENT, Dordrecht: Martinus Nijhoff Publishers, 1988

Carrillo-Suárez, Arturo, *Hors de Logique: Contemporary Issues in International Humanitarian Law as Applied to Internal Armed Conflict,* 15 AMERICAN UNIVERSITY INTERNATIONAL LAW REVIEW 1 (1999)

CASSESE, ANTONIO, (ED.), THE NEW HUMANITARIAN LAW OF ARMED CONFLICT, Naples: Editoriale Scientifica, 1979

—— *The Geneva Protocols of 1977 on the Humanitarian Law of Armed Conflict and Customary International Law*, 3 UNIVERSITY OF CALIFORNIA LOS ANGELES PACIFIC BASIN LAW JOURNAL 55 (1984)

Chuang, Janie, *Redirecting the Debate over Trafficking in Women: Definitions, Paradigms, and Contexts*, 11 HARVARD HUMAN RIGHTS JOURNAL 65 (1998)

Consard, Michel, *Quelques observations sur les décisions de la Chambre des Lords du 25 novembre 1998 et du 24 mars 1999 dans l'affaire Pinochet*, 103 REVUE GÉNÉRALE DE DROIT INTERNATIONAL PUBLIC 309 (1999)

Cotler, Irwin, *International Decisions: Regina v. Finta*, 90 AMERICAN JOURNAL OF INTERNATIONAL LAW 460 (1996)

Crockett, Clyde H., *Toward A Revision of the International Law of Piracy*, 26 DEPAUL LAW REVIEW 78 (1976)

D'Zurilla, William T., *Individual Responsibility for Torture under International Law*, 56 TULANE LAW REVIEW 186 (1981)

Damrosch, Lori F., Kurdish Genocide Case—Legal Memorandum for Governments, June 4, 1993 (memorandum for Middle East Watch) (on file with authors)

Dautricourt, Joseph Y., *Crime Against Humanity: European Views on Its Conception and Its Future*, 40 JOURNAL OF CRIMINAL LAW AND CRIMINOLOGY 170 (1949)

Demleitner, Nora V., *Forced Prostitution: Naming an International Offense*, 18 FORDHAM INTERNATIONAL LAW JOURNAL 163 (1994)

DINSTEIN, YORAM, THE DEFENSE OF 'OBEDIENCE TO SUPERIOR ORDERS' IN INTERNATIONAL LAW, Leiden: A. W. Sijthoff, 1965

—— *The Right to Life, Physical Integrity, and Liberty, in* THE INTERNATIONAL BILL OF RIGHTS: THE COVENANT ON CIVIL AND POLITICAL RIGHTS 114 (Louis Henkin (ed.)), New York: Columbia University Press, 1981

—— *International Criminal Law*, 20 ISRAEL LAW REVIEW 206 (1985)

—— WAR, AGGRESSION AND SELF-DEFENCE, Cambridge: Grotius Publications, 1988

Doswald-Beck, Louise, and Vité, Sylvain, *International Humanitarian Law and Human Rights Law*, 293 INTERNATIONAL REVIEW OF THE RED CROSS 94 (1993)

Draft Code of Offenses Against the Peace and Security of Mankind, 1986 AMERICAN SOCIETY OF INTERNATIONAL LAW PROCEEDINGS 120

Draper, G. I. A. D., *The Geneva Conventions of 1949*, 114 RECUEIL DES COURS 59 (1965–I)

—— *Wars of National Liberation and War Criminality*, *in* RESTRAINTS ON WAR: STUDIES IN THE LIMITATION OF ARMED CONFLICT 135 (Michael Howard (ed.)), Oxford: Oxford University Press, 1979

Duffy, P. J., *Article 3 of the European Convention on Human Rights*, 32 INTERNATIONAL AND COMPARATIVE LAW QUARTERLY 316 (1983)

Edwards, Joseph F., *Major Global Treaties for the Protection and Enjoyment of Art and Cultural Objects*, 22 TOLEDO LAW REVIEW 919 (1991)

Ehard, Hans, *The Nuremberg Trial Against the Major War Criminals and International Law*, 43 AMERICAN JOURNAL OF INTERNATIONAL LAW 223 (1949)

FALK, RICHARD A. (ED.), THE INTERNATIONAL LAW OF CIVIL WAR, Baltimore, Mld.: Johns Hopkins University Press, 1971

Farer, Tom, *Humanitarian Law and Armed Conflicts: Toward the Definition of 'International Armed Conflict'*, 71 COLUMBIA LAW REVIEW 37 (1971)

Farrior, Stephanie, *The International Law on Trafficking in Women and Children for Prostitution: Making it Live Up to its Potential*, 10 HARVARD HUMAN RIGHTS JOURNAL 213 (1997)

Fenrick, W. J., *Some International Law Problems Related to Prosecutions Before the International Criminal Tribunal for the Former Yugoslavia*, 6 DUKE JOURNAL OF COMPARATIVE AND INTERNATIONAL LAW 103 (1995)

Fenwick, C. G., and Potter, Pitman P., *Draft Code of Offenses Against the Peace and Security of Mankind*, 46 AMERICAN JOURNAL OF INTERNATIONAL LAW 98 (1953)

Ferencz, Benjamin B., *The Draft Code of Offenses Against the Peace and Security of Mankind*, 75 AMERICAN JOURNAL OF INTERNATIONAL LAW 674 (1981)

Finch, George A., *The Nuremberg Trial and International Law*, 41 AMERICAN JOURNAL OF INTERNATIONAL LAW 20 (1947)

Francillon, Jacques, *Crimes de Guerre, Crimes Contre l'Humanité*, JURIS-CLASSEURS, Fasc. 410 (1983)

Frankowska, Maria, *The United States Should Withdraw its Reservations to the Genocide Convention: A Response to Professor Paust's Proposal*, 12 MICHIGAN JOURNAL OF INTERNATIONAL LAW 141 (1990)

Garner, James W., *Punishment of Offenders Against the Laws and Customs of War*, 14 AMERICAN JOURNAL OF INTERNATIONAL LAW 70 (1920)

Gasser, Hans-Peter, *International Non-International Armed Conflicts: Case Studies of Afghanistan, Kampuchea, and Lebanon*, 31 AMERICAN UNIVERSITY LAW REVIEW 911 (1982)

The Genocide Convention after Fifty Years: Contemporary Strategies for Combating a Crime against Humanity, 1998 AMERICAN SOCIETY OF INTERNATIONAL LAW PROCEEDINGS 1

Genocide: The Convention, Domestic Laws, and State Responsibility, 1989 AMERICAN SOCIETY OF INTERNATIONAL LAW PROCEEDINGS 314

GINSBURGS, GEORGE, and KUDRIAVTSEV, V. N. (EDS.), THE NUREMBERG TRIAL AND INTERNATIONAL LAW, Dordrecht: Martinus Nijhoff Publishers, 1990

GLASER, STÉFAN, DROIT INTERNATIONAL PÉNAL CONVENTIONNEL, Brussels: E. Bruylant, 1970

Glueck, Sheldon, *The Nuernberg Trial and Aggressive War*, 59 HARVARD LAW REVIEW 396 (1946)

Goldberg, Arthur J., *The Status of Apartheid Under International Law*, 13 HASTINGS CONSTITUTIONAL LAW QUARTERLY 1 (1985)

Goldenberg, Sydney L., *Crimes Against Humanity—1945–1970*, 10 UNIVERSITY OF WESTERN ONTARIO LAW REVIEW 1 (1971)

Goodheart, A. L., *Questions and Answers Concerning the Nuremberg Trials*, 41 AMERICAN JOURNAL OF INTERNATIONAL LAW 525 (1947)

Graditzky, Thomas, *Individual criminal responsibility for violations of international humanitarian law committed in non-international armed conflicts*, 322 INTERNATIONAL REVIEW OF THE RED CROSS 29 (1998)

Graven, Jean, *Les Crimes Contre l'Humanité*, 76 RECUEIL DES COURS 427 (1950–I)

GRAVIER, BRUNO, and ELCHARDUS, JEAN-MARC (EDS.), LE CRIME CONTRE L'HUMANITÉ, Ramonville Saint-Agne: Erès, 1996

Green, L. C., *International Crimes and the Legal Process*, 29 INTERNATIONAL AND COMPARATIVE LAW QUARTERLY 567 (1980)

—— ESSAYS ON THE MODERN LAW OF WAR, Dobbs Ferry, NY: Transnational Publishers, 1985

—— *Canadian Law, War Crimes and Crimes Against Humanity*, 59 BRITISH YEAR BOOK OF INTERNATIONAL LAW 217 (1988)

—— *Superior Orders and Command Responsibility*, 27 CANADIAN YEARBOOK OF INTERNATIONAL LAW 167 (1989)

—— THE CONTEMPORARY LAW OF ARMED CONFLICT, Manchester: Manchester University Press, 1993

—— *Command Responsibility in International Humanitarian Law*, 5 TRANSNATIONAL LAW AND CONTEMPORARY PROBLEMS 319 (1995)

—— *Strengthening Legal Protection in Internal Conflicts: Low-Intensity Conflict and the Law*, 3 ILSA JOURNAL OF INTERNATIONAL AND COMPARATIVE LAW 493 (1997)

Greenawalt, Alexander K.A., *Rethinking Genocidal Intent: The Case for a Knowledge-Based Interpretation*, 99 COLUMBIA LAW REVIEW 2259 (1999)

Greenwood, Christopher, *International Humanitarian Law and the Tadic Case*, 7 EUROPEAN JOURNAL OF INTERNATIONAL LAW 265 (1996)

Greppi, Edoardo, *The evolution of criminal responsibility under international law*, 81 INTERNATIONAL REVIEW OF THE RED CROSS 531 (1999)

Gross, Leo, *Some Observations on the United Nations Draft Code of Offenses Against the Peace and Security of Mankind*, 13 ISRAEL YEAR BOOK ON HUMAN RIGHTS 9 (1983)

—— *Some Observations on the United Nations Draft Code of Offenses Against the Peace and Security of Mankind*, 15 ISRAEL YEAR BOOK ON HUMAN RIGHTS 224 (1985)

Gross, Leo, *Draft Code of Offenses Against the Peace and Security of Mankind*, 16 ISRAEL YEAR BOOK ON HUMAN RIGHTS 162 (1986)

Gross, Oren, *The Grave Breaches System and the Armed Conflict in the Former Yugoslavia*, 16 MICHIGAN JOURNAL OF INTERNATIONAL LAW 783 (1995)

GUTMAN, ROY, and RIEFF, DAVID (EDS.), CRIMES OF WAR: WHAT THE PUBLIC SHOULD KNOW, New York: W.W. Norton and Company, 1999

Gutteridge, Joyce A. C., *The Geneva Conventions of 1949*, 26 BRITISH YEAR BOOK OF INTERNATIONAL LAW 294 (1949)

Handl, Günther, *The Pinochet Case, Foreign State Immunity and the Changing Constitution of the International Community*, *in* DEVELOPMENT AND DEVELOPING INTERNATIONAL AND EUROPEAN LAW: ESSAYS IN HONOUR OF KONRAD GINTHER ON THE OCCASION OF HIS 65TH BIRTHDAY 59 (W. Benedek (ed.)), Frankfurt am Main: Peter Lang, 1999

Harvard Research in International Law, *Part IV—Piracy*, 26 AMERICAN JOURNAL OF INTERNATIONAL LAW (Supp.) 739 (1932)

HEATH, JAMES, TORTURE AND ENGLISH LAW, London: Greenwood Press, 1982

HENRY DUNANT INSTITUTE (ED.), INTERNATIONAL DIMENSIONS OF HUMANITARIAN LAW, Dordrecht: Martinus Nijhoff, 1988

Herzog, Jacques-Bernard, *Contribution à l'Etude de la Définition de Crime contre l'Humanité*, 18 REVUE INTERNATIONAL DE DROIT PÉNAL 155 (1947)

Johnson, D. H. N., *The Draft Code of Offences Against the Peace and Security of Mankind*, 4 INTERNATIONAL AND COMPARATIVE LAW QUARTERLY 445 (1955)

JONGMAN, ALBERT J. (ED.), CONTEMPORARY GENOCIDES: CAUSES, CASES, CONSEQUENCES, Leiden: PIOOM, 1996

Kader, David, *Law and Genocide: A Critical Annotated Bibliography*, 11 HASTINGS INTERNATIONAL AND COMPARATIVE LAW REVIEW 381 (1988)

KALSHOVEN, FRITS, THE LAW OF WARFARE: A SUMMARY OF ITS RECENT HISTORY AND TRENDS IN DEVELOPMENT, Leiden: A. W. Sijthoff, 1973

KAPLAN, JOHN, WEISBERG, ROBERT, and BINDER, GUYORA, CRIMINAL LAW: CASES AND MATERIALS (3d edn.), Boston, Mass.: Little, Brown and Company, 1996

Kelsen, Hans, *Will the Judgement in the Nuremberg Trial Constitute a Precedent in International Law?*, 1 INTERNATIONAL LAW QUARTERLY 153 (1947)

Koessler, Maximilian, *American War Crimes Trials in Europe*, 39 GEORGETOWN LAW JOURNAL 18 (1950)

KUPER, LEO, THE PREVENTION OF GENOCIDE, New Haven, Conn.: Yale University Press, 1985

LAEL, RICHARD L., THE YAMASHITA PRECEDENT: WAR CRIMES AND COMMAND RESPONSIBILITY, Wilmington, Del.: Scholarly Resources Inc., 1982

Lane, Eric, *Mass Killing by Governments: Lawful in the World Legal Order?*, 12 NEW YORK UNIVERSITY JOURNAL OF INTERNATIONAL LAW AND POLITICS 239 (1978)

Lauterpacht, Hersch, *The Law of Nations and the Punishment of War Crimes*, 21 BRITISH YEAR BOOK OF INTERNATIONAL LAW 58 (1944)

LAWS OF MANU (THE) (Wendy Doniger and Brian K. Smith (trans.)), New York: Penguin Books, 1991

LeBlanc, Lawrence J., *The Intent to Destroy Groups in the Genocide Convention:*

The Proposed U.S. Understanding, 78 AMERICAN JOURNAL OF INTERNATIONAL LAW 369 (1984)

—— *The ICJ, the Genocide Convention, and the United States*, 6 WISCONSIN INTERNATIONAL LAW JOURNAL 43 (1987)

—— *The United Nations Genocide Convention and Political Groups: Should the United States Propose an Amendment?*, 13 YALE JOURNAL OF INTERNATIONAL LAW 268 (1988)

LEMKIN, RAPHAËL, AXIS RULE IN OCCUPIED EUROPE, Washington, DC: Carnegie Endowment for International Peace, Division of International Law, 1944

Levasseur, Georges, *Les crimes contre l'humanité et le problème de leur prescription*, 93 JOURNAL DE DROIT INTERNATIONAL 259 (1966)

Lippman, Matthew, *The Drafting of the 1948 Convention on the Prevention and Punishment of the Crime of Genocide*, 3 BOSTON UNIVERSITY INTERNATIONAL LAW JOURNAL 1 (1985)

—— *The Other Nuremberg: American Prosecutions of Nazi War Criminals in Occupied Germany*, 3 INDIANA INTERNATIONAL AND COMPARATIVE LAW REVIEW 1 (1992)

—— *The Development and Drafting of the United Nations Convention Against Torture and Other Cruel, Inhuman or Degrading Treatment or Punishment*, 17 BOSTON COLLEGE INTERNATIONAL AND COMPARATIVE LAW REVIEW 275 (1994)

—— *The 1948 Convention on the Prevention and Punishment of the Crime of Genocide: Forty-Five Years Later*, 8 TEMPLE INTERNATIONAL AND COMPARATIVE LAW JOURNAL 1 (1994)

—— *War Crimes Trials of German Industrialists: The 'Other Schindlers'*, 9 TEMPLE INTERNATIONAL AND COMPARATIVE LAW JOURNAL 173 (1995)

—— *Conundrums of Armed Conflict: Criminal Defenses to Violations of the Humanitarian Law of War*, 15 DICKINSON JOURNAL OF INTERNATIONAL LAW 1 (1996)

—— *The Convention on the Prevention and Punishment of the Crime of Genocide: Fifty Years Later*, 15 ARIZONA JOURNAL OF INTERNATIONAL AND COMPARATIVE LAW 415 (1998)

MacKinnon, Catherine A., *Rape, Genocide, and Women's Human Rights*, 17 HARVARD WOMEN'S LAW JOURNAL 5 (1994)

Marchisio, Sergio, *The* Priebke *Case Before the Italian Military Tribunals: A Reaffirmation of the Principle of Non-Applicability of Statutory Limitations to War Crimes and Crimes Against Humanity*, 1 YEARBOOK OF INTERNATIONAL HUMANITARIAN LAW 344 (1998)

McCormack, Timothy L. H., and Simpson, Gerry J., *The International Law Commision's Draft Code of Crimes against the Peace and Security of Mankind: An Appraisal of the Substantive Provisions*, 5 CRIMINAL LAW FORUM 1 (1994)

—— and —— (EDS.), THE LAW OF WAR CRIMES: NATIONAL AND INTERNATIONAL APPROACHES, The Hague: Kluwer Law International, 1997

—— and Robertson, Sue, *Jurisdictional Aspects of the Rome Statute for the New International Criminal Court*, 23 MELBOURNE UNIVERSITY LAW REVIEW 635 (1999)

McCoubrey, Hilaire, and White, Nigel D., International Law and Armed Conflict, Aldershot: Dartmouth, 1992

Meron, Theodor, *The Geneva Conventions as Customary Law*, 81 American Journal of International Law 348 (1987)

—— Human Rights and Humanitarian Norms as Customary Law, Oxford: Clarendon Press, 1989

—— *Rape as a Crime under International Humanitarian Law*, 87 American Journal of International Law 424 (1993)

—— *War Crimes in Yugoslavia and the Development of International Law*, 88 American Journal of International Law 78 (1994)

—— *International Criminalization of Internal Atrocities*, 89 American Journal of International Law 554 (1995)

—— *The Continuing Role of Custom in the Formation of International Humanitarian Law*, 90 American Journal of International Law 238 (1996)

—— *Is International Law Moving towards Criminalization?*, 9 European Journal of International Law 18 (1998)

—— *The Humanization of Humanitarian Law*, 94 American Journal of International Law 239 (2000)

Meyer, David A., *The 1954 Hague Cultural Property Convention and Its Emergence into Customary International Law*, 11 Boston University International Law Journal 349 (1993)

Meyerowitz, Henri, La Répression par les Tribunaux Allemands des Crimes Contre L'Humanité et de l'Appartenance à une Organisation Criminelle, Paris: Librairie Générale de Droit et de Jurisprudence, 1960

Miller, Richard I. (ed.), The Law of War, Lexington, Mass.: Lexington Books, 1975

Miller, Robert H., *The Convention on the Non-Applicability of Statutory Limitations to War Crimes and Crimes Against Humanity*, 65 American Journal of International Law 476 (1971)

Monson, Robert A., *The West German Statute of Limitations on Murder: A Political, Legal, and Historical Exposition*, 30 American Journal of Comparative Law 605 (1982)

Moore, John Norton (ed.), Law and Civil War in the Modern World, Baltimore, Mld.: Johns Hopkins University Press, 1974

Morris, Scott R., *Killing Egyptian Prisoners of War: Does the Phrase 'Lest We Forget' Apply to Israeli War Criminals?*, 29 Vanderbilt Journal of Transnational Law 903 (1996)

Mueller, Gerhard O. W., and Wise, Edward M. (eds.), International Criminal Law, London: Sweet & Maxwell, 1965

Nafziger, James A. R., *International Penal Aspects of Protecting Cultural Property*, 19 International Lawyer 835 (1985)

Osiel, Mark J., Obeying Orders: Atrocity, Military Discipline & the Law of War, New Brunswick, NJ: Transaction Publishers, 1999

Parks, William H., *Command Responsibility for War Crimes*, 62 Military Law Review 1 (1973)

Parry, Clive, *Some Considerations Upon the Content of a Draft Code of Offences*

Against the Peace and Security of Mankind, 3 INTERNATIONAL LAW QUARTERLY 208 (1950)

Paust, Jordan J., *Legal Aspects of the My Lai Incident—A Response to Professor Rubin, in* THE VIETNAM WAR AND INTERNATIONAL LAW (Vol. 3) 359 (Richard A. Falk (ed.)), Princeton, NJ: Princeton University Press, 1972

—— *My Lai and Vietnam: Norms, Myths and Leader Responsibility*, 57 MILITARY LAW REVIEW 99 (1972)

—— *Aggression Against Authority: The Crime of Oppression, Politicide and Other Crimes Against Human Rights*, 18 CASE WESTERN RESERVE JOURNAL OF INTERNATIONAL LAW 283 (1986)

—— *Congress and Genocide: They're Not Going to Get Away with It*, 11 MICHIGAN JOURNAL OF INTERNATIONAL LAW 90 (1989)

—— *Applicability of International Criminal Laws to Events in the Former Yugoslavia*, 9 AMERICAN UNIVERSITY JOURNAL OF INTERNATIONAL LAW AND POLICY 499 (1994)

—— *It's No Defense: Nullum Crimen, International Crime and the Gingerbread Man*, 60 ALBANY LAW REVIEW 657 (1997)

Petchsiri, Apirat, EASTERN IMPORTATION OF WESTERN CRIMINAL LAW: THAILAND AS A CASE STUDY, Littleton, Colo.: Fred B. Rothman, 1987

PICTET, JEAN S., COMMENTARY, IV GENEVA CONVENTION RELATIVE TO THE PROTECTION OF CIVILIAN PERSONS IN TIME OF WAR, Geneva: International Committee of the Red Cross, 1958

—— HUMANITARIAN LAW AND THE PROTECTION OF WAR VICTIMS, Leiden: A. W. Sijthoff, 1975

Plattner, Denise, *The Penal Repression of Violations of International Humanitarian Law Applicable in Non-international Armed Conflicts*, 30 INTERNATIONAL REVIEW OF THE RED CROSS 409 (1990)

Prott, Lyndel V., *International Penal Aspects of Cultural Protection Law*, 7 CRIMINAL LAW JOURNAL 207 (1983)

Rassam, A. Yasmine, *Contemporary Forms of Slavery and the Evolution of the Prohibition of Slavery and the Slave Trade Under Customary International Law*, 39 VIRGINIA JOURNAL OF INTERNATIONAL LAW 303 (1999)

Ratner, Steven R., *The Schizophrenias of International Criminal Law*, 33 TEXAS INTERNATIONAL LAW JOURNAL 237 (1998)

—— and Slaughter, Anne-Marie (eds.), *Symposium on Method in International Law*, 93 AMERICAN JOURNAL OF INTERNATIONAL LAW 291 (1999)

REISMAN, W. MICHAEL, and BAKER, JAMES E., REGULATING COVERT ACTION, New Haven, Conn.: Yale University Press, 1992

Rikhof, Joseph, *Crimes against Humanity, Customary International Law and International Tribunals for Bosnia and Rwanda*, 6 NATIONAL JOURNAL OF CONSTITUTIONAL LAW 233 (1996)

Robbins, James S., *War Crimes: The Case of Iraq*, FLETCHER FORUM OF WORLD AFFAIRS, Summer/Fall 1994, at 45

ROBERTS, ADAM, and GUELFF, RICHARD (EDS.), DOCUMENTS ON THE LAWS OF WAR (3d edn.), Oxford: Oxford University Press, 2000

Robinson, Darryl, *Defining 'Crimes against Humanity' at the Rome Conference*, 93 AMERICAN JOURNAL OF INTERNATIONAL LAW 43 (1999)

ROBINSON, NEHEMIAH, THE GENOCIDE CONVENTION: A COMMENTARY, New York: Institute of Jewish Affairs, World Jewish Congress, 1960

Roch, Michael P., *Forced Displacement in the Former Yugoslavia: A Crime Under International Law?,* 14 DICKINSON JOURNAL OF INTERNATIONAL LAW 1 (1995)

ROLPH, JOHN W., PERFECTING AN INTERNATIONAL CODE OF CRIMES (Department of the Army Pamphlet 27–50–235) (1992)

Rowe, Peter, *Duress as a Defence to War Crimes after* Erdemovic: *A Laboratory for a Permanent Court?,* 1 YEARBOOK OF INTERNATIONAL HUMANITARIAN LAW 210 (1998)

—— *The International Criminal Tribunal for Yugoslavia: The Decision of the Appeals Chamber on the Interlocutory Appeal on Jurisdiction in the* Tadic *Case*, 45 INTERNATIONAL AND COMPARATIVE LAW QUARTERLY 691 (1996)

SANDOZ, YVES, SWINARSKI, CHRISTOPHE, and ZIMMERMANN, BRUNO (EDS.) COMMENTARY ON THE ADDITIONAL PROTOCOLS OF 8 JUNE 1977 TO THE GENEVA CONVENTIONS OF 12 AUGUST 1949, Geneva: International Committee of the Red Cross, 1987

Sassòli, Marco, *La première décision de la chambre d'appel du Tribunal Penal International pour l'ex-Yougoslavie: Tadic (Competence)*, 100 REVUE GÉNÉRALE DE DROIT INTERNATIONAL PUBLIC 101 (1996)

Schiller, Barry M., *Life in a Symbolic Universe: Comments on the Genocide Convention and International Law*, 9 SOUTHWESTERN UNIVERSITY LAW REVIEW 47 (1977)

Schindler, Dietrich, *The Different Types of Armed Conflicts According to the Geneva Conventions and Protocols*, 163 RECUEIL DES COURS 117 (1979–II)

—— and TOMAN, JIRÍ (EDS.), THE LAWS OF ARMED CONFLICTS: A COLLECTION OF CONVENTIONS, RESOLUTIONS, AND OTHER DOCUMENTS, Leiden: A.W. Sijthoff, 1973

Schwarzenberger, Georg, *The Problem of an International Criminal Law*, 3 CURRENT LEGAL PROBLEMS 263 (1950)

Schwelb, Egon, *Crimes Against Humanity*, 23 BRITISH YEAR BOOK OF INTERNATIONAL LAW 178 (1946)

—— *The International Convention on the Elimination of All Forms of Racial Discrimination,* 15 INTERNATIONAL AND COMPARATIVE LAW QUARTERLY 996 (1966)

Sellers, Patricia Viseur, and Okuizumi, Kaoru, *International Prosecution of Sexual Assaults*, 7 TRANSNATIONAL LAW AND CONTEMPORARY PROBLEMS 45 (1997)

SIOTIS, JEAN, LE DROIT DE LA GUERRE ET LES CONFLITS ARMÉS D'UN CARACTÈRE NON-INTERNATIONAL, Paris: Librairie Générale de Droit et de Jurisprudence, 1958

Slye, Ronald C., *Apartheid as a Crime Against Humanity: A Submission to the South African Truth and Reconciliation Commission*, 20 MICHIGAN JOURNAL OF INTERNATIONAL LAW 267 (1999)

Solf, Waldemar A., and Cummings, Edward R., *A Survey of Penal Sanctions Under Protocol I to the Geneva Conventions of August 12, 1949*, 9 CASE WESTERN RESERVE JOURNAL OF INTERNATIONAL LAW 205 (1977)

Starkman, Paul, *Genocide and International Law: Is There a Cause of Action?*, 8 American Society of International Law Students International Law Journal 1 (1984)

Stefani, Gaston, Levasseur, Georges, and Bouloc, Bernard, Droit Pénal Général (15th edn.), Paris: Dalloz, 1995

——, —— and —— Procédure Pénale (17th edn.), Paris: Dalloz, 2000

Stewart, David P., *The Torture Convention and the Reception of International Criminal Law within the United States*, 15 Nova Law Review 449 (1991)

Sun Tzu, The Art of War (Samuel B. Griffith (ed.)), Oxford: Clarendon Press, 1963

Sunga, Lyal S., Individual Responsibility in International Law for Serious Human Rights Violations, Dordrecht: Martinus Nijhoff Publishers, 1992

Suter, Keith, An International Law of Guerrilla Warfare: The Global Politics of Law-Making, New York: St. Martin's Press, 1984

Symposium, *Genocide, War Crimes, and Crimes Against Humanity*, 23 Fordham International Law Journal 275 (1999)

Turns, David, *War Crimes Without War?—The Applicability of International Humanitarian Law to Atrocities in Non-International Armed Conflicts*, 7 African Journal of International and Comparative Law 804 (1995)

—— *The International Criminal Tribunal for the Former Yugoslavia: The Erdemovic Case*, 47 International and Comparative Law Quarterly 461 (1998)

Van Schaak, Beth, *The Definition of Crimes Against Humanity: Resolving the Incoherence*, 37 Columbia Journal of Transnational Law 787 (1999)

Vetter, Greg R., *Command Responsibility of Non-Military Superiors in the International Criminal Court*, 25 Yale Journal of International Law 89 (2000)

Watts, Arthur, *The Legal Position in International Law of Heads of States, Heads of Governments and Foreign Ministers*, 247 Recueil des Cours 9 (1994-III)

Webb, John, *Genocide Treaty—Ethnic Cleansing—Substantive and Procedural Hurdles in the Application of the Genocide Convention to Alleged Crimes in the Former Yugoslavia*, 23 Georgia Journal of International and Comparative Law 377 (1993)

Weiler, Joseph H. H., Cassese, Antonio, and Spinedi, Marina (eds.), International Crimes of State: A Critical Analysis of the ILC's Draft Article 19 on State Responsibility, Berlin: Walter de Gruyter, 1989

Weissbrodt, David, and Mahoney, Georgiana, *International Legal Action Against Apartheid*, 4 Law and Inequality 485 (1986)

Wembou, Michel-Cyr Djiena, *La répression des crimes de guerre et des autres violations graves du droit humanitaire*, 11 African Journal of International and Comparative Law 375 (1999)

Wexler, Leila Sadat, *The Interpretation of the Nuremberg Principles by the French Court of Cassation: From Touvier to Barbie and Back Again*, 32 Columbia Journal of Transnational Law 289 (1994)

Williams, Sharon A., The International and National Protection of Movable Cultural Property: A Comparative Study, Dobbs Ferry, NY: Oceana Publications, 1978

Wright, Lord, *War Crimes Under International Law*, 62 LAW QUARTERLY REVIEW 40 (1946)

Wright, Quincy, *The Law of the Nuremberg Trial*, 41 AMERICAN JOURNAL OF INTERNATIONAL LAW 38 (1947)

—— *Legal Positivism and the Nuremberg Judgment*, 42 AMERICAN JOURNAL OF INTERNATIONAL LAW 405 (1948)

—— *The Scope of International Criminal Law: A Conceptual Framework*, 15 VIRGINIA JOURNAL OF INTERNATIONAL LAW 561 (1975)

Wu, Timothy, and Kang, Yong-Sung, *Criminal Liability for the Actions of Subordinates—The Doctrine of Command Responsibility and its Analogues in United States Law*, 38 HARVARD INTERNATIONAL LAW JOURNAL 272 (1997)

Yarnold, Barbara M., *Doctrinal Basis for the International Criminalization Process*, 8 TEMPLE INTERNATIONAL AND COMPARATIVE LAW JOURNAL 85 (1994)

Zoller, Elisabeth, *La Définition des Crimes contre l'Humanité*, 120 JOURNAL DE DROIT INTERNATIONAL 549 (1993)

Mechanisms for Accountability

Affolder, Natasha A., *Tadic, the Anonymous Witness and the Sources of International Procedural Law*, 19 MICHIGAN JOURNAL OF INTERNATIONAL LAW 445 (1998)

Akhavan, Payam, *Enforcement of the Genocide Convention Through the Advisory Opinion Jurisdiction of the International Court of Justice*, 12 HUMAN RIGHTS LAW JOURNAL 285 (1991)

—— *Enforcement of the Genocide Convention: A Challenge to Civilization*, 8 HARVARD HUMAN RIGHTS JOURNAL 229 (1995)

—— *The International Criminal Tribunal for Rwanda: The Politics and Pragmatics of Punishment*, 90 AMERICAN JOURNAL OF INTERNATIONAL LAW 501 (1996)

—— *The Yugoslav Tribunal at a Crossroads: The Dayton Peace Agreement and Beyond*, 18 HUMAN RIGHTS QUARTERLY 259 (1996)

—— *Justice in The Hague, Peace in the Former Yugoslavia?: A Commentary on the United Nations War Crimes Tribunal*, 20 HUMAN RIGHTS QUARTERLY 737 (1998)

Aldrich, George H., *Jurisdiction of the International Criminal Tribunal for the Former Yugoslavia*, 90 AMERICAN JOURNAL OF INTERNATIONAL LAW 64 (1996)

Allen, Jonathan, *Balancing Justice and Social Unity: Political Theory and the Idea of a Truth and Reconciliation Commission*, 49 UNIVERSITY OF TORONTO LAW JOURNAL 315 (1999)

Alvarez, José E., *Nuremberg Revisited: The Tadic Case*, 7 EUROPEAN JOURNAL OF INTERNATIONAL LAW 245 (1996)

—— *Rush to Closure: Lessons of the Tadic Judgement*, 96 MICHIGAN LAW REVIEW 2031 (1998)

—— *Crimes of States/Crimes of Hate: Lessons from Rwanda*, 24 YALE JOURNAL OF INTERNATIONAL LAW 365 (1999)

Ambos, Kai, *Impunity and International Criminal Law: A Case Study on Colombia, Peru, Bolivia, Chile, and Argentina*, 18 HUMAN RIGHTS LAW JOURNAL 1 (1997)

—— *Aktuelle Probleme der deutschen Verfolgung von 'Kriegsverbrechen' in Bosnien-Herzegowina*, 5 NEUE ZEITSCHRIFT FÜR STRAFRECHT 226 (1999)

AMERICAN LAW INSTITUTE, RESTATEMENT (THIRD) OF THE FOREIGN RELATIONS LAW OF THE UNITED STATES (Vol. 1), St. Paul, Minn.: American Law Institute Publishers, 1987

AMERICAS WATCH, HUMAN RIGHTS AND THE 'POLITICS OF AGREEMENTS', New York: Human Rights Watch, 1991

—— TRUTH AND PARTIAL JUSTICE IN ARGENTINA: AN UPDATE, New York: Human Rights Watch, 1991

AMNESTY INTERNATIONAL, ARGENTINA: THE MILITARY JUNTA AND HUMAN RIGHTS: REPORT OF THE TRIAL OF THE FORMER JUNTA MEMBERS, London: Amnesty International, 1987

—— ETHIOPIA, ACCOUNTABILITY PAST AND PRESENT: HUMAN RIGHTS IN TRANSITION, New York: Amnesty International, 1995

—— RWANDA AND BURUNDI: A CALL FOR ACTION BY THE INTERNATIONAL COMMUNITY, New York: Amnesty International, 1995

—— RWANDA AND BURUNDI, THE RETURN HOME: RUMOURS AND REALITIES, New York: Amnesty International, 1996

—— RWANDA: THE TROUBLED COURSE OF JUSTICE (Apr. 2000), available at www.amnesty.org

Andries, André, *Investigations et Poursuites des Violations du Droit des Conflits Armés, Partie I: Lois et Procédures Nationales*, 37 REVUE DE DROIT MILITAIRE ET DE DROIT DE LA GUERRE 179 (1998)

Arbour, Louise, *Access to Justice: The Prosecution of International Crimes: Prospects and Pitfalls*, 1 WASHINGTON UNIVERSITY JOURNAL OF LAW AND POLICY 13 (1999)

—— *The Status of the International Criminal Tribunals for the Former Yugoslavia and Rwanda: Goals and Results*, 3 HOFSTRA LAW AND POLICY SYMPOSIUM 37 (1999)

Ash, Timothy Garton, *True Confessions*, NEW YORK REVIEW OF BOOKS, July 17, 1997, at 33

ASPEN INSTITUTE (ED.), STATE CRIMES: PUNISHMENT OR PARDON, Queenstown, Mld.: The Aspen Institute, 1989

Association of American Law Schools, *Panel on the International Criminal Court*, 36 AMERICAN CRIMINAL LAW REVIEW 223 (1999)

Bassiouni, M. Cherif, *Nuremberg Forty Years After: An Introduction*, 18 CASE WESTERN RESERVE JOURNAL OF INTERNATIONAL LAW 261 (1986)

—— INTERNATIONAL EXTRADITION: UNITED STATES LAW AND PRACTICE (3d edn., Dobbs Ferry, NY: Oceana Publications, 1996

—— THE STATUTE OF THE INTERNATIONAL CRIMINAL COURT: A DOCUMENTARY HISTORY, Ardsley, NY: Transnational Publishers, 1998

—— *Combating Impunity for International Crimes*, 71 UNIVERSITY OF COLORADO LAW REVIEW 409 (2000)

—— and Blakesley, Christopher L., *The Need for an International Criminal*

Court in the New International World Order, 25 VANDERBILT JOURNAL OF TRANSNATIONAL LAW 151 (1992)

Bassiouni, M. Cherif and MANIKAS, PETER, THE LAW OF THE INTERNATIONAL CRIMINAL TRIBUNAL FOR THE FORMER YUGOSLAVIA, Irvington-on-Hudson, NY: Transnational Publishers, 1996

—— and Morris, Madeline M. (eds.), *Symposium: Accountability for International Crimes and Serious Violations of Human Rights*, 59 LAW AND CONTEMPORARY PROBLEMS 1 (1996)

—— and WISE, EDWARD M., AUT DEDERE AUT JUDICARE: THE DUTY TO EXTRADITE OR PROSECUTE IN INTERNATIONAL LAW, Dordrecht: Martinus Nijhoff Publishers, 1995

Baxter, Richard R., *The Municipal and International Law Basis of Jurisdiction Over War Crimes*, 28 BRITISH YEAR BOOK OF INTERNATIONAL LAW 382 (1951)

Benedetti, Fanny, and Washburn, John L., *Drafting the International Criminal Court Treaty: Two Years to Rome and an Afterword on the Rome Diplomatic Conference*, 5 GLOBAL GOVERNANCE 1 (1999)

Beres, Louis René, *Iraqi Crimes and International Law: The Imperative to Punish*, 21 DENVER JOURNAL OF INTERNATIONAL LAW AND POLICY 335 (1993)

—— *Iraqi Crimes During and After the Gulf War: The Imperative Response of International Law*, 15 LOYOLA OF LOS ANGELES INTERNATIONAL AND COMPARATIVE LAW JOURNAL 675 (1993)

Beresford, Stuart, *The International Criminal Tribunal for the Former Yugoslavia: The First Four Years*, 9 OTAGO LAW REVIEW 557 (1999)

Blum, Jeffrey M., and Steinhardt, Ralph G., *Federal Jurisdiction Over International Human Rights Claims: The Alien Tort Claims Act after Filartiga v. Peña-Irala*, 22 HARVARD INTERNATIONAL LAW JOURNAL 53 (1981)

Boed, Roman, *An Evaluation of the Legality and Efficacy of Lustration as a Tool of Transitional Justice*, 37 COLUMBIA JOURNAL OF TRANSNATIONAL LAW 357 (1999)

Boelaert-Suominen, Sonja, *The International Criminal Tribunal for the former Yugoslavia and the Kosovo conflict*, 82 INTERNATIONAL REVIEW OF THE RED CROSS 217 (2000)

—— *Grave Breaches, Universal Jurisdiction and Internal Armed Conflicts: Is Customary Law Moving Towards a Uniform Enforcement Mechanism for all Armed Conflicts?*, 5 JOURNAL OF CONFLICT AND SECURITY LAW 63 (2000)

Bolton, John R., *Courting Danger: What's Wrong with the International Criminal Court*, THE NATIONAL INTEREST, Winter 1998/99, at 60

BORAINE, ALEX, LEVY, JANET, and SCHEFFER, RONEL (EDS.), DEALING WITH THE PAST: TRUTH AND RECONCILIATION IN SOUTH AFRICA, Cape Town: IDASA, 1994

—— and LEVY, JANET (EDS.), THE HEALING OF A NATION?, Cape Town: Justice in Transition, 1995

BRACKMAN, ARNOLD C., THE OTHER NUREMBERG: THE UNTOLD STORY OF THE TOKYO WAR CRIMES TRIALS, New York: Morrow, 1987

Bridge, John W., *The Case for an International Court of Criminal Justice and the Formulation of International Criminal Law*, 13 INTERNATIONAL AND COMPARATIVE LAW QUARTERLY 1255 (1964)

Brower, Charles N., *Evidence Before International Tribunals: The Need for Some Standard Rules*, 28 INTERNATIONAL LAWYER 47 (1994)

Brown, Bartram S., *U.S. Objections to the Statute of the International Criminal Court: A Brief Response*, 31 NEW YORK UNIVERSITY JOURNAL OF INTERNATIONAL LAW AND POLITICS 855 (1999)

Buergenthal, Thomas, *The United Nations Truth Commission for El Salvador*, 27 VANDERBILT JOURNAL OF TRANSNATIONAL LAW 498 (1994)

Carnegie, A. R., *Jurisdiction Over Violations of the Laws and Customs of War*, 39 BRITISH YEAR BOOK OF INTERNATIONAL LAW 402 (1963)

Carter, Edward F., *The Nurnberg Trials: A Turning Point in the Enforcement of International Law*, 28 NEBRASKA LAW REVIEW 370 (1949)

Cassel, Douglass W., Jr., *International Truth Commissions and Justice*, 5 ASPEN INSTITUTE QUARTERLY 77 (1993)

Cavicchia, Joel, *The Prospects for an International Criminal Court in the 1990s*, 10 DICKINSON JOURNAL OF INTERNATIONAL LAW 223 (1992)

CHANDLER, PELEG W., AMERICAN CRIMINAL TRIALS (Vol. 1, 1841), Boston, Mass.: Little, Brown & Company, 1970

Cissé, Catherine, *The End of a Culture of Impunity in Rwanda? Prosecution of Genocide and War Crimes before Rwandan Courts and the International Criminal Tribunal for Rwanda*, 1 YEARBOOK OF INTERNATIONAL HUMANITARIAN LAW 161 (1998)

Clark, Roger S., and Nanda, Ved P. (eds.), *Symposium: International Criminal Law*, 5 TRANSNATIONAL LAW AND CONTEMPORARY PROBLEMS 237 (1995)

Cogan, Jacob Katz, *The Problem of Obtaining Evidence for International Criminal Courts*, 22 HUMAN RIGHTS QUARTERLY 404 (2000)

Cohen, Stanley, *State Crimes of Previous Regimes: Knowledge, Accountability, and the Policing of the Past*, 20 LAW AND SOCIAL INQUIRY 7 (1995)

Cole, David, Lobel, Jules, and Koh, Harold Hongju, *Interpreting the Alien Tort Statute: Amicus Curiae Memorandum of International Law Scholars and Practitioners in Trajano v. Marcos*, 12 HASTINGS INTERNATIONAL AND COMPARATIVE LAW REVIEW 1 (1988)

COMMISSION NATIONALE CONSULTATIVE DES DROITS DE L'HOMME and INTERNATIONAL COMMISSION OF JURISTS (EDS.), JUSTICE NOT IMPUNITY: INTERNATIONAL MEETING ON IMPUNITY OF PERPETRATORS OF GROSS HUMAN RIGHTS, Dijon-Chenôve: Abrax, 1993

Coombs, Mary, *International Decisions: In re Surrender of Ntakirutimana*, 94 AMERICAN JOURNAL OF INTERNATIONAL LAW 171 (2000)

Correa S., Jorge, *Dealing with Past Human Rights Violations: The Chilean Case After Dictatorship*, 67 NOTRE DAME LAW REVIEW 1455 (1992)

Creta, Vincent M., *The Search for Justice in the Former Yugoslavia and Beyond: Analyzing the Rights of the Accused Under the Statute and the Rules of Procedure and Evidence of the International Criminal Tribunal for the Former Yugoslavia*, 20 HOUSTON JOURNAL OF INTERNATIONAL LAW 381 (1998)

D'Amato, Anthony, *Peace vs. Accountability in Bosnia*, 88 AMERICAN JOURNAL OF INTERNATIONAL LAW 500 (1994)

DAMROSCH, LORI F. (ED.), THE INTERNATIONAL COURT OF JUSTICE AT A CROSSROADS, Dobbs Ferry, NY: Transnational Publishers, 1987

DASSIN, JOAN (ED.), TORTURE IN BRAZIL: A REPORT BY THE ARCHDIOCESE OF SÃO PAULO, New York: Vintage Books, 1986

DAVIDSON, SCOTT, THE INTER-AMERICAN COURT OF HUMAN RIGHTS, Aldershot: Dartmouth, 1992

de Gouttes, Régis, *Un exemple de poursuites de crimes contre l'humanité devant les jurisdictions nationales: le procès des criminels de l'ancien régime du colonel Menghistu en Éthiopie*, 1998 REVUE DE SCIENCE CRIMINELLE ET DE DROIT PÉNAL COMPARÉ 697 (1998)

DE WAAL, ALEXANDER, EVIL DAYS: THIRTY YEARS OF WAR AND FAMINE IN ETHIOPIA, New York: Human Rights Watch, 1991

Diessenbacher, Hartmut, *Explaining the Genocide in Rwanda*, 52 LAW AND STATE 59 (1995)

DINSTEIN, YORAM, and TABORY, MALA (EDS.), WAR CRIMES IN INTERNATIONAL LAW, The Hague: Martinus Nijhoff, 1996

Drumbl, Mark A., *Rule of Law Amid Lawlessness: Counselling the Accused in Rwanda's Domestic Genocide Trials*, 29 COLUMBIA HUMAN RIGHTS LAW REVIEW 545 (1998)

Dugard, John, *Reconciliation and Justice: The South African Experience*, 8 TRANSNATIONAL LAW AND CONTEMPORARY PROBLEMS 277 (1998)

—— *Dealing With Crimes of a Past Regime: Is Amnesty Still an Option?*, 12 LEIDEN JOURNAL OF INTERNATIONAL LAW 1001 (1999)

Dzubow, Jason A., *The International Response to the Civil War in Rwanda*, 8 GEORGETOWN IMMIGRATION LAW JOURNAL 513 (1994)

Edelenbos, Carla, *Human Rights Violations: A Duty to Prosecute?*, 7 LEIDEN JOURNAL OF INTERNATIONAL LAW 5 (1994)

Engelschiøn, Tore Sverdrup, *Ethiopia: War Crimes and Violations of Human Rights,* 34 REVUE DE DROIT MILITAIRE ET DE DROIT DE LA GUERRE 9 (1995)

Ensalaco, Mark, *Truth Commissions for Chile and El Salvador: A Report and Assessment*, 16 HUMAN RIGHTS QUARTERLY 656 (1994)

Falk, Richard A., *Nuremberg: Past, Present, and Future*, 80 YALE LAW JOURNAL 1501 (1971)

Featherstone, Y.M.O., *The International Criminal Tribunal for the Former Yugoslavia: Recent Develpments in Witness Protection*, 10 LEIDEN JOURNAL OF INTERNATIONAL LAW 179 (1997)

FERENCZ, BENJAMIN B., AN INTERNATIONAL CRIMINAL COURT: A STEP TOWARD WORLD PEACE (2 vols.), New York: Oceana Publications, 1980

Ferstman, Carla J., *Domestic Trials for Genocide and Crimes Against Humanity: The Example of Rwanda*, 9 AFRICAN JOURNAL OF INTERNATIONAL AND COMPARATIVE LAW 857 (1997)

Forsythe, David P., *Politics and the International Tribunal for the Former Yugoslavia*, 5 CRIMINAL LAW FORUM 401 (1994)

Forty Years After the Nuremberg and Tokyo Tribunals: The Impact of the War Crimes Trials on International and National Law, 1986 AMERICAN SOCIETY OF INTERNATIONAL LAW PROCEEDINGS 56

Gabriel, Manfred J., *Coming to Terms with the East German Border Guards Cases*, 38 Columbia Journal of Transnational Law 375 (1999)

Gaeta, Paola, *Is NATO Authorized or Obliged to Arrest Persons Indicted by the International Criminal Tribunal for the Former Yugoslavia?*, 9 European Journal of International Law 174 (1998)

Garro, Alejandro M., *Nine Years of Transition to Democracy in Argentina: Partial Failure or Qualified Success?*, 31 Columbia Journal of Transnational Law 1 (1993)

—— and Dahl, Henry, *Legal Accountability for Human Rights Violations in Argentina: One Step Forward and Two Steps Backward*, 8 Human Rights Law Journal 283 (1987)

Gery, Yoav, *The Torture Victim Protection Act: Raising Issues of Legitimacy*, 26 George Washington Journal of International Law and Economics 597 (1993)

Gibson, Lauren, and Roht-Arriaza, Naomi, *The Developing Jurisprudence on Amnesty*, 20 Human Rights Quarterly 843 (1998)

Goldstone, Richard J., *The International Tribunal for the Former Yugoslavia: A Case Study in Security Council Action*, 6 Duke Journal of Comparative and International Law 5 (1995)

Gordon, Charles, and Mailman, Stanley, Immigration Law and Procedure (Vol. 4), New York: Matthew Bender, 2000

Gravier, Bruno, and Elchardus, Jean-Marc (eds.), Le Crime contre L'Humanité, Ramonville Saint-Agne: Erès, 1996

Gross, Leo, *The Punishment of War Criminals: The Nuremberg Trial*, 2 Netherlands International Law Review 356 (1955)

Guillaume, Gilbert, *The Future of International Judicial Institutions*, 44 International and Comparative Law Quarterly 848 (1995)

Hampson, Françoise J., *The International Criminal Tribunal for the Former Yugoslavia and the Reluctant Witness*, 47 International and Comparative Law Quarterly 50 (1998)

Harvard Law School Human Rights Program (ed.), Truth Commissions: A Comparative Assessment, Cambridge, Mass: Harvard Law School, 1997

Harris, Kenneth J., and Kushen, Robert, *Surrender of Fugitives to the War Crimes Tribunals for Yugoslavia and Rwanda: Squaring International Legal Obligations with the United States Constitution*, 7 Criminal Law Forum 561 (1996)

Hayner, Priscilla, *Fifteen Truth Commissions—1974 to 1994: A Comparative Study*, 16 Human Rights Quarterly 597 (1994)

Helsinki Watch, Procedural and Evidentiary Issues for the Yougoslav War Crimes Tribunal: Resource Allocation, Evidentiary Questions and Protection of Witnesses, New York: Human Rights Watch, 1993

Herdegen, Matthias J., *Unjust Laws, Human Rights, and the German Constitution: Germany's Recent Confrontation with the Past*, 32 Columbia Journal of Transnational Law 591 (1995)

Howland, Todd, and Calathes, William, *The UN's International Criminal Tribunal, Is it Justice or Jingoism for Rwanda? A Call for Transformation*, 39 Virginia Journal of International Law 135 (1998)

HUMAN RIGHTS WATCH, SPECIAL ISSUE NO.4: ACCOUNTABILITY FOR PAST HUMAN RIGHTS ABUSES, New York: Human Rights Watch, 1989

—— CHILE: WHEN TYRANTS TREMBLE: THE PINOCHET CASE, New York: Human Rights Watch, 1999

—— and INTERNATIONAL FEDERATION OF HUMAN RIGHTS, RWANDA: THE CRISIS CONTINUES, New York: Human Rights Watch, 1995

HUMAN RIGHTS WATCH/AFRICA, ETHIOPIA: RECKONING UNDER THE LAW, New York: Human Rights Watch, 1994

HUNTINGTON, SAMUEL P., THE THIRD WAVE: DEMOCRATIZATION IN THE LATE TWENTIETH CENTURY, Norman, Okla.: University of Oklahoma Press, 1991

Huyse, Luc, *Justice After Transition: On the Choices Successor Elites Make in Dealing with the Past*, 20 LAW AND SOCIAL INQUIRY 51 (1995)

IGNATIEFF, MICHAEL, THE WARRIOR'S HONOR: ETHNIC WAR AND THE MODERN CONSCIENCE, New York: Metropolitan Books, 1997

The Internationalization of Criminal Law, 1995 AMERICAN SOCIETY OF INTERNATIONAL LAW PROCEEDINGS 297

JONES, JOHN R.W.D., THE PRACTICE OF THE INTERNATIONAL CRIMINAL TRIBUNALS FOR THE FORMER YUGOSLAVIA AND RWANDA (2d edn.), Ardsley, NY: Transnational Publishers, 2000

Jones, Robert H., *Jurisdiction and Extradition Under the Convention, in The United States and the 1948 Genocide Convention*, 16 HARVARD INTERNATIONAL LAW JOURNAL 683 (1975)

Josipović, Ivo, *Implementing Legislation for the Application of the Law on the International Criminal Tribunal for the Former Yugoslavia and Criteria for its Evaluation,* 1 YEARBOOK OF INTERNATIONAL HUMANITARIAN LAW 35 (1998)

Joyner, Christopher C., *Enforcing Human Rights Standards in the Former Yugoslavia: The Case for an International War Crimes Tribunal*, 22 DENVER JOURNAL OF INTERNATIONAL LAW AND POLICY 235 (1994)

—— *Strengthening Enforcement of Humanitarian Law: Reflections on the International Criminal Tribunal for the Former Yugoslavia*, 6 DUKE JOURNAL OF COMPARATIVE AND INTERNATIONAL LAW 79 (1995)

Keegan, Michael J., *Prosecuting International Crimes: An Inside View: The Preparation of Cases for the ICTY*, 7 TRANSNATIONAL LAW AND CONTEMPORARY PROBLEMS 119 (1997)

KIRCHHEIMER, OTTO, POLITICAL JUSTICE: THE USE OF LEGAL PROCEDURE FOR POLITICAL ENDS, Princeton: Princeton University Press, 1961

Kirsch, Philippe, and Holmes, John T., *The Rome Conference on an International Criminal Court: The Negotiating Process*, 93 AMERICAN JOURNAL OF INTERNATIONAL LAW 2 (1999)

Kopelman, Elizabeth S., *Ideology and International Law: The Dissent of the Indian Justice at the Tokyo War Crimes Trial*, 23 NEW YORK UNIVERSITY JOURNAL OF INTERNATIONAL LAW AND POLITICS 373 (1991)

Kovács, Péter, *Correspondents Reports*, 1 YEARBOOK OF INTERNATIONAL HUMANITARIAN LAW 451 (1998)

Kozinski, Alex, *Sanhedrin II: The Case of Ivan Demjanjuk*, NEW REPUBLIC, September 13, 1993, at 16

KRITZ, NEIL J. (ED.), TRANSITIONAL JUSTICE (3 vols.), Washington, DC: United States Institute of Peace Press, 1995

—— *Coming to Terms with Atrocities: A Review of Accountability Mechanisms for Mass Violations of Human Rights,* 59 LAW AND CONTEMPORARY PROBLEMS 127 (1996)

Kunstle, David P., *Kadic v. Karadzic: Do Private Individuals Have Enforceable Rights and Obligations Under the Alien Tort Claims Act?*, 6 DUKE JOURNAL OF COMPARATIVE AND INTERNATIONAL LAW 319 (1996)

Kushen, Robert, and Harris, Kenneth J., *Surrender of Fugitives by the United States to the War Crimes Tribunals for Yugoslavia and Rwanda*, 90 AMERICAN JOURNAL OF INTERNATIONAL LAW 510 (1996)

Laber, Jeri, and Nizich, Ivana, *The War Crimes Tribunal for the Former Yugoslavia: Problems and Prospects*, FLETCHER FORUM OF WORLD AFFAIRS, Summer/Fall 1994, at 7

Lansing, Paul, and King, Julie C., *South Africa's Truth and Reconciliation Commission: The Conflict between Individual Justice and National Healing in the Post-Apartheid Age*, 15 ARIZONA JOURNAL OF INTERNATIONAL AND COMPARATIVE LAW 753 (1998)

LEE, ROY S. (ED.), THE INTERNATIONAL CRIMINAL COURT: THE MAKING OF THE ROME STATUTE, The Hague: Kluwer Law International, 1999

LEIGH, MONROE, and BLAKESLEE, MERRITT R. (EDS.), NATIONAL TREATY LAW AND PRACTICE, Washington, DC: American Society of International Law, 1995

Leigh, Monroe, *The Yugoslav Tribunal: Use of Unnamed Witnesses Against Accused*, 90 AMERICAN JOURNAL OF INTERNATIONAL LAW 235 (1996)

LESCURE, KARINE, and TRINTIGNAC, FLORENCE, INTERNATIONAL JUSTICE FOR FORMER YUGOSLAVIA: THE WORKING OF THE INTERNATIONAL CRIMINAL TRIBUNAL OF THE HAGUE, The Hague: Kluwer Law International, 1996

Llewellyn, Jennifer J., and Howse, Robert, *Institutions for Restorative Justice: The South African Truth and Reconciliation Commission*, 49 UNIVERSITY OF TORONTO LAW JOURNAL 355 (1999)

LOWE, VAUGHAN, and FITZMAURICE, MALGOSIA (EDS.), FIFTY YEARS OF THE INTERNATIONAL COURT OF JUSTICE, Cambridge: Grotius Publications, 1996

MACDONALD, R. ST. J., MATSCHER, F., and PETZOLD, H. (EDS.), THE EUROPEAN SYSTEM FOR THE PROTECTION OF HUMAN RIGHTS, Dordrecht: Martinus Nijhoff Publishers, 1993

Maison, Rafaëlle, *Les premiers cas d'application des dispositions pénales des Conventions de Genève par les jurisdictions internes*, 6 EUROPEAN JOURNAL OF INTERNATIONAL LAW 260 (1995)

MALAMUD-GOTI, JAIME, GAME WITHOUT END: STATE TERROR AND THE POLITICS OF JUSTICE, Norman, Okla.: University of Oklahoma Press, 1996

—— *Transitional Governments in the Breach: Why Punish State Criminals?,* 12 HUMAN RIGHTS QUARTERLY 1 (1990)

Marquadt, Paul D., *Law without Borders: The Constitutionality of an International Criminal Court*, 33 COLUMBIA JOURNAL OF TRANSNATIONAL LAW 73 (1995)

Matas, David, *Prosecuting in Canada for Crimes Against Humanity*, 11 NEW YORK LAW SCHOOL JOURNAL OF INTERNATIONAL AND COMPARATIVE LAW 347 (1990)

May, Richard, and Wierda, Marieke, *Trends in International Criminal Evidence: Nuremberg, Tokyo, The Hague, and Arusha*, 37 Columbia Journal of Transnational Law 725 (1999)

Mayfield, Julie V., *The Prosecution of War Crimes and Respect for Human Rights: Ethiopia's Balancing Act*, 9 Emory International Law Review 553 (1995)

McCarthy, Emily H., *South Africa's Amnesty Process: A Viable Route Toward Truth and Reconciliation?*, 3 Michigan Journal of Race and Law 183 (1997)

Méndez, Juan E., *Accountability for Past Abuses*, 19 Human Rights Quarterly 255 (1997)

Meron, Theodor, *The Case for War Crimes Trials in Yugoslavia*, Foreign Affairs, Summer 1993, at 122

Meyer, Michael A., *Liability of Prisoners of War for Offenses Committed Prior to Capture: The Astiz Affair*, 32 International and Comparative Law Quarterly 948 (1983)

Mignone, Emilio Fermin, Estlund, Cynthia L., and Issacharoff, Samuel, *Dictatorship on Trial: Prosecution of Human Rights Violations in Argentina*, 10 Yale Journal of International Law 118 (1984)

Minear, Richard H., Victor's Justice: The Tokyo War Crimes Trial, Princeton, NJ: Princeton University Press, 1971

Minow, Martha, Between Vengeance and Forgiveness: Facing History after Genocide and Mass Violence, Boston, Mass: Beacon Press, 1998

Mitchell, Andrew D., *Genocide, Human Rights Implementation and the Relationship Between International and Domestic Law:* Nulyarimma v Thompson, 24 Melbourne University Law Review 15 (2000)

Morris, Madeline H., *The Trials of Concurrent Jurisdiction: The Case of Rwanda*, 7 Duke Journal of Comparative and International Law 349 (1997)

Morris, Virginia, and Scharf, Michael P., An Insider's Guide to the International Criminal Tribunal for the Former Yugoslavia, Irvington-on-Hudson, NY: Transnational Publishers, 1995

Murphy, John F., *Civil Liability for the Commission of International Crimes as an Alternative to Criminal Prosecution*, 12 Harvard Human Rights Journal 1 (1999)

Murphy, Peter (ed.), Blackstone's Criminal Practice, London: Blackstone Press, 1994

Murphy, Sean, *Progress and Jurisprudence of the International Criminal Tribunal for the Former Yugoslavia*, 93 American Journal of International Law 57 (1999)

Murray, Matthew H., *The Torture Victim Protection Act: Legislation to Promote Enforcement of the Human Rights of Aliens in U.S. Courts*, 25 Columbia Journal of Transnational Law 673 (1987)

Muther, Thomas F., *The Extradition of International Criminals: A Changing Perspective*, 24 Denver Journal of International Law and Policy 221 (1995)

Nagan, Winston P., *International Criminal Law and the Ad Hoc Tribunal for*

Former Yugoslavia, 6 Duke Journal of Comparative and International Law 127 (1995)

Neier, Aryeh, *What Should be Done About the Guilty?*, New York Review of Books, February 1, 1990, at 32

—— War Crimes: Brutality, Genocide, Terror, and the Struggle for Justice, New York: Times Books, 1998

Niang, Mame Mandiaye, *Le tribunal pénal international pour le Rwanda. Et si la contumace était possible!*, 103 Revue Générale de Droit International Public 379 (1999)

Nino, Carlos S., *The Duty to Punish Past Abuses of Human Rights Put Into Context: The Case of Argentina*, 100 Yale Law Journal 2619 (1991)

Nino, Carlos Santiago, Radical Evil on Trial, New Haven, Conn.: Yale University Press, 1996

Nouvel, Yves, *Précisions sur le pouvoir du Tribunal pour l'ex-Yougoslavie d'ordonner la production des preuves et la comparution des témoins: L'Arrêt de la Chambre d'appel du 29 octobre 1997 dans L'affaire Blaškić*, 102 Revue Général de Droit International Public 157 (1998)

O'Brien, James C., *The International Tribunal for Violations of International Humanitarian Law in the Former Yugoslavia*, 87 American Journal of International Law 639 (1993)

Orentlicher, Diane F., *Settling Accounts: The Duty to Prosecute Human Rights Violations of a Prior Regime*, 100 Yale Law Journal 2537 (1991)

—— *A Reply to Professor Nino*, 100 Yale Law Journal 2641 (1991)

Osiel, Mark J., *Ever Again, Legal Remembrance of Administrative Massacre*, 144 University of Pennsylvania Law Review 463 (1995)

Osofsky, Hari M., *Domesticating International Criminal Law: Bringing Human Rights Violators to Justice*, 107 Yale Law Journal 191 (1997)

Parker, Peter, *The Politics of Indemnities, Truth Telling and Reconciliation in South Africa*, 17 Human Rights Law Journal 1 (1996)

Pasqualucci, Jo M., *The Whole Truth and Nothing But the Truth: Truth Commissions, Impunity, and the Inter-American Human Rights System*, 12 Boston University International Law Journal 321 (1994)

Paust, Jordan J., *Suing Saddam: Private Remedies for War Crimes and Hostage-Taking*, 31 Virginia Journal of International Law 351 (1991)

Pejic, Jelena, *Creating a Permanent International Criminal Court: The Obstacles to Independence and Effectiveness*, 29 Columbia Human Rights Law Review 291 (1998)

Penrose, Mary Margaret, *Lest We Fail: The Importance of Enforcement in International Criminal Law*, 15 American University International Law Review 321 (2000)

Popkin, Margaret, and Roht-Arriaza, Naomi, *Truth as Justice: Investigatory Commissions in Latin America*, 20 Law and Social Inquiry 79 (1995)

The Protection of Human Rights Through International Criminal Law: A Conversation with Madam Justice Louise Arbour, Chief Prosecutor for the International Criminal Tribunals for the Former Yugoslavia and Rwanda, 57 University of Toronto Faculty of Law Review 83 (1999)

PRUNIER, GÉRARD, THE RWANDA CRISIS, 1959–1994: HISTORY OF A GENOCIDE, London: Hurst & Co., 1995

Quint, Peter E., *Judging the Past: The Prosecution of East German Border Guards and the GDR Chain of Command*, 61 REVIEW OF POLITICS 303 (1999)

Randall, Kenneth C., *Universal Jurisdiction Under International Law*, 66 TEXAS LAW REVIEW 785 (1988)

Ratner, Steven R., *New Democracies, Old Atrocities: An Inquiry in International Law,* 87 GEORGETOWN LAW JOURNAL 707 (1999)

Reisman, W. Michael, *Institutions and Practices for Restoring and Maintaining Public Order*, 6 DUKE JOURNAL OF COMPARATIVE AND INTERNATIONAL LAW 175 (1995)

Reydams, Luc, *Universal Jurisdiction over Atrocities in Rwanda: Theory and Practice*, 4 EUROPEAN JOURNAL OF CRIME, CRIMINAL LAW AND CRIMINAL JUSTICE 18 (1996)

—— *International Decisions*, 93 AMERICAN JOURNAL OF INTERNATIONAL LAW 700 (1999)

ROHT-ARRIAZA, NAOMI (ED.), IMPUNITY AND HUMAN RIGHTS IN INTERNATIONAL LAW AND PRACTICE, New York: Oxford University Press, 1995

RÖLING, B. V. A., THE TOKYO TRIAL AND BEYOND: REFLECTIONS OF A PEACEMONGER (Antonio Cassese (ed.)), Cambridge: Polity Press, 1993

RONIGER, LUIS, AND SZNAJDER, MARIO, THE LEGACY OF HUMAN-RIGHTS VIOLATIONS IN THE SOUTHERN CONE: ARGENTINA, CHILE, AND URUGUAY, New York: Oxford University Press, 1999

ROSENBERG, TINA, THE HAUNTED LAND: FACING EUROPE'S GHOSTS AFTER COMMUNISM, New York: Random House, 1995

—— *Overcoming the Legacies of Dictatorship*, FOREIGN AFFAIRS, May/June 1995, at 134

—— *Recovering from Apartheid*, THE NEW YORKER, November 18, 1996, at 86

ROSENNE, SHABTAI, PROCEDURE IN THE INTERNATIONAL COURT, Dordrecht: Martinus Nijhoff Publishers, 1983

—— THE LAW AND PRACTICE OF THE INTERNATIONAL COURT, 1920–1996 (4 vols., 3d edn.), The Hague: Martinus Nijhoff Publishers, 1997

Rosenstock, Robert, *The Forty-Fourth Session of the International Law Commission*, 87 AMERICAN JOURNAL OF INTERNATIONAL LAW 138 (1993)

—— *The Forty-Seventh Session of the International Law Commission*, 90 AMERICAN JOURNAL OF INTERNATIONAL LAW 106 (1996)

Rubin, Alfred P., *An International Criminal Tribunal for Former Yugoslavia?,* 6 PACE INTERNATIONAL LAW REVIEW 7 (1994)

—— *A Critical View of the Proposed International Criminal Court*, 23 FLETCHER FORUM OF WORLD AFFAIRS 139 (1999)

Rydberg, Åsa, *The Protection of the Interests of Witnesses — The ICTY in Comparison to the Future ICC*, 12 LEIDEN JOURNAL OF INTERNATIONAL LAW 455 (1999)

Sachs, Albie, *Truth and Reconciliation*, 52 SOUTHERN METHODIST UNIVERSITY LAW REVIEW 1563 (1999)

Sadat, Leila Nadya, and Carden, S. Richard, *The New International Criminal Court: An Uneasy Revolution,* 88 GEORGETOWN LAW JOURNAL 381 (2000)

SANDIFER, DURWARD V., EVIDENCE BEFORE INTERNATIONAL TRIBUNALS, Charlottesville, Vir.: University Press of Virginia, 1975

Sarooshi, Danesh, *The Statute of the International Criminal Court*, 48 INTERNATIONAL AND COMPARATIVE LAW QUARTERLY 387 (1999)

Schabas, William A., *Justice, Democracy, and Impunity in Post-genocide Rwanda: Searching for Solutions to Impossible Problems*, 7 CRIMINAL LAW FORUM 523 (1996)

—— *International Decisions*, 93 AMERICAN JOURNAL OF INTERNATIONAL LAW 529 (1999)

—— *International Decisions:* Barayagwiza v. Prosecutor, 94 AMERICAN JOURNAL OF INTERNATIONAL LAW 563 (2000)

Scharf, Michael, P., *The Politics of Establishing an International Criminal Court*, 6 DUKE JOURNAL OF COMPARATIVE AND INTERNATIONAL LAW 167 (1995)

—— *Swapping Amnesties for Peace: Was There A Duty to Prosecute International Crimes in Haiti?*, 31 TEXAS INTERNATIONAL LAW JOURNAL 1 (1996)

—— The Prosecutor v. Slavko Dokmanović: *Irregular Rendition and the ICTY*, 11 LEIDEN JOURNAL OF INTERNATIONAL LAW 369 (1998)

Schrag, Minna, *The Yugoslav Crimes Tribunal: A Prosecutor's Views*, 6 DUKE JOURNAL OF COMPARATIVE AND INTERNATIONAL LAW 187 (1995)

Schwartz, Herman, *Lustration in Eastern Europe*, 1 PARKER SCHOOL JOURNAL OF EAST EUROPEAN LAW 141 (1994)

SHKLAR, JUDITH, LEGALISM: LAW, MORALS, AND POLITICAL TRIALS, Cambridge, Mass: Harvard University Press, 1986

Shraga, Daphna, and Zacklin, Ralph, *The International Criminal Tribunal for the Former Yugoslavia*, 5 EUROPEAN JOURNAL OF INTERNATIONAL LAW 360 (1994)

—— and ——, *The International Criminal Tribunal for Rwanda*, 7 EUROPEAN JOURNAL OF INTERNATIONAL LAW 501 (1996)

Simon, Jean-Marie, *The Alien Tort Claims Act: Justice or Show Trials?*, 11 BOSTON UNIVERSITY INTERNATIONAL LAW JOURNAL 1 (1993)

Sluiter, Göran, *Obtaining Evidence for the International Criminal Tribunal for the Former Yugoslavia: An Overview and Assessment of Domestic Implementing Legislation*, 45 NETHERLANDS INTERNATIONAL LAW REVIEW 87 (1998)

Slye, Ronald C., *Amnesty, Truth, and Reconciliation, in* TRUTH V. JUSTICE: THE MORAL EFFICACY OF TRUTH COMMISSIONS IN SOUTH AFRICA AND BEYOND (Robert I. Rotberg and Dennis Thompson (eds.), Princeton, NJ: Princeton University Press, 2000

STEPHENS, BETH, and RATNER, MICHAEL, INTERNATIONAL HUMAN RIGHTS LITIGATION IN U.S. COURTS, Irvington-on-Hudson, NY: Transnational Publishers, 1996

Stern, Brigitte, *La compétence universelle en France: le cas des crimes commis en ex-Yugoslavie et au Rwanda*, 40 GERMAN YEARBOOK OF INTERNATIONAL LAW 280 (1997)

—— *À propos de la compétence universelle, in* LIBER AMICORUM JUDGE MOHAMMED BEDJAOUI 735 (Emile Yakpo and Tahar Boumedra (eds.)), The Hague: Kluwer Law International, 1999

Stern, Brigitte, *International Decisions*, 93 AMERICAN JOURNAL OF INTERNATIONAL LAW 696 (1999)

Symposium, *The International Criminal Court*, 8 DETROIT COLLEGE OF LAW AT MICHIGAN STATE UNIVERSITY JOURNAL OF INTERNATIONAL LAW AND PRACTICE 1 (1999)

Symposium, *The International Criminal Court: Consensus and Debate on the International Adjudication of Genocide, Crimes Against Humanity, War Crimes, and Aggression*, 32 CORNELL INTERNATIONAL LAW JOURNAL 437 (1999)

Symposium, *International Law Enforcement, Extradition, and Mutual Legal Assistance in the 21st Century*, 23 FORDHAM INTERNATIONAL LAW JOURNAL (2000)

Symposium, *Nuremberg and the Rule of Law: A Fifty-Year Verdict*, 149 MILITARY LAW REVIEW 1 (1995)

Symposium, *1945–1995: Critical Perspectives on the Nuremberg Trials and State Accountability*, 12 NEW YORK LAW SCHOOL JOURNAL OF HUMAN RIGHTS 453 (1995)

Symposium, *War Crimes Tribunals: The Record and the Prospects*, 13 AMERICAN UNIVERSITY INTERNATIONAL LAW REVIEW 1383 (1998)

Szasz, Paul C., *The Proposed War Crimes Tribunal for Ex-Yugoslavia*, 25 NEW YORK UNIVERSITY JOURNAL OF INTERNATIONAL LAW AND POLITICS 405 (1993)

TAYLOR, TELFORD, THE ANATOMY OF THE NUREMBERG TRIALS, New York: Alfred A. Knopf, 1992

Thieroff, Mark, and Aimley, Edward A., Jr., *Proceeding to Justice and Accountability in the Balkans: The International Criminal Tribunal for the Former Yugoslavia and Rule 61*, 23 YALE JOURNAL OF INTERNATIONAL LAW 231 (1998)

Tomuschat, Christian, *Between National and International Law: Guatemala's Historical Clarification Commission*, *in* LIBER AMICORUM GÜNTHER JAENICKE—ZUM 85. GEBURTSTAG 991 (Christiane Philipp (ed.)), Berlin: Springer, 1998

TUSA, ANN, and TUSA, JOHN, THE NUREMBERG TRIAL, New York: McGraw-Hill, 1983

UNITED STATES INSTITUTE OF PEACE, RWANDA: ACCOUNTABILITY FOR WAR CRIMES AND GENOCIDE, Washington, DC: United States Institute of Peace Press, 1994

Van den Wyngaert, Christine, and Stessens, Guy, *The International* non bis in idem *Principle: Resolving Some of the Unanswered Questions*, 48 INTERNATIONAL AND COMPARATIVE LAW QUARTERLY 779 (1999)

VILLA-VICENCIO, CHARLES, AND VERWOERD, WILHELM (EDS.), LOOKING BACK, REACHING FORWARD: REFLECTIONS ON THE TRUTH AND RECONCILIATION COMMISSION OF SOUTH AFRICA, London: Zed Books, 2000

VON HEBEL, HERMAN A.M., LAMMERS, JOHAN G., and SCHUKKING, JOLIEN (EDS.), REFLECTIONS ON THE INTERNATIONAL CRIMINAL COURT: ESSAYS IN HONOUR OF ADRIAAN BOS, The Hague: T.M.C. Asser Press, 1999

Wagner, J. Martin, *U.S. Prosecution of Past and Future War Criminals and Criminals Against Humanity: Proposals for Reform Based on the Canadian and Australian Experience*, 29 VIRGINIA JOURNAL OF INTERNATIONAL LAW 887 (1989)

Walsh, James, *Can Justice Ever Be Done?*, TIME, May 22, 1995, at 19

Wedgwood, Ruth, *War Crimes in the Former Yugoslavia: Comments on the International War Crimes Tribunal*, 34 VIRGINIA JOURNAL OF INTERNATIONAL LAW 267 (1994)

—— *International Criminal Tribunals and State Sources of Proof: The Case of Tihomir Blaškić*, 11 LEIDEN JOURNAL OF INTERNATIONAL LAW 635 (1998)

—— *Fiddling in Rome: America and the International Criminal Court*, FOREIGN AFFAIRS, November/December 1998, at 20

Weissbrodt, David, and Fraser, Paul W., *Book Review: Report of the Chilean National Commission on Truth and Reconciliation*, 14 HUMAN RIGHTS QUARTERLY 601 (1992)

WESCHLER, LAWRENCE, A MIRACLE, A UNIVERSE: SETTLING ACCOUNTS WITH TORTURERS, New York: Pantheon Books, 1990

WIGMORE, JOHN HENRY, EVIDENCE IN TRIALS AT COMMON LAW (Vol. 9), Boston, Mass.: Little, Brown & Company, 1981

Wilson, Richard J., *Prosecuting Pinochet: International Crimes in Spanish Domestic Law*, 21 HUMAN RIGHTS QUARTERLY 927 (1999)

Woods, Jeanne M., *Reconciling Reconciliation*, 3 UCLA JOURNAL OF INTERNATIONAL LAW AND FOREIGN AFFAIRS 81 (1998)

Zacklin, Ralph, *Bosnia and Beyond*, 34 VIRGINIA JOURNAL OF INTERNATIONAL LAW 277 (1994)

Zalaquett, José, *Confronting Human Rights Violations Committed by Former Governments: Principles Applicable and Political Constraints*, 13 HAMLINE LAW REVIEW 623 (1990)

ZOBEL, HILLER B., THE BOSTON MASSACRE, New York: W. W. Norton, 1970

Cambodia and the Khmer Rouge

ABRAMS, JASON S., and RATNER, STEVEN R., STRIVING FOR JUSTICE: ACCOUNTABILITY AND THE CRIMES OF THE KHMER ROUGE (1995) (consultants' study prepared for U.S. Department of State)

AMNESTY INTERNATIONAL, KINGDOM OF CAMBODIA: DIMINISHING RESPECT FOR HUMAN RIGHTS, New York: Amnesty International, 1996

BECKER, ELIZABETH, WHEN THE WAR WAS OVER: THE VOICES OF CAMBODIA'S REVOLUTION AND ITS PEOPLE, New York: Simon & Schuster, 1986

Bureaucracy of Death: Documents from Inside Pol Pot's Torture Machine, NEW STATESMAN, May 2, 1980, at 668

CHANDA, NAYAN, BROTHER ENEMY: THE WAR AFTER THE WAR, San Diego, Cal.: Harcourt Brace Jovanovich, 1986

CHANDLER, DAVID P., THE TRAGEDY OF CAMBODIAN HISTORY: POLITICS, WAR AND REVOLUTION SINCE 1945, New Haven, Conn.: Yale University Press, 1991

—— A HISTORY OF CAMBODIA, Boulder, Colo.: Westview Press, 1992

—— and KIERNAN, BEN (EDS.), REVOLUTION AND ITS AFTERMATH IN KAMPUCHEA: EIGHT ESSAYS, New Haven, Conn.: Yale University South East Asia Studies, 1983

Donovan, Dolores A., *The Cambodian Legal System: An Overview, in*

REBUILDING CAMBODIA: HUMAN RESOURCES, HUMAN RIGHTS, AND LAW (Frederick Z. Brown (ed.)), Washington, DC: Paul H. Nitze School of Advanced International Studies, 1992

—— *Cambodia: Building a Legal System from Scratch*, 27 INTERNATIONAL LAWYER 445 (1993)

Hannum, Hurst, *International Law and Cambodian Genocide: The Sounds of Silence*, 11 HUMAN RIGHTS QUARTERLY 82 (1989)

Hawk, David, *International Human Rights Law and Democratic Kampuchea*, 16 INTERNATIONAL JOURNAL OF POLITICS (1986)

—— *The Cambodian Genocide, in* GENOCIDE: A CRITICAL BIBLIOGRAPHIC REVIEW 137 (Israel W. Charny (ed.)), New York: Facts on File Publications, 1988

HUMAN RIGHTS WATCH/ASIA and HUMAN RIGHTS WATCH ARMS PROJECT, CAMBODIA AT WAR, New York: Human Rights Watch, 1995

JACKSON, KARL D. (ED.), CAMBODIA 1975–1978: RENDEZVOUS WITH DEATH, Princeton, NJ: Princeton University Press, 1989

Kiernan, Ben, *New Light on the Origins of the Vietnam-Kampuchea Conflict*, 12 BULLETIN OF CONCERNED ASIAN SCHOLARS 61 (1980)

—— HOW POL POT CAME TO POWER: A HISTORY OF COMMUNISM IN KAMPUCHEA, London: Verso, 1985

—— CAMBODIA: THE EASTERN ZONE MASSACRES, New York: Center for the Study of Human Rights, Columbia University, 1986

—— *Genocidal Targeting: Two Groups of Victims in Pol Pot's Cambodia, in* STATE ORGANIZED TERROR: THE CASE OF VIOLENT INTERNAL REPRESSION 207 (P. Timothy Bushnell, Vladimir Shlapentokh, Christopher K. Vanderpool, and Jeyaratan Sundram (eds.)), Boulder, Colo.: Westview Press, 1991

—— (ED.), GENOCIDE AND DEMOCRACY IN CAMBODIA, New Haven, Conn.: Yale University South East Asia Studies, 1993

—— THE POL POT REGIME, New Haven, Conn.: Yale University Press, 1996

LAWYERS COMMITTEE FOR HUMAN RIGHTS, CAMBODIA: THE JUSTICE SYSTEM AND VIOLATIONS OF HUMAN RIGHTS, New York: Lawyers Committee for Human Rights, 1992

LIBRARY OF CONGRESS, FEDERAL RESEARCH DIVISION, CAMBODIA: A COUNTRY STUDY (Russell R. Ross (ed.)), Washington, DC: United States Government Printing Office, 1990

Marks, Stephen P., *Forgetting 'The Policies and Practices of the Past': Impunity in Cambodia*, FLETCHER FORUM OF WORLD AFFAIRS, Summer/Fall 1994, at 17

—— *The New Cambodian Constitution: From Civil War to a Fragile Democracy*, 26 COLUMBIA HUMAN RIGHTS LAW REVIEW 45 (1994)

NGOR, HAING, A CAMBODIAN ODYSSEY, New York: Warner Books, 1987

PONCHAUD, FRANÇOIS, CAMBODIA: YEAR ZERO (Nancy Amphoux (trans.)), New York: Holt Rinehart & Winston, 1978

Railsback, Kathryn, *A Genocide Convention Action Against the Khmer Rouge: Preventing a Resurgence of the Killing Fields*, 5 CONNECTICUT JOURNAL OF INTERNATIONAL LAW 457 (1990)

Rasy, Douc, Remarks on the Punishment of Genocide in Cambodia, June 23, 1995 (on file with authors)

Ratner, Steven R., *The Cambodia Settlement Agreements*, 87 AMERICAN JOURNAL OF INTERNATIONAL LAW 1 (1993)

—— THE NEW UN PEACEKEEPING: BUILDING PEACE IN LANDS OF CONFLICT AFTER THE COLD WAR, New York: St. Martin's Press, 1995

—— *The United Nations Group of Experts for Cambodia*, 93 AMERICAN JOURNAL OF INTERNATIONAL LAW 948 (1999)

SHAWCROSS, WILLIAM, SIDESHOW: KISSINGER, NIXON AND THE DESTRUCTION OF CAMBODIA (rev. edn.), New York: Simon & Schuster, 1987

—— *Tragedy in Cambodia*, NEW YORK REVIEW OF BOOKS, November 14, 1996, at 41

Significant Official Reports

(in chronological order)

United Nations and Other Intergovernmental Reports

Commission on the Responsibility of the Authors of the War and on Enforcement of Penalties, *Report Presented to the Preliminary Peace Conference, March 29, 1919, reprinted in* 14 AMERICAN JOURNAL OF INTERNATIONAL LAW 95 (1920)

UNITED NATIONS WAR CRIMES COMMISSION, HISTORY OF THE UNITED NATIONS WAR CRIMES COMMISSION AND THE DEVELOPMENT OF THE LAWS OF WAR, London: Her Majesty's Stationery Office, 1948

SECRETARY-GENERAL OF THE UNITED NATIONS, THE CHARTER AND JUDGMENT OF THE NÜRNBERG TRIBUNAL: HISTORY AND ANALYSIS (1949), UN Doc. A/CN.4/5, UN Sales No. 1949.V.7

Reports of the International Law Commission to the General Assembly for 1949–54, 1983–96, *reprinted in* Yearbook of the International Law Commission for those years

Study of the Question of the Prevention and Punishment of the Crime of Genocide, prepared by Nicodème Ruhashyamiko, July 4, 1978, UN Doc. E/CN.4/Sub.2/416

Revised and updated report on the question of the prevention and punishment of the crime of genocide, prepared by B. Whitaker, July 2, 1985, UN Doc. E/CN.4/Sub.2/1985/6

Report of the Secretary-General pursuant to paragraph 2 of Security Council Resolution 808 (1993), May 3, 1993, UN Doc. S/25704

Final Report of the Commission of Experts Established Pursuant to Security Council Resolution 780 (1992), May 27, 1994, UN Doc. S/1994/674

Final Report of the Commission of Experts established pursuant to Security Council Resolution 935 (1994), December 9, 1994, UN Doc. S/1994/1405

Question of the impunity of perpetrators of human rights violations (civil and political): Revised final report prepared by Mr. Joinet pursuant to subcommission decision, 1996/119, October 2, 1997, UN Doc. E/CN.4/Sub.2/1997/20 Rev. 1

Report of the Group of Experts for Cambodia established pursuant to General Assembly resolution 52/135, March 16, 1999, UN Doc. A/53/850-S/1999/321

Individual States

TAYLOR, TELFORD, FINAL REPORT TO THE SECRETARY OF THE ARMY ON THE NUERNBERG WAR CRIMES TRIALS UNDER CONTROL COUNCIL LAW NO. 10, Washington, DC: United States Government Printing Office, 1949

UNITED STATES DEPARTMENT OF THE ARMY, THE LAW OF LAND WARFARE (Field Manual 27–10), Ann Arbor, Mich.: Judge Advocate General's School, 1956

ARGENTINE NATIONAL COMMISSION ON THE DISAPPEARED, NUNCA MÁS: THE REPORT OF THE ARGENTINE NATIONAL COMMISSION ON THE DISAPPEARED (1984), New York: Farrar Straus Giroux, 1986

HETHERINGTON, THOMAS, and CHALMERS, WILLIAM, WAR CRIMES: REPORT OF THE WAR CRIMES INQUIRY, London: Her Majesty's Stationery Office, 1989

CHILEAN NATIONAL COMMISSION ON TRUTH AND RECONCILIATION, REPORT OF THE CHILEAN NATIONAL COMMISSION ON TRUTH AND RECONCILIATION (Phillip E. Berryman, trans.), Notre Dame, Ind.: Notre Dame Press, 1993

TRUTH AND RECONCILIATION COMMISSION OF SOUTH AFRICA: FINAL REPORT, London: Macmillan, 1999, available at www.mg.co.za/mg/projects/trc

COMISIÓN PARA EL ESCLARECIMIENTO HISTÓRICO, GUATEMALA: MEMORIA DEL SILENCIO, Guatemala City: Historical Clarification Commission, 1999, available at http://hrdata.aaas.org/ceh

Index